ACCA

Paper F9

Financial Management

Complete Text

British library cataloguing-in-publication data

A catalogue record for this book is available from the British Library.

Published by:
Kaplan Publishing UK
Unit 2 The Business Centre
Molly Millars Lane
Wokingham
Berkshire
RG41 2QZ

ISBN 978-1-78415-217-8

The text in this material and any others made available by any Kaplan Group company does not amount to advice on a particular matter and should not be taken as such. No reliance should be placed on the content as the basis for any investment or other decision or in connection with any advice given to third parties. Please consult your appropriate professional adviser as necessary. Kaplan Publishing Limited and all other Kaplan group companies expressly disclaim all liability to any person in respect of any losses or other claims, whether direct, indirect, incidental, consequential or otherwise arising in relation to the use of such materials.

Printed and bound in Great Britain.

Acknowledgements

We are grateful to the Association of Chartered Certified Accountants and the Chartered Institute of Management Accountants for permission to reproduce past examination questions. The answers have been prepared by Kaplan Publishing.

Kaplan Publishing are constantly finding new ways to make a difference to your studies and our exciting online resources really do offer something different to students looking for exam success.

This book comes with free MyKaplan online resources so that you can study anytime, anywhere

Having purchased this book, you have access to the following online study materials:

CONTENT	ACCA (including FFA,FAB,FMA)		FIA (excluding FFA,FAB,FMA)	
	Text	Kit	Text	Kit
iPaper version of the book	✓	✓	✓	✓
Interactive electronic version of the book	✓			
Progress tests with instant answers	✓			
Material updates	✓	✓	✓	✓
Latest official ACCA exam questions*		✓		
Extra question assistance using the signpost icon*		✓		
Timed questions with an online tutor debrief using the clock icon*		✓		
Interim assessment including questions and answers	✓		✓	
Technical articles	✓	✓	✓	✓

* Excludes F1, F2, F3, FFA, FAB, FMA

How to access your online resources

Kaplan Financial students will already have a MyKaplan account and these extra resources will be available to you online. You do not need to register again, as this process was completed when you enrolled. If you are having problems accessing online materials, please ask your course administrator.

If you are already a registered MyKaplan user go to www.MyKaplan.co.uk and log in. Select the 'add a book' feature and enter the ISBN number of this book and the unique pass key at the bottom of this card. Then click 'finished' or 'add another book'. You may add as many books as you have purchased from this screen.

If you purchased through Kaplan Flexible Learning or via the Kaplan Publishing website you will automatically receive an e-mail invitation to MyKaplan. Please register your details using this email to gain access to your content. If you do not receive the e-mail or book content, please contact Kaplan Flexible Learning.

If you are a new MyKaplan user register at www.MyKaplan.co.uk and click on the link contained in the email we sent you to activate your account. Then select the 'add a book' feature, enter the ISBN number of this book and the unique pass key at the bottom of this card. Then click 'finished' or 'add another book'.

Your Code and Information

This code can only be used once for the registration of one book online. This registration and your online content will expire when the final sittings for the examinations covered by this book have taken place. Please allow one hour from the time you submit your book details for us to process your request.

NOT AVAILABLE

KAPLAN PUBLISHING

Contents

chapter

roduction

How to Use the Materials

These Kaplan Publishing learning materials have been carefully designed to make your learning experience as easy as possible and to give you the best chances of success in your examinations.

The product range contains a number of features to help you in the study process. They include:

(1) Detailed study guide and syllabus objectives

(2) Description of the examination

(3) Study skills and revision guidance

(4) Complete text or essential text

(5) Question practice

The sections on the study guide, the syllabus objectives, the examination and study skills should all be read before you commence your studies. They are designed to familiarise you with the nature and content of the examination and give you tips on how to best to approach your learning.

The **complete text or essential text** comprises the main learning materials and gives guidance as to the importance of topics and where other related resources can be found. Each chapter includes:

- The **learning objectives** contained in each chapter, which have been carefully mapped to the examining body's own syllabus learning objectives or outcomes. You should use these to check you have a clear understanding of all the topics on which you might be assessed in the examination.
- The **chapter diagram** provides a visual reference for the content in the chapter, giving an overview of the topics and how they link together.
- The **content** for each topic area commences with a brief explanation or definition to put the topic into context before covering the topic in detail. You should follow your studying of the content with a review of the illustration/s. These are worked examples which will help you to understand better how to apply the content for the topic.
- **Test your understanding** sections provide an opportunity to assess your understanding of the key topics by applying what you have learned to short questions. Answers can be found at the back of each chapter.

- **Summary diagrams** complete each chapter to show the important links between topics and the overall content of the paper. These diagrams should be used to check that you have covered and understood the core topics before moving on.
- **Question practice** is provided at the back of each text.

Quality and accuracy are of the utmost importance to us so if you spot an error in any of our products, please send an email to mykaplanreporting@kaplan.com with full details, or follow the link to the feedback form in MyKaplan.

Our Quality Co-ordinator will work with our technical team to verify the error and take action to ensure it is corrected in future editions.

Icon Explanations

Definition – Key definitions that you will need to learn from the core content.

Key Point – Identifies topics that are key to success and are often examined.

New – Identifies topics that are brand new in papers that build on, and therefore also contain, learning covered in earlier papers.

Expandable Text – Expandable text provides you with additional information about a topic area and may help you gain a better understanding of the core content. Essential text users can access this additional content on-line (read it where you need further guidance or skip over when you are happy with the topic)

Test Your Understanding – Exercises for you to complete to ensure that you have understood the topics just learned.

Illustration – Worked examples help you understand the core content better.

Tricky topic – When reviewing these areas care should be taken and all illustrations and test your understanding exercises should be completed to ensure that the topic is understood.

On-line subscribers

Our on-line resources are designed to increase the flexibility of your learning materials and provide you with immediate feedback on how your studies are progressing. Ask your local customer services staff if you are not already a subscriber and wish to join.

If you are subscribed to our on-line resources you will find:

(1) On-line referenceware: reproduces your Complete or Essential Text on-line, giving you anytime, anywhere access.

(2) On-line testing: provides you with additional on-line objective testing so you can practice what you have learned further.

(3) On-line performance management: immediate access to your on-line testing results. Review your performance by key topics and chart your achievement through the course relative to your peer group.

Syllabus

Aim

The aim of ACCA Paper F9, Financial management, is to develop the knowledge and skills expected of a financial manager, relating to issues affecting investment, financing, and dividend policy decisions.

Main capabilities

- Discuss the role and purpose of the financial management function.
- Assess and discuss the impact of the economic environment on financial management.
- Discuss and apply working capital management techniques.
- Carry out effective investment appraisal.
- Identify and evaluate alternative sources of business finance.
- Explain and calculate cost of capital and the factors which affect it.
- Discuss and apply principles of business and asset valuations.
- Explain and apply risk management techniques in business.

Core areas of the syllabus

- Financial management function.
- Financial management environment.
- Working capital management.
- Investment appraisal.
- Business finance.
- Cost of capital.
- Business valuations.
- Risk management.

Syllabus objectives

We have reproduced the ACCA's study guide below, showing where the objectives are explored within this book.

Within the chapters, we have broken down the extensive information found in the study guide into easily digestible and relevant sections, called Content Objectives. These correspond to the objectives at the beginning of each chapter.

Syllabus learning objective and Chapter reference:

A FINANCIAL MANAGEMENT FUNCTION

1 The nature and purpose of financial management

(a) Explain the nature and purpose of financial management.[1] **Ch. 1**

(b) Explain the relationship between financial management and financial and management accounting.[1] **Ch. 1**

2 Financial objectives and the relationship with corporate strategy

(a) Discuss the relationship between financial objectives, corporate objectives and corporate strategy.[2] **Ch. 1**

(b) Identify and describe a variety of financial objectives, including: [2] **Ch.1**

- (i) shareholder wealth maximisation
- (ii) profit maximisation
- (iii) earnings per share growth.

3 Stakeholders and impact on corporate objectives

(a) Identify the range of stakeholders and their objectives.[2] **Ch. 1**

(b) Discuss the possible conflict between stakeholder objectives.[2]**Ch. 1**

(c) Discuss the role of management in meeting stakeholder objectives, including the application of agency theory.[2]**Ch. 1**

(d) Describe and apply ways of measuring achievement of corporate objectives including:[2] **Ch. 19**

- (i) ratio analysis using appropriate ratios such as return on capital employed, return on equity, earnings per share and dividend per share
- (ii) changes in dividends and share prices as part of total shareholder return.

(e) Explain ways to encourage the achievement of stakeholder objectives, including:[2] **Ch. 1**

(i) managerial reward schemes such as share options and performance-related pay

(ii) regulatory requirements such as corporate governance codes of best practice and stock exchange listing regulations

4 Financial and other objectives in not-for-profit organisations

(a) Discuss the impact of not-for-profit status on financial and other objectives.[2] **Ch. 1**

(b) Discuss the nature and importance of Value for Money as an objective in not-for-profit organisations.[2] **Ch. 1**

(c) Discuss ways of measuring the achievement of objectives in not-for-profit organisations.[2] **Ch. 1**

B FINANCIAL MANAGEMENT ENVIRONMENT

1 The economic environment for business

(a) Identify and explain the main macroeconomic policy targets.[1] **Ch. 11**

(b) Define and discuss the role of fiscal, monetary, interest rate and exchange rate policies in achieving macroeconomic policy targets.[1] **Ch. 11**

(c) Explain how government economic policy interacts with planning and decision-making in business.[2] **Ch. 11**

(d) Explain the need for and the interaction with planning and decision-making in business of:[1] **Ch. 11**

(i) competition policy

(ii) government assistance for business

(iii) green policies

(iv) corporate governance regulation.[2]

2 The nature and role of financial markets and institutions

(a) Identify the nature and role of money and capital markets, both nationally and internationally.[2] **Ch. 12**

(b) Explain the role of financial intermediaries.[1] **Ch. 12**

(c) Explain the functions of a stock market and a corporate bond market.[2] **Ch. 12**

(d) Explain the nature and features of different securities in relation to the risk/return trade-off.[2] **Ch. 15**

3 The nature and role of the money market

(a) Describe the role of the money markets in:[1] **Ch. 12 / 13 / 14**

(i) Providing short-term liquidity to industry and the public sector

(ii) Providing short-term trade finance

(iii) Allowing an organisation to manage its exposure to foreign currency risk and interest rate risk

(b) Explain the role of banks and other financial institutions in the operation of the money markets.[2] **Ch. 12**

(c) Explain the characteristics and role of the principal money market instruments:[2] **Ch. 12**

(i) Interest-bearing instruments

(ii) Discount instruments

(iii) Derivative products.

C WORKING CAPITAL MANAGEMENT

1 The nature, elements and importance of working capital

(a) Describe the nature of working capital and identify its elements. [1] **Ch. 7**

(b) Identify the objectives of working capital management in terms of liquidity and profitability, and discuss the conflict between them. [2] **Ch. 7**

(c) Discuss the central role of working capital management in financial management.[2] **Ch. 7**

2 Management of inventories, accounts receivable, accounts payable and cash

(a) Explain the cash operating cycle and the role of accounts payable and receivable.[2] **Ch. 7**

(b) Explain and apply relevant accounting ratios, including:[2] **Ch. 7**

(i) current ratio and quick ratio

(ii) inventory turnover ratio, average collection period and average payable period

(iii) sales revenue/net working capital ratio.

(c) Discuss, apply and evaluate the use of relevant techniques in managing inventory, including the Economic Order Quantity model and Just-in-Time techniques.[2] **Ch. 8**

(d) Discuss, apply and evaluate the use of relevant techniques in managing accounts receivable, including: **Ch. 9**

(i) assessing creditworthiness[1]

(ii) managing accounts receivable[1]

(iii) collecting amounts owing[1]

(iv) offering early settlement discounts[2]

(v) using factoring and invoice discounting[2]

(vi) managing foreign accounts receivable.[2]

(e) Discuss and apply the use of relevant techniques in managing accounts payable, including: **Ch. 9**

(i) using trade credit effectively[1]

(ii) evaluating the benefits of discounts for early settlement and bulk purchase[2]

(iii) managing foreign accounts payable.[1]

(f) Explain the various reasons for holding cash, and discuss and apply the use of relevant techniques in managing cash, including:[2] **Ch. 10**

(i) preparing cash flow forecasts to determine future cash flows and cash balances

(ii) assessing the benefits of centralised treasury management and cash control

(iii) cash management models, such as the Baumol model and the Miller-Orr model

(iv) investing short-term

3 Determining working capital needs and funding strategies

(a) Calculate the level of working capital investment in current assets and discuss the key factors determining this level, including:[2] **Ch.7**

(i) the length of the working capital cycle and terms of trade

(ii) an organisation's policy on the level of investment in current assets

(iii) the industry in which the organisation operates.

(b) Describe and discuss the key factors in determining working capital funding strategies, including:[2] **Ch.7**
   (i) the distinction between permanent and fluctuating current assets
   (ii) the relative cost and risk of short-term and long-term finance
   (iii) the matching principle
   (iv) the relative costs and benefits of aggressive, conservative and matching funding policies management attitudes to risk, previous funding decisions and organisation size.[1]
   (v) management attitudes to risk, previous funding decisions and organisation size:[1]

D INVESTMENT APPRAISAL

1 Investment appraisal process techniques

(a) Identify and calculate relevant cash flows for investment projects. [2] **Ch.2**

(b) Calculate payback period and discuss the usefulness of payback as an investment appraisal method.[2] **Ch.2**

(c) Calculate return on capital employed (accounting rate of return) and discuss its usefulness as an investment appraisal method.[2] **Ch.2**

(d) Calculate net present value and discuss its usefulness as an investment appraisal method.[2] **Ch.3**

(e) Calculate internal rate of return and discuss its usefulness as an investment appraisal method.[2] **Ch.3**

(f) Discuss the superiority of DCF methods over non-DCF methods. [2] **Ch.3**

(g) Discuss the relative merits of NPV and IRR.[2] **Ch. 3**

(h) Calculate discounted payback and discuss its usefulness as an investment appraisal method.[2] **Ch. 6**

2 Allowing for inflation and taxation in DCF

(a) Apply and discuss the real-terms and nominal-terms approaches to investment appraisal.[2] **Ch.4**

(b) Calculate the taxation effects of relevant cash flows, including the tax benefits of tax-allowable depreciation and the tax liabilities of taxable profit.[2] **Ch.4**

(c) Calculate and apply before- and after-tax discount rates.[2] **Ch.17**

3 Adjusting for risk and uncertainty in investment appraisal

(a) Describe and discuss the difference between risk and uncertainty in relation to probabilities and increasing project life.[2] **Ch.6**

(b) Apply sensitivity analysis to investment projects and discuss the usefulness of sensitivity analysis in assisting investment decisions.[2] **Ch.6**

(c) Apply probability analysis to investment projects and discuss the usefulness of probability analysis in assisting investment decisions.[2] **Ch.6**

(d) Apply and discuss other techniques of adjusting for risk and uncertainty in investment appraisal, including: **Ch.6**

- (i) simulation[1]
- (ii) adjusted payback[1]
- (iii) risk-adjusted discount rates.[2]

4 Specific investment decisions (Lease or buy, asset replacement, capital rationing, etc)

(a) Evaluate leasing and borrowing to buy using the before-and after-tax costs of debt.[2] **Ch.5**

(b) Evaluate asset replacement decisions using equivalent annual cost.[2] **Ch.5**

(c) Evaluate investment decisions under single-period capital rationing, including:[2] **Ch.5**

- (i) the calculation of profitability indexes for divisible investment projects
- (ii) the calculation of the NPV of combinations of non-divisible investment projects
- (iii) a discussion of the reasons for capital rationing.

E BUSINESS FINANCE

1 Sources of and raising business finance

(a) Identify and discuss the range of short-term sources of finance available to businesses, including:[2] **Ch.15**

- (i) overdraft
- (ii) short-term loan
- (iii) trade credit
- (iv) lease finance.

(b) Identify and discuss the range of long-term sources of finance available to businesses, including:[2] **Ch.15**

(i) equity finance

(ii) debt finance

(iii) lease finance

(iv) venture capital.

(c) Identify and discuss methods of raising equity finance, including: [2] **Ch.15**

(i) rights issue

(ii) placing

(iii) public offer

(iv) stock exchange listing.

(d) Identify and discuss methods of raising short and long term Islamic finance including: [1] **Ch.15**

(i) major difference between Islamic finance and other forms of business finance

(ii) The concept of Riba (interest) and how returns are made by Islamic financial securities

(iii) Islamic financial instruments available to businesses including

(iv) murabaha (trade credit)

(v) Ijara (lease finance)

(vi) mudaraba (equity finance)

(vii) sukuk (debt finance)

(viii)musharaka (venture capital)

(note calculations are not required)

(e) Identify and discuss internal sources of finance, including:[2] **Ch.15**

(i) retained earnings

(ii) increasing working capital management efficiency.

(iii) the relationship between the dividend decision and the financing decision[2] **Ch.16**

(iv) the theoretical approaches to, and the practical influences on, the dividend decision, including legal constraints, liquidity, shareholding expectations and alternatives to cash dividends [2] **Ch.16**

2 Estimating the cost of capital

(a) Estimate the cost of equity, including:[2] **Ch.17**
   (i) Application of the dividend growth model and discussion of its weaknesses
   (ii) Explanation and discussion of systematic and unsystematic risk
   (iii) Relationship between portfolio theory and the capital asset pricing model (CAPM)
   (iv) Application of the CAPM, its assumptions, advantages and disadvantages.

(b) Estimating the cost of debt[2] **Ch.17**
   (i) irredeemable debt
   (ii) redeemable debt
   (iii) convertible debt
   (iv) preference shares
   (v) bank debt.

(c) Estimating the overall cost of capital, including:[2] **Ch.17**
   (i) Distinguishing between average and marginal cost of capital
   (ii) Calculating the weighted average cost of capital (WACC) using book value and market value weightings.

3 Sources of finance and their relative costs

(a) Describe the relative risk-return relationship and the relative costs of equity and debt.[2] **Ch.17**

(b) Describe the creditor hierarchy and its connection with the relative costs of sources of finance.[2] **Ch.17**

(c) Identify and discuss the problem of high levels of gearing.[2] **Ch.18**

(d) Assess the impact of sources of finance on financial position, financial risk and shareholder wealth using appropriate measures, including: **Ch.19**
   (i) ratio analysis using statement of financial position gearing, operational and financial gearing, interest coverage ratio and other relevant ratios[2]
   (ii) cash flow forecasting[2]
   (iii) leasing or borrowing to buy.[2]

(e) Impact of cost of capital on investments, including:[2] **Ch.17**

(i) the relationship between company value and cost of capital

(ii) the circumstances under which WACC can be used in investment appraisal

(iii) the advantages of the CAPM over WACC in determining a project-specific cost of capital

(iv) application of CAPM in calculating a project specific discount rate.

4 Capital structure theories and practical considerations

(a) Describe the traditional view of capital structure and its assumptions. [2] **Ch.18**

(b) Describe the views of Miller and Modigliani on capital structure, both without and with corporate taxation, and their assumptions.[2] **Ch.18**

(c) Identify a range of capital market imperfections and describe their impact on the views of Miller and Modigliani on capital structure. [2] **Ch.18**

(d) Explain the relevance of pecking order theory to the selection of sources of finance.[1] **Ch.18**

5 Finance for small and medium-sized entities (SMEs)

(a) Describe the financing needs of small businesses.[2] **Ch.15**

(b) Describe the nature of the financing problem for small businesses in terms of the funding gap, the maturity gap and inadequate security. [2] **Ch.15**

(c) Explain measures that may be taken to ease the financing problems of SMEs, including the responses of government departments and financial institutions.[1] **Ch.15**

(d) Identify appropriate sources of finance for SMEs and evaluate the financial impact of different sources of finance on SMEs.[2] **Ch.15**

F BUSINESS VALUATIONS

1 Nature and purpose of the valuation of business and financial assets

(a) Identify and discuss reasons for valuing businesses and financial assets.[2]**Ch.20**

(b) Identify information requirements for valuation and discuss the limitations of different types of information.[2] **Ch.20**

2 Models for the valuation of shares

(a) Asset-based valuation models, including:[2] **Ch.20**
  (i) net book value (statement of financial position basis).
  (ii) net realisable value basis.
  (iii) net replacement cost basis.

(b) Income-based valuation models, including:[2] **Ch.20**
  (i) price/earnings ratio method
  (ii) earnings yield method

(c) Cash flow-based valuation models, including: [2] **Ch.20**
  (i) dividend valuation model and the dividend growth model
  (ii) discounted cash flow basis.

3 The valuation of debt and other financial assets

(a) Apply appropriate valuation methods to:[2] **Ch.20**
  (i) irredeemable debt
  (ii) redeemable debt
  (iii) convertible debt
  (iv) preference shares.

4 Efficient market hypothesis (EMH) and practical considerations in the valuation of shares

(a) Distinguish between and discuss weak form efficiency, semi-strong form efficiency and strong form efficiency.[2] **Ch.20**

(b) Discuss practical considerations in the valuation of shares and businesses, including:[2] **Ch.20**
  (i) marketability and liquidity of shares
  (ii) availability and sources of information
  (iii) market imperfections and pricing anomalies
  (iv) market capitalisation.

(c) Describe the significance of investor speculation and the explanations of investor decisions offered by behavioural finance. [1] **Ch.20**

G RISK MANAGEMENT

1 The nature and types of risk and approaches to risk management

(a) Describe and discuss different types of foreign currency risk: [2] **Ch.13**

- (i) translation risk
- (ii) transaction risk
- (iii) economic risk.

(b) Describe and discuss different types of interest rate risk:[1] **Ch.14**

- (i) gap exposure
- (ii) basis risk

2 Causes of exchange rate differences and interest rate fluctuations

(a) Describe the causes of exchange rate fluctuations, including: **Ch.13**

- (i) balance of payments[1]
- (ii) purchasing power parity theory[2]
- (iii) interest rate parity theory[2]
- (iv) four-way equivalence.[2]

(b) Forecast exchange rates using:[2] **Ch.13**

- (i) purchasing power parity
- (ii) interest rate parity.

(c) Describe the causes of interest rate fluctuations, including: [2] **Ch.14**

- (i) structure of interest rates and yield curves
- (ii) expectations theory
- (iii) liquidity preference theory
- (iv) market segmentation.

3 Hedging techniques for foreign currency risk

(a) Discuss and apply traditional methods of foreign currency risk management, including: **Ch.13**

(i) currency of invoice[1]

(ii) netting and matching[2]

(iii) leading and lagging[2]

(iv) forward exchange contracts[2]

(v) money market hedging[2]

(vi) asset and liability management.[1]

(b) Compare and evaluate traditional methods of foreign currency risk management.[2] **Ch.13**

(c) Identify the main types of foreign currency derivates used to hedge foreign currency risk and explain how they are used in hedging.[1] (No numerical questions will be set on this topic)**Ch.13**

4 Hedging techniques for interest rate risk

(a) Discuss and apply traditional methods of interest rate risk management, including: **Ch.14**

(i) matching and smoothing[1]

(ii) asset and liability management[1]

(iii) forward rate agreements.[2]

(b) Identify the main types of interest rate derivates used to hedge interest rate risk and explain how they are used in hedging.[1] (No numerical questions will be set on this topic) **Ch.14**

The superscript numbers in square brackets indicate the intellectual depth at which the subject area could be assessed within the examination. Level 1 (knowledge and comprehension) broadly equates with the Knowledge module, Level 2 (application and analysis) with the Skills module and Level 3 (synthesis and evaluation) to the Professional level. However, lower level skills can continue to be assessed as you progress through each module and level.

The examination

Examination format

The syllabus for Paper F9, Financial Management, has the aim of developing in students the skills expected from a financial manager who is responsible for the finance function of a business. The paper also prepares candidates for more advanced and specialist study in Paper P4, Advanced financial management. All questions are compulsory. The paper will contain both computational and discursive elements. Some questions will adopt a scenario/ case study approach.

Section A of the exam comprises 20 multiple choice questions of 2 marks each. Section B of the exam comprises three 10 mark questions and two 15 mark questions. The two 15 mark questions will come from working capital management, investment appraisal and business finance areas of the syllabus. The section A questions and the other questions in section B can cover any areas of the syllabus. Candidates are provided with a formulae sheet and tables of discount factors and annuity factors.

Number of marks 100. Total time allowed: 3 hours and 15 minutes reading time.

Paper-based examination tips

Spend the fifteen minutes of reading time **reading the paper** and planning your answers. During the reading time you may annotate the question paper but not write in the answer booklet. In particular you should use this time to ensure that you understand the requirements, highlighting key verbs, consider which parts of the syllabus are relevant and plan key calculations.

Divide the time you spend on questions in proportion to the marks on offer. One suggestion for this examination is to allocate 1 and 4/5 minutes to each mark available, so a 10-mark question should be completed in approximately 18 minutes.

Unless you know exactly how to answer the question, spend some time **planning** your answer. Stick to the question and **tailor your answer** to what you are asked. Pay particular attention to the verbs in the question.

Spend the last five minutes reading through your answers and making any additions or corrections.

If you **get completely stuck** with a question, leave space in your answer book and **return to it later**.

If you do not understand what a question is asking, state your assumptions. Even if you do not answer in precisely the way the examiner hoped, you should be given some credit, if your assumptions are reasonable.

You should do everything you can to make things easy for the marker. The marker will find it easier to identify the points you have made if your answers are legible.

Essay questions: Some questions may contain short essay-style requirements. Your essay should have a clear structure. It should contain a brief introduction, a main section and a conclusion. Be concise. It is better to write a little about a lot of different points than a great deal about one or two points.

Computations: It is essential to include all your workings in your answers. Many computational questions require the use of a standard format. Be sure you know these formats thoroughly before the exam and use the layouts that you see in the answers given in this book and in model answers.

Case studies: Most questions will be based on specific scenarios. To write a good case study, first identify the area in which there is a problem, outline the main principles/theories you are going to use to answer the question, and then apply the principles/theories to the case.

Reports, memos and other documents: some questions ask you to present your answer in the form of a report or a memo or other document. So use the correct format – there could be easy marks to gain here.

Study skills and revision guidance

This section aims to give guidance on how to study for your ACCA exams and to give ideas on how to improve your existing study techniques.

Preparing to study

Set your objectives

Before starting to study decide what you want to achieve – the type of pass you wish to obtain. This will decide the level of commitment and time you need to dedicate to your studies.

Devise a study plan

Determine which times of the week you will study.

Split these times into sessions of at least one hour for study of new material. Any shorter periods could be used for revision or practice.

Put the times you plan to study onto a study plan for the weeks from now until the exam and set yourself targets for each period of study – in your sessions make sure you cover the course, course assignments and revision.

If you are studying for more than one paper at a time, try to vary your subjects as this can help you to keep interested and see subjects as part of wider knowledge.

When working through your course, compare your progress with your plan and, if necessary, re-plan your work (perhaps including extra sessions) or, if you are ahead, do some extra revision/practice questions.

Effective studying

Active Reading

You are not expected to learn the text by rote, rather, you must understand what you are reading and be able to use it to pass the exam and develop good practice. A good technique to use is SQ3Rs – Survey, Question, Read, Recall, Review:

(1) **Survey** the chapter – look at the headings and read the introduction, summary and objectives, so as to get an overview of what the chapter deals with.

(2) **Question** – whilst undertaking the survey, ask yourself the questions that you hope the chapter will answer for you.

(3) **Read** through the chapter thoroughly, answering the questions and making sure you can meet the objectives. Attempt the exercises and activities in the text, and work through all the examples.

(4) **Recall** – at the end of each section and at the end of the chapter, try to recall the main ideas of the section/chapter without referring to the text. This is best done after a short break of a couple of minutes after the reading stage.

Review – check that your recall notes are correct. You may also find it helpful to re-read the chapter to try to see the topic(s) it deals with as a whole.

Note-taking

Taking notes is a useful way of learning, but do not simply copy out the text. The notes must:

- be in your own words
- be concise
- cover the key points
- be well-organised
- be modified as you study further chapters in this text or in related ones.

Three ways of taking notes:

Summarise the key points of a chapter.

Make linear notes – a list of headings, divided up with subheadings listing the key points. If you use linear notes, you can use different colours to highlight key points and keep topic areas together. Use plenty of space to make your notes easy to use.

Try a diagrammatic form – the most common of which is a mind-map. To make a mind-map, put the main heading in the centre of the paper and put a circle around it. Then draw short lines radiating from this to the main sub-headings, which again have circles around them. Then continue the process from the sub-headings to sub-sub-headings, advantages, disadvantages, etc.

Highlighting and underlining

You may find it useful to underline or highlight key points in your study text – but do be selective. You may also wish to make notes in the margins.

Revision

The best approach to revision is to revise the course as you work through it. Also try to leave four to six weeks before the exam for final revision. Make sure you cover the whole syllabus and pay special attention to those areas where your knowledge is weak. Here are some recommendations:

Read through the text and your notes again and condense your notes into key phrases. It may help to put key revision points onto index cards to look at when you have a few minutes to spare.

Review any assignments you have completed and look at where you lost marks – put more work into those areas where you were weak.

Practise exam standard questions under timed conditions. If you are short of time, list the points that you would cover in your answer and then read the model answer, but do try to complete at least a few questions under exam conditions.

Also **practise producing answer plans** and comparing them to the model answer.

If you are **stuck** on a topic find somebody (a tutor) to explain it to you.

Read good newspapers and professional journals, especially ACCA's Student Accountant – this can give you an advantage in the exam.

Ensure you know the structure of the exam – how many questions and of what type you will be expected to answer. During your revision attempt all the different styles of questions you may be asked.

Further reading

You can find further reading and technical articles under the student section of ACCA's website.

FORMULAE AND TABLES

Economic order quantity

$$= \sqrt{\frac{2C_oD}{C_H}}$$

Miller-Orr Model

Return point = Lower limit + ($\frac{1}{3}$ × spread)

$$\text{Spread} = 3\left[\frac{\frac{3}{4} \times \text{transaction cost} \times \text{variance of cashflows}}{\text{interest rate}}\right]^{\frac{1}{3}}$$

The Capital Asset Pricing Model

$$E(r_i) = R_f + \beta_i(E(r_m) - R_f)$$

The asset beta formula

$$\beta_a = \left[\frac{V_e}{(V_e + V_d(1-T))}\beta_e\right] + \left[\frac{V_d(1-T)}{V_e + V_d(1-T))}\beta_d\right]$$

The Growth Model

$$P_0 = \frac{D_0(1+g)}{(r_e - g)}$$

Gordon's growth approximation

$$g = br_e$$

The weighted average cost of capital

$$\text{WACC} = \left[\frac{V_e}{V_e + V_d}\right]k_e + \left[\frac{V_d}{V_e + V_d}\right]k_d(1-T)$$

The Fisher formula

$$(1+i) = (1+r)(1+h)$$

Purchasing power parity and interest rate parity

$$S_1 = S_0 \text{x} \frac{(1+h_c)}{(1+h_b)} \qquad F_0 = S_0 \text{x} \frac{(1+i_c)}{(1+i_b)}$$

Present value table

Present value of 1, i.e. $(1 + r)^{-n}$

Where r = discount rate

n = number of periods until payment

Periods (n)	Discount rate (r)									
	1%	2%	3%	4%	5%	6%	7%	8%	9%	10%
1	0.990	0.980	0.971	0.962	0.952	0.943	0.935	0.926	0.917	0.909
2	0.980	0.961	0.943	0.925	0.907	0.890	0.873	0.857	0.842	0.826
3	0.971	0.942	0.915	0.889	0.864	0.840	0.816	0.794	0.772	0.751
4	0.961	0.924	0.888	0.855	0.823	0.792	0.763	0.735	0.708	0.683
5	0.951	0.906	0.863	0.822	0.784	0.747	0.713	0.681	0.650	0.621
6	0.942	0.888	0.837	0.790	0.746	0.705	0.666	0.630	0.596	0.564
7	0.933	0.871	0.813	0.760	0.711	0.665	0.623	0.583	0.547	0.513
8	0.923	0.853	0.789	0.731	0.677	0.627	0.582	0.540	0.502	0.467
9	0.914	0.837	0.766	0.703	0.645	0.592	0.544	0.500	0.460	0.424
10	0.905	0.820	0.744	0.676	0.614	0.558	0.508	0.463	0.422	0.386
11	0.896	0.804	0.722	0.650	0.585	0.527	0.475	0.429	0.388	0.350
12	0.887	0.788	0.701	0.625	0.557	0.497	0.444	0.397	0.356	0.319
13	0.879	0.773	0.681	0.601	0.530	0.469	0.415	0.368	0.326	0.290
14	0.870	0.758	0.661	0.577	0.505	0.442	0.388	0.340	0.299	0.263
15	0.861	0.743	0.642	0.555	0.481	0.417	0.362	0.315	0.275	0.239

Periods (n)	Discount rate (r)									
	11%	12%	13%	14%	15%	16%	17%	18%	19%	20%
1	0.901	0.893	0.885	0.877	0.870	0.862	0.855	0.847	0.840	0.833
2	0.812	0.797	0.783	0.769	0.756	0.743	0.731	0.718	0.706	0.694
3	0.731	0.712	0.693	0.675	0.658	0.641	0.624	0.609	0.593	0.579
4	0.659	0.636	0.613	0.592	0.572	0.552	0.534	0.516	0.499	0.482
5	0.593	0.567	0.543	0.519	0.497	0.476	0.456	0.437	0.419	0.402
6	0.535	0.507	0.480	0.456	0.432	0.410	0.390	0.370	0.352	0.335
7	0.482	0.452	0.425	0.400	0.376	0.354	0.333	0.314	0.296	0.279
8	0.434	0.404	0.376	0.351	0.327	0.305	0.285	0.266	0.249	0.233
9	0.391	0.361	0.333	0.308	0.284	0.263	0.243	0.225	0.209	0.194
10	0.352	0.322	0.295	0.270	0.247	0.227	0.208	0.191	0.176	0.162
11	0.317	0.287	0.261	0.237	0.215	0.195	0.178	0.162	0.148	0.135
12	0.286	0.257	0.231	0.208	0.187	0.168	0.152	0.137	0.124	0.112
13	0.258	0.229	0.204	0.182	0.163	0.145	0.130	0.116	0.104	0.093
14	0.232	0.205	0.181	0.160	0.141	0.125	0.111	0.099	0.088	0.078
15	0.209	0.183	0.160	0.140	0.123	0.108	0.095	0.084	0.074	0.065

Annuity table

Present value of an annuity of 1, i.e. $\frac{1-(1+r)^{-n}}{r}$

Where r = discount rate

n = number of periods

Periods (n)	Discount rate (r) 1%	2%	3%	4%	5%	6%	7%	8%	9%	10%
1	0.990	0.980	0.971	0.962	0.952	0.943	0.935	0.926	0.917	0.909
2	1.970	1.942	1.913	1.886	1.859	1.833	1.808	1.783	1.759	1.736
3	2.941	2.884	2.829	2.775	2.723	2.673	2.624	2.577	2.531	2.487
4	3.902	3.808	3.717	3.630	3.546	3.465	3.387	3.312	3.240	3.170
5	4.853	4.713	4.580	4.452	4.329	4.212	4.100	3.993	3.890	3.791
6	5.795	5.601	5.417	5.242	5.076	4.917	4.767	4.623	4.486	4.355
7	6.728	6.472	6.230	6.002	5.786	5.582	5.389	5.206	5.033	4.868
8	7.652	7.325	7.020	6.733	6.463	6.210	5.971	5.747	5.535	5.335
9	8.566	8.162	7.786	7.435	7.108	6.802	6.515	6.247	5.995	5.759
10	9.471	8.983	8.530	8.111	7.722	7.360	7.024	6.710	6.418	6.145
11	10.368	9.787	9.253	8.760	8.306	7.887	7.499	7.139	6.805	6.495
12	11.255	10.575	9.954	9.385	8.863	8.384	7.943	7.536	7.161	6.814
13	12.134	11.348	10.635	9.986	9.394	8.853	8.358	7.904	7.487	7.103
14	13.004	12.106	11.296	10.563	9.899	9.295	8.745	8.244	7.786	7.367
15	13.865	12.849	11.938	11.118	10.380	9.712	9.108	8.559	8.061	7.606

Periods (n)	Discount rate (r) 11%	12%	13%	14%	15%	16%	17%	18%	19%	20%
1	0.901	0.893	0.885	0.877	0.870	0.862	0.855	0.847	0.840	0.833
2	1.713	1.690	1.668	1.647	1.626	1.605	1.585	1.566	1.547	1.528
3	2.444	2.402	2.361	2.322	2.283	2.246	2.210	2.174	2.140	2.106
4	3.102	3.037	2.974	2.914	2.855	2.798	2.743	2.690	2.639	2.589
5	3.696	3.605	3.517	3.433	3.352	3.274	3.199	3.127	3.058	2.991
6	4.231	4.111	3.998	3.889	3.784	3.685	3.589	3.498	3.410	3.326
7	4.712	4.564	4.423	4.288	4.160	4.039	3.922	3.812	3.706	3.605
8	5.146	4.968	4.799	4.639	4.487	4.344	4.207	4.078	3.954	3.837
9	5.537	5.328	5.132	4.946	4.772	4.607	4.451	4.303	4.163	4.031
10	5.889	5.650	5.426	5.216	5.019	4.833	4.659	4.494	4.339	4.192
11	6.207	5.938	5.687	5.453	5.234	5.029	4.836	4.656	4.486	4.327
12	6.492	6.194	5.918	5.660	5.421	5.197	4.988	4.793	4.611	4.439
13	6.750	6.424	6.122	5.842	5.583	5.342	5.118	4.910	4.715	4.533
14	6.982	6.628	6.302	6.002	5.724	5.468	5.229	5.008	4.802	4.611
15	7.191	6.811	6.462	6.142	5.847	5.575	5.324	5.092	4.876	4.675

chapter

1

The financial management function

Chapter learning objectives

Upon completion of this chapter you will be able to:

- explain the nature and purpose of financial management
- distinguish between financial management and financial and management accounting
- discuss the relationship between financial objectives, corporate objectives and corporate strategy
- identify and describe a variety of financial objectives, including:
  - shareholder wealth maximisation
  - profit maximisation
  - earnings per share growth
- identify stakeholders, their objectives and possible conflicts
- discuss the possible conflict between stakeholder objectives
- discuss the role of management in meeting stakeholder objectives, including the use of agency theory
- explain ways to encourage the achievement of stakeholder objectives, including:
  - managerial reward schemes
  - regulatory requirements
- discuss the impact of not-for-profit status on financial and other objectives
- discuss the nature and importance of Value for Money as an objective in not-for-profit organisations
- discuss ways of measuring the achievement of objectives in not-for-profit organisations.

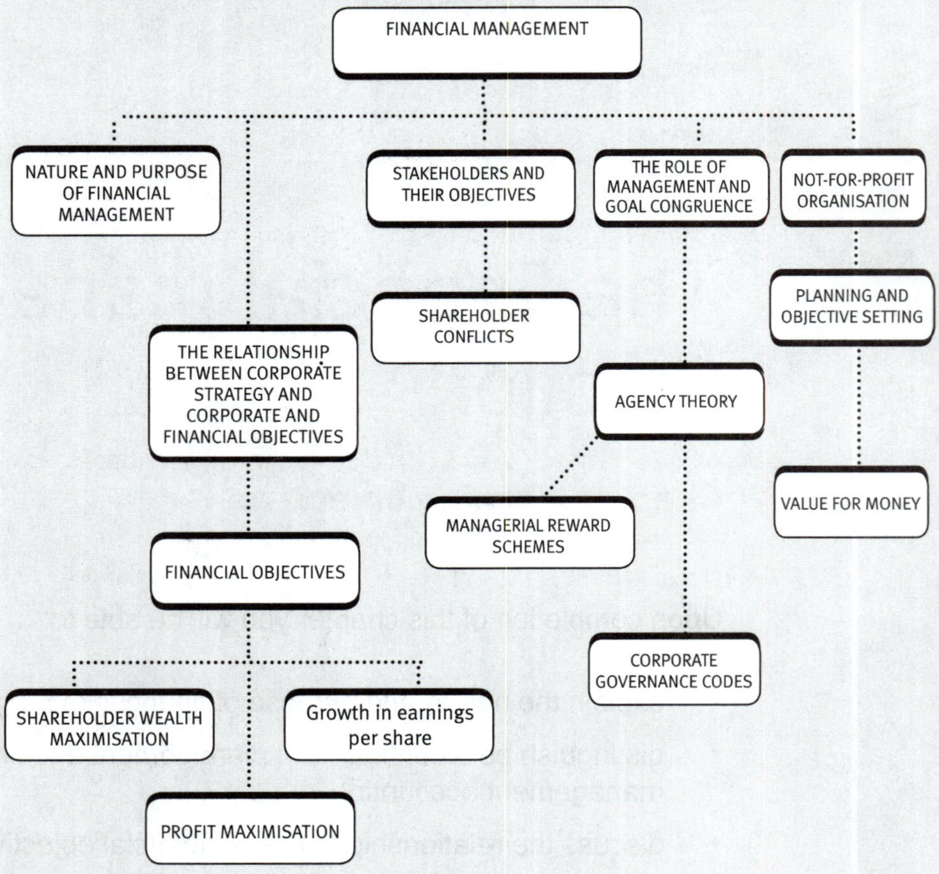

1 The nature and purpose of financial management

Financial management is concerned with the efficient acquisition and deployment of both short- and long-term financial resources, to ensure the objectives of the enterprise are achieved.

Decisions must be taken in three key areas:

- investment – both long-term investment in non-current assets and short-term investment in working capital;
- finance – from what sources should funds be raised?
- dividends – how should cash funds be allocated to shareholders and how will the value of the business be affected by this?

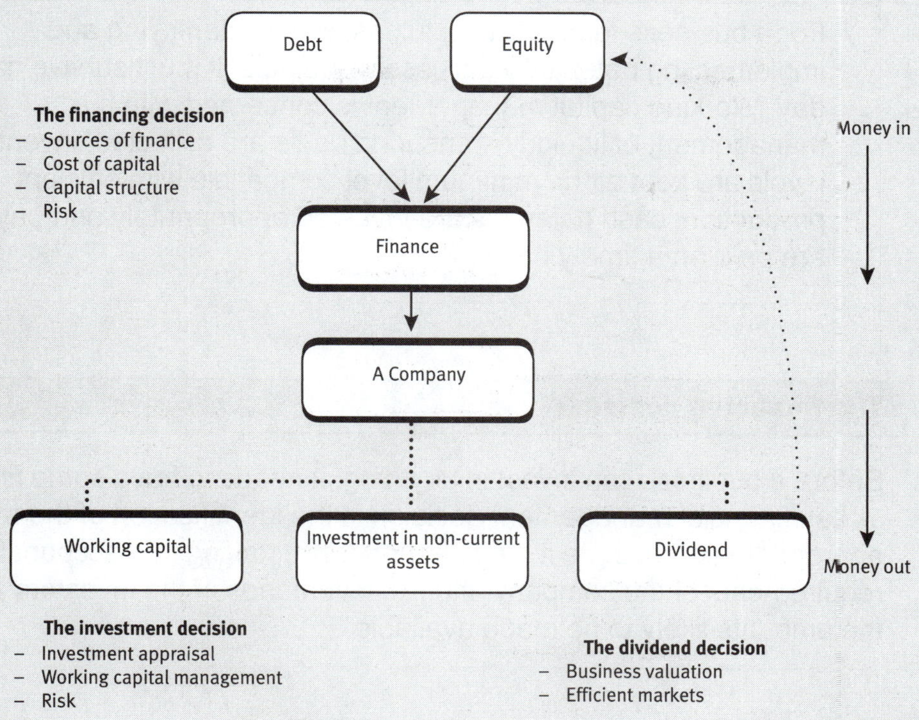

An understanding of these three key areas is fundamental for the examination.

In taking these decisions, the financial manager will need to take account of:

- the organisation's commercial and financial objectives
- the broader economic environment in which the business operates
- the potential risks associated with the decision and methods of managing that risk.

The F9 syllabus covers all these key aspects of financial management.

The investment decision

To operate, all business will need finance and part of the financial manager's role is to ensure this finance is used efficiently and effectively to ensure the organisation's objectives are achieved. This can be further broken down into two elements:

- Investment appraisal considers the long-term plans of the business and identifies the right projects to adopt to ensure financial objectives are met. The projects undertaken will nearly always involve the purchase of non-current assets at the start of the process.

- For a business to be successful, as well as identifying and implementing potentially successful projects, it must survive day to day. Working capital management is concerned with the management of liquidity – ensuring debts are collected, inventory levels are kept at the minimum level compatible with efficient production, cash balances are invested appropriately and payables are paid on a timely basis.

The financing decision

Before a business can invest in anything, it needs to have some finance. A key financial management decision is the identification of the most appropriate sources (be it long or short term), taking into account the requirements of the company, the likely demands of the investors and the amounts likely to be made available.

The dividend decision

Having invested wisely, a business will hopefully be profitable and generate cash. The final key decision for the financial manager is whether to return any of that cash to the owners of the business (in the form of dividends) and if so, how much.

The alternative is to retain some of the cash in the business where it can be invested again to earn further returns. This decision is therefore closely linked to the financing decision.

The decision on the level of dividends to be paid can affect the value of the business as a whole as well the ability of the business to raise further finance in the future.

Financial management should be distinguished from other important financial roles:

- management accounting – concerned with providing information for the more day to day functions of control and decision making
- financial accounting – concerned with providing information about the historical results of past plans and decisions.

Financial roles

Management accounting and financial management are both concerned with the use of resources to achieve a given target. Much of the information used and reported is common to both functions.

The main difference is in the time scales. **Financial management** is concerned with the **long-term raising of finance** and the **allocation and control of resources**; it involves targets, or objectives, that are generally long-term by nature, whilst management accounting usually operates within a 12-month time horizon.

Management accounting is concerned with **providing information** for the more **day-to-day** functions of **control and decision making**. This will involve budgeting, cost accounting, variance analysis, and evaluation of alternative uses of short-term resources.

Financial accounting is not directly involved in the day-to-day planning, control and decision making of an organisation. Rather, it is concerned with **providing information** about the **historical results** of past plans and decisions. Its purpose is to keep the owners (shareholders) and other interested parties informed of the overall financial position of the business, and it will not be concerned with the detailed information used internally by management accountants and financial managers.

The following table illustrates the distinction between some of the tasks carried out by each of these financial roles:

	Management accounting	**Financial management**	**Financial accounting**
Review of overtime spending	√		
Depreciation of non-current assets			√
Establishing dividend policy		√	
Evaluating proposed expansion plans		√	
Apportioning overheads to cost units	√		
Identifying accruals and prepayments			√

2 The relationship between corporate strategy and corporate and financial objectives

Objectives/targets define **what** the organisation is trying to achieve. Strategy considers **how** to go about it.

Objectives and strategy

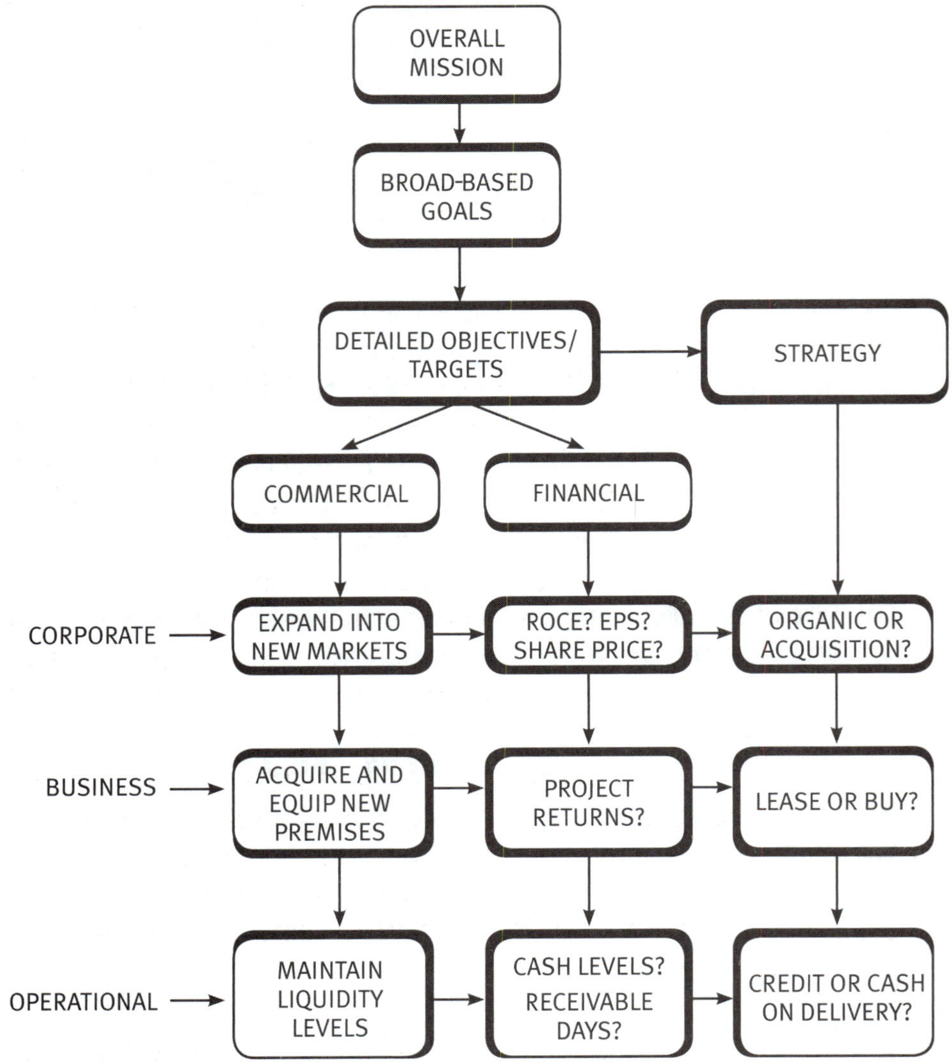

The diagram above is key to understanding how financial management fits into overall business strategy

The business should recognise its overriding purpose or mission and develop broad-based goals for the business to pursue to ensure it fulfils that purpose.

Each goal is then further broken down into detailed commercial and financial objectives, each of which should have appropriate identifiable, measurable targets so that progress towards them can be monitored.

The distinction between 'commercial' and 'financial' objectives is to emphasise that not all objectives can be expressed in financial terms and that some objectives derive from commercial marketplace considerations

These are then cascaded down throughout the organisation through the setting of targets so that all parts of the business are working to achieve the same overall goal. For example, the receivables days target of the credit control department should be linked to the cash needs of the investment projects, and the projects should be selected to achieve the overall corporate aim such as improving the share price. This in turn then satisfies the shareholders by increasing their wealth.

Once objectives and targets are set, the enterprise must then work to achieve them by developing and implementing appropriate strategies. Strategies will be developed at all levels of the business.

- Corporate strategy concerns the decisions made by senior management about matters such as the particular business the company is in, whether new markets should be entered or whether to withdraw from current markets. Such decisions can often have important financial implications. If, for example, a decision is taken to enter a new market, an existing company in that market could be bought, or a new company be started from scratch.
- Business strategy concerns the decisions to be made by the separate strategic business units within the group. Each unit will try to maximise its competitive position within its chosen market. This may involve for example choosing whether to compete on quality or cost.
- Operational strategy concerns how the different functional areas within a strategic business unit plan their operations to satisfy the corporate and business strategies being followed. We are, of course, most interested in the decisions facing the finance function. These day-to-day decisions include all aspects of working capital management.

Almost all strategies developed by the business will have financial implications and the financial manager has a key role to play in helping business strategies succeed.

Additional question – Objectives and strategy

The following list contains some commercial objectives/targets, some financial objectives/targets and some strategies, all at different levels of the business. Identify which is which.

- Implement a Just-In-Time (JIT) inventory system.
- Increase earnings per share (EPS) by 5% on prior year.
- Acquire a rival in a share-for-share purchase.
- Buy four new cutting machines for $250,000 each.
- Achieve returns of 15% on new manufacturing investment.
- Improve the ratio of current assets to current liabilities from 1.7 to 1.85.
- Reduce unsold inventory items by 12%.
- Update manufacturing capacity to incorporate new technology.
- Improve brand awareness within the UK.

	Commercial objectives /targets	**Financial objectives /targets**	**Strategies**
Corporate level			
Business level			
Operational level			

The answer to this question can be found after the chapter summary diagram at the end of this chapter.

3 Financial objectives

Shareholder wealth maximisation

Shareholder wealth maximisation is a fundamental principle of financial management. You should seek to understand the different aspects of the syllabus (e.g. finance, dividend policy, investment appraisal) within this unifying theme.

Many other objectives are also suggested for companies including:

- profit maximisation
- growth
- market share
- social responsibilities

Financial objectives

Shareholder wealth maximisation

If strategy is developed in response to the need to achieve objectives, it is obviously important to be clear about what those objectives are.

Most companies are owned by shareholders and originally set up to make money for those shareholders. The primary objective of most companies is thus to maximise shareholder wealth. (This could involve increasing the share price and/or dividend payout.)

Profit maximisation

In financial management we assume that the objective of the business is to maximise shareholder wealth. This is not necessarily the same as maximising profit.

Firms often find that share prices bear little relationship to reported profit figures (e.g. biotechnology companies and other 'new economy' ventures).

There are a number of potential problems with adopting an objective of profit maximisation:

- Long-run versus short-run issues: In any business it is possible to boost short-term profits at the expense of long-term profits. For example discretionary spending on training, advertising, repairs and research and development (R&D) may be cut. This will improve reported profits in the short-term but damage the long-term prospects of the business. The stock exchange will normally see through such a tactic and share prices will fall.

- Quality (risk) of earnings: A business may increase its reported profits by taking a high level of risk. However the risk may endanger the returns available to shareholders. The stock exchange will then generally regard these earnings as being of a poor quality and the more risk-averse shareholders may sell. Once again the share price could fall.
- Cash: Accounting profits are just a paper figure. Dividends are paid with cash. Investors will therefore consider cash flow as well as profit.

Earnings per share (EPS) growth

A widely used measure of corporate success is EPS as it provides a measure of return to equity. EPS growth is therefore a commonly pursued objective.

However it is a measure of profitability, not wealth generation, and it is therefore open to the same criticisms as profit maximisation above.

The disadvantage of EPS is that it does not represent income of the shareholder. Rather, it represents that investor's share of the income generated by the company according to an accounting formula.

Whilst there is obviously a correlation between earnings and the wealth received by individual shareholders, they are not the same.

Maximising and satisficing

A distinction must be made between maximising and satisficing:

- maximising – seeking the maximum level of returns, even though this might involve exposure to risk and much higher management workloads.
- satisficing – finding a merely adequate outcome, holding returns at a satisfactory level, avoiding risky ventures and reducing workloads.

Within a company, management might seek to maximise the return to some groups (e.g. shareholders) and satisfy the requirements of other groups (e.g. employees). The discussion about objectives is really about which group's returns management is trying to maximise.

4 Stakeholder objectives and conflicts

A stakeholder group is one with a vested interest in the company.

Typical stakeholders for an organisation would include:

Internal

- company employees
- company managers/directors

Connected

- equity investors (ordinary shareholders)
- customers
- suppliers
- finance providers (debt holders / bankers)
- competitors

External

- the government
- the community at large
- pressure groups
- regulators.

Many argue that managers should balance the needs and objectives of all stakeholders.

Conflict between and within groups of stakeholders and the need for management to balance the various interests is a key issue.

The stakeholder view

We've already stated that the primary objective of a company is to maximise the wealth of shareholders. However, modern organisations vary in type, and talk of pursuing single objectives is perhaps a little simplistic. Many argue that a business must adopt the **stakeholder view**, which involves balancing the competing claims of a wide range of stakeholders, and taking account of broader economic and social responsibilities.

Professor Charles Handy is a prominent advocate of this view, arguing that maximisation of shareholder wealth, while important, cannot be the single overall objective of organisations, and account must be taken of broader economic and social responsibilities. Increasing globalisation, and the fact that some multinational companies have revenue in excess of the incomes of small countries, puts these responsibilities sharply into focus. Typical stakeholders for an organisation might include the following.

- Equity investors (ordinary shareholders) – within any economic system, the equity investors provide the risk finance. There is a very strong argument for maximising the wealth of equity investors. In order to attract funds, the company has to compete with risk-free investment opportunities, e.g. government securities. The attraction is the accrual of any surplus to the equity investors. In effect, this is the risk premium which is essential for the allocation of resources to relatively risky investments in companies.
- Company managers/directors – such senior employees are in an ideal position to follow their own aims at the expense of other stakeholders. Their goals will be both long-term (defending against takeovers, sales maximisation) and short-term (profit margins leading to increased bonuses).
- Company employees – obviously, many trade unionists would like to see their members as the residual beneficiaries of any surplus the company creates. Certainly, there is no measurement problem: returns = wages or salaries. However, maximising the returns to employees does assume that risk finance can be raised purely on the basis of satisficing, i.e. providing no more than an adequate return to shareholders.
- Customers – satisfaction of customer needs will be achieved through the provision of value-for-money products and services. There remains, of course, the requirement for organisations to accurately identify precisely what those needs are.

- Suppliers – suppliers to the organisation will have short-term goals such as prompt payment terms alongside long-term requirements including contracts and regular business. The importance of the needs of suppliers will depend upon both their relative size and the number of suppliers.
- Finance providers – providers of finance (banks, loan creditors) will primarily be interested in the ability of the organisation to repay the finance including interest. As a result it will be the organisation's ability to generate cash both long- and short-term that will be the basis of interest to these providers.
- The government – the government will have political and financial interests in the organisation. Politically they will wish to increase exports and decrease imports whilst monitoring companies via the Competition and Markets Authority (formerly the Office of Fair Trading). Financially they require long-term profits to maximise taxation income. Equally importantly the government via its own agencies or via the legal system will seek to ensure that organisations observe health and safety, planning and minimum wage legislation. Also, on behalf of the community at large, the government must consider modifying the behaviour of both individuals and organisations for environmental/health reasons, e.g. banning smoking in certain public places and restricting the advertising of tobacco companies.
- The community at large – this is a particularly important group for public sector enterprises and will have, in particular, environmental expectations from private sector or regulated organisations, such as organic foods, safe trains and cleaner petrol. For organisations there are problems of measurement – what are returns to the community at large? The goals of the community will be broad but will include such aspects as legal and social responsibilities, pollution control and employee welfare.

Critics of the stakeholder view argue that while the interests of these other groups must obviously be balanced and managed, only shareholders have a relationship with organisations which is one of risk and return, and so practically the long-term financial objective of a private sector organisation is to maximise the wealth of equity investors. The debate will continue, but there seems to be an acceptance that organisations need to have a greater awareness of the societies in which they operate and this is reflected in the later debate on ethics.

Additional question – Stakeholder conflicts

Suggest the potential conflicts in objectives which could arise between the following groups of stakeholders in a company.

Stakeholders			Potential conflict
Employees	⇔	Shareholders	
Customers	⇔	Community at large	
Shareholders	⇔	Finance providers	
Customers	⇔	Shareholders/ managers	
Government	⇔	Shareholders	
Shareholders	⇔	Managers	

The answer to this question can be found after the chapter summary diagram at the end of this chapter.

5 The role of management and goal congruence

Agency theory

Agency theory is often used to describe the relationships between the various interested parties in a firm and can help to explain the various duties and conflicts that occur:

Agency relationships occur when one party, **the principal**, employs another party, **the agent**, to perform a task on their behalf. In particular, directors (agents) act on behalf of shareholders (principals).

How to reduce the problems caused by agency relationships

Finding ways to reduce the problems of the agency relationship and ensure that managers take decisions which are consistent with the objectives of shareholders is a key issue.

Agency theory

Agency theory can help to explain the actions of the various interest groups in the corporate governance debate.

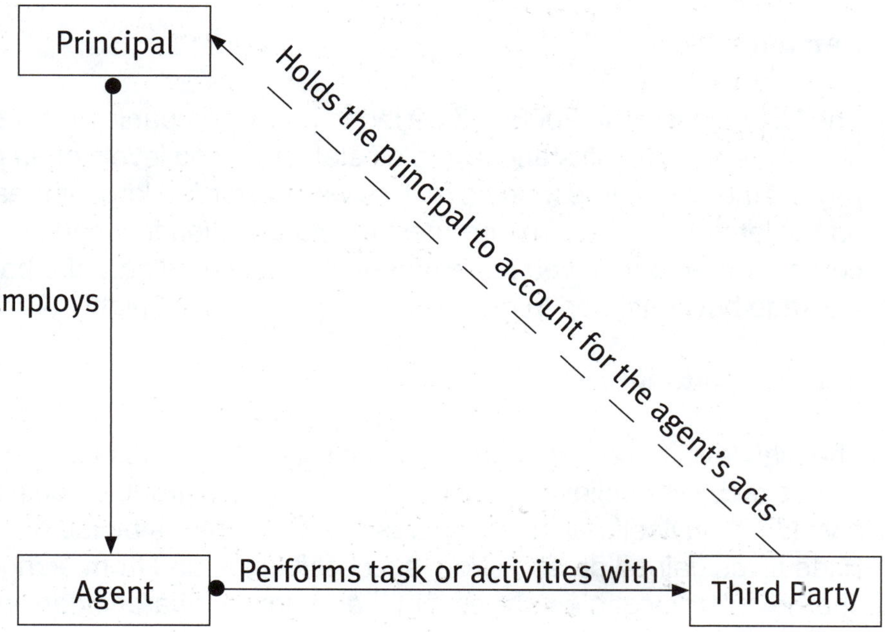

For example, managers can be seen as the agents of shareholders, employees as the agents of managers, managers and shareholders as the agents of long- and short-term creditors, etc. In most of these principal-agent relationships, conflicts of interest will exist.

The problem lies in the fact that once the agent has been appointed he is able to act in his own selfish interests rather than pursuing the objectives of the principal.

The divorce of ownership and control

By far the most important conflict of those mentioned above is that between the interests of shareholders who own the company and the directors/managers who run it.

- Shareholders are reliant upon the management of the company to understand and pursue the objectives set for them.
- Although shareholders can intervene via resolutions at general meeting, the managers are usually left alone on a day-to-day basis.
- Management are uniquely placed to make decisions to maximise their own wealth or happiness rather than the wealth of the shareholders.

During the past 20 years or so, and particularly following the Maxwell scandal and others, attention has focused increasingly on the activities of directors. There has been an allegation that directors have been making corporate decisions in their own interests rather than for the benefit of the company as a whole and the shareholders in particular. Examples include the following:

Remuneration

The UK recession in 2008 – 2009 led to many companies reporting sharply reduced profits and laying off staff or cutting levels of employee pay. At the same time many directors were awarded large increases in pay or large bonuses. The greatest media attention focused on the companies who received government assistance as part of a bail-out package but continued to reward their top executives highly.

Empire building

The high level of corporate takeover activity in the 1980s led to many chief executives believing that building as large a group as possible was a valid aim in itself, an objective described as empire building. Executives gained prestige from successful bids and from being in charge of large conglomerates, but the returns to shareholders were often disappointing.

Creative accounting

The directors are responsible for selecting the accounting policies to be used by their company, subject to accounting standards and the opinion of the auditors. Despite the constraints upon them, the directors are still free to use creative accounting techniques to flatter their published accounts and perhaps artificially boost the share price. Examples of such techniques are: capitalising expenses on the balance sheet (e.g. development expenditure, advertising expenditure), not depreciating non-current assets, maximising the value of intangibles on the balance sheet (e.g. putting a value to brands), recognising revenue on long-term contracts at the earliest possible time, and other forms of off-balance-sheet financing (see below).

Those charged with setting accounting standards have a continuing work programme that aims to cut out creative accounting practices as much as is practically possible.

Off-balance-sheet finance refers to ways of financing assets where the method of funding is not recorded on the balance sheet.

One example is the use of leased, rather than purchased, assets. In the UK, before SSAP 21 a lessee's obligation to the lessor was omitted from the lessee's balance sheet and he could therefore report a lower gearing ratio and raise new funds at lower interest rates. SSAP 21 required that assets acquired under finance leases must be capitalised on the lessee's balance sheet together with the corresponding obligation to the lessor. The introduction of FRS 5 aimed to restrict off-balance-sheet finance still further, for example by requiring quasi subsidiaries to be consolidated into the group accounts. The collapse of Enron in the US in late 2001 has put the spotlight on the various forms of off-balance-sheet finance used, and further scrutiny and regulation is inevitable.

Takeover bids

Boards of directors often spend considerable amounts of time and money attempting to defend their companies against takeover bids, even when it appears that the takeover would be in the best interests of the target company's shareholders. These directors are accused of trying to protect their own jobs, fearing that they will be retired if their company is taken over. Directors of public companies must now comply with the City Code on Takeovers and Mergers during a bid period.

Unethical activities

Unethical activities might not be prohibited by the Companies Acts or stock exchange regulations, but are believed by many to be undesirable to society as a whole. Examples are trading with countries ruled by dictatorships, testing products on animals, emitting pollution or carrying out espionage against competitors. The importance of **good business ethics** and **corporate social responsibility** (CSR) has been recognised in recent years and it is hoped that further progress is being made in the new millennium.

Although directors are supposed to be acting in the interests of the shareholders of their company, they stand accused in recent years of having made decisions on the basis of their own self-interest.

Managerial reward schemes

One way to help ensure that managers take decisions which are consistent with the objectives of shareholders is to introduce carefully designed remuneration packages. The schemes should:

- be clearly defined, impossible to manipulate and easy to monitor
- link rewards to changes in shareholder wealth
- match managers' time horizons to shareholders' time horizons
- encourage managers to adopt the same attitudes to risk as shareholders.

Common types of reward schemes include:

- remuneration linked to:
  - minimum profit levels
  - economic value added (EVA)
  - revenue growth
- executive share option schemes (ESOP).

Managerial reward schemes

Types of remuneration schemes include:

Remuneration linked to minimum profit levels

This scheme would be easy to set up and monitor.

Disadvantages are that the scheme may lead to managers taking decisions that would result in profits being earned in the short-term at the expense of long-term profitability. It could also lead to managers under-achieving, i.e. relaxing as soon as the minimum is achieved. The scheme might also tempt managers to use creative accounting to boost the profit figure.

Remuneration linked to economic value added (EVA)

EVA is a measure of the increase in the value of shareholder wealth in the period. Schemes such as these are therefore designed to more closely align the interests of the employee and the shareholder.

A potential disadvantage is that calculating the bonus may be complex.

Remuneration linked to revenue growth

Growth of the business and higher production levels can lead to economies of scale which in turn can help the business compete more successfully on price.

However, revenue growth could be achieved at the expense of profitability, e.g. by reducing selling prices or by selecting high revenue product lines which may not necessarily be the most profitable. Maximising revenue is therefore unlikely to maximise shareholder wealth.

An executive share option scheme (ESOP)

This scheme has the advantage that it will encourage managers to maximise the value of the shares of the company, i.e. the wealth of the shareholders. When an executive is awarded share options, the theory is that it is in their interests for the share price to rise, so they will do whatever possible to improve the share price. Their interests will be best served by working towards a goal that is also in the interests of the shareholders.

Such schemes are normally set up over a relatively long period thereby encouraging managers to make decisions to invest in positive return projects which should result in an increase in the price of the company shares. However, efficient managers may be penalised at times when share prices in general are falling.

There are several criticisms of ESOPs.

- When directors exercise their share options, they tend to sell the shares almost immediately to cash in on their profit. Unless they are awarded more share options, their interest in the share price therefore ends when the option exercise date has passed.
- If the share price falls when options have been awarded, and the options go 'underwater' and have no value, they cannot act as an incentive.
- If a company issues large quantities of share options, there could be some risk of excessive dilution of the equity interests of the existing shareholders. As a result, it has been suggested that companies should recognise the cost of share options to their shareholders, by making some form of charge for options in the statement of profit or loss.
- Directors may distort reported profits (creative accounting) to protect the share price and the value of their share options.

Additional question – Managerial reward schemes

Gretsch Inc, a listed company, has developed a highly successful new product and is thus growing rapidly. However, with this growth the firm is experiencing cash flow problems. Managers are currently awarded bonuses if there is growth in reported earnings per share (EPS).

Comment on the current remuneration scheme.

The answer to this question can be found after the chapter summary diagram at the end of this chapter.

Corporate governance codes

The director/shareholder conflict has also been addressed by the requirements of a number of corporate governance codes. The following key areas relate to this conflict.

- Non-executive directors (NEDs)
  - important presence on the board
  - must give obligation to spend sufficient time with the company
  - should be independent.
- Executive directors
  - separation of chairman and chief executive officer (CEO)
  - submit for re-election
  - clear disclosure of financial rewards
  - outnumbered by the NEDs.
- Remuneration committees.
- Nomination committees.
- Annual general meeting (AGM).

Corporate governance codes

After a number of high-profile firms collapsed, concerns over how the companies had been run led to a determination to ensure good corporate governance in future. A number of committees met and produced reports containing recommendations on how to improve corporate governance procedures. One of the areas addressed was the conflict between director and shareholder interests. Below is a selection of the current requirements:

NEDs

- At least half of the members of the board, excluding the chairman, should be independent NEDs. These are directors who do not take part in the running of the business. They attend board meetings, provide advice, listen to what is said and are generally meant to act as a control on the actions of the executive directors. Independence means they are free of any business or other relationship, which could materially interfere with the exercise of their independent judgement. Boards should disclose in the annual report which of the NEDs are considered to be independent.
- NEDs should get extra fees for chairing company committees but should not hold share options in their company. There was concern that allowing NEDs to hold share options in a company could encourage corporate excess or wrongdoing.
- One of the independent NEDs should be appointed a senior independent NED who would act as a champion for the interests of shareholders.
- Prospective NEDs should conduct due diligence before accepting the role. They should satisfy themselves that they have the knowledge, skills, experience and time to make a positive contribution to the company board.
- On appointment, the NEDs would also undertake that they have the time to meet their obligations. Company nomination committees would examine their performance, and make an assessment of whether they were devoting enough time to their duties.

Executive directors

- The chairman and the CEO roles should be separate, and a CEO should not become chairman of the same company.
- The chairman should be independent at the time of his appointment. Note that the effect of this, combined with the point about independent NEDs making up at least half of the board, will be to place independent NEDs in a majority on the board.
- All directors should submit themselves for re-election at least every three years.
- There should be clear disclosure of directors' total emoluments and those of the chairman and highest-paid UK director.
- Boards should set as their objective the reduction of directors' contract periods to one year or less.

Remuneration committees

- Executive directors' pay should be subject to the recommendations of a remuneration committee made up wholly of independent NEDs.
- Remuneration committees should objectively determine executive remuneration and individual packages for each executive director.
- The broad framework and cost of remuneration should be a matter for the board on the advice of the remuneration committee.

Nomination committees

- This committee will consist of NEDs with the aim of bringing an independent view to the selection and recruitment of both executive directors and NEDs.
- It will meet when required and effectively 'headhunt' directors. It will be a high-profile committee so as to demonstrate to stakeholders that a reasonable degree of objectivity exists in the selection process.

AGM

- Companies whose AGMs are well attended should consider providing a business presentation, with a question and answer session.
- Shareholders should be able to vote separately on each substantially separate issue; and the practice of 'bundling' unrelated proposals in a single resolution should cease.

Stock exchange listing requirements and other regulations

Although adherence to the principles of the corporate governance codes is voluntary, they are often referred to in the listing requirements of stock exchanges.

Other regulations

Stock exchange listing requirements

The UK Corporate Governance Code is attached to the UK Listing Rules so that listed companies in the UK are under pressure to comply. Under an amendment to the UK Listing Rules, listed companies must:

- disclose how they have applied the principles and complied with the Code's provisions in their annual report and accounts
- state and explain any deviation from the recommended best practice.

Similarly some aspects of governance have moved into the statute books.

The Directors' Remuneration Report Regulations 2002 in the UK amends the Companies Act 2006 and apply to quoted companies. The main provisions of the Regulations are as follows:

- a directors' remuneration report must be produced each year containing details of:
  - the remuneration for the year of each individual director
  - 'golden handshakes'
  - payments into a pension scheme for a director
  - details of share option arrangements
- the report should be submitted to the shareholders for approval by vote at the AGM.

6 Measuring achievement of corporate objectives

It is necessary for managers, shareholders and other stakeholders to have ways of measuring the progress of the company towards its objectives. This is commonly done via ratio analysis.

Ratio analysis compares and quantifies relationships between financial variables.

Ratio analysis can be grouped into four main categories:

- Profitability and return
- Debt and gearing
- Liquidity
- Investor

The specific ratios covered in the F9 syllabus will be looked at in detail in chapter 19 although some of them may already be familiar to you from previous papers.

7 Objective setting in not for profit organisations

The primary objective of not for profit organisations (NFPs or NPOs) is not to make money but to benefit prescribed groups of people.

As with any organisation, NFPs will use a mixture of financial and non-financial objectives.

However, with NFPs the non-financial objectives are often more important and more complex because of the following.

- Most key objectives are very difficult to quantify, especially in financial terms, e.g. quality of care given to patients in a hospital.
- Multiple and conflicting objectives are more common in NFPs, e.g. quality of patient care versus number of patients treated.

Objective setting in NFPs

A number of factors influence the way in which management objectives are determined in NFPs, which distinguish them from commercial businesses:

- wide range of stakeholders
- high level of interest from stakeholder groups
- significant degree of involvement from funding bodies and sponsors
- little or no financial input from the ultimate recipients of the service
- funding often provided as a series of advances rather than as a lump sum
- projects typically have a longer-term planning horizon
- may be subject to government influence/government macroeconomic policy.

For a company listed on the stock market we can take the maximisation of shareholder wealth as a working objective and know that the achievement of this objective can be monitored with reference to share price and dividend payments.

For an NFP the situation is more complex. There are two questions to be answered:

- in whose interests is it run?
- what are the objectives of the interested parties?

Many such organisations are run in the interests of society as a whole and therefore we should seek to attain the position where the gap between the benefits they provide to society and the costs of their operation is the widest (in positive terms).

The cost is relatively easily measured in accounting terms. However, many of the benefits are intangible. For example, the benefits of such bodies as the National Health Service (NHS) or local education authorities (LEAs) are almost impossible to quantify.

Because of the problem of quantifying the non-monetary objectives of such organisations most public bodies operate under objectives determined by the government (and hence ultimately by the electorate).

Value for money (VFM) and the 3 Es

VFM can be defined as 'achieving the desired level and quality of service at the most economical cost'.

VFM

Because a significant number of NFPs are funded from the public purse, the lack of clear financial performance measures has been seen as a particular problem. It is argued that the public are entitled to reassurance that their money (in the form of taxes for public sector organisations or donations for charities) is being properly spent.

In addition, the complex mix of objectives with no absolute priority has also led to concern that the money may be being directed towards the wrong ends.

These issues, along with a growth in the perceived need for greater accountability among public officials, led to the development of the concept of evaluating VFM in public sector organisations. The principles developed are now widely applied in NFPs.

Systems analysis

A more detailed analysis of what is meant by VFM can be achieved by viewing the organisation as a system set up to achieve its objectives by means of processing inputs into outputs.

The organisation as a system

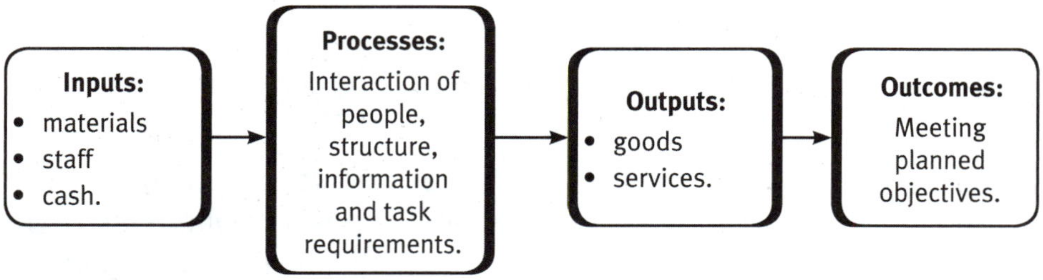

The three Es

Assessing whether the organisation provides value for money involves looking at all functioning aspects of the organisation. Performance measures have been developed to permit evaluation of each part separately.

VFM

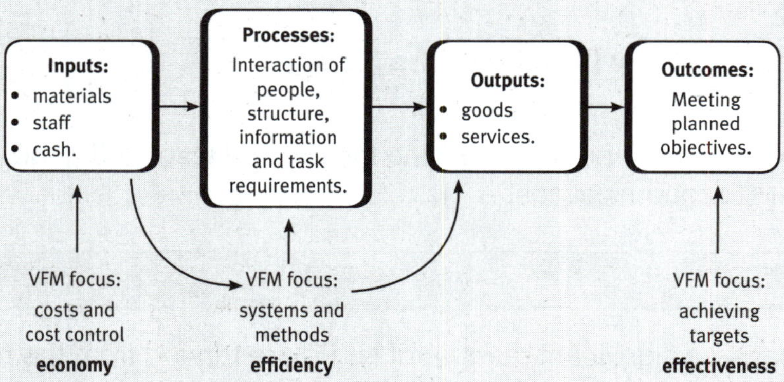

Economy: Minimising the costs of inputs required to achieve a defined level of output.

Efficiency: Ratio of outputs to inputs – achieving a high level of output in relation to the resources put in (input driven) or providing a particular level of service at reasonable input cost (output driven)

Effectiveness: Whether outputs are achieved that match the predetermined objectives.

Use of the 3Es as a performance measure and a way to assess VFM is a key issue for examination questions that relate to NFPs and public sector organisations.

3Es

Known as the 3 Es these measures are fundamental to an understanding of VFM. An organisation achieving economy, efficiency and effectiveness in each part of the system is considered to be providing good VFM.

Public sector organisations are subject to regular VFM (or best value) reviews and the results have important impacts on future plans and funding decisions.

Economy

Acquiring resources of appropriate quality and quantity at the lowest cost. Note that whilst obtaining low prices is an important consideration it is not the only one. Achieving true economy will include ensuring the purchases are fit for purpose and meet any predetermined standards.

Efficiency

Maximising the useful output from a given level of resources, or minimising the inputs required to produce the required level of output.

Some public services fall within the first definition as they try to provide as much of a service as possible with strictly limited resources and few opportunities to generate further income sources. This is defined as 'input-driven' efficiency. This would include services such as library provision.

However in many areas, there is a statutory obligation to provide a particular standard of service, for example prison services, which cannot be significantly reduced or withdrawn. In this case the obligation is to provide the service at a reasonable cost and is known as 'output-driven' efficiency.

In both areas, the key consideration is whether the resources used were put to good use and the methods and processes carried out represent best practice.

Effectiveness

Ensuring that the output from any given activity is achieving the desired result.

For example the cheapest site on which to build and run a sports centre may be a disused brownfield site on the edge of town. However, if the council's objectives included reduction in car use and accessible opportunities for health improvement, then the output of the building process – the sports centre, even if built economically and efficiently, would not be considered effective as it failed to meet the stated objectives.

Measuring the achievement of objectives in NFPs

Since the services provided are limited primarily by the funds available, key financial objectives for NFPs will be to:

- raise as large a sum as possible
- spend funds as effectively as possible.

Targets may then be set for different aspects of each accounting period's finances such as:

- total to be raised in grants and voluntary income
- maximum percentage of this total that fund-raising expenses represents
- amounts to be spent on specified projects or in particular areas
- maximum permitted administration costs
- meeting budgets
- breaking even in the long run.

The actual figures achieved can then be compared with these targets and control action taken if necessary.

Test your understanding 1 – Not for profit organisations

A subsidised college canteen service is to be evaluated by the local council to assess amongst other things, whether it is financially sound and offers value for money.

Suggest appropriate measures of achievement that could be set for the service.

Test your understanding 2

Which of the following is NOT one of the three main types of decision facing the financing manager in a company?

A Dividend decision

B Investment decision

C Economic decision

D Financing decision

Test your understanding 3

The agency problem is a driving force behind the growing importance attached to sound corporate governance.

In this context, the 'agents' are the:

A Customers

B Shareholders

C Managers

D Auditors

Test your understanding 4

Which of the following is an example of a financial objective that a company might choose to pursue?

A Provision of good wages and salaries

B Dealing honestly and fairly with customers on all occasions

C Producing environmentally friendly products

D Restricting the level of gearing to below a specified target level

Test your understanding 5

In the context of managing performance in 'not for profit' organisations, which of the following definitions is incorrect?

A Value for money means providing a service in a way which is economical, efficient and effective

B Economy means doing things cheaply: not spending $2 when the same thing can be bought for $1

C Efficiency means doing things quickly: minimising the amount of time that is spent on a given activity

D Effectiveness means doing the right things: spending funds so as to achieve the organisation's objectives

Test your understanding 6

Which of the following is a problem associated with managerial reward schemes?

A By rewarding performance, an effective scheme creates an organisation focused on continuous improvement

B Schemes based on shares can motivate employees/ managers to act in the long-term interests of the company

C Self-interested performance may be encouraged at the expense of team work

D Effective schemes attract and keep the employees valuable to an organisation

Chapter summary

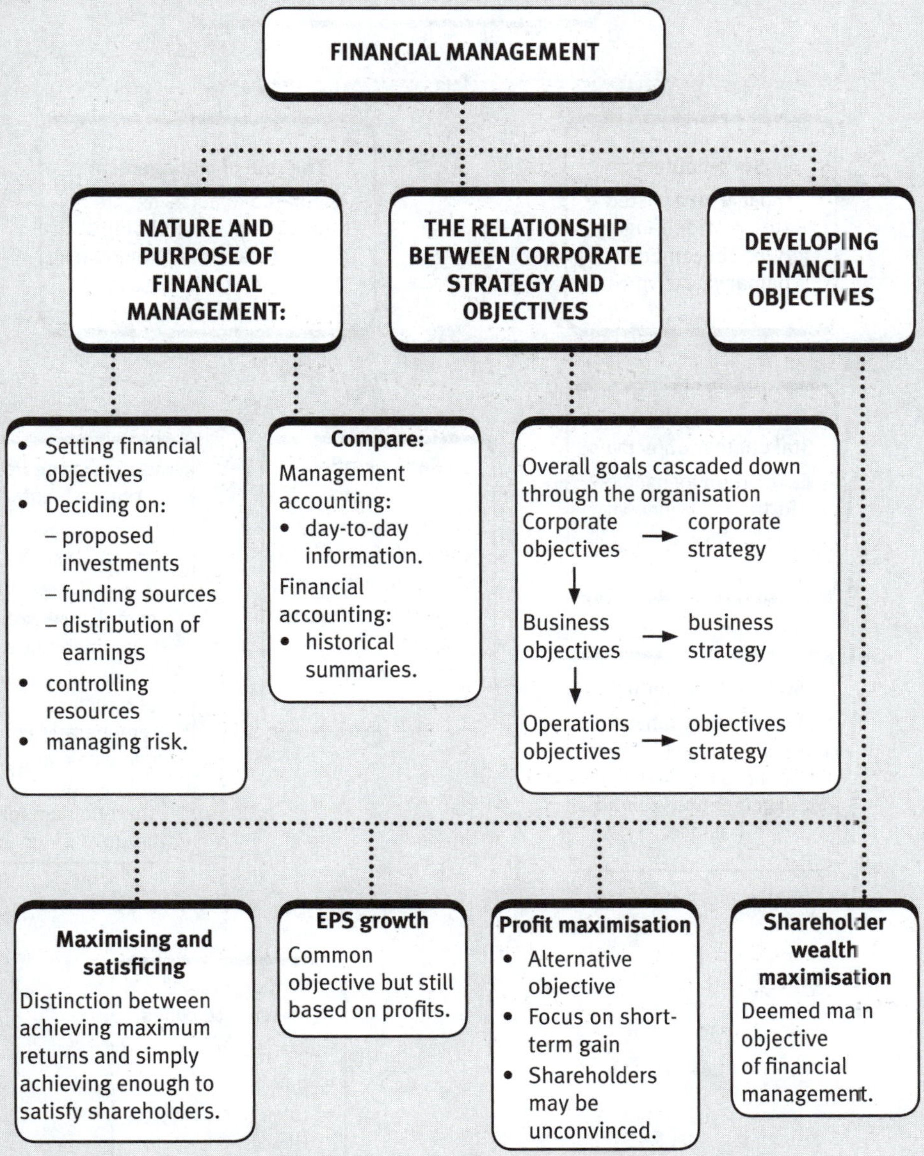

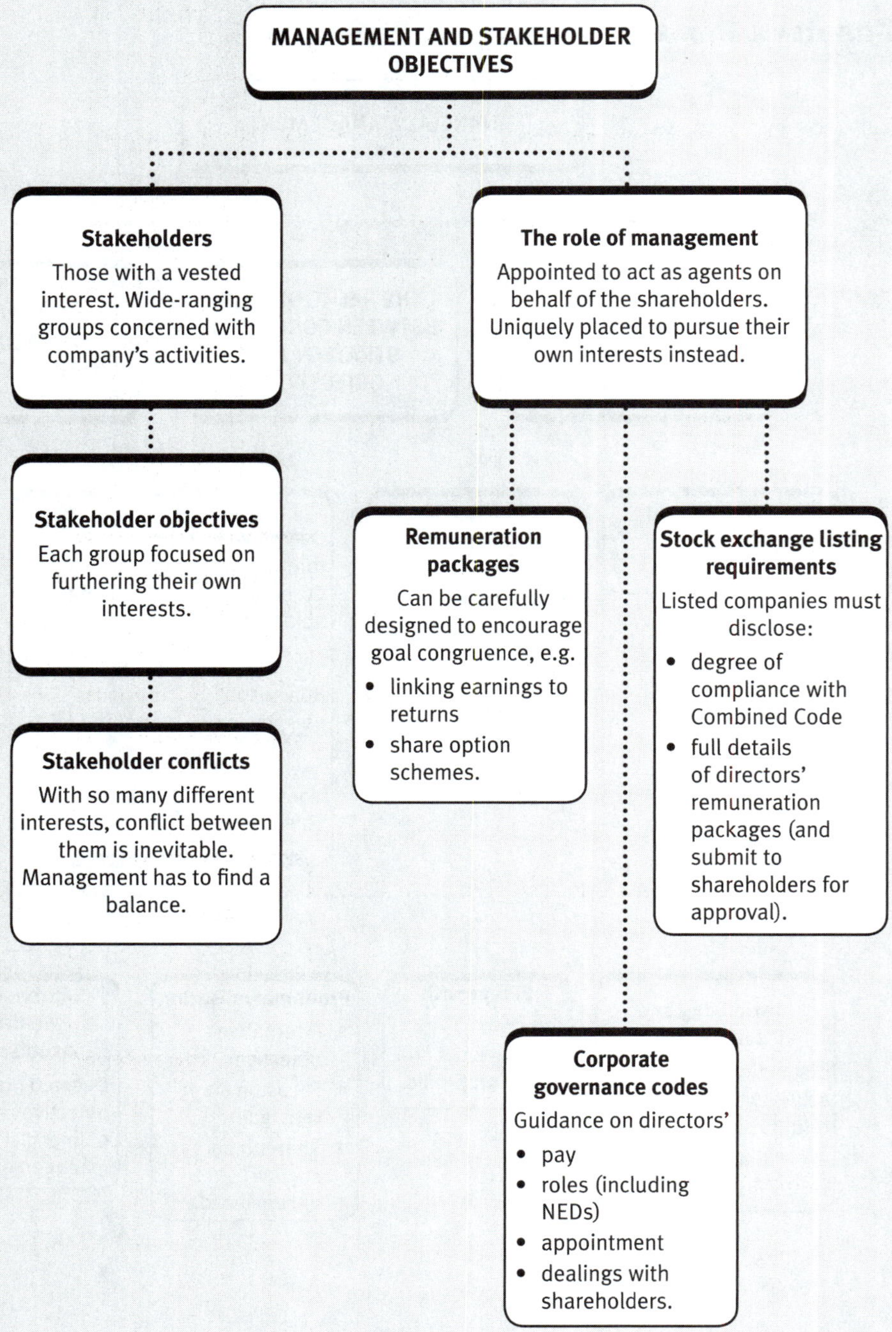
MANAGEMENT AND STAKEHOLDER OBJECTIVES
Stakeholders
Those with a vested interest. Wide-ranging groups concerned with company's activities.
Stakeholder objectives
Each group focused on furthering their own interests.
Stakeholder conflicts
With so many different interests, conflict between them is inevitable. Management has to find a balance.
The role of management
Appointed to act as agents on behalf of the shareholders. Uniquely placed to pursue their own interests instead.
Remuneration packages
Can be carefully designed to encourage goal congruence, e.g.
• linking earnings to returns
• share option schemes.
Stock exchange listing requirements
Listed companies must disclose:
• degree of compliance with Combined Code
• full details of directors' remuneration packages (and submit to shareholders for approval).
Corporate governance codes
Guidance on directors'
• pay
• roles (including NEDs)
• appointment
• dealings with shareholders.

Objectives in not-for-profit organisations

e.g. charities, public services, local government, trade unions, sports associations, professional institutes.

Impact of not-for-profit status on non-financial objectives

- Wide-ranging high-interest stakeholders
- Involvement of sponsors
- No 'price' for end user
- Funding in tranches.

Impact of not-for-profit status on financial objectives

Limited funds so targets set on:

- total to be raised
- amount spent on fund-raising
- amount to be spent on specified projects
- adminisration spending
- staying within budget
- breaking even.

Understanding VFM

Achieving the desired level and quality of service at the most economical cost.

Measuring VFM

Economy
Efficiency
Effectiveness.

Setting objectives in NFPs

Set financial targets and targets in each of the 3 Es for all parts of the system.

Answer to additional question – Objectives and strategy

	Commercial objectives /targets	**Financial objectives /targets**	**Strategies**
Corporate level	Improve brand awareness within the UK.	Increase EPS by 5% on prior year.	Acquire rival chain in a share-for-share purchase.
Business level	Update manufacturing capacity to incorporate new technology.	Achieve returns of 15% on new manufacturing investment.	Buy four new cutting machines for $250,000 each.
Operational level	Reduce unsold inventory items by 12%.	Improve the ratio of current assets to current liabilities from 1.7 to 1.85.	Implement a JIT inventory system.

Answer to additional question – Stakeholder conflicts

Stakeholders			Potential conflict
Employees	⇔	Shareholders	Employees may resist the introduction of automated processes which would improve efficiency but cost jobs. Shareholders may resist wage rises demanded by employees as uneconomical.
Customers	⇔	Community at large	Customers may demand lower prices and greater choice, but in order to provide them a company may need to squeeze vulnerable suppliers or import products at great environmental cost.
Shareholders	⇔	Finance providers	Shareholders may encourage management to pursue risky strategies in order to maximise potential returns, whereas finance providers prefer stable lower-risk policies that ensure liquidity for the payment of debt interest.
Customers	⇔	Shareholders/ managers	Customers may require higher service levels (such as 24 rather than 48 hour delivery) which are resisted by shareholders as too expensive or by management due to increased workload.
Government	⇔	Shareholders	Government will often insist upon levels of welfare (such as the minimum wage and health and safety practices) which would otherwise be avoided as an unnecessary expense.
Shareholders	⇔	Managers	Shareholders are concerned with the maximisation of their wealth. Managers may instead pursue strategies focused on growth as these may bring the greatest personal rewards.

Note: You may have come up with different suggestions. The point is to recognise that there is a huge range of potential conflicts of interest and senior management will need to work to achieve a balance.

Answer to additional question – Managerial reward schemes

Advantages

- Goal congruence – managers will work to achieve growth in EPS, which will make shareholders feel that their wealth is increasing.
- The figure is difficult (but not impossible!) to manipulate from one period to another as it will be audited.

Disadvantages

- There is little incentive for managers to control working capital and cash flow – a pressing problem. Growth may be at the expense of liquidity and ultimately compromise the firm's future survival.
- Managers may gain bonuses simply because of the products concerned rather than their own efforts. A target growth in EPS would be better.
- Long-term shareholder value and EPS are not well correlated.
- There is only one measure that focuses on final effects rather than operational causes.

Test your understanding answers

Test your understanding 1 – Not for profit organisations

Financial measures:

- proportion of overall funds spent on administration costs
- ability to stay within budget/break even
- revenue targets met.

Economy targets:

- costs of purchasing provisions of suitable nutritional quality
- costs of negotiating for and purchasing equipment
- negotiation of bulk discounts
- pay rates for staff of appropriate levels of qualification.

Efficiency targets:

- numbers of portions produced
- cost per meal sold
- levels of wastage of unprepared and of cooked food
- staff utilisation
- equipment life.

Effectiveness targets:

- numbers using the canteen
- customer satisfaction ratings
- nutritional value of meals served.

Test your understanding 2

Answer C

Financial management aims to ensure that the money is available to finance profitable projects and to select those projects which the company should undertake. Once profits have been made the decision then needs to be made about how much to distribute to the owners and how much to re-invest for the future.

Test your understanding 3

Answer C

The separation of ownership and control creates a situation where managers act as the agents of the owners (shareholders).

Test your understanding 4

Answer D

This is a financial objective that relates to the level of risk that the company accepts.

Test your understanding 5

Answer C

Efficiency means doing things well: getting the best use out of what money is spent on.

Test your understanding 6

Answer C

This identifies a typical problem associated with many managerial reward schemes.

chapter

2

Basic investment appraisal techniques

Chapter learning objectives

Upon completion of this chapter you will be able to:

- define a relevant cash flow (and distinguish it from an accounting profit)
- identify and calculate relevant cash flows in a scenario
- calculate the payback period and use it to appraise an investment
- discuss the usefulness of payback as an investment appraisal method
- calculate return on capital employed (ROCE) (accounting rate of return) and use it to appraise an investment
- discuss the usefulness of ROCE as an investment appraisal method.

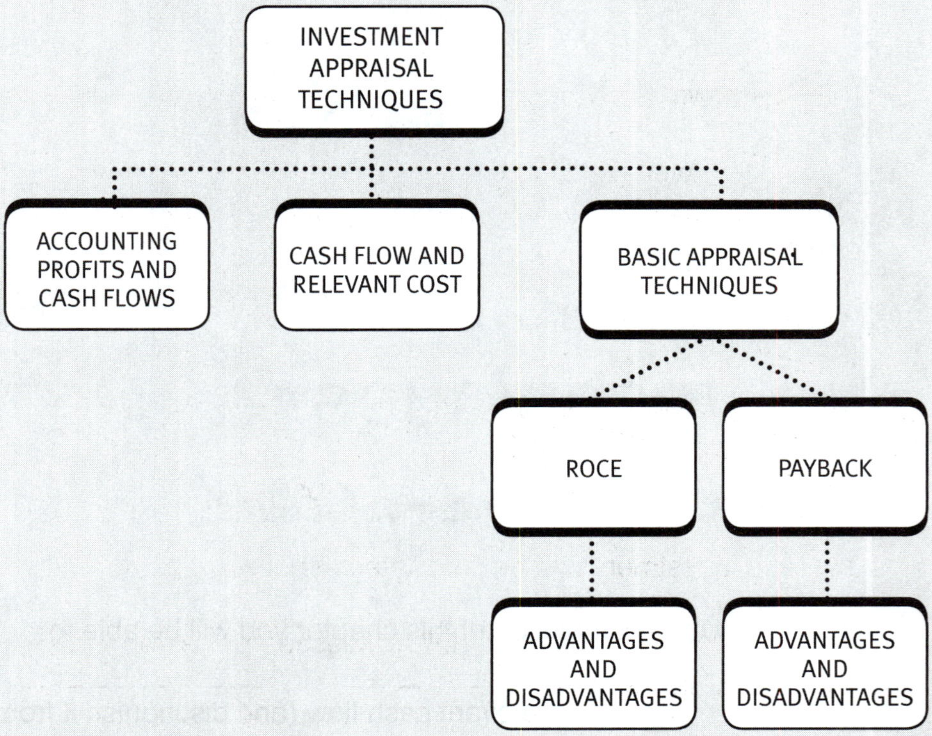

1 Investment appraisal process

One stage in the capital budgeting process is **investment appraisal**. This appraisal has the following features:

- assessment of the level of expected returns earned for the level of expenditure made
- estimates of future costs and benefits over the project's life.

Two basic appraisal techniques are covered in this chapter:

- ROCE
- Payback.

More sophisticated methods of investment appraisal are dealt with in the next chapter.

Examination questions may ask you to compare and contrast the use of these two basic techniques.

2 ROCE

This is also known as accounting rate of return (ARR).

$$\text{ROCE} = \frac{\text{Average annual profits before interest and tax}}{\text{Initial capital costs}} \times 100\%$$

or alternatively:

$$\text{ROCE} = \frac{\text{Average annual profits before interest and tax}}{\text{Average capital investment}} \times 100\%$$

The average investment can be calculated as:

$$\text{Average capital investment} = \frac{\text{Initial investment } + \text{ scrap value}}{2}$$

In the exam you should use the initial capital cost unless you are told otherwise. However, the ROCE calculation based on the average capital investment is the method most commonly asked for in the exam. This will be made clear in the question.

Decision rule:

- If the expected ROCE for the investment is greater than the target or hurdle rate (as decided by management) then the project should be accepted.

Test your understanding 1 – ROCE

A project involves the immediate purchase of an item of plant costing $110,000. It would generate annual cash flows of $24,400 for five years, starting in Year 1. The plant purchased would have a scrap value of $10,000 in five years, when the project terminates. Depreciation is on a straight-line basis.

Determine the project's ROCE using:

(a) initial capital costs

(b) average capital investment

Test your understanding 2 – ROCE

A project requires an initial investment of $800,000 and then earns net cash inflows as follows:

Year	1	2	3	4	5	6	7
Cash inflows ($000)	100	200	400	400	300	200	150

In addition, at the end of the seven-year project the assets initially purchased will be sold for $100,000.

Determine the project's ROCE using:

(a) initial capital costs

(b) average capital investment.

Initial capital cost

The initial capital cost could comprise any or all of the following:

- cost of new assets bought
- net book value (NBV) of existing assets to be used in the project
- investment in working capital
- capitalised R&D expenditure (**NB** ensure this is amortised against profit).

3 Advantages and disadvantages of ROCE

Advantages include:

- simplicity
- links with other accounting measures.

Disadvantages include:

- no account is taken of project life
- no account is taken of timing of cash flows

- it varies depending on accounting policies
- it may ignore working capital
- it does not measure absolute gain
- there is no definitive investment signal.

In the examination it is important that you can discuss the features of ROCE as an investment appraisal technique, in addition to being able to calculate it.

Advantages and disadvantages of ROCE

Advantages

Simplicity – being based on widely-reported measures of return (profits) and asset (statement of financial position values), it is easily understood and easily calculated.

Links with other accounting measures – annual ROCE, calculated to assess a business or sector of a business (and therefore the investment decisions made by that business), is a widely used measure. It is expressed in percentage terms with which managers and accountants are familiar.

Disadvantages

It fails to take account of either the project life or the timing of cash flows within that life. This therefore ignores the time value of money (see next chapter).

It will vary with specific accounting policies, and the extent to which project costs are capitalised. Profit measurement is thus 'subjective', and ROCE figures for identical projects would vary from business to business.

It might ignore working capital requirements.

Like all rate of return measures, it is not a measurement of absolute gain in wealth for the business owners.

There is no definite investment signal. The decision to invest or not remains subjective in view of the lack of an objectively set target ROCE.

4 Accounting profits and cash flows

In capital investment appraisal it is more appropriate to evaluate future cash flows than accounting profits, because:

- profits cannot be spent
- profits are subjective
- cash is required to pay dividends.

Profits versus cash flows

Cash flows are a better measure of the suitability of a capital investment because:

- cash is what ultimately counts – profits are only a guide to cash availability: they cannot actually be spent
- profit measurement is subjective – the time period in which income and expenses are recorded, and so on, are a matter of judgement
- cash is used to pay dividends – dividends are the ultimate method of transferring wealth to equity shareholders.

In practice, the cash flow effects of a project are likely to be similar to the project's effects on profits. Major differences in cash and profit flows will be linked to the following:

- changes in working capital
- asset purchase and depreciation
- deferred taxation
- capitalisation of research and development expenditure.

5 Cash flows and relevant costs

For all methods of investment appraisal, with the exception of ROCE, only relevant cash flows should be considered. These are:

- future
- incremental
- cash-based.

Ignore:

- sunk costs
- committed costs
- non-cash items
- allocated costs.

Relevant costs

The only cash flows that should be taken into consideration in capital investment appraisal (with the exception of ROCE) are:

- cash flows that will happen in the future, and
- cash flows that will arise only if the capital project goes ahead.

These cash flows are direct revenues from the project and relevant costs. Relevant costs are future costs that will be incurred or saved as a direct consequence of undertaking the investment.

- Costs that have already been incurred are not relevant to a current decision. For example, suppose a company makes a non-returnable deposit as a down payment for an item of equipment, and then reconsiders whether it wants the equipment after all. The money that has already been spent cannot be recovered and so is not relevant to the current decision about obtaining the equipment.
- Costs that will be incurred anyway, whether or not a capital project goes ahead, cannot be relevant to a decision about investing in the project. Fixed cost expenditures are an example of 'committed costs'. For the purpose of investment appraisal, a project should not be charged with an amount for a share of fixed costs that will be incurred in any event.
- Non-cash items of cost can never be relevant to investment appraisal. In particular, the depreciation charges on a non-current asset are not relevant costs for analysis because depreciation is not a cash expenditure.
- Accounting treatment of costs is often irrelevant (e.g. depreciation, inventory valuation, methods of allocating overheads) because it has no bearing on cash flows, except to the extent that it may affect taxation payable. Overheads attributed to projects should, in the examination, be taken as absorbed figures unless specified otherwise. It should be assumed there is no change to actual overhead paid, and thus no relevant cash flow.

Test your understanding 3 – Relevant costs

A manufacturing company is considering the production of a new type of widget. Each widget will take two hours to make.

Fixed overheads are apportioned on the basis of $1 per labour hour.

If the new widgets are produced, the company will have to employ an additional supervisor at a salary of $15,000 pa. The company will produce 10,000 widgets pa.

What are the relevant cash flows?

Additional question – Relevant costs

A company is evaluating a proposed expenditure on an item of equipment that would cost $160,000.

A technical feasibility study has been carried out by consultants, at a cost of $15,000, into benefits from investing in the equipment.

It has been estimated that the equipment would have a life of four years, and annual profits would be $8,000, after deducting annual depreciation of $40,000 and an annual charge of $25,000 for a share of the existing fixed cost of the company.

What are the relevant cash flows for this?

The answer to this question can be found after the chapter summary diagram at the end of this chapter.

6 Payback method of appraisal

The **payback** period is the time a project will take to pay back the money spent on it. It is based on expected cash flows and provides a measure of liquidity.

Decision rule:

- only select projects which pay back within the specified time period
- choose between options on the basis of the fastest payback

Constant annual cash flows

$$\text{Payback period} = \frac{\text{initial investment}}{\text{annual cash flow}}$$

Test your understanding 4 – Payback with constant annual cash

An expenditure of $2 million is expected to generate net cash inflows of $500,000 each year for the next seven years.

What is the payback period for the project?

A payback period may not be for an exact number of years. To calculate the payback in years and months you should multiply the decimal fraction of a year by 12 to the number of months.

Test your understanding 5 – Payback in years and months

A project will involve spending $1.8 million now. Annual cash flows from the project would be $350,000.

What is the expected payback period?

Uneven annual cash flows

In practice, cash flows from a project are unlikely to be constant. Where cash flows are uneven, payback is calculated by working out the cumulative cash flow over the life of the project.

Test your understanding 6 – Payback with uneven cash flows

A project is expected to have the following cash flows:

Year	Cash flow
	$000
0	(1,900)
1	300
2	500
3	600
4	800
5	500

What is the expected payback period?

Test your understanding 7 – Payback with uneven cash flows

Calculate the payback period in years and months for the following project:

Year	Cash flow
	$000
0	(3,100)
1	1,000
2	900
3	800
4	500
5	500

7 Advantages and disadvantages of payback

Advantages include:

- it is simple
- it is useful in certain situations:
  - rapidly changing technology
  - improving investment conditions

- it favours quick return:
  - helps company growth
  - minimises risk
  - maximises liquidity
- it uses cash flows, not accounting profit.

Disadvantages include:

- it ignores returns after the payback period
- it ignores the timings of the cash flows
- it is subjective – no definitive investment signal
- it ignores project profitability.

In the examination it is important that you can discuss the features of payback as an investment appraisal technique as well as being able to do the calculation.

Advantages and disadvantages of payback

Advantages

Simplicity – as a concept, it is easily understood and is easily calculated.

Rapidly changing technology – If new plant is likely to be scrapped in a short period because of obsolescence, a quick payback is essential.

Improving investment conditions – When investment conditions are expected to improve in the near future, attention is directed to those projects which will release funds soonest, to take advantage of the improving climate.

Payback favours projects with a quick return – It is often argued that these are to be preferred for three reasons:

(1) Rapid project payback leads to rapid company growth, but in fact such a policy will lead to many profitable investment opportunities being overlooked because their payback period does not happen to be particularly swift.

(2) Rapid payback minimises risk (the logic being that the shorter the payback period, the less there is that can go wrong). Not all risks are related to time, but payback is able to provide a useful means of assessing time risks (and only time risks). It is likely that earlier cash flows can be estimated with greater certainty.

(3) Rapid payback maximises liquidity – but liquidity problems are best dealt with separately, through cash forecasting.

Cash flows – Unlike the other traditional methods it uses cash flows, rather than profits, and so is less likely to produce an unduly optimistic figure distorted by assorted accounting conventions which might permit certain costs to be carried forward and not affect profit initially.

Disadvantages

Project returns may be ignored – cash flows arising after the payback period are totally ignored. Payback ignores profitability and concentrates on cash flows and liquidity.

Timing ignored – cash flows are effectively categorised as pre-payback or post-payback, but no more accurate measure is made. In particular, the time value of money is ignored.

Lack of objectivity – there is no objective measure as to what length of time should be set as the minimum payback period. Investment decisions are therefore subjective.

Project profitability is ignored – payback takes no account of the effects on business profits and periodic performance of the project, as evidenced in the financial statements. This is critical if the business is to be reasonably viewed by users of the accounts.

Test your understanding 8

Which of the following is an example of a relevant cash flow to be considered in an investment appraisal process for a new project?

A Market research expenditure already incurred

B Additional tax that will be paid on extra profits generated

C Centrally-allocated overheads that are not a consequence of undertaking the project

D Tax-allowable depreciation

Test your understanding 9

Garfield plc is considering whether to enter into a new project. The machinery which would be used to produce the goods for the contract was purchased seven years ago at a cost of $80,000, with an estimated life of ten years. Depreciation is on a straight-line basis. The machinery has been idle for some time, and if not used on this contract would be scrapped and sold immediately for an estimated $5,000. After use on this contract the machinery would have no value, and would have to be dismantled and disposed of at a cost of $1,500.

Ignoring the time value of money (covered later in Chapter 3), what is the relevant cost of the machine to the new contract?

A $3,500

B $5,000

C $6,500

D $24,500

Test your understanding 10

Which of the following is an advantage of the payback method of investment appraisal?

A It takes account of the timing of the cash flows within the payback period

B It uses accounting profits rather than cash flows

C It takes account of the cash flows after the end of the payback period and therefore the total project return

D It can be used as a screening device as a first stage in eliminating obviously inappropriate projects prior to more detailed evaluation

Test your understanding 11

Which of the following statements is not true?

A The return on capital employed method of investment appraisal takes account of the length of the project

B Focus on an early payback period can enhance liquidity

C Investment risk is increased if the payback period is longer

D Shorter term forecasts are likely to be more reliable

Test your understanding 12

Acorn plc is considering purchasing a new machine at a cost of $110,400 that will be operated for four years, after which time it will be sold for an estimated $9,600. Acorn uses a straight-line policy for depreciation.

Forecast operating profits to be generated by the machine are as follows:

Year	$
1	39,600
2	19,600
3	22,400
4	32,400

Select the payback period (PP) and the average return on capital employed (ROCE), calculated as average annual profits divided by the average investment.

A **PP:** 2.02 years **ROCE:** 47.5%

B **PP:** 3.89 years **ROCE:** 25.8%

C **PP:** 3.89 years **ROCE:** 47.5%

D **PP:** 2.02 years **ROCE:** 25.8%

Chapter summary

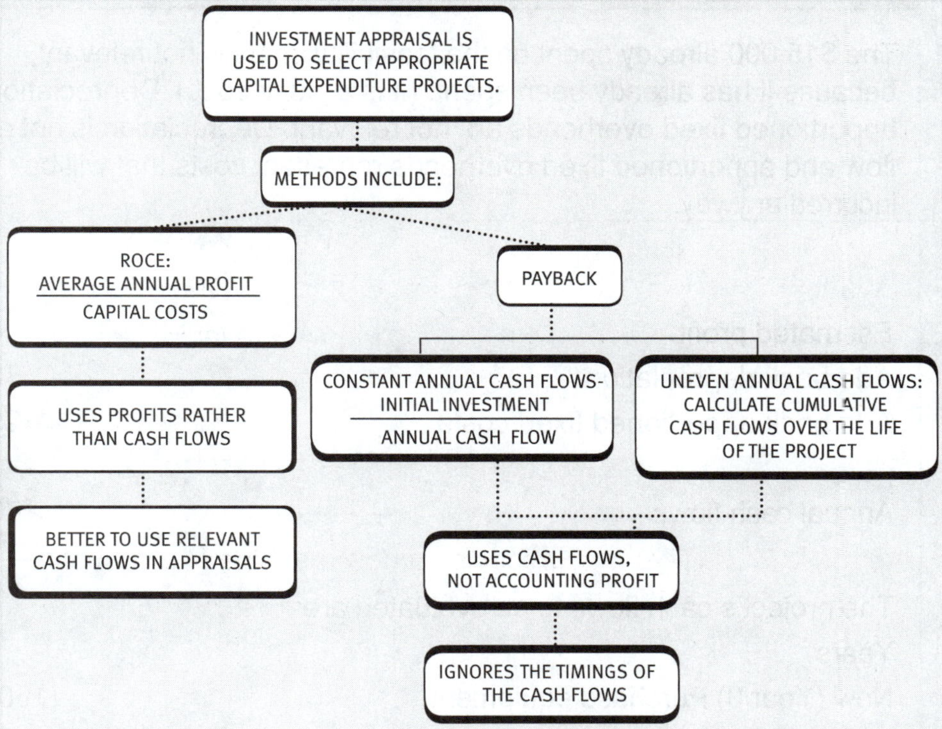

Answer to additional question – Relevant costs

The $15,000 already spent on the feasibility study is not relevant, because it has already been spent. (It is a 'sunk cost'). Depreciation and apportioned fixed overheads are not relevant. Depreciation is not a cash flow and apportioned fixed overheads represent costs that will be incurred anyway.

	$
Estimated profit	8,000
Add back depreciation	40,000
Add back apportioned fixed costs	25,000
Annual cash flows	73,000

The project's cash flows to be evaluated are:

Years	$
Now (Year 0) Purchase equipment	(160,000)
1–4 Cash flow from profits	73,000 each year

Test your understanding answers

Test your understanding 1 – ROCE

Annual cash flows are taken to be profit before depreciation.

Average annual depreciation = (\$110,000 – \$10,000) ÷ 5

= \$20,000

Average annual profit = \$24,400 – \$20,000

= \$4,400

Using initial cost:

$$ROCE = \frac{\text{Average annual profit}}{\text{Initial capital cost}} \times 100\%$$

$$= \frac{\$4,400}{\$110,000} \times 100\% = 4\%$$

Using average capital investment:

Average annual profits (as before) = \$4,400

$$\text{Average book value of assets} = \frac{\text{Initial cost + Final scrap value}}{2}$$

$$= \frac{\$110,000 + \$10,000}{2} = \$60,000$$

$$ROCE = \frac{\text{Average annual profit}}{\text{Average book value of assets}} \times 100\%$$

$$= \frac{\$4,400}{\$60,000} \times 100\% = 7.33\%$$

Test your understanding 2 – ROCE

This uses profits rather than cash flows.

Average annual inflows = \$1,750,000 ÷ 7 = \$250,000
Average annual depreciation = (\$800,000 – \$100,000) ÷ 7 = \$100,000
(A net \$700,000 is being written off as depreciation over 7 years.)
Average annual profit = \$250,000 – \$100,000 = \$150,000
The average capital invested is (800,000 + 100,000) ÷ 2 = \$450,000

(a)

$$\text{ROCE} = \frac{\text{Average annual profit}}{\text{Initial capital cost}} \times 100 = \frac{\$150{,}000}{\$800{,}000} \times 100 = 18.75\%$$

(b)

$$\text{ROCE} = \frac{\text{Average annual profit}}{\text{Average capital investment}} \times 100 = \frac{\$150{,}000}{\$450{,}000} \times 100 = 33.33\%$$

Test your understanding 3 – Relevant costs

Only the \$15,000 salary is relevant. The fixed overheads are not incremental to the decision and should be ignored.

Test your understanding 4 – Payback with constant annual cash

$$\text{Payback period} = \frac{\$2{,}000{,}000}{\$500{,}000} = 4 \text{ years}$$

Test your understanding 5 – Payback in years and months

$$\text{Payback} = \frac{\$1{,}800{,}000}{\$350{,}000} = 5.1429 \text{ years}$$

0.1429 of a year × 12 months = 1.7 months (rounded = 2 months)

The answer can therefore be stated as either:

- 5.1 years
- 5 years 2 months

assuming cash flows occur evenly throughout the year.

Test your understanding 6 – Payback with uneven cash flows

Year	Cash flow	Cumulative cash flow
	$000	$000
0	(1,900)	(1,900)
1	300	(1,600)
2	500	(1,100)
3	600	(500)
4	800	300
5	500	800

In the table above a column is added for cumulative cash flows for the project to date. Figures in brackets are negative cash flows.

Each year's cumulative figure is simply the cumulative figure at the start of the year plus the figure for the current year. The cumulative figure each year is therefore the expected position as at the end of that year.

Payback is between the end of Year 3 and the end of Year 4 – that is during Year 4. This is the point at which the cumulative cash flow changes from being negative to positive. If we assume a constant rate of cash flow throughout the year, we could estimate that payback will be three years plus ($500/800) of Year 4. This is because the cumulative cash flow is minus $500 at the start of the year and the Year 4 cash flow would be $800.

$500/800 = 0.625

Therefore payback is after 3.625 years.

Payback in years and months is calculated by multiplying the decimal fraction of a year by 12 months. In this example, 0.625 years = 7.5 months (0.625 × 12 months), which is rounded to 8 months. So therefore, payback occurs after 3 years 8 months.

Note that if cash flows were deemed to arise at the end of the year then the payback period would be 4 years.

Test your understanding 7 – Payback with uneven cash flows

The payback period would be calculated as follows.

Year	**Cash flow**	**Cumulative cash flow**
	$000	$000
0	(3,100)	(3,100)
1	1,000	(2,100)
2	900	(1,200)
3	800	(400)
4	500	100
5	500	600

Payback is between the end of Year 3 and the end of Year 4, in other words during Year 4.

If we assume a constant rate of cash flow through the year, we could estimate that payback will be three years, plus ($400/500) of Year 4, which is 3.8 years.

0.8 years = 10 months (0.8 × 12)

We could therefore estimate that payback would be after 3 years 10 months.

Test your understanding 8

Answer B

Any cost incurred in the past (A), or any committed costs which will be incurred regardless of whether or not an investment is undertaken (C), are not relevant cash flows. They have occurred, or will occur, whatever investment decision is taken. Any costs which do not represent an actual cash flow (D) should also be ignored.

Test your understanding 9

Answer C

	$
Loss of opportunity to gain revenue	5,000
Pay for dismantle	1,500
	6,500

Test your understanding 10

Answer D

The payback method ignores both the timing of the cash flows within the payback period (A) and the cash flows after the end of the payback period (C). The payback method uses cash flows rather than accounting profits (B).

Test your understanding 11

Answer A

The ROCE method fails to take account of the life of the project.

Test your understanding 12

Answer A

PP:

Depreciation must be added back to the annual profit figure to derive the annual cash flows.

Annual depreciation – ($110,400 – $9,600)/4 years = $25,200

Adding $25,200 to each year's profit figure produces the following cash flows.

	Cash flow	**Cumulative cash flow**
	$	$
Initial investment	(110,400)	(110,400)
Year 1	64,800	(45,600)
Year 2	44,800	(800)
Year 3	47,600	46,800

Payback period = 2 years + (800/(47,600) × 1 year) = 2.02 years

If you selected a payback period of 3.89 years you based your calculations on the accounting profits after the deduction of depreciation. The calculation of the payback period should be based on cash flows.

ROCE:

Average profit = $(39,600 + 19,600 + 22,400 + 32,400)/4 = $28,500
Average investment = $(110,400 + 9,600)/2 = $60,000
ROCE = $(28,500/60,000) × 100% = 47.5%

If you selected a ROCE of 25.8% you calculated the ROCE using the opening investment rather than the average investment.

chapter

3

Investment appraisal – discounted cash flow techniques

Chapter learning objectives

Upon completion of this chapter you will be able to:

- explain the concept of the time value of money
- calculate the future value of a sum by compounding
- calculate the present value (PV) of a single sum using a formula
- calculate the PV of a single sum using discount tables
- calculate the PV of an annuity using a formula
- calculate the PV of an annuity using annuity tables
- calculate the PV of a perpetuity using a formula
- calculate the PV of advanced annuities and perpetuities
- calculate the PV of delayed annuities and perpetuities
- explain the basic principle behind the concept of a cost of capital
- calculate the net present value (NPV) of an investment and use it to appraise the proposal
- discuss the usefulness of NPV as an investment appraisal method and its superiority over non-discounted cash flows (DCF) methods
- calculate the internal rate of return (IRR) of an investment and use it to appraise the proposal
- discuss the usefulness of IRR as an investment appraisal method and its superiority over non-DCF methods
- discuss the relative merits of NPV and IRR.

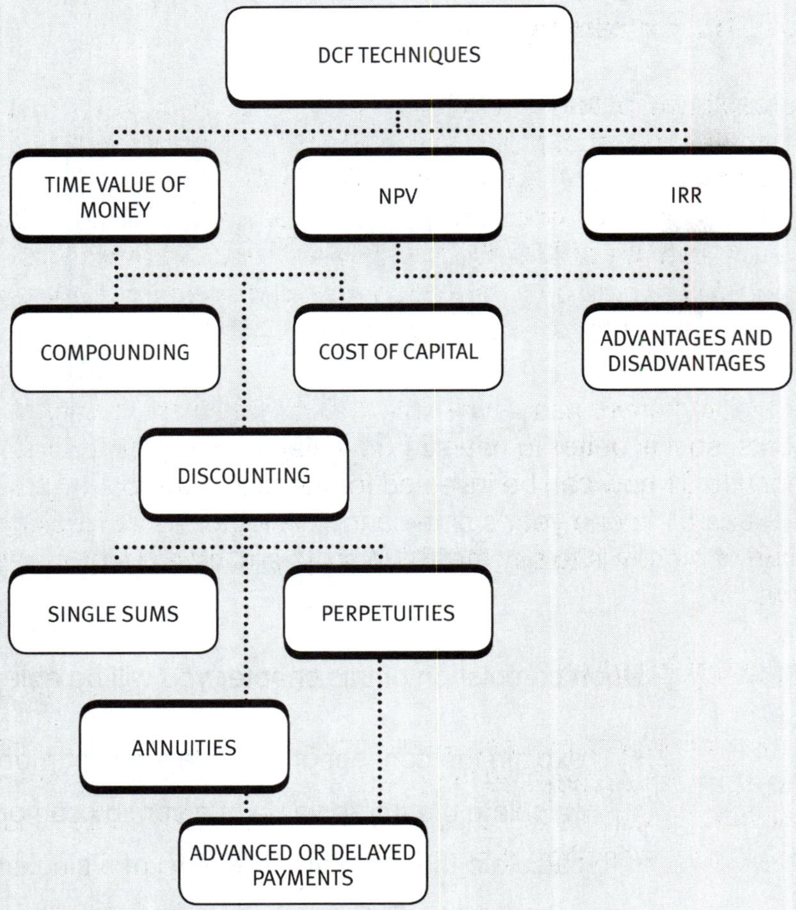

1 The time value of money

Money received today is worth more than the same sum received in the future, i.e. it has a **time value.**

This occurs for three reasons:

- potential for earning interest/cost of finance
- impact of inflation
- effect of risk.

This is a key concept throughout the F9 syllabus.

Discounted cash flow (DCF) techniques take account of this time value of money when appraising investments.

The time value of money

Potential for earning interest

If a capital investment is to be justified, it needs to earn at least a minimum amount of profit, so that the return compensates the investor for both the amount invested and also for the length of time before the profits are made. For example, if a company could invest $80,000 now to earn revenue of $82,000 in one week's time, a profit of $2,000 in seven days would be a very good return. However, if it takes four years to earn the money, the return would be very low.

Therefore money has a time value. It can be invested to earn interest or profits, so it is better to have $1 now than in one year's time. This is because $1 now can be invested for the next year to earn a return, whereas $1 in one year's time cannot. Another way of looking at the time value of money is to say that $1 in six years' time is worth less than $1 now.

Impact of inflation

In most countries, in most years prices rise as a result of inflation. Therefore funds received today will buy more than the same amount a year later, as prices will have risen in the meantime. The funds are subject to a loss of purchasing power over time.

Risk

The earlier cash flows are due to be received, the more certain they are – there is less chance that events will prevent payment. Earlier cash flows are therefore considered to be more valuable.

2 Compounding

A sum invested today will earn interest. Compounding calculates the future or terminal value of a given sum invested today for a number of years.

To compound a sum, the figure is increased by the amount of interest it would earn over the period.

Illustration 1 – Compounding

An investment of $100 is to be made today. What is the value of the investment after two years if the interest rate is 10%?

Solution

		$
Value after one year	100 × 1.1 =	110
Value after two years	110 × 1.1 =	121

The $100 will be worth $121 in two years at an interest rate of 10%.

This is a fairly straightforward calculation. However, if the question asked for the value of the investment after 20 years, it would take a lot longer.

So, to speed up the process, we can use a formula to calculate the future value of a sum invested now. The formula is:

$F = P(1 + r)^n$

where F = Future value after n periods

P = Present or Initial value

r = Rate of interest per period

n = Number of periods

The terminal value is the value, in n years' time, of a sum invested now, at an interest rate of r%.

Test your understanding 1 – Compounding

You have $5,000 to invest now for six years at an interest rate of 5% pa.

What will be the value of the investment after six years?

3 Discounting

In a potential investment project, cash flows will arise at many different points in time. To make a useful comparison of the different flows, they must all be converted to a common point in time, usually the present day, i.e. the cash flows are discounted.

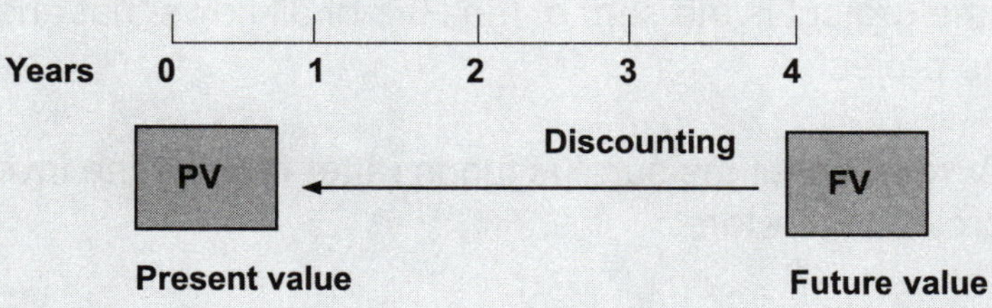

Discounting a single sum

The present value (PV) is the cash equivalent now of money receivable/payable at some future date.

The PV of a future sum can be calculated using the formula:

$$P = \frac{F}{(1+r)^n} = F \times (1+r)^{-n}$$

This is just a re-arrangement of the formula we used for compounding.

$(1 + r)^{-n}$ is called the discount factor (DF).

Test your understanding 2 – Discounting a single sum

What is the PV of $115,000 receivable in nine years' time if r = 6%?

4 The cost of capital

In the above discussions we referred to the rate of interest. There are a number of alternative terms used to refer to the rate a firm should use to take account of the time value of money:

- cost of capital
- discount rate
- required return.

Whatever term is used, the rate of interest used for discounting reflects the cost of the finance that will be tied up in the investment.

5 The Net Present Value (NPV)

To appraise the overall impact of a project using DCF techniques involves discounting all the relevant cash flows associated with the project back to their PV.

If we treat outflows of the project as negative and inflows as positive, the NPV of the project is the sum of the PVs of all flows that arise as a result of doing the project.

The NPV represents the surplus funds (after funding the investment) earned on the project, therefore:

- if the NPV is positive – the project is financially viable
- if the NPV is zero – the project breaks even
- if the NPV is negative – the project is not financially viable
- if the company has two or more mutually exclusive projects under consideration it should choose the one with the highest NPV
- the NPV gives the impact of the project on shareholder wealth.

What does the NPV actually mean?

Suppose, in an investment problem, we calculate the NPV of certain cash flows at 12% to be – $97, and at 10% to be zero, and yet at 8% the NPV of the same cash flows is + $108. Another way of expressing this is as follows.

- If the funds were borrowed at 12% the investor would be $97 out of pocket – i.e. the investment earns a yield below the cost of capital.
- If funds were borrowed at 10% the investor would break even – i.e. the investment yields a return equal to the cost of capital.
- If funds were borrowed at 8% the investor would be $108 in pocket – i.e. the investment earns a return in excess of the cost of capital.

In other words, a positive NPV is an indication of the surplus funds available to the investor now as a result of accepting the project.

Assumptions used in discounting

Unless the examiner tells you otherwise, the following assumptions are made about cash flows when calculating the net present value:

- all cash flows occur at the start or end of a year
- initial investments occur T_0
- other cash flows start one year after that (T_1).

Also note, you should never include interest payments within an NPV calculation as these are taken account of by the cost of capital.

Assumptions used in discounting

- All cash flows occur at the start or end of a year.

Although in practice many cash flows accrue throughout the year, for discounting purposes they are all treated as occurring at the start or end of a year. Note also that if today (T_0) is 01/01/20X0, the dates 31/12/20X1 and 01/01/20X2, although technically separate days, can be treated for discounting as occurring at the same point in time, i.e. at T_1.

- Initial investments occur at once (T_0), other cash flows start in one year's time (T_1).

In project appraisal, the investment needs to be made before the cash flows can accrue. Therefore, unless the examiner specifies otherwise, it is assumed that investments occur in advance. The first cash flows associated with running the project are therefore assumed to occur one year after the project begins, i.e. at T_1.

Test your understanding 3 – Net present value

The cash flows for a project have been estimated as follows:

Year	$
0	(25,000)
1	6,000
2	10,000
3	8,000
4	7,000

The cost of capital is 6%.

Convert these cash flows to a PV.

Calculate the net present value (NPV) of the project to assess whether it should be undertaken.

Test your understanding 4 – Net present value

An organisation is considering a capital investment in new equipment. The estimated cash flows are as follows.

Year	**Cash flow**
	$
0	(240,000)
1	80,000
2	120,000
3	70,000
4	40,000
5	20,000

The company's cost of capital is 9%.

Calculate the NPV of the project to assess whether it should be undertaken.

6 Advantages and disadvantages of using NPV

Advantages

Theoretically the NPV method of investment appraisal is superior to all others. This is because it:

- considers the time value of money
- is an absolute measure of return
- is based on cash flows not profits
- considers the whole life of the project
- should lead to maximisation of shareholder wealth.

Disadvantages

- It is difficult to explain to managers
- It requires knowledge of the cost of capital
- It is relatively complex.

Advantages and disadvantages of NPV

When appraising projects or investments, NPV is considered to be superior (in theory) to most other methods. This is because it:

- considers the time value of money – discounting cash flows to PV takes account of the impact of interest, inflation and risk over time. (See later sessions for more on inflation and risk.) These significant issues are ignored by the basic methods of payback and annual rate of return (ARR)
- is an absolute measure of return – the NPV of an investment represents the actual surplus raised by the project. This allows a business to plan more effectively
- is based on cash flows not profits – the subjectivity of profits makes them less reliable than cash flows and therefore less appropriate for decision making. Neither ARR nor payback is an absolute measure
- considers the whole life of the project – methods such as payback only consider the earlier cash flows associated with the project. NPV takes account of all relevant flows associated with the project. Discounting the flows takes account of the fact that later flows are less reliable which ARR ignores

- should lead to maximisation of shareholder wealth. If the cost of capital reflects the investors' (i.e. shareholders') required return, then the NPV reflects the theoretical increase in their wealth (see session 18 later). For a company, this is considered to be the primary objective of the business.

However, there are some potential drawbacks:

- It is difficult to explain to managers. To understand the meaning of the NPV calculated requires an understanding of discounting. The method is not as intuitive as techniques such as payback.
- It requires knowledge of the cost of capital. As we will see later (session 18), the calculation of the cost of capital is, in practice, more complex than identifying interest rates. It involves gathering data and making a number of calculations based on that data and some estimates. The process may be deemed too protracted for the appraisal to be carried out.
- It is relatively complex. For the reasons explained above, NPV may be rejected in favour of simpler techniques.

7 Time-saving in the exam

Although you will be able to perform almost any NPV calculation using the above information, there are a number of time-saving techniques that can help you in the exam.

Present Value Tables

$(1 + r)^{-n}$ is called the discount factor (DF). In the exam you will be provided with a Present Value table that gives the discount factors for various different discount rates over various time period. So, to find the DF, for example if r = 10% and n = 5, you can:

The 5-year DF at 10%

Formula or **Tables** (given in examination)

$$\frac{1}{(1.10)^5} = 0.621$$

You can simply find the DF from the PV table by locating the DF at the 10% column and the 5-year row, i.e. 0.621

Test your understanding 5 – Discounting using tables

What amount should be invested now to receive $10,000 in four years' time if r = 8% pa.

Show your workings using the formula approach and then compare this with using the present value table.

Discounting annuities

An annuity is a constant annual cash flow for a number of years.

Illustration 2 – Discounting annuities

A payment of $1,000 is to be made every year for 3 years, the first payment occurring in one year's time. The interest rate is 10%. What is the PV of the annuity?

Solution

The PV of an annuity could be found by adding the PVs of each payment separately.

Time	Payment	DF @ 10% (from tables)	PV
	$		$
T_1	1,000	0.909	909
T_2	1,000	0.826	826
T_3	1,000	0.751	751
		2.486	2,486

However, you can see from the table that the sum of all the DF is 2.486.

Therefore the PV can be found more quickly:

$1,000 × 2.486= $2,486.

The **annuity factor** (AF) is the name given to the sum of the individual DF.

The PV of an annuity can therefore be quickly found using the formula:

PV = Annual cash flow × AF

Like with calculating a discount factor, the AF can be found using a formula.

The formula is:

$$AF = \frac{1 - (1+r)^{-n}}{r}$$

Test your understanding 6 – Discounting annuities

A payment of $3,600 is to be made every year for seven years, the first payment occurring in one year's time. The interest rate is 8%. What is the PV of the annuity.

Annuity Tables

Just as you are provided with a Present Value Table in the exam showing pre-calculated discount factors, you will also be provided with an Annuity Table (sometimes referred to as a Cumulative Present Value Table), which provides pre-calculated annuity factors for various different discount rates over various periods.

So again, you have a choice. For example, for a three-year annuity at 10%:

The AF

Formula or **Tables** (given in examination)

Formula:

$$\frac{1 - (1+r)^{-n}}{r}$$

$$= \frac{1 - (1.1)^{-3}}{0.1}$$

=2.486

Tables (given in examination):

You can simply find the AF from the annuity table by locating the DF at the 10% column and the three-year row, i.e. 2.486

Note: there might be a small difference due to roundings.

The tables should not be used as a substitute for knowing how to use the formula. Remember, the tables only cover a small range of discount rates and time periods and you may be required to calculate a discount factor or annuity factor for variables outside of this range.

Test your understanding 7 – Discounting annuities using tables

A payment of $11,400 is to be made every year for 13 years, the first payment occurring in one year's time. The interest rate is 5%. What is the PV of the annuity.

Show you workings using both the formula approach and the annuity table.

Discounting perpetuities

A perpetuity is an annual cash flow that occurs forever.

It is often described by examiners as a cash flow continuing 'for the foreseeable future'.

The PV of a **perpetuity** is found using the formula

$$PV = \frac{\text{cash flow}}{r}$$

or

$$PV = \text{cash flow} \times \frac{1}{r}$$

$\frac{1}{r}$ is known as the perpetuity factor.

The PV of a **growing perpetuity** is found using the formula

$$PV = \text{cash flow at } T_1 \times \frac{1}{r - g}$$

$\frac{1}{r-g}$ is known as the perpetuity factor, with growth

Test your understanding 8 – Discounting perpetuities

Calculate the present value of the following, assuming a discount rate of 10%.

(1) $3,000 received in one year's time and for ever

(2) $3,000 received in one year's time, then growing by 2% per annum in perpetuity

Advanced and delayed annuities and perpetuities

The use of annuity factors and perpetuity factors both assume that the first cash flow will be occurring in one year's time. Annuity or perpetuity factors will therefore discount the cash flows back to give the value one year before the first cash flow arose. For standard annuities and perpetuities this gives the present (T_0) value since the first cash flow started at T_1.

Be careful: if this is not the case, you will need to adjust your calculation.

Advanced annuities and perpetuities

Some regular cash flows may start now (at T_0) rather than in one year's time (T_1).

Calculate the PV by ignoring the payment at T_0 when considering the number of cash flows and then adding one to the annuity or perpetuity factor.

Advanced annuities: An illustration

A 5-year $600 annuity is starting today. Interest rates are 10%. Find the PV of the annuity.

Solution

This is essentially a standard 4-year annuity with an additional payment at T_0. The PV could be calculated as follows:

	T_0		T_1	T_2	T_3	T_4
CF	600		600	600	600	600
	↓		↘	↓	↓	↙
PV	600	+	600 × 4-year 10% AF			

PV = 600 + 600 × 3.17 = 600 + 1902 = $2,502

The same answer can be found more quickly by adding 1 to the AF:

PV = 600 × (1 + 3.17) = 600 × 4.17 = $2,502.

Advanced perpetuities: An illustration

A perpetuity of $2,000 is due to commence immediately. The interest rate is 9%. What is the PV?

Solution

This is essentially a standard perpetuity with an additional payment at T_0. The PV could be calculated as follows:

T_0	T_1	T_2	T_3	T_4 ....
2,000	2,000 → ∞			

$$PV\left(2000\right) + \left(2000 \text{ x } 9\% \text{ perpetuity formula}\right)$$

Again, the same answer can be found more quickly by adding 1 to the perpetuity factor.

$$2000 \times \left(1 + \frac{1}{0.09}\right) = 2000 \quad \times 12.111 = \$24{,}222$$

Additional question – Advanced annuities and perpetuities

Find the present value of the following cash flows:

(1) A fifteen year annuity of $300 starting at once. Interest rates are 6%.

(2) A seven year annuity of $450 starting immediately. Interest rates are 11%

(3) A perpetuity of $33,000 commencing immediately. Interest rates are 22%

(4) A perpetuity of $14,000 starting at once. Interest rates are 12.5%

The answer to this question can be found after the chapter summary diagram at the end of this chapter.

Delayed annuities and perpetuities

Some regular cash flows may start later than T_1.

These are dealt with by:

(1) applying the appropriate factor to the cash flow as normal

(2) discounting your answer back to T_0.

Delayed annuities: An illustration

For delayed cash flows, applying the standard annuity factor will find the value of the cash flows one year before they began, which in this illustration is T_2. To find the PV, an additional calculation is required – the value must be discounted back to T_0.

Illustration – Delayed annuities and perpetuities

What is the PV of $200 incurred each year for four years, starting in three year's time, if the discount rate is 5%?

Solution

Method: A four-year annuity starting at T_3

(1-4)

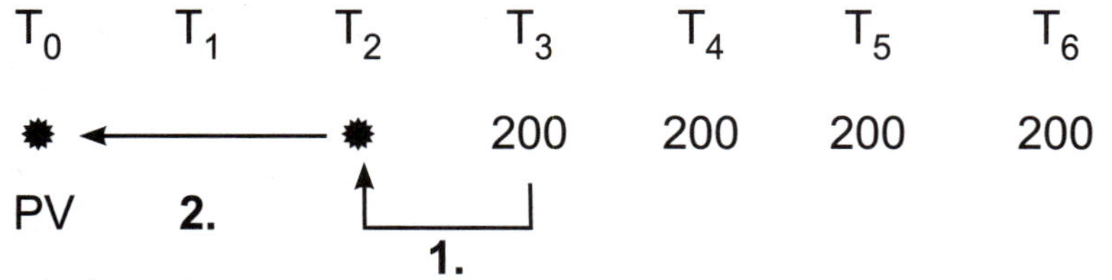

Step 1. Discount the annuity as usual

200 × 4yr 5% AF = 200 × 3.546 = 709.2

Note that this gives the value of the annuity at T_2

Step 2. Discount the answer back to T_0

709.2 × 2yr 5% DF = 709.2 × 0.907 = $643

Care must be taken to discount back the appropriate number of years. The figure here was discounted back two years because the first step gave the value at T_2. It can help to draw a timeline as above and mark on the effect of the first step (as shown with a 1. here) to help you remember.

Additional question – Delayed annuities and perpetuities

Find the present value of the following cash flows:

(1) A fifteen year annuity of $300 starting at T_3. Interest rates are 6%.

(2) A seven year annuity of $450 starting in five year's time. Interest rates are 11%

(3) A perpetuity of $33,000 commencing at T_2. Interest rates are 22%

(4) A perpetuity of $14,000 starting in ten year's time. Interest rates are 12.5%

(5) A perpetuity of $2,000 starting in six year's time, growing at 3% per annum. Interest rates are 10%

The answer to this question can be found after the chapter summary diagram at the end of this chapter.

8 The Internal Rate of Return (IRR)

The IRR is another project appraisal method using DCF techniques.

The IRR represents the discount rate at which the NPV of an investment is zero. As such it represents a breakeven cost of capital.

Decision rule:

- projects should be accepted if their IRR is greater than the cost of capital.

IRR

Using the NPV method, PVs are calculated by discounting cash flows at a given cost of capital, and the difference between the PV of costs and the PV of benefits is the NPV. In contrast, the IRR method of DCF analysis is to calculate the exact DCF rate of return that the project is expected to achieve.

If an investment has a positive NPV, it means it is earning more than the cost of capital. If the NPV is negative, it is earning less than the cost of capital. This means that if the NPV is zero, it will be earning exactly the cost of capital.

Conversely, the percentage return on the investment must be the rate of discount or cost of capital at which the NPV equals zero. This rate of return is called the IRR, or the DCF yield and if it is higher than the target rate of return then the project is financially worth undertaking.

Calculating the IRR using linear interpolation

The steps in linear interpolation are:

(1) Calculate two NPVs for the project at two different costs of capital

(2) Use the following formula to find the IRR:

$$IRR = L + \left[\frac{N_L}{N_L - N_H} \times (H - L) \right]$$

where:

L = Lower rate of interest

H = Higher rate of interest

N_L = NPV at lower rate of interest

N_H = NPV at higher rate of interest.

The diagram below shows the IRR as estimated by the formula.

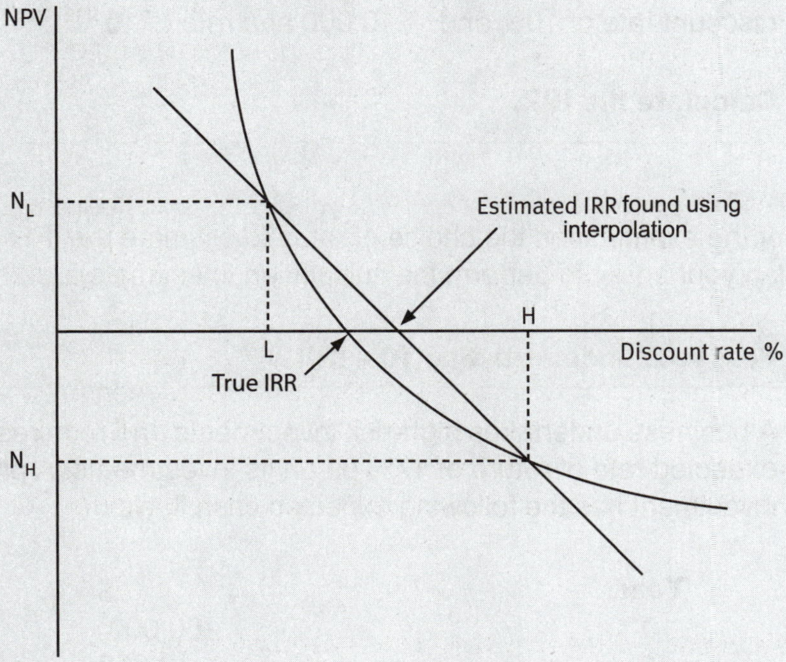

Calculating the IRR

The IRR may be calculated by a linear interpolation, i.e. by assuming a linear relationship between the NPV and the discount rate. Plotting a graph would give an approximate IRR, but the same point can also be found using a formula.

Step 1 Calculate two NPVs for the project at two different costs of capital. You can choose any costs of capital and get a fair result. However, it helps to find two costs of capital for which the NPV is close to 0, because the IRR will be a value close to them. Ideally, you should use one cost of capital where the NPV is positive and the other cost of capital where the NPV is negative, although this is not essential. You should not waste time in the exam

Step 2 Once the two NPVs have been calculated, they and their associated costs of capital can be used to calculate the IRR. In other words, we can estimate the IRR by finding the point where a line joining these points would cross the x-axis (the point where the NPV is zero) in a graph plotting the project NPV against various discount rates.

To calculate the exact IRR requires a more complex technique, best carried out using an Excel spreadsheet. This will not be expected in the exam.

Test your understanding 9 – IRR

A potential project's predicted cash flows give a NPV of $50,000 at a discount rate of 10% and –$10,000 at a rate of 15%.

Calculate the IRR.

For the examination the choice of rates to estimate the IRR is less important than your ability to perform the calculation to estimate it.

Test your understanding 10 – IRR

A business undertakes high-risk investments and requires a minimum expected rate of return of 17% pa on its investments. A proposed capital investment has the following expected cash flows:

Year	$
0	(50,000)
1	18,000
2	25,000
3	20,000
4	10,000

(1) Calculate the NPV of the project if the cost of capital is 15%.

(2) Calculate the NPV of the project if the cost of capital is 20%.

(3) Use the NPVs you have calculated to estimate the IRR of the project.

(4) Recommend, on financial grounds alone, whether this project should go ahead.

Calculating the IRR with even cash flows

There is a simpler technique available, using annuity tables, if the project cash flows are annuities.

(1) Find the cumulative DF, Initial investment ÷ Annual inflow

(2) Find the life of the project, n.

(3) Look along the n year row of the cumulative DF until the closest value is found.

(4) The column in which this figure is found is the IRR.

Illustration – Calculating IRR of a project with even cash flows

Find the IRR of a project with an initial investment of $1.5 million and three years of inflows of $700,000 starting in one year.

Solution

NPV calculation:

		Cash flow	DF (c) %	PV
		$000		$000
Time				
0	Investment	(1,500)	1	(1,500)
1–3	Inflow	700	(b)	(a)
NPV				Nil

- The aim is to find the discount rate (c) that produces an NPV of nil.
- Therefore the PV of inflows (a) must equal the PV of outflows, $1,500,000.
- If the PV of inflows (a) is to be $1,500,000 and the size of each inflow is $700,000, the DF required (b) must be 1,500,000 ÷ 700,000 = 2.143.
- The discount rate (c) for which this is the 3-year factor can be found by looking along the 3-year row of the cumulative DFS shown in the annuity table.
- The figure of 2.140 appears under the 19% column suggesting an IRR of 19% is the closest.

Calculating the IRR with perpetuities

$$\text{IRR of a perpetuity} = \frac{\text{Annual inflow}}{\text{Initial investment}} \times 100$$

Illustration – Calculating IRR where cash flows are perpetuities

Find the IRR of an investment that costs $20,000 and generates $1,600 for an indefinitely long period.

Solution

$$\text{IRR} = \frac{\text{Annual inflow}}{\text{Initial investment}} \times 100 = \frac{\$1,600}{\$20,000} \times 100 = 8\%$$

Test your understanding 11 – IRR with even cash flows

Find the IRR of an investment of $50,000 if the inflows are:

(a) $5,000 in perpetuity

(b) $8,060 for eight years.

9 Advantages and disadvantages of IRR

Advantages

The IRR has a number of benefits, e.g. it:

- considers the time value of money
- is a percentage and therefore easily understood
- uses cash flows not profits
- considers the whole life of the project
- means a firm selecting projects where the IRR exceeds the cost of capital should increase shareholders' wealth

Disadvantages

- It is not a measure of absolute profitability.
- Interpolation only provides an estimate and an accurate estimate requires the use of a spreadsheet programme.
- It is fairly complicated to calculate.
- Non-conventional cash flows may give rise to multiple IRRs which means the interpolation method can't be used.

Advantages and disadvantages of IRR

Advantages:

- IRR considers the time value of money. The current value earned from an investment project is therefore more accurately measured. As discussed above this is a significant improvement over the basic methods.
- IRR is a percentage and therefore easily understood. Although managers may not completely understand the detail of the IRR, the concept of a return earned is familiar and the IRR can be simply compared with the required return of the organisation.
- IRR uses cash flows not profits. These are less subjective as discussed above.
- IRR considers the whole life of the project rather than ignoring later flows (which would occur with payback for example).
- IRR a firm selecting projects where the IRR exceeds the cost of capital should increase shareholders' wealth. This holds true provided the project cash flows follow the standard pattern of an outflow followed by a series of inflows, as in the investment examples above.

However there are a number of difficulties with the IRR approach:

- It is not a measure of absolute profitability. A project of $1,000 invested now and paying back $1,100 in a year's time has an IRR of 10%. If a company's required return is 6%, then the project is viable according to the IRR rule but most businesses would consider the absolute return too small to be worth the investment.
- Interpolation only provides an estimate (and an accurate estimate requires the use of a spreadsheet programme). The cost of capital calculation itself is also only an estimate and if the margin between required return and the IRR is small, this lack of accuracy could actually mean the wrong decision is taken.

- For example if the cost of capital is found to be 8% (but is actually 8.7%) and the project IRR is calculated as 9.2% (but is actually 8.5%) the project would be wrongly accepted. Note that where such a small margin exists, the project's success would be considered to be sensitive to the discount rate (see session 12 on risk).
- Non-conventional cash flows may give rise to no IRR or multiple IRRs. For example a project with an outflow at T0 and T2 but income at T1 could, depending on the size of the cash flows, have a number of different profiles on a graph (see below). Even where the project does have one IRR, it can be seen from the graph that the decision rule would lead to the wrong result as the project does not earn a positive NPV at any cost of capital.

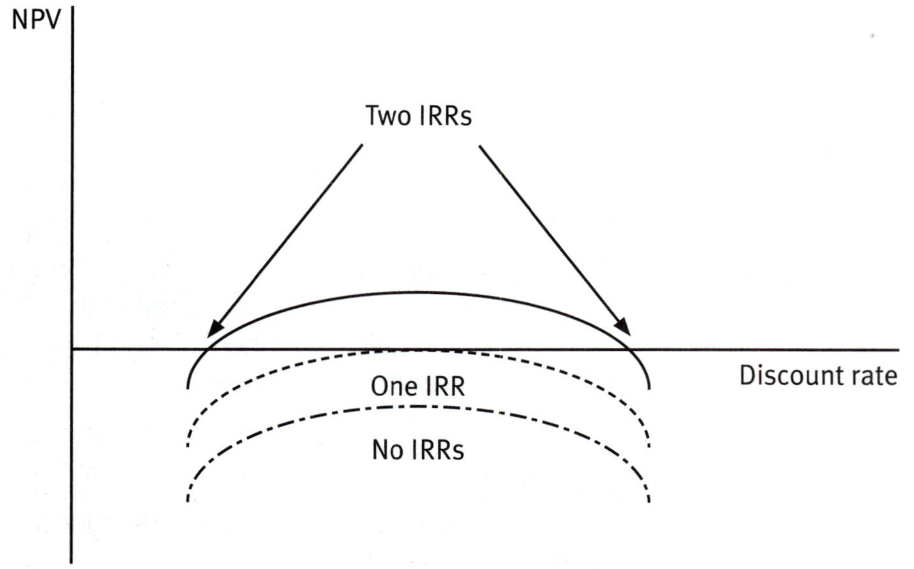

10 NPV versus IRR

Both NPV and IRR are investment appraisal techniques which discount cash flows and are superior to the basic techniques discussed in the previous session. However only NPV can be used to distinguish between two mutually-exclusive projects, as the diagram below demonstrates:

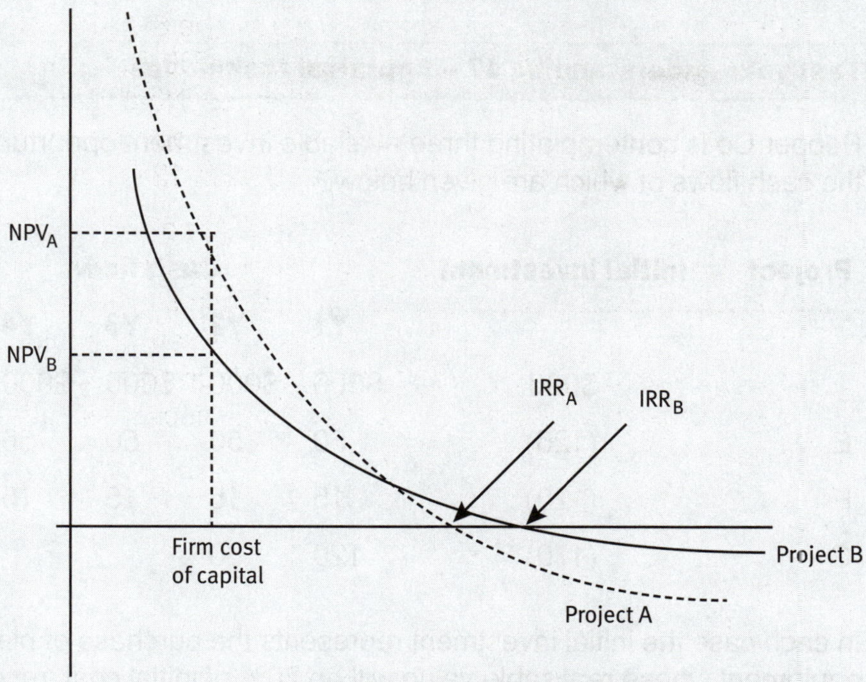

The profile of project A is such that it has a lower IRR and applying the IRR rule would prefer project B. However in absolute terms, A has the higher NPV at the company's cost of capital and should therefore be preferred.

NPV is therefore the better technique for choosing between projects.

The advantage of NPV is that it tells us the absolute increase in shareholder wealth as a result of accepting the project, at the current cost of capital. The IRR simply tells us how far the cost of capital could increase before the project would not be worth accepting.

Test your understanding 12 – Appraisal techniques

Pepper Co is contemplating three available investment opportunities, the cash flows of which are given below.

Project	Initial investment	Cash flow				
		Y1	Y2	Y3	Y4	Y5
	$000	$000	$000	$000	$000	$000
E	(125)	50	50	50	50	
F	(120)	15	15	15	15	200
G	(170)	120	80			

In each case the initial investment represents the purchase of plant and equipment whose realisable value will be 20% of initial cost, receivable in addition to the above flow at the end of the life of the project.

Required:

For each of the three projects:

(a) Calculate the accounting rate of return (based on the average investment method)

(b) Calculate the payback period

(c) Calculate the net present value using a discount rate of 10%

(d) Calculate the internal rate of return

Test your understanding 13

The higher risk of a project can be recognised by decreasing

A the cost of the initial investment of the project

B the estimates of future cash inflows from the project

C the internal rate of return of the project

D the required rate of return of the project

Test your understanding 14

Which of the following statements about net present value (NPV) and internal rate of return (IRR) methods are correct?

(i) An investment with a positive NPV is financially viable

(ii) NPV is a superior method of investment appraisal to IRR

(iii) The graph of NPV against discount rate has a negative slope for most projects

(iv) NPV is the present value of expected future net cash receipts less the cost of the investment

A (i) and (ii) only

B (ii) and (iv) only

C (i), (ii) and (iii) only

D (i), (ii), (iii) and (iv)

Test your understanding 15

Which of the following is not an advantage of the IRR?

A It considers the whole life of the project

B It uses cash flows not profits

C It is a measure of absolute return

D It considers the time value of money

Test your understanding 16

Arbury plc has made an investment with a net present value (NPV) of $42,000 at 10% and an NPV of ($22,000) at 20%.

What is the internal rate of return of the project?

A 31.0%

B 16.6%

C 15.0%

D 13.4%

Test your understanding 17

A company is considering a two-year project which has two annual internal rates of return, namely 10% and 25%. The sum of the undiscounted cash flows is positive.

The project will necessarily have a positive net present value, when the annual cost of capital is

A More than 25%

B More than 10%

C Between 10% and 25%

D Less than 25%

Chapter summary

DCF TECHNIQUES

Time value of money

- interest
- inflation
- risk.

Compounding:

Calculates a terminal value: $F = P(1 + r)^n$

Discounting:

Calculates a present ie T_0 value

PV of a single sum:

$$P = \frac{F}{(1+r)^n} = F(1+r)^{-n}$$

PV of an annuity:

Annuity x AF where AF is $\frac{1-(1+r)^{-n}}{r}$

PV of a perpetuity:

Perpetuity x 1/r

Advanced annuities/ perpetuities:

- ignore T_0 flow
- add 1 to the annuity/ perpetuity factor

Delayed annuities/ perpetuities:

- apply factor as normal
- discount back to T_0.

NPV:

Gives the net surplus earned for investors.

Advantages:

- DCF technique
- absolute returns

Disadvantage:

- complex.

IRR:

- Gives the DCF return earned on the project
- is the rate at which NPV=0
- Found through interpolation

$$IRR = L + \left[\frac{N_L}{N_L - N_H} \times (H - L)\right]$$

- quick method for annuities and perpetuities.

Advantages:

- DCF technique
- % ∴ understood.

Disadvantages:

- estimate
- complex
- may mislead where
  - choice
  - unusual cfs.

Answer to additional question – advanced

(1) This is a standard 14-year annuity with one additional payment at T_0.

Step 1: Look up the 14-year AF : AF = 9.295

Step 2: Add 1 : 9.295 + 1 = 10.295

Step 3: Calculate the PV : 300 × 10.295 = $3,088.50

(2) This is a standard 6-year annuity with one additional payment at T_0.

Step 1: Look up the 6-year AF : AF = 4.231

Step 2: Add 1 : 4.231 + 1 = 5.231

Step 3: Calculate the PV : 450 × 5.231= $2,353.95

(3) This is simply a standard perpetuity with one additional payment at T_0.

Step 1: Calculate the perpetuity factor : 1/0.22 = 4.545

Step 2: Add 1 : 4.545 + 1 = 5.545

Step 3: Calculate the PV : 33,000 × 5.545 = $182,985

(4) This is simply a standard perpetuity with one additional payment at T_0.

Step 1: Calculate the perpetuity factor : 1/0.125 = 8

Step 2: Add 1 : 8+ 1 = 9

Step 3: Calculate the PV : 14,000 × 9 = $126,000

Answer to additional question – delayed

(1) A fifteen year annuity of $300 starting at T_3.

Step 1: Look up the 15-year AF : AF = 9.712

Step 2: Discount the annuity as usual : 300 × 9.712= $2,913.60

Note that this gives the value of the annuity at T_2

Step 3: Discount the answer back to T_0 :$2,913.60 × 0.890 = $2,593.10

(2) A seven year annuity of $450 starting in five year's time.

Step 1: Look up the 7-year AF : AF = 4.712

Step 2: Discount the annuity as usual : 450 × 4.712= $2,120 40

Note that this gives the value of the annuity at T_4

Step 3: Discount the answer back to T_0 : 2,120.40 × 0.659= $1,397.34

(3) A perpetuity of $33,000 commencing at T_2.

Step 1: Calculate the perpetuity factor : 1/0.22 = 4.545

Step 2: Discount the perpetuity as usual : 33,000 × 4.545 = $149,985

Note that this gives the value of the perpetuity at T_1

Step 3: Calculate the PV : 149,985 × (1 / 1.22) = $122,939

(4) A perpetuity of $14,000 starting in ten year's time.

Step 1: Calculate the perpetuity factor : 1/0.125 = 8

Step 2: Discount the perpetuity as usual : 14,000 × 8= $112,000

Note that this gives the value of the perpetuity at T_9

Step 3: Calculate the PV : 112,000 × (1 / 1.125^9) = $38,801

(5) A perpetuity of $2,000 starting in six year's time, growing at 3% per annum.

Step 1: Calculate the perpetuity factor, with growth : 1/(0.10 – 0.03) = 14.286

Step 2: Discount the perpetuity as usual : 2,000 × 14.286 = $28,572

Note that this gives the value of the perpetuity at T_5

Step 3: Calculate the PV : 28,572 × (1 / 1.10^5) = $17,743

Test your understanding answers

Test your understanding 1 – Compounding

$F = \$5,000\ (1 + 0.05)^6$

$= \$5,000 \times 1.3401$

$= \$6,700$

Test your understanding 2 – Discounting a single sum

$$P = \frac{F}{(1+r)^n} = \frac{115,000}{(1+0.06)^9} = \$68,068$$

Test your understanding 3 – Net present value

Year	Cash flow	DF	PV
	$	at 6%	$
0	(25,000)	1.000	(25,000)
1	6,000	0.943	5,658
2	10,000	0.890	8,900
3	8,000	0.840	6,720
4	7,000	0.792	5,544
			1,822

The NPV of the project is positive at $1,822. The project should therefore be accepted.

Test your understanding 4 – Net present value

Year	Cash flow	DF at 9%	PV
	$		$
0	(240,000)	1.000	(240,000)
1	80,000	0.917	73,360
2	120,000	0.842	101,040
3	70,000	0.772	54,040
4	40,000	0.708	28,320
5	20,000	0.650	13,000
NPV			+ 29,760

The PV of cash inflows exceeds the PV of cash outflows by $29,760, which means that the project will earn a DCF return in excess of 9%, i.e. it will earn a surplus of $29,760 after paying the cost of financing. It should therefore be undertaken.

Test your understanding 5 – Discounting using tables

The amount to be invested is the PV of the future sum.

$P = \$10,000/(1.08)^4 = \$7,350$

$P = \$10,000 \times 0.735 = \$7,350$ (using tables).

Test your understanding 6 – Discounting annuities

Using the formula:

$$\frac{1-(1+r)^{-n}}{r} = \frac{1-(1.08)^{-7}}{0.08} = 5.206$$

$\$3,600 \times 5.206 = \$18,741.60$

Test your understanding 7 – Discounting annuities using tables

Using the formula:

$$\frac{1-(1+r)^{-n}}{r} = \frac{1-(1.05)^{-13}}{0.05} = 9.394$$

$11,400 × 9.394= $107,091.60

From the annuity factor tables, the AF = 9.394.

Test your understanding 8 – Discounting perpetuities

(1) $$PV = \frac{\$3{,}000}{0.1} = \$30{,}000$$

(2) $$PV = \frac{\$3{,}000}{0.1 - 0.02} = \$37{,}500$$

Test your understanding 9 – IRR

$$IRR = 10\% + \frac{50{,}000}{50{,}000-(-10{,}000)} \times (15\%-10\%) = 14.17\%$$

Test your understanding 10 – IRR

Year	**Cash flow**	**DF @ 15%**	**PV @ 15%**	**DF @ 20%**	**PV @ 20%**
	$		$		$
0	(50,000)	1.000	(50,000)	1.000	(50,000)
1	18,000	0.870	15,660	0.833	14,994
2	25,000	0.756	18,900	0.694	17,350
3	20,000	0.658	13,160	0.579	11,580
4	10,000	0.572	5,720	0.482	4,820
NPV			+ 3,440		(1,256)

The IRR is above 15% but below 20%.

Using the interpolation method:

(1) The NPV is + 3,440 at 15%.

(2) The NPV is – 1,256 at 20%.

(3) The estimated IRR is therefore:

$$\text{IRR} = 15\% + \frac{3,440}{(3,440 - (-1,256))} \times (20 - 15)\%$$

$$= 15\% + 3.7\%$$

$$= 18.7\%$$

(4) The project is expected to earn a DCF return in excess of the target rate of 17%, so on financial grounds (ignoring risk) it is a worthwhile investment.

Test your understanding 11 – IRR with even cash flows

(a) $\text{IRR} = \dfrac{\text{Annual inflow}}{\text{Initial investment}} \times 100 = \dfrac{\$5{,}000}{\$50{,}000} \times 100 = 10\%$

(b) NPV calculation

		Cash flow	DF(c) %	PV
		$		$
Time				
0	Investment	(50,000)	1	(50,000)
1–8	Inflow	8,060	(b)	(a)
			NPV	Nil

– The aim is to find the discount rate (c) that produces an NPV of nil.

– Therefore the present value of inflows (a) must equal the present value of outflows, $50,000.

– If the present value of inflows (a) is to be $50,000 and the size of each inflow is $8,060, the discount factor required must be 50,000 ÷ 8,060 = 6.203.

– The discount rate (c) for which this is the 8-year factor can be found by looking along the 8-year row of the cumulative discount factors shown in the annuity table.

– The figure of $6.210 appears under the 6% column suggesting an IRR of 6% is the closest.

Test your understanding 12 – Appraisal techniques

(a) **Accounting rate of return**

For each project the ARR has been calculated as:

$$ARR = \frac{(\text{Total cash flows} - \text{depreciation}) \div \text{project life}}{(\text{Initial investment} + \text{scrap value}) \div 2} \times 100\%$$

and depreciation has been calculated as initial investment – scrap value.

Project E

$$ARR = \frac{(\$200k - \$100k) \div 4}{(\$125k + \$25k) \div 2} \times 100\% = 33.3\%$$

Project F

$$ARR = \frac{(\$260k - \$96k) \div 5}{(\$120k + \$24k) \div 2} \times 100\% = 45.6\%$$

Project G

$$ARR = \frac{(\$200k - \$136k) \div 2}{(\$170k + \$34k) \div 2} \times 100\% = 31.4\%$$

(b) **Payback**

Project E

$$\text{Payback} = \frac{\$125k}{\$50k} = 2.5 \text{ years}$$

Project F

$120k – (4 × $15k) = $60k

$60k ÷ ($200k + $24k) = 0.268

Payback therefore happens after 4.268 years or approx 4 years and 3 months

Project G

$170k – $120k = $50k

$50k ÷ ($80k + $34) = 0.439

Payback therefore happens after 1.439 years, or approx 1 years and 5 months

(c) **NPV @ 10%**

Project E

NPV = ($125k) + $50k × 3.170 + $25k × 0.683 = $50.6k

Project F

NPV = ($120k) + $15k × 3.170 + $200k × 0.621 + $24k × 0.621 = $66.7k

Project G

NPV = ($170k) + $120k × 0.909 + $80k × 0.826 + $34k × 0.826 = $33.2k

(d) **Internal rate of return**

NPV @ 20%

Project E

NPV = ($125k) + $50k × 2.589+ $25k × 0.482 = $16.5k

Project F

NPV = ($120k) + $15k × 2.589 + $200k × 0.402 + $24k × 0.402 = $8.9k

Project G

NPV = ($170k) + $120k × 0.833 + $80k × 0.694 + $34k × 0.694 = $9.1k

IRRs =

Project E

$$IRR = 10\% + \frac{\$50.6k}{\$50.6k - \$16.5k} \times (20\%–10\%) = 24.8\%$$

Project F

$$IRR = 10\% + \frac{\$66.7k}{\$66.7k - \$8.9k} \times (20\%–10\%) = 21.5\%$$

Project G

$$IRR = 10\% + \frac{\$33.2k}{\$33.2k - \$9.1k} \times (20\%–10\%) = 23.8\%$$

Test your understanding 13

Answer B

The internal rate of return (C) and the cost of the initial investment (A) are independent of the risk of the project. The higher the risk of the project, the greater (not less) is the required rate of return (D).

Test your understanding 14

Answer D

All four statements are correct. The NPV method is extensively used in practice to ascertain whether a project is a viable investment or not.

Test your understanding 15

Answer C

IRR is based on discounted cash flow principles. It therefore considers all of the cash flows in a project (A), does not include notional accounting costs such as depreciation (B) and it considers the time value of money (D).

It is not an absolute measure of return, however, as the IRR is expressed as a percentage. Two projects can have the same IRR but very different cash flows. C is therefore an incorrect statement.

Test your understanding 16

Answer B

The IRR can be calculated using the following formula.

If:

a = 10%
b = 20%
A = $42,000
B = ($22,000)

Then:
IRR = a% + (A/(A–B)) × (b-a)% = 10 + 0.66 × 10 = 16.6%

If you selected 31.0% you did not account correctly for the fact that the NPV was negative at a discount rate of 20%. You treated the $22,000 NPV as a positive figure in the calculation. If you selected 13.4% you swapped A and B round in the formula, using A = $22,000 and B = $42,000. If you selected 15.0% you have simply calculated the mid point of the two rates instead of using the IRR formula.

Test your understanding 17

Answer A

The graph would be U-shaped with a negative NPV between 10% and 25% and positive NPVs at less than 10% or more than 25%.

chapter

4

Investment appraisal – further aspects of discounted cash flows

Chapter learning objectives

Upon completion of this chapter you will be able to:

- explain the impact of inflation on interest rates and define and distinguish between real and nominal (money) interest rates
- explain the difference between the real terms and nominal terms approaches to investment appraisal
- use the nominal (money) terms approach to appraise an investment
- use the real terms approach to appraise an investment
- explain the impact of tax on DCF appraisals
- calculate the tax cash flows associated with tax-allowable depreciation and incorporate them into net present values (NPV) calculations
- calculate the tax cash flows associated with taxable profits and incorporate them into NPV calculations
- explain the impact of working capital on an NPV calculation and incorporate working capital flows into NPV calculations.

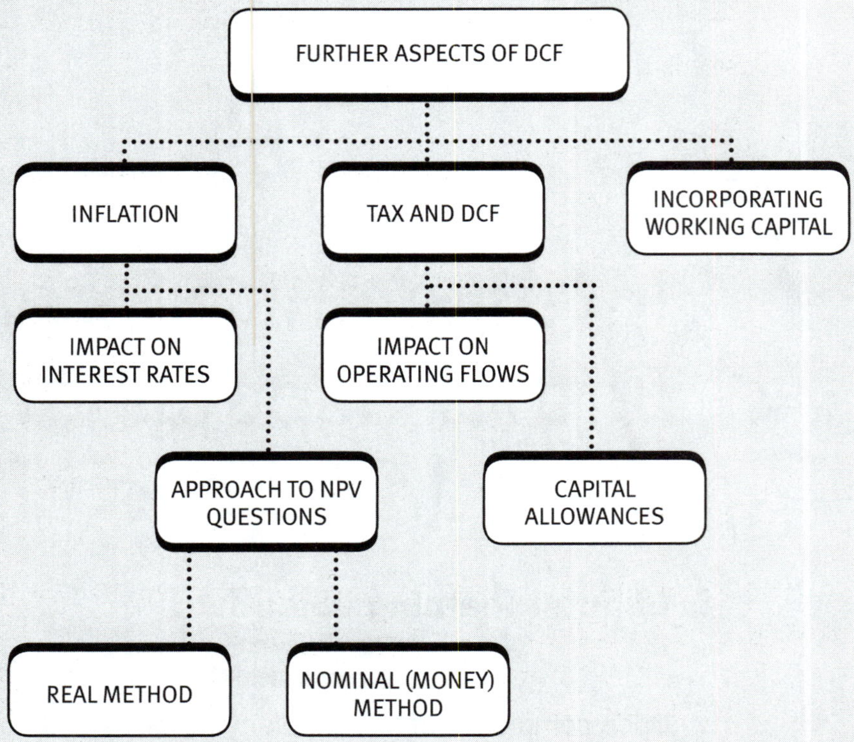

1 The impact of inflation on interest rates

Inflation is a general increase in prices leading to a general decline in the real value of money.

In times of inflation, the fund providers will require a return made up of two elements:

- real return for the use of their funds (i.e. the return they would want if there were no inflation in the economy)
- additional return to compensate for inflation.

The overall required return is called the money or nominal rate of return.

The real and money (nominal) returns are linked by the formula:

$$(1 + i) = (1 + r)(1 + h)$$

where

i = money rate

r = real rate

h = inflation

Illustration of relationship between inflation and interest rates

An investor is prepared to invest $100 for one year.

He requires a real return of 10% pa.

In addition, he requires compensation for loss of purchasing power resulting from inflation which is currently running at 5% pa.

What money rate of return will he require?

Solution

Just to compensate for inflation, his money needs to increase by 5%, to $100 × 1.05 = $105.

To give a real return on top of this, it must further increase by 10%, to $105 × 1.1 = $115.50.

Thus his money must increase overall by 1.05 × 1.1 = 1.155, i.e. by 15.5%.

So the investor's actual required return is 15.5%.

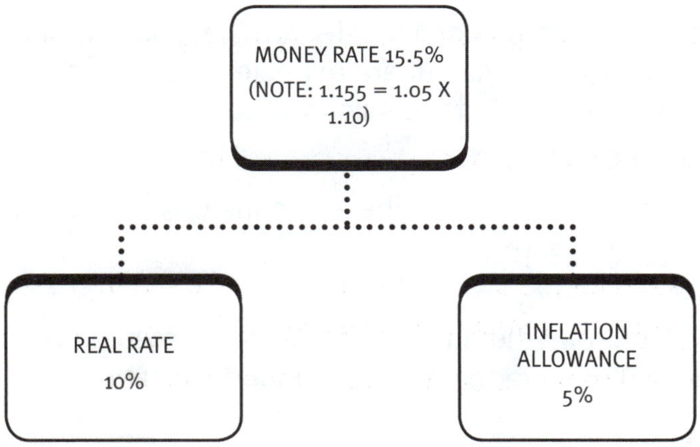

Test your understanding 1 – Money and real returns

$1,000 is invested in an account that pays 10% interest pa. Inflation is currently 7% pa.

Find the real return on the investment.

Test your understanding 2 – Money and real returns

If the real rate of interest is 8% and the rate of inflation is 5%, what should the money rate of interest be?

2 The impact of inflation on cash flows

Where cash flows have not been increased for expected inflation they are described as being in **current prices**, or **today's prices**.

Where cash flows have been increased to take account of expected inflation they are known as **money cash flows**, or **nominal cash flows**. Remember, if they do take inflation into account, they represent expected flows of money, hence the term 'money cash flows'.

You can assume that cash flows you are given in the exam are the money cash flows unless told otherwise.

If the examiner specifies that the cash flows are in current price terms you will generally need to put these in money terms before you can discount them (although see "other methods of dealing with inflation" below).

- For example if the question tells you that sales for the next 3 years are $100 in current terms but are expected to inflate by 10%, then what he actually means is that the sales will be:

  Year 1: $110
  Year 2: $121 } i.e. these are the cash flows in money terms
  Year 3: $133.10

Make sure you read the question carefully. Sometimes you will be given the cash flows in Year 1 terms with subsequent inflation.

- For example if the question says "Sales will be $100 in the first year, but are they going to inflate by 10% for the next two years", then the sales will be:

  Year 1: $100
  Year 2: $110 } compare these to the previous example – make sure
  Year 3: $121 you understand why they are different!

The impact of inflation can be dealt with in two different ways - both methods give the same NPV.

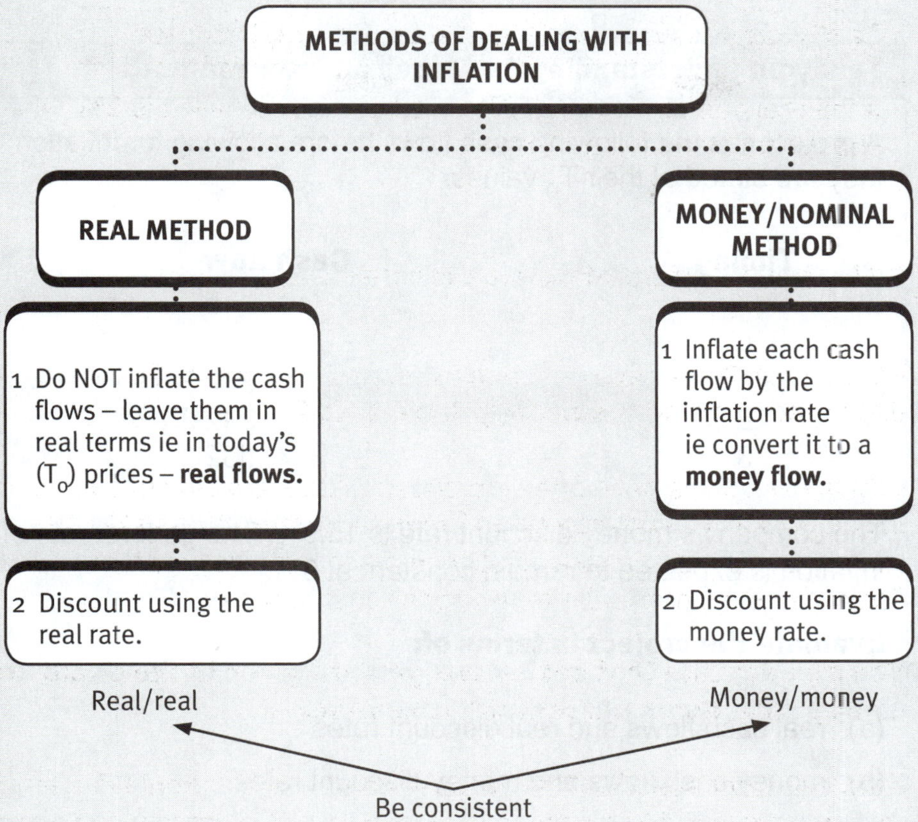

Test your understanding 3 – Money and real methods

Storm Co is evaluating Project X, which requires an initial investment of $50,000. Expected net cash flows are $20,000 per annum for four years at today's prices. However these are expected to rise by 5.5% pa because of inflation. The firm's money cost of capital is 15%.

Find the NPV by:

(a) discounting money cash flows

(b) discounting real cash flows.

Test your understanding 4 – Money and real methods

A project has the following cash flows before allowing for inflation, i.e. they are stated at their T_0 values.

Timing	Cash flow
	$
0	(750)
1	330
2	242
3	532

The company's money discount rate is 15.5%. The general rate of inflation is expected to remain constant at 5%.

Evaluate the project in terms of:

(a) real cash flows and real discount rates

(b) money cash flows and money discount rates.

3 Specific and general inflation rates

The TYUs given above had all cash flows inflating at the general rate of inflation. In practice, inflation does not affect all costs to the same extent. In some investment appraisal questions you may be given information on more than one inflation rate. In these situations you will have information on both specific inflation rates and general inflation rates.

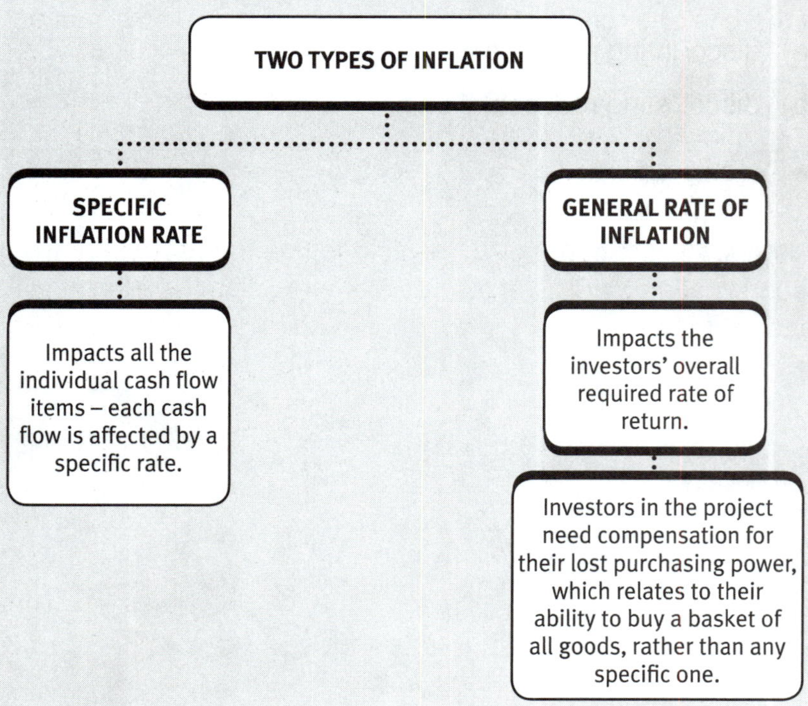

In situations where you are given a number of specific inflation rates, the real method outlined above cannot be used.

The following gives a useful summary of how to approach examination questions.

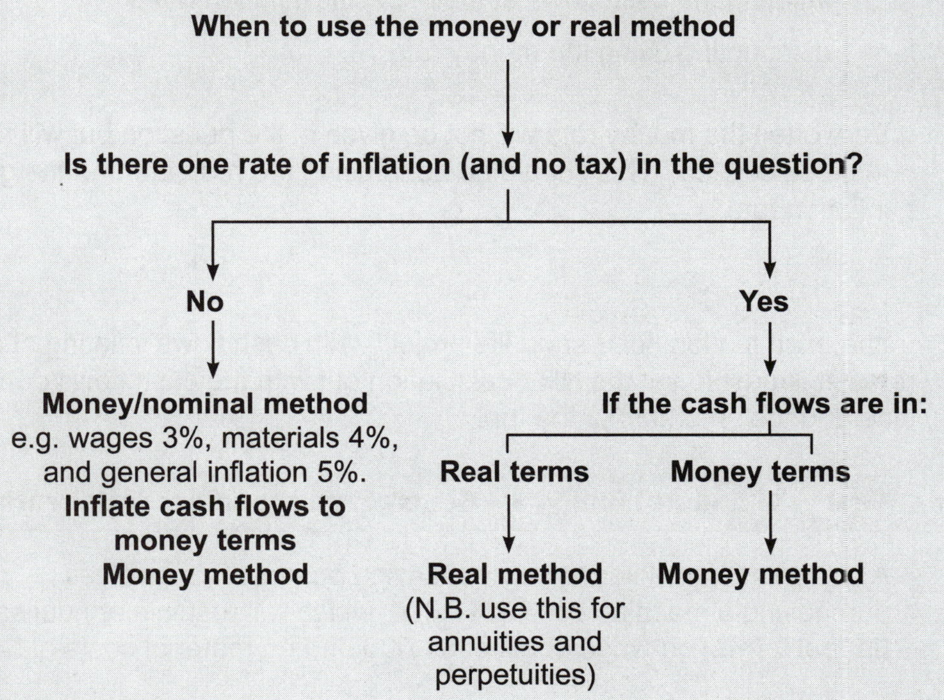

If a question contains both tax and inflation, it is advisable to use the money method.

Specific and general inflation rates

If there is one rate of inflation in the question both the real and money method will give the same answer. However it is easier to adjust one discount rate, rather than all the cash flows over a number of years. This is particularly true where the cash flows are annuities. The real method is the only possible method where they are perpetuities.

Although it is theoretically possible to use the real method in questions incorporating tax, it is extremely complex. It is therefore much safer (and easier) to use the money/nominal method in all questions where tax is taken into account.

To use the real method when cash flows inflate at different rates (specific rates) is extremely complex and would involve a lot of calculations. It is therefore advisable to always use the money method in these situations. This involves:

- inflating the cash flows at their specific inflation rates
- discounting using the money rate

Very often the money rate will not be given in the question but will need to be calculated. This should be done using the real rate and the general inflation rate.

In the examination, for a short life project, with cash flows inflating at different rates, it is best to set the NPV calculation out with the cash flows down the side and the time across the top.

Test your understanding 5 – General and specific inflation rates

A company is considering a cost-saving project. This involves purchasing a machine costing $7,000, which will result in annual savings (in real terms) on wage costs of $1,000 and on material costs of $400.

The following forecasts are made of the rates of inflation each year for the next five years:

Wage costs	10%
Material costs	5%
General prices	6%

The cost of capital of the company, in real terms, is 8.5%.

Evaluate the project, assuming that the machine has a life of five years and no scrap value.

4 Dealing with tax in NPV calculations

Since most companies pay tax, the impact of corporation tax must be considered in any investment appraisal.

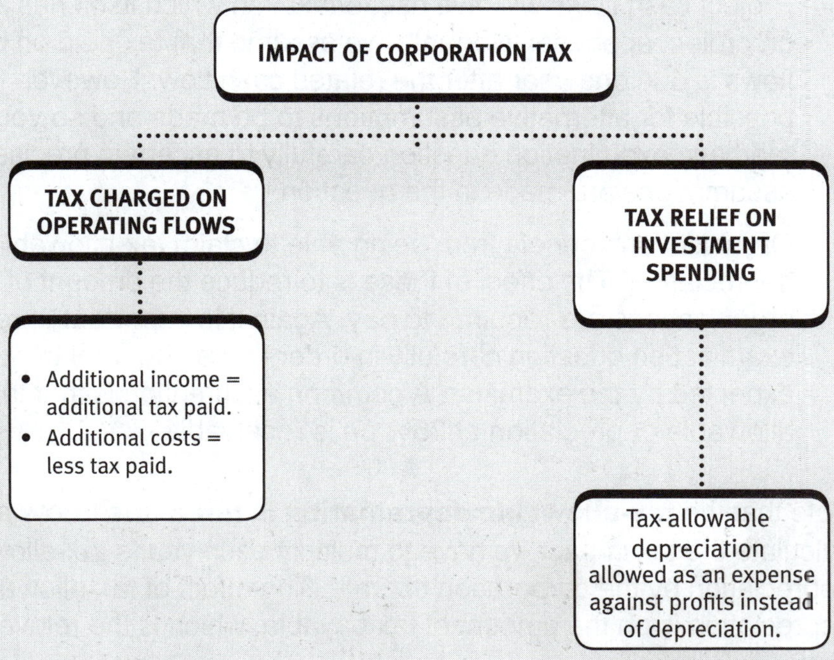

The impact of taxation on cash flows

Corporation tax charged on a company's profits is a relevant cash flow for NPV purposes. It is assumed, unless otherwise stated in the question, that:

- operating cash inflows will be taxed at the corporation tax rate
- operating cash outflows will be tax deductible and attract tax relief at the corporation tax rate
- investment spending attracts tax-allowable depreciation
- the company is earning net taxable profits overall (this avoids any issues of carrying losses forwards to reduce future taxation).
- tax is paid one year after the related operating cash flow is earned (unless told otherwise)

The impact of taxation on cash flows

Taxation has the following effects on an investment appraisal problem:

- Project cash flows will give rise to taxation which itself has an impact on project appraisal. Normally we assume that tax paid on operating flows is due one year after the related cash flow. However, it is possible for alternative assumptions to be made and so you should read any examination question carefully to ascertain precisely what assumptions are made in the question.
- Organisations benefit from being able to claim tax-allowable depreciation. The effect of these is to reduce the amount of tax that organisations are required to pay. Again it is important to read any examination question carefully in order to identify what treatment is expected by the examiner. A common assumption is that tax-allowable depreciation at 25% pa is receivable.

Note that the **tax-allowable depreciation is not a cash flow** and to calculate the tax impact we have to multiply each year's tax-allowable depreciation by the corporation tax rate. The effect of tax-allowable depreciation is on the amount of tax payable, which is the relevant cash flow.

In dealing with these tax effects it is always assumed that where a tax loss arises from the project, there are sufficient taxable profits elsewhere in the organisation to allow the loss to reduce any relevant (subsequent) tax payment (and it may therefore be treated as a cash inflow) and that the company has sufficient taxable profits to obtain full benefit from tax-allowable depreciation.

In practice, the effects of taxation are complex, and are influenced by a number of factors including the following:

- the taxable profits and tax rate
- the company's accounting period and tax payment dates
- tax-allowable depreciation
- losses available for set-off

but many of these issues are ignored or simplified for the purposes of NPV investment appraisal.

Tax-allowable depreciation

For tax purposes, a business may not deduct the cost of an asset from its profits as depreciation (in the way it does for financial accounting purposes).

Instead the cost must be deducted from taxable profits in the form of tax-allowable depreciation. The basic rules are as follows:

- tax-allowable depreciation is calculated based on the written down value of the assets (this will either be on a reducing balance or straight line basis – read the question carefully)
- the total amount of tax-allowable depreciation given over the life of an asset will equate to its fall in value over the period (i.e. the cost less any scrap proceeds)
- tax-allowable depreciation is claimed as early as possible
- tax-allowable depreciation is given for every year of ownership except the year of disposal
- in the year of sale or scrap a balancing allowance (BA) or balancing charge arises (BC).

	$
Original cost of asset	X
Cumulative tax-allowable depreciation claimed	(X)
Written down value of the asset	X
Disposal value of the asset	(X)
Balancing allowance or balancing charge	X

Tax-allowable depreciation

If a business buys a capital asset in one year and sells it several years later, the total tax relief it will receive is the tax on the cost of the asset less its eventual disposal value.

For example, if a business buys equipment for $100,000 in Year 0 and disposes of it in Year 5 for $20,000, it will receive tax relief on the net cost of $80,000. If the rate of corporation tax is 30%, the reduction in tax payments over the five years would be 30% × $80,000 = $24,000.

Balancing allowances are given as a final deduction to ensure the full fall in value has been allowed. Balancing charges occur where the total tax-allowable depreciation claimed exceeds the fall in value of the asset. The excess claimed is treated as a taxable amount in the year of disposal.

Test your understanding 6 – Balancing allowance or charge

An asset is bought for $10,000 and will be used on a project for four years after which it will be disposed of. Tax is payable at 30%, one year in arrears, and tax-allowable depreciation is available at 25% reducing balance.

Required:

(a) Calculate the tax-allowable depreciation and hence the tax savings for each year if the proceeds on disposal of the asset are $2,500.

(b) How would your answer change if the asset was sold for $5,000?

(c) If net trading income from the project is $8,000 pa, based on your answer to part (a) and a cost of capital of 10%, calculate the NPV of the project.

For tax purposes care must be taken to identify the exact time of asset purchase relative to the accounting period end. However, unless you are told otherwise in the exam you should assume that an asset is purchased on the first day of an accounting period (T_0) and that the first amount of tax-allowable depreciation is given one year later at T_1

Timing of asset purchase and sale

Assets are always assumed to be bought at T_0. However, this could be the very end of an accounting period (e.g. 31/12/X1) or the start of another (e.g. 1/1/X2).

There is no distinction between these dates for discounting, but there is for tax.

Although the total value of tax-allowable depreciation will not alter, the timing of the asset purchase relative to the accounting period affects how much of the total fall in value is claimed in each tax year. This is because tax-allowable depreciation will be awarded for any asset owned by a company at the end of its accounting period, regardless of how long it has owned that asset.

- If an asset is bought at T_0 on 1/1/X2 (let's say this is the start of an accounting period), the first year of ownership is the period 1/1/X2 – 31/12/X2, and the first tax-allowable depreciation deduction will be set off against profits earned in that period. Since for NPV purposes cash flows are deemed to occur at year end, the tax-allowable depreciation deduction will be claimed at T_1. Corresponding tax relief will therefore occur one year later at T_2.

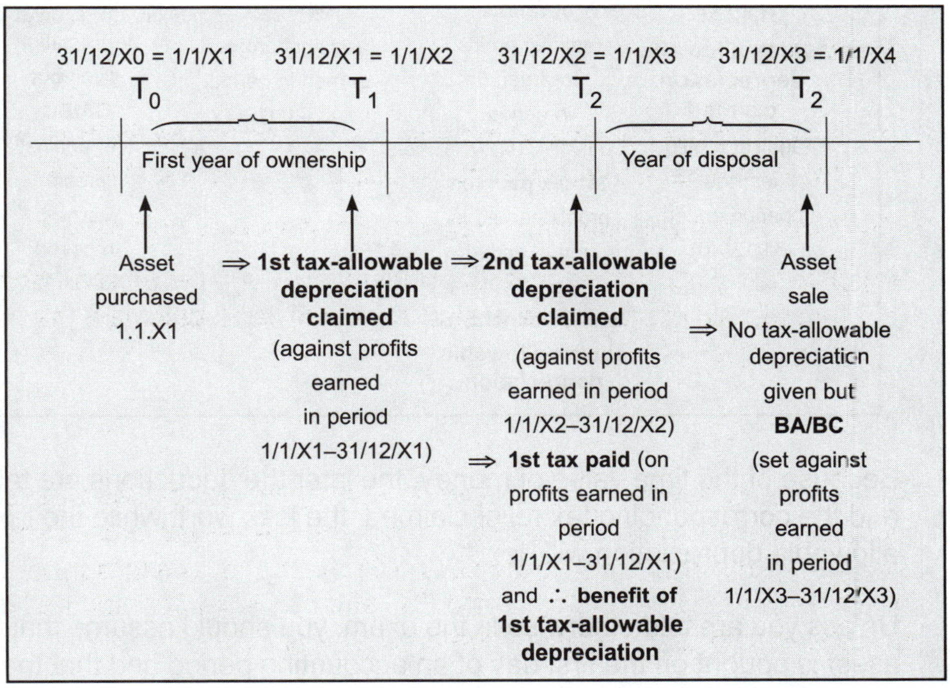

- However, if the asset is bought, still at T_0, but at the end of an accounting period, e.g. on 31/12/X1, the first amount of tax-allowable depreciation will be allowed for set-off against profits earned in the accounting period 1/1/X1 – 31/12/X1 (i.e. a period earlier that in the past example) since this is now the first year of ownership, even though the asset was owned for only one day of the year. This means the tax-allowable depreciation is claimed at T_0, at the same time as the purchase. The corresponding tax relief will therefore occur a year earlier than before at T_1.

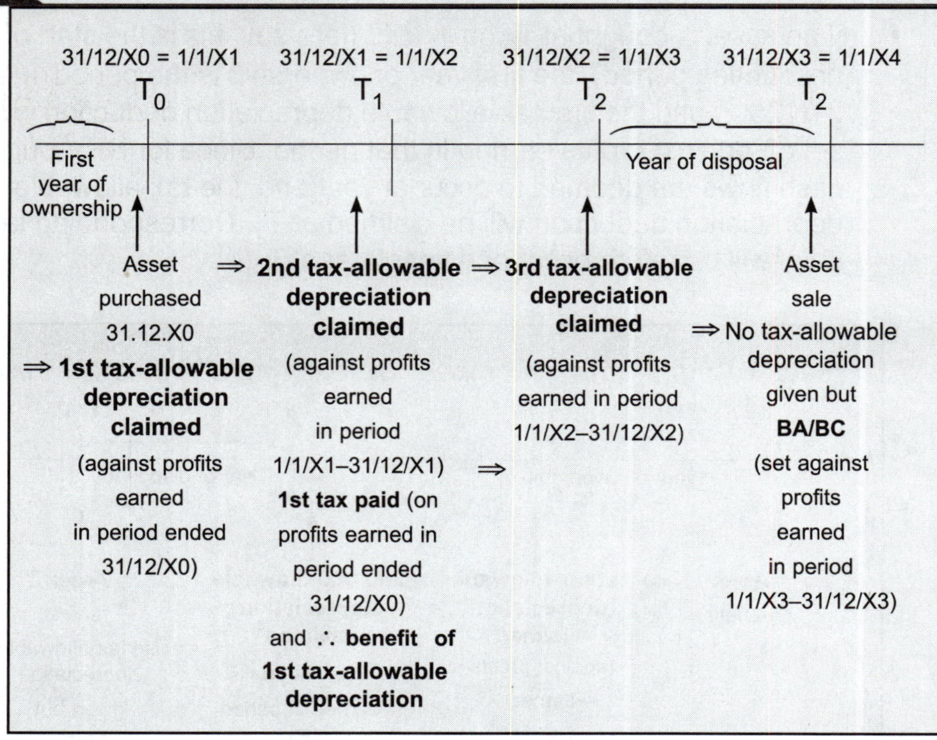

Because of the time value of money, the later the deductions are taken, and the corresponding tax relief claimed, the less worthwhile the tax-allowable depreciation will be.

Unless you are told otherwise in the exam, you should assume that the asset is bought on the first day of an accounting period and that the first amount of tax-allowable depreciation will therefore be given at T_1.

Additional question: Timing of asset purchase and sale

A company buys an asset on the first day of the accounting period for $26,000. It will be used on a project for three years after which it will be disposed of. Tax is payable at 30% one year in arrears, and tax-allowable depreciation is available at 25% reducing balance.

(a) Calculate the tax-allowable depreciation and hence the tax savings for each year if the proceeds on disposal of the asset are $12,500.

(b) If net trading income from the project is $16,000 pa and the cost of capital is 8% calculate the NPV of the project.

(c) How would your answer change if the asset was bought on the last day of the accounting period?

5 Incorporating working capital

Investment in a new project often requires an additional investment in working capital, i.e. the difference between short-term assets and liabilities.

The treatment of working capital is as follows:

- initial investment is a cost at the start of the project
- if the investment is increased during the project, the **increase** is a relevant cash outflow
- at the end of the project all the working capital is 'released' and treated as a cash inflow.

To calculate the working capital cash flows you should:

Step 1: Calculate the absolute amounts of working capital needed in each period

Step 2: Work out the incremental cash flows required each year

Test your understanding 7 – Working capital

A company expects sales for a new project to be $225,000 in the first year growing at 5% pa. The project is expected to last for 4 years Working capital equal to 10% of annual sales is required and needs to be in place at the start of each year.

Calculate the working capital flows for incorporation into the NPV calculation.

If you have a question including both working capital and inflation, you should always adopt the money method (inflating the cash flows). Calculate the actual money amount of the factor on which working capital is dependent (often sales or contribution) before calculating the working capital requirements.

Test your understanding 8 – Working capital

A company anticipates sales for the latest venture to be 100,000 units per year. The selling price is expected to be $3 per unit in the first year, inflating by 8% pa over the three-year life of the project. Working capital equal to 10% of annual sales is required and needs to be in place at the start of each year.

Calculate the working capital flows.

6 Laying out long NPV questions

For the majority of investment appraisal questions, the following pro-forma is recommended:

YEAR	0	1	2	3
	Add an extra year (if tax is delayed) ↗			

(1) Net trading revenue The inflows and outflows from trading (e.g. sales minus operating cash flows)	Inflated where necessary
(2) Tax payable The net trading revenue × tax rate (normally delayed by one year)	Calculated as normal on the money flows
(3) Investment	Shouldn't need inflating!
(4) Residual/scrap value	May need inflating but usually given in money terms
(5) Tax relief on tax-allowable depreciation	Calculated as normal
(6) Working capital flows	Calculate using money figures

7 Dealing with questions with both tax and inflation

Combining tax and inflation in the same question does not make it any more difficult than keeping them separate.

Questions with both tax and inflation are best tackled using the money method.

- Inflate costs and revenues, where necessary, before determining their tax implications.
- Ensure that the cost and disposal values have been inflated (if necessary) before calculating tax-allowable depreciation.
- Always calculate working capital on these inflated figures, unless given.
- Use a post-tax money discount rate.

Test your understanding 9 – NPV with tax and inflation

Ackbono Co is considering a potential project with the following forecasts:

	Now	T_1	T_2	T_3
Initial investment ($million)	(1,000)			
Disposal proceeds ($million)				200
Demand (millions of units)		5	10	6

The initial investment will be made on the first day of the new accounting period.

The selling price per unit is expected to be $100 and the variable cost $30 per unit. Both of these figures are given in today's terms.

Tax is paid at 30%, one year after the accounting period concerned.

Working capital will be required equal to 10% of annual sales. This will need to be in place at the start of each year.

Tax-allowable depreciation is available at 25% reducing balance.

The company has a real required rate of return of 6.8%.

General inflation is predicted to be 3% pa but the selling price is expected to inflate at 4% and variable costs by 5% pa

Determine the NPV of the project.

N.B. work in $ millions and round all numbers to the nearest whole million.

Test your understanding 10

A project has an annual net cash inflow (in current terms) of $3 million, occurring at the end of each year of the project's two-year life. An investment of $3.5 million is made at the outset. All cash inflows are subject to corporation tax of 30%, payable when the cash is received. There is no tax-allowable depreciation on the initial investment. An average inflation rate of 5% per annum is expected to affect the inflows of the project.

The cost of capital in money terms is 15.5%

What is the expected net present value of the project (to the nearest $100,000)?

A $93,000

B $147,000

C $287,000

D $367,000

Test your understanding 11

A company has a 'money' cost of capital of 16.55% per annum. The 'real' cost of capital is 11% per annum.

What is the inflation rate?

A 5%

B 5.55%

C 11%

D 16.55

Test your understanding 12

Data of relevance to the evaluation of a particular project is given below.

Cost of capital in real terms 10% per annum
Expected inflation 5% per annum
Expected increase in the project's annual cash inflow 6% per annum
Expected increase in the project's annual cash outflow 4% per annum

Which one of the following sets of adjustments will lead to the correct NPV being calculated?

	Cash inflow	*Cash outflow*	*Discount percentage*
A	Unadjusted	Unadjusted	10.0%
B	5% pa increase	5% pa increase	15.5%
C	6% pa increase	4% pa increase	15.0%
D	6% pa increase	4% pa increase	15.5%

Test your understanding 13

An asset costing $40,000 is expected to last for three years, after which is can be sold for $16,000. The corporation tax rate is 30%, tax-allowable depreciation at 25% is available, and the cost of capital is 10%. Tax is payable at the end of each financial year.

Capital expenditure occurs on the last day of a financial year, and the tax-allowable depreciation is claimed as early as possible.

What is the cash flow in respect of tax-allowable depreciation that will be used at time 2 of the net present value calculation?

A $1,688

B $2,250

C $5,624

D $7,500

Test your understanding 14

A new project is expected to generate sales of 55,000 units per year. The selling price is expected to be $3.50 per unit in the first year, growing at 6% pa. The project is expected to last for three years. Working capital equal to 12% of annual sales is required and needs to be in place at the start of each year.

What is the cash flow in respect of working capital that will be used at time 2 of the net present value calculation?

A $(25,955)

B $(24,486)

C $(1,386)

D $(1,469)

Chapter summary

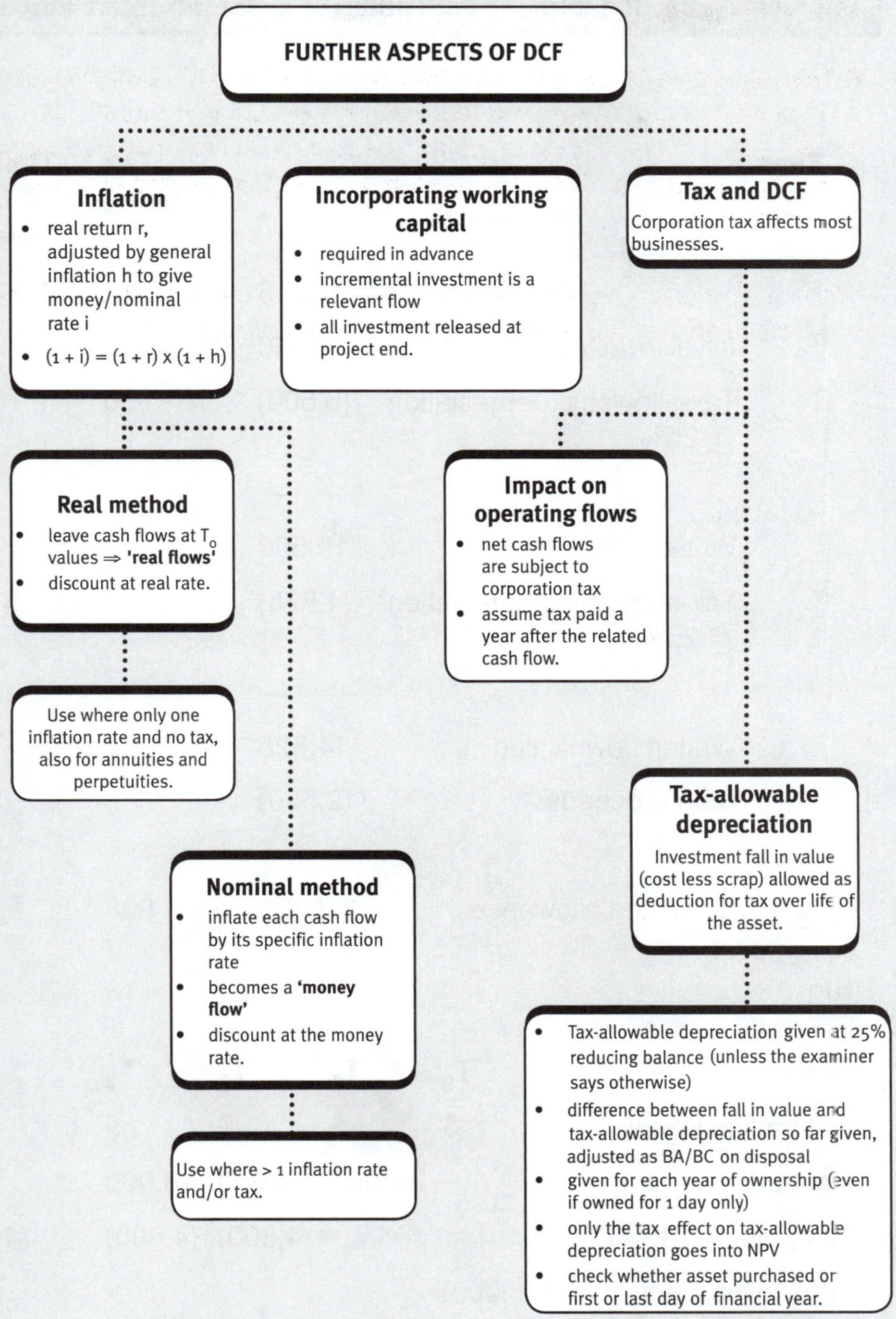

Answer to additional question: Timing of asset purchase and sale

(a)

Time		$	$	Tax saving @30%	Timing of tax relief
T_0	Initial investment		26,000		
T_1	Tax-allowable depreciation @ 25%		(6,500)	1,950	T_2
	Written down value		19,500		
T_2	Tax-allowable depreciation @ 25%		(4,875)	1,463	T_3
	Written down value		14,625		
	Sale proceeds		(12,500)		
T_3	Balancing allowance		2,125	638	T_4

(b)

Time	T_0	T_1	T_2	T_3	T_4
Net trading inflows	$	$	$	$	$
Net trading inflows		16,000	16,000	16,000	
Tax payable (30%)			(4,800)	(4,800)	(4,800)
Initial investment	(26,000)				
Scrap proceeds				12,500	
Tax relief on tax-allowable depreciation			1,950	1,463	638
Net cash flows	(26,000)	16,000	13,150	25,163	(4,162)
DF @ 8%	1.000	0.926	0.857	0.794	0.735
PV	(26,000)	14,816	11,270	19,979	(3,059)
NPV					$17,006

(c) **Time**		$	$	**Tax saving @ 30%**	**Timing of tax relief**
T_0	Initial investment		26,000		
T_0	Tax-allowable depreciation @ 25%		(6,500)	1,950	T_1
	Written down value		19,500		
T_1	Tax-allowable depreciation @ 25%		(4,875)	1,463	T_2
	Written down value		14,625		
T_2	Tax-allowable depreciation @ 25%		(3,656)	1,097	T_3
	Written down value		10,969		
	Sale proceeds		(12,500)		
T_3	Balancing charge		(1,531)	(459)	T_4

Time	T_0	T_1	T_2	T_3	T_4
	$	$	$	$	$
Net trading inflows		16,000	16,000	16,000	
Tax payable (30%)			(4,800)	(4,800)	(4,800)
Initial investment	(26,000)				
Scrap proceeds				12,500	
Tax relief on tax-allowable depreciation		1,950	1,463	1,097	(459)
Net cash flows	(26,000)	17,950	12,663	24,797	(5,259)
DF @ 8%	1.000	0.926	0.857	0.794	0.735
PV	(26,000)	16,622	10,852	19,689	(3,865)
				NPV	$17,298

The NPV is higher as a result of the purchase being made one day earlier.

Test your understanding answers

Test your understanding 1 – Money and real returns

(1 + r) = (1 + i) / (+ h) = 1.10/1.07 = 1.028.

r = 0.028 or 2.8%.

Test your understanding 2 – Money and real returns

(1 + i) = (1 + r)(1 + h) = 1.08 × 1.05 = 1.134

Money rate (i) = 13.4%.

Test your understanding 3 – Money and real methods

Discounting the money cash flows at the money rate – the money method

Discounting money cash flow at the money rate: The cash flows at today's prices are inflated by 5.5% for every year to convert them into money flows. They are then discounted using the money cost of capital.

The money cash flows are therefore:

Time	Working	Money cash flow
		$
0	(50,000)	= (50,000)
1	20,000 × 1.055	= 21,100
2	20,000 × $(1.055)^2$	= 22,261
3	20,000 × $(1.055)^3$	= 23,485
4	20,000 × $(1.055)^4$	= 24,776

Note: The question simply refers to the 'firm's cost of capital'. You can assume this is the money rate – if you are given a real rate the examiner will always specify.

Time	Money cash flow	Discount rate	PV
	$	15%	$
0	(50,000)	1	(50,000)
1	21,100	0.870	18,357
2	22,261	0.756	16,829
3	23,485	0.658	15,453
4	24,776	0.572	14,172
		NPV =	14,811

Discounting the real cash flows at the real rate – the real method.

Calculate the real rate by removing the general inflation from the money cost of capital:

$$(1+r) = \frac{(1+i)}{(1+h)}$$

$$(1+r) = \frac{(1+0.15)}{(1+0.055)}$$

$$(1+r) = 1.09$$

Therefore $r = 0.09$ i.e. 9.%

The real rate can now be applied to the real flows without any further adjustments.

Year	Real cash flow	Discount rate	PV
	$	**9%**	$
0	(50,000)	1	(50,000)
1–4	20,000	3.240	64,800
		NPV =	14,800

Note: Differences due to rounding.

Test your understanding 4 – Money and real methods

(a) **Real cash flows and real discount rates**

Discount rate as per the question of 15.5% includes investor's/lender's inflation expectation of 5%. Hence 'real' discount rate, r, is given by:

$$1+r = \frac{1+i}{1+h}$$

$$1+r = \frac{1+0.155}{1 + 0.05} = 1.10$$

Therefore r is 0.10 or 10%

Timing	**Cash flow**	**Discount factor**	**PV**
$	$	@ 10%	$
0	(750)	1.000	(750)
1	330	0.909	300
2	242	0.826	200
3	532	0.751	400
NPV			150

(b) **Money cash flows and money discount rates**

The discount rate as per the question of 15.5% is the money discount rate.

To convert real cash flows into money flows they will need to be increased by 5% each year from year 0, to allow for inflation.

Timing	Real/ cash flow	Inflation factor	Money cash flow	DF @ 15.5%	PV
	(a)	(b)	(a) × (b)		
	$		$		$
0	(750)	1	(750)	1.000	(750)
1	330	1 + 0.05	346.5	0.866*	300
2	242	$(1 + 0.05)^2$	266.8	0.750	200
3	532	$(1 + 0.05)^3$	615.9	0.649	400
NPV					150

*$1/1.155 = 0.866$

$1/1.155^2 = 0.750$

$1/1.155^3 = 0.649$

Note: that either approach yields identical conclusions (allowing for rounding).

Test your understanding 5 – General and specific inflation rates

Since the question contains both specific and general inflation rates, the money method should be used

Step 1

The money method needs to be calculated using the information provided on the real rate of return and the general rate of inflation

$(1 + i) = (1 + r)(1 + h)$

$(1 + i) = (1.085)(1.06)$

$i = 15\%$

Step 2

Inflate the cash flows using the specific inflation rates and discount using the money rate calculated above.

	T_0	T_1	T_2	T_3	T_4	T_5
	$	$	$	$	$	$
Investment	(7,000)					
Wages savings (inflating @ 10%)		1,100	1,210	1,331	1,464	1,610
Materials savings (inflating @ 5%)		420	441	463	486	510
Net cash flow	(7,000)	1,520	1,651	1,794	1,950	2,120
Discount factor @ 15%	1.000	0.870	0.756	0.658	0.572	0.497
PV of cash flow	(7,000)	1,322	1,248	1,180	1,115	1,054

Therefore NPV = $(1,081) which suggests the project is not worthwhile.

Test your understanding 6 – Balancing allowance or charge

(a)

Time		$	Tax saving @ 30%	Timing of tax relief
T_0	Initial investment	10,000		
T_1	Tax-allowable depreciation @ 25%	(2,500)	750	T_2
	Written down value	7,500		
T_2	Tax-allowable depreciation @ 25%	(1,875)	563	T_3
	Written down value	5,625		
T_3	Tax-allowable depreciation @ 25%	(1,406)	422	T_4
	Written down value	4,219		
T_4	Sale proceeds	(2,500)		
T_4	Balancing Allowance	1,719	516	T_5

Note:

- total tax-allowable depreciation = 2,500 + 1,875 + 1,406 + 1,719 = 7,500 = fall in value of the asset
- total tax relief = 750 + 563 + 422 + 516 = 2251 ≈ 7,500 × 30% (tax-allowable depreciation x tax rate)

(b) If the scrap proceeds had been $5,000, there would be a balancing charge in T4 of $5,000 – $4,219 = $781 and additional tax of $234 ($781 × 30%) would be payable in T5.

Note:

- total tax-allowable depreciation = 2,500 + 1,875 + 1,406 – 781= 5,000 = fall in value of the asset
- total tax relief = 750 + 563 + 422 – 234 = 1,501 ≈ 5,000 × 30% (tax-allowable depreciation x tax rate)

(c)

Time	T_0	T_1	T_2	T_3	T_4	T_5
	$	$	$	$	$	$
Net trading inflows		8,000	8,000	8,000	8,000	
Tax payable (30%)			(2,400)	(2,400)	(2,400)	(2,400)
Initial investment	(10,000)					
Scrap proceeds					2,500	
Tax relief on tax-allowable depreciation			750	563	422	516
Net cash flows	(10,000)	8,000	6,350	6,163	8,522	(1,884)
DF @ 10%	1.000	0.909	0.826	0.751	0.683	0.621
PV	(10,000)	7,272	5,245	4,628	5,821	(1,170)
					NPV	$11,796

Test your understanding 7 – Working capital

Step 1: Calculate the absolute amounts of working capital needed over the project:

	T_0	T_1	T_2	T_3	T_4
	$	$	$	$	$
Sales		225,000	236,250	248,063	260,466
Working capital required(10% sales)	22,500	23,625	24,806	26,047	

Step 2: Work out the **incremental** investment required each year (remember that the full investment is released at the end of the project):

	T_0	T_1	T_2	T_3	T_4
	$	$	$	$	$
Working	22,500 – 0	23,625 – 22,500	24,806 – 23,625	26,047 – 24,806	26,047 – 0
Working capital investment	(22,500)	(1,125)	(1,181)	(1,241)	26,047

Test your understanding 8 – Working capital

Step 1: Calculate the absolute amounts of working capital needed over the project:

	T_0	T_1	T_2	T_3
	$	$	$	$
Selling price (inflating at 8% p.a.)		3.00	3.24	3.4992
Sales value (based on 100,000 units)		300,000	324,000	349,920
Working capital required	30,000	32,400	34,992	

Step 2: Work out the incremental investment required each year remembering to release all the working capital at the end of the project

	T_0	T_1	T_2	T_3
	$	$	$	$
Working		32,400 – 30,000	34,992 – 32,400	
Capital investment	(30,000)	(2,400)	(2,592)	34,992

Test your understanding 9 – NPV with tax and inflation

$ millions	T_0	T_1	T_2	T_3	T_4
Sales (W1)		520	1082	675	
Variable costs (W1)		(158)	(331)	(208)	
Net trading inflows		362	751	467	
Tax payable (30%)			(109)	(225)	(140)
Initial investment	(1,000)				
Scrap proceeds				200	
Tax relief on tax-allowable depreciation (W2)			75	56	109
Working capital (W3)	(52)	(56)	40	68	
Net cash flows	(1,052)	306	757	566	(31)
DF @ 10% (W4)	1	0.909	0.826	0.751	0.683
PV	(1,052)	278	625	425	(21)
				NPV	255

(W1) **revenue and costs**

Revenue and costs need to be expressed in money terms.

e.g. revenue at T_2 = $10m × 100 × $(1.04)^2$ = $1,081.6m.

(W2) **Tax-allowable depreciation**

Time		$m	**Tax saving**	**Timing of tax relief**
			$m	
T_0	Initial investment	1000		
T_1	Tax-allowable depreciation @ 25%	(250)	75	T_2
		——		
	Written down value	750		
T_2	Tax-allowable depreciation @ 25%	(188)	56	T_3
		——		
	Written down value	562		
	Sale proceeds	(200)		
		——		
T_3	Balancing Allowance	362	109	T_4

(W3) **Working capital requirements**

Step 1: Calculate the absolute amounts of working capital needed over the project:

$ millions	T_0	T_1	T_2	T_3
Sales		520	1,082	675
Working capital required	52	108	68	

Step 2: Work out the incremental investment required each year, remembering to release all the working capital at the end of the project

	T_0	T_1	T_2	T_3
Working		52 – 108	108 – 68	
Capital investment	(52)	(56)	40	68

(W4) **Discount rate**

(1+i) = (1+r) × (1+h) = 1.068 × 1.03 = 1.10, giving a money rate (i) = 10%.

Test your understanding 10

Answer B

Time	0	1	2
	$000	$000	$000
Investment	(3,500)		
Revenue		3,150	3,308
Tax		(945)	(992)
Net cash flow	(3,500)	2,205	2,316
Discount factor @ 15.5%	1	0.866	0.750
PV @ 15.5%	(3,500)	1,910	1,737

NPV = $147,000

Test your understanding 11

Answer A

(1 + Money rate) = (1 + Real rate) × (1 + Inflation rate)

1.1655 = (1.11) × (1 + Inflation rate)

Inflation rate = 5%

Test your understanding 12

Answer D

As there are different rates of inflation the 'money approach' must be used, i.e. the cash flows must be inflated at their specific rates and discounted at the money cost of capital.

(1 + Money rate) = (1 + Real rate) × (1 + Inflation rate) = 1.1 × 1.05 = 1.155

Test your understanding 13

Answer A

Time		$m	**Tax saving**	**Timing of tax relief**
			$m	
T_0	Initial investment	40,000		
T_0	Tax-allowable depreciation @ 25%	(10,000)	3,000	T_0
	Written down value	30,000		
T_1	Tax-allowable depreciation @ 25%	(7,500)	2,250	T_1
	Written down value	22,500		
T_2	Tax-allowable depreciation @ 25%	5,625	1,688	T_2

Test your understanding 14

Answer D

Step 1: Calculate the absolute amounts of working capital needed over the project:

	T_0	T_1	T_2	T_3
	$	$	$	$
Selling price (inflating at 6% p.a.)		3.50	3.71	3.9326
Sales value (based on 55,000 units)		192,500	204,050	216,293
Working capital required (12%)	23,100	24,486	25,955	

Step 2: Work out the incremental investment required each year, remembering to release all the working capital at the end of the project

	T_0	T_1	T_2	T_3
	$	$	$	$
Working		24,486 – 23,100	25,955 – 24,486	
Capital investment	(23,100)	(1,386)	(1,469)	25,955

chapter

5

Asset investment decisions and capital rationing

Chapter learning objectives

Upon completion of this chapter you will be able to:

- evaluate the choice between leasing an asset and borrowing to buy using the before- and after-tax costs of debt
- define and calculate an equivalent annual cost (EAC)
- evaluate asset replacement decisions using EACs
- explain the reasons why capital rationing might be required
- define and distinguish between divisible and indivisible projects
- calculate profitability indexes for divisible investment projects and use them to evaluate investment decisions
- calculate the net present value (NPV) of combinations of non-divisible investment projects and use the results to evaluate investment decisions.

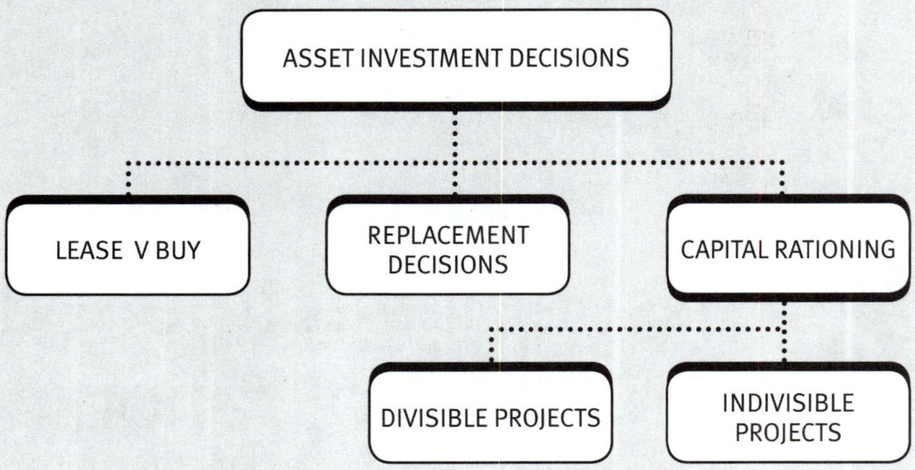

1 Lease versus buy

Once the decision has been made to acquire an asset for an investment project, a decision still needs to be made as to how to finance it. The choices that we will consider are:

- lease
- buy.

The NPVs of the financing cash flows for both options are found and compared and the lowest cost option selected.

The finance decision is considered separately from the investment decision. The operating costs and revenues from the investment will be common in each case.

Only the relevant cash flows arising as a result of the type of finance are included in the NPV calculation.

Leasing

The asset is never 'owned' by the user company from the perspective of the taxman.

Implications

- The finance company receives the tax-allowable depreciation as the owner of the asset.
- The user receives no tax-allowable depreciation but is able to offset the full rental payment against tax.

The relevant cash flows would thus be:

- the lease payments
- tax relief on the lease payments.

Buying

The assumption is that buying requires the use of a bank loan (for the sake of comparability). The user is the owner of the asset.

Implication

- The user will receive tax-allowable depreciation on the asset and tax relief for the interest payable on the loan.

The relevant cash flows would be:

- the purchase cost
- any residual value
- any associated tax implications due to tax-allowable depreciation.

Do not include the interest payments or the tax relief arising on them in the NPV calculation, as this is dealt with via the cost of capital (see below).

Cost of capital

As the interest payments attract tax relief we must use the post-tax cost of borrowing as our discount rate. As all financing cash flows are considered to be risk-free, this rate is used for both leasing and buying.

Post-tax cost of borrowing = Cost of borrowing × (1 – Tax rate).

(**Note:** in some questions you may find that a company is not paying tax and so the pre-tax rate would be appropriate.)

Lease versus buy

Where the use of an asset is required for a new project, there are effectively two decisions to be made:

- Is the project worthwhile?
- If so, should the asset be leased or bought with a loan?

If the project has been approved in principle then you need to calculate the NPVs of the two sets of financing cash flows for buying and leasing.

To be consistent with the earlier calculations, you could use the company's existing cost of capital to discount these cash flows.

However, the decision of whether to lease or borrow to buy is actually a financing decision as opposed to an investment decision. Therefore, the appropriate discount rate is the borrowing cost (cost of debt) of the company, whether on a before or after-tax basis.

Test your understanding 1 – Leasing calculations

Walshey Co has already decided to accept a project and is now considering how to finance it.

The asset could be leased over four years at a rental of $36,000 pa, payable at the start of each year.

Tax is payable at 30%, one year in arrears. The post-tax cost of borrowing is 10%.

Required:

Calculate the net present value of the leasing option.

Test your understanding 2 – Lease versus buy

A firm has decided to acquire a new machine to neutralise the toxic waste produced by its refining plant. The machine would cost $6.4 million and would have an economic life of five years.

Tax-allowable depreciation of 25% pa on a reducing balance basis is available for the investment.

Taxation of 30% is payable on operating cash flows, one year in arrears.

The firm intends to finance the new plant by means of a five-year fixed interest loan at a pre-tax cost of 11.4% pa, principal repayable in five years' time.

As an alternative, a leasing company has proposed a finance lease over five years at $1.42 million pa payable in advance.

Scrap value of the machine under each financing alternative will be zero.

Evaluate the two options for acquiring the machine and advise the company on the best alternative.

Other considerations

There may be other issues to consider before a final decision is made to lease or buy, for example:

- Who receives the residual value in the lease agreement?
- Any restrictions associated with the taking on of leased equipment, e.g. leases may restrict a firm's borrowing capacity.
- Any additional benefits associated with lease agreement, e.g. maintenance or other support services.

See chapter 15 for further details.

2 Replacement decisions using equivalent annual cost and equivalent annual benefit

Once the decision has been made to acquire an asset for a long-term project, it is quite likely that the asset will need to be replaced periodically throughout the life of the project.

Where there are competing replacements for a particular asset we must compare the possible replacement strategies available.

A problem arises where

- equivalent assets available are likely to last for different lengths of time or
- an asset, once bought, must be replaced at regular intervals.

The decision we are concerned with here is – how often should the asset be replaced?

Equivalent annual costs (EACs)

In order to deal with the different time-scales, the NPV of each option is converted into an annuity or an EAC.

The EAC is the equal annual cash flow (annuity) to which a series of uneven cash flows is equivalent in PV terms.

The formula used is:

$$EAC = \frac{\text{PV of costs}}{\text{Annuity factor}}$$

The **optimum replacement period (cycle)** will be the period that has the lowest EAC, although in practice other factors may influence the final decision.

The method can be summarised as:

(1) calculate the NPV of each strategy or replacement cycle

(2) calculate the EAC for each strategy

(3) choose the strategy with the lowest EAC.

Key assumptions

- Cash inflows from trading are ignored since they will be similar regardless of the replacement decision. In practice using an older asset may result in lower quality, which in turn could affect sales.
- The operating efficiency of machines will be similar with differing machines or with machines of differing ages.
- The assets will be replaced in perpetuity or at least into the foreseeable future.
- In most questions tax and inflation are ignored.
- As with all NPV calculations non-financial aspects such as pollution and safety are ignored. An older machine may have a higher chance of employee accidents and may produce more pollution.

Replacement decisions

The factors to be considered when making replacement decisions are as follows:

- Capital cost of new equipment – the higher cost of equipment will have to be balanced against known or possible technical improvements.
- Operating costs – operating costs will be expected to increase as the machinery deteriorates over time. This is referred to as operating inferiority, and is the result of:
  - increased repair and maintenance costs
  - loss of production due to 'down time' resulting from increased repair and maintenance time
  - lower quality and quantity of output.
- Resale value – the extent to which old equipment can be traded in for new.
- Taxation and investment incentives.
- Inflation – both the general price level change, and relative movements in the prices of input and outputs.

Determining the optimum replacement period (cycle) will largely be influenced by:

- the capital cost/resale value of the asset – the longer the period, the less frequently these will occur
- the annual operating costs of running the asset – the longer the period, the higher these will become.

The timescale problems

A special feature of replacement problems is that it involves comparisons of alternatives with different timescales. If the choice is between replacing an item of machinery every two years or every three years, it would be meaningless simply to compare the NPV of the two costs.

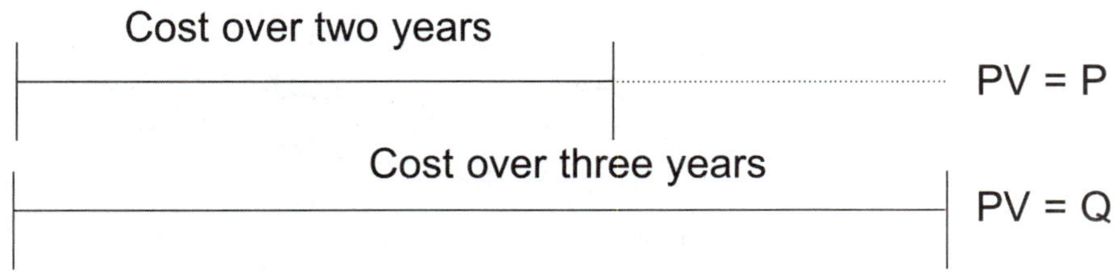

Almost certainly $P < Q$. However, this does not take account of the cost of providing an asset for the third year. One way of comparing asset replacement options is to convert the PV of cost over one replacement cycle to an equivalent annual PV of cost.

In other words, we compute the PV of costs over one cycle and then turn it into an EAC using the AF for the number of years in the replacement cycle.

Thus, the costs associated with any particular cycle can be considered as equivalent to having to pay this EAC every year throughout the cycle and throughout subsequent cycles.

Test your understanding 3 – Equivalent annual costs

A machine costs $20,000.

The following information is also available:

Running costs (payable at the end of the year):

Year 1	$5,000
Year 2	$5,500

Trade-in allowance

Disposal after 1 year:	$16,000
Disposal after 2 years:	$13,000

Calculate the optimal replacement cycle if the cost of capital is 10%.

Test your understanding 4 – Equivalent annual costs

A decision has to be made on replacement policy for vans. A van costs $12,000 and the following additional information applies:

Asset sold at end of year	Trade-in allowance	Asset kept for	Maintenance cost at end of year
	$		$
1	9,000	1 year	0
2	7,500	2 years	1,500 in 1st year
3	7,000	3 years	2,700 in 2nd year

Calculate the optimal replacement policy at a cost of capital of 15%.

Note that the asset is only maintained at the end of the year if it is to be kept for a further year, i.e. there are no maintenance costs in the year of replacement.

Ignore taxation and inflation.

Limitations of replacement analysis

The model assumes that when an asset is replaced, the replacement is in all practical respects identical to the last one and that this process will continue for the foreseeable future. However in practice this will not hold true owing to:

- changing technology
- inflation
- changes in production plans.

Limitations of replacement analysis

The replacement analysis model assumes that the firm replaces like with like each time it needs to replace an existing asset.

However this assumption ignores:

- Changing technology – machines fast become obsolete and can only be replaced with a more up-to-date model which will be more efficient and perhaps perform different functions.
- Inflation – the increase in prices over time alters the cost structure of the different assets, meaning that the optimal replacement cycle can vary over time.
- Changes in production plans – firms cannot predict with accuracy the market environment they will be facing in the future and whether they will even need to make use of the asset at that time.

Equivalent annual benefits

The equivalent annual benefit (EAB) is the annual annuity with the same value as the net present value of an investment project.

It can be calculated using a similar formula to that used for the equivalent annual cost:

$$EAB = \frac{\text{NPV of project}}{\text{Annuity factor}}$$

Calculating the EAB is particularly useful when trying to compare projects with unequal lives. The project with the highest EAB would be preferred.

3 Capital rationing

An introduction

Shareholder wealth is maximised if a company undertakes all possible positive NPV projects. Capital rationing is where there are insufficient funds to do so. This implies that where investment capital is rationed, shareholder wealth is not being maximised.

Ensure you are able to discuss the difference between hard (external) and soft (internal) capital rationing.

Hard capital rationing: An absolute limit on the amount of finance available is imposed by the lending institutions.

Soft capital rationing: A company may impose its own rationing on capital. This is contrary to the rational view of shareholder wealth maximisation.

Reasons for hard or soft capital rationing

Hard capital rationing	**Soft capital rationing**
Reasons for hard capital rationing: • Industry-wide factors limiting funds. • Company-specific factors, such as: – lack of or poor track record – lack of asset security – poor management team.	Reasons for soft capital rationing: • Limited management skills available. • Desire to maximise return of a limited range of investments. • Limited exposure to external finance. • Encourages acceptance of only substantially profitable business.

Single and multi-period capital rationing

Single-period capital rationing: Shortage of funds for this period only.

Multi-period capital rationing: Shortage of funds in more than one period (outside syllabus)

The method for dealing with single-period capital rationing is similar to the limiting factor analysis used elsewhere in decision making.

The profitability index (PI) and divisible projects

If a project is divisible, any fraction of the project may be undertaken and the returns from the project are expected to be generated in exact proportion to the amount of investment undertaken. Projects cannot however be undertaken more than once.

The aim when managing capital rationing is to maximise the NPV earned per $1 invested in projects.

Where the projects:

- are divisible (i.e. can be done in part)
- earn corresponding returns to scale

it is achieved by:

(1) calculating a PI for each project (see below)

(2) ranking the projects according to their PI

(3) allocating funds according to the projects' rankings until they are used up.

The formula is:

$$PI = \frac{NPV}{Investment}$$

Test your understanding 5 – Divisible projects

A company has $100,000 available for investment and has identified the following 5 investments in which to invest. All investments must be started now (Yr 0).

Project	**Initial investment (Yr 0)** $000	**NPV** $000
C	40	20
D	100	35
E	50	24
F	60	18
G	50	(10)

Required:

Determine which projects should be chosen to maximise the return to the business.

Indivisible projects – trial and error

If a project is indivisible it must be done in its entirety or not at all.

Where projects cannot be done in part, the optimal combination can only be found by trial and error.

Test your understanding 6 – Indivisible projects

A Co has the same problem as before but this time the projects are indivisible.

The information is reproduced below:

A company has $100,000 available for investment and has identified the following 5 investments in which to invest. All investments must be started now (Yr 0).

Project	**Initial investment (Yr 0)** $000	**NPV** $000
C	40	20
D	100	35
E	50	24
F	60	18
G	50	(10)

Required:

Determine the optimal project selection.

The key in the examination is to ascertain whether or not the projects are divisible.

Divisible projects can be ranked using the PI. Combinations of indivisible projects must be considered on a trial and error basis.

Mutually-exclusive projects

Sometimes the taking on of projects will preclude the taking on of another, e.g. they may both require use of the same asset.

In these circumstances, each combination of investments is tried to identify which earns the higher level of returns.

Test your understanding 7 – Mutually exclusive projects

Using the same company information for A Co (divisible projects) the additional factor to be considered is that projects C and E are mutually exclusive.

The information is reproduced below.

A company has $100,000 available for investment and has identified the following 5 investments in which to invest. All investments must be started now (Yr 0).

Project	**Initial investment (Yr 0)** $000	**NPV** $000	**PI NPV/** $
C	40	20	0.5
D	100	35	0.35
E	50	24	0.48
F	60	18	0.3
G	50	(10)	not worth while

Required:

Determine the optimal project selection.

Test your understanding 8

Sarratt plc has calculated the following NPVs relating to two mutually-exclusive projects, X and Y.

	X	Y
NPV at 10%	100	35
NPV/$ invested	50	24

The company's cost of capital is 10%.

If the objective of Sarratt plc is the maximisation of shareholder wealth, which project(s), if any, should it accept?

A Neither project

B Project Y only

C Project X only

D Both projects

Test your understanding 9

Which of the following is not a reason for hard capital rationing?

A Lending institutions may consider the company to be too risky

B There are restrictions on lending due to government control

C The costs associated with making small issues of capital may be too great

D Desire to maximise return of a limited range of investments

Test your understanding 10

A company has a number of projects available to it but has a limit of $20,000 on its capital investment funds. Each project has an initial outlay followed by a constant annual cash inflow in perpetuity, commencing in one year's time. The projects are as follows.

Project	*Initial outlay*	*Inflow per year*
	$	$
E	6,000	900
F	8,000	1,000
G	10,000	3,500
H	12,000	3,600
I	20,000	4,600

The company's cost of capital is 10% per year and all projects are independent and indivisible.

What is the maximum net present value that can be generated?

A $26,000

B $27,000

C $28,000

D $45,000

Test your understanding 11

A machine costing $150,000 has a useful life of eight years, after which time its estimated resale value will be $30,000. Annual running costs will be $6,000 for the first three years of use and $8,000 for each of the next five years. All running costs are payable on the last days of the year to which they relate.

Using a discount rate of 20% per annum, what is the equivalent annual cost (to the nearest $100) of using the machine if it were bought and replaced every eight years in perpetuity?

A $21,100

B $34,000

C $44,200

D $46,600

Test your understanding 12

Which of the following statements is incorrect?

A The optimum replacement period (cycle) will be the period that has the highest equivalent annual cost, although in practice, other factors may influence the final decision

B The replacement analysis model assumes that the firm replaces like with like each time it needs to replace an existing asset

C The replacement analysis model ignores inflation, meaning that the optimal replacement cycle can vary over time

D The replacement analysis model ignores the fact that firms cannot predict whether they will even need to make use of the asset in the future

Chapter summary

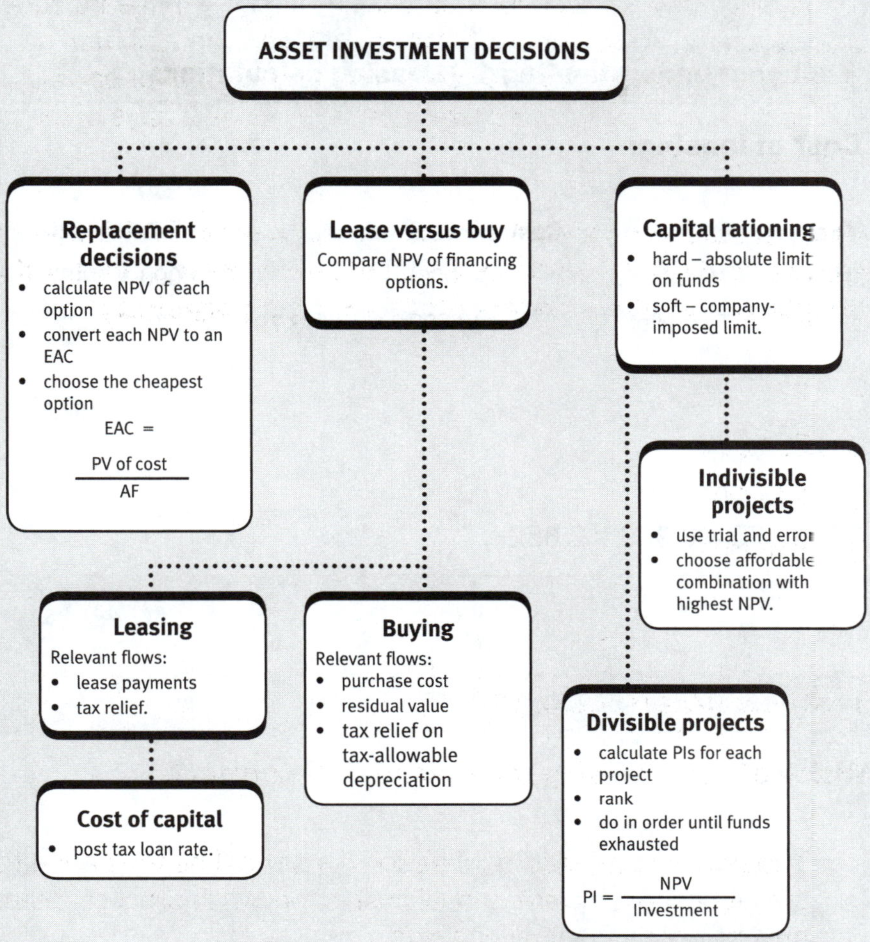

Test your understanding answers

Test your understanding 1 – Leasing calculations

Cost of leasing:

Year		Cash flows $	DF @10%	PV $
0–3	Rentals	(36,000)	1.000 + 2.487	(125,532)
2–5	Tax relief	10,800	3.791 – 0.909 = 2.882*	31,126
			NPV	(94,406)

*Or 3.170 × 0.909 = 2.882

Test your understanding 2 – Lease versus buy

(W1) Calculation of the tax relief on tax-allowable depreciation if asset bought:

Year	Narrative	Written down value	Tax saved/ (extra tax paid) at 30%	Timing of tax flow
		$m	$m	
0	Cost	6.400		
1	Tax-allowable depreciation	1.600	0.480	2
		4.800		
2	Tax-allowable depreciation	1.200	0.360	3
		3.600		
3	Tax-allowable depreciation	0.900	0.270	4
		2.700		
4	Tax-allowable depreciation	0.675	0.203	5
		2.025		
5	Disposal proceeds	0.000		
	Balancing allowance	2.025	0.608	6

Note: The asset is bought at time t=0 as usual with the first amount of tax-allowable depreciation in the year ended time one. Given the one-year time lag on the tax, the first tax effect is at time t=2.

(W2) Calculation of the post-tax cost of borrowing.

The pre-tax cost of borrowing is 11.4%.

The post-tax cost of borrowing can be approximated by multiplying this by (1 – tax rate), i.e. 11.4% × (1 – 0.3) = 7.98%, say 8% (strictly this ignores the impact of a one-year time delay on tax relief, but this is acceptable).

Cost of borrowing to buy:

Time	**0**	**1**	**2**	**3**	**4**	**5**	**6**
	$m	$m	$m	$m	$m	$m	$m
Asset	(6.400)						
Tax relief on tax-allowable depreciation			0.480	0.360	0.270	0.203	0.608
	(6.400)	0.000	0.480	0.360	0.270	0.203	0.608
(W1) PV factor @ 8%	1.000	0.926	0.857	0.794	0.735	0.681	0.630
(W2) PV	(6.400)	0	0.411	0.286	0.198	0.138	0.383

NPV = $(4.984)m

Cost of leasing:

Timing	**Narrative**	**Cash flow**	**DF @ 8%**	**PV**
		$m		$m
0–4	Lease payments	(1.420)	1+ 3.312	(6.123)
2–6	Tax savings	0.426	3.993 × 0.926	1.575
	NPV			(4.548)

The cost of leasing is lower than the cost of buying and the asset should therefore be acquired under a finance lease.

Test your understanding 3 – Equivalent annual costs

Note: in contrast to the maintenance costs in the above illustration, running costs (e.g. petrol) are incurred in every year of ownership.

One-year replacement cycle:

	0	**1**
	$	$
Buy asset	(20,000)	
Running costs		(5,000)
Trade-in		16,000
Net cash flow	(20,000)	11,000
DF@10%	1	0.909
PV	(20,000)	9,999
NPV	(10,001)	

$$\text{Equivalent annual cost} = \frac{\$10,001}{\text{1 yr AF}} = \frac{\$10,001}{0.909} = \$11,002$$

Two-year replacement cycle:

	0	**1**	**2**
	$	$	$
Buy asset	(20,000)		
Running costs		(5,000)	(5,500)
Trade-in			13,000
Net cash flow	(20,000)	(5,000)	7,500
DF@10%	1	0.909	0.826
PV	(20,000)	(4,545)	6,195
NPV	(18,350)		

$$\text{Equivalent annual cost} = \frac{\$18,350}{\text{2 yr AF}} = \frac{\$18,350}{1.736} = \$10,570$$

The machine should therefore be replaced after two years.

Test your understanding 4 – Equivalent annual costs

The costs incurred over a single cycle are computed and the EAC is found as follows.

(1) **Replace every year**

	0	1	2	3
	$	$	$	$
Buy asset	(12,000)			
Maintenance costs		0		
Trade-in		9,000		
Net cash flow	(12,000)	9,000		
DF@15%	1	0.870		
PV	(12,000)	7,830		
NPV	(4,170)			

$$\text{EAC} = \frac{\text{PV of costs}}{\text{1 year AF}} = \frac{(4{,}170)}{0.870} = (\$4{,}793)$$

(2) **Replace every two years**

	0	1	2	3
Buy asset	(12,000)			
Maintenance costs		(1,500)		
Trade-in			7,500	
Net cash flow	(12,000)	(1,500)	7,500	
DF@15%	1	0.870	0.756	
PV	(12,000)	(1,305)	5,670	
NPV	(7,635)			

$$\text{EAC} = \frac{\text{PV of costs}}{\text{2 year AF}} = \frac{(7{,}635)}{1.626} = (\$4{,}696)$$

(3) **Replace every three years**

	0	1	2	3
Buy asset	(12,000)			
Maintenance costs		(1,500)	(2,700)	
Trade-in				7,000
Net cash flow	(12,000)	(1,500)	(2,700)	7,000
DF@15%	1	0.870	0.756	0.658
PV	(12,000)	(1,305)	(2,041)	4,606
NPV	(10,740)			

$$EAC = \frac{\text{PV of costs}}{\text{3 year AF}} = \frac{(10{,}740)}{2.283} = (\$4{,}704)$$

Here, the optimal replacement period is every two years.

Note that the EAC is that sum that could be paid annually in arrears to finance the three replacement cycles. It is equivalent to the budget accounts that various public services encourage customers to open to spread the cost of those services more evenly. The PV of annual sums equal to the EAC is the same as the PV of the various receipts and payments needed to buy and maintain a van.

Test your understanding 5 – Divisible projects

Solution

Project	Working	PI	Ranking
C	20/40	= 0.5	1
D	35/100	= 0.35	3
E	24/50	= 0.48	2
F	18/60	= 0.3	4
G	Not worth while		

Funds available	Projects undertaken	NPV earned
$		$
100,000		
(40,000)	Project C	20,000
60,000		
(50,000)	Project E	24,000
10,000		
(10,000)	10/100 = 10% project D	3,500
Nil	Total NPV	47,500

Test your understanding 6 – Indivisible projects

Solution

Alternatives Mix	Investment	NPV earned
	$	$
C,F	100,000	38,000
D	100,000	35,000
C,E	90,000	44,000*

*C and E is the best mix. There is a problem however relating to the unused funds. The assumption is that the un-utilised funds will earn a return equivalent to the cost of capital and hence will generate an NPV of 0. This may or may not be the case.

Test your understanding 7 – Mutually exclusive projects

Solution

Mix	**Investment**	**NPV**
	$	$
Project C mix	$100,000	S41,000 (20 + 0.6 × 35)
C, 60 % D		
Project E mix	$100,000	$41,500* (24 + 0.5 × 35)
E, 50% D		

* The best mix

Note that F is not considered as it ranks below project D according to the PI.

Test your understanding 8

Answer C

The correct answer (based on NPVs) is project X.

Test your understanding 9

Answer D

This is an example of soft capital rationing.

Soft capital rationing is brought about by internal factors. Hard capital rationing is brought about by external factors.

Test your understanding 10

Answer C

Project		**NPV**
		$
E	–6,000 + 900/0.1	3,000
F	–8,000 + 1,000/0.1	2,000
G	–10,000 + 3,500/0.1	25,000
H	–12,000 + 3,600/0.1	24,000
I	–20,000 + 4,600/0.1	26,000

	NPV
	$
E + F	5,000
E + G	28,000
E + H	27,000
F + G	27,000
F + H	26,000
I	26,000

The best combination is E + G, where NPV = $28,000

Test your understanding 11

Answer C

$$\text{NPV} = \frac{-\$150{,}000 + \$30{,}000 \times 0.233 - \$6{,}000 \times 2.106 - \$8{,}000 \times 2.991 \times 0.579}{3.837} = 44{,}175$$

Test your understanding 12

Answer A

The optimum replacement period (cycle) will be the period that has the lowest (not the highest) equivalent annual cost, although in practice other factors may influence the final decision.

chapter

6

Investment appraisal under uncertainty

Chapter learning objectives

Upon completion of this chapter you will be able to:

- distinguish between risk and uncertainty in investment appraisal
- define sensitivity analysis and discuss its usefulness in assisting investment decisions
- apply sensitivity analysis to investment projects and explain the meaning of the findings
- define an expected value (EV) and discuss the usefulness of probability analysis in assisting investment decisions
- apply probability analysis to investment projects and explain the meaning of the findings
- discuss the use of simulation to take account of risk and uncertainty in investment appraisal
- discuss the use of adjusted payback in investment appraisal
- calculate the discounted payback and discuss its usefulness as an investment appraisal method
- explain the principle of adjusting discount rates to take account of risk.

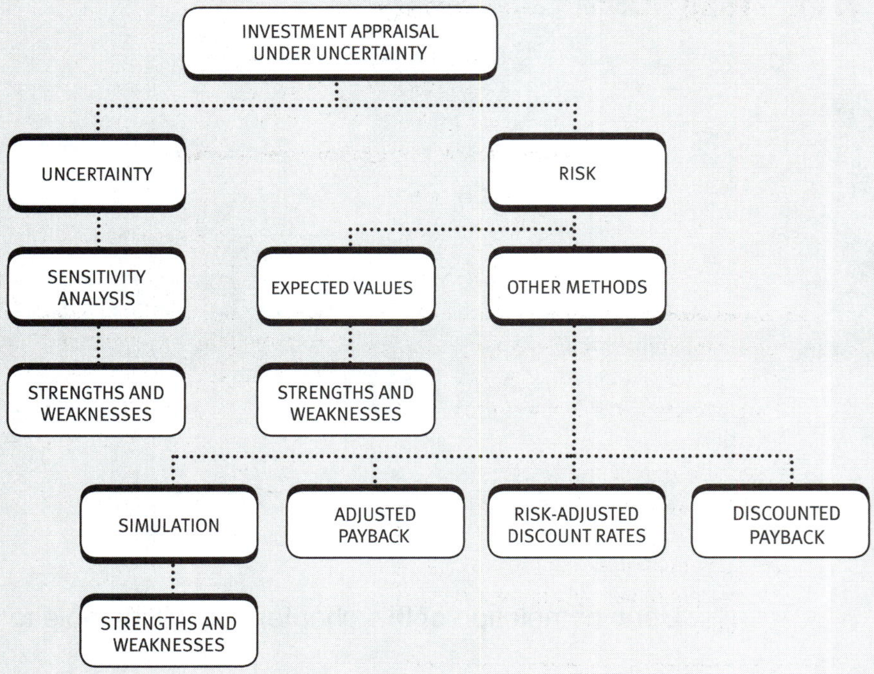

1 Risk and uncertainty

The difference between risk and uncertainty

Investment appraisal faces the following problems:

- all decisions are based on forecasts
- all forecasts are subject to uncertainty
- this uncertainty needs to be reflected in the financial evaluation.

The decision maker must distinguish between:

- **risk** – quantifiable – possible outcomes have associated probabilities, thus allowing the use of mathematical techniques
- **uncertainty** – unquantifiable – outcomes cannot be mathematically modelled.

In investment appraisal the areas of concern are therefore the accuracy of the estimates concerning:

- project life
- predicted cash flows and associated probabilities
- discount rate used.

Incorporating risk and uncertainty

INVESTMENT APPRAISAL UNDER UNCERTAINTY

Uncertainty

- set a minimum payback period
- make prudent estimates of cash flows to assess the worst possible situation
- assess both best and worst possible situations to obtain a range of net present values (NPVs)
- use sensitivity analysis to measure the 'margin of safety' on input data (see below).

Risk

- expected values (below)
- simulation models (below)
- adjusted payback (below)
- risk-adjusted discount rates (below).

2 Sensitivity analysis

- Sensitivity analysis typically involves posing 'what if?' questions.
- For example, what if demand fell by 10% compared to our original forecasts? Would the project still be viable?
- Ideally we want to know how much demand could fall before the project should be rejected or, equivalently, the breakeven demand that gives an NPV of zero. We could then assess the likelihood of forecast demand being that low.

Calculating sensitivity

This maximum possible change is often expressed as a percentage:

$$\text{Sensitivity margin} = \frac{\text{NPV}}{\text{Present value (PV) of flow under consideration}} \times 100\%$$

This would be calculated for each input individually.

The lower the sensitivity margin, the more sensitive the decision to the particular parameter being considered, i.e. small changes in the estimate could change the project decision from accept to reject.

NB Because we will need the PV of each cash flow separately, the following tabular approach is the preferred layout for the NPV calculation:

Time	Cash flow	Discount factor (DF) at x%	PV

Test your understanding 1 – Sensitivity analysis

An investment of $40,000 today is expected to give rise to annual contribution of $25,000. This is based on selling one product, with a sales volume of 10,000 units, selling price of $12.50 and variable costs per unit of $10. Annual fixed cost of $10,000 will be incurred for the next four years; the discount rate is 10%.

Required:

(a) Calculate the NPV of this investment.

(b) Calculate the sensitivity of your calculation to the following:

(i) initial investment

(ii) selling price per unit

(iii) variable cost per unit

(iv) sales volume

(v) fixed costs

(vi) discount rate

Test your understanding 2 – Sensitivity analysis

Bacher Co is considering investing $500,000 in equipment to produce a new type of ball. Sales of the product are expected to continue for three years, at the end of which the equipment will have a scrap value of $80,000. Sales revenue of $600,000 pa will be generated at a variable cost of $350,000. Annual fixed costs will increase by $40,000.

(a) Determine whether, on the basis of the estimates given, the project should be undertaken, assuming that all cash flows occur at annual intervals and that Bacher Co has a cost of capital of 15%.

(b) Find the percentage changes required in the following estimates for the investment decision to change:

(i) initial investment

(ii) scrap value

(iii) selling price

(iv) unit variable cost

(v) annual fixed cost

(vi) sales volume

(vii) cost of capital.

Advantages and disadvantages of sensitivity analysis

Advantages

- simple
- provides more information to allow management to make subjective judgements
- identifies critical estimates.

Disadvantages:

- assumes variables change independently of each other
- does not assess the likelihood of a variable changing
- does not directly identify a correct decision.

Advantages and disadvantages of sensitivity analysis

Strengths of sensitivity analysis

- No complicated theory to understand.
- Information will be presented to management in a form which facilitates subjective judgement to decide the likelihood of the various possible outcomes considered.
- Identifies areas which are crucial to the success of the project. If the project is chosen, those areas can be carefully monitored.
- Indicates just how critical are some of the forecasts which are considered to be uncertain.

Weaknesses of sensitivity analysis

- It assumes that changes to variables can be made independently, e.g. material prices will change independently of other variables. This is unlikely. If material prices went up the firm would probably increase selling price at the same time and there would be little effect on NPV. A technique called simulation (see later) allows us to change more than one variable at a time.
- It only identifies how far a variable needs to change. It does not look at the probability of such a change. In the above analysis, sales volume appears to be the most crucial variable, but if the firm were facing volatile raw material markets a 65% change in raw material prices would be far more likely than a 29% change in sales volume.
- It is not an optimising technique. It provides information on the basis of which decisions can be made. It does not point directly to the correct decision.

Sensitivity analysis – the certainty equivalent approach

An alternative method of performing sensitivity analysis is the certainty equivalent approach.

With this approach the cash flows of the project are calculated as per normal but then adjusted downwards by a certain equivalent factor. This in effect decreases the cash flow. The cash flows are then discounted at the risk-free rate.

Illustration

Year	**Cash flow**	**Certainty equivalent factor**	**Risk-free discount factor (6%)**	**Present value**
	$000			$000
0	(1,000)	1.00	1	(1,000)
1	900	0.95	0.943	806
2	750	0.90	0.890	601

Total NPV = $407,000

In practice the major problem is that the use of certainty equivalents is subjective.

3 Probability analysis

When there are several possible outcomes for a decision and probabilities can be assigned to each, a probability distribution of expected cash flows can often be estimated, recognising there are several possible outcomes, not just one. This could then be used to:

(1) Calculate an expected value (EV);

(2) Measure risk by:

(a) calculating the worst possible outcome and its probability;

(b) calculating the probability that the project will fail (for example, that a negative NPV will result);

(c) assessing the standard deviation of the outcomes.

The EV is the weighted average of all the possible outcomes, with the weightings based on the probability estimates.

The standard deviation is a statistical measure of the variability of a distribution around its mean (i.e. it measures the dispersion of possible outcomes about the EV). The tighter the distribution, the lower this measure will be. It is a measure of risk – the wider the dispersion the riskier the situation.

Calculating an EV

The formula for calculating an EV is:

$EV = \sum px$

where

p = the probability of an outcome

x = the value of an outcome.

The EV is not the most likely result. It may not even be a possible result, but instead it finds the long-run average outcome.

Expected values

The EV is the weighted average of the outcomes, with the weightings based on the probability estimates.

The EV does not necessarily represent what the outcome will be, nor does it represent the most likely result. What it really represents is the average pay-off per occasion if the project were repeated many times (i.e. a 'long-run' average).

There are two main problems with using EV to make decisions in this way:

- The project will only be carried out once. It could result in a sizeable loss and there may be no second chance to win our money back.
- The probabilities used are simply subjective estimates of our belief, on a scale from 0 to 1. There is probably little data on which to base these estimates.

Test your understanding 3 – Expected values

A firm has to choose between three mutually exclusive projects, the outcomes of which depend on the state of the economy. The following estimates have been made:

State of the economy	**Recession**	**Stable**	**Growing**
Probability	0.5	0.4	0.1
	NPV ($000)	NPV ($000)	NPV ($000)
Project A	100	200	1,400
Project B	0	500	600
Project C	180	190	200

Determine which project should be selected on the basis of expected market values.

Using EVs in larger NPV calculations

The EV technique can be used to simplify the available data in a larger investment appraisal question.

Test your understanding 4 – Expected values in larger NPV

Dralin Co is considering an investment of $460,000 in a non-current asset expected to generate substantial cash inflows over the next five years. Unfortunately the annual cash flows from this investment are uncertain, but the following probability distribution has been established:

Annual cash flow ($)	Probability
50,000	0.3
100,000	0.5
150,000	0.2

At the end of its five-year life, the asset is expected to sell for $40,000. The cost of capital is 5%.

Should the investment be undertaken?

Using EVs with decision matrices

EVs are also used to deal with situations where the same conditions are faced many times. The problems involve construction of a 'decision matrix'.

Using EVs with decision matrices

Illustration – Using expected values with decision matrices

A newsagent sells a weekly magazine which advertises local second-hand goods. The owner can buy the magazines for 15c each and sell them at the retail price of 25c. At the end of each week unsold magazines are obsolete and have no value.

The owner estimates a probability distribution for weekly demand which looks like this:

Weekly demand in units	Probability
10	0.20
15	0.55
20	0.25
	1.00

(a) What is the EV of demand?

(b) If the owner is to order a fixed quantity of magazines per week how many should that be? Assume no seasonal variations in demand.

Solution

(a) EV of demand = (10 × 0.20) + (15 × 0.55) + (20 × 0.25) = 15.25 units per week.

(b) **Step 1**: Set up a decision matrix of possible strategies (numbers bought) and possible demand, as follows:

	(Number demanded)		
Strategy (Number bought)	10	15	20
10			
15			
20			

Step 2: The 'payoff' from each combination of action and outcome is then computed:

No sale → loss of 15c per magazine.

Sale → profit of 25c − 15c = 10c per magazine.

– Payoffs are shown for each combination of strategy and outcome:

Workings

(i) If 10 magazines are bought, then 10 are sold no matter how many are demanded and the payoff is always 10 × 10c = 100c.

(ii) If 15 magazines are bought and 10 are demanded, then 10 are sold at a profit of 10 × 10c = 100c, and 5 are scrapped at a loss of 5 × 15c = 75c, making a net profit of 25c.

(iii) The other contributions are similarly calculated.

Step 3: Probabilities are then applied to compute the expected value resulting from each possible course of action.

Alternatively, in the same matrix, probability × payoff can be inserted in each cell and totalled to give the expected payoff.

		(Number demanded)			
		p = 0.2	p = 0.55	p = 0.25	
Strategy		10	15	20	EV
(Number bought)	10	100	100	100	100
	15	25	150	150	125
	20	(50)	75	200	81.25

From this matrix we can see that the best alternative is to buy 15 magazines each week.

What does this EV mean?

It means that if the strategy is followed for many weeks, then on average the profit will be 125c per week.

What actually happens is that eight weeks out of ten the payoff is likely to be 150c and two weeks out of ten it drops to 25c.

This strategy produces the highest long-run profit for the firm.

Strengths and weaknesses of EVs

Strengths

- Deals with multiple outcomes.
- Quantifies probabilities.
- Relatively simple calculation.
- Assists decision making.

Weaknesses

- Subjective probabilities.
- Answer is only a long-run average.
- Ignores variability of payoffs.
- Risk neutral decision, i.e. ignores investor's attitude to risk.

Using EVs as a basis for decision making is appropriate if three conditions are met or nearly met:

- there is a reasonable basis for making the forecasts and estimating the probability of different outcomes
- the decision is relatively small in relation to the business, so risk is small in magnitude
- the decision is for a category of decisions that are often made.

The EV technique is best suited to a problem which is repetitive and involves relatively small investments.

Advantages and limitations of EVs

Advantages of EVs

- The technique recognises that there are several possible outcomes and is, therefore, more sophisticated than single value forecasts.
- Enables the probability of the different outcomes to be quantified.
- Leads directly to a simple optimising decision rule by reducing a range of possible outcomes into one number. However, care should be taken (see below)
- Calculations are relatively simple.

Limitations of EVs

- By asking for a series of forecasts the whole forecasting procedure is complicated. Inaccurate forecasting is already a major weakness in project evaluation. The probabilities used are also usually very subjective.
- The EV is merely a weighted average of the probability distribution, indicating the average payoff if the project is repeated many times.
- The EV gives no indication of the dispersion of possible outcomes about the EV. The more widely spread out the possible results are, the more risky the investment is usually seen to be. The EV ignores this aspect of the probability distribution.
- In ignoring risk, the EV technique also ignores the investor's attitude to risk. Some investors are more likely to take risks than others.

Conclusions on EVs

The simple EV decision rule is appropriate if three conditions are met or nearly met:

- there is a reasonable basis for making the forecasts and estimating the probability of different outcomes
- the decision is relatively small in relation to the business. Risk is then small in magnitude
- the decision is for a category of decisions that are often made.

A technique which maximises average payoff is then valid.

4 Further techniques for adjusting for risk and uncertainty

Simulation

Sensitivity analysis considers the effect of changing one variable at a time. Simulation improves on this by looking at the impact of many variables changing at the same time.

Using mathematical models, it produces a distribution of the possible outcomes from the project. The probability of different outcomes can then be calculated.

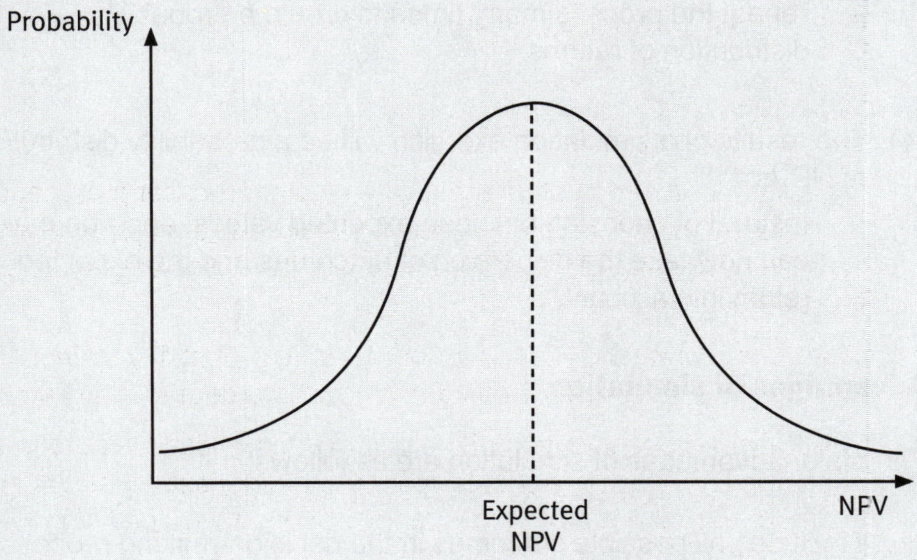

You will never be expected to carry out a simulation exercise in the exam although you may be asked to interpret the output.

Simulation

The four stages of a simulation exercise

There are four stages involved in carrying out a simulation exercise:

(1) Specify major variables, e.g.:
- Market details
- Investment costs
- Operating costs

(2) Specify the relationships between variables to calculate an NPV, e.g.:

Sales revenue = market size × market share × selling price.

Net cash flow = sales revenue − (variable costs + fixed costs + taxation), etc.

(3) Simulate the environment:

- select different values of each variable within the parameters set and compute an NPV
- repeat the process many times to create a probability distribution of returns.

(4) The results of a simulation exercise will be a probability distribution of NPVs.

- Instead of choosing between expected values, decision makers can now take the dispersion of outcomes and the expected return into account.

Advantages of simulation

The major advantages of simulation are as follows:

- it includes all possible outcomes in the decision-making process
- it is a relatively easily understood technique
- it has a wide variety of applications (inventory control, component replacement, corporate models, etc.).

Drawbacks of simulation

However, it does have some significant drawbacks:

- models can become extremely complex and the time and costs involved in their construction can be more than is gained from the improved decisions
- probability distributions may be difficult to formulate.

Adjusted payback

We looked at the payback form of investment appraisal in the chapter on basic investment appraisal.

One way of dealing with risk is to shorten the payback period required. This places more emphasis on the earlier cash flows, which are considered to be less risky.

However, given the disadvantages of payback as a method of investment appraisal, adjusted payback is rarely recommended as a method of adjusting for risk.

Discounted payback

It is also possible to reflect risk by using discounted cash flows in the calculation of a discounted payback period. The cash flows are first discounted using an appropriate discount rate that reflects the risk profile of the project. The cumulative discounted cash flow can then be calculated in the same manner as the cumulative cash flow is for the standard payback calculation.

The discounted payback method has the same advantages and disadvantages as for the traditional payback method except that the shortcoming of failing to account for the time value of money has been overcome.

e.g

Illustration 1 Discounted Payback Period

A project with the following cash flows is under consideration:

T_0	T_1	T_2	T_3	T_4
(20,000)	8,000	12,000	4,000	2,000

Cost of capital 8%

Required:

Calculate the Discounted Payback Period.

Solution

Year	**Working**		**Discounted cash flow** $	**Cumulative discounted cashflow** $
0			(20,000)	(20,000)
1	8,000/(1.08)	=	7,407	(12,593)
2	$12{,}000/(1.08)^2$	=	10,288	(2,305)
3	$4{,}000/(1.08)^3$	=	3,175	870

Hence discounted payback period = 2 years + (2,305/3,175) = 2.73 years

Risk-adjusted discount rates

The discount rate we have assumed so far is the rate that reflects either:

- the cost of borrowing funds in the form of a loan rate or
- the underlying required return of the business (i.e. the return required by the shareholder),
- or a mix of both.

If an individual investment or project is perceived to be more risky than existing investments, the increased risk could be used as a reason to adjust the discount rate.

This is a key concept in investment appraisal. Applying the existing discount rate or cost of capital to an investment assumes that the existing business and gearing risk of the company will remain unchanged. If the project is significant in size and likely to result in additional risks then a project specific or risk-adjusted discount rate should be used.

The application of an increased discount rate is often successful in eliminating marginal projects. The addition to the usual discount rate is called the risk premium. The method used is examined further in the cost of capital chapter.

Test your understanding 5

A company is currently evaluating a project which requires investments of $12,000 now, and $4,800 at the end of year 1. The cash inflow from the project will be $16,800 at the end of year 2 and $14,400 at the end of year 3. The cost of capital is 15%.

What is the discounted payback period (DPP) and the net present value (NPV)?

	DPP	NPV
A	2.0 years	$6,000
B	2.36 years	$4,440
C	2.0 years	$4,440
D	2.36 years	$6,000

Test your understanding 6

Petra is contemplating purchasing a machine for $275,000 which she will use to produce 50,000 units of a product per annum for five years. These products will be sold for $10 each and unit variable costs are expected to be $6. Incremental fixed costs will be $70,000 per annum for production costs and $25,000 per annum for selling and distribution costs. Petra has a required rate of return of 10% per annum.

By how many units must the estimate of production and sale volume fall for the project to be regarded as not worthwhile?

A 2,875

B 6,465

C 8,115

D 12,315

Test your understanding 7

When using the expected value criterion, it is assumed that the individual wants to

A Minimise risk for a given level of return

B Maximise return for a given level of risk

C Minimise risk irrespective of the level of return

D Maximise return irrespective of the level of risk

Test your understanding 8

Which of the following statements is incorrect?

A Sensitivity analysis assesses how responsive the project's NPV is to changes in the variables used to calculate that NPV

B When calculating the sensitivity of each variable, the lower the percentage, the less sensitive is the NPV to that project variable

C Management should review critical variables to assess whether or not there is a strong possibility of events occurring which will lead to a negative NPV

D Sensitivity analysis does not provide a decision rule. Parameters defining acceptability must be laid down by managers

Test your understanding 9

A distinction should be made between the terms risk and uncertainty.

Which of the following statements is true?

Statement 1: Risk can be applied to a situation where there are several possible outcomes and, on the basis of past relevant experience, probabilities can be ass gned to the various outcomes that could prevail.

Statement 2: Uncertainty can be applied to a situation where there are several possible outcomes but there is little past relevant experience to enable the probability of the possible outcomes to be predicted.

	Statement 1	*Statement 2*
A	True	True
B	True	False
C	False	True
D	False	False

Chapter summary

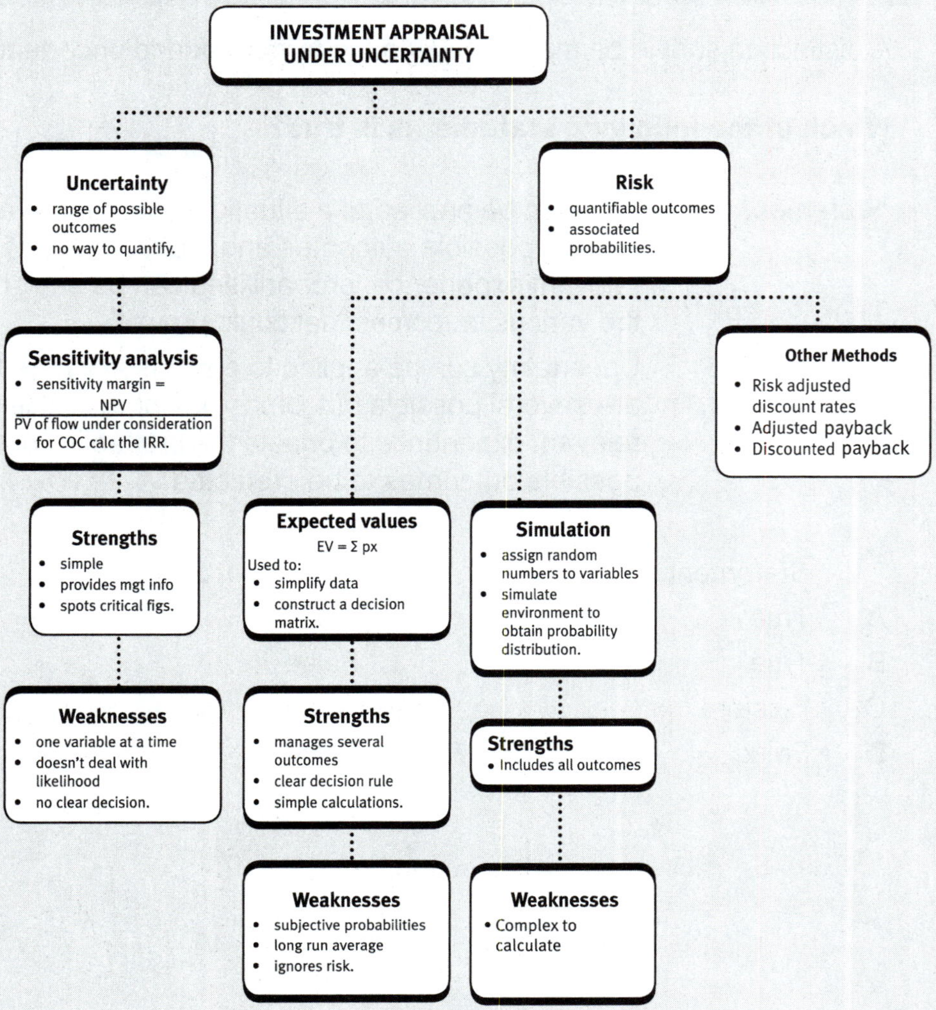

Test your understanding answers

Test your understanding 1 – Sensitivity analysis

Solution

(a)

Time	Narrative	Cash flow	DF	PV
		$	**10%**	$
0	Investment	(40,000)	1.000	(40,000)
1–4	Contribution	25,000	3.170	79,250
1–4	Fixed costs	(10,000)	3.170	(31,700)
			NPV =	7,550

Therefore the decision should be to accept the investment.

(b)

(i) Sensitivity to initial investment = $\frac{7,550}{40,000} \times 100 = 18.9\%$

i.e. an 18.9% increase in the cost of the initial investment would cause the NPV to fall to zero.

(ii) Sensitivity to selling price per unit

If selling price changes, the revenue will change, so the relevant cash flow will be revenue.

PV of revenue = $12.50 × 10,000 × 3.170 = 396,250

Sensitivity margin = $\frac{7,550}{396,250} \times 100 = 1.9\%$

i.e. if price per unit falls by more than 1.9%, the project will make a loss.

(iii) Sensitivity to variable cost per unit

If the variable cost per unit changes, the total variable cost will change, so the relevant cash flow will be total variable cost.

PV of total variable cost = $10 × 10,000 × 3.170 = 317,000

$$\text{Sensitivity margin} = \frac{7,550}{317,000} \times 100 = 2.4\%$$

i.e. if cost per unit increases by more than 2.4%, the project will make a loss.

(iv) Sensitivity to sales volume

As sales volume affects both sales revenue and variable costs, being asked to find the sensitivity to sales volume is the same as sensitivity to contribution.

PV of contribution = ($12.50 – $10.00) × 10,000 × 3.170 = 79,250

$$\text{Sensitivity margin} = \frac{7,550}{79,250} \times 100 = 9.5\%$$

i.e. a 9.5% decrease in the level of contribution would cause the NPV to fall to zero.

(v) Sensitivity to fixed cost

$$\text{Sensitivity margin} = \frac{7,550}{31,700} \times 100 = 23.8\%$$

(vi) Sensitivity to the discount rate

To calculate the sensitivity to the discount rate, it is necessary to find the rate at which the project NPV is zero, i.e. the internal rate of return (IRR) of the project.

Time	**Cash flow**	**DF**	**PV**
	$	%	$
0	(40,000)	1.000	(40,000)
1–4	15,000	2.667 (W1)	40,000
		NPV =	0

(W1)

If the project NPV is set to zero, the PV of the net cash inflows would need to be $40,000. Hence the discount factor needed to make the NPV go down to 0 is 40,000 ÷ 15,000 = 2.667.

From tables, at four years, the closest annuity rate to 2.667 occurs at approximately 18%. This is therefore the breakeven discount rate, i.e. the IRR.

This quick method of finding the IRR will only work if all the inflows are in the form of annuities. Otherwise the usual linear interpolation route must be followed.

Test your understanding 2 – Sensitivity analysis

Although part (a) could be completed most efficiently by finding the PV of net annual inflows ($600,000 – $350,000 – $40,000), i.e. of $210,000, part (b) would be most effectively negotiated if the separate PVs were found.

NPV calculation

Time		**Cash flow**	**15% DF**	**PV**
		$000		$000
0	Equipment	(500)	1	(500)
1–3	Revenue	600	2.283	1,370
1–3	Variable costs	(350)	2.283	(799)
1–3	Fixed costs	(40)	2.283	(91)
3	Scrap value	80	0.658	53
NPV				33

The project should, on the basis of these estimates, be accepted.

(a) **Sensitivity analysis**

(i) Initial investment

For the decision to change, the NPV must fall by $33,000. For this to occur, the cost of the equipment must rise by $33,000.

This is a rise of: $\frac{33}{500} \times 100 = 6.6\%$

(ii) Scrap value

If the NPV is to fall by $33,000, the PV of scrap proceeds must fall by $33,000. The PV of scrap proceeds is currently $53,000. It must fall by: 33÷53 × 100 = 62.26%, say 62%

(iii) Selling price

If sales price varies, sales revenue will vary (assuming no effect on demand). If the NPV of the project is to fall by $33,000, the selling price must fall by:

$$\frac{33}{1,370} \times 100 = 2.4\%$$

(iv) Unit variable cost

The project's NPV must fall by $33,000 therefore the PV of the variable costs must rise by $33,000. Since the PV of variable costs is $799,000, a rise of $33,000 is an increase of:

$$\frac{33}{799} \times 100 = 4.1\%$$

(v) Annual fixed costs

Since the PV of fixed costs is $91,000, a rise of $33,000 is an increase of:

$$\frac{33}{91} \times 100 = 36\%$$

(vi) Sales volume

If sales volume falls, revenue and variable costs fall (contribution falls). If the NPV is to fall by $33,000, volume must fall by:

$$\frac{33}{1,370 - 799} \times 100 = 5.8\%$$

(vii) Cost of capital

If NPV is to fall, cost of capital must rise. The figure which the cost of capital must rise to, that gives an NPV of zero, is the project's IRR.

To find the IRR, which is probably not much above 15%, the NPV at 20% can be found using the summarised cash flows.

NPV ($000) = − 500 + [210 × 2.106] + [80 × 0.579] = −11. The IRR is therefore a little closer to 20% than 15%, but the formula can be used.

$$IRR \approx 15 + \frac{33}{33 + 11} \times (20 - 15)$$

≈ 18.75%

The cost of capital would have to increase from 15% to 18.75% before the investment decision changes.

Test your understanding 3 – Expected values

Project A

State of the economy	**Probability (p)**	**Project NPV (x)**	**px**
		$000	$000
Recession	0.5	100	50
Stable	0.4	200	80
Growing	0.1	1,400	140
Expected value			270

Project B

State of the economy	**Probability (p)**	**Project NPV (x)**	**px**
		$000	$000
Recession	0.5	0	0
Stable	0.4	500	200
Growing	0.1	600	60
Expected value			260

Project C

State of the economy	**Probability (p)**	**Project NPV (x)**	**px**
		$000	$000
Recession	0.5	180	90
Stable	0.4	190	76
Growing	0.1	200	20
Expected value			186

On the basis of expected values Project A should be selected.

However it should be noted that Project A is also the most risky option as it has the widest range of potential outcomes.

Test your understanding 4 – Expected values in larger NPV

Expected annual cash flows are:

	Annual cash flow	Probability	px
	(x)	(p)	
	50,000	0.3	15,000
	100,000	0.5	50,000
	150,000	0.2	30,000
Expected value			95,000

NPV calculation:

Time	Cash flow	DF 5%	PV
	$		$
0	(460,000)	1.000	(460,000)
1–5	95,000	4.329	411,255
5	40,000	0.784	31,360
		NPV =	(17,385)

As the expected NPV is negative, the project should not be undertaken.

An alternative approach would be to calculate three separate NPVs and then combine them, giving the following figures:

Annual cash flow	NPV working	NPV
$		$
50,000	($460k) + $50k ×4.329 + $40k × 0.784 =	(212,190)
100,000	($460k) + $100k ×4.329 + $40k × 0.784 =	4,260
150,000	($460k) + $150k ×4.329 + $40k × 0.784 =	220,710

Expected NPV = 0.3 × (–$212,190) + 0.5 × $4,260 + 0.2 × $220,710 = ($17,385)

Even though the expected NPV is negative these figures show that there is a 70% chance of the project giving a positive NPV. Some investors may consider the project acceptable on this basis.

Test your understanding 5

Answer D

DPP is 2.36 years and NPV is $6,000

Year	Present value (PV)	Discount factor	Cumulative PV
	$	@ 15%	$
0	(12,000)	1.000	(12,000)
1	(4,800)	0.870	(4,176)
2	16,800	0.756	12,701
3	14,400	0.658	9,475

Net present value (NPV) = $6,000

If you selected an NPV of $4,400 you treated the $12,000 cash flow as occurring in year 1 and discounted it. Cash flows occurring 'now' should not be discounted.

Year	Present value (PV)	Cumulative PV
	$	$
0	(12,000)	(12,000)
1	(4,176)	(16,176)
2	12,701	(3,475)
3	9,475	6,000

DPP = 2 years + (3,475/(3,475 + 6,000) × 1 year) = 2.36 years

If you selected 2.0 years you calculated the non-discounted payback period.

Test your understanding 6

Answer C

	Cash flow $	Discount factor @ 10%	PV $
Time 0 machine	(275,000)	1.000	(275,000)
Time 1–5 contribution	200,000	3.791	758,200
Time 1–5 fixed costs	(95,000)	3.791	(360,145)
NPV			123,055

PV of contribution must fall by $123,055

Sales volume must fall by $123,055/758,200 = 16.23%

Fall in sales volume = 0.1623 × 50,000 = 8,115

Test your understanding 7

Answer D

The expected value criterion is irrespective of risk.

Test your understanding 8

Answer B

When calculating the sensitivity of each variable, the lower the percentage, the more (not less) sensitive is the NPV to that project variable.

Test your understanding 9

Answer A

A risky situation is one where we can say that there is a 70% probability that returns from a project will be in excess of $100,000 but a 30% probability that returns will be less than $100,000. If, however, no information can be provided on the returns from the project, we are faced with an uncertain situation.

chapter

7

Working capital management

Chapter learning objectives

Upon completion of this chapter you will be able to:

- define working capital and identify its elements
- explain the objectives of working capital management in terms of liquidity and profitability, and discuss the conflict between them
- explain the importance of working capital management to good financial management
- describe the principle and components of the cash operating cycle including the impact on it of accounts payable and receivable
- calculate the length of the cash operating cycle from supplied data
- calculate the current ratio and explain its relevance
- calculate the quick ratio and explain its relevance
- calculate the inventory turnover ratio and the inventory holding period and explain their relevance
- calculate the average collection period for receivables and explain its relevance
- calculate the average payable period for payables and explain its relevance
- calculate the length of a company's cash operating cycle by selecting relevant data from the company's accounts and discuss the implications for the company
- calculate the sales revenue/net working capital ratio and explain its relevance
- calculate the level of working capital investment in current assets from supplied data

- discuss the effect of a business' terms of trade on the length of the working capital cycle
- explain the policies a company may adopt on the level of investment in current assets
- discuss the effect of the industry in which the organisation operates on the length of the working capital cycle
- calculate the level of working capital investment in current assets by selecting relevant data from the company's accounts and discuss the implications for the company.

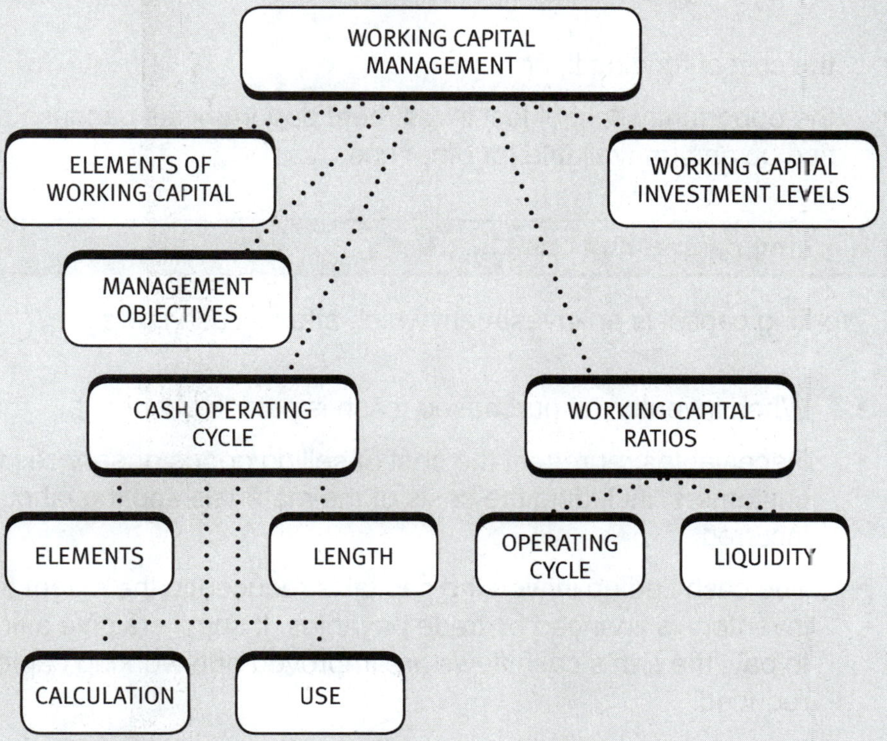

1 The elements of working capital

Working capital is the capital available for conducting the day-to-day operations of an organisation; normally the excess of current assets over current liabilities.

Working capital management is the management of all aspects of both current assets and current liabilities, to minimise the risk of insolvency while maximising the return on assets.

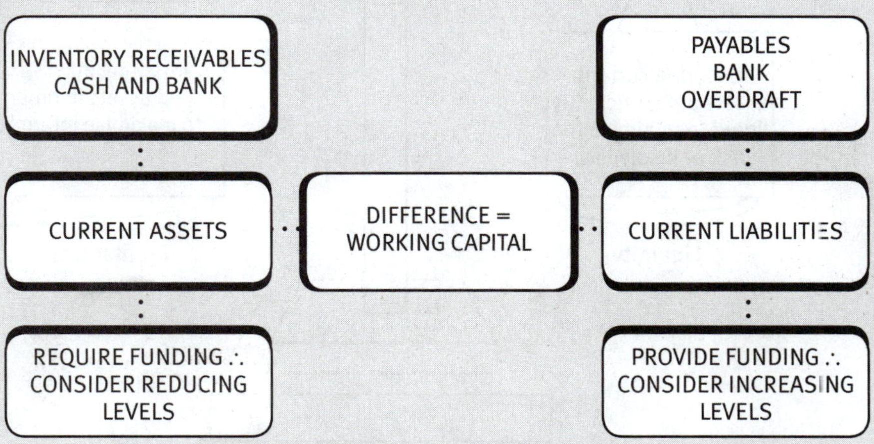

Investing in working capital has a cost, which can be expressed either as:

- the cost of funding it, or
- the opportunity cost of lost investment opportunities because cash is tied up and unavailable for other uses.

Working capital and cash flows

Working capital is an investment which affects cash flows.

- When inventory is purchased, cash is paid to acquire it.
- Receivables represent the cost of selling goods or services to customers, including the costs of the materials and the labour incurred.
- The cash tied up in working capital is reduced to the extent that inventory is financed by trade payables. If suppliers give a firm time to pay, the firm's cash flows are improved and working capital is reduced.

2 The objectives of working capital management

The main objective of working capital management is to get the balance of current assets and current liabilities right.

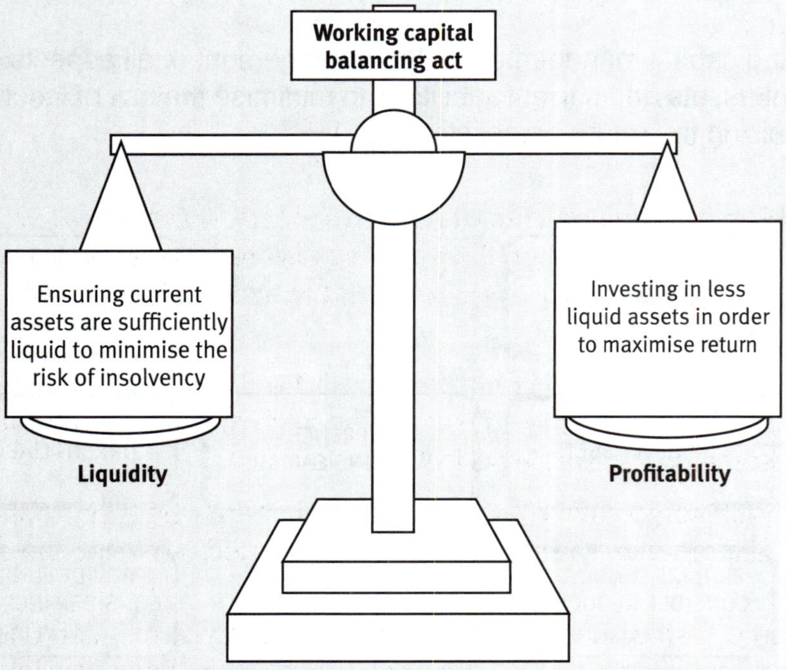

This can also be seen as the trade-off between cash flow versus profits.

Current assets are a major financial position statement item and especially significant to smaller firms. Mismanagement of working capital is therefore a common cause of business failure, e.g.:

- inability to meet bills as they fall due
- demands on cash during periods of growth being too great (overtrading)
- overstocking.

Working capital management is a key factor in an organisation's long-term success. The trade-off between liquidity and profitability and its role in determining a business' overall investment in working capital is fundamental to your understanding of working capital management for the examination.

Profitability v liquidity

The decision regarding the level of overall investment in working capital is a cost/benefit trade-off – **liquidity versus profitability**, or **cash flow versus profits**.

Cash flow versus profit

It is worth while stressing the difference between cash flow and profits. Cash flow is as important as profit. Unprofitable companies can survive if they have liquidity. Profitable companies can fail if they run out of cash to pay their liabilities (wages, amounts due to suppliers, overdraft interest, etc.).

Some examples of transactions that have this 'trade-off' effect on cash flows and on profits are as follows:

(a) Purchase of non-current assets for cash. The cash will be paid in full to the supplier when the asset is delivered; however profits will be charged gradually over the life of the asset in the form of depreciation.

(b) Sale of goods on credit. Profits will be credited in full once the sale has been confirmed; however the cash may not be received for some considerable period afterwards.

(c) With some payments such as tax there may be a significant timing difference between the impact on reported profit and the cash flow.

Clearly, cash balances and cash flows need to be monitored just as closely as trading profits. The need for adequate cash flow information is vital to enable management to fulfil this responsibility.

Profitability versus liquidity

Liquidity in the context of working capital management means having enough cash or ready access to cash to meet all payment obligations when these fall due. The main sources of liquidity are usually:

- cash in the bank
- short-term investments that can be cashed in easily and quickly
- cash inflows from normal trading operations (cash sales and payments by receivables for credit sales)
- an overdraft facility or other ready source of extra borrowing.

The basis of the trade off is where a company is able to improve its profitability but at the expense of tying up cash. For example:

- Receiving a bulk purchase discount (improved profitability) for buying more inventory than is currently required (reduced liquidity)
- Offering credit to customers (attracts more customers so improves profitability but reduces liquidity)

Sometimes, the opposite situation can be seen where a company can improve its liquidity position but at the expense of profitability. For example. offering an early settlement discount to customers.

Additional question – Profitability v liquidity

Fill in the blanks in the table to identify the advantages of having more or less working capital.

Advantages of keeping it high		Advantages of keeping it low
	INVENTORY	
	+	
	RECEIVABLES	
	+	
	CASH	
	=	
	CURRENT ASSETS	
	–	
	TRADE PAYABLES	
	=	
	WORKING CAPITAL	

The answer to this question can be found after the chapter summary diagram at the end of this chapter.

3 Policies regarding working capital management

Aggressive versus conservative approach

A firm choosing to have a lower level of working capital than rivals is said to have an **'aggressive'** approach, whereas a firm with a higher level of working capital has a **'conservative'** approach.

An aggressive approach will result in higher profitability and higher risk, while a conservative approach will result in lower profitability and lower risk.

Over-capitalisation and working capital

If there are excessive inventories, accounts receivable and cash, and very few accounts payable, there will be an over-investment by the company in current assets. Working capital will be excessive and the company will be over-capitalised.

Overtrading

Cash flow is the lifeblood of the thriving business. Effective and efficient management of the working capital investment is essential to maintaining control of business cash flow. Management must have full awareness of the profitability versus liquidity trade-off.

For example, healthy trading growth typically produces:

- increased profitability
- the need to increase investment in non-current assets and working capital.

In contrast to over-capitalisation, if the business does not have access to sufficient capital to fund the increase, it is said to be "overtrading". This can cause serious trouble for the business as it is unable to pay its business creditors.

In the exam, you might be expected to diagnose overtrading from information given about a company. You should look out for the following:

- A rapid increase in revenue
- A rapid increase in the volume of current assets
- Most of the increase in assets being financed by credit
- A dramatic drop in the liquidity ratios (see next section)

4 Working capital ratios – liquidity

Two key measures, the current ratio and the quick ratio, are used to assess short-term liquidity. Generally a higher ratio indicates better liquidity.

Current ratio

Measures how much of the total current assets are financed by current liabilities.

$$\text{Current ratio} = \frac{\text{Current assets}}{\text{Current liabilities}}$$

A measure of 2:1 means that current liabilities can be paid twice over out of existing current assets.

Quick (acid test) ratio

The quick or acid test ratio:

- measures how well current liabilities are covered by liquid assets
- is particularly useful where inventory holding periods are long.

$$\text{Quick ratio (acid test)} = \frac{\text{Current assets – Inventory}}{\text{Current liabilities}}$$

A measure of 1:1 means that the company is able to meet existing liabilities if they all fall due at once.

Liquidity ratios

These liquidity ratios are a guide to the risk of cash flow problems and insolvency. If a company suddenly finds that it is unable to renew its short-term liabilities (for instance if the bank suspends its overdraft facilities) there will be a danger of insolvency unless the company is able to turn enough of its current assets into cash quickly.

In general, high current and quick ratios are considered 'good' in that they mean that an organisation has the resources to meet its commitments as they fall due. However, it may indicate that working capital is not being used efficiently, for example that there is too much idle cash that should be invested to earn a return.

Conventional wisdom has it that an ideal current ratio is 2 and an ideal quick ratio is 1. It is very tempting to draw definite conclusions from limited information or to say that the current ratio should be 2, or that the quick ratio should be 1.

However, this is not very meaningful without taking into account the type of ratio expected in a similar business or within a business sector. Any assessment of working capital ratios must take into account the nature of the business involved.

For example a supermarket business operating a JIT system will have little inventory and since most of sales are for cash they will have few receivables. In addition the ability to negotiate long credit periods with suppliers can result in a large payables figure. This can result in net current liabilities and a current ratio below 1 – but does not mean the business has a liquidity problem.

Some companies use an overdraft as part of their long-term finance, in which case the current and quick ratios may appear worryingly low. In such questions you could suggest that the firm reschedule the overdraft as a loan. Not only would this be cheaper but it would also improve liquidity ratios.

5 The cash operating cycle

The elements of the operating cycle

The cash operating cycle is the length of time between the company's outlay on raw materials, wages and other expenditures and the inflow of cash from the sale of goods.

The faster a firm can 'push' items around the cycle the lower its investment in working capital will be.

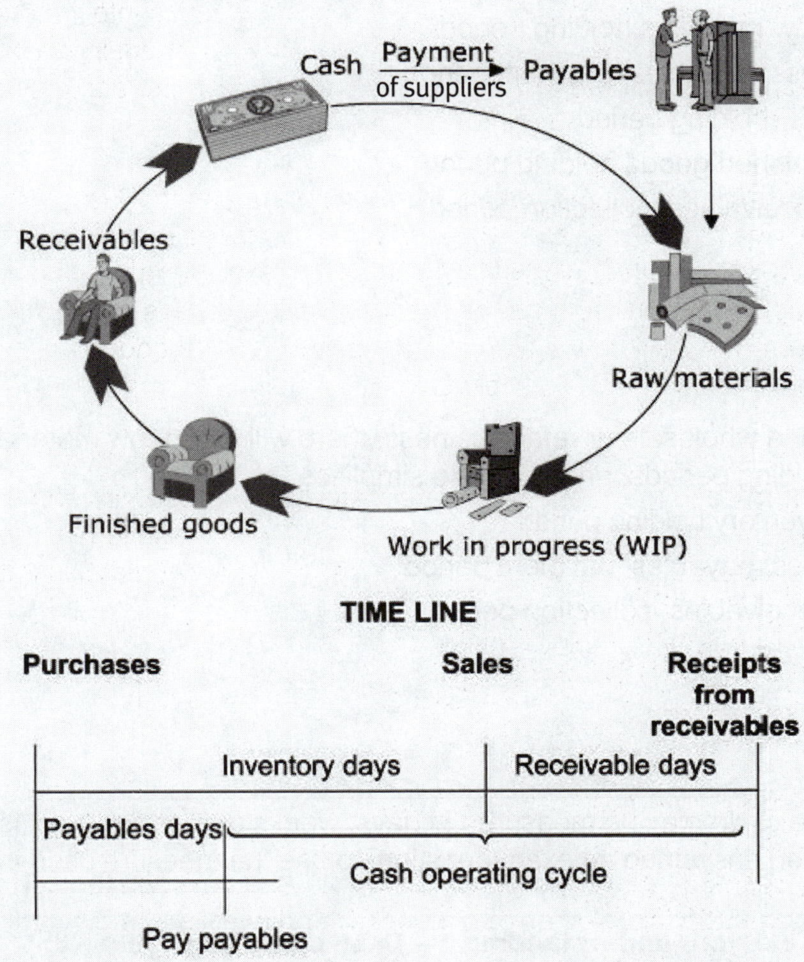

The cash operating cycle

The cash operating cycle reflects a firm's investment in working capital as it moves through the production process towards sales. The investment in working capital gradually increases, first being only in raw materials, but then in labour and overheads as production progresses. This investment must be maintained throughout the production process, the holding period for finished goods and up to the final collection of cash from trade receivables.

(**Note:** The net investment can be reduced by taking trade credit from suppliers.)

Calculation of the cash operating cycle

For a manufacturing business, the cash operating cycle is calculated as:

Raw materials holding period	x
Less: payables' payment period	(x)
WIP holding period	x
Finished goods holding period	x
Receivables' collection period	x
	x

For a wholesale or retail business, there will be no raw materials or WIP holding periods, and the cycle simplifies to:

Inventory holding period	x
Less: payables' payment period	(x)
Receivables' collection period	x
	x

The cycle may be measured in days, weeks or months and it is advisable, when answering an exam question, to use the measure used in the question.

Test your understanding 1 – Cash operating cycle

A company has provided the following information:

Receivables collection period	56 days
Raw material inventory holding period	21 days
Production period (WIP)	14 days
Suppliers' payment period	42 days
Finished goods holding period	28 days

Calculate the length of the operating cycle

Factors affecting the length of the operating cycle

Length of the cycle depends on:

- liquidity versus profitability decisions
- terms of trade
- management efficiency
- industry norms, e.g. retail versus construction.

The optimum level of working capital is the amount that results in no idle cash or unused inventory, but that does not put a strain on liquid resources.

The length of the cycle

The length of the cycle depends on how the balancing act between liquidity and profitability is resolved, the efficiency of management and the nature of the industry.

The optimum level is the amount that results in no idle cash or unused inventory, but that does not put a strain on liquid resources. Trying to shorten the cash cycle may have detrimental effects elsewhere, with the organisation lacking the cash to meet its commitments and losing sales since customers will generally prefer to buy from suppliers who are prepared to extend trade credit, and who have items available when required.

Additionally, any assessment of the acceptability or otherwise of the length of the cycle must take into account the nature of the business involved.

A supermarket chain will tend to have a very low or negative cycle – they have very few, if any, credit customers, they have a high inventory turnover and they can negotiate quite long credit periods with their suppliers.

A construction company will have a long cycle – their projects tend to be long-term, often extending over more than a year, and whilst progress payments may be made by the customer (if there is one), the bulk of the cash will be received towards the end of the project.

The amount of cash required to fund the operating cycle will increase as either:

- the cycle gets longer
- the level of activity/sales increases.

This can be summed up as follows:

Activity/sales	Length of cycle	Funds needed increase proportionate to:
Stays constant =	Increases ↑	Days in cycle
Increase ↑	Stays constant =	Sales

Where level of activity (sales) is constant and the number of days of the operating cycle increase the amount of funds required for working capital will increase in approximate proportion to the number of days.

Where the cycle remains constant but activity (sales) increase the funds required for working capital will increase in approximate proportion to sales.

By monitoring the operating cycle the manager gains a macro view of the relative efficiency of the working capital utilisation. Further it may be a key target to reduce the operating cycle to improve the efficiency of the business.

6 Working capital ratios – operating cycle

The periods used to determine the cash operating cycle are calculated by using a series of working capital ratios.

The ratios for the individual components (inventory, receivables and payables) are normally expressed as the number of days/weeks/months of the relevant statement of profit or loss figure they represent.

e.g

Illustration 1 – Working capital ratios – operating cycle

X Co has the following figures from its most recent accounts:

	$m
Receivables	4
Trade payables	2
Inventory	4.3
Sales (80% on credit)	30
Materials purchases (all on credit)	18
Cost of sales	25

Required:

Calculate the relevant working capital ratios. Round your answers to the nearest day.

Inventory holding period

The length of time inventory is held between purchase and sale.

Calculated as:

$$= \frac{\text{Inventory}}{\text{Cost of sales}} \times 365$$

Solution to Illustration

Solution 1 to illustration 1

$$\frac{\$4.3\text{m}}{\$25\text{m}} \times 365 = 63 \text{ days}$$

In some questions, a more detailed breakdown of inventory may be provided, with values given for raw materials, work-in-progress and finished goods stock. Where this is the case, more detailed calculations can be performed as follows:

Raw material inventory holding period

The length of time raw materials are held between purchase and being used in production.

Calculated as:

$$= \frac{\text{Raw material inventory}}{\text{Material usage}} \times 365$$

NB. Where usage cannot be calculated, purchases gives a good approximation.

Solution to illustration

Solution 2 to illustration 1

Suppose you are told that raw materials inventory was $1m of the total inventory held and that materials usage was $20m. The raw material inventory holding period could be calculated as:

$$\frac{\$1\text{m}}{\$20\text{m}} \times 365 \qquad = 18 \text{ days}$$

WIP holding period

The length of time goods spend in production.

Calculated as:

$$= \frac{\text{Work-in-progress inventory held}}{\text{Production cost}} \times 365$$

NB. Where production cost cannot be calculated, cost of goods sold gives a good approximation.

Solution to illustration

Solution 3 to illustration 1

If you were told this company had a WIP balance of $1.3m and a total production cost of $23m, the WIP holding period could be calculated as:

$$\frac{\$1.3m}{\$23m} \times 365 = 21 \text{ days}$$

Finished goods inventory period

The length of time finished goods are held between completion or purchase and sale.

Calculated as:

$$= \frac{\text{Finished goods inventory held}}{\text{Cost of goods sold}} \times 365$$

For all inventory period ratios, a low ratio is usually seen as a sign of good working capital management. It is very expensive to hold inventory and thus minimum inventory holding usually points to good practice.

Solution to illustration

Solution 4 to illustration 1

If you were told that the remaining inventory of $2m was finished goods inventory, you could calculate the finished goods holding period as:

$$\frac{\$2m}{\$25m} \times 365 = 29 \text{ days}$$

Note: the total of the three individual holding periods calculated is slightly more than the one calculated as an overall inventory holding period. This is because the more detailed approach allows us to take account of the costs within each element by using materials usage and production cost within the calculation rather than just cost of sales. The more detailed approach is more accurate but won't always be possible due to the information available.

Inventory turnover

For each ratio, the corresponding turnover ratio can be calculated as:

$$\text{Inventory turnover (no of times)} = \frac{\text{Cost}}{\text{Average inventory held}}$$

Generally this is less useful in the examination.

Using finished goods information from illustration 1:

$$\text{Inventory turnover} = \frac{\$25\text{m}}{\$2\text{m}} = 12.5 \text{ times}$$

Thus finished goods inventory turns round/is turned into sales 12.5 times in the year.

Trade receivables days

The length of time credit is extended to customers.

Calculated as:

$$= \frac{\text{Receivables}}{\text{Credit sales}} \times 365$$

Generally shorter credit periods are seen as financially sensible but the length will also depend upon the nature of the business.

Solution to illustration

Solution 5 to illustration 1

$$\frac{\$4\text{m}}{\$30\text{m} \times 80\%} \times 365 = 61 \text{ days}$$

Interpreting trade receivables collection periods

Businesses which sell goods on credit terms specify a credit period. Failure to send out invoices on time or to follow up late payers will have an adverse effect on the cash flow of the business. The receivables collection period measures the average period of credit allowed to customers.

In general, the shorter the collection period the better because receivables are effectively 'borrowing' from the company. Remember, however, that the level of receivables reflects not only the ability of the credit controllers but also the sales and marketing strategy adopted, and the nature of the business. Any change in the level of receivables must therefore be assessed in the light of the level of sales.

Trade payables days

The average period of credit extended by suppliers.

Calculated as:

$$= \frac{\text{Trade payables}}{\text{Credit purchases}} \times 365$$

Solution to illustration

Solution 6 to illustration 1

$$\frac{\$2\text{m}}{\$18\text{m}} \times 365 = 41 \text{ days}$$

Generally, increasing payables days suggests advantage is being taken of available credit but there are risks:

- losing supplier goodwill
- losing prompt payment discounts
- suppliers increasing the price to compensate.

The operating cycle

The ratios can then be brought together to produce the cash operating cycle.

	Days
Inventory days	63
Trade payables days	(41)
Receivables days	61
Length of cash operating cycle	83

The cash operating cycle tells us it takes X Co 83 days between paying out for material inventories and eventually receiving cash back from customers.

As always this must then be compared with prior periods or industry average for meaningful analysis.

Additional points for calculating ratios

The ratios may be needed to provide analysis of a company's performance or simply to calculate the length of the operating cycle.

There are a few simple points to remember which will be of great use in the examination:

- Where the period is required in days, the multiple in the ratios is 365, for months the multiple is 12, or 52 for weeks.
- To avoid getting a result that is unduly influenced by unusual balances at a period in time, your calculations should ideally use average balances for inventory, receivables and payables. If not given, these could be calculated by taking the opening and closing financial position statement figures and dividing by two. If you are required to compare ratios between two financial position statements, it is acceptable to base each holding period on financial position statement figures, rather than an average, in order to see whether the ratio has increased or decreased.
- For each ratio calculated above, the corresponding turnover ratio can be calculated by inverting the ratio given and removing the multiple.
- When using the ratios to appraise performance, it is essential to compare the figure with others in the industry or identify the trend over a number of periods.

- Ratios have their limitations and care must be taken because:
  - the financial position statement values at a particular time may not be typical
  - balances used for a seasonal business may not represent average levels, e.g. a fireworks manufacturer
  - ratios can be subject to window dressing/manipulation
  - ratios concern the past (historic) not the future
  - figures may be distorted by inflation and/or rapid growth.

Working capital turnover

One final ratio that relates to working capital is the working capital turnover ratio and is calculated as:

$$\frac{\text{Sales revenue}}{\text{Net working capital}}$$

This measures how efficiently management is utilising its investment in working capital to generate sales and can be useful when assessing whether a company is overtrading.

It must be interpreted in the light of the other ratios used.

Test your understanding 2 – Calculation of cash operating cycle

Marlboro Co estimates the following figures for the coming year.

Sales – all on credit	$3,600,000
Receivables	$306,000
Gross profit margin *	25% on sales
Finished goods	$200,000
Work in progress	$350,000
Raw materials (balance held)	$150,000
Trade payables	$130,000

Inventory levels are constant.

* Raw materials are 80% of cost of sales – all on credit.

Required:

Calculate the cash operating cycle.

From an examination point of view, calculating the ratios is only the start – interpretation is the key to a good answer. Try to build a cumulative picture, e.g. the current ratio looks good until we find out from calculating the inventory holding period that there are high levels of illiquid inventory.

Do not be afraid to point out further information that may be required to provide a better interpretation of your calculations, e.g. the company credit policy, industry benchmarks, etc.

Test your understanding 3 – Appraisal of working capital

You have been given the following information for a company:

Summarised statements of financial position at 30 June

	20X7		20X6	
	$000	$000	$000	$000
Non-current assets (carrying value)		130		139
Current assets:				
Inventory	42		37	
Receivables	29		23	
Bank	3		5	
		74		65
Total assets		204		204
Equity and liabilities				
Ordinary share capital (50 cent shares)		35		35
Share premium account		17		17
Revaluation reserve		10		–
Profit and loss account		31		22
		93		74
Non-current liabilities				
5% secured loan notes		40		40
8% Preference shares ($1 shares)		25		25
Current liabilities				
Trade payables	36		55	
Taxation	10		10	
		46		65
Total equity and liabilities		204		204

Summarised statements of profit or loss for the year ended 30 June

	20X7		20X6	
	$000	$000	$000	$000
Revenue		209		196
Opening inventory	37		29	
Purchases	162		159	
	199		188	
Closing inventory	42		37	
		157		151
Gross profit		52		45
Finance costs	2		2	
Depreciation	9		9	
Sundry expenses	14		11	
		25		22
Operating profit		27		23
Taxation		10		10
Profit after taxation		17		13
Dividends:				
Ordinary shares	6		5	
Preference shares	2		2	
		8		7
Retained profit		9		6

Required:

(a) Calculate the liquidity ratios in 20X6 and 20X7

(b) Calculate the length of the cash operating cycle in 20X6 and 20X7

(c) Comment on your results and appraise how effectively the working capital is being managed

7 Working capital investment levels

The working capital ratios shown above can be used to predict the future levels of investment (the financial position statement figure) required. This is done by re-arranging the formulas. For example:

$$\text{Trade receivables balance} = \frac{\text{Trade receivables days}}{365} \times \text{Credit sales}$$

Working capital investment levels

The level of working capital required is affected by the following factors:

(1) The nature of the business, e.g. manufacturing companies need more inventory than service companies.

(2) Uncertainty in supplier deliveries. Uncertainty would mean that extra inventory needs to be carried in order to cover fluctuations.

(3) The overall level of activity of the business. As output increases, receivables, inventory, etc. all tend to increase.

(4) The company's credit policy. The tighter the company's policy the lower the level of receivables.

(5) The length of the operating cycle. The longer it takes to convert material into finished goods into cash the greater the investment in working capital

(6) The credit policy of suppliers. The less credit the company is allowed to take, the lower the level of payables and the higher the net investment in working capital.

Test your understanding 4 – Working capital investment levels

X plc has the following expectations for the forthcoming period.

	$m
Sales	10
Materials	(6)
Other costs	(2)
Profit	2

The following working capital ratios are expected to apply.

Inventory days	30 days
Receivables days	60 days
Payables days	40 days

Required:

Compute the working capital requirement.

Additional question – Working capital inv levels (1)

A company's annual sales are $8 million with a mark-up on cost of 60%. It normally settles payables two months after purchases are made, holding one month's worth of demand in inventory. It allows receivables 1½ months' credit and its cash balance currently stands at $1,250,000.

What are its current and quick ratios?

The answer to this question can be found after the chapter summary diagram at the end of this chapter.

Additional question – Working capital inv levels (2)

The following data relate to Mugwump Co, a manufacturing company.

Sales revenue for year:	$1,500,000
Costs as percentage of sales:	30%
Direct materials	
Direct labour	25%
Variable overheads	10%
Fixed overheads	15%
Selling and distribution	5%

Average statistics relating to working capital are as follows:

- receivables take 2½ months to pay
- raw materials are in inventory for three months
- WIP represents two months' half-produced goods
- finished goods represent one month's production
- credit is taken
  - Materials — 2 months
  - Direct labour — 1 week
  - Variable overheads — 1 month
  - Fixed overheads — 1 month
  - Selling and distribution — ½ month

WIP and finished goods are valued at the cost of material, labour and variable expenses.

Compute the working capital requirement of Mugwump Co assuming that the labour force is paid for 50 working weeks in each year.

The answer to this question can be found after the chapter summary diagram at the end of this chapter.

Test your understanding 5

A company has a liquidity ratio equal to 0.5. The directors believe that the company has to reduce its bank overdraft and have agreed to alter the company's credit terms to customers from two months to one month.

What would be the effects on the company's cash operating cycle and liquidity ratio if this change were to be achieved?

	Cash operating cycle	*Liquidity ratio*
A	Decrease	Decrease
B	Decrease	No change
C	Decrease	Increase
D	Increase	Increase

Test your understanding 6

The key trade-off that lies at the heart of working capital management is that between

A Business stability and solvency

B Debtors and creditors

C Current assets and current liabilities

D Liquidity and profitability

Test your understanding 7

Which of the following is not a typical symptom of overtading?

A A rapid increase in sales revenue

B A bank overdraft which may reach the limit of the facilities agreed by the bank

C An decrease in the current ratio and the quick ratio

D An decrease in trade payables days

Test your understanding 8

Archie plc manufactures plastic cutlery. The company buys raw materials from suppliers that allow the company 2.5 months credit. The raw materials remain in inventory for 2 months and it takes Archie plc 2 months to produce the goods, which are sold immediately production is completed. Customers take an average of 1.5 months to pay.

What is Archie plc's cash operating cycle?

A 2 month

B 2.5 months

C 3 months

D 7 months

Test your understanding 9

Which of the following will shorten the cash operating cycle?

A An increase in the raw materials inventory holding period

B An increase in the trade payables days

C An increase in the trade receivables days

D An increase in the production period

Chapter summary

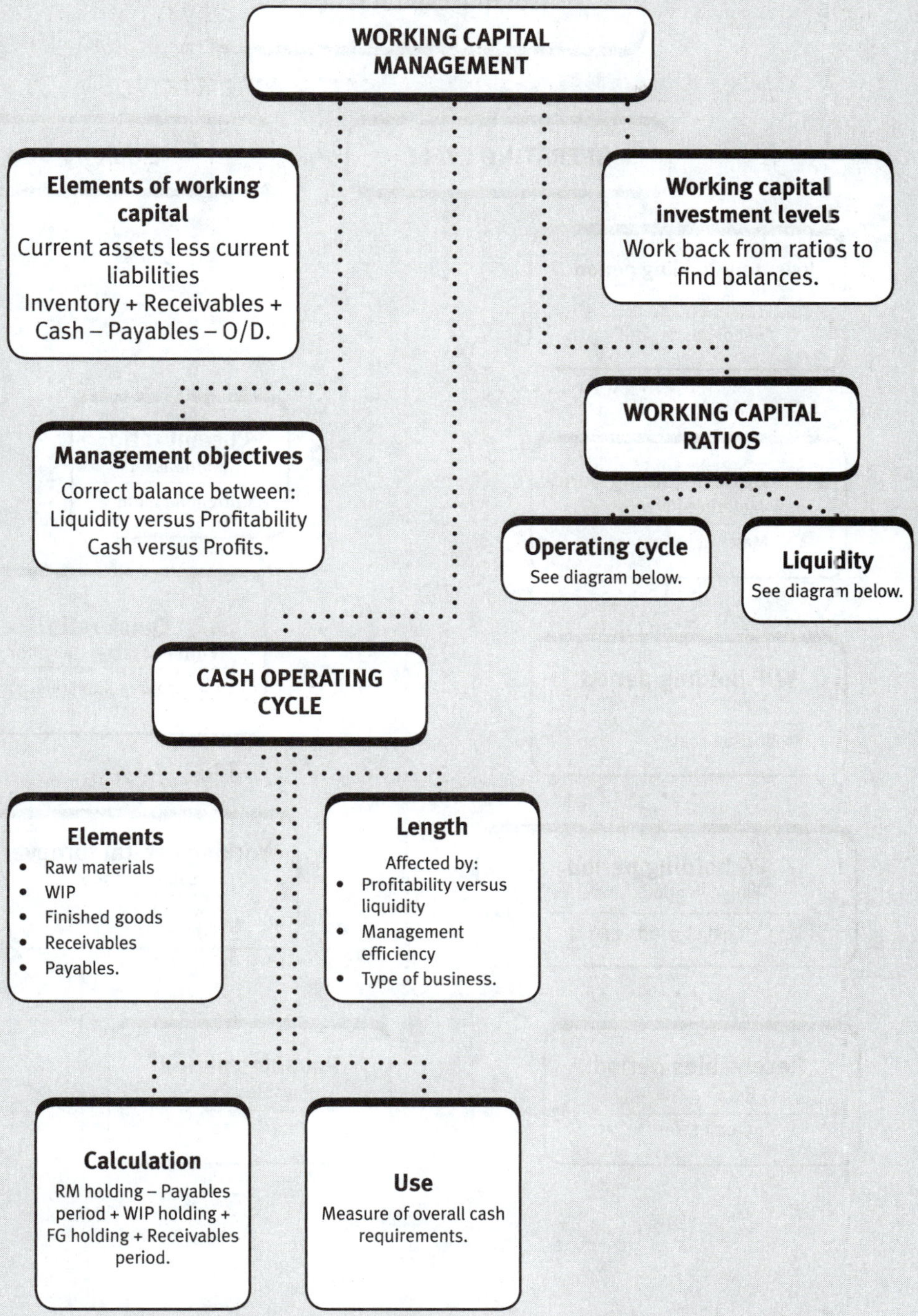

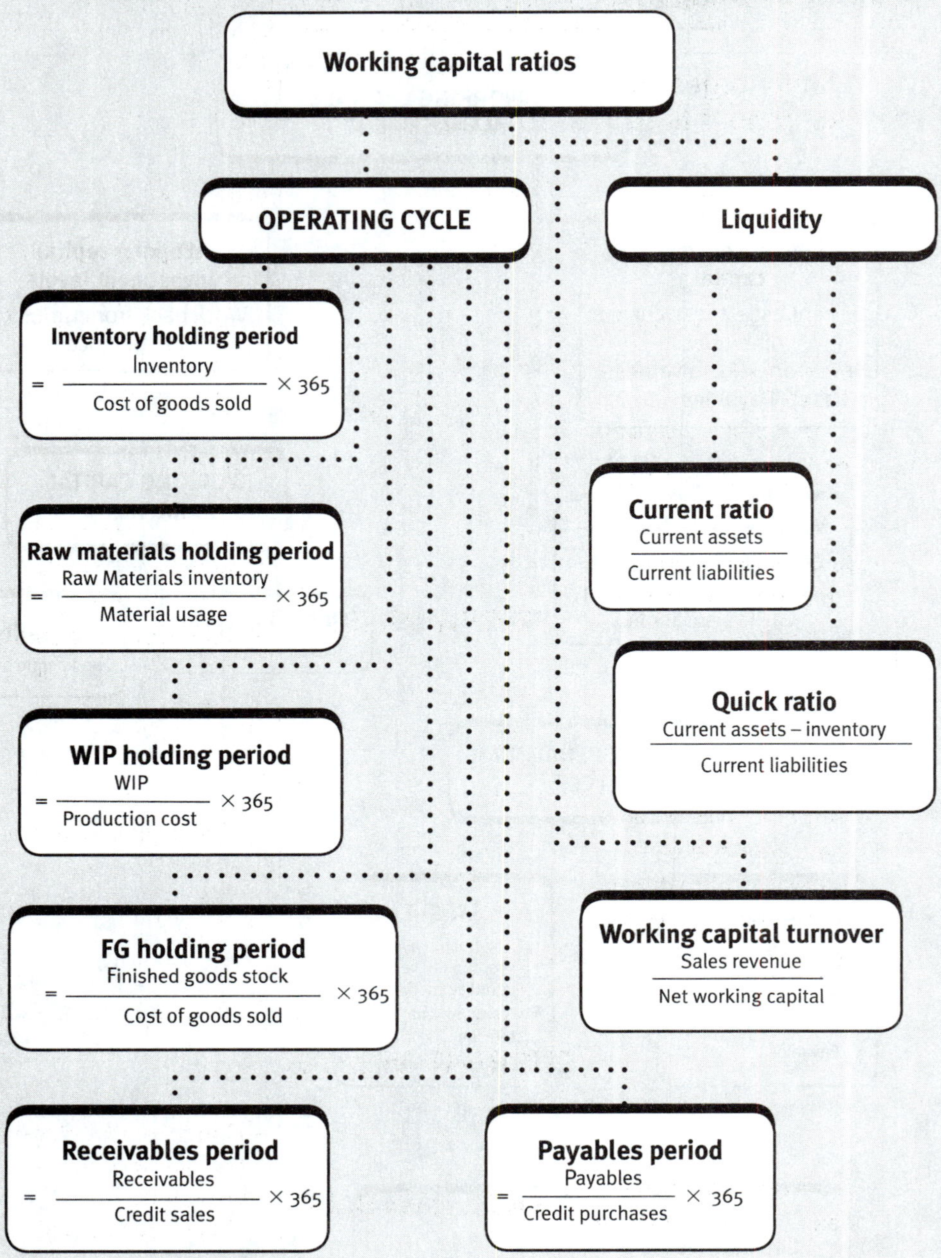
Working capital ratios
OPERATING CYCLE
Liquidity
Inventory holding period
= Inventory / Cost of goods sold × 365
Raw materials holding period
= Raw Materials inventory / Material usage × 365
WIP holding period
= WIP / Production cost × 365
FG holding period
= Finished goods stock / Cost of goods sold × 365
Receivables period
= Receivables / Credit sales × 365
Payables period
= Payables / Credit purchases × 365
Current ratio
Current assets / Current liabilities
Quick ratio
Current assets – inventory / Current liabilities
Working capital turnover
Sales revenue / Net working capital

Answer to additional question – Profitability v liquidity

Advantages of keeping it high ↑		Advantages of keeping it low ↓
– Few stockouts – Bulk purchase discounts – Reduced ordering costs	**INVENTORY**	– Less cash tied up in inventory – Lower storage costs – Flexibility
	+	
– Customers like credit – ∴ profitable as attracts more sales	**RECEIVABLES**	– Less cash tied up – Less chance of – irrecoverable debts – Reduced costs of credit control
	+	
– Able to pay bills on time – Take advantage of unexpected opportunities – Avoid high borrowing costs	**CASH**	– Can invest surplus to earn higher returns – Less vulnerable to takeover
	=	
	CURRENT ASSETS	
– Preserves own cash – cheap source of finance	– **TRADE PAYABLES**	– Can take advantage of prompt payment discounts – Retain good credit status – Move favourable supplier treatment
	=	
	WORKING CAPITAL	

Answer to additional question – Working capital inv levels (1)

Step 1 Calculate annual cost of sales, using the cost structure.

	%	$m
Sales	160	8
Cost of sales (COS)	100	5
Gross profit	60	3

Step 2 Calculate payables, receivables and inventory.

20X6 20X5

$$\text{Payables} = \frac{2}{12} \times \text{annual COS} = \frac{2}{12} \times \$5\text{m} = \$0.833\text{m}$$

$$\text{Receivables} = \frac{1.5}{12} \times \text{annual sales} = \frac{1.5}{12} \times \$8\text{m} = \$1\text{m}$$

$$\text{Inventory} = \frac{1}{12} \times \text{annual COS} \quad \frac{1}{12} \times \$5\text{m} = \$0.417\text{m}$$

Step 3 Calculate the ratios.

$$\text{Current ratio} = \frac{\text{Inventory + receivables + cash}}{\text{Payables}} = \frac{0.417 + 1 + 1.25}{0.833} = 3.2$$

$$\text{Quick ratio} = \frac{\text{Receivables + cash}}{\text{Payables}} = \frac{1 + 1.25}{0.833} = 2.7$$

Answer to additional question – Working capital inv levels (2)

(1) Costs incurred

		$
Direct materials 30% of $1,500,000		450,000
Direct labour 25% of $1,500,000		375,000
Variable overheads 10% of $1,500,000		150,000
Fixed overheads 15% of $1,500,000		225,000
Selling and distribution 5% of $1,500,000		75,000

(2) Average value of current assets

	$	$
Finished goods 1/12 × $975,000		81,250
Raw materials 3/12 × $450,000		112,500
WIP:		
(2 months @ half produced –		
1 month equivalent cost)		
Materials		
1/12 × $450,000	37,500	
Labour 1/12 × $375,000	31,250	
Variable overheads 1/12 × $150,000	12,500	
		81,250
Receivables 2 ½ /12 × $1,500,000		312,500
		587,500

(3) Average value of current liabilities

Materials 2/12 × $450,000	75,000	
Labour 1/50 × $375,000	7,500	
Variable overheads 1/12 × $150,000	12,500	
Fixed overheads 1/12 × $225,000	18,750	
Selling and distribution 1/24 × $75,000	3,125	
		(116,875)

(4) Working capital required 470,625

Test your understanding answers

Test your understanding 1 – Cash operating cycle

	Days
Raw materials inventory holding period	21
Less: suppliers' payment period	(42)
WIP holding period	14
Finished goods holding period	28
Receivables' collection period	56
Operating cycle (days)	77

Test your understanding 2 – Calculation of cash operating cycle

Statement of profit or loss

	$	$
Revenue		3,600,000
Cost of sales		
Materials – 80% (given)	2,160,000	
Other (balancing figure)	540,000	
		2,700,000
Gross profit – 25% (given)		900,000

Cash operating cycle

Raw materials holding period

$$\frac{\$150,000}{\$2,160,000} \times 365 = 25 \text{ days}$$

Trade payables days

$$\frac{\$130{,}000}{\$2{,}160{,}000} \times 365 = (22) \text{ days}$$

WIP holding days

$$\frac{\$350{,}000}{\$2{,}700{,}000} \times 365 = 48 \text{ days}$$

Finished goods holding period

$$\frac{\$200{,}000}{\$2{,}700{,}000} \times 365 = 27 \text{ days}$$

Receivables collection period

$$\frac{\$306{,}000}{\$3{,}600{,}000} \times 365 = 31 \text{ days}$$

109 days

Test your understanding 3 – Appraisal of working capital

The current ratio:

20X7

$$\frac{74}{46} = 1.6$$

20X6

$$\frac{65}{65} = 1.0$$

The quick (or acid test) ratio:

20X7

$$\frac{32}{46} = 0.7$$

20X6

$$\frac{28}{65} = 0.4$$

Both of these ratios show an improvement. The extent of the change between the two years seems surprising and would require further investigation. It would also be useful to know how these ratios compare with those of a similar business, since typical liquidity ratios for supermarkets, say, are quite different from those for heavy engineering firms.

In 20X7 current liabilities were well covered by current assets. Liabilities payable in the near future are 70% covered by cash and receivables (a liquid asset, close to cash).

To better understand the liquidity ratios we can then look at each individual component of working capital:

The inventory holding period:

20X7

$$\frac{(\tfrac{1}{2}(37 + 42) \times 365 \text{ days})}{157} = 92 \text{ days}$$

20X6

$$\frac{(\tfrac{1}{2}(29 + 37) \times 365 \text{ days})}{151} = 80 \text{ days}$$

The inventory holding period has lengthened. In general, the shorter the stock holding period the better. It is very expensive to hold stock and thus minimum stock holding usually points to good management.

The current ratio calculation now seems less optimistic, considering the holding period for inventory of 92 days. Inventory that takes nearly four months to sell is not very liquid! It would be better to focus attention on the acid test ratio.

Receivables days:

	20X7		20X6	
Average daily sales	$209,000 / 365	= $573	$196,000 / 365	= $537
Closing trade receivables	$29,000		$23,000	
Receivables days	$29,000 / $573	= 51 days	$23,000 / $537	= 43 days

Or more quickly:

20X7

$$\frac{29{,}000}{209{,}000} \times 365 \text{ days} = 50.6 \text{ days}$$

20X6

$$\frac{23{,}000}{196{,}000} \times 365 = 42.8 \text{ days}$$

Compared with 20X6, the receivables collection period has worsened in 20X7. It would be important to establish the company policy on credit allowed. If the average credit allowed to customers was, say, 30 days, then something is clearly wrong. Further investigation might reveal delays in sending out invoices or failure to 'screen' new customers.

This situation suggests yet a further review of the liquidity ratios. The acid test ratio ignores inventory but still assumes receivables are liquid. If debt collection is a problem then receivables too are illiquid and the company could struggle to pay its current liabilities were they all to fall due in a short space of time.

Payables days:

	20X7		20X6	
Average daily purchases	$162,000 / 365	= $444	$159,000 / 365	= $436
Closing trade receivables	$36,000		$55,000	
Payables' payment period	81 days		126 days	

Or more quickly:

20X6

$$\frac{36{,}000}{162{,}000} \times 365 \text{ days} = 81.1 \text{ days}$$

20X6

$$\frac{55{,}000}{159{,}000} \times 365 = 126.3 \text{ days}$$

The payables' payment period has reduced substantially from last year. It is, however, in absolute terms still a high figure. Often, suppliers request payment within 30 days. The company is taking nearly three months. Trade creditors are thus financing much of the working capital requirements of the business, which is beneficial to the company.

A high level of creditor days may be good in that it means that all available credit is being taken, but there are three potential disadvantages of taking extended credit:

- Future supplies may be endangered.
- Availability of cash discounts is lost.
- Suppliers may quote a higher price for the goods knowing the company takes extended credit.

Additionally when viewed alongside the previous ratios calculated, this might suggest a cash flow problem causing suppliers to be left unpaid.

Length of the operating cycle:

	20X7 days	**20X6 days**
Inventory holding period	92	80
+		
Receivables' collection period	51	43
–		
Payables' payment period	(81)	(126)
=		
Cash operating cycle	62 days	(3 days)

Our example shows that, in 20X7, there is approximately a 62-day gap between paying cash to suppliers for goods, and receiving the cash back from customers. However, in 20X6, there was the somewhat unusual situation where cash was received from the customers, on average, more than 3 days before the payment to suppliers was needed.

Test your understanding 4 – Working capital investment levels

We need to use the ratios to calculate financial position statement values in order to construct the projected working capital position.

				$m
Inventory	=	30 ÷ 365	× $6m	= 0.49
Receivables	=	60 ÷ 365	× $10m	1.64
Trade payables	=	40 ÷ 365	× $6m	= (0.66)
Working capital required				1.47

Test your understanding 5

Answer A

Cash operating cycle decreases, liquidity ratio decreases.

The reduction in the amount of time taken for customers to pay their bills would reduce the cash operating cycle.

The reduction in receivables and in the overdraft mean that the numerator and denominator of the liquidity ratio would both reduce by the same amount. Therefore the ratio would decrease.

Test your understanding 6

Answer D

All businesses face a trade-off between being profitable (providing a return) and being liquid (staying in business).

Test your understanding 7

Answer D

Overtrading happens when a business tries to do too much too quickly with too little long-term capital The business tries to support too large a volume of trade with the capital resources at its disposal. As such, the payment period to accounts payable is likely to lengthen (not shorten).

Test your understanding 8

Answer C

	Months
The average time the raw materials are in inventory	2.0
Less: The time taken to pay suppliers	(2.5)
Time taken to produce the goods	2.0
Time taken by customers to pay for the goods	1.5
Total	3.0

Test your understanding 9

Answer B

The calculation of trade payables days gives the average period of credit extended to suppliers. As this amount increases, the cash operating cycle will shorten.

chapter

8

Working capital management – inventory control

Chapter learning objectives

Upon completion of this chapter you will be able to:

- explain the objective of inventory management
- define and explain lead time and buffer inventory
- explain and apply the basic economic order quantity (EOQ) formula to data provided
- calculate the EOQ taking account of quantity discounts and calculate the financial implications of discounts for bulk purchases
- define and calculate the re-order level where demand and lead time are known
- describe and evaluate the main inventory management systems including Just-In-Time (JIT) techniques
- suggest appropriate inventory management techniques for use in a scenario.

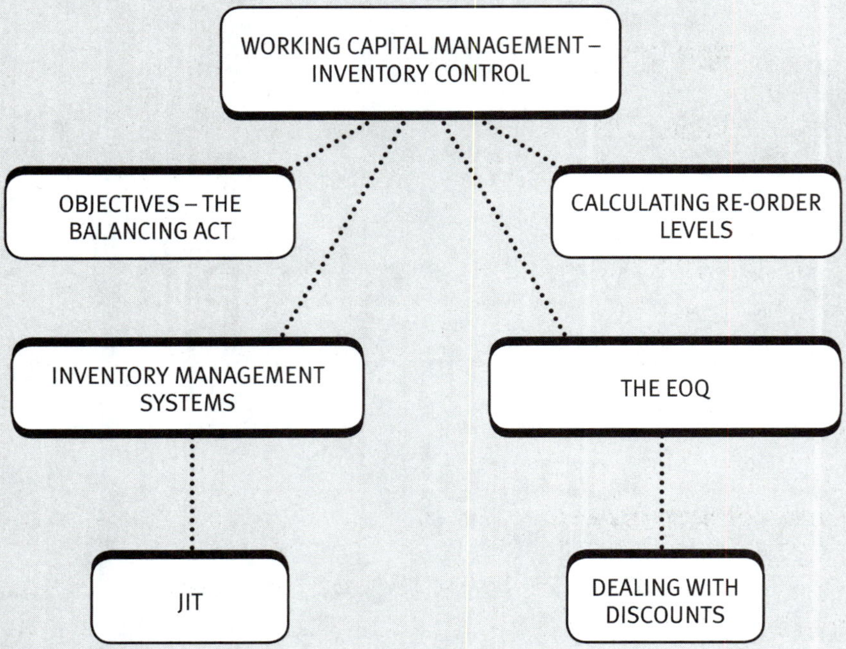

1 The objectives of inventory management

Inventory is a major investment for many companies. Manufacturing companies can easily be carrying inventory equivalent to between 50% and 100% of the revenue of the business. It is therefore essential to reduce the levels of inventory held to the necessary minimum.

The balancing act

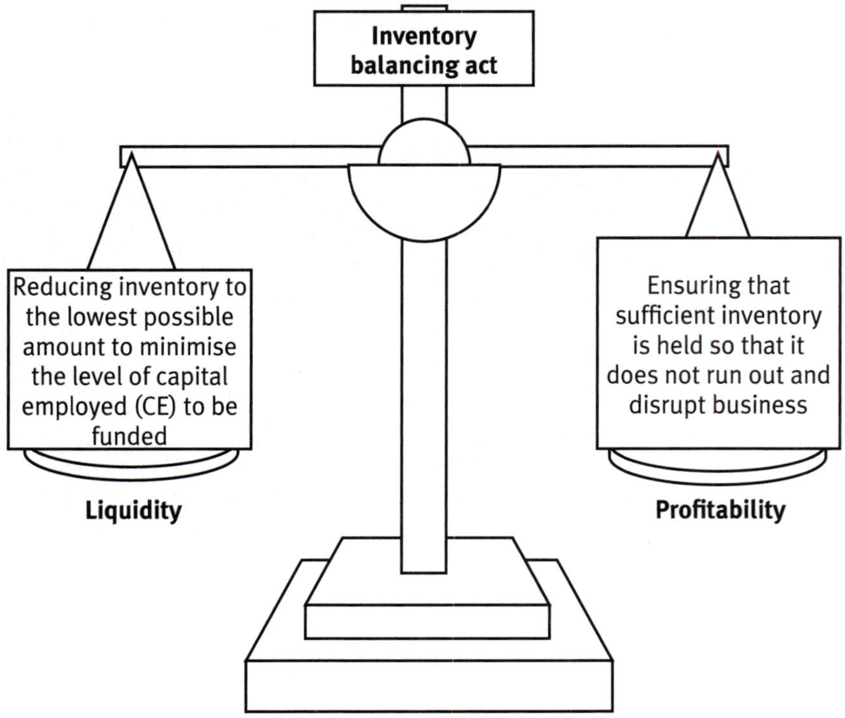

Costs of high inventory levels

Keeping inventory levels high is expensive owing to:

- purchase costs
- holding costs:
  - storage
  - stores administration
  - risk of theft/damage/obsolescence.

Costs of high inventory levels

Carrying inventory involves a major working capital investment and therefore levels need to be very tightly controlled. The cost is not just that of purchasing the goods, but also storing, insuring, and managing them once they are in inventory.

Purchase costs: once goods are purchased, capital is tied up in them and until sold on (in their current state or converted into a finished product), the capital earns no return. This lost return is an opportunity cost of holding the inventory.

Storage and stores administration: in addition, the goods must be stored. The company must incur the expense of renting out warehouse space, or if using space they own, there is an opportunity cost associated with the alternative uses the space could be put to. There may also be additional requirements such as controlled temperature or light which require extra funds.

Other risks: once stored, the goods will need to be insured. Specialist equipment may be needed to transport the inventory to where it is to be used. Staff will be required to manage the warehouse and protect against theft and if inventory levels are high, significant investment may be required in sophisticated inventory control systems.

The longer inventory is held, the greater the risk that it will deteriorate or become out of date. This is true of perishable goods, fashion items and high-technology products, for example.

Costs of low inventory levels

If inventory levels are kept too low, the business faces alternative problems:

- stockouts:
  - lost contribution
  - production stoppages
  - emergency orders
- high re-order/setup costs
- lost quantity discounts.

Costs of low inventory levels

Stockout: if a business runs out of a particular product used in manufacturing it may cause interruptions to the production process – causing idle time, stockpiling of work-in-progress (WIP) or possibly missed orders. Alternatively, running out of goods held for onward sale can result in dissatisfied customers and perhaps future lost orders if custom is switched to alternative suppliers. If a stockout looms, the business may attempt to avoid it by acquiring the goods needed at short notice. This may involve using a more expensive or poorer quality supplier.

Re-order/setup costs: each time inventory runs out, new supplies must be acquired. If the goods are bought in, the costs that arise are associated with administration – completion of a purchase requisition, authorisation of the order, placing the order with the supplier, taking and checking the delivery and final settlement of the invoice. If the goods are to be manufactured, the costs of setting up the machinery will be incurred each time a new batch is produced.

Lost quantity discounts: purchasing items in bulk will often attract a discount from the supplier. If only small amounts are bought at one time in order to keep inventory levels low, the quantity discounts will not be available.

The challenge

The objective of good inventory management is therefore to determine:

- the optimum re-order level – how many items are left in inventory when the next order is placed, and
- the optimum re-order quantity – how many items should be ordered when the order is placed

for all material inventory items.

In practice, this means striking a balance between holding costs on the one hand and stockout and re-order costs on the other.

The balancing act between liquidity and profitability, which might also be considered to be a trade-off between holding costs and stockout/re-order costs, is key to any discussion on inventory management.

Terminology

Other key terms associated with inventory management include

- lead time – the lag between when an order is placed and the item is delivered
- buffer inventory – the basic level of inventory kept for emergencies. A buffer is required because both demand and lead time will fluctuate and predictions can only be based on best estimates.

Ensure you can distinguish between the various terms used: re-order level, re-order quantity, lead time and buffer inventory.

2 Economic order quantity (EOQ)

For businesses that do not use just in time (JIT) inventory management systems (discussed in more detail below), there is an optimum order quantity for inventory items, known as the EOQ.

The challenge

The aim of the EOQ model is to minimise the total cost of holding and ordering inventory.

EOQ explanation

To minimise the total cost of holding and ordering inventory, it is necessary to balance the relevant costs. These are:

- the variable costs of holding the inventory
- the fixed costs of placing the order

Holding costs

The model assumes that it costs a certain amount to hold a unit of inventory for a year (referred to as C_H in the formula). Therefore, as the average level of inventory increases, so too will the total annual holding costs incurred.

Because of the assumption that demand per period is known and is constant (see below), conclusions can be drawn over the average inventory level in relationship to the order quantity.

When new batches or items of inventory are purchased or made at periodic intervals, the inventory levels are assumed to exhibit the following pattern over time.

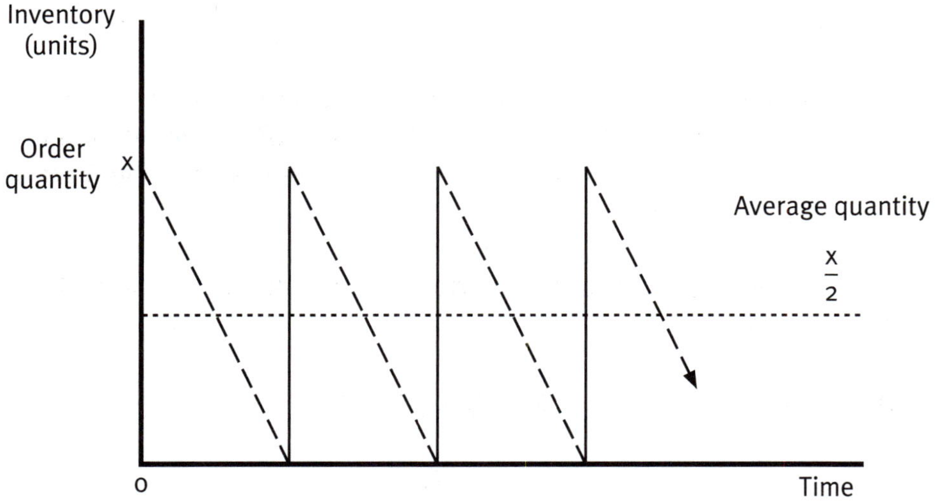

If x is the quantity ordered, the annual holding cost would be calculated as:

Holding cost per unit × Average inventory:

$$C_H \times \frac{x}{2}$$

We therefore see an upward sloping, linear relationship between the re-order quantity and total annual holding costs.

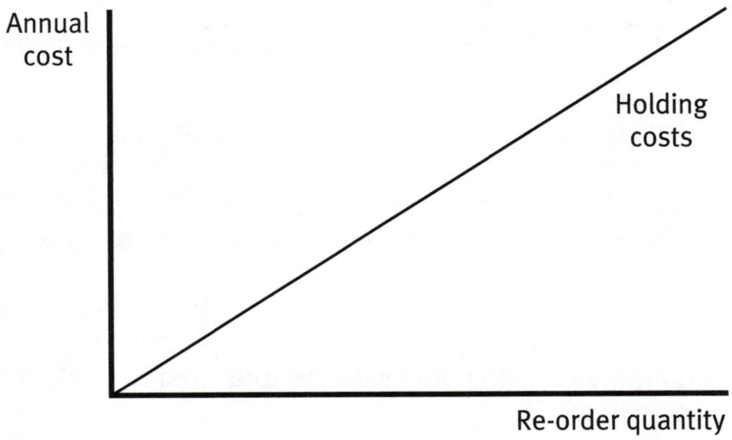

Ordering costs

The model assumes that a fixed cost is incurred every time an order is placed (referred to as C_O in the formula). Therefore, as the order quantity increases, there is a fall in the number of orders required, which reduces the total ordering cost.

If D is the annual expected sales demand, the annual order cost is calculated as:

Order cost per order × no. of orders per annum.

$$C_O \times \frac{D}{x}$$

However, the fixed nature of the cost results in a downward sloping, curved relationship.

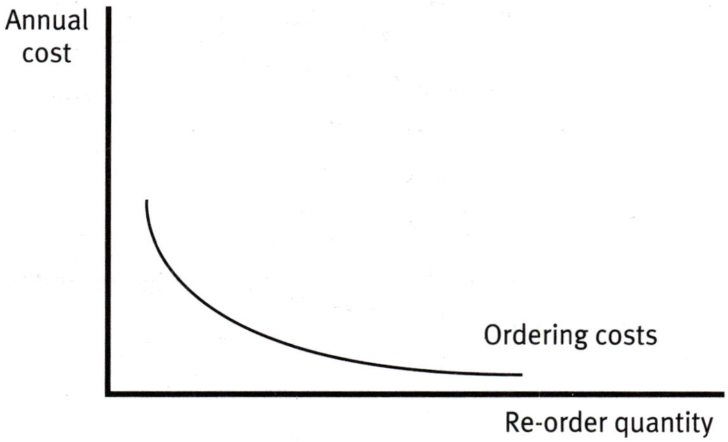

Because you are trying to balance these two costs (one which increases as re-order quantity increases and one which falls), total costs will always be minimised at the point where the total holding costs equals the total ordering costs. This point will be the economic order quantity.

When the re-order quantity chosen minimises the total cost of holding and ordering, it is known as the EOQ.

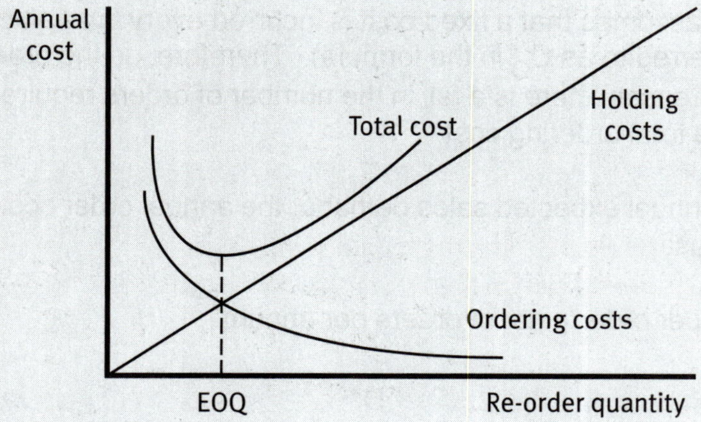

Assumptions

The following assumptions are made:

- demand and lead time are constant and known
- purchase price is constant
- no buffer inventory held (not needed).

These assumptions are critical and should be discussed when considering the validity of the model and its conclusions, e.g. in practice, demand and/or lead time may vary.

The calculation

The EOQ can be more quickly found using a formula (given in the examination):

$$EOQ = \sqrt{\frac{2C_O D}{C_H}}$$

where:

C_O = cost per order

D = annual demand

C_H = cost of holding one unit for one year.

Test your understanding 1 – EOQ I

A company requires 1,000 units of material X per month. The cost per order is $30 regardless of the size of the order. The holding costs are $2.88 per unit pa.

Required:

Investigate the total cost of buying the material in quantities of 400, 500, or 600 units at one time. What is the cheapest option?

Use the EOQ formula to prove your answer is correct.

Test your understanding 2 – EOQ II

Monthly demand for a product is 10,000 units. The purchase price is \$10/unit and the company's cost of finance is 15% pa. Warehouse storage costs per unit pa are \$2/unit. The supplier charges \$200 per order for delivery.

Calculate the EOQ.

Dealing with quantity discounts

Discounts may be offered for ordering in large quantities. If the EOQ is smaller than the order size needed for a discount, should the order size be increased above the EOQ?

To work out the answer you should carry out the following steps:

Step 1: Calculate EOQ, ignoring discounts.

Step 2: If the EOQ is below the quantity qualifying for a discount, calculate the total annual inventory cost arising from using the EOQ.

Step 3: Recalculate total annual inventory costs using the order size required to just obtain each discount.

Step 4: Compare the cost of Steps 2 and 3 with the saving from the discount, and select the minimum cost alternative.

Step 5: Repeat for all discount levels.

Test your understanding 3 – EOQ with discounts I

W Co is a retailer of barrels. The company has an annual demand of 30,000 barrels. The barrels cost \$2 each. Fresh supplies can be obtained immediately, with ordering and transport costs amounting to \$200 per order. The annual cost of holding one barrel in stock is estimated to be \$1.20.

A 2% discount is available on orders of at least 5,000 barrels and a 2.5% discount is available if the order quantity is 7,500 barrels or above.

Required:

Calculate the EOQ ignoring the discount and determine if it would change once the discount is taken into account.

Test your understanding 4 – EOQ with discounts II

D Co uses component V22 in its construction process. The company has a demand of 45,000 components pa. They cost $4.50 each There is no lead time between order and delivery, and ordering costs amount to $100 per order. The annual cost of holding one component in inventory is estimated to be $0.65.

A 0.5% discount is available on orders of at least 3,000 components and a 0.75% discount is available if the order quantity is 6,000 components or above.

Calculate the optimal order quantity.

3 Calculating the re-order level (ROL)

Known demand and lead time

Having decided how much inventory to re-order, the next problem is when to re-order. The firm needs to identify a level of inventory which can be reached before an order needs to be placed.

The **ROL** is the quantity of inventory on hand when an order is placed.

When demand and lead time are known with certainty the ROL may be calculated exactly, i.e. ROL = demand in the lead time.

Test your understanding 5 – Calculating the re-order level I

Using the data for W Co, assume that the company adopts the EOQ as its order quantity and that it now takes two weeks for an order to be delivered.

How frequently will the company place an order? How much inventory will it have on hand when the order is placed?

Test your understanding 6 – Calculating the re-order level II

Using the data relating to D Co, and ignoring discounts, assume that the company adopts the EOQ as its order quantity and that it now takes three weeks for an order to be delivered.

(a) How frequently will the company place an order?

(b) How much inventory will it have on hand when the order is placed?

ROL with variable demand or variable lead time

When lead time and demand are known with certainty, ROL = demand during lead time. Where there is uncertainty, an optimum level of buffer inventory must be found. This depends on:

- variability of demand
- cost of holding inventory
- cost of stockouts.

You will not be required to perform this calculation in the examination.

Re-order levels

If there were certainty, then the last unit of inventory would be sold as the next delivery is made. In the real world, this ideal cannot be achieved. Demand will vary from period to period, and ROL must allow some buffer (or safety) inventory, the size of which is a function of maintaining the buffer (which increases as the levels increase), running out of inventory (which decreases as the buffer increases) and the probability of the varying demand levels.

4 Inventory management systems

A number of systems have been developed to simplify the inventory management process:

- bin systems
- periodic review
- JIT.

Bin systems

A simple visual reminder system for re-ordering is to use a bin system.

Two-bin system

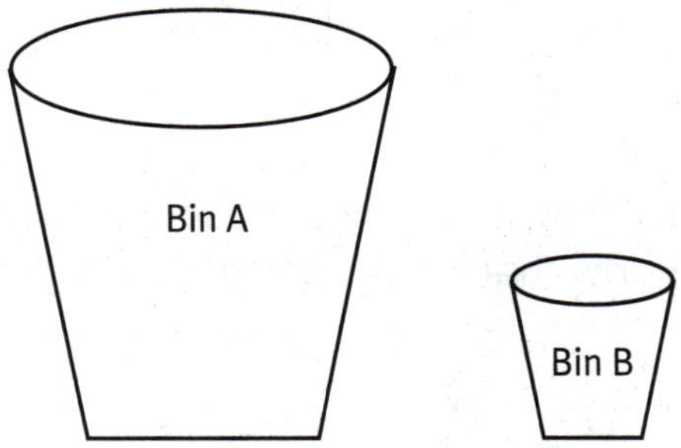

One-bin system

Two-bin system

This system utilises two bins, e.g. A and B. Inventory is taken from A until A is empty. An order for a fixed quantity is placed and, in the meantime, inventory is used from B. The standard inventory for B is the expected demand in the lead time (the time between the order being placed and the inventory arriving), plus some 'buffer' inventory.

When the new order arrives, B is filled up to its standard level and the rest is placed in A. Inventory is then drawn as required from A, and the process is repeated.

One-bin system

The same sort of approach is adopted by some firms for a single bin with a red line within the bin indicating the ROL.

These methods rely on accurate estimates of:

- lead time
- demand in lead time.

Action must therefore be taken if inventory levels:

- fall below a preset minimum
- exceed a preset maximum.

Control levels

Minimum inventory level usually corresponds with buffer inventory. If inventory falls below that level, emergency action to replenish may be required.

Maximum inventory level would represent the normal peak holding, i.e. buffer inventory plus the re-order quantity. If the maximum is exceeded, a review of estimated demand in the lead time is needed.

The levels would also be modified according to the relative importance/cost of a particular inventory item.

Periodic review system (constant order cycle system)

Inventory levels are reviewed at fixed intervals, e.g. every four weeks. The inventory in hand is then made up to a predetermined level, which takes account of:

- likely demand before the next review
- likely demand during the lead time.

Thus a four-weekly review in a system where the lead time was two weeks would demand that inventory be made up to the likely maximum demand for the next six weeks.

Additional question – Periodic review systems

A company has estimated that for the coming season weekly demand for components will be 80 units. Suppliers take three weeks on average to deliver goods once they have been ordered and a buffer inventory of 35 units is held.

If the inventory levels are reviewed every six weeks, how many units will be ordered at a review where the count shows 250 units in inventory?

The answer to this question can be found after the chapter summary diagram at the end of this chapter.

Bin systems versus periodic review

Advantage of bin systems	Advantage of periodic review system
Inventory can be kept at a lower level because of the ability to order whenever inventory falls to a low level, rather than having to wait for the next re-order date.	Order office load is more evenly spread and easier to plan. For this reason the system is popular with suppliers.

Slow moving inventory

Certain items may have a high individual value, but be subject to infrequent demand.

In most organisations, about 20% of items held make up 80% of total usage (the 80/20 rule).

Slow-moving inventory

Management need to review inventory usage to identify slow-moving inventory. An aged inventory analysis should be produced and reviewed regularly so that action can be taken. Actions could include:

- elimination of obsolete items
- slow-moving inventory items only ordered when actually needed (unless a minimum order quantity is imposed by the supplier)
- review of demand level estimates on which re-order decisions are based.

A regular report of slow-moving items is useful in that management is made aware of changes in demand and of possible obsolescence. Arrangements may then be made to reduce or eliminate inventory levels or, on confirmation of obsolescence, for disposal.

Just in Time (JIT) systems

JIT is a series of manufacturing and supply chain techniques that aim to minimise inventory levels and improve customer service by manufacturing not only at the exact time customers require, but also in the exact quantities they need and at competitive prices.

In JIT systems the balancing act is dispensed with. Inventory is reduced to an absolute minimum or eliminated altogether.

Aims of JIT are:

- a smooth flow of work through the manufacturing plant
- a flexible production process which is responsive to the customer's requirements
- reduction in capital tied up in inventory.

This involves the elimination of all activities performed that do not add value = waste.

Just in time systems

JIT extends much further than a concentration on inventory levels. It centres around the elimination of waste. Waste is defined as any activity performed within a manufacturing company which does not add value to the product. Examples of waste are:

- raw material inventory
- WIP inventory
- finished goods inventory
- materials handling
- quality problems (rejects and reworks, etc.)
- queues and delays on the shop floor
- long raw material lead times
- long customer lead times
- unnecessary clerical and accounting procedures.

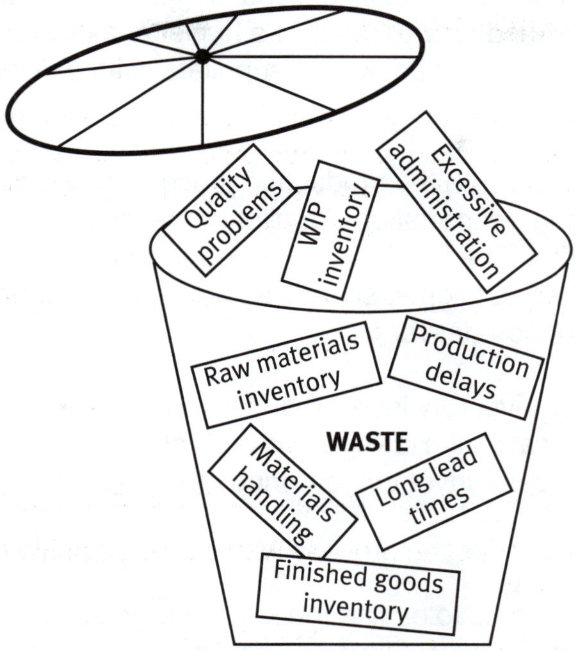

JIT attempts to eliminate waste at every stage of the manufacturing process, notably by the elimination of:

- WIP, by reducing batch sizes (often to one)
- raw materials inventory, by the suppliers delivering direct to the shop floor JIT for use
- scrap and rework, by an emphasis on total quality control of the design, of the process, and of the materials
- finished goods inventory, by reducing lead times so that all products are made to order
- material handling costs, by re-design of the shop floor so that goods move directly between adjacent work centres.

The combination of these concepts in JIT results in:

- a smooth flow of work through the manufacturing plant
- a flexible production process which is responsive to the customer's requirements
- reduction in capital tied up in inventory.

A JIT manufacturer looks for a single supplier who can provide **high quality**, **frequent** and **reliable** deliveries, rather than the lowest price. In return, the supplier can expect more business under **long-term purchase orders**, thus providing **greater certainty** in forecasting activity levels. Very often the suppliers will be located close to the company.

Long-term contracts and single sourcing strengthen buyer-supplier relationships and tend to result in a higher quality product. Inventory problems are shifted back onto suppliers, with deliveries being made as required.

The spread of JIT in the production process inevitably affects those in delivery and transportation. Smaller, more frequent loads are required at shorter notice. The haulier is regarded as almost a partner to the manufacturer, but tighter schedules are required of hauliers, with penalties for non-delivery.

Reduction in inventory levels reduces the time taken to count inventory and the clerical cost. However with JIT, although inventory holding costs are close to zero, inventory ordering costs are high.

You need to be able to outline the key features of each stock control system and the impact they may have on ordering and holding costs and/or order dates and quantities. Ensure you can discuss the implications of JIT for production processes and supplier relationships as well as inventory levels.

Test your understanding 7

Gogo plc is a retailer of large storage boxes. The company has an annual demand of 120,000 units. The costs incurred each time an order is placed are $200. The carrying cost per unit of the item each month is estimated at $3. The purchase price of each unit is $4. The economic order quantity formula is:

$$EOQ = \sqrt{\frac{2C_OD}{C_H}}$$

When using this formula to find the optimal quantity to be ordered, which of the following amounts are not included in the calculation?

A Cost per order ($200)

B Carrying cost per unit ($3)

C Purchase price per unit ($4)

D Estimated usage of the inventory item over a particular period (120,000 units per annum)

Test you understanding 8

The Economic Order Quantity (EOQ):

A is a formula that calculates a realistic purchase price for an item

B determines the lowest order quantity by balancing the cost of ordering against the cost of holding inventory

C is used to calculate how much safety inventory should be carried

D should be calculated once a year

Test your understanding 9

Which of the following statements is true?

Statement 1: The re-order level is the measure of inventory at which a replenishment order should be made.

Statement 2: Use of a re-order level builds in a measure of safety inventory and minimises the risk of the organisation running out of inventory.

	Statement 1	*Statement 2*
A	True	True
B	True	False
C	False	True
D	False	False

Test you understanding 10

Periodic review means

A Ordering inventory at a fixed and regular time interval

B Ordering inventory when it falls below the designated safety inventory level

C Ordering inventory in consultation with suppliers relative to their available capacity

D Ordering inventory at a pre-determined re-order level

Test you understanding 11

A number of systems have been developed to simplify the inventory management process.

What is a two-bin system?

A A system in which orders are placed when only one complete bin of inventory is remaining

B A system in which everything is split between two storage bins

C A system in which suppliers deliver two bins of inventory at the same time

D A system in which two full bins of an item are always kept in inventory

Chapter summary

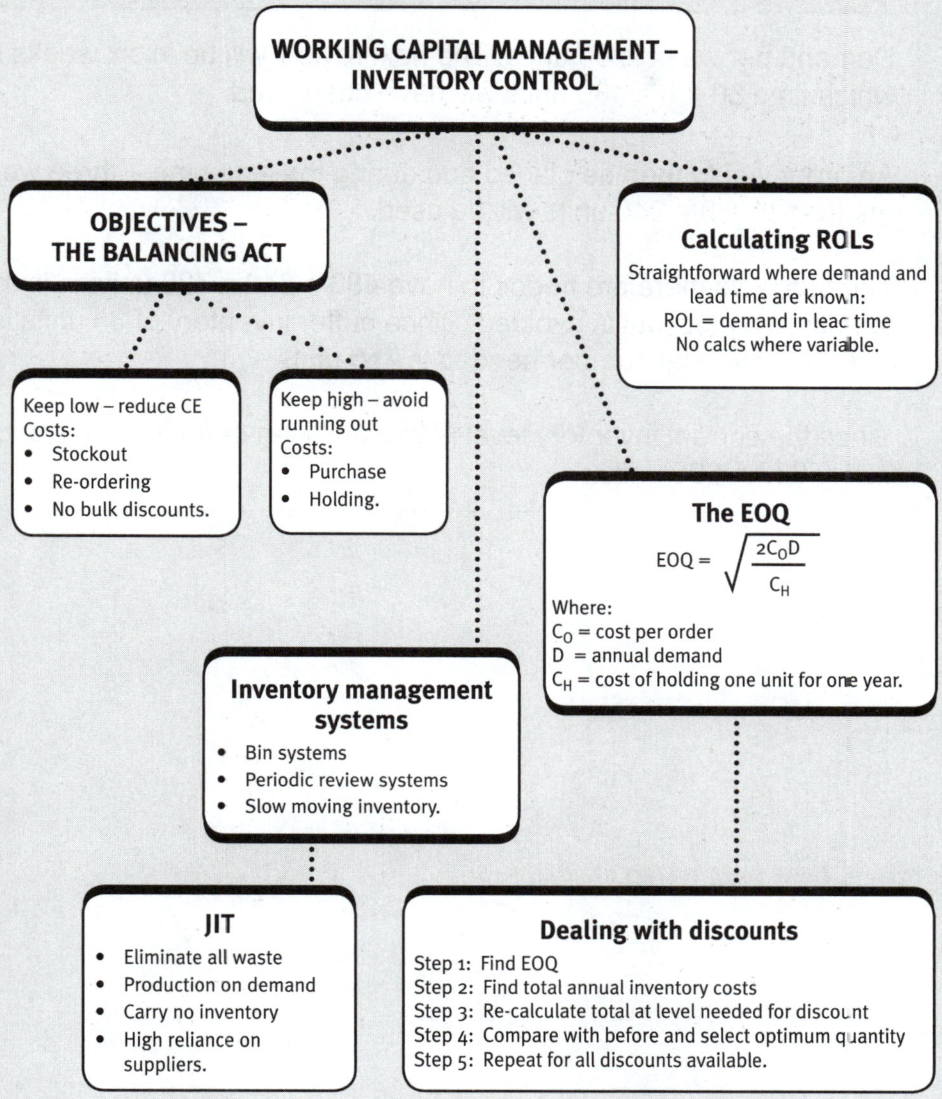

Answer to additional question – Periodic review systems

Demand per week is 80 units. The next review will be in six weeks by which time 80 × 6 = 480 units will have been used.

An order would then be placed and during the lead time – three weeks – another 80 × 3 = 240 units will be used.

The business therefore needs to have 480 + 240 = 720 units in inventory to ensure a stockout is avoided. Since buffer inventory of 35 units is required, the total number needed is 755 units.

Since the current inventory level is 250 units, an order must be placed for 755 – 250 = 505 units.

Test your understanding answers

Test your understanding 1 – EOQ I

Solution:

	Order quantity		
	400 units	**500 units**	**600 units**
Average inventory	200	250	300
No. of orders pa	30	24	20
Holding cost – average units × \$2.88	\$576	\$720	\$864

	Order quantity		
	400 units	500 units	600 units
Ordering cost – no. of orders × \$30	\$900	\$720	\$600
Total cost	\$1,476	\$1,440	\$1,464

Therefore the best option is to order 500 units each time.

Note: that this is the point at which total cost is minimised and the holding costs and order costs are equal.

Solution using the formula:

$$EOQ = \sqrt{\frac{2C_OD}{C_H}}$$

$C_O = 30$

$D = 1{,}000 \times 12 = 12{,}000$

$C_H = 2.88$

$$EOQ = \sqrt{\frac{2 \times 30 \times 12{,}000}{2.88}} = 500 \text{ units per order}$$

Test your understanding 2 – EOQ II

$$EOQ = \sqrt{\frac{2C_oD}{C_H}}$$

C_O = $200

D = 10,000 units × 12 = 120,000 units per annum

C_H = (10 × 0.15) + 2 = $3.5 per unit per annum

$$EOQ = \sqrt{\frac{2 \times 200 \times 120{,}000}{3.5}} = 3{,}703 \text{ units per order}$$

Test your understanding 3 – EOQ with discounts I

Solution

Step 1 Calculate EOQ, ignoring discounts.

$$EOQ = \sqrt{\frac{2C_OD}{C_H}}$$

C_O = $200

D = 30,000 barrels per annum

C_H = $1.20 per barrel per annum

$$EOQ = \sqrt{\frac{2 \times 200 \times 30{,}000}{1.2}} = 3{,}162 \text{ barrels per order}$$

Step 2 As this is below the level for discounts, calculate total annual inventory costs.

Total annual costs for the company will comprise holding costs plus re-ordering costs.

$$= (\text{Average inventory} \times C_H) + (\text{Number of re-orders pa} \times C_O)$$

$$= \frac{3,162}{2} \times \$1.20 + \frac{30,000}{3,162} \times \$200$$

= \$1,897.20 + \$1,897.53
= \$3,794.73
= \$3,795 per annum

Step 3 Recalculate total annual inventory costs using the order size required to just obtain the discount.

At order quantity 5,000, total costs are as follows.

$$= (\text{Average inventory} \times C_H) + (\text{Number of re-orders pa} \times C_O)$$

$$= \frac{5,000}{2} \times \$1.20 + \frac{30,000}{5,000} \times \$200$$

= \$3,000 + \$1,200

= \$4,200 per annum

	\$
Extra costs of ordering in batches of 5,000 (4,200 – 3,795)	(405)
Less: Saving on discount 2% × \$2 × 30,000	1,200
Step 4 Net cost saving	795

Hence batches of 5,000 are worthwhile.

Step 3 (again)

At order quantity 7,500, total costs are as follows:

$$= (\text{Average inventory} \times C_H) + (\text{Number of re-orders pa} \times C_O)$$

$$= \frac{7{,}500}{2} \times \$1.20 + \frac{30{,}000}{7{,}500} \times \$200$$

$$= \$4{,}500 + \$800$$

$$= \$5{,}300 \text{ per annum}$$

Extra costs of ordering in batches of 7,500 (5,300 – 4,200)	(1,100)
Less: Saving on extra discount (2.5% – 2%) × $2 × 30,000)	300
Step 4 Net additional cost	(800)

So a further cost saving cannot be made on orders of 7,500 units. The company should therefore opt for buying 5,000 units in order to maximise the benefit.

Note: If Step 1 produces an EOQ at which a discount would have been available, and the holding cost would be reduced by taking the discount, i.e. where C_H is based on the purchase price × the cost of finance, the EOQ must be recalculated using the new C_H before the above steps are followed.

Test your understanding 4 – EOQ with discounts II

Step 1

$$EOQ = \sqrt{\frac{2C_OD}{C_H}}$$

C_O = $100 per order

D = 45,000 components per annum

C_H = $0.65 per component per annum

$$EOQ = \sqrt{\frac{2 \times 100 \times 45{,}000}{0.65}}$$ = 3,721, components per order which would qualify for a 0.5% discount

Step 2

Total annual costs for the company will comprise holding costs plus re-ordering costs.

= (Average inventory × C_H) + (Number of re-orders pa × C_O)

$$= \left(\frac{3{,}721}{2} \times \$0.65\right) + \left(\frac{45{,}000}{3{,}721} \times \$100\right)$$

= $2,419 per annum

Step 3

At an order quantity of 6,000 components, total costs are as follows.

(6,000 × $0.65/2) + (45,000 × $100 ÷ 6,000) = $2,700

	$
Extra costs of ordering in batches of 6,000 (2,700 – 2,419)	(281)
Less: Saving on extra discount	
(0.75% – 0.5%) × $4.5 × 45,000	506.25

Step 4

Net cost saving	225.25

So a saving can be made on orders of 6,000 components.

Test your understanding 5 – Calculating the re-order level I

- Annual demand is 30,000. The original EOQ is 3,162 barrels per order. The company will therefore place an order once every

  3,162 ÷ 30,000 × 365 days = 38 days

- The company must be sure that there is sufficient inventory on hand when it places an order to last the two weeks' lead time. It must therefore place an order when there is two weeks' worth of demand in inventory:

  i.e. Re-order level = 2 ÷ 52 × 30,000 = 1,154 barrels remaining in inventory

Test your understanding 6 – Calculating the re-order level II

(a) Annual demand is 45,000 components. The original EOQ is 3,721 components per order.

The company will therefore place an order once every
3,721 ÷ 45,000 × 365 days = 30 days

(b) The company must be sure that there is sufficient inventory on hand when it places an order to last the three weeks' lead time. It must therefore place an order when there is three weeks' worth of demand in inventory:

3/52 × 45,000 = 2,596 components in inventory.

Test your understanding 7

Answer C

In the formula, C = the cost of placing one order; D = the estimated usage of an inventory item over a particular period; and H = the cost of holding one unit of inventory for that period.

The purchase price per unit is not a constituent part of the formula.

Test you understanding 8

Answer B

The EOQ is the optimal ordering quantity for an item of inventory which will minimise costs.

Test your understanding 9

Answer A

The re-order level is the quantity of inventory on hand when an order is placed. The level will depend on variability of demand. cost of holding inventory and cost of stockouts.

Test you understanding 10

Answer A

Inventory levels are reviewed at fixed time. The inventory in hand is then made up to a predetermined level.

Test you understanding 11

Answer A

When items in the first bin are finished, an order is place to replace these items. The second bin should have enough items to last until the placed order arrives.

chapter

9

Working capital management – accounts receivable and payable

Chapter learning objectives

Upon completion of this chapter you will be able to:

- explain how to establish and implement a credit policy for accounts receivable
- explain the administration involved in collecting amounts owing from accounts receivable
- explain the pros and cons of offering early settlement discounts to accounts receivable
- calculate the financial implications of offering discounts for early settlement
- define and explain the features of factoring
- discuss the advantages and disadvantages of factoring
- define and explain the features of invoice discounting
- suggest and evaluate suitable techniques for managing accounts receivable within a scenario question
- explain the factors involved in the effective management of trade credit
- calculate the effective cost of an early settlement discount offered on an account payable
- discuss the advantages and disadvantages of trade credit as a source of short-term finance
- explain the specific factors to be considered when managing foreign accounts receivable and payable.

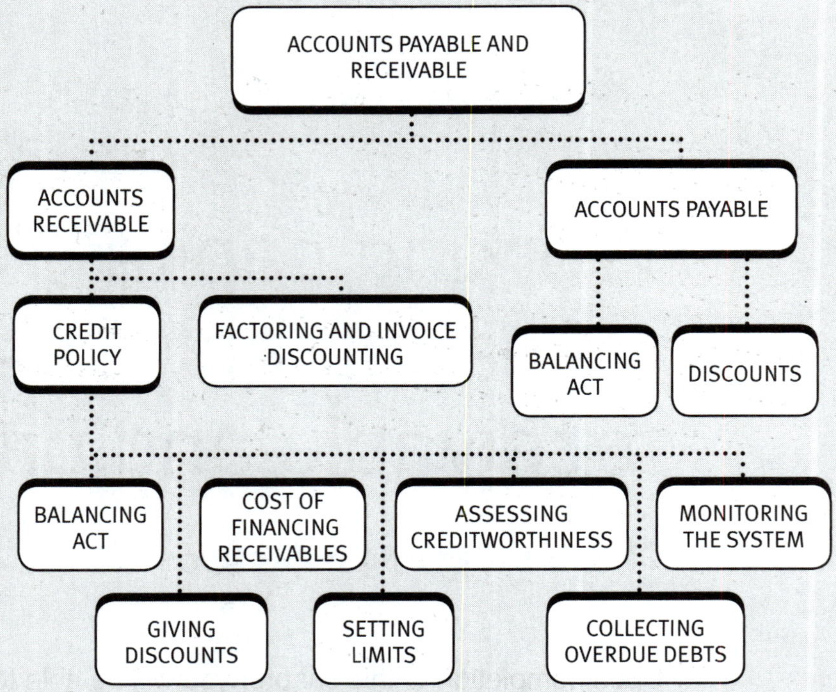

1 The objectives of accounts receivable management

The optimum level of trade credit extended represents a balance between two factors:

- profit improvement from sales obtained by allowing credit
- the cost of credit allowed.

The balancing act

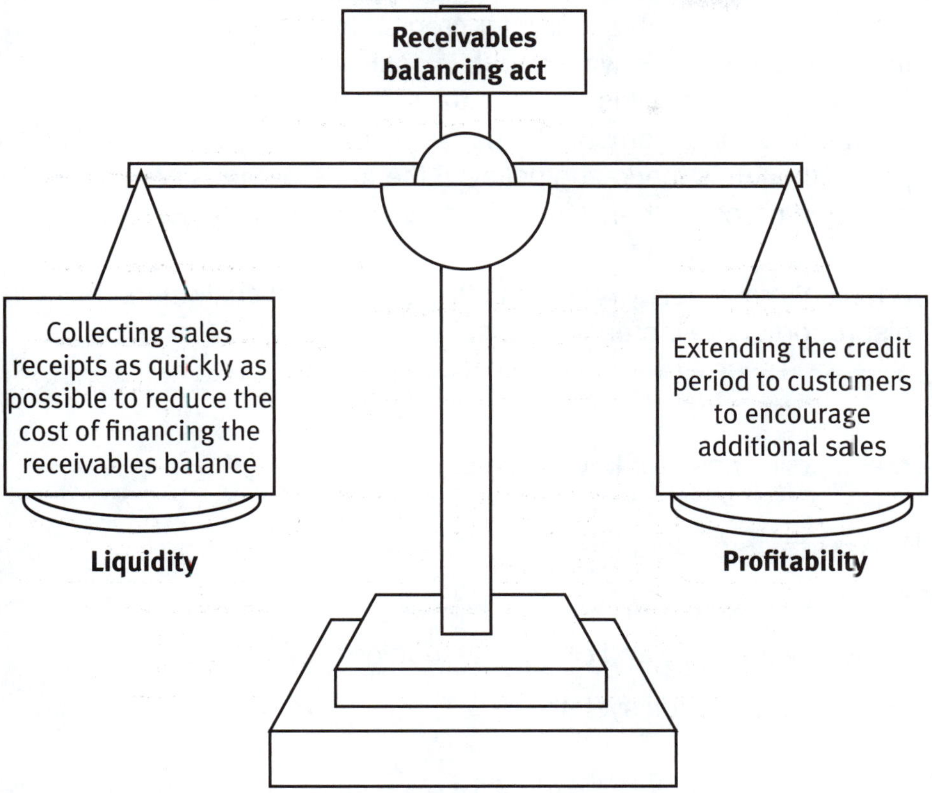

Remember this trade-off is a key factor in determining the company's working capital investment.

2 Accounts receivable – establishing a credit policy

Management must establish a credit policy.

For accounts receivable, the company's policy will be influenced by:

- demand for products
- competitors' terms
- risk of irrecoverable debts
- financing costs
- costs of credit control.

Why have a credit policy?

A firm must establish a policy for credit terms given to its customers. Ideally the firm would want to obtain cash with each order delivered, but that is impossible unless substantial settlement (or cash) discounts are offered as an inducement. It must be recognised that credit terms are part of the firm's marketing policy. If the trade or industry has adopted a common practice, then it is probably wise to keep in step with it.

A lenient credit policy may well attract additional customers, but at a disproportionate increase in cost.

A credit policy has four key aspects:

(1) Assess creditworthiness.

(2) Credit limits.

(3) Invoice promptly and collect overdue debts.

(4) Monitor the credit system.

This is a useful structure to adopt for examination questions that ask about the management of receivables.

Assessing creditworthiness

A firm should assess the creditworthiness of:

- all new customers immediately
- existing customers periodically.

Information may come from:

- bank references
- trade references
- competitors
- published information
- credit reference agencies
- company sales records
- credit scoring.

Assessing creditworthiness

To minimise the risk of irrecoverable debts occurring, a company should investigate the creditworthiness of all new customers (credit risk), and should review that of existing customers from time to time, especially if they request that their credit limit should be raised. Information about a customer's credit rating can be obtained from a variety of sources.

These include:

- Bank references – A customer's permission must be sought. These tend to be fairly standardised in the UK, and so are not perhaps as helpful as they could be.
- Trade references – Suppliers already giving credit to the customer can give useful information about how good the customer is at paying bills on time. There is a danger that the customer will only nominate those suppliers that are being paid on time.
- Competitors – in some industries such as insurance, competitors share information on customers, including creditworthiness.
- Published information – The customer's own annual accounts and reports will give some idea of the general financial position of the company and its liquidity.
- Credit reference agencies – Agencies such as Dunn & Bradstreet publish general financial details of many companies, together with a credit rating. They will also produce a special report on a company if requested. The information is provided for a fee.
- Company's own sales records – For an existing customer, the sales ledgers will show how prompt a payer the company is, although they cannot show the ability of the customer to pay.
- Credit scoring – Indicators such as family circumstances, home ownership, occupation and age can be used to predict likely creditworthiness. This is useful when extending credit to the public where little other information is available. A variety of software packages is available which can assist with credit scoring.

Credit limits

Credit limits should be set to reflect both the:

- amount of credit available
- length of time allowed before payment is due.

The ledger account should be monitored to take account of orders in the pipeline as well as invoiced sales, before further credit is given.

Invoicing and collecting overdue debts

A credit period only begins once an invoice is received so prompt invoicing is essential. If debts go overdue, the risk of default increases, therefore a system of follow-up procedures is required.

Invoicing and collecting overdue debts

The longer a debt is allowed to run, the higher the probability of eventual default. A system of follow-up procedures is required, bearing in mind the risk of offending a valued customer to such an extent that their business is lost.

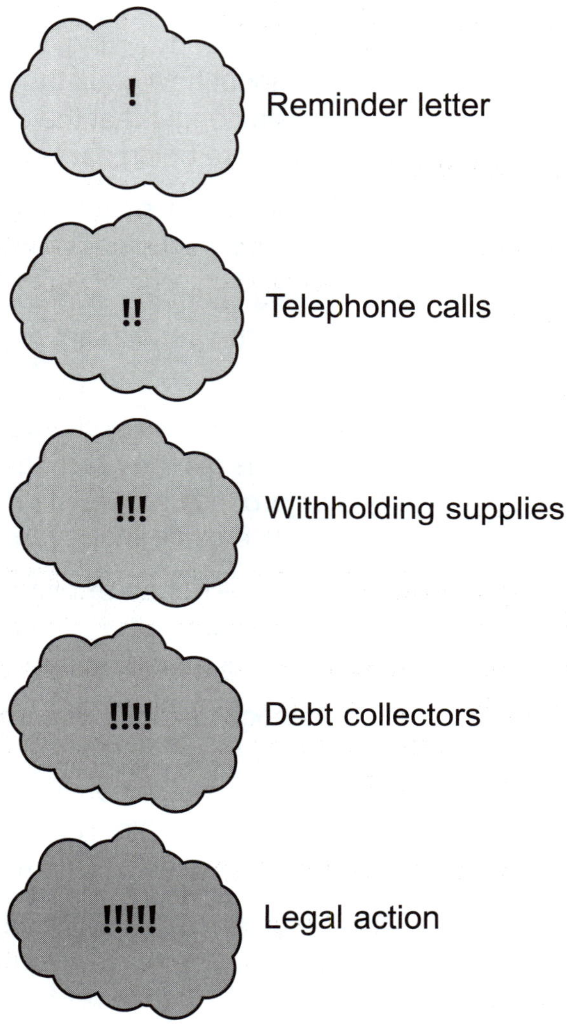

Techniques for 'chasing' overdue debts include the following:

- Reminder letters: these are often regarded as being a relatively poor way of obtaining payment, as many customers simply ignore them. Sending reminders by fax or email is usually more productive than using the post.

- Telephone calls: these are more expensive than reminder letters but where large sums are involved they can be an efficient way of speeding payment.
- Withholding supplies: putting customers on the 'stop list' for further orders or spare parts can encourage rapid settlement of debts.
- Debt collection agencies and trade associations: these offer debt collection services on a fixed fee basis or on 'no collection no charge' terms. The quality of service provided varies considerably and care should be taken in selecting an agent.
- Legal action: this is often seen as a last resort. A solicitor's letter often prompts payment and many cases do not go to court. Court action is usually not cost effective but it can discourage other customers from delaying payment.

Monitoring the system

The position of receivables should be regularly reviewed as part of managing overall working capital and corrective action taken when needed. Methods include:

- age analysis
- ratios
- statistical data.

Monitoring the system

Management will require regular information to take corrective action and to measure the impact of giving credit on working capital investment. Typical management reports on the credit system will include the following points.

- Age analysis of outstanding debts.
- Ratios, compared with the previous period or target, to indicate trends in credit levels and the incidence of overdue and irrecoverable debts.
- Statistical data to identify causes of default and the incidence of irrecoverable debts among different classes of customer and types of trade.

3 Accounts receivable – calculations

Costs of financing receivables

Key working:

Finance cost = Receivable balance × Interest (overdraft) rate

$$\text{Receivable balance} = \text{Credit sales} \times \frac{\text{Receivable days}}{365}$$

Test your understanding 1 – Cost of financing receivables

Paisley Co has sales of $20 million for the previous year, receivables at the yearend were $4 million, and the cost of financing receivables is covered by an overdraft at the interest rate of 12% pa.

Required:

(a) calculate the receivables days for Paisley

(b) calculate the annual cost of financing receivables.

Early settlement discounts

Cash discounts are given to encourage early payment by customers. The cost of the discount is balanced against the savings the company receives from having less capital tied up due to a lower receivables balance and a shorter average collection period. Discounts may also reduce the number of irrecoverable debts.

The calculation of the annual cost can be expressed as a formula:

$$\text{Annual cost of discount} = \left[1 + \frac{\text{discount}}{\text{amount left to pay}}\right]^{\text{no.of periods}} - 1$$

where no. of periods = $\dfrac{365 / 52 / 12}{\text{no. of days / weeks / months earlier the money is received.}}$

Notice that the annual cost calculation is always based on the amount left to pay, i.e. the amount net of discount.

If the cost of offering the discount exceeds the rate of overdraft interest then the discount should not be offered.

Test your understanding 2 – Early settlement discounts I

A company is offering a cash discount of 2.5% to receivables if they agree to pay debts within one month. The usual credit period taken is three months.

What is the effective annualised cost of offering the discount and should it be offered, if the bank would loan the company at 18% pa?

The above calculation gives a quick and easy way to evaluate the annual cost and reach a decision on whether to offer an early settlement discount. This method should be used in all situations where all customers are expected to take advantage of the discount, or when the question does not specify the expected take up (as in test your understanding 2).

However, in many scenarios, you may be provided with more in-depth information, in particular information relating to the proportion of customers that are expected to take up the offer. In these situations it is necessary to perform a longer calculation.

The calculation involves comparing the cost of offering the discount with the benefit that will be received (the lower financing costs resulting from the reduced receivables balance)

Test your understanding 3 – Early settlement discounts II

Paisley Co has sales of $20 million for the previous year, receivables at the year end of $4 million and the cost of financing receivables is covered by an overdraft at the interest rate of 12% pa. It is now considering offering a cash discount of 2% for payment of debts within 10 days. Should it be introduced if 40% of customers will take up the discount?

4 Accounts receivable – invoice discounting and factoring

Invoice discounting and factoring are both ways of speeding up the receipt of funds from accounts receivable.

Invoice discounting

Invoice discounting is a method of raising finance against the security of receivables without using the sales ledger administration services of a factor.

While specialist invoice discounting firms exist, this is a service also provided by a factoring company. Selected invoices are used as security against which the company may borrow funds. This is a temporary source of finance, repayable when the debt is cleared. The key advantage of invoice discounting is that it is a confidential service, and the customer need not know about it.

In some ways it is similar to the financing part of the factoring service without control of credit passing to the factor.

Ensure you can explain the difference between factoring and invoice discounting, and the situations where one may be more appropriate than the other.

Invoice discounting

Typical arrangement

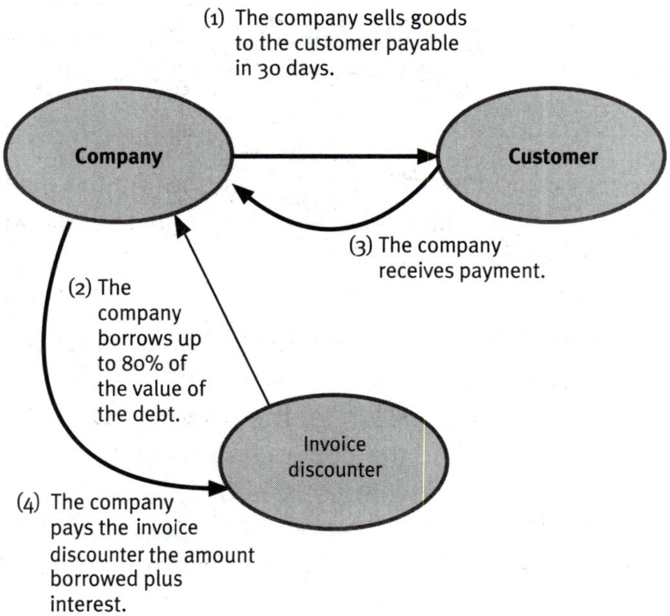

Invoice discounting is a method of raising finance against the security of receivables without using the sales ledger administration services of a factor. With invoice discounting, the business retains control over its sales ledger, and confidentiality in its dealings with customers. Firms of factors will also provide invoice discounting to clients.

The method works as follows:

- The business sends out invoices, statements and reminders in the normal way, and collects the debts. With 'confidential invoice discounting', its customers are unaware that the business is using invoice discounting.
- The invoice discounter provides cash to the business for a proportion of the value of the invoice, as soon as it receives a copy of the invoice and agrees to discount it. The discounter will advance cash up to 80% of face value.
- When the business eventually collects the payment from its customer, the money must be paid into a bank account controlled by the invoice discounter. The invoice discounter then pays the business the remainder of the invoice, less interest and administration charges.

Invoice discounting can help a business that is trying to improve its cash flows, but does not want a factor to administer its sales ledger and collect its debts. It is therefore equivalent to the financing service provided by a factor.

Administration charges for this service are around 0.5–1% of a client's revenue. It is more risky than factoring since the client retains control over its credit policy. Consequently, such facilities are usually confined to established companies with high sales revenue, and the business must be profitable. Finance costs are usually in the range 3–4% above base rate, although larger companies and those which arrange credit insurance may receive better terms.

The invoice discounter will check the sales ledger of the client regularly, perhaps every three months, to check that its debt collection procedures are adequate.

Illustration of the invoice discounting process

At the beginning of August, Basildon plc sells goods for a total value of $300,000 to regular customers but decides that it requires payment earlier than the agreed 30-day credit period for these invoices.

A discounter agrees to finance 80% of their face value, i.e. $240,000, at an interest cost of 9% pa.

The invoices were due for payment in early September, but were subsequently settled in mid-September, exactly 45 days after the initial transactions. The invoice discounter's service charge is 1% of invoice value. A special account is set up with a bank, into which all payments are made.

The sequence of cash flows is:

August	Basildon receives cash advance of $240,000.	
Mid-September	Customers pay $300,000.	
	Invoice discounter receives the full $300,000 paid into the special bank account.	
	Basildon receives the balance payable, less charges, i.e.	
	Service fee = 1% × $300,000 =	$3,000
	Finance cost = 9% × $240,000 × 45/365 =	$2,663
	Total charges	$5,663
	Basildon receives:	
	Balance of payment from customer	$60,000
	Less charges	$5,663
		$54,337
Summary	Total receipts by Basildon: $240,000 + $54,337	$294,337
	Invoice discounter's fee and interest charges	$5,663
	Total amount invoiced	$300,000

Factoring

Factoring is the outsourcing of the credit control department to a third party.

The debts of the company are effectively sold to a factor (normally owned by a bank). The factor takes on the responsibility of collecting the debt for a fee. The company can choose some or all of the following three services offered by the factor:

(1) debt collection and administration – recourse or non-recourse

(2) financing

(3) credit insurance.

These are of particular value to:

- smaller firms
- fast growing firms.

Make sure you can discuss the various services offered and remember that non-recourse factoring is more expensive as the factor bears the costs of any irrecoverable debts.

Factoring

Debt collection and administration – the factor takes over the whole of the company's sales ledger, issuing invoices and collecting debts.

Financing provision – in addition to the above, the factor will advance up to 80% of the value of a debt to the company; the remainder (minus finance costs) being paid when the debts are collected. The factor becomes a source of finance. Finance costs are usually 1.5% to 3% above bank base rate and charged on a daily basis.

Credit insurance – the factor agrees to insure the irrecoverable debts of the client. The factor would then determine to whom the company was able to offer credit.

Some companies realise that, although it is necessary to extend trade credit to customers for competitive reasons, they need payment earlier than agreed in order to assist their own cash flow. Factors exist to help such companies.

Factoring is most suitable for:

- small and medium-sized firms which often cannot afford sophisticated credit and sales accounting systems, and
- firms that are expanding rapidly. These often have a substantial and growing investment in inventory and receivables, which can be turned into cash by factoring the debts. Factoring debts can be a more flexible source of financing working capital than an overdraft or bank loan.

Factoring is primarily designed to allow companies to accelerate cash flow, providing finance against outstanding trade receivables. This improves cash flow and liquidity.

Factoring can be arranged on either a 'without recourse' basis or a 'with recourse' basis.

- When factoring is without recourse or 'non-recourse', the factor provides protection for the client against irrecoverable debts. The factor has no 'comeback' or recourse to the client if a customer defaults. When a customer of the client fails to pay a debt, the factor bears the loss and the client receives the money from the debt.
- When the service is with recourse ('recourse factoring'), the client must bear the loss from any irrecoverable debt, and so has to reimburse the factor for any money it has already received for the debt.

Credit protection is provided only when the service is non-recourse and this is obviously more costly.

Typical factoring arrangements

Administration and debt collection

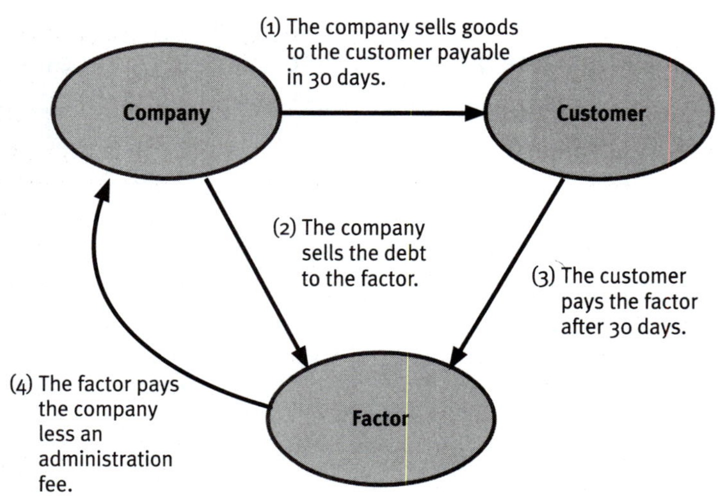

Including financing

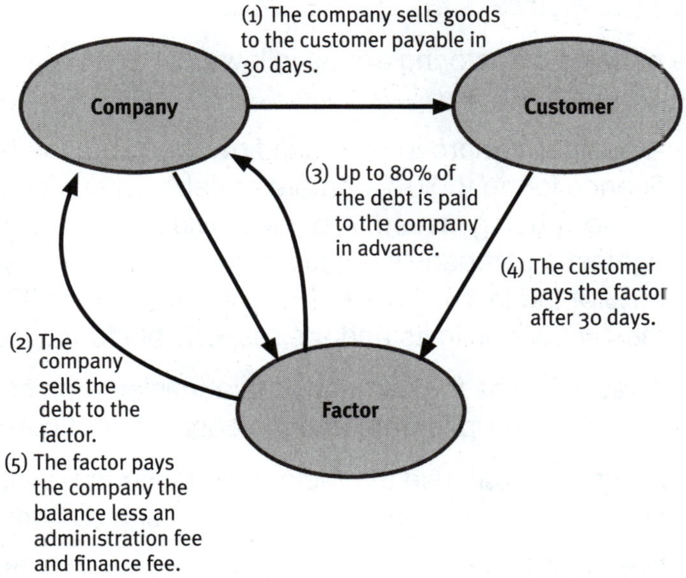

Advantages	**Disadvantages**
(1) Saving in administration costs. (2) Reduction in the need for management control. (3) Particularly useful for small and fast growing businesses where the credit control department may not be able to keep pace with volume growth.	(1) Likely to be more costly than an efficiently run internal credit control department. (2) Factoring has a bad reputation associated with failing companies; using a factor may suggest your company has money worries. (3) Customers may not wish to deal with a factor. (4) Once you start factoring it is difficult to revert easily to an internal credit control system. (5) The company may give up the opportunity to decide to whom credit may be given (non-recourse factoring).

Benefits and problems with factoring

The benefits of factoring are as follows.

- A business improves its cash flow, because the factor provides finance for up to 80% or more of debts within 24 hours of the invoices being issued. A bank providing an overdraft facility secured against a company's unpaid invoices will normally only lend up to 50% of the invoice value. (Factors will provide 80% or so because they set credit limits and are responsible for collecting the debts.)
- A factor saves the company the administration costs of keeping the sales ledger up to date and the costs of debt collection.
- A business can use the factor's credit control system to assess the creditworthiness of both new and existing customers.
- Non-recourse factoring is a convenient way of obtaining insurance against irrecoverable debts.

Problems with factoring

- Although factors provide valuable services, companies are sometimes wary about using them. A possible problem with factoring is that the intervention of the factor between the factor's client and the debtor company could endanger trading relationships and damage goodwill. Customers might prefer to deal with the business, not a factor.
- When a non-recourse factoring service is used, the client loses control over decisions about granting credit to its customers.
- For this reason, some clients prefer to retain the risk of irrecoverable debts, and opt for a 'with recourse' factoring service. With this type of service, the client and not the factor decides whether extreme action (legal action) should be taken against a non-payer.
- On top of this, when suppliers and customers of the client find out that the client is using a factor to collect debts, it may arouse fears that the company is beset by cash flow problems, raising fears about its viability. If so, its suppliers may impose more stringent payment terms, thus negating the benefits provided by the factor.
- Using a factor can create problems with customers who may resent being chased for payment by a third party, and may question the supplier's financial stability.

Test your understanding 4 – Factoring arrangements

Edden is a medium-sized company producing a range of engineering products, which it sells to wholesale distributors. Recently, its sales have begun to rise rapidly due to economic recovery. However, it is concerned about its liquidity position and is looking at ways of improving cash flow.

Its sales are $16 million pa, and average receivables are $3.3 million (representing about 75 days of sales).

One way of speeding up collection from receivables is to use a factor.

Required:

Determine the relative costs and benefits of using the factor in each of the following scenarios.

(a) The factor will operate on a service-only basis, administering and collecting payment from Edden's customers. This is expected to generate administrative savings of $100,000 each year.

The factor has undertaken to pay outstanding debts after 45 days, regardless of whether the customers have actually paid or not. The factor will make a service charge of 1.75% of Edden's revenue. Edden can borrow at an interest rate of 8% pa.

(b) It is now considering a factoring arrangement with a different factor where 80% of the book value of invoices is paid immediately, with finance costs charged on the advance at 10% pa.

Suppose that this factor will charge 1% of sales as their fee for managing the sales ledger, that there will be administrative savings of $100,000 as before, but that outstanding balances will be paid after 75 days (i.e. there is no change in the typical payment pattern by customers this time).

5 Accounts payable – managing trade credit

Trade credit is the simplest and most important source of short-term finance for many companies.

Again it is a balancing act between liquidity and profitability.

The balancing act

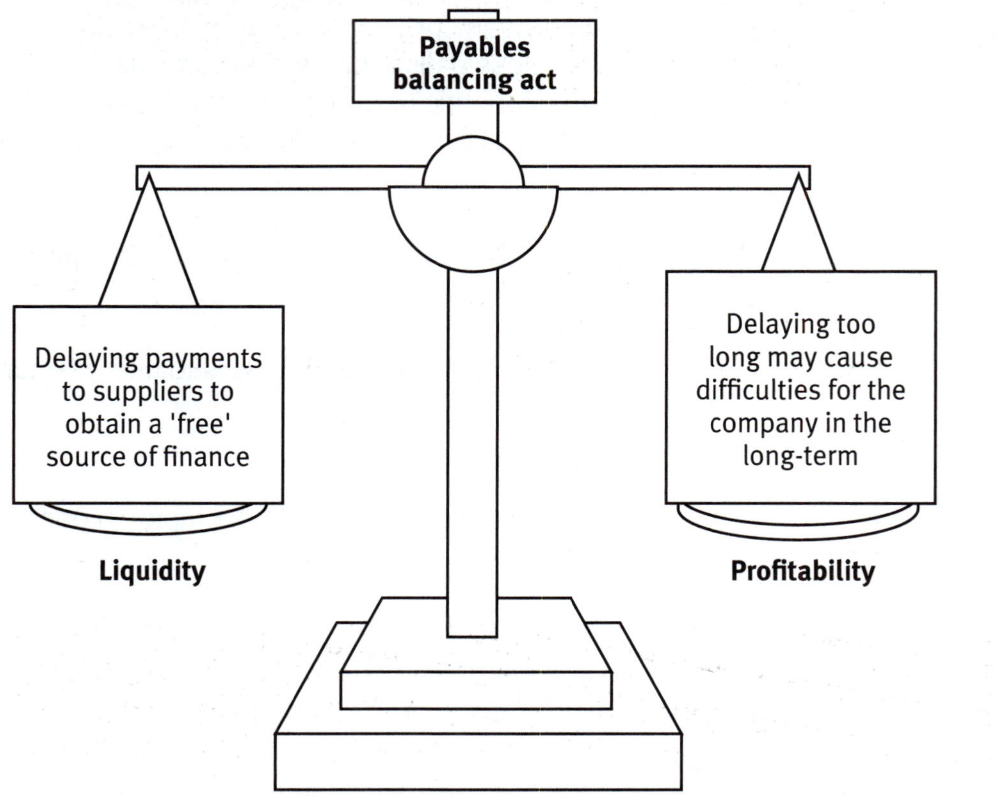

By delaying payment to suppliers companies face possible problems:

- supplier may refuse to supply in future
- supplier may only supply on a cash basis
- there may be loss of reputation
- supplier may increase price in future.

Trade credit is normally seen as a 'free' source of finance. Whilst this is normally true, it may be that the supplier offers a discount for early payment. In this case delaying payment is no longer free, since the cost will be the lost discount.

In the examination, you need to be able to calculate the cost of this discount foregone.

It can be done using the same techniques we saw under accounts receivable.

Test your understanding 5 – Discount for early payment

One supplier has offered a discount to Box Co of 2% on an invoice for $7,500, if payment is made within one month, rather than the three months normally taken to pay. If Box's overdraft rate is 10% pa, is it financially worthwhile for them to accept the discount and pay early?

Test your understanding 6 – Equivalent annual cost of discount

Work out the equivalent annual cost of the following credit terms: 1.75% discount for payment within three weeks; alternatively, full payment must be made within eight weeks of the invoice date. Assume there are 50 weeks in a year.

Hint: Consider a $100 invoice.

Trade payables

Under **trade credit** a firm is able to obtain goods (or services) from a supplier without immediate payment, the supplier accepting that the firm will pay at a later date.

Trade credit periods vary from industry to industry and each industry will have what is a generally accepted norm which would be from seven days upwards. The usual terms of credit range from four weeks to the period between the date of purchase and the end of the month following the month of purchase.

However, considerable scope for flexibility exists and longer credit periods are sometimes offered, particularly where the type of business activity requires a long period to convert materials into saleable products, e.g. farming.

A proportion of the firm's suppliers will normally offer early **settlement discounts** which should be taken up where possible by ensuring prompt payment within the specified terms where settlement discount is allowed. However, if the firm is short of funds, it might wish to make maximum use of the credit period allowed by suppliers regardless of the settlement discounts offered.

It is a mistake to reduce working capital by holding on to creditors' money for a longer period than is allowed as, in the long-term, this will affect the supplier's willingness to supply goods and raw materials, and cause further embarrassment to the firm.

Favourable credit terms are one of several factors which influence the choice of a supplier. Furthermore, the act of accepting settlement discounts has an opportunity cost, i.e. the cost of finance obtained from another source to replace that not obtained from creditors.

Whilst trade credit may be seen as a source of **free credit** , there will be **costs** associated with extending credit taken beyond the norm – lost discounts, loss of supplier goodwill, more stringent terms for future sales.

In order to compare the cost of different sources of finance, all costs are usually converted to a rate per annum basis. The cost of extended trade credit is usually measured by loss of discount, but the calculation of its cost is complicated by such variables as the number of alternative sources of supply, and the general economic conditions.

Certain assumptions have to be made concerning (a) the maximum delay in payment which can be achieved before the supply of goods is withdrawn by the supplier, and (b) the availability of alternative sources of supply.

6 Accounts receivable and payable – managing foreign trade

Overseas accounts receivable and payable bring additional risks that need to be managed:

Export credit risk is the risk of failure or delay in collecting payments due from foreign customers.

Foreign exchange risk is the risk that the value of the currency will change between the date of contract and the date of settlement. For more details see chapter 13.

Risks of overseas trades

Whilst all of the basic management principles and techniques discussed so far apply equally to overseas receivables and payables, there are additional risks that will need to be managed, including:

- export credit risk; and
- foreign exchange transaction exposure.

Possible causes of loss from export credit risk, which apply to all export trade of whatever size, include the following.

- Illiquidity or insolvency of the customer. This also occurs in domestic trading. When an export customer cannot pay however, suppliers have extra problems in protecting their positions in a foreign legal and banking system.
- Bankruptcy or failure of a bank in the remittance chain.
- A poorly-specified remittance channel.
- Inconvertibility of the customer's currency, and lack of access to the currency in which payment is due. This can be caused by deliberate exchange controls or by an unplanned lack of foreign exchange in the customer's central bank.
- Political risks. Their causes can be internal (change of regime, civil war) or external (war, blockade) to the country concerned.

Exporters can protect themselves against these risks by the following means.

- Use banks in both countries to act as the collecting channel for the remittance and to control the shipping documents so that they are only released against payment or acceptance of negotiable instruments (bills of exchange or promissory notes).
- Commit the customer's bank through an international letter of credit (ILC).
- Require the ILC to be confirmed (effectively guaranteed) by a first class bank in the exporter's country. This makes the ILC a confirmed ILC (CILC).

- Obtain support from third parties, e.g.:
  - get a guarantee of payment from a local bank
  - get a letter from the local finance ministry or central bank confirming availability of foreign currency.
- Take out export credit cover.
- Use an intermediary such as a confirming, export finance, factoring or forfeiting house to handle the problems on their behalf; or possibly by giving no credit or selling only through agents who accept the credit risk (del credere agents) and are themselves financially strong.

None of these devices will enable the exporter to escape from certain hard facts of life.

- The need to avoid giving credit to uncreditworthy customers. Weak customers cannot obtain an ILC from their own bank, nor would they be cleared for credit by a credit insurer or intermediary.
- The need to negotiate secure payment terms, procedures and mechanisms which customers do not find congenial. An ILC and especially a CILC are costly to customers, and restrict their flexibility: if they are short of cash at the end of the month, they must still pay out if their bank is committed.
- Exporters can only collect under a letter of credit if they present exactly the required documents. They will not be able to do this if they have sent the goods by air and the credit requires shipping documents; or if they need to produce the customer's inspection certificates and the customer's engineer is mysteriously unavailable to inspect or sign.
- The need to insist that payment is in a convertible currency and in a form which the customer's authorities will permit to become effective as a remittance to where the exporters need to have the funds, usually in their own country. Often this means making the sale subject to clearance under exchange controls or import licensing regulations.

Introductory points about foreign exchange:

Many companies trade in foreign currencies, either buying from abroad in a foreign currency or denominating sales to export customers in a foreign currency.

If so they might need to:

- buy foreign currency to pay a supplier, or
- convert foreign currency receipts into domestic currency.

Like domestic trade, foreign trade is arranged on credit terms. Companies usually know in advance what foreign currency they will need to pay out and what currencies they will be receiving. Foreign exchange risk arises in these situations:

- If a company has to obtain foreign currency at a future date to make a payment there is a risk that the cost of buying the currency will rise (from what it would cost now) if the exchange rate moves and the currency strengthens in value.
- If a company will want to convert currency earnings into a domestic currency at a future date, there is a risk that the value of the currency will fall (from its current value) if the exchange rate moves and the currency falls in value.

Exposures to these risks of adverse changes in an exchange rate are known as 'foreign exchange transaction exposures'. These exposures can be 'hedged' (reduced or offset). The methods available to hedge the risks are covered in chapter 13.

In a question that deals with overseas receivables and payables remember to consider export credit risk and foreign transaction exposure as well as the normal points on the management of receivables and payables.

Test you understanding 7

In order to improve operational cash flows, indicate whether a company would need to increase or decrease their receivables balance and payables balance.

	Receivables	*Payables*
A	Increase	Increase
B	Increase	Decrease
C	Decrease	Decrease
D	Decrease	Increase

Test your understanding 8

Olive plc usually takes 2 months to collect its debts from credit customers. It has just issued an invoice to Alfie plc for $100 and offers a cash discount of 2% if payment is made within 1 month.

What is the effective annualised cost of the discount if Alfie plc does settle within 1 month?

A 27.4%

B 34.4%

C 20.0%

D 32.6%

Test you understanding 9

The main aspects of debt factoring include

(1) Administration of the client's invoicing, sales accounting and debt collection service

(2) Making payments to the client in advance of collecting the debts

(3) Credit protection when the service is non-recourse

A (1) only

B (1) and (2) only

C (2) and (3) only

D All of the above

Test you understanding 10

Which of the following statements, concerning invoice discounting, are true?

(1) Invoice discounting is the purchase of a selection of invoices (by the provider of the discounting service) of trade debts at a discount

(2) With 'confidential discounting' the client's customers are unaware that the business is using invoice discounting

(3) The invoice discounter does not take over the administration of the client's sales ledger

A (1) only

B (1) and (2) only

C (2) and (3) only

D All of the above

Test you understanding 11

Which of the following statements, concerning receivables management, is incorrect?

A Credit limits should be reviewed periodically

B Credit analysis depends on the provision of relevant information, for example trade references

C Delaying payment of invoices is likely to make receivables management more effective

D Longer-term credit may increase revenue but also increases the risk of bad debts

Chapter summary

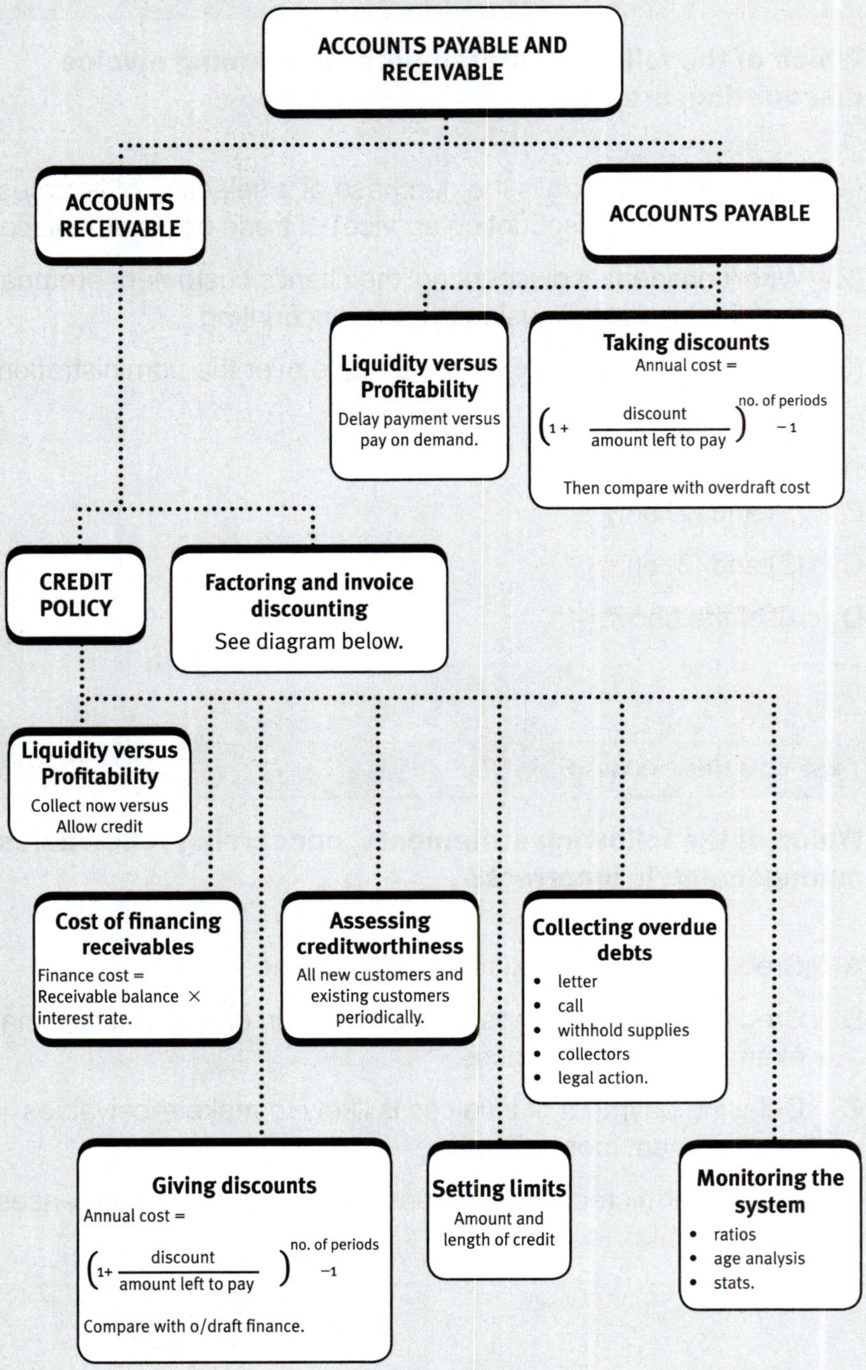

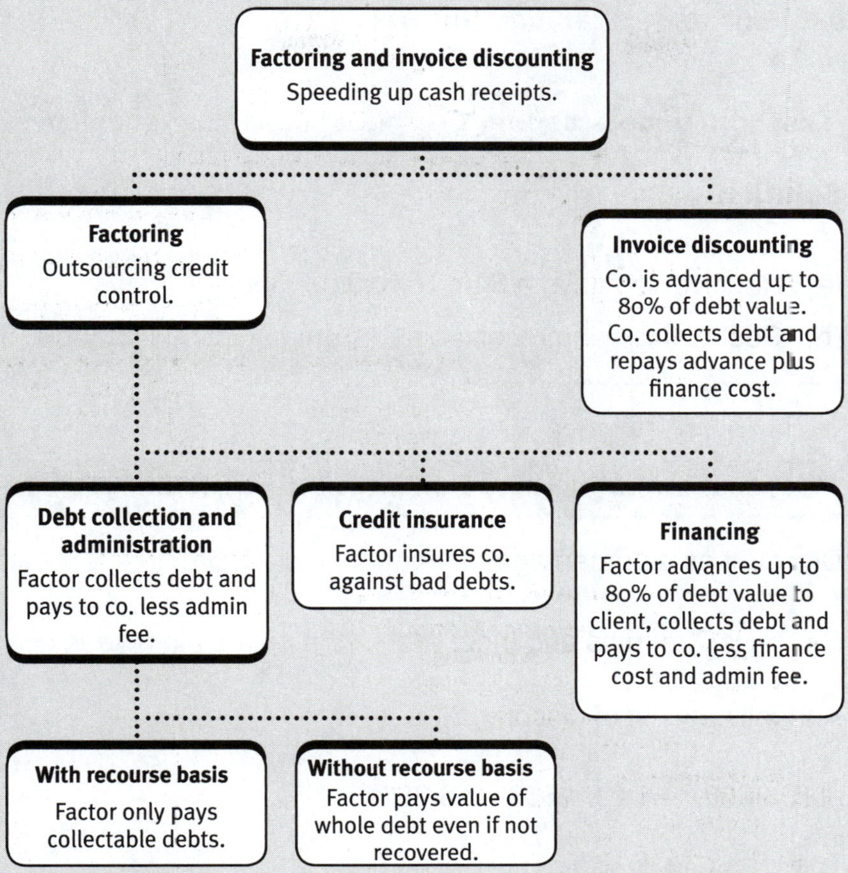
Factoring and invoice discounting
Speeding up cash receipts.
Factoring
Outsourcing credit control.
Invoice discounting
Co. is advanced up to 80% of debt value. Co. collects debt and repays advance plus finance cost.
Debt collection and administration
Factor collects debt and pays to co. less admin fee.
Credit insurance
Factor insures co. against bad debts.
Financing
Factor advances up to 80% of debt value to client, collects debt and pays to co. less finance cost and admin fee.
With recourse basis
Factor only pays collectable debts.
Without recourse basis
Factor pays value of whole debt even if not recovered.

Test your understanding answers

Test your understanding 1 – Cost of financing receivables

Solution

(a) Receivables days = $4m ÷ $20m × 365 = 73 days

(b) Cost of financing receivables = $4m × 12% = $480,000.

Test your understanding 2 – Early settlement discounts I

Discount as a percentage of amount paid = 2.5/97.5 = 2.56%

Saving is 2 months and there are 12/2 = periods in a year.

Annualised cost of discount % is

$(1+0.0256)^6 - 1 = 0.1638 = 16.38\%$.

The loan rate is 18%.

It would therefore be worthwhile offering the discount.

Test your understanding 3 – Early settlement discounts II

To determine if the early settlement discount should be introduced, a comparison must be made between the cost and the benefit.

Cost

$20m of revenue × 40% take up × 2% discount = **$160,000**

Benefit

The benefit is a reduction in the receivables balance which will result in a higher cash balance, thereby reducing interest payable (say, on an overdraft balance). The value can be found by:

(1) Calculate the current level of receivables & receivables days

(2) Calculate the cost of financing this

(3) Calculate the new level of receivables & receivables days

(4) Calculate the cost of financing this new level

(5) Compare the old cost with the new cost to determine the benefit

Step 1 – Calculate the current level of receivables & receivables days

The current receivables balance is $4m (per the question). This implies receivables days of:
$4m/$20m × 365 = 73 days

Step 2 – Calculate the cost of financing this

$4m × 12% interest = $480,000 p.a.

Step 3 – Calculate the new level of receivables & receivables days

Since 40% of customers will now pay within 10 days, and the remaining 60% will continue paying as before (i.e. taking 73 days), the new level of receivables can be assumed to be:

10/365 × $20m × 40% =$219,178
73/365 × $20m × 60% = $2,400,000

Total $2,619,178

Step 4 – Calculate the cost of financing this new level

$2,619,178 × 12% interest = $314,301

Step 5 – Compare the old cost with the new cost to determine the benefit

The benefit of the lower receivables balance is therefore $480,000 – $314,301 = $165,699.

Comparison of cost and benefit

Now we can compare the cost of offering the discount with the benefit.

Cost = $160,000

Benefit = $165,699

Net benefit = $5,699

The conclusion is that this discount should be offered.

Test your understanding 4 – Factoring arrangements

(a) **Reduction in receivables days = 75 – 45 = 30 days**

Reduction in receivables	= 30 ÷ 365 × $16m	= $1,315,068
Saving in finance cost	= (8% × $1,315,068)	= $105,205
		say $105,000
Administrative savings		= $100,000
Service charge	= (1.75% × $16m)	= $280,000

Summary

	$
Service charge	(280,000)
Finance cost saved by reducing receivables	105,000
Administration costs saved	100,000
Net annual cost of the service	(75,000)

Edden will have to balance this cost against the security offered by improved cash flows and greater liquidity.

(b)

	Costs of factoring	**Savings**
	$	$
Sales ledger administration 1% × $16m	160,000	
Administration cost savings		100,000
Cost of factor finance 10% × 80% × $3.3m	264,000	
Overdraft finance costs 8% × 80% × $3.3m saved		211,200
Total	424,000	311,200
Net cost of factoring	112,800	

As before the firm will have to balance this cost against the security offered by improved cash flows and greater liquidity.

Test your understanding 5 – Discount for early payment

Discount saves 2% of $7,500 =$150

Financed by overdraft for extra two months in order to pay early:

Cost = $10\% \times \frac{2}{12} \times \$7,500$ = ($125)

Net saving = $25

It is worth accepting the discount.

Alternatively :

Discount as a percentage of amount paid = $\frac{150}{7,350}$ = 2.04%

Saving is 2 months and there are $\frac{12}{2}$ = 6 periods in a year

Annualised cost of not taking the discount (and therefore borrowing from the supplier) is: $(1+0.0204)^6 - 1$

= 0.1288 = 12.88%

The overdraft rate is 10%.

It would be cheaper to borrow the money from the bank to pay early and accept the discount.

Test your understanding 6 – Equivalent annual cost of discount

Step 1

Work out the discount available and the amount due if the discount were taken.

Discount available on a \$100 invoice = 1.75% × \$100 = \$1.75.

Amount due after discount = \$100 × \$1.75 = \$98.25

Step 2

The effective interest cost of not taking the discount is:

1.75 ÷ 98.25 = 0.0178

for an 8 – 3 = five-week period.

Step 3

Calculate the equivalent annual rate. There are ten five-week periods in a year.

The equivalent interest annual rate is $(1 + 0.018)^{10} - 1 = 0.195$ or 19.5%.

Test you understanding 7

Answer D

In order to improve cash flow, a business needs to decrease receivables and increase the credit period taken from suppliers.

Test your understanding 8

Answer A

Discount as a percentage of the amount paid = 2/98 = 2.04%

Saving is 1 month and there are 12/1 = periods in a year.

Annualised cost of discount % is

$(1 + 0.0204)^{12} - 1 = 27.4\%$

Test you understanding 9

Answer D

The main aspects of debt factoring include administration, financing and credit insurance.

Test you understanding 10

Answer D

Invoice discounting is related to factoring and many factors will provide an invoice discounting service. In some ways, invoice discounting is similar to the financing parts of the factoring service without the control of credit passing to the factor.

Test you understanding 11

Answer C

Delaying payment of invoices is an action relating to payables management, not receivables management.

chapter

10

Working capital management – cash and funding strategies

Chapter learning objectives

Upon completion of this chapter you will be able to:

- explain the main reasons for a business to hold cash
- define and explain the use of cash budgets and cash flow forecasts
- prepare a cash flow forecast to determine future cash flows and cash balances
- explain the points addressed by the Baumol cash management model
- calculate the optimum cash management strategy using the Baumol cash management model
- explain the logic of the Miller-Orr cash management model
- calculate the optimum cash management strategy using the Miller-Orr cash management model
- explain the ways in which a firm can invest cash short-term
- explain the ways in which a firm can borrow cash short-term
- calculate the level of working capital investment in current assets from supplied data
- explain the main strategies available for the funding of working capital
- explain the distinction between permanent and fluctuating current assets
- explain the relative costs and risks of short-term and long-term finance

- explain the logic behind matching short- and long-term assets and funding
- explain the relative costs and benefits of aggressive, conservative and matching funding policies
- explain the impact that factors such as management attitudes to risk, previous funding decisions and organisation size might have on the strategy chosen to fund working capital.
- discuss the advantages and disadvantages of an overdraft as a source of short-term finance
- discuss the advantages and disadvantages of a short-term loan as a source of short-term finance

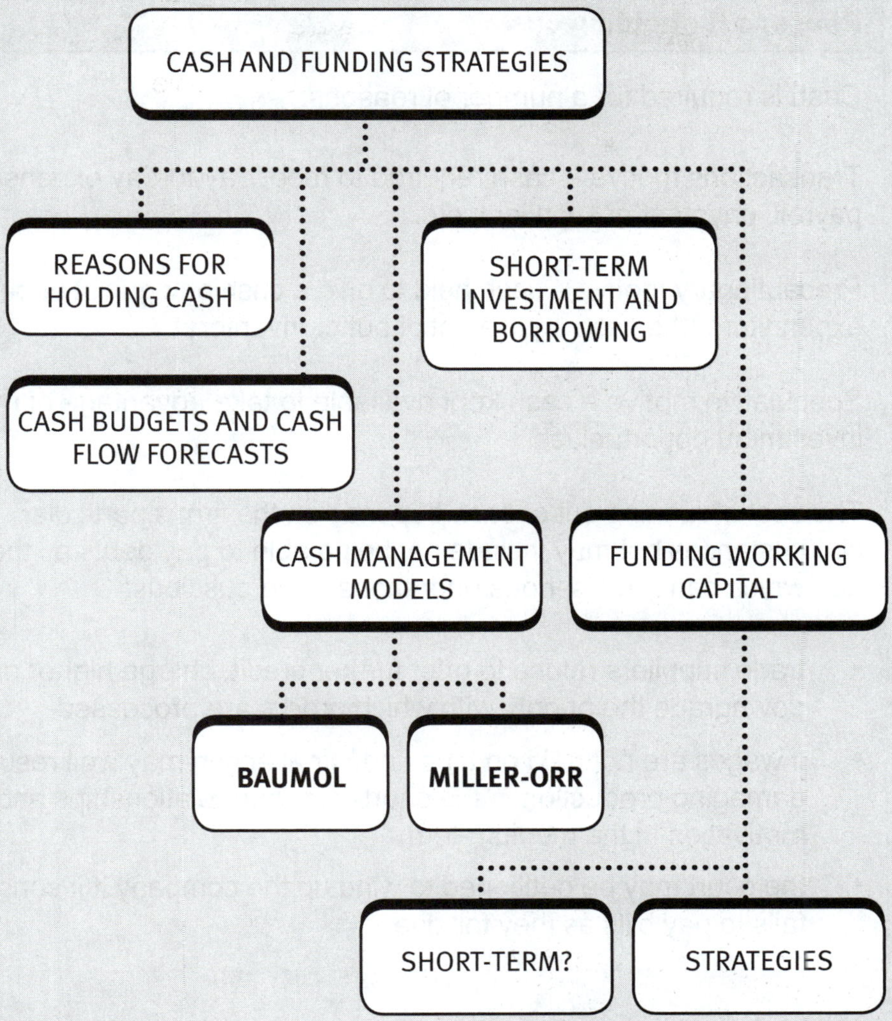

1 Reasons for holding cash

Although cash needs to be invested to earn returns, businesses need to keep a certain amount readily available. The reasons include:

- transactions motive
- precautionary motive
- investment motive.

Failure to carry sufficient cash levels can lead to:

- loss of settlement discounts
- loss of supplier goodwill
- poor industrial relations
- potential liquidation.

Reasons for holding cash

Cash is required for a number of reasons:

Transactions motive – cash required to meet day-to-day expenses, e.g. payroll, payment of suppliers, etc.

Precautionary motive – cash held to give a cushion against unplanned expenditure (the cash equivalent of buffer inventory).

Speculative motive – cash kept available to take advantage of market investment opportunities.

The cost of running out of cash depends on the firm's particular circumstances but may include not being able to pay debts as they fall due which can have serious operational repercussions:

- trade suppliers refuse to offer further credit, charge higher prices or downgrade the priority with which orders are processed
- if wages are not paid on time, industrial action may well result, damaging production in the short-term and relationships and motivation in the medium-term
- the court may be petitioned to wind up the company if it consistently fails to pay bills as they fall due.

Once again therefore the firm faces a balancing act between liquidity and profitability.

The balancing act

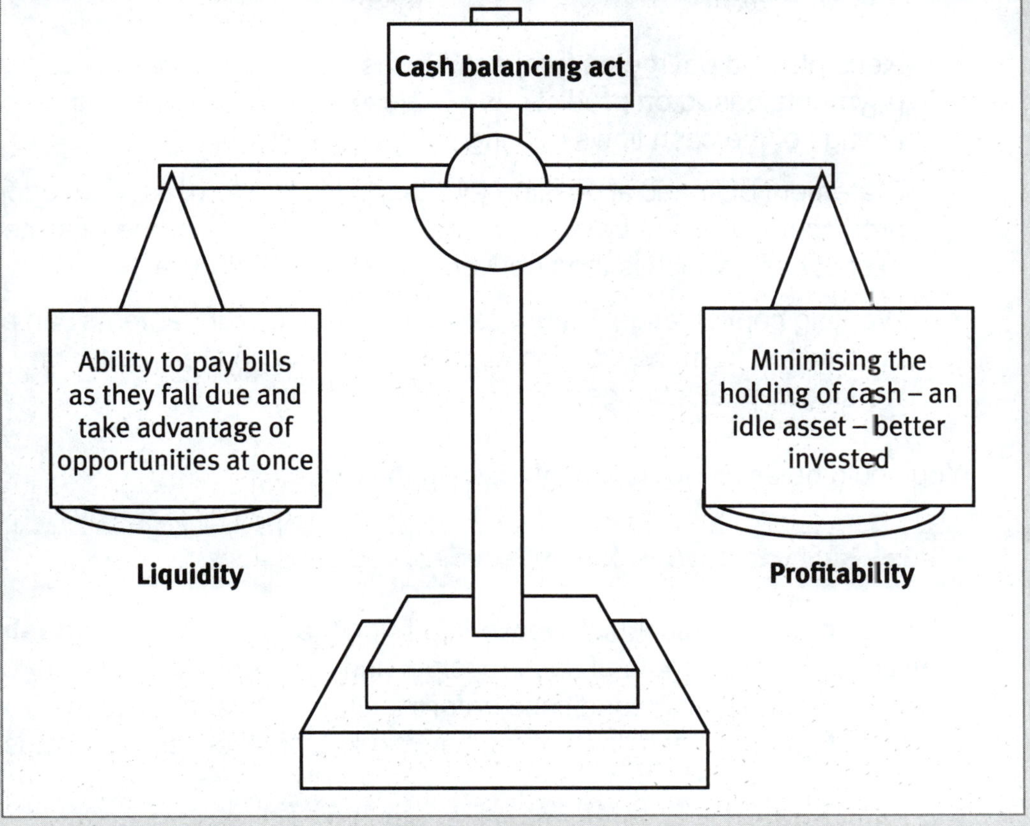

Remember to consider the three motives for holding cash and the liquidity/profitability trade-off in a question that asks for a discussion of cash management.

2 Cash budgets and cash flow forecasts

A **cash forecast** is an estimate of cash receipts and payments for a future period under existing conditions.

A **cash budget** is a commitment to a plan for cash receipts and payments for a future period after taking any action necessary to bring the forecast into line with the overall business plan.

Cash budgets are used to:

- assess and integrate operating budgets
- plan for cash shortages and surpluses
- compare with actual spending.

Cash forecasts can be prepared based on:

- Receipts and payments forecast. This is a forecast of cash receipts and payments based on predictions of sales and cost of sales and the timings of the cash flows relating to these items.
- Statement of financial position forecast. This is a forecast derived from predictions of future balance sheets. Predictions are made of all items except cash, which is then derived as a balancing figure.
- Working capital ratios. Future cash and funding requirements can be determined from the working capital ratios seen in the chapter on working capital management.

You could be asked to do any of these in the exam.

Cash budgets and cash flow forecasts

It is important to distinguish between a budget and a forecast. A **cash forecast** is an estimate of cash receipts and payments for a future period under existing conditions before taking account of possible actions to modify cash flows, raise new capital, or invest surplus funds.

A **cash budget** is a commitment to a plan for cash receipts and payments for a future period after taking any action necessary to bring the preliminary cash forecast into conformity with the overall plan of the business.

Companies are likely to prepare a cash budget as part of the annual master budget, but then to continually prepare revised cash forecasts throughout the year, as a means of monitoring and managing cash flows.

Using planned receipts and payments

Preparing a cash flow forecast from receipts and payments

Every type of cash inflow and receipt, along with their timings, must be forecast. Note that cash receipts and payments differ from sales and cost of sales in the statement of profit or loss because:

- not all cash receipts or payments affect the statement of profit or loss, e.g. the issue of new shares or the purchase of a non-current asset
- some statement of profit or loss items are derived from accounting conventions and are not cash flows, e.g. depreciation or the profit/loss on the sale of a non-current asset

- the timing of cash receipts and payments does not coincide with the statement of profit or loss accounting period, e.g. a sale is recognised in the statement of profit or loss when the invoice is raised, yet the cash payment from the receivable may not be received until the following period or later.

The following approach should be adopted for examination questions.

Step 1 – Prepare a proforma

Month:	1	2	3	4
	$	$	$	$
Receipts	X	X	X	X
(few lines)	X	X	X	X
Sub total	X	X	X	X
Payments	X	X	X	X
(Many lines)	X	X	X	X
	X	X	X	X
Sub total	X	X	X	X
Net cash flow	X	X	X	X
Opening balance	X	X	X	X
Closing balance	X	X	X	X

Step 2 – Fill in the simple figures

Some payments need only a small amount of work to identify the correct figure and timing and can be entered straight into the proforma. These would usually include:

- wages and salaries
- fixed overhead expenses
- dividend payments
- purchase of non-current assets.

Step 3 – Work out the more complex figures

The information on sales and purchases can be more time consuming to deal with, e.g.:

- timings for both sales and purchases must be found from credit periods
- variable overheads may require information about production levels
- purchase figures may require calculations based on production schedules and inventory balances.

Additional question – Full cash flow forecast

In the near future a company will purchase a manufacturing business for $315,000, this price to include goodwill ($150,000), equipment and fittings ($120,000), and inventory of raw materials and finished goods ($45,000).

A delivery van will be purchased for $15,000 as soon as the business purchase is completed. The delivery van will be paid for in the second month of operations.

The following forecasts have been made for the business following purchase:

(i) Sales (before discounts) of the business's single product, at a mark-up of 60% on production cost will be:

Month	1	2	3	4	5	6
($000)	96	96	92	96	100	104

25% of sales will be for cash; the remainder will be on credit, for settlement in the month following that of sale. A discount of 10% will be given to selected credit customers, who represent 25% of gross sales.

(ii) Production cost will be $5 per unit. The production cost will be made up of:

Raw materials	$2.50
Direct labour	$1.50
Fixed overhead	$1.00

(iii) Production will be arranged so that closing inventory at the end of any month is sufficient to meet sales requirements in the following month. A value of $30,000 is placed on the inventory of finished goods, which was acquired on purchase of the business. This valuation is based on the forecast of production cost per unit given in (ii) above.

(iv) The single raw material will be purchased so that inventory at the end of a month is sufficient to meet half of the following month's production requirements. Raw material inventory acquired on purchase of the business ($15,000) is valued at the cost per unit that is forecast as given in (ii) above. Raw materials will be purchased on one month's credit.

(v) Costs of direct labour will be met as they are incurred in production.

(vi) The fixed production overhead rate of $1.00 per unit is based upon a forecast of the first year's production of 150,000 units. This rate includes depreciation of equipment and fittings on a straight-line basis over the next five years. Fixed production overhead is paid in the month incurred.

(vii) Selling and administration overheads are all fixed, and will be $208,000 in the first year. These overheads include depreciation of the delivery van at 30% pa on a reducing balance basis. All fixed overheads will be incurred on a regular basis, and paid in the month incurred, with the exception of rent and rates. $25,000 is payable for the year ahead in month one for rent and rates.

Required:

(a) Prepare a monthly cash flow forecast. You should include the business purchase and the first four months of operations following purchase.

(b) Calculate the inventory, receivables, and payables balances at the end of the four-month period. Comment briefly upon the liquidity situation.

The answer to this question can be found after the chapter summary diagram at the end of this chapter.

Using a statement of financial position

Preparing a cash flow forecast from a statement of financial position

Used to predict the cash balance at the end of a given period, this method will typically require forecasts of:

- changes to non-current assets (acquisitions and disposals)
- future inventory levels
- future receivables levels
- future payables levels
- changes to share capital and other long-term funding (e.g. bank loans)
- changes to retained profits.

Additional question – Statement of financial position

Zed Co has the following statement of financial position at 30 June 20X3:

	$	$
Non-current assets:		
Plant and machinery		192,000
Current assets:		
Inventory	16,000	
Receivables	80,000	
Bank	2,000	
		98,000
Total assets		290,000
Equity and liabilities:		
Issued share capital		216,000
Retained profits		34,000
		250,000

Current liabilities		
Trade payables	10,000	
Dividend payable	30,000	
		40,000
Total equity and liabilities		290,000

(a) The company expects to acquire further plant and machinery costing $8,000 during the year to 30 June 20X4.

(b) The levels of inventories and receivables are expected to increase by 5% and 10% respectively by 30 June 20X4, due to business growth.

(c) Trade payables and dividend liabilities are expected to be the same at 30 June 20X4.

(d) No share issue is planned, and retained profits for the year to 30 June 20X4 are expected to be $42,000.

(e) Plant and machinery is depreciated on a reducing balance basis, at the rate of 20% pa, for all assets held at the balance sheet date.

Required:

Produce a financial position statement forecast as at 30 June 20X4, and predict what the cash balance or bank overdraft will be at that date.

The answer to this question can be found after the chapter summary diagram at the end of this chapter.

Using working capital ratios

Preparing a cash flow forecast from working capital ratios

Working capital ratios can also be used to forecast future cash requirements.

The first stage is to use the ratios to work out the working capital requirement, as we have already seen in the working capital management chapter.

This technique is used to help forecast overall cash flow. The proforma below is used.

		$
	Operating profit	X
	Add: Depreciation	X
	Cash flow from operations	X
Add:	Cash from sale of non-current assets	X
	Long-term finance raised	X
Less:	Purchase of non-current assets	(X)
	Redemption of long-term funds	(X)
	Interest paid	(X)
	Tax paid	(X)
	Dividend paid	(X)
	Increase in working capital	(X)
	Net cash flow	X

Note that the proforma given is not strictly in accordance with International Accounting Standards, which govern the production of cash flow statements in a company's financial statements. However, here we are calculating projected future cash flows rather that the historical cash flow that is covered by the standards.

Additional question – Forecasts from working capital ratios

X Co had the following results for last year.

Statement of profit or loss	$m
Sales	200
Cost of sales (including $20m depreciation)	120
Operating profit	80
Interest	5
Profit before tax	75
Tax	22
Profit after tax	53
Dividend proposed	10
Retained earnings	43

Statement of financial position (extract)

	$m	$m
Non-current assets		400
Current assets:		
Inventory	25	
Receivables	33	
Cash	40	
		98
Current liabilities:		
Trade payables	20	
Dividend payable	10	
Tax payable	22	
		52
Long term loan @ 10%		50

X Co expects the following for the forthcoming year.

Sales will increase by	10%
Plant and machinery will be purchased costing	$12m
Inventory days	80 days
Receivables days	75 days
Trade payables days	50 days
Depreciation will be	$15m

Required:

Prepare a cash flow projection for the forthcoming period.

The answer to this question can be found after the chapter summary diagram at the end of this chapter.

3 Cash management models

Cash management models are aimed at minimising the total costs associated with movements between:

- a current account (very liquid but not earning interest) and
- short-term investments (less liquid but earning interest).

The models are devised to answer the questions:

- at what point should funds be moved?
- how much should be moved in one go?

The Baumol cash management model

Baumol noted that cash balances are very similar to inventory levels, and developed a model based on the economic order quantity (EOQ).

Assumptions:

- cash use is steady and predictable
- cash inflows are known and regular
- day-to-day cash needs are funded from current account
- buffer cash is held in short-term investments.

The formula calculates the amount of funds to inject into the current account or to transfer into short-term investments at one time:

$$Q = \sqrt{\frac{2C_OD}{C_H}}$$

where:

C_O = transaction costs (brokerage, commission, etc.)

D = demand for cash over the period

C_H = cost of holding cash.

The model suggests that when interest rates are high, the cash balance held in non-interest-bearing current accounts should be low. However its weakness is the unrealistic nature of the assumptions on which it is based.

Explanation of terminology

C_O = transaction costs are the costs of making a trade in securities or moving funds in and out of interest-bearing deposit accounts.

D = the demand for cash over the period relates to cash needs for day-to-day transactions.

C_H = the cost of holding cash will be the opportunity cost relating to either the return it could have earned in marketable securities or deposit accounts or the cost of borrowing in order to acquire cash.

Test your understanding 1 – Baumol

A company generates $10,000 per month excess cash, which it intends to invest in short-term securities. The interest rate it can expect to earn on its investment is 5% pa. The transaction costs associated with each separate investment of funds is constant at $50.

Required:

(a) What is the optimum amount of cash to be invested in each transaction?

(b) How many transactions will arise each year?

(c) What is the cost of making those transactions pa?

(d) What is the opportunity cost of holding cash pa?

Test your understanding 2 – Baumol

A company faces a constant demand for cash totalling $200,000 pa. It replenishes its current account (which pays no interest) by selling constant amounts of treasury bills which are held as an investment earning 6% pa. The cost per sale of treasury bills is a fixed $15 per sale.

What is the optimum amount of treasury bills to be sold each time an injection of cash is needed in the current account, how many transfers will be needed and what will the overall transaction cost be?

The Miller-Orr cash management model

The **Miller-Orr** model controls irregular movements of cash by the setting of upper and lower control limits on cash balances.

The **Miller-Orr** model is used for setting the target cash balance.

It has the advantage of incorporating uncertainty in the cash inflows and outflows.

The diagram below shows how the model works over time.

- The model sets higher and lower control limits, H and L, respectively, and a target cash balance, Z.
- When the cash balance reaches H, then (H-Z) dollars are transferred from cash to marketable securities, i.e. the firm buys (H-Z) dollars of securities.
- Similarly when the cash balance hits L, then (Z-L) dollars are transferred from marketable securities to cash.

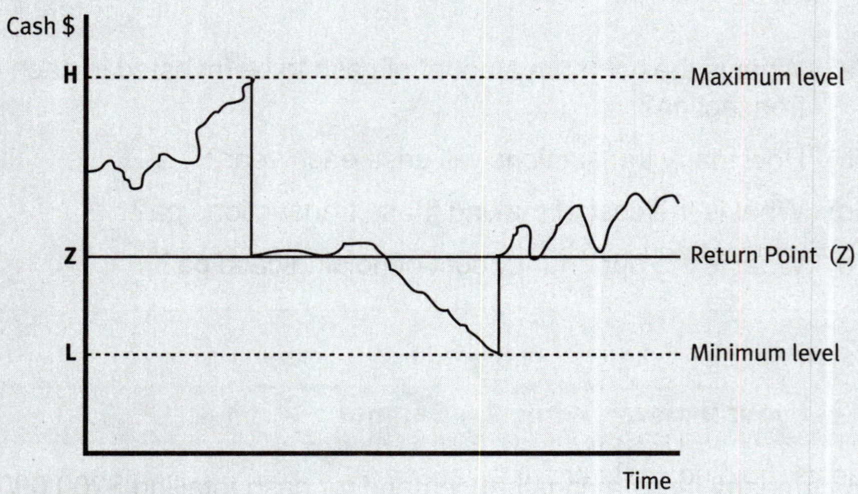

The lower limit, L is set by management depending upon how much risk of a cash shortfall the firm is willing to accept, and this, in turn, depends both on access to borrowings and on the consequences of a cash shortfall.

The formulae (given in the examination) for the **Miller-Orr** model are:

Return point = Lower limit + (1/3 × spread)

Spread = 3 [(3/4 × Transaction cost × Variance of cash flows) ÷ Interest rate] $^{1/3}$

Note: variance and interest rates should be expressed in daily terms. If the question provides you with the standard deviation of daily cash flows, you will need to square this number to obtain the variance.

Miller Orr

The **Miller-Orr** model controls irregular movements of cash by the use of upper and lower limits on cash balances.

The lower limit has to be specified by the firm and the upper limit is calculated by the model. The cash balance of the firm is allowed to vary freely between the two limits but if the cash balance on any day goes outside these limits, action must be taken.

If the cash balance reaches the lower limit it must be replenished in some way, e.g. by the sale of marketable securities or withdrawal from a deposit account. The size of this withdrawal is the amount required to take the balance back to the return point. It is the distance between the return point (usually set in **Miller-Orr** as the lower limit plus one third of the distance up to the upper limit) and the lower limit.

If the cash balance reaches the upper limit, an amount must be invested in marketable securities or placed in a deposit account, sufficient to reduce the balance back to the return point. Again, this is calculated by the model as the distance between the upper limit and the return point.

The minimum cost upper limit is calculated by reference to brokerage costs, holding costs and the variance of cash flows. The model has some fairly restrictive assumptions, e.g. normally distributed cash flows but, in tests, **Miller and Orr** found it to be fairly robust and claim significant potential cost savings for companies.

Test your understanding 3 – Miller Orr

The minimum cash balance of $20,000 is required at Miller-Orr Co, and transferring money to or from the bank costs $50 per transaction. Inspection of daily cash flows over the past year suggests that the standard deviation is $3,000 per day, and hence the variance (standard deviation squared) is $9 million. The interest rate is 0.03% per day.

Calculate:

(i) the spread between the upper and lower limits

(ii) the upper limit

(iii) the return point.

Test your understanding 4 – Miller Orr

A company sets its minimum cash balance at $5,000 and has estimated the following:

- transaction cost = $15 per sale or purchase of gilts
- standard deviation of cash flows = $1,200 per day (i.e. variance = $1.44 million per day)
- interest rate = 7.3% pa = 0.02% per day.

(i) What is the spread between the upper and lower limits?

(ii) What is the upper limit?

(iii) What is the return point?

4 Short-term investment and borrowing solutions

The cash management models discussed above assumed that funds could be readily obtained when required either by liquidating short-term investments or by taking out short-term borrowing.

A company must choose from a range of options to select the most appropriate source of investment/funding.

Short-term cash investments

Short-term cash investments are used for temporary cash surpluses. To select an investment, a company has to weigh up three potentially conflicting objectives and the factors surrounding them.

The objectives can be categorised as follows:

Liquidity: the cash must be available for use when needed.

Safety: no risk of loss must be taken.

Profitability: subject to the above, the aim is to earn the highest possible after-tax returns.

Ensure you can discuss the three key objectives affecting the choice of short-term investment.

Short-term investment

Short-term investment opportunities present themselves when cash surpluses arise. The company's attitude to risk and working capital management will determine the planned cash holdings. This section deals with the practical aspects of the management of a portfolio of short-term investments.

Surplus cash comprises liquid balances held by a business, which are neither needed to finance current business operations nor held permanently for short-term investment. The availability of surplus cash is temporary, awaiting employment either in existing operations or in new investment opportunities (whether already identified or not). The 'temporary' period can be of any duration, from one day to the indefinite future date at which the new investment opportunity may be identified and seized.

Where balances are held temporarily for conversion to other, more important, business uses, absolute priority must be given to the avoidance of risk over maximising returns. The usual principle of finding the optimal mix between risk and return does not apply here, because the investment is secondary and incidental to the ultimate business use of the asset, not an end in itself.

Objectives in the investment of surplus cash

Each of the three objectives raises problems.

The liquidity problem

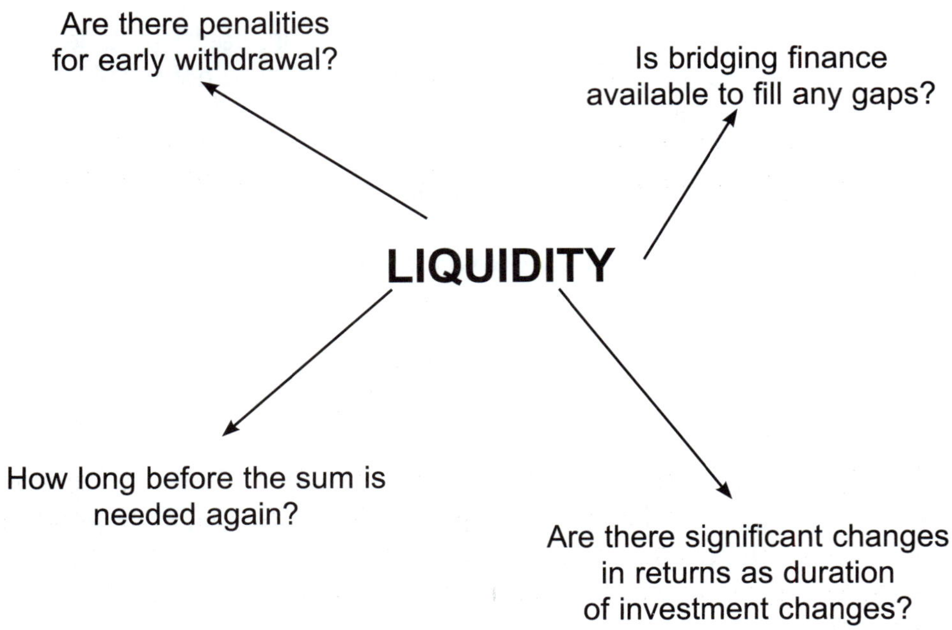

At first sight this problem is simple enough. If a company knows that it will need the funds in three days (or weeks or months), it simply invests them for just that period at the best rate available with safety. The solution is to match the maturity of the investment with the period for which the funds are surplus. However there are a number of factors to consider:

- The exact duration of the surplus period is not always known. It will be known if the cash is needed to meet a loan instalment, a large tax payment or a dividend. It will not be known if the need is unidentified, or depends on the build-up of inventory, the progress of construction work, or the hammering out of an acquisition deal.
- Expected future trends in interest rates (see below) affect the maturity of investments.
- Bridging finance may be available to bridge the gap between the time when the cash is needed and the subsequent date on which the investment matures.
- An investment may not need to be held to maturity, if either an earlier withdrawal is permitted by the terms of the instrument without excessive penalty, or there is a secondary market and its disposal in that market causes no excessive loss.
- A good example of such an investment is a certificate of deposit (CD), where the investor 'lends' the bank a stated amount for a stated period, usually between one and six months. As evidence of the debt and its promise to pay interest, the bank gives the investor a CD. There is an active market for CDs issued by the commercial banks and turning a CD into cash is easy and cheap.

The safety problem

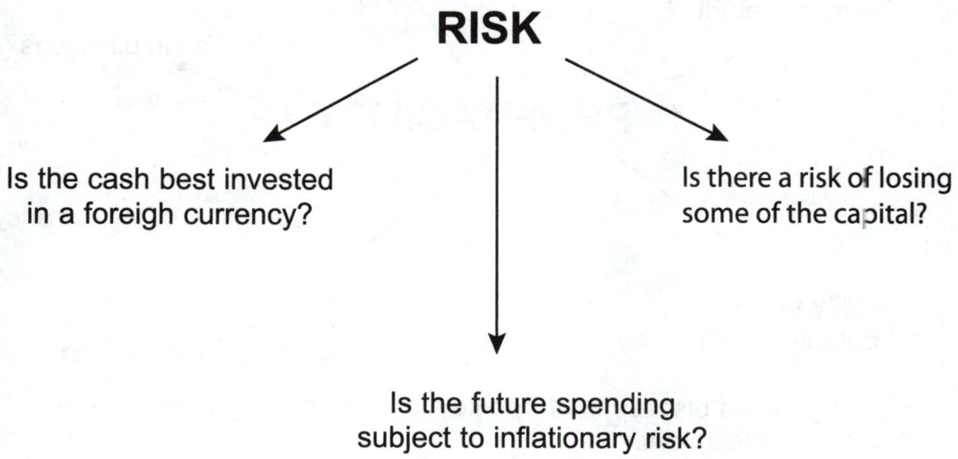

Safety means there is no risk of capital loss. Superficially this again looks simple. The concept certainly includes the absence of credit risk. For example, the firm should not deposit with a bank which might conceivably fail within the maturity period and thus not repay the amount deposited.

However, safety is not necessarily to be defined as certainty of getting the original investment repaid at 100% of its original home currency value. If the purpose for which the surplus cash is held is not itself fixed in the local currency, then other criteria of safety may apply.

Examples

If the cash is being held to meet a future commitment, the ultimate amount of the commitment may be subject to inflationary rises (e g. payment to building contractors for a new factory). In this case a safer investment instrument may be an index-linked gilt-edged bond with a maturity date close to the expected date of the payment.

The profitability problem

If the cash is being held to meet a future payment in a foreign currency, the only riskless investment would be one denominated in that currency.

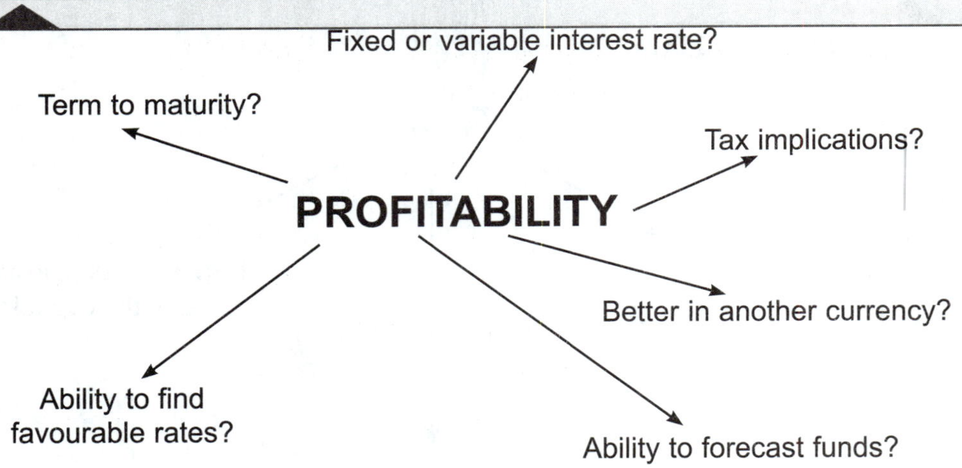

Ensure you can discuss the three key factors affecting the choice of short-term investment.

The profitability objective looks deceptively simple at first: go for the highest rate of return subject to the overriding criteria of safety and liquidity. However, here there are even more complications.

Factor being considered	**Rule of thumb course of action**
Fixed or variable rates	Invest long (fixed interest investments with late maturity dates – subject to the liquidity rule) if there are good reasons to expect interest rates to fall.
Term to maturity	Invest short (fixed interest investments with early maturity dates) or at variable rates if there are good grounds for expecting rates to go up.
Tax effects	Aim to optimise net cash flows after tax. Tax payments are a cash outflow. There are many tax-efficient investments for surplus cash, e.g. use of tax havens, or government securities which may be exempt from capital gains tax (CGT).
Use of other currencies	Investing in currencies other than the company's operating currency in which it has the bulk of its assets and in which it reports to its owners is clearly incompatible with the overriding requirement of safety, except in two possible sets of circumstances: • the investment is earmarked for a payment due in another currency (as seen earlier) or • both principal and interest are sold forward or otherwise hedged against the operating currency (hedging is covered in greater detail later in Chapter 14).

Difficulty in forecasting available funds	Segregate receipts and payments into the following categories: • The steadier and more forecastable flows, such as cash takings in retail trades. There may be predictable peaks, say at the end of the week and in the pre-Christmas period. • The less predictable but not individually large items. • Controllable items such as payments to normal suppliers. • Items such as collections from major customers, which are individually so large that it pays to spend some management time on them. This segregation can even be taken to the point where separate bank accounts are used for the different categories.
Difficulty in finding the most favourable rates	Know the available instruments and their current relative benefits. Shop around for the 'best buy' among investees who offer the most appropriate instrument.

Short-term borrowing

Short-term cash requirements can also be funded by borrowing from the bank. There are two main sources of bank lending:

- bank overdraft
- bank loans.

Bank overdrafts are mainly provided by the clearing banks and are an important source of company finance.

Advantages

- Flexibility
- Only pay for what is used, so cheaper

Disadvantages

- Repayable on demand
- May require security
- Variable finance costs

Bank loans are a contractual agreement for a specific sum, loaned for a fixed period, at an agreed rate of interest. They are less flexible and more expensive than overdrafts but provide greater security.

Short-term borrowing

Finance costs on bank loans and overdrafts are normally variable, i.e. they alter in line with base rates. Fixed rate loans are available, but are less popular with firms (and providers of finance).

Bank overdrafts

A common source of short-term financing for many businesses is a bank overdraft. These are mainly provided by the clearing banks and represent permission by the bank to write cheques even though the firm has insufficient funds deposited in the account to meet the cheques.

An overdraft limit will be placed on this facility, but provided the limit is not exceeded, the firm is free to make as much or as little use of the overdraft as it desires. The bank charges interest on amounts outstanding at any one time, and the bank may also require repayment of an overdraft at any time.

The advantages of overdrafts are the following.

- Flexibility – they can be used as required.
- Cheapness – interest is only payable on the finance actually used, usually at 2-5% above base rate (and all loan interest is a tax deductible expense).

The disadvantages of overdrafts are as follows.

- Overdrafts are legally repayable on demand. Normally, however, the bank will give customers assurances that they can rely on the facility for a certain time period, say six months.
- Security is usually required by way of fixed or floating charges on assets or sometimes, in private companies and partnerships, by personal guarantees from owners.
- Interest costs vary with bank base rates. This makes it harder to forecast and exposes the business to future increases in interest rates.

Overall, bank overdrafts are one of the most important sources of short-term finance for industry.

Bank loans

A bank loan represents a formal agreement between the bank and the borrower, that the bank will lend a specific sum for a specific period (one to seven years being the most common). Interest must be paid on the whole of this sum for the duration of the loan.

This source is, therefore, liable to be more expensive than the overdraft and is less flexible but, on the other hand, there is no danger that the source will be withdrawn before the expiry of the loan period. Interest rates and requirements for security will be similar to overdraft lending.

Comparison of bank loans and overdrafts

Consider a company that requires a maximum of $600 over the next four months. However, it is only halfway through month four that it actually requires the full amount.

The difference can be shown as follows:

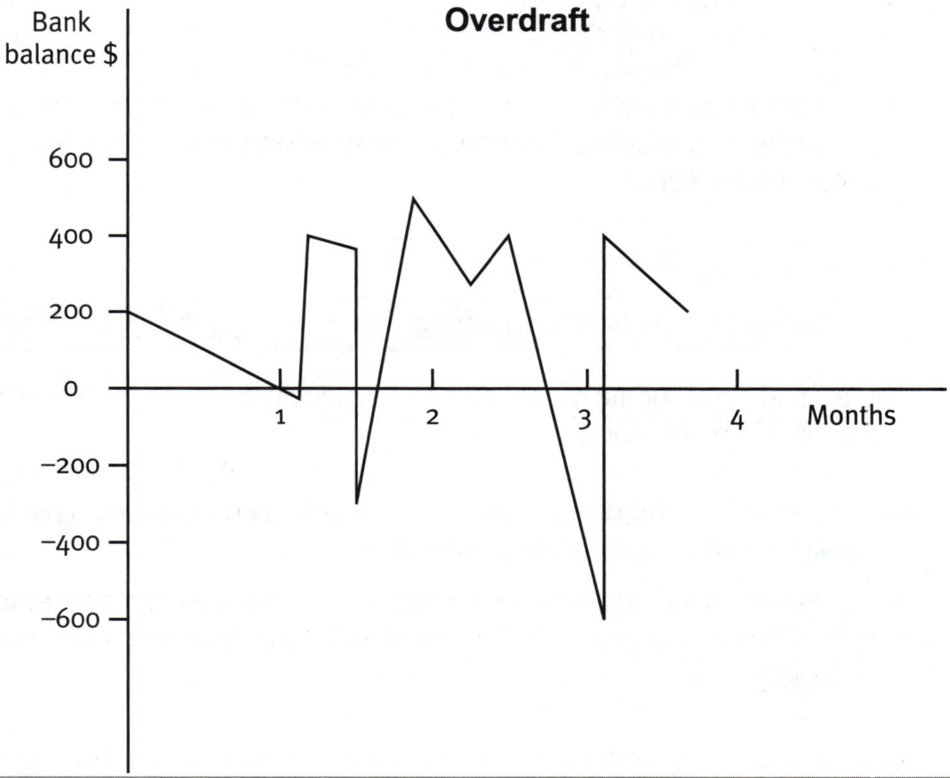

Bank loan

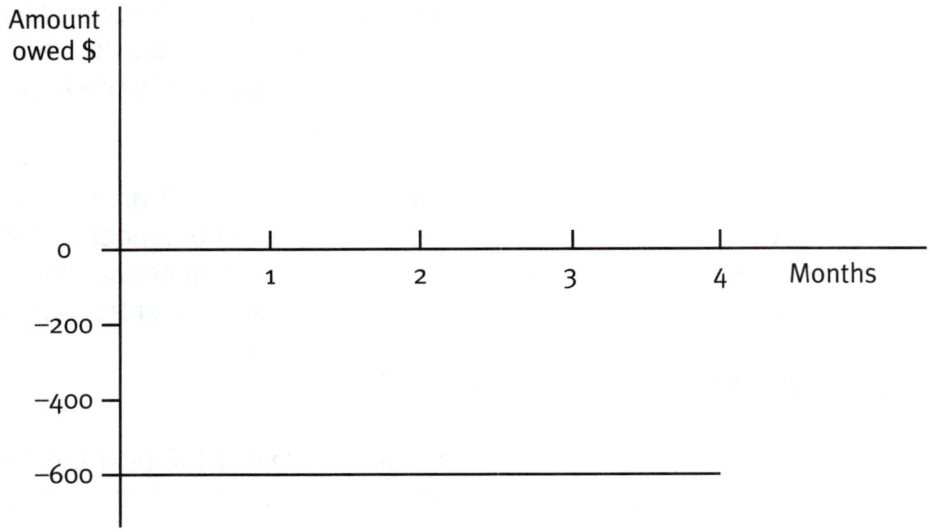

If an overdraft is used, the company will pay interest on the maximum amount part way through month 4. For the remainder of the period it will pay interest on an overdraft of substantially less than that, or it will pay no interest at all as it has a positive bank balance. If it borrows $600 by way of a bank loan at the beginning of the four months, it must pay interest for four months on the amount borrowed, despite the fact that it rarely requires the full sum.

Calculation of repayment on a loan

The annual repayments on a loan can be calculated using the annuity factors seen in chapter 3.

For example, a $100,000 loan taken out by a business at a rate of 7%, repayable over 5 years will have annual repayments of:

$$\text{Annual payment} = \frac{\$100{,}000}{4.100} = \$24{,}390.25$$

where 4.100 is the 7 year, 5% annuity factor.

Each payment can then be split between the repayment of capital and interest on the outstanding balance.

Year	Balance b/f	Interest @ 7%	Annual payment	Balance c/f
	$	$	$	$
1	100,000	7,000	24,390	82,610
2	82,610	5,783	24,390	64,003
3	64,003	4,480	24,390	44,093
4	44,093	3,087	24,390	22,790
5	22,790	1,600*	24,390	0

* Rounding difference

5 Strategies for funding working capital

In the same way as for long-term investments, a firm must make a decision about what source of finance is best used for the funding of working capital requirements.

The decision about whether to choose short- or long-term options depends upon a number of factors:

- the extent to which current assets are permanent or fluctuating
- the costs and risks of short-term finance
- the attitude of management to risk

Permanent or fluctuating current assets

In most businesses a proportion of the current assets are fixed over time, i.e. 'permanent'. For example:

- buffer inventory,
- receivables during the credit period,
- minimum cash balances.

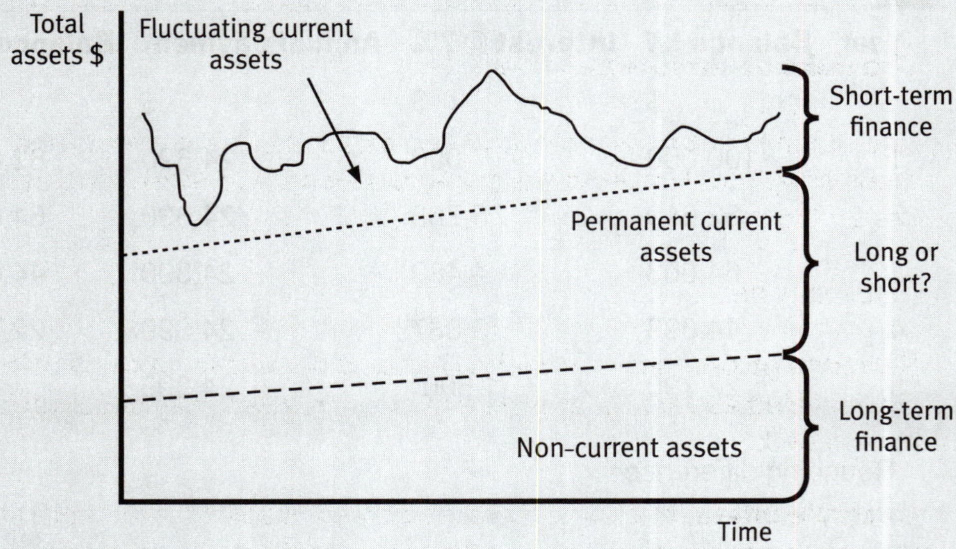

The choice of how to finance the permanent current assets is a matter for managerial judgement, but includes an analysis of the cost and risks of short-term finance.

Costs and risks of short-term finance

The cost of short-term finance

Short-term finance is usually **cheaper** than long-term finance. This is largely due to the risks taken by creditors. For example, if a bank were considering two loan applications, one for one year and the other for 20 years, all other things being equal it would demand a higher interest rate on the 20-year loan. This is because it feels more exposed to risk on long-term loans, as more could go wrong with the borrower over a period of twenty years than a period of one year (although it should be noted that occasionally this situation is reversed, with rates of return being higher on short-term finance).

Short-term finance also tends to be more flexible. For example, if funds are raised on overdraft and used to finance a fluctuating investment in current assets, they can be paid off when not required and interest saved. On the other hand, if funds were borrowed for the long term, early repayment may not be possible, or, if allowed, early repayment penalties may be experienced. The flexibility of short-term finance may, therefore, reduce its overall cost.

Short-term finance includes items such as trade payables, which are normally regarded as low cost funds, whereas long-term finance will include debt and equity. Equity finance is particularly expensive, its required returns being high, and non-tax deductible.

The risks of short-term finance

Short-term financing has already been established as generally 'the cheaper option'. However, the price paid for reduced cost is increased risk for the borrower.

There may be:

Renewal problems – short-term finance may need to be continually renegotiated as various facilities expire and renewal may not always be guaranteed.

Unstable interest rates – if the company constantly has to renew its funding arrangements, it will be at the mercy of fluctuations in short-term interest rates.

Working capital investment levels v working capital financing

Working capital investment policy is concerned with the level of investment in current assets, with one company being compared with another. Working capital financing policy is concerned with the relative proportions of short-term and long-term finance used by a company.

While working capital investment policy is therefore assessed on an inter-company comparative basis, assessment of working capital financing policy involves analysis of financial information for one company alone.

Both working capital investment policy and working capital financing policy use the terms conservative, moderate and aggressive. In investment policy, the terms are used to indicate the comparative level of investment in current assets on an inter-company basis. One company has a more aggressive approach compared to another company if it has a lower level of investment in current assets, and vice versa for a conservative approach to working capital investment policy. In working capital financing policy, the terms are used to indicate the way in which fluctuating current assets and permanent current assets are matched to short-term and long-term finance sources.

The attitude of management to risk: aggressive, conservative and matching funding policies

There is no ideal funding package, but three approaches may be identified.

- Aggressive – finance most current assets, including 'permanent' ones, with short-term finance. Risky but profitable.
- Conservative – long-term finance is used for most current assets, including a proportion of fluctuating current assets. Stable but expensive.
- Matching – the duration of the finance is matched to the duration of the investment.

The attitude of management to risk

Illustration – Aggressive, conservative and matching funding policies

The following three companies have current asset financing structures that may be considered as aggressive, matching and conservative:

Statement of financial position	**Aggressive**	**Matching**	**Conservative**
	$000	$000	$000
Non-current assets	50	50	50
Current assets	50	50	50
	100	100	100
Equity (50,000 $1 shares)	50	50	50
Long-term debt (average cost 10% pa)	–	25	40
Current liabilities (average cost 3% pa)	50	25	10
	100	100	100
Current ratio	1:1	2:1	5:1

Statement of profit or loss	$	$	$
EBIT	15,000	15,000	15,000
Less: Interest	1,500	3,250	4,300
Earnings before tax	13,500	11,750	10,700
Corporation tax @ (say) 40%	5,400	4,700	4,280
Earnings available to equity	8,100	7,050	6,420
Earnings per share (EPS)	16.2c	14.1c	12.84c

The aggressive company is so termed as it is prepared to take the risk of financing more of its business investment with short-term credit. The defensive company, at the other 'extreme', takes on board a high proportion of longer-term debt with, consequently, less short-term credit risk.

It can be seen that the aggressive company returns a higher profit but at the cost of greater risk. It is interesting to note that this higher risk is revealed in its relatively poor current ratio.

Essentially the final choice of working capital funding is down to the management of the individual companies, bearing in mind:

- the size of the organisation
- the willingness of creditors to lend
- the risks of their commercial sector
- previous funding decisions (past experiences will improve the managers' ability to anticipate the effect of working capital fluctuations and proactively make decision to curtail the negative impact of such fluctuations)

Funding strategies for smaller companies

Smaller companies may, by necessity, finance almost all their needs from short-term finance, since long-term debt and equity may be difficult to raise without marketable shares and a good track record.

If the commercial sector in which the company operates has volatile earnings, management may consider it best to take a conservative approach to funding to avoid particular problems in problem years.

The attitude to risk of the decision maker will ultimately determine the decision taken (see chapter 17 for more analysis of attitude to risk), and this in turn may be influenced by the attitudes and decisions of those who have gone before.

Test your understanding 5

Which of the following should not be included in a cash flow forecast?

A Funds from the issue of share capital

B Repayment of a bank loan

C Receipts of dividends from outside the business

D Revaluation of a non-current asset

Test your understanding 6

Roger plc's projected revenue for 20X4 is $350,000. It is forecast that 12% of sales will occur in January and remaining sales will be equally spread among the other eleven months. All sales are on credit. Receivables accounts are settled 50% in the month of sale, 45% in the following month, and 5% are written off as bad debts after two months.

Which of the following amounts represents the budgeted cash collections for March?

A $24,500

B $26,600

C $28,000

D $32,900

Test your understanding 7

Which of the following actions would be appropriate if the cash budget identified a short-term cash deficit?

A Issue shares

B Pay suppliers early

C Arrange an overdraft

D Invest in a short-term deposit account

Test your understanding 8

In the Miller-Orr cash management model

Return point = Lower limit + ... × spread

A One half

B One third

C One quarter

D One fifth

Test your understanding 9

Which of the following statements is true?

Statement 1: An aggressive working capital investment policy aims to finance most of its current assets with long-term finance.

Statement 2: A conservative working capital investment policy aims to finance most of its current assets with short-term finance.

	Statement 1	*Statement 2*
A	True	True
B	True	False
C	False	True
D	False	False

Chapter summary

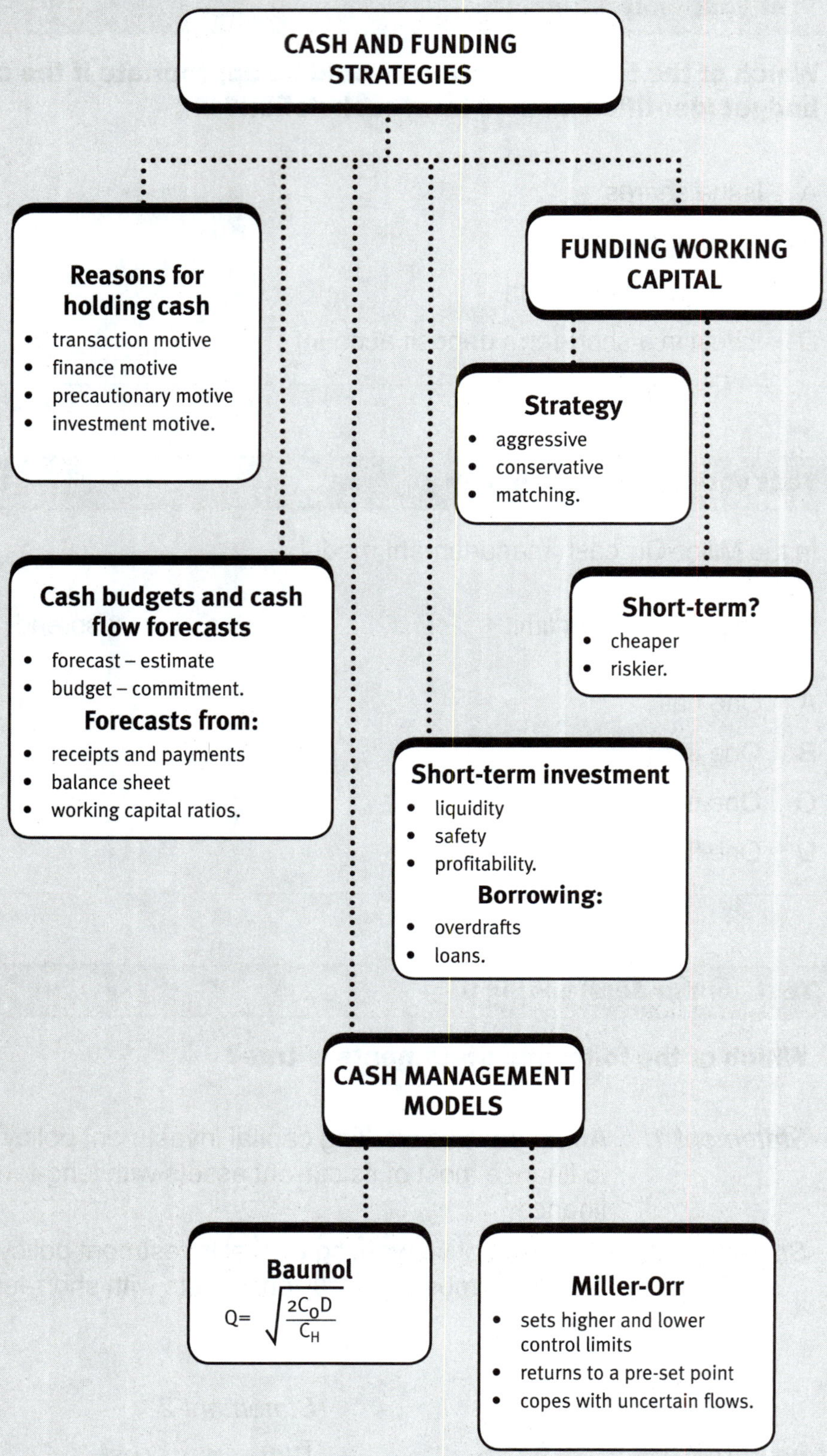

Answer to additional question – Full cash flow forecast

(a) **Monthly cash budget**

	Month 1	Month 2	Month 3	Month 4
	$	$	$	$
Cash inflows:				
Cash sales	24,000	24,000	23,000	24,000
Credit sales		72,000	72,000	69,000
Less: Discounts		(2,400)	(2,400)	(2,300)
Total inflow	24,000	93,600	92,600	90,700
Cash outflows:				
Purchases (W1)	–	44,375	29,375	30,625
Labour (W1)	27,000	17,250	18,000	18,750
Production overhead (W2)	10,500	10,500	10,500	10,500
Selling and administration overhead (W3)	39,875	14,875	14,875	14,875
Purchase of business	315,000	–	–	–
Purchase of van	–	15,000	–	–
Total outflow	392,375	102,000	72,750	74,750
Net cash flow for month	(368,375)	(8,400)	19,850	15,950
Opening balance	0	(368,375)	(376,775)	(356,925)
Closing balance	(368,375)	(376,775)	(356,925)	(340,975)

Workings

(W1)

	Month 1	Month 2	Month 3	Month 4	Month 5	Month 6
Sales ($)	96,000	96,000	92,000	96,000	100,000	104,000
Sales units	12,000	12,000	11,500	12,000	12,500	13,000
+ Closing inventory	12,000	11,500	12,000	12,500	13,000	
– Opening inventory	6,000	12,000	11,500	12,000	12,500	13,000
Production (units)	18,000	11,500	12,000	12,500	13,000	
Raw material usage (Production × $2.50)	45,000	28,750	30,000	31,250	32,500	
+ Closing inventory	14,375	15,000	15,625	16,250		
– Opening inventory	15,000	14,375	15,000	15,625		
Purchases (one month delay)	44,375	29,375	30,625	31,875		
Labour cost (production × $1.50)	27,000	17,250	18,000	18,750		

(W2) **Production overheads**

	$
Annual overheads (150,000 × $1)	150,000
Depreciation (120,000/5)	(24,000)
	126,000
Monthly cash outflow (126,000/12)	10,500

(W3) **Selling and administration overheads**

	$
Annual overheads	208,000
Depreciation (15,000 × 0.3)	(4,500)
	203,500
Less: Rent and rates in month 1	25,000
Monthly cash outflow – months 2, 3, 4 (178500/12)	178,500
Month 1: 25,000 + 14,875	14,875
	39,875

(b) **Closing balances:**

	$
Inventory:	
Finished goods (12,500 × $5)	62,500
Raw materials	16,250
	78,750
Receivables:	
Month 4 credit sales (96,000 × 0.75)	72,000
Less: Discount (10% × 0.25 × 96,000)	(2,400)
	69,600
Payables	31,875

Apart from the purchase of the business, which will require separate long-term finance, the cash flow forecast suggests that there will be sufficient cash inflows to meet the cash outflows on an ongoing basis. The current assets and receivables provide sufficient funds to cover the payables.

Answer to additional question – Statement of financial position

Zed Co – Statement of financial position at 30 June 20X4

	$	$
Non-current assets:		
Plant and machinery[(192,000 + 8,000) × 80%]		160,000
Current assets:		
Inventory (16,000 × 105%)	16,800	
Receivables (80,000 × 110%)	88,000	
Bank (balancing figure)	67,200	
		172,000
Total assets		332,000
Equity and liabilities		
Issued share capital		216,000
Retained profits (34,000 + 42,000)		76,000
		292,000
Current liabilities:		
Trade payables	10,000	
Dividend payable	30,000	
		40,000
Total equity and liabilities		332,000

The forecast is that the bank balance will increase by $65,200 (i.e. $67,200 – $2,000). This can be reconciled as follows:

	$	$
Retained profit		42,000
Add: Depreciation (20% of ($192,000 + $8,000))		40,000
		82,000
Less: Non-current asset acquired		(8,000)
		74,000
Increase in inventory	800	
Increase in receivables	8,000	
		(8,800)
Increase in cash balance		65,200

Answer to additional question – Forecasts from working capital

Here we will assume that the gross profit percentage will remain unaltered in cash terms.

	$m
Last year	
Sales	200
Cost of sales less depreciation	100
Operating cash flow	100
Gross profit percentage	50%

	$m
This year	
Sales 110% × $200m	220
Cost of sales 50% × $220m	110
Operating cash flow	110

Next we calculate the working capital requirements (to the nearest $m).

		$m
Inventory	80 ÷ 365 × $110m =	24
Receivables	75 ÷ 365 × $220m =	45
Trade payables	50 ÷ 365 × $110m =	15

Now we assemble the information in the proforma given earlier.

Note		$m
1	Operating cash flow	110
2	Interest	(5)
3	Tax	(22)
3	Dividend	(10)
4	Purchase of plant and machinery	(12)
5	Reduction in inventory ($24m ÷ $25m)	1
5	Increase in receivables ($45m × $33m)	(12)
5	Reduction in trade payables ($15m × $20m)	(5)
	Net cash flow	45

Notes

(1) We have already calculated operating cash flow so do not need to adjust for depreciation of $15m.

(2) It is assumed that this is the same as last period, as the loans have not changed.

(3) The tax and dividend payables in last year's balance sheet will be paid in the forthcoming period

(4) This was given in the question.

(5) Increases in current assets are an outflow, reductions are an inflow. The reverse is the case for trade payables.

Test your understanding answers

Test your understanding 1 – Baumol

Solution

$$Q \text{ (cash investment)} = \sqrt{\left(\frac{2 \times 50 \times 10{,}000 \times 12}{0.05}\right)} = \$15{,}492$$

(b) Number of transactions pa = $\frac{120{,}000}{15{,}492}$ = 7.75

(c) Annual transaction cost = 7.75 × $50 = $387

(d) Annual opportunity cost = (holding cost) 5 % × $\frac{15{,}492}{2}$ = $387

Test your understanding 2 – Baumol

The optimum amount of treasury bills sold, Q, for each cash injection into the current account will be:

Q = √(2 x 200,000 × 15 ÷ 0.06) = $10,000

The total number of transactions will be

200,000 ÷ 10.000 = 20

and the total transaction cost will be 20 × $15 = $300.

Test your understanding 3 – Miller Orr

(i) Spread = 3 (3/4 × 50 × 9,000,000/0.0003)$^{1/3}$ = $31,200

(ii) Upper limit = 20,000 + 31,200 = $51,200

(iii) Return point = 20,000 + 31,200/3 = $30,400

Test your understanding 4 – Miller Orr

The spread is calculated as:

$3 \times [(3/4 \times 15 \times 1.44m) \div 0.0002]^{1/3}$

= 3 × $4,327

= $12,981

Therefore:

- lower limit (set by the company) = $5,000
- upper limit = 5,000 + 12,981 = $17,981
- return point = 5,000 + (1/3 × 12,981) = $9,327.

Test your understanding 5

Answer D

Revaluation of a non-current asset does not represent a cash flow.

Test your understanding 6

Answer B

January sales are $350,000 × 12% = $42,000.

Sales in each of the other months are ($350,000 – $42,000)/11 = $28,000.

March cash collections will be:

50% of March sales = $28,000 × 50% = $14,000

45% of February sales = $28,000 × 45% = $12,600

Total = $14,000 + $12,600 = $26,600

If you incorrectly calculated the cash collections in March as $28,000 then you probably calculated the collections using 50% on both March and February sales.

If you incorrectly calculated the cash collection in March as $32,900 then you probably used January sales of $42,000 × 45% and February sales of $28,000 × 50% in error.

Test your understanding 7

Answer C

Arranging short-term finance in the form of an overdraft will alleviate the short-term cash deficit problem.

Test your understanding 8

Answer B

One third.

Test your understanding 9

Answer D

A conservative working capital investment policy aims to reduce the risk of system breakdown by holding high levels of working capital.

An aggressive working capital investment policy aims to reduce financing costs and increase profitability by reducing inventories, speeding up collections from customers and delaying payments to suppliers.

chapter

11

The economic environment for business

Chapter learning objectives

Upon completion of this chapter you will be able to:

- explain the main objectives of macroeconomic policy
- explain the potential conflict between the main objectives of macroeconomic policy and its impact on policy targets
- explain the impact of general macroeconomic policy on planning and decision making in the business sector
- define monetary policy and explain the main tools used
- discuss the general role of monetary policy in the achievement of macroeconomic policy targets
- discuss use of interest rates in the achievement of macroeconomic policy targets
- define exchange rate policy and discuss its role in the achievement of macroeconomic policy targets
- explain the impact of specific economic policies on planning and decision making in the business sector
- define fiscal policy and explain the main tools used
- discuss the role of fiscal policy in the achievement of macroeconomic policy targets.
- explain the need for competition policy and its interaction with business planning and decision making
- explain the need for government assistance for business and its interaction with business planning and decision making

- explain the need for green policies and their interaction with business planning and decision making
- explain the need for corporate governance regulation and its interaction with business planning and decision making

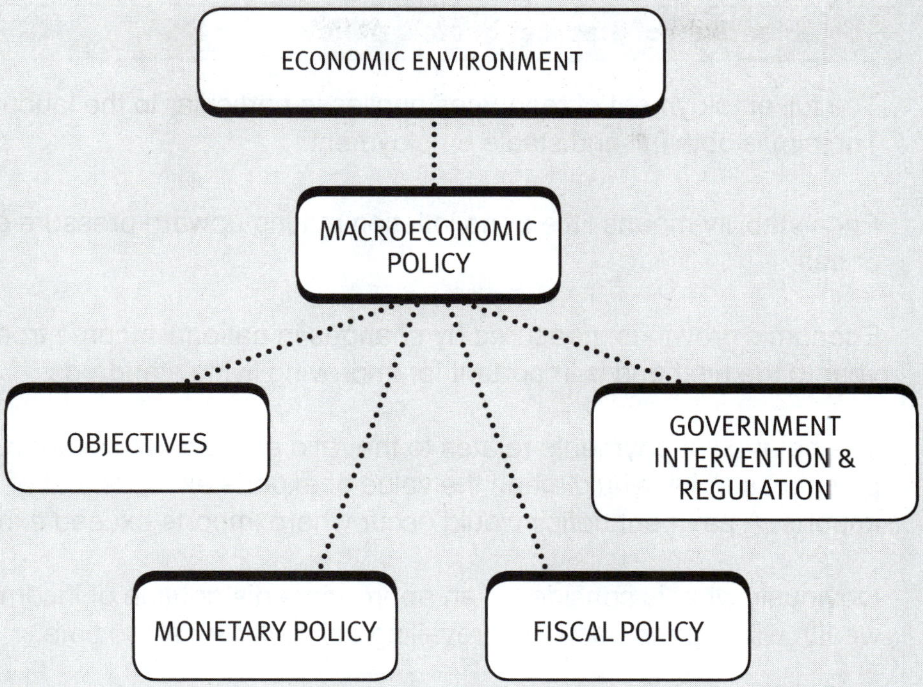

1 Macroeconomic policy

The objectives of macroeconomic policy

Macroeconomic policy is the management of the economy by government in such a way as to influence the performance and behaviour of the economy as a whole.

The principal objectives of macroeconomic policy will be to achieve the following:

- full employment of resources
- price stability
- economic growth
- balance of payments equilibrium
- an appropriate distribution of income and wealth.

The objectives of macroeconomic policy

The full employment of resources applies in particular to the labour force. The aim is both full and stable employment.

Price stability means little or no inflation putting upward pressure on prices.

Economic growth is measured by changes in national income from one year to the next and is important for improving living standards.

The balance of payments relates to the ratio of imports to exports. A payment surplus would mean the value of exports exceeds that of imports. A payment deficit would occur where imports exceed exports.

Obviously what is considered an appropriate distribution of income and wealth will depend upon the prevailing political view at the time.

Potential for conflict

The pursuit of macroeconomic objectives may involve trade-offs – where one objective has to be sacrificed for the sake of another, e.g.:

Full employment	**versus**	**Price stability**
Economic growth	**versus**	**Balance of payments**

Potential for conflict

Both economic theory and the experience of managing the economy suggest that the simultaneous achievement of all macroeconomic objectives may be extremely difficult. Two examples of possible conflict may be cited here.

There may be conflict between full employment and price stability. It is suggested that inflation and employment are inversely related. The achievement of full employment may therefore lead to excessive inflation through an excess level of aggregate demand in the economy.

Rapid economic growth may, in the short-term at least, have damaging consequences for the balance of payments since rapidly rising incomes may lead to a rising level of imports.

Government reputation and business confidence will both be damaged if the government is seen to be pursuing policy targets which are widely regarded as incompatible.

Policy objectives may conflict and hence governments have to consider trade-offs between objectives. The identification of targets for policy should reflect this.

Making an impact – how macroeconomic policy affects the business sector

In order for macroeconomic policy to work, its instruments must have an impact on economic activity. This means that it must affect the business sector. It does so in two broad forms:

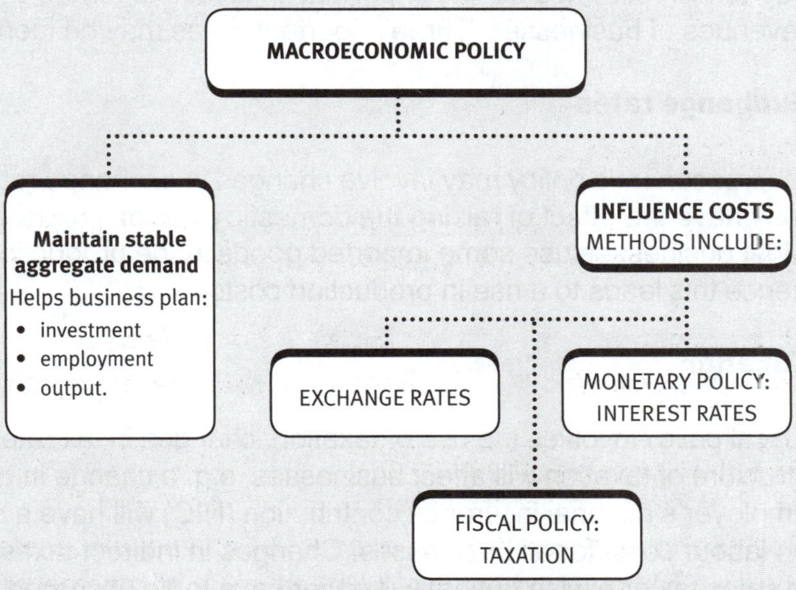

Aggregate demand

Aggregate Demand (AD) is the total demand for goods and services in the economy.

Note: National income is AD that has been satisfied by the provision of goods and services, etc.

The broad thrust of macroeconomic policy is to influence the level of AD in the economy. This is because the level of AD is central to the determination of the level of unemployment and the rate of inflation. If AD is too low, unemployment might result; if AD is too high, inflation induced by excess demand might result.

Changes in AD will affect all businesses to varying degrees.

Thus effective business planning requires that businesses can:

- predict the likely thrust of macroeconomic policy in the short- to medium-term
- predict the consequences for sales growth of the overall stance of macroeconomic policy and any likely changes in it.

The more stable government policy is, the easier it is for businesses to plan, especially in terms of investment, employment and future output capacity.

Business costs

Macroeconomic policy may influence the costs of the business sector.

Not only will the demand for goods and services be affected by macro-economic policy, it also has important implications for the costs and revenues of businesses. Three important areas may be identified:

Exchange rates

Macroeconomic policy may involve changes in exchange rates. This may have the effect of raising the domestic price of imported goods. Most businesses use some imported goods in the production process; hence this leads to a rise in production costs.

Taxation

Fiscal policy involves the use of taxation: changes in tax rates or the structure of taxation will affect businesses, e.g. a change in the employer's national insurance contribution (NIC) will have a direct effect on labour costs for all businesses. Changes in indirect taxes (e.g. a rise in sales tax or excise duties) will either have to be absorbed or the business will have to attempt to pass on the tax to its customers.

Interest rates

Monetary policy involves changes in interest rates. These changes will directly affect firms in two ways:

- Costs of servicing debts will change, especially for highly-geared firms.
- The viability of investment will be affected since all models of investment appraisal include the rate of interest as one, if not the main, variable.

2 Monetary policy

Monetary policy is concerned with influencing the overall monetary conditions in the economy in particular:

- the volume of money in circulation – the money supply
- the price of money – interest rates.

Monetary policy

It is clear that money is crucial to the way in which a modern economy functions. **Money** is any financial asset which has liquidity and fulfils the task of a medium of exchange.

Monetary policy is concerned with influencing the overall monetary conditions in the economy.

Two particular problems with the use of monetary policy are:

- the choice of targets
- the effects of interest rate changes.

The choice of targets

A fundamental problem of monetary policy concerns the choice of variable to operate on. The ultimate objective of monetary policy is to influence some important variable in the economy – the level of demand, the rate of inflation, the exchange rate for the currency, etc. However monetary policy has to do this by targeting some intermediate variable which, it is believed, influences, in some predictable way, the ultimate object of the policy.

The broad choice here is between targeting the **stock of money** or the **rate of interest:**

(a) The volume of money in circulation. The stock of money in the economy (the 'money supply') is believed to have important effects on the volume of expenditure in the economy. This in turn may influence the level of output in the economy or the level of prices.

(b) The **price** of money. The price of money is the rate of interest. If governments wish to influence the amount of money held in the economy or the demand for credit, they may attempt to influence the level of interest rates.

The monetary authorities may be able to control either the supply of money in the economy or the level of interest rates but cannot do both simultaneously. In practice, attempts by governments to control the economy by controlling the money supply have failed and have been abandoned. However, growth in the money supply is monitored, because excessive growth could be destabilising.

The measurement of the money supply (stock)

Currently, in the UK, two measures of money supply are monitored.

(a) **M0:** a **narrow** money measure, incorporating:

   (1) notes and coins in circulation with the public

   (2) till money held by banks and building societies

   (3) operational balances held by commercial banks at the Bank of England.

(b) **M4:** a **broad** money measure, incorporating:

   (1) notes and coins in circulation with the public

   (2) all sterling deposits held by the private sector at UK banks and building societies.

The effects of interest rates

The problem for the monetary authorities is that controlling the level of interest rates is rather easier than controlling the overall stock of money but the effects of doing so are less certain.

If governments choose to target interest rates as the principal means of conducting monetary policy, this may have a series of undesirable effects. These principally relate to the indiscriminate nature of interest rate changes and to the external consequences of monetary policy.

When interest rates are changed, it is expected that the general level of demand in the economy will be affected. Thus a rise in interest rates will discourage expenditure, by raising the cost of credit. However, the effects will vary:

(1) **Investment may be affected more than consumption.** The rate of interest is the main cost of investment whether it is financed by internal funds or by debt. However, most consumption is not financed by credit and hence is less affected by interest rate changes. Since the level of investment in the economy is an important determinant of economic growth and international competitiveness there may be serious long-term implications arising from high interest rates.

(2) Even where consumption is affected by rising interest rates, the **effects are uneven.** The demand for consumer durable goods and houses is most affected since these are normally credit-based purchases. Hence active interest policy may induce instability in some sectors of business.

The second problem arises from the openness of modern economies and their economic interdependence. There is now a very high degree of capital mobility between economies: large sums of short-term capital move from one financial centre to another in pursuit of higher interest rates. Changes in domestic interest rates relative to those in other financial centres will produce large inflows and outflows of short-term capital. Inflows of capital represent a demand for the domestic currency and hence push up the exchange rate. Outflows represent sales of the domestic currency and hence depress the exchange rate. This may bring about unacceptable movements in the exchange rate.

Monetary policy in the UK

It is useful to look at the current monetary policy in the UK. Similar policies are pursued in the US and the Euro-zone countries.

In the UK, the central bank has been given responsibility by the government for controlling short-term interest rates. Short-term interest rates are controlled with a view to influencing the rate of inflation in the economy, over the long-term. In broad terms, an increase in interest rates is likely to reduce demand in the economy and so lower inflationary pressures, whereas a reduction in interest rates should give a boost to spending in the economy, but could result in more inflation. The aim of economic policy is to find a suitable balance between economic growth and the risks from inflation.

Central governments can control short-term interest rates through their activities in the money markets. This is because the commercial banks need to borrow regularly from the central bank. The central bank lends to the commercial banks at a rate of its own choosing (a rate known in the UK as the repo rate). This borrowing rate for banks affects the interest rates that the banks set for their own customers. Action by a central bank to raise or lower interest rates normally results in an immediate increase or reduction in bank base rates.

Interest rate smoothing

Interest rate smoothing is the policy of some central banks to move official interest rates in a sequence of relatively small steps in the same direction, rather than waiting until making a single larger change.

This is usually for the following reasons:

- economic (e.g. to avoid instability and the need for reversals in policy) and
- political (e.g. higher rates are broken to the electorate gently).

Impact of monetary policy on business decision making

Factors affected	**Achieved by controlling supply**	**Achieved by increasing interest rates**
Availability of finance	Credit restrictions ⇨small businesses struggle to raise funds	
Cost of finance	Reduced supply pushes up the cost of funds ⇨ discourages expansion	Shareholders require higher returns ⇨ if not met, share price falls
Level of consumer demand	Too difficult to raise funds to spend	Saving becomes more attractive
Exchange rates		High interest rates attracts foreign investment ⇨ increase in exchange rates: • exports dearer • imports cheaper.

All the above factors will also therefore influence inflation, which has a significant impact on business cash flows and profits. Inflation may be:

- demand-pull inflation – excess demand
- cost-push inflation – high production costs.

Both can have negative impact on cash flows and profits.

Impact of monetary policy

Changes in monetary policy will influence the following factors.

The availability of finance. Credit restrictions achieved via the banking system or by direct legislation will reduce the availability of loans. This can make it difficult for small- or medium-sized new businesses to raise finance. The threat of such restrictions in the future will influence financial decisions by companies, making them more likely to seek long-term finance for projects.

The cost of finance. Any restrictions on the stock of money, or restrictions on credit, will raise the cost of borrowing, making fewer investment projects worth while and discouraging expansion by companies. Also, any increase in the level of general interest rates will increase shareholders' required rate of return so unless companies can increase their return, share prices will fall as interest rates rise. Thus, in times of 'tight' money and high interest rates, organisations are less likely to borrow money and will probably contract rather than expand operations.

The level of consumer demand. Periods of credit control and high interest rates reduce consumer demand. Individuals find it more difficult and more expensive to borrow to fund consumption, whilst saving becomes more attractive. This is another reason for organisations to have to contract operations.

The level of exchange rates. Monetary policy which increases the level of domestic interest rates is likely to raise exchange rates as capital is attracted into the country. Very many organisations now deal with both suppliers and customers abroad and thus cannot ignore the effect of future exchange rate movements. Financial managers must consider methods of hedging exchange rate risk and the effect of changes in exchange rates on their positions as importers and exporters.

The level of inflation. Monetary policy is often used to control inflation. Rising price levels and uncertainty as to future rates of inflation make financial decisions more difficult and more important. As prices of different commodities change at different rates, the timing of purchase, sale, borrowing and repayment of debt becomes critical to the success of organisations and their projects. This is discussed further below:

Impact of inflation on business cash flows and profits

The real effects on the level of profits and the cash flow position of a business of a sustained rate of inflation depend on the form that inflation is taking and the nature of the markets in which the company is operating. One way of analysing inflation is to distinguish between demand-pull inflation and cost-push inflation.

Demand-pull inflation might occur when excess aggregate monetary demand in the economy and hence demand for particular goods and services enable companies to raise prices and expand profit margins.

Cost-push inflation will occur when there are increases in production costs independent of the state of demand, e.g. rising raw material costs or rising labour costs. The initial effect is to reduce profit margins and the extent to which these can be restored depends on the ability of companies to pass on cost increases as price increases for customers.

One would expect that the effect of cost-push inflation on company profits and cash flow would always be negative, but that with demand-pull inflation, profits and cash flow might be increased, at least in nominal terms and in the short run. In practice, however, even demand-pull inflation may have negative effects on profits and cash flow.

Demand-pull inflation may in any case work through cost. This is especially true if companies use pricing strategies in which prices are determined by cost plus some mark-up.

- Excess demand for goods leads companies to expand output.
- This leads to excess demand for factors of production, especially labour, so costs (e.g. wages) rise.
- Companies pass on the increased cost as higher prices.
- In most cases inflation will reduce profits and cash flow, especially in the long run.

3 Fiscal policy

Fiscal policy is the manipulation of the government budget in order to influence the level of aggregate demand and therefore the level of activity in the economy. It covers:

- government spending
- taxation
- government borrowing

which are linked as follows:

public expenditure = taxes raised + government borrowing (+ sundry other income)

Fiscal policy

The role of the Chancellor is to balance the budget:

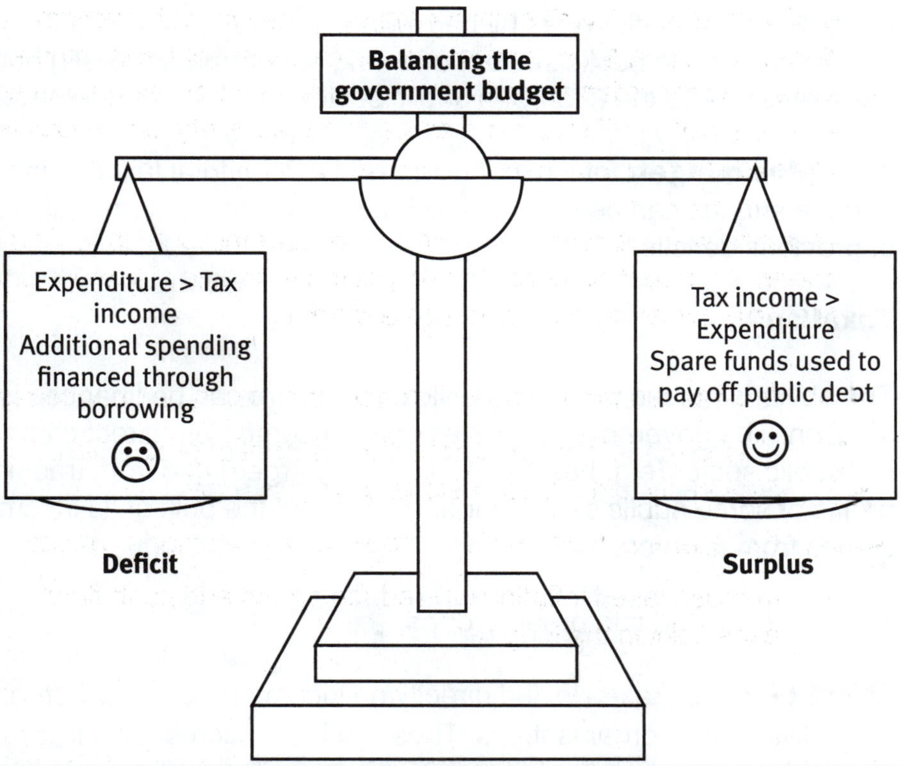

Balancing the budget

All governments engage in public expenditure, although levels vary somewhat from country to country. This expenditure must be financed either by taxation or by borrowing. Thus the existence of public expenditure itself raises issues of policy, notably how to tax and whom to tax. But, in addition, the process of expenditure and taxation permits the use of fiscal policy in a wider sense: the government budget can be manipulated to influence the level of AD in the economy and hence the level of economic activity.

The government budget (including central and local government) is a statement of public expenditure and income over a period of one year. Expenditure can be financed either by taxation or by borrowing. The relationship of expenditure to taxation indicates the state of the budget.

Three budget positions can be identified.

A **balanced budget:** total expenditure is matched by total taxation income.

A **deficit budget:** total expenditure exceeds total taxation income and the deficit must be financed by borrowing. In the UK the budget deficit was known as the public sector borrowing requirement (PSBR) but has been renamed to the (PSNCR) public sector net cash requirement.

A **surplus budget:** total expenditure is less than total taxation income and the surplus can be used to pay back public debt incurred as a result of previous deficits.

Taxation

The obvious means by which public expenditure can be financed is by taxation. The government receives some income from direct charges in the public sector (e.g. health prescription charges) and from trading profits of some public sector undertakings, but the bulk of its income comes from taxation.

Taxes are divided into broad groups.

Direct taxes are taxes levied directly on income receivers whether they are individuals or organisations. These include income tax, NICs, corporation tax, and inheritance tax.

Indirect taxes are levied on one set of individuals or organisations but may be partly or wholly passed on to others and are largely related to consumption not income. These include VAT and excise duties. By their very nature, indirect taxes tend to be regressive which means they have a relatively greater impact on individuals with lower incomes.

Impacts of excessive taxation

Taxation can raise very large flows of income for the government. However excessive taxation may have undesirable economic consequences. Those most frequently cited are as follows

- Personal disincentives to work and effort: this may be related mainly to the form of taxation, e.g. progressive income tax (earn more, pay more), rather than the overall level of taxation.
- Discouragement to business, especially the disincentive to invest and engage in research and development (R&D), which results from high business taxation.
- Disincentive to foreign investment: multinational firms may be dissuaded from investing in economies with high tax regimes.
- A reduction in tax revenue may occur if taxpayers are dissuaded from undertaking extra income-generating work and are encouraged to seek tax-avoidance schemes.

If the tax rate exceeds a certain level, the total tax revenue falls. It should be noted that these disincentive effects, while apparently clear in principle, are difficult to identify in the real world and hence their impact is uncertain.

Government borrowing

Broadly the government can undertake two types of borrowing:

It can borrow directly or indirectly **from the public** by issuing relatively illiquid debt. This includes National Savings certificates, premium bonds, and long-term government bonds. This is referred to as 'funding' the debt.

It can borrow **from the banking system** by issuing relatively liquid debt such as Treasury bills. This is referred to as 'unfunded' debt.

Long-term government bonds (gilts) are issued for long-term financing requirements, whereas Treasury bills are issued to fund short-term cash flow requirements.

Problems of fiscal policy

Two difficulties associated with fiscal policy have dominated debates about macroeconomic management in recent years:

- the problem of 'crowding out'
- the incentive effects of taxation.

Both have had a major impact on the way in which fiscal policy has been conducted, especially in the US and UK .

Crowding out

It is suggested that fiscal policy can lead to 'financial crowding out', whereby government borrowing leads to a fall in private investment. This occurs because increased borrowing leads to higher interest rates by creating a greater demand for money and loanable funds and hence a higher 'price'.

The private sector, which is sensitive to interest rates, will then reduce investment due to a lower rate of return. This is the investment that is crowded out. The weakening of fixed investment and other interest-sensitive expenditure counteracts the economy boosting benefits of government spending. More importantly, a fall in fixed investment by business can hurt long-term economic growth.

Doubts exist over the likely size of any crowding out effect of government borrowing on other borrowers but a very large PSNCR may well lead to a fall in private investment.

However, when the economy is depressed, and there is not much new private sector investment, government spending programmes could help to give a boost to the economy.

Incentives

It is likely that all taxes have some effect. Indeed, the structure of taxes is designed to influence particular economic activities: in particular, taxes on spending are used to alter the pattern of consumption. Here are two examples.

- High excise duties on alcohol and tobacco products reflect social and health policy priorities.
- Policies to use excise duties to raise the real price of petrol over time are designed to discourage the use of private cars because of the environmental effects.

Thus taxes as instruments of fiscal policy can fulfil a variety of useful functions.

However, there has been a growing concern among some economists that taxes have undesirable side effects on the economy, notably on incentives. As we have seen, it is argued that high taxes, especially when they are steeply progressive, act as a disincentive to work.

Moreover some taxes have more specific effects. For example employer national insurance (NI) payments raise the cost of labour and probably reduce employment.

4 Government intervention and regulation

As well as the general measures to impact business operations discussed above, governments can also take more specific measures to regulate business.

These measures will cover aspects such as:

- Competition policy
- Provision of government assistance
- Green policies
- Corporate governance guidelines

Competition policy

It is not the government's place to set prices for goods and services provided by businesses in the private sector. In a competitive marketplace, prices will be set within the industry according to demand and supply. All producers have to accept the prevailing market price, unless they are able to add distinguishing features to their products (e.g. branding, superior technology) that enable them to charge higher prices.

However, some markets are characterised by various degrees of market power, in particular monopolies, whereby producers become price **makers** rather than price **takers.**

(A **monopoly** is where a firm has a sufficient share of the market to enable it to restrict output and raise prices.)

The absence of competition results in disadvantages to the economy as a whole.

- Economic inefficiency: output is produced at a higher cost than necessary. For example, there may be no incentive to reduce costs by improving technology used.
- Monopolies may be able to engage in price discrimination: charging different prices to different customers for the same goods or services, e.g. peak and off-peak pricing. This may act against the interests of customers.
- Disincentive to innovate: the absence of competition may reduce the incentive to develop new products or new production processes.
- Pricing practices: monopolies may adopt pricing practices to make it uneconomic for new firms to enter the industry, thus reducing competition in the long run.

These potential problems of companies with monopoly power must be considered in the light of some possible advantages that may be associated with such firms:

- Large firms may secure economies of scale: it is possible that there are significant economies of scale, reducing production costs, but that these require large firms and hence the number of firms in an industry is restricted. In this case the benefits of economies of scale may offset the inefficiencies involved.
- The special case of natural monopolies: this is the case where the economies of scale in the provision of some basic infrastructure are so great that only one producer is feasible. This may be the case of the public utilities in energy and water.
- Research and development: it may be that monopoly profits are both the reward and the source of finance, which then enable technological and organisational innovation. Thus some disadvantages have to be accepted in order to ensure a dynamic and innovative business sector.

Economic theory concludes that, all other things being equal, economic welfare is maximised when markets are competitive.

Government responses

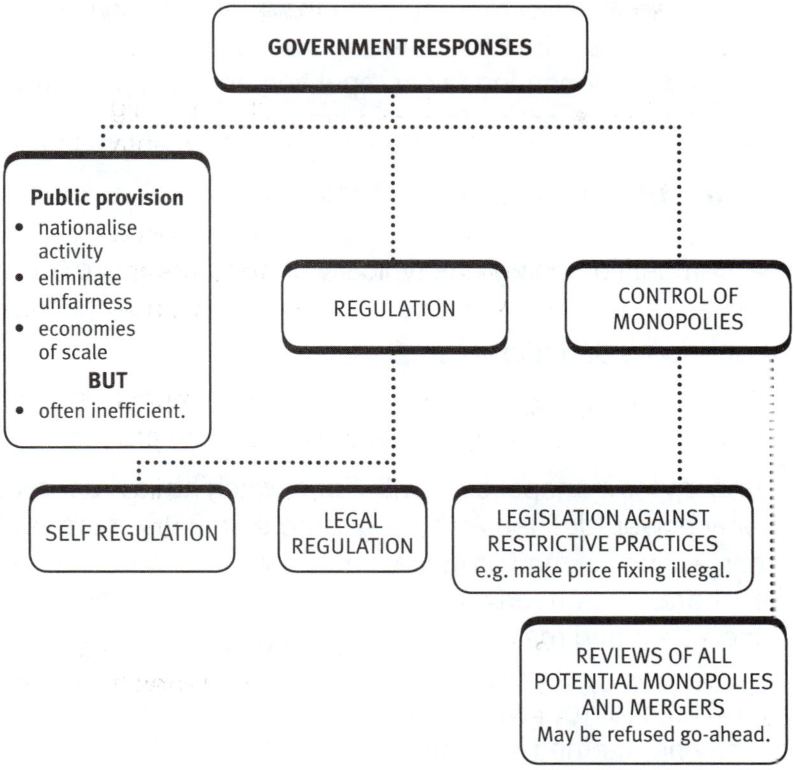

Fair competition: public provision and regulation

The response to the problems associated with monopoly power can take a variety of forms. The first of these is public provision. This is where an economic activity is nationalised. The advantages of this are as follows:

- unfair pricing practices and/or excessive prices can be eliminated
- cost advantages of economies of scale can be reaped.

Traditionally, public utilities have presented the most convincing case for nationalisation because they are natural monopolies. However, nationalised industries may have disadvantages, notably a greater potential for cost-inefficiency.

The alternative response to the dangers of monopoly is regulation.

Self-regulation is common in many professions where the profession itself establishes codes of conduct and rules of behaviour (e.g. the Law Society, the British Medical Association).

The alternative is some form of **public or legal regulation.** An example in the UK is the establishment of regulatory bodies for the privatised utilities such as OFTEL and OFGAS. These were established in recognition of the monopoly power of the privatised utilities and have a degree of power over both prices and services in these industries.

Another UK regulatory body is the Financial Services Authority (FSA) which has responsibility for regulating the financial services, banking and insurance markets. The FSA does not have to control monopolies, but it is concerned with ensuring fair competition and protecting the public against unfair treatment by financial organisations.

Fair competition: the control of monopoly

Formal competition policy has typically centred upon two broad issues.

- monopolies and mergers
- restrictive practices.

The concern for monopolies is with firms which have a degree of monopoly power (defined as having more than 25% of the market) or with mergers which may produce a new company with more than 25% of market share. The underlying presumption is that monopolies are likely to be inefficient and may act against the interests of customers.

The concern over restrictive practices is with trading practices of firms which may be deemed to be uncompetitive and act against the interests of consumers.

Legislation typically prohibits:

(a) anti-competitive agreements (such as price-fixing cartels); and

(b) abuse of a dominant position in a market.

Government assistance

The political and social objectives of a government, as well as its economic objectives, could be pursued through official aid intervention such as grants and subsidies. The government provides support to businesses both financially, in the form of grants, and through access to networks of expert advice and information.

For example to:

- boost enterprise
- encourage innovation

- speed urban renewal
- revive flagging industries
- train labour force
- sponsor important research.

There is always strong competition for the grants and the criteria for awards are stringent. These vary but are likely to include the location, size and industry sector of the business.

Green policies

When a firm appraises a project it may, rationally, only include those costs it will itself incur. However, for the good of society, external costs (such as damage to wildlife) need to be taken into account.

This has led to:

- green legislation
- punitive taxation on damaging practices

which force companies to consider the negative impacts of potential projects in any appraisals.

Externalities are costs (benefits) which are not paid (received) by the producers or consumers of the product but by other members of society.

The need for green policies arises from the existence of external environmental costs associated with some forms of production or consumption. An example of each is given below:

- production: river pollution from various manufacturing processes
- consumption: motor vehicle emissions causing air pollution and health hazards.

If external costs (and benefits) exist in the production or consumption process and if they are large in relation to private costs and benefits, the price system may be a poor mechanism for the allocation of resources. This is because private producers and consumers ignore (and indeed may be unaware of) the external effects of their activities.

Thus the price system, in which prices are determined by the interaction of supply and demand and which determines the allocation of resources, may lead to a misallocation of resources.

It is likely that policies to control damage to the environment will become more and more common as concern for the environment increases. Many countries already have a differential tax on leaded and unleaded petrol with governments taking the decision to use taxes to raise the real price of petrol each year. There is also a continuing debate in the EU over the possible introduction of a wider 'carbon tax'.

Externalities lead to a **misallocation of resources** and imply the need for policies to correct this. In particular, **green policies** are needed to tackle externalities that affect the **environment.**

Corporate governance

Corporate governance is defined as 'the system by which companies are directed and controlled' and covers issues such as ethics, risk management and stakeholder protection.

Regulation

Following the collapse of several large businesses and widespread concern about the standard of corporate governance across the business community, a new corporate governance framework was introduced.

A variety of rules have been introduced in different countries but the principles, common to all, contain regulations on:

- separation of the supervisory function and the management function
- transparency in the recruitment and remuneration of the board
- appointment of non-executive directors (NEDs)
- establishment of an audit committee and a remuneration committee
- establishment of risk control procedures to monitor strategic, business and operational activities.

Corporate governance was also discussed in the chapter on the financial management function.

Key issues in corporate governance

A further constraint on a company's activities is the system of corporate governance regulation which has been introduced to improve the standard of corporate governance in companies. The framework was introduced following a series of high profile international business collapses. There was widespread belief that the traditional systems with the board of directors responsible for a company and the auditors appointed by the shareholders but remunerated by the directors, was insufficient to control modern companies.

Governance reports, codes and legislation vary from country to country but typically cover the following:

- Membership of the board to achieve a suitable balance of power. The chairman and chief executive officer (CEO) should not be the same individual. There should be a sufficient number of non-executive directors on the board, and most of these should be independent.
- NEDs on the board should prevent the board from being dominated by the executive directors. The role of the NEDs is seen as critical in preventing a listed company from being run for the personal benefit of its senior executive directors.
- A remuneration committee to be established to decide on the remuneration of executive directors. Service contracts for directors should not normally exceed one year. There have also been efforts to give shareholders greater influence over directors' remuneration.
- The role of the audit committee of the board. This should consist of NEDs, and should work with the external auditors.
- The responsibility of the board of directors for monitoring all aspects of risk, not just the internal control system. For example, the Turnbull Committee was set up by the ICAEW to report on the risk management element of corporate governance.

The Turnbull report produced recommendations, and a risk report is now provided by listed companies in their annual report and accounts.

Audit committees

Many global listed companies now have an audit committee, or equivalent.

An audit committee:

- is a committee of the board of directors, normally three to five
- is made up of NEDs with no operating responsibility
- has a primary function to assist the board to fulfil its stewardship responsibilities by reviewing the:
  - systems of internal control
  - audit process
  - financial information which is provided to shareholders.

Test your understanding 1

The policies pursued by a government may serve various objectives.

Which of the following is not one of the principle objectives of macroeconomic policy?

A Economic growth

B Price stability

C Balance of payments surplus

D Full employment

Test your understanding 2

Which of the following statements is true?

Statement 1: Monetary policy seeks to regulate the economy by influencing such variables as the level of interest rates and conditions for availability of credit.

Statement 2: Fiscal policy seeks to influence the economy by managing the amounts which the government spends and the amounts it collects through taxation.

	Statement 1	*Statement 2*
A	True	True
B	True	False
C	False	True
D	False	False

Test your understanding 3

Which of the following statements is correct?

A A surplus budget occurs when total expenditure is less than total taxation income

B Indirect taxes include income tax, corporation tax and inheritance tax

C Direct taxes include VAT and excise duties

D Cost-push inflation might occur when excess aggregate monetary demand enables companies to raise prices and expand profit margins

Test your understanding 4

Which of the following is not a commonly cited factor which can influence the level of exchange rates?

A Comparative inflation rates

B Comparative interest rates

C Speculation

D Government borrowing

Test your understanding 5

What is the situation called where a firm has sufficient share of the market to enable it to restrict output and raise prices?

A Duopoly

B Oligopoly

C Monopoly

D Totopoly

Chapter summary

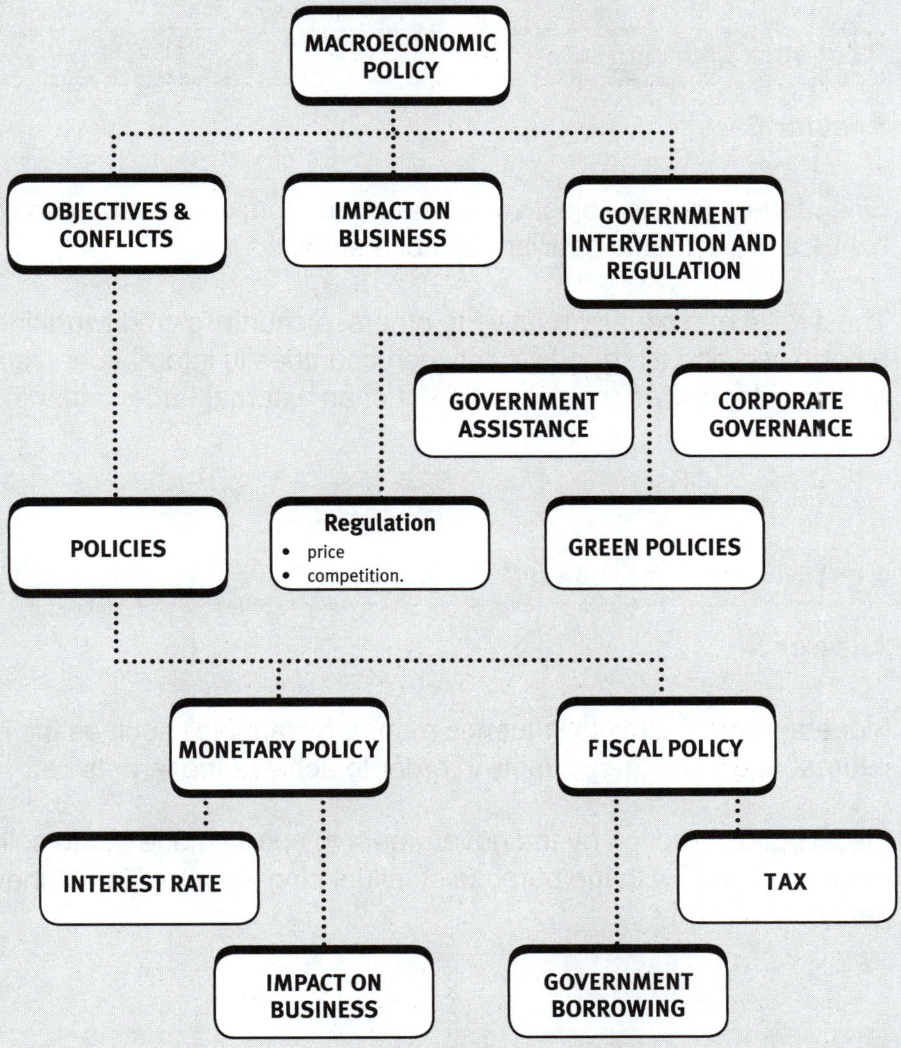

Test your understanding answers

Test your understanding 1

Answer C

One of the principle objectives of macroeconomic policy is to achieve a balance of payments equilibrium, not a surplus.

The wealth of a country relative to others, a country's creditworthiness as a borrower, and the goodwill between countries in international relations might all depend on the achievement of an external trade balance over time.

Test your understanding 2

Answer A

Monetary policy aims to influence monetary variables such as the rate of interest and the money supply in order to achieve the targets set.

Fiscal policy is action by the government to spend money or to collect money in taxes, with the purpose of influencing the condition of the national economy.

Test your understanding 3

Answer A

Direct taxes include income tax, corporation tax and inheritance tax (B).

Indirect taxes include VAT and excise duties (C).

Demand-pull inflation might occur when excess aggregate monetary demand in the economy and hence demand for particular goods and services enables companies to raise prices and expand profit margins.

Test your understanding 4

Answer D

The exchange rate between two currencies is determined primarily by supply and demand in the foreign exchange markets. Supply and demand in turn are subject to a number of influences such as the rate of inflation, compared with the rate of inflation in other countries (A); interest rates, compared with interest rates in other countries (B); and speculation (C).

Test your understanding 5

Answer C

chapter

12

Financial markets and the treasury function

Chapter learning objectives

Upon completion of this chapter you will be able to:

- identify the nature and role of capital markets, both nationally and internationally
- identify the nature and role of money markets, both nationally and internationally
- explain the role of financial intermediaries
- explain the main functions of a stock market
- explain the main functions of a corporate bond market
- describe the role of the money markets in providing short-term liquidity to industry and the public sector
- describe the role of the money markets in providing short-term trade finance
- describe the role of the money markets in allowing an organisation to manage its exposure to foreign currency and interest rate risk
- explain the role of the banks and other financial institutions in the operation of the money markets
- explain the characteristics of interest-bearing and discount instruments and their use in the money markets
- explain the characteristics of derivatives and their use in the money markets
- discuss the advantages and disadvantages of centralised treasury management and cash control

1 Introduction – the financial system

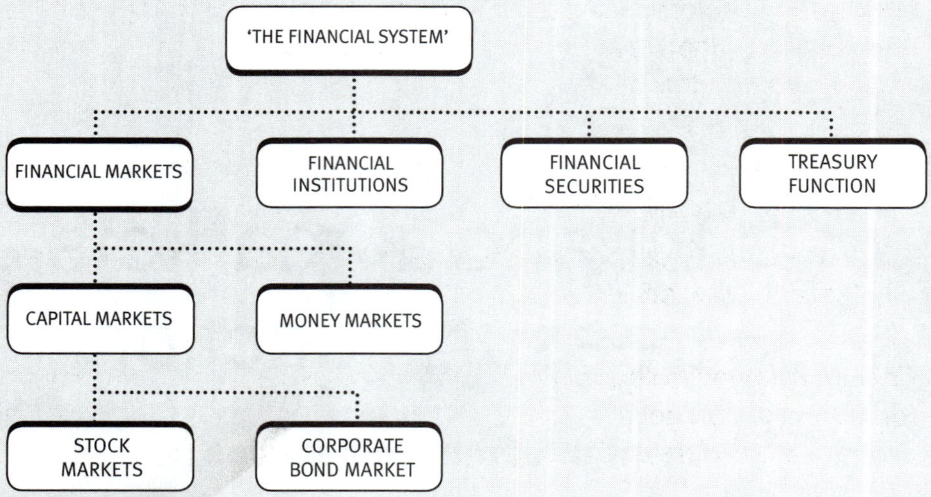

'The financial system' is an umbrella term covering the following:

- Financial markets – e.g. stock exchanges, money markets.
- Financial institutions – e.g. banks, building societies, insurance companies and pension funds.
- Financial securities – e.g. mortgages, bonds, bills and equity shares.

Collectively the financial system does the following:

(1) Channels funds from lenders to borrowers.

(2) Provides a mechanism for payments – e.g. direct debits, cheque clearing system.

(3) Creates liquidity and money – e.g. banks create money through increasing their lending.

(4) Provides financial services such as insurance and pensions.

(5) Offers facilities to manage investment portfolios – e.g. to hedge risk.

The term **security** is a generic term for a medium of investment, for example, a share, a corporate bond or a money market instrument (see later for a definition of this). Many securities are traded on a market.

For every security there is a buyer (the investor who is providing the finance) and a seller (the receivor of the finance).

Some examples would be an individual (the buyer) investing in the shares (the security) of a listed company (the seller) or a bank (the buyer) investing in some treasury bills (the security) issued by the government (the seller).

2 The role of financial markets

Within each sector of the economy (households, firms and governmental organisations) there are times when there are cash surpluses and times when there are deficits.

- In the case of surpluses the party concerned will seek to invest/deposit/lend funds to earn an economic return.
- In the case of deficits the party will seek to borrow funds to manage their liquidity position.

The financial markets are mechanisms where those requiring finance (deficit units) can get in touch with those able to supply it (surplus units), i.e. allowing the buyers and sellers of finance to get together.

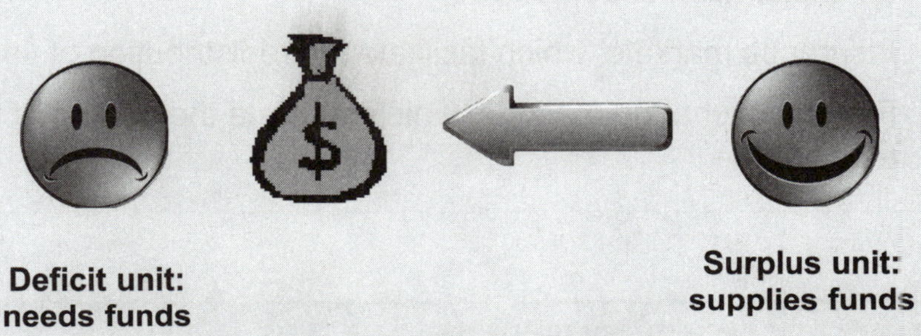

There are two main types of financial market: capital and money markets, and within each of these are primary and secondary markets:

Primary market – deals in new securities

Secondary market – deals in 'second-hand' securities

Details of financial markets

The financial markets can be divided into different types, depending on the products being issued/bought/sold:

- Capital markets which consist of stock-markets for shares and bond markets.
- Money markets, which provide short-term (< 1 year) debt financing and investment.
- Commodity markets, which facilitate the trading of commodities (e.g. oil, metals and agricultural produce).
- Derivatives markets, which provide instruments for the management of financial risk, such as options and futures contracts (see later for an explanation of derivatives).
- Insurance markets, which facilitate the redistribution of various risks.
- Foreign exchange markets, which facilitate the trading of foreign exchange.

Primary and secondary markets

Primary markets provide a focal point for borrowers and lenders to meet. The forces of supply and demand should ensure that funds find their way to their most productive usage. Primary markets deal in new issues of loanable funds. They raise new finance for the deficit units.

Secondary markets allow holders of financial claims (surplus units) to realise their investments before the maturity date by selling them to other investors. They therefore increase the willingness of surplus units to invest their funds. A well-developed secondary market should also reduce the price volatility of securities, as regular trading in 'second-hand' securities should ensure smoother price changes. This should further encourage investors to supply funds.

Secondary markets help investors achieve the following ends.

(a) **Diversification**

By giving investors the opportunity to invest in a wide range of enterprises, it allows them to spread their risk. This is the familiar 'Don't put all your eggs in one basket' strategy.

(b) **Risk shifting**

Deficit units, particularly companies, issue various types of security on the financial markets to give investors a choice of the degree of risk they take. For example company loan stocks secured on the assets of the business offer low risk with relatively low returns, whereas equities carry much higher risk with correspondingly higher returns.

(c) **Hedging**

Financial markets offer participants the opportunity to reduce risk through hedging, which involves taking out counterbalancing contracts to offset existing risks, e.g. if a UK exporter is awaiting payment in euros from a French customer he is subject to the risk that the euro may decline in value over the credit period. To hedge this risk he could enter a counterbalancing contract and arrange to sell the euros forward (agree to exchange them for pounds at a fixed future date at a fixed exchange rate). In this way he has used the foreign exchange market to insure his future sterling receipt. Similar hedging possibilities are available on interest rates (see chapter 14).

(d) **Arbitrage**

Arbitrage is the process of buying a security at a low price in one market and simultaneously selling in another market at a higher price to make a profit.

Although it is only the primary markets that raise new funds for deficit units, well-developed secondary markets are required to fulfil the above roles for lenders and borrowers. Without these opportunities more surplus units would be tempted to keep their funds 'under the bed' rather than putting them at the disposal of deficit units.

However, the emergence of disintermediation (reduction in the use of intermediaries) and securitisation (conversion into marketable securities), where companies lend and borrow funds directly between themselves, has provided a further means of dealing with cash flow surpluses and deficits.

Division of sources of finance

For the deficit units (those requiring finance), the source of finance can be divided between short- and long-term:

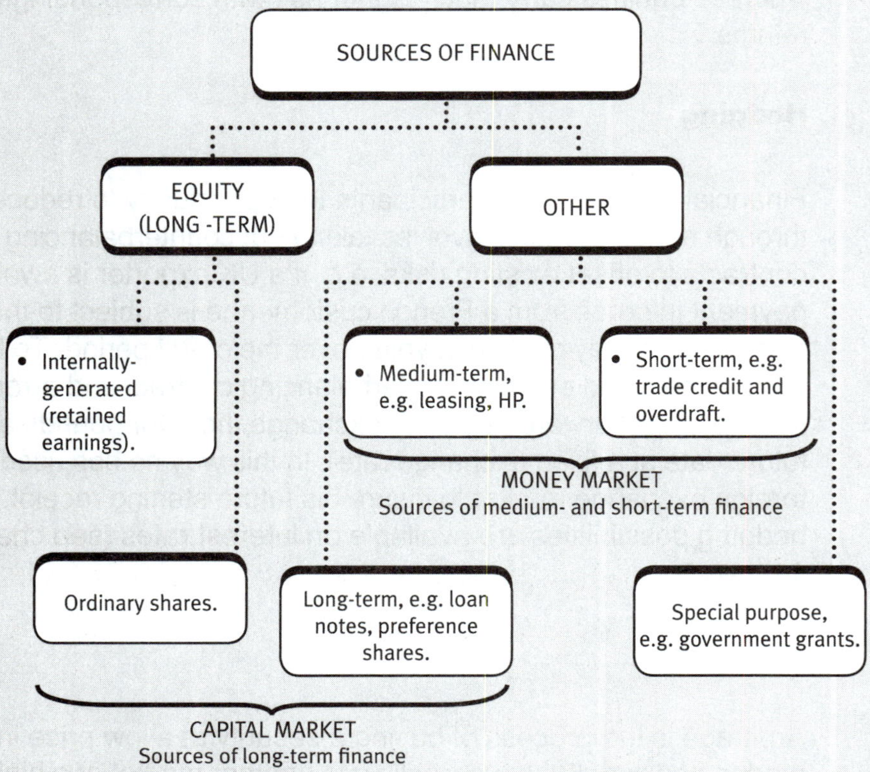

Durations of each are roughly:

Short-term	up to one year.
Medium-term	1–7 years
Long-term	7 years or more

As you can see from the above diagram, which financial market the deficit unit will need will depend on the duration of the funds required.

Equally, for the surplus unit (the provider of finance / investor), which market they deal in will depend on how long they are willing to invest for.

The money markets

Money markets deal in short-term funds and transactions are conducted by phone or telex. It is not one single market but a number of closely-connected markets.

Participants include

- central banks
- finance houses
- building societies
- unit trusts
- large companies
- private individuals
- local authorities
- investment trusts
- commercial banks

All the markets in a money market closely inter-mesh with each other and in that way the market may be regarded as an entity. The players are the same and they pass the ball between each other.

However, since the global "credit crunch" of 2008, the liquidity in the money markets has reduced as the different players have begun to view each other with suspicion.

e.g

Illustration 1

- A large company might deposit \$500,000 with Bull's Bank, which issues it with a Certificate of Deposit (CD).
- Bull's Bank then looks at the local authority market, decides that rates there are rather low, and instead lends the money for a week on the inter-bank market to another bank that is short of funds.
- A week later local authority rates have improved and Bull's Bank lends the \$500,000 to a big city council.
- Meanwhile, the large company has decided to bring forward an investment project and wants its \$500,000 quickly to help pay for some sophisticated new electronic equipment. It sells the CD to a bank, which might either carry it to maturity or sell it to any of the banks – except Bull's Bank.

All these transactions, with the possible exception of the CD deals, will have taken place through a broker who sits at the end of a telephone switching the funds from one market to another as rates move and potential borrowers and lenders acquaint the broker with information about their requirements.

Money markets play a key role in:

- providing short-term liquidity to companies, banks and the public sector (see expandable text below)
- providing short-term trade finance (see expandable text below)
- allowing an organisation to manage its exposure to foreign currency risk and interest rate risk (see chapters on foreign exchange and interest rate risk)

Money markets: Providing short-term liquidity to the private

Companies

- For many companies bank borrowing is the simplest method of short-term finance.
  - Loans are usually fixed term, may be for variable or fixed rates and are normally secured, overdrafts variable rate and unsecured.
  - Rates will depend on perceived credit risk.
- Factoring can be useful where sales are made to low risk customers.
- Companies with high credit ratings often take advantage of commercial paper markets, where they may be able to borrow at lower rates than those offered by banks.

Banks

- Banks participate in 'inter-bank markets', either lending to other banks, or borrowing from them. Recently they have been joined by the larger building societies.
- This is a very important source of funds to banks. For example, the London Inter-Bank Offered Rate (or LIBOR) is now used instead of base rate to determine the interest payable on some types of company borrowing.

Local authorities

Local authorities obtain their borrowing requirements from:

- central government and money markets
- stock exchanges, and
- from advertising for loans from the general public.

Money markets: Providing short-term trade finance

As well as having routine cash surpluses /deficits that need managing, firms often need short-term finance for individual (usually large) trade deals. A supplier faces two problems in such cases:

- Default risk from the customer.
- The time delay between cash outflows to make the product and receipt of payment.

The most common way of managing these is by using banker's acceptances by creating a 'letter of credit'.

Letter of credit illustration

Step 1 Initial trade deal

- Company A agrees to buy goods from Company B for $10 million (say), payable in 30 days' time.

Step 2 Create letter of credit (LOC)

- Co. A agrees payment terms with their bank (Bank A).
- Bank A issues Co. B's bank (Bank B) with a letter of credit, stating that it will pay the $10m in 30 days.
- Bank B informs Company B of the receipt.

Step 3 Supply of goods

- Co. B then ships the goods to Co. A.
- Co. B passes shipping and other necessary documents to Bank B.

Step 4 Create banker's acceptance

- Bank B passes the letter of credit and supporting documentation back to Bank A.
- If all is in order, Bank A 'accepts' the letter of credit, accepting responsibility for payment. This creates the 'banker's acceptance', which is passed back to Bank B.

Step 5 Options for using the banker's acceptance.

Bank B could:

- wait until payment in 30 days
- request immediate payment (of the discounted value) from Bank A – effectively selling it back to Bank A
- sell the acceptance (at its discounted value) to the money markets.

Step 6 Banker's acceptance redeemed

- After 30 days Bank A redeems the acceptance, paying the then holder.

The capital markets

Capital markets deal in longer-term finance, mainly via a stock exchange.

The major types of securities dealt on capital markets are as follows:

- public sector and foreign stocks
- company securities (shares and corporate bonds)
- Eurobonds.

Eurobonds are bonds denominated in a currency other than that of the national currency of the issuing company (nothing to do with Europe or the Euro!). They are also called international bonds.

International capital markets

An international financial market exists where domestic funds are supplied to a foreign user or foreign funds are supplied to a domestic user. The currencies used need not be those of either the lender or the borrower.

International capital markets

The most important international markets are:

- the Euromarkets
- the foreign bond markets.

Eurocurrency is money deposited with a bank outside its country of origin, e.g. money in a US dollar account with a bank in London is Eurodollars.

Note that these deposits need not be with European banks, although originally most of them were.

Once in receipt of these Eurodeposits, banks then lend them to other customers and a Euromarket in the currency is created.

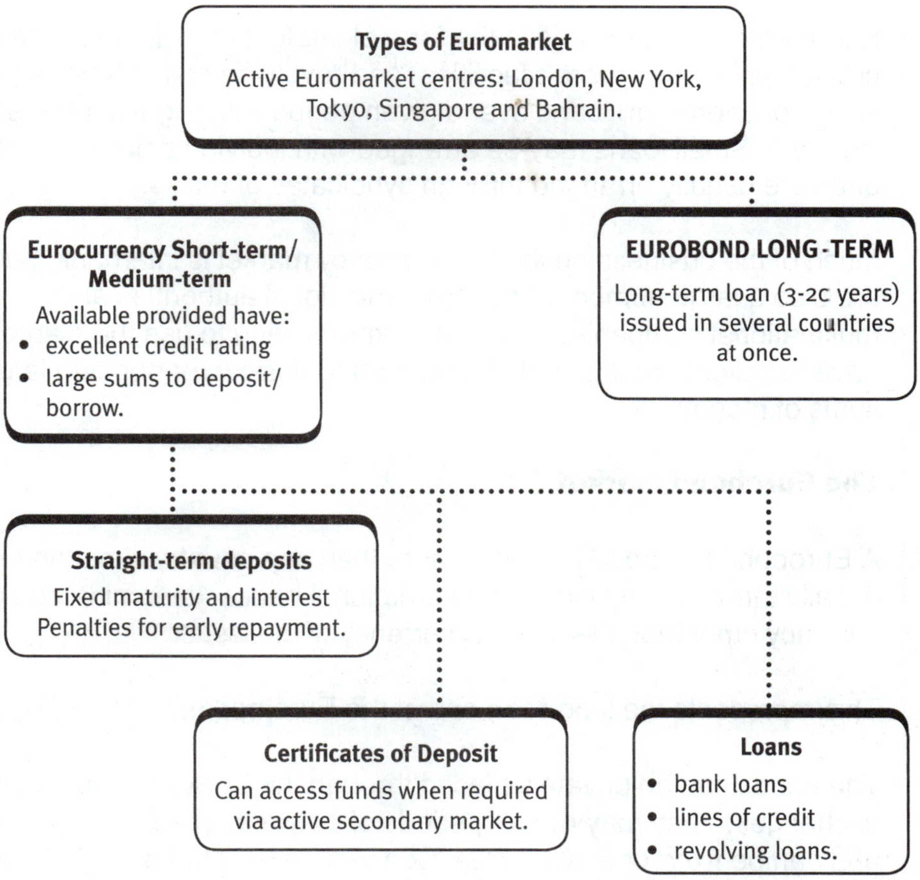

The Eurocurrency market

This incorporates the short- to medium-term end of the Euromarket. It is a market for borrowing and lending Eurocurrencies. Various types of deposits and loans are available.

Deposits vary from overnight to five years. Deposits can be in the form of straight-term deposits, with funds placed in a bank for a fixed maturity at a fixed interest rate. However, these carry the problem of interest rate penalties if early repayment is required.

Alternatively, deposits can be made in the form of negotiable Certificates of Deposit (CDs). There is an active secondary market in CDs and investors are therefore able to have access to their funds when required. Deposits can be made in individual currencies or in the form of 'currency cocktails' to allow depositors to take a diversified currency position. One common cocktail is the Special Drawing Right, consisting of US dollars, yen, Euros and sterling.

Euromarket loans may be in the form of straight bank loans, lines of credit (similar to overdraft facilities) and revolving commitments (a series of short-term loans over a given period with regular interest rate reviews). Small loans may be arranged with individual banks, but larger ones are usually arranged through syndicates of banks.

Much of the business on the Eurocurrency market is interbank, but there are also a large number of governments, local authorities and multinational companies involved. Firms wishing to use the market must have excellent credit standing and wish to borrow (or deposit) large sums of money.

The Eurobond market

A Eurobond is a bond issued in more than one country simultaneously, usually through a syndicate of international banks, denominated in a currency other than the national currency of the issuer.

This represents the long-term end of the Euromarket.

The bonds can be privately placed through the banks or quoted on stock exchanges. They may run for periods of between three and 20 years, and can be fixed or floating rate. Convertible Eurobonds (similar to domestic convertible loan stocks) and Option Eurobonds (giving the holder the option to switch currencies for repayment and interest) are also used.

The major borrowers are large companies, international institutions like the World Bank, and the EC. The most common currencies are the US dollar, the Euro, the Swiss franc, and to a lesser extent sterling.

Stock markets and Corporate bond markets

The syllabus does not require you to have a detailed knowledge of any specific country's stock market or securities exchanges. We may, however, make reference to the markets that operate in the UK for illustration purposes.

The role of the stock market is to:

- facilitate trade in stocks such as:
  - issued shares of public companies
  - corporate bonds
  - government bonds
  - local authority loans.
- allocate capital to industry
- determine a fair price for the assets traded.

Speculative trading on the market can assist by:

- smoothing price fluctuations
- ensuring shares are readily marketable.

Market-makers:

- maintain stocks of securities in a number of quoted companies
- continually quote prices for buying and prices for selling the securities (bid and offer prices)
- generate income by the profits they make from the difference (or 'spread') between the bid and offer prices.

Countries may have more than one stock market. In the UK there are three:

(1) London Stock Exchange – main market

(2) Alternative Investment Market (AIM) – for smaller companies

(3) Ofex (off exchange) – trade via specialist brokers.

Stock markets

A country's stock market is the institution that embodies many of the processes of the capital market. Essentially it is the market for the issued securities of public companies, government bonds, loans issued by local authority and other publicly-owned institutions, and some overseas stocks. Without the ability to sell long-term securities easily, few people would be prepared to risk making their money available to business or public authorities.

A stock market assists the allocation of capital to industry; if the market thinks highly of a company, that company's shares will rise in value and it will be able to raise fresh capital through the new issue market at relatively low cost. On the other hand, less popular companies will have difficulty in raising new capital. Thus, successful firms are helped to grow and the unsuccessful will contract.

The role of speculation

Any consideration of a stock market has to face up to the problem of speculation, i.e. gambling. It is suggested that speculation can perform the following functions:

It smoothes price fluctuations. Speculators, to be successful, have to be a little ahead of the rest of the market. The skilled speculator will be buying when others are still selling and selling when others are still buying. The speculator, therefore, removes the peaks and troughs of inevitable price fluctuations and so makes price changes less violent.

Speculation ensures that shares are readily marketable. Almost all stock can be quickly bought and sold, at a price. Without the chance of profit there would be no professional operator willing to hold stock or agree to sell stock that is not immediately available. The fact that there are always buyers and sellers is of considerable importance to the ordinary individual investor, who may have to sell unexpectedly at any time with little warning.

Stock markets help in the determination of a fair price for assets, and ensure that assets are readily marketable.

Buying and selling shares or loan notes

An investor will contact a broker in order to buy and sell securities. The broker may act as agent for the investor by contacting a market-maker (see below) or he may act as principal if he makes a market in them himself (i.e. buys and sells on his own behalf). In the latter case he is a broker-dealer.

Trading via a broker-dealer

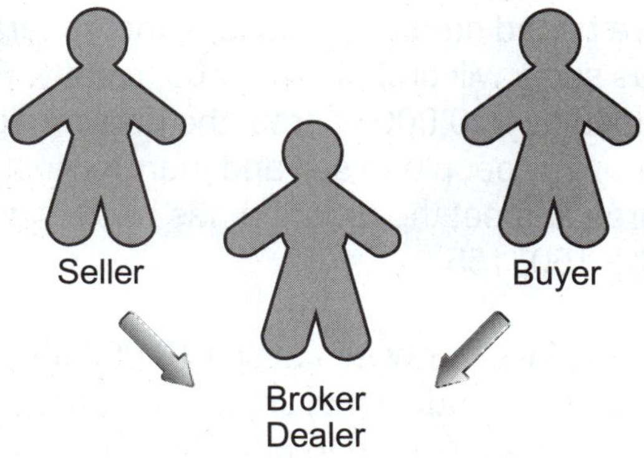

Trading via a broker and a market-maker

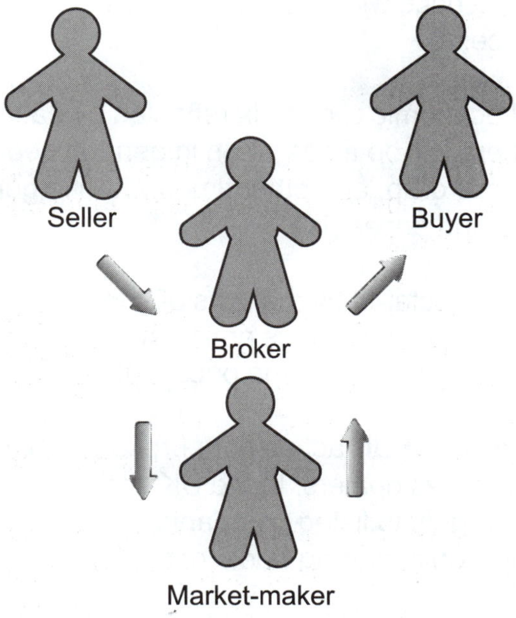

Market-makers maintain stocks of securities in a number of quoted companies, appropriate to the level of trading in that security, and their income is generated by the profits they make by dealing in securities. A market-maker undertakes to maintain an active market in shares that it trades, by continually quoting prices for buying and prices for selling (bid and offer prices).

If security prices didn't move, their profits would come from the difference (or 'spread') between the bid and offer prices. This profit is approximately represented by the difference between the 'bid' and 'offered' price for a given security – the price at which a market-maker is prepared to buy the stock and the price at which he would be prepared to sell it.

For example, assume a quotation in respect of the shares of a fictitious company, Clynch Co.

The dealer might quote 145, 150.

This means he will buy the shares at $1.45 each and sell at $1.50 each.

Quotations are based on expectations of the general marketability of the shares and, as such, will probably vary constantly. For example, if an investor wants to buy 10,000 shares, the dealer might decide to raise his prices to encourage people to sell and thereby ensure that he will have sufficient shares to meet the order he has just received. Thus, his next quote might be 150, 155.

Conversely, if the investor wants to sell 10,000 shares, the dealer will be left with that number of additional shares, and he may wish to reduce his quotation to encourage people to buy; thus he may quote 140, 145.

If sufficient numbers of people wish to buy and sell the shares of Clynch Co, eventually a price will be found at which only marginal transactions are taking place.

If the general economic climate is reflected by each company's shares, it follows that there will be times when in general people wish to sell shares and hence prices drop, and other times when in general people are buying shares and prices rise.

Share prices are dictated by the laws of supply and demand. If the future return/risk profile of the share is anticipated to improve, the demand for that share will be greater and the price higher.

Broker-dealers in the UK act as both brokers for clients and trade on their own account as dealers. In the UK, their activities in share dealing are restricted largely to listed companies whose shares are traded on SETS, the electronic 'trading book' of the London Stock Exchange.

Types of stock market

A country may have more than one securities market in operation. For illustration, the UK has the following:

The London Stock Exchange – the main UK market for securities, on which the shares of large public companies are quoted and dealt. Costs of meeting entry requirements and reporting regulations are high.

The AIM – a separate market for the securities of smaller companies. Entry and reporting requirements are significantly less than those for the main market of the London Stock Exchange.

An 'Ofex' (off exchange) market in which shares in some public companies are traded, but through a specialist firm of brokers and not through a stock exchange.

3 The role of financial institutions

Faced with a desire to lend or borrow, there are three choices open to the end-users of the financial system:

(1) Lenders and borrowers contact each other directly.

This is rare due to the high costs involved, the risks of default and the inherent inefficiencies of this approach.

(2) Lenders and borrowers use an organised financial market.

For example, an individual may purchase corporate bonds from a recognised bond market. If this is a new issue of bonds by a company looking to raise funds, then the individual has effectively lent money to the company.

If the individual wishes to recover their funds before the redemption date on the bond, then they can sell the bond to another investor.

(3) Lenders and borrowers use financial institutions as intermediaries.

In this case the lender obtains an asset which cannot usually be traded but only returned to the intermediary. Such assets could include a bank deposit account, pension fund rights, etc.

The borrower will typically have a loan provided by an intermediary.

Intermediation refers to the process whereby potential borrowers are brought together with potential lenders by a third party, the intermediary.

Financial intermediaries have a number of important roles.

- Risk reduction
- Aggregation
- Maturity transformation
- Financial intermediation

Intermediaries: What they do

Risk reduction

By lending to a wide variety of individuals and businesses financial intermediaries reduce the risk of a single default resulting in total loss of assets.

Aggregation

By pooling many small deposits, financial intermediaries are able to make much larger advances than would be possible for most individuals.

Maturity transformation

Most borrowers wish to borrow in the long term whilst most savers are unwilling to lock up their money for the long term. Financial intermediaries, by developing a floating pool of deposits, are able to satisfy both the needs of lenders and borrowers.

Financial intermediation

Financial intermediaries bring together lenders and borrowers through a process known as financial intermediation.

There are many types of institutions and other organisations that act as intermediaries in matching firms and individuals who need finance with those who wish to invest.

Intermediaries: Who they are

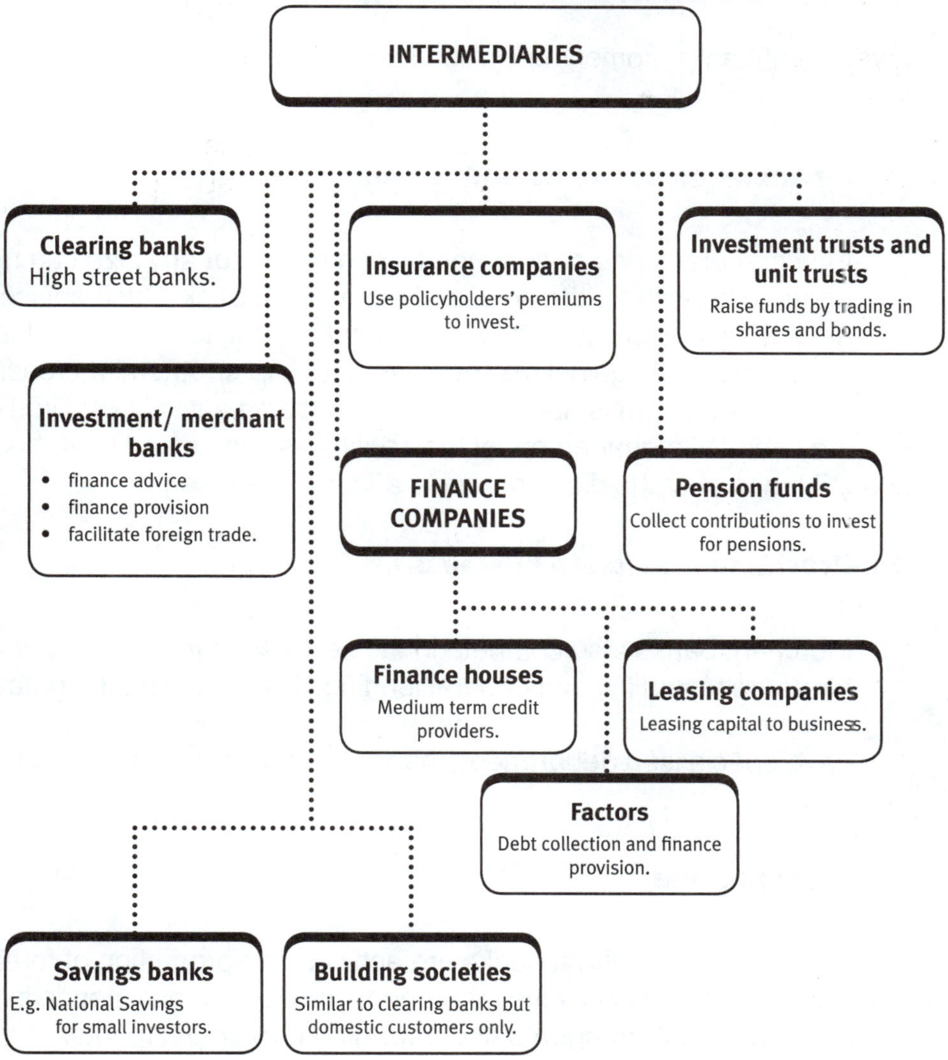

Clearing banks

The familiar high street banks provide a payment and cheque clearing mechanism. They offer various accounts to investors and provide large amounts of short- to medium-term loans to the business sector and the personal sector. They also offer a wide range of financial services to their customers.

Investment banks

Investment banks, sometimes called merchant banks, concentrate on the following.

(a) **Financial advice to business firms**

Few manufacturing or commercial companies of any size can now afford to be without the advice of a merchant bank. Such advice is necessary in order to obtain investment capital, to invest surplus funds, to guard against takeover, or to take over others. Increasingly, the merchant banks have themselves become actively involved in the financial management of their business clients and have had an influence over the direction these affairs have taken.

(b) **Providing finance to business**

Merchant banks also compete in the services of leasing, factoring, hire-purchase (HP) and general lending. They are also the gateway to the capital market for long-term funds because they are likely to have specialised departments handling capital issues as 'issuing houses'.

(c) **Foreign trade**

A number of merchant banks are active in the promotion of foreign trade by providing marine insurance, credits, and assistance in appointing foreign agents and arranging foreign payments.

Not all merchant banks are large and not all offer a wide range of services: the term is now rather misused. However, it is expected that a merchant bank will operate without the large branch network necessary for a clearing bank. It will work closely with its business clients, and will be more ready to take business risks and promote business enterprise than a clearing bank. It is probably fair to say that a merchant bank is essentially in the general business of creating wealth and of helping those who show that they are capable of successful business enterprise.

Savings banks

Public sector savings banks (e.g. the National Savings Bank in the UK) are used to collect funds from the small personal saver, which are then mainly invested in government securities.

Building societies

These take deposits from the household sector and lend to individuals buying their own homes. They also provide many of the services offered by the clearing banks. They are not involved, however, in providing funds for the business sector. Over recent years, many have converted to banks.

Finance companies

These come in three main varieties:

(a) Finance houses, providing medium-term instalment credit to the business and personal sector. These are usually owned by business sector firms or by other financial intermediaries. The trend is toward them offering services similar to the clearing banks.

(b) Leasing companies, leasing capital equipment to the business sector. They are usually subsidiaries of other financial institutions.

(c) Factoring companies, providing loans to companies secured on trade debtors, are usually bank subsidiaries. Other debt collection and credit control services are generally on offer.

Pension funds

These collect funds from employers and employees to provide pensions on retirement or death. As their outgoings are relatively predictable they can afford to invest funds for long periods of time.

Insurance companies

These use premium income from policyholders to invest mainly in long-term assets such as bonds, equities and property. Their outgoings from their long-term business (life assurance and pensions) and their short-term activities (fire, accident, motor insurance, etc.) are once again relatively predictable and therefore they can afford to tie up a large proportion of their funds for a long period of time.

Investment trusts and unit trusts

Investment trusts are limited liability companies collecting funds by selling shares and bonds and investing the proceeds, mainly in the ordinary shares of other companies. Funds at their disposal are limited to the amount of securities in issue plus retained profits, and hence they are often referred to as 'closed end funds'. Unit trusts on the other hand, although investing in a similar way, find that their funds vary according to whether investors are buying new units or cashing in old ones. Both offer substantial diversification opportunities to the personal investor.

4 Money market instruments

A money market instrument is a type of security that is traded in the money market.

A financial manager needs to understand the characteristics of the following money market instruments:

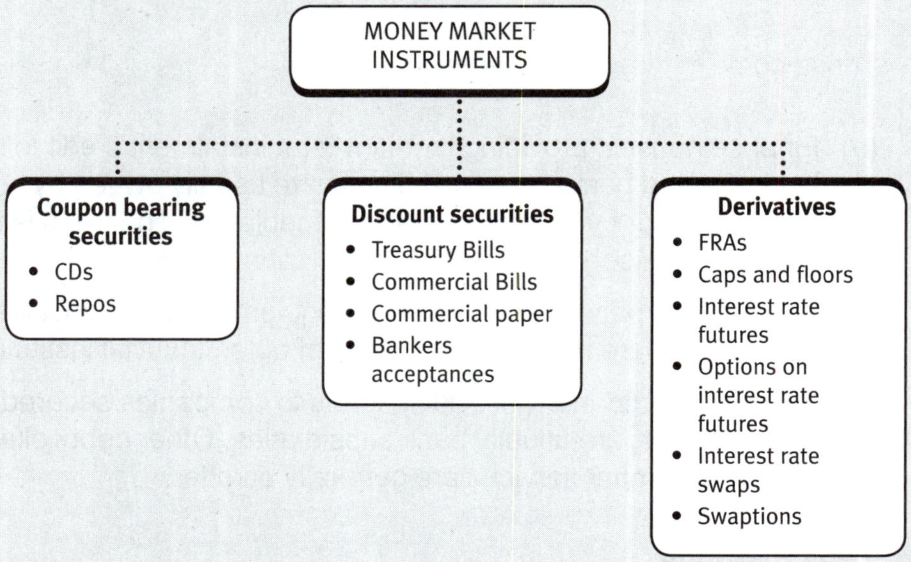

Coupon bearing instruments

Coupon bearing securities have a fixed maturity and a specified rate of interest.

Certificates of deposit (CDs)

- CDs are evidence of a deposit with an issuing bank (or building society).
- They are fully negotiable and hence attractive to the depositor since they ensure instant liquidity if required.
- They provide the bank with a deposit for a fixed period at a fixed rate of interest.

Sale and repurchase agreements ('repos')

- In a repo transaction, X sells certain securities (treasury bills, bank bills etc) to Y and simultaneously agrees to buy them back at a later date at a higher price.

- This could be arranged through the repo desk of a major bank, for example.
- In effect, a repo is a secured short-term loan and the higher repurchase price reflects the interest on the loan.
- Central banks often fix the short-term repo interest rate, which in turn affects all other short-term interest rates (e.g. base rates, LIBOR).

Illustration of repos

Reaper Co enters a repo agreement as follows:

(1) Sell £4 million (nominal) UK Treasury Bills for £3.94 million.

(2) Buy them back 45 days later for £3.96 million.

Determine the effective interest rate.

Solution

Interest rate = ((3.96 – 3.94)/(3.94)) × 365/45 = 0.0411, or 4.11%

This could be compared with the borrowing rate offered by banks, for example.

Note: In some areas, notably the USA, a 360 day count is used instead of 365.

Discount instruments

In the discount market, funds are raised by issuing bills at a discount to their eventual redemption or maturity value.

Bills have the following characteristics:

- Issued in large denominations.
- Highly liquid – due to short maturity and highly organised market for buying/selling.
- Reward for the lender comes as a capital gain.
- Effectively fixed-interest as redemption value fixed.

Treasury bills

- Issued mainly by governments via central banks.
- Usually one or three month maturity.

Commercial bills

- Similar to treasury bills except issued by large corporations.

Commercial paper

- Initial maturity usually between seven and forty-five days.
- May be unsecured so credit ratings important.
- High issue costs so only suitable for larger amounts.

Banker's acceptances

- These are discussed in more detail below under trade finance.

Illustration of commercial paper

CP Co wishes to issue $10 million of commercial paper for 90 days at an implicit interest rate of 5% pa.

(**Note:** this could be expressed as stating that the paper will be issued 'at a discount of 5%'.)

Determine the issue price.

Solution

Issue price = present value of future redemption

= $10m × 1/(1 + 0.05 × 90/365) = $9,878,213

Derivatives

- A derivative is an asset whose performance (and hence value) is derived from the behaviour of the value of an underlying asset (the 'underlying').
- The most common underlyings are commodities (e.g. tea, pork bellies), shares, bonds, share indices, currencies and interest rates.
- Derivatives are contracts that give the right and sometimes the obligation, to buy or sell a quantity of the underlying or benefit in some other way from a rise or fall in the value of the underlying.

- Derivatives include the following:
  - Forwards.
  - Forward rate agreements ('FRAs').
  - Futures.
  - Options.
  - Swaps.
- Forwards, FRAs and futures effectively fix a future price. Options give you the right without the obligation to fix a future price.
- The legal right is an asset with its own value that can be bought or sold.
- Derivatives are not fixed in volume of supply like normal equity or bond markets. Their existence and creation depends on the existence of counterparties, market participants willing to take alternative views on the outcome of the same event.
- Some derivatives (esp. futures and options) are traded on exchanges where contracts are standardised and completion guaranteed by the exchange. Such contracts will have values and prices quoted. Exchange-traded instruments are of a standard size thus ensuring that they are marketable.
- Other transactions are over the counter ('OTC'), where a financial intermediary puts together a product tailored precisely to the needs of the client. It is here where valuation issues and credit risk may arise.

Specific details of some of the above instruments are discussed in more detail within the foreign exchange and interest rate risk chapters.

The role of money market instruments for short term financing

While some firms encounter a mixture of short-term cash surpluses and deficits, many can be classified as either cash generators or cash consumers.

- Cash generators (e.g. many retailers) will look to lay off cash on short-term markets or return surplus funds to investors (e.g. via a dividend).
- Cash consumers (e.g. young, fast growing firms) will look to borrow short-term.

Test your understanding 1

By considering the product lifecycle, comment as to whether a major drugs company is likely to be a cash generator or a cash consumer?

Test your understanding 2

What do you consider to be the key factors to consider when choosing which instruments to use?

5 The role of the treasury function

The treasury function of a firm usually has the following roles:

Short-term management of resources

- Short-term cash management – lending/borrowing funds as required.
- Currency management.

Long-term maximisation of shareholder wealth

- Raising long-term finance, including equity strategy, management of debt capacity and debt and equity structure.
- Investment decisions, including investment appraisal, the review of acquisitions and divestments and defence from takeover.
- Dividend policy.

Risk management

- Assessing risk exposure.
- Interest rate risk management.
- Hedging of foreign exchange risk.

Many larger organisations will often operate a separate treasury department, separate from the finance department. In smaller companies though, the treasury function will form part of the responsibilities of the finance team.

Treasury management

All treasury management activities are concerned with managing the liquidity of a business, the importance of which to the survival and growth of a business cannot be over-emphasised.

Why have a treasury department?

The functions carried out by the treasurer have always existed, but have been absorbed historically within other finance functions. A number of reasons may be identified for the modern development of separate treasury departments:

- size and internationalisation of companies: these factors add to both the scale and the complexity of the treasury functions
- size and internationalisation of currency, debt and security markets: these make the operations of raising finance, handling transactions in multiple currencies and investing, much more complex. They also present opportunities for greater gains
- sophistication of business practice: this process has been aided by modern communications, and as a result the treasurer is expected to take advantage of opportunities for making profits or minimising costs which did not exist a few years ago.

For these reasons, most large international corporations have moved towards setting up a separate treasury department.

Treasury departments tend to rely heavily on new technology for information.

Treasury responsibilities

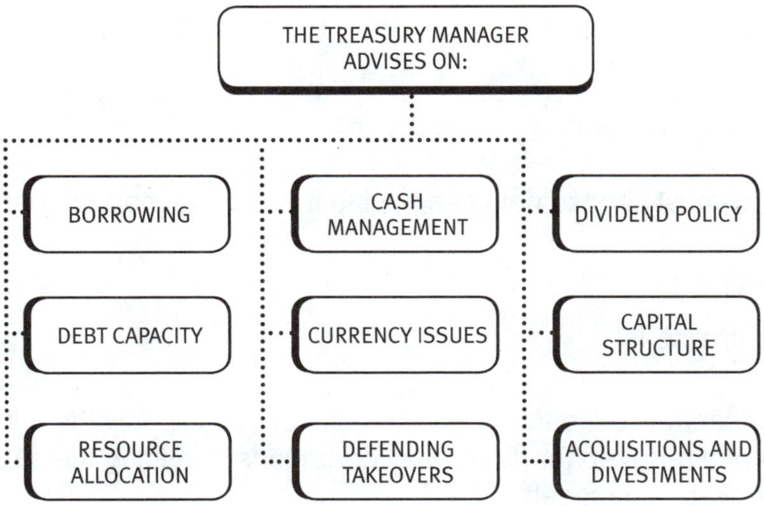

The treasurer will generally report to the finance director (financial manager), with a specific emphasis on borrowing and cash and currency management. The treasurer will have a direct input into the finance director's management of debt capacity, debt and equity structure, resource allocation, equity strategy and currency strategy.

The treasurer will be involved in investment appraisal, and the finance director will often consult the treasurer in matters relating to the review of acquisitions and divestments, dividend policy and defence from takeover.

Treasury departments are not large, since they are not involved in the detailed recording of transactions.

The international treasury function

The corporate treasurer in an international group of companies will be faced with problems relating specifically to the international spread of investments.

- Setting transfer prices to reduce the overall tax bill.
- Deciding currency exposure policies and procedures.
- Transferring of cash across international borders.
- Devising investment strategies for short-term funds from the range of international money markets and international marketable securities.
- Netting and matching currency obligations.

Test your understanding 3

Compare and contrast the roles of the treasury and finance departments with respect to a proposed investment.

The case for centralising treasury management

A company must choose between having its treasury management:

- centralised
- decentralised

If they are centralised, each operating company holds only the minimum cash balance required for day-to-day operations, remitting the surplus to the centre for overall management.

If they are decentralised, each operating company must appoint an officer responsible for that company's own treasury operations.

The centralisation of treasury activities

The question arises in a large international group of whether treasury activities should be centralised or decentralised.

- If centralised, then each operating company holds only the minimum cash balance required for day to day operations, remitting the surplus to the centre for overall management. This process is sometimes known as cash pooling, the pool usually being held in a major financial centre or a tax haven country.
- If decentralised, each operating company must appoint an officer responsible for that company's own treasury operations.

Advantages of centralisation

- No need for treasury skills to be duplicated throughout the group. One highly trained central department can assemble a highly skilled team, offering skills that could not be available if every company had their own treasury.
- Necessary borrowings can be arranged in bulk, at keener interest rates than for smaller amounts. Similarly bulk deposits of surplus funds will attract higher rates of interest than smaller amounts.
- The group's foreign currency risk can be managed much more effectively from a centralised treasury since only they can appreciate the total exposure situation. A total hedging policy is more efficiently carried out by head office rather than each company doing their own hedging.
- One company does not borrow at high rates while another has idle cash.
- Bank charges should be lower since a situation of carrying both balances and overdraft in the same currency should be eliminated.
- A centralised treasury can be run as a profit centre to raise additional profits for the group.
- Transfer prices can be established to minimise the overall group tax bill.
- Funds can be quickly returned to companies requiring cash via direct transfers.

Advantages of decentralisation

- Greater autonomy leads to greater motivation. Individual companies will manage their cash balances more attentively if they are responsible for them rather than simply remitting them up to head office.
- Local operating units should have a better feel for local conditions than head office and can respond more quickly to local developments.

Test your understanding 4

Which of the following is least likely to be a reason for seeking a stock market listing?

A Access to a wider pool of finance

B Improving existing owners' control over the business

C Transfer of capital to other users

D Enhancement of company's image

Test your understanding 5

Which of the following statements is correct?

A Money markets are markets for long- term capital

B Capital markets are markets for short-term capital

C Primary markets enable existing investors to sell their investments

D A financial intermediary links those with surplus funds to those with fund deficits

Test your understanding 6

International capital markets are available for larger companies wishing to raise larger amounts of finance.

Which of the following statements is incorrect?

A Eurobonds are bonds denominated in a currency which often differs from that of the country of issue

B Eurocurrency is a currency which is held by individuals and institutions outside the country of issue of that currency

C Eurobonds are short-term loans raised by international companies or other institutions

D Eurobonds are sold to investors in several countries at the same time

Test your understanding 7

Which of the following is not a role typically performed by financial intermediaries?

A Risk reduction

B Aggregation

C Securitisation

D Maturity transformation

Test your understanding 8

A large organisation will have a treasury department to manage liquidity, short-term investment, borrowings, foreign exchange and other specialised areas.

Which of the following is not an advantage of having a centralised treasury department?

A Greater autonomy can be given to subsidiaries and divisions

B No need for treasury skills to be duplicated through the group

C Necessary borrowings can be arranged in bulk, at lower interest rates than for smaller borrowings

D The group's currency risk can be managed more effectively as the overall exposure to the group can be appreciated

6 Chapter summary

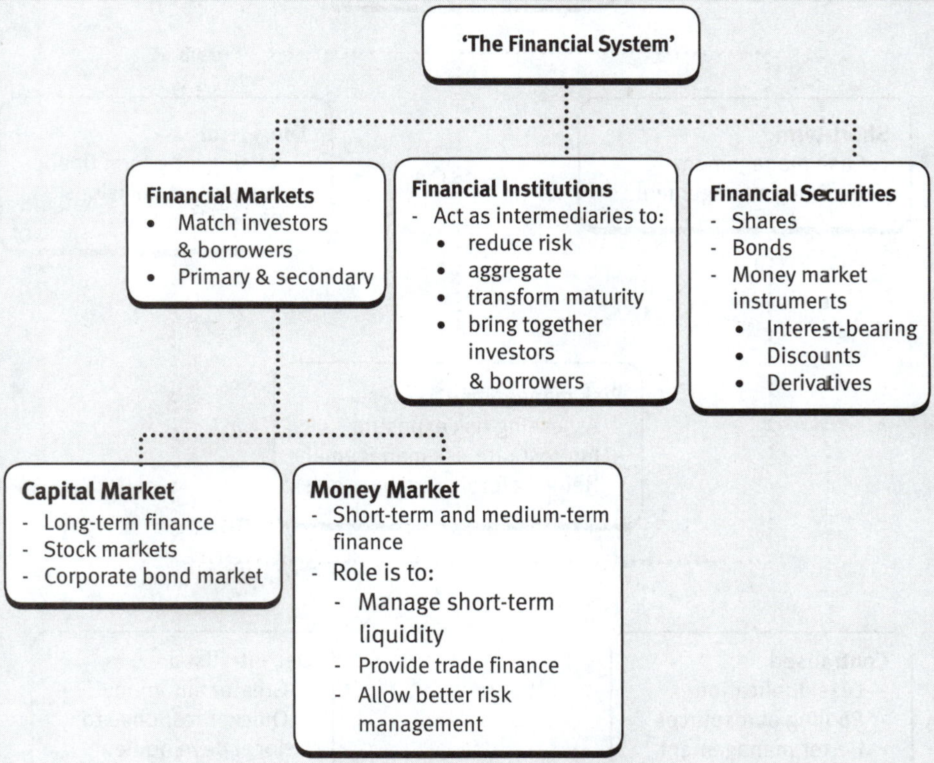

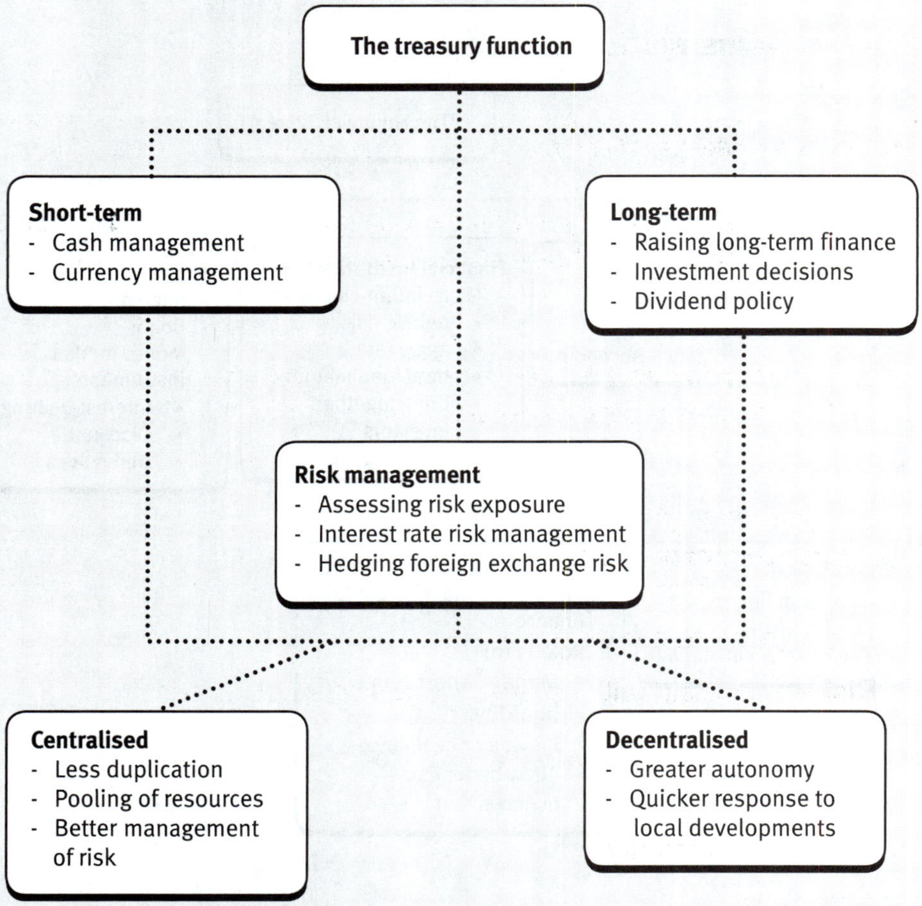
The treasury function
Short-term
- Cash management
- Currency management
Long-term
- Raising long-term finance
- Investment decisions
- Dividend policy
Risk management
- Assessing risk exposure
- Interest rate risk management
- Hedging foreign exchange risk
Centralised
- Less duplication
- Pooling of resources
- Better management of risk
Decentralised
- Greater autonomy
- Quicker response to local developments

Test your understanding answers

Test your understanding 1

In the drug development stage of the product lifecycle, the firm will be a cash consumer due to the huge sums that need to be spent on research and development.

If patent protection can be established, then high prices should ensure that the company is a cash generator until the patent expires.

Test your understanding 2

- Effective interest rate – linked to default risk.
- Risk – especially with regard to investing surplus cash.
- Amounts.
- Marketability/liquidity.
- Timescales/maturity.
- Availability.

Test your understanding 3

Treasury is the function concerned with the provision and use of finance and thus handles the acquisition and custody of funds whereas the Finance Department has responsibility for accounting, reporting and control. The roles of the two departments in the proposed investment are as follows:

Evaluation

- Treasury will quantify the cost of capital to be used in assessing the investment.
- The finance department will estimate the project cash flows.

Implementation

- Treasury will establish corporate financial objectives, such as wanting to restrict gearing to 40%, and will identify sources and types of finance.
- Treasury will also deal with currency management – dealing in foreign currencies and hedging currency risks – and taxation.
- The finance department will be involved with the preparation of budgets and budgetary control, the preparation of periodic financial statements and the management and administration of activities such as payroll and internal audit.

Interaction

- The Treasury Department has main responsibility for setting corporate objectives and policy and Financial Control has the responsibility for implementing policy and ensuring the achievement of corporate objectives. This distinction is probably far too simplistic and, in reality, both departments will make contributions to both determination and achievement of objectives.
- There is a circular relationship in that Treasurers quantify the cost of capital, which the Financial Controllers use as the criterion for the deployment of funds; Financial Controllers quantify projected cash flows which in turn trigger Treasurers' decisions to employ capital.

Test your understanding 4

Answer B

A stock market listing is likely to involve a significant loss of control to a wider circle of investors.

Test your understanding 5

Answer D

Money markets are markets for short-term capital (A). Capital markets are markets for long-term capital (B). Primary markets enable organisations to raise new finance. Secondary markets enable exisiting investors to sell their investments (C).

Test your understanding 6

Answer C

Eurobonds represent the long-term end of the Euromarket.

Test your understanding 7

Answer C

Securitisation is the process of converting illiquid assets into marketable asset-backed securities. The development of securitisation has led to disintermediation and a reduction in the role of financial intermediaries as borrowers can reach lenders directly.

Test your understanding 8

Answer A

Less (not more) autonomy can be given to subsidiaries and divisions if a centralised treasury department exists.

chapter

13

Foreign exchange risk

Chapter learning objectives

Upon completion of this chapter you will be able to:

- explain the meaning and causes of translation risk
- explain the meaning and causes of transaction risk
- explain the meaning and causes of economic risk
- describe how the balance of payments can cause exchange rate fluctuations
- explain the impact of purchasing power parity on exchange rate fluctuations
- explain the impact of interest rate parity on exchange rate fluctuations
- use purchasing power parity theory (PPPT) to forecast exchange rates
- use interest rate parity theory (IRPT) to forecast exchange rates
- explain the principle of four-way equivalence and the impact on exchange rate fluctuations
- explain the significance of the currency of an invoice on foreign currency risk management
- discuss and apply netting and matching as a form of foreign currency risk management
- discuss and apply leading and lagging as a form of foreign currency risk management
- define a forward exchange contract
- calculate the outcome of a forward exchange contract
- define money market hedging
- calculate the outcome of a money market hedge used by an exporter

- calculate the outcome of a money market hedge used by an importer
- explain the significance of asset and liability management on foreign currency risk management
- compare and evaluate traditional methods of foreign currency risk management
- define the main types of foreign currency derivates and explain how they can be used to hedge foreign currency risk.

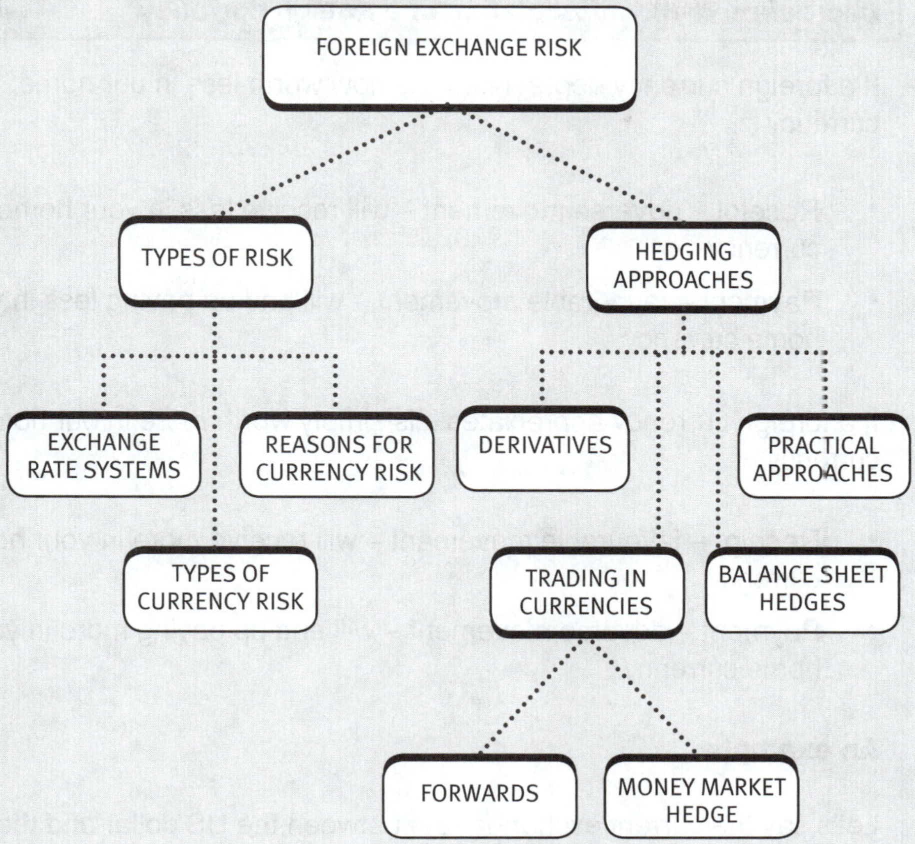

1 Foreign currency risk

Unlike when trading domestically, foreign currency risk arises for companies that trade internationally.

In a floating exchange rate system:

- the authorities allow the forces of supply and demand to continuously change the exchange rates without intervention
- the future value of a currency vis-à-vis other currency is uncertain
- the value of foreign trades will be affected.

Depreciation and appreciation of a foreign currency

If a foreign currency depreciates it is now worth less in our home currency.

- Receipt – adverse movement – will receive less in your home currency.
- Payment – favourable movement – will end up paying less in your home currency.

If a foreign currency appreciates it is simply worth more in our home currency.

- Receipt – favourable movement – will receive more in your home currency.
- Payment – adverse movement – will end up paying more in your home currency.

An example

Let's say the current exchange rate between the US dollar and the UK pound is $1.60/£. This means that a $10m cash flow would equate to £6.25m.

Now let's say the exchange rate moves to $1.50/£. In this case, the $ has **appreciated** (you would have to sell fewer $s to get one pound). The same $10m cash flow now equates to £6.67m. If you are a UK company receiving $10m, this is obviously good news. However, if you are needing to pay $10m, this will not cost you more.

A movement in the opposite direction, to say $1.70/£ reflects a **depreciation** in the US dollar (you would need to sell more $s to get one pound). The $10m cash flow now equates to £5.88m. For a UK company, this would be bad news if you were receiving the money but good news if you were making a payment.

The currency blues

If a currency appreciates, companies complain that they cannot sell their goods abroad and workers agitate about losing their jobs.

If a currency depreciates, consumers are unhappy because inflation is imported and their money travels less far when they go abroad.'

Additional question – Foreign currency implications

What would a strong pound mean for companies in the UK pricing transactions in foreign currency if they were a:

- **UK exporter?**
- **UK importer?**

What would a weak Euro mean for companies in the Eurozone pricing transactions in foreign currency if they were a:

- **European exporter?**
- **European importer?**

The answer to this question can be found after the chapter summary diagram at the end of this chapter.

Exchange rate systems

The world's leading currencies such as:

- US dollar
- Japanese yen
- British pound
- European euro

float against each other. However only a minority of currencies use this system.

Other systems include.

- Fixed exchange rates
- Freely floating exchange rates
- Managed floating exchange rates.

Exchange rate systems

Although the world's leading trading currencies, like the US dollar, Japanese yen, British pound and European Euro are floating against the other currencies, a minority of countries use floating exchange rates. The main exchange rate systems include:

(a) **Fixed exchange rates**

This involves publishing the target parity against a single currency (or a basket of currencies), and a commitment to use monetary policy (interest rates) and official reserves of foreign exchange to hold the actual spot rate within some trading band around this target.

Fixed against a single currency

This is where a country fixes its exchange rate against the currency of another country's currency. More than 50 countries fix their rates in this way, mostly against the US dollar. Fixed rates are not permanently fixed and periodic revaluations and devaluations occur when the economic fundamentals of the country concerned strongly diverge (e.g. inflation rates).

Fixed against a basket of currencies

Using a basket of currencies is aimed at fixing the exchange rate against a more stable currency base than would occur with a single currency fix. The basket is often devised to reflect the major trading links of the country concerned.

Historical perspective: British pound previously used a fixed rate system

The pound was fixed against the US dollar from 1945 to 1972, and more recently was part of the European Exchange Rate Mechanism (ERM) between 1990 and 1992. The rules of the ERM were complicated, UK membership of the ERM involved a target rate of 2.95 DM against the £ with a +/– 6% trading band: in other words, a minimum spot rate of around 2.77DM. To hold sterling above this rate in 1992, the government used a significant amount of the UK's foreign currency reserves and a high interest rate policy. Following its failure to defend the pound within the system, the UK left the ERM in September 1992.

(b) **Freely floating exchange rates (sometimes called a 'clean float')**

A genuine free float would involve leaving exchange rates entirely to the vagaries of supply and demand on the foreign exchange markets, and neither intervening on the market using official reserves of foreign exchange nor taking exchange rates into account when making interest rate decisions. The Monetary Policy Committee of the Bank of England clearly takes account of the external value of sterling in its decision-making process, so that although the pound is no longer in a fixed exchange rate system, it would not be correct to argue that it is on a genuinely free float.

(c) **Managed floating exchange rates (sometimes called a 'dirty float')**

The central bank of countries using a managed float will attempt to keep currency relationships within a predetermined range of values (not usually publicly announced), and will often intervene in the foreign exchange markets by buying or selling their currency to remain within the range.

2 Types of foreign currency risk

Since firms regularly trade with firms operating in countries with different currencies, and may operate internationally themselves, it is essential to understand the impact that foreign exchange rate changes can have on the business.

Transaction risk

Transaction risk is the risk of an exchange rate changing between the transaction date and the subsequent settlement date, i.e. it is the gain or loss arising on conversion.

It arises on any future transaction involving conversion between two currencies (for example, if a UK company were to invest in USD bonds, the interest receipts would be subject to transaction risk). The most common area where transaction risk is experienced relates to imports and exports.

Test your understanding 1 – Transaction risk

On 1 January a UK firm enters into a contract to buy a piece of equipment from the US for $300,000. The invoice is to be settled on 31 March.

The exchange rate on 1 January is $1.6/£ (i.e. $1.6 = £1).

However by 31 March, the pound may have

(1) strengthened to $1.75/£ or

(2) depreciated to $1.45/£.

Explain the risk faced by the UK firm.

A firm may decide to hedge – take action to minimise – the risk, if it is:

- a material amount
- over a material time period
- thought likely exchange rates will change significantly.

We will see more on hedging later in this chapter.

Economic risk

Economic risk is the variation in the value of the business (i.e. the present value of future cash flows) due to unexpected changes in exchange rates. It is the long-term version of transaction risk.

For an export company it could occur because:

- the home currency strengthens against the currency in which it trades
- a competitor's home currency weakens against the currency in which it trades.

A favoured but long-term solution is to diversify all aspects of the business internationally so the company is not overexposed to any one economy in particular.

Test your understanding 2 – Economic risk

A US exporter sells one product in Europe on a cost plus basis.

The selling price is based on a US price of $16 to cover costs and provide a profit margin.

The current exchange rate is €1.26/$.

What would be the effect on the exporter's business if the dollar strengthened to €1.31/$?

Economic risk

Transaction exposure focuses on relatively short-term cash flows effects; economic exposure encompasses these, plus the longer-term effects of changes in exchange rates on the market value of a company. Basically this means a change in the present value of the future after-tax cash flows due to changes in exchange rates.

There are two ways in which a company is exposed to economic risk

Directly: If your firm's home currency strengthens then foreign competitors are able to gain sales at your expense because your products have become more expensive (or you have reduced your margins) in the eyes of customers both abroad and at home.

Indirectly: Even if your home currency does not move vis-à-vis your customer's currency, you may lose competitive position. For example suppose a South African firm is selling into Hong Kong and its main competitor is a New Zealand firm. If the New Zealand dollar weakens against the Hong Kong dollar the South African firm has lost some competitive position.

Economic risk is difficult to quantify but a favoured strategy is to diversify internationally, in terms of sales, location of production facilities, raw materials and financing. Such diversification is likely to significantly reduce the impact of economic exposure relative to a purely domestic company, and provide much greater flexibility to react to real exchange rate changes.

Translation risk

Where the reported performance of an overseas subsidiary in home-based currency terms is distorted in consolidated financial statements because of a change in exchange rates.

NB. This is an accounting risk rather than a cash-based one.

Translation risk

The financial statements of overseas subsidiaries are usually translated into the home currency in order that they can be consolidated into the group's financial statements. Note that this is purely a paper-based exercise – it is the translation not the conversion of real money from one currency to another.

The reported performance of an overseas subsidiary in home-based currency terms can be severely distorted if there has been a significant foreign exchange movement.

'If initially the exchange rate is given by $1/£ and an American subsidiary is worth $500,000, then the UK parent company will anticipate a statement of financial position value of £500,000 for the subsidiary. A depreciation of the US dollar to $2/£ would result in only £250,000 being translated.'

Unless managers believe that the company's share price will fall as a result of showing a translation exposure loss in the company's accounts, translation exposure will not normally be hedged. The company's share price, in an efficient market, should only react to exposure that is likely to have an impact on cash flows.

Make sure you are able to distinguish between the three types of foreign currency risk: transaction, economic and translation.

3 Trading in currencies

The foreign exchange market

The foreign exchange or forex market is an international market in national currencies. It is highly competitive and virtually no difference exists between the prices in one market (e.g. New York) and another (e.g. London).

Bid and offer prices

Banks dealing in foreign currency quote two prices for an exchange rate:

- a lower 'bid' price
- a higher 'offer' price.

For example, a dealer might quote a price for US$/£ of 1.340 – 1.345:

- The lower rate, 1.340, is the rate at which the dealer will sell the variable currency (US$) in exchange for the base currency (sterling).
- The higher rate, 1.345, is the rate at which the dealer will buy the variable currency (US$) in exchange for the base currency (sterling).

This quote might also be written as a mid price with an adjustment, for example:

US$/£ 1.3425 ± 0.0025

This tells you to add $0.0025 to get the buying rate ($1.3425 + $0.0025 = $1.345) or subtract $0.0025 to get the selling rate ($1.3425 – $0.0025 = $1.340).

To remember which of the two prices is relevant to any particular foreign exchange (FX) transaction, remember the bank will always trade at the rate that is more favourable to itself.

If in doubt, work out which rate most favours the bank or remember the rules:

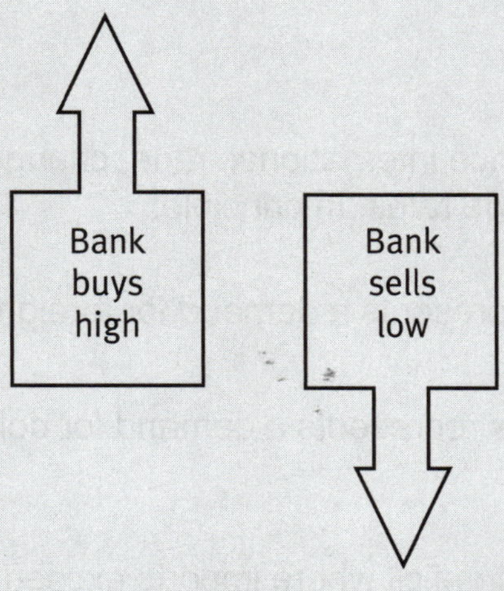

Test your understanding 3 – Bid and offer prices

The US$ rate per £ is quoted as 1.4325 – 1.4330.

Company A wants to buy $100,000 in exchange for sterling.

Company B wants to sell $200,000 in exchange for sterling.

What rate will the bank offer each company?

The spot market

The spot market is where you can buy and sell a currency now (immediate delivery), i.e. the spot rate of exchange.

The forward market

The forward market is where you can buy and sell a currency, at a fixed future date for a predetermined rate, by entering into a forward exchange contract.

Why exchange rates fluctuate

Changes in exchange rates result from changes in the demand for and supply of the currency. These changes may occur for a variety of reasons, e.g. due to changes in international trade or capital flows between economies.

Balance of payments

Since currencies are required to finance international trade, changes in trade may lead to changes in exchange rates. In principle:

- demand for imports in the US represents a demand for foreign currency or a supply of dollars
- overseas demand for US exports represents a demand for dollars or a supply of the currency.

Thus a country with a current account deficit where imports exceed exports may expect to see its exchange rate depreciate, since the supply of the currency (imports) will exceed the demand for the currency (exports).

Any factors which are likely to alter the state of the current account of the balance of payments may ultimately affect the exchange rate.

Capital movements between economies

There are also **capital movements between economies**. These transactions are effectively switching bank deposits from one currency to another. These flows are now more important than the volume of trade in goods and services.

Thus supply/demand for a currency may reflect events on the capital account. Several factors may lead to inflows or outflows of capital:

- changes in interest rates: rising (falling) interest rates will attract a capital inflow (outflow) and a demand (supply) for the currency
- inflation: asset holders will not wish to hold financial assets in a currency whose value is falling because of inflation.

These forces which affect the demand and supply of currencies and hence exchange rates have been incorporated into a number of formal models.

4 The causes of exchange rate fluctuations

Purchasing Power Parity Theory (PPPT)

PPPT claims that the rate of exchange between two currencies depends on the relative inflation rates within the respective countries.

PPPT is based on:

'the law of one price'.

In equilibrium, identical goods must cost the same, regardless of the currency in which they are sold.

e.g

Illustration 1 – PPPT

An item costs $3,000 in the US.

Assume that sterling and the US dollar are at PPPT equilibrium, at the current spot rate of $1.50/£, i.e. the sterling price x current spot rate of $1.50 = dollar price.

The spot rate is the rate at which currency can be exchanged today.

	The US market		The UK market
Cost of item now	$3,000	$1.50	£2,000
Estimated inflation	5%		3%
Cost in one year	$3,150		£2,060

The 'law of one price' states that the item must always cost the same. Therefore in one year:

$3,150 must equal £2,060

and so the expected future spot rate can be calculated:

$3,150/2,060 = $1.5291

Rule: PPPT predicts that the country with the higher inflation will be subject to a depreciation of its currency.

If you need to estimate the expected future spot rates, simply apply the following formula:

$$S_1 = S_0 \times \frac{(1+h_c)}{(1+h_b)}$$

Where:

S_0 = Current spot

S_1 = Expected future spot

h_b = Inflation rate in country for which the spot is quoted (base currency)

h_c = Inflation rate in the other country. (counter currency)

This formula is given to you in the exam.

Test your understanding 4 – PPPT

The dollar and sterling are currently trading at $1.72/£.

Inflation in the US is expected to grow at 3% pa, but at 4% pa in the UK.

Predict the future spot rate in a year's time.

PPPT can be used as our best predictor of future spot rates; however it suffers from the following major limitations:

- the future inflation rates are only estimates
- the market is dominated by speculative transactions (98%) as opposed to trade transactions; therefore purchasing power theory breaks down
- government intervention: governments may manage exchange rates, thus defying the forces pressing towards PPPT.

PPPT

The main function of an exchange rate is to provide a means of translating prices expressed in one currency into another currency. The implication is that the exchange will be determined in some way by the relationship between these prices. This arises from the law of one price.

The law of one price states that in a free market with no barriers to trade and no transport or transactions costs, the competitive process will ensure that there will only be one price for any given good. If price differences occurred they would be removed by arbitrage; entrepreneurs would buy in the low market and resell in the high market. This would eradicate the price difference.

If this law is applied to international transactions, it suggests that exchange rates will always adjust to ensure that only one price exists between countries where there is relatively free trade.

Thus if a typical set of goods cost $1,000 in the USA and the same set cost £500 in the UK, free trade would produce an exchange rate of £1 to $2.

How does this result come about?

Let us suppose that the rate of exchange was $1.5 to £1: the sequence of events would be:

- US purchasers could buy UK goods more cheaply (£500 at $1.5 to £1 is $750).
- There would be a flow of UK exports to the US: this would represent demand for sterling.
- The sterling exchange rate would rise.
- When the exchange rate reached $2 to £1, there would be no extra US demand for UK exports since prices would have been equalised: purchasing power parity would have been established.

The clear prediction of the purchasing power parity model of exchange rate determination is that if a country experiences a faster rate of inflation than its trading partners, it will experience a depreciation in its exchange rate. It follows that if inflation rates can be predicted, so can movements in exchange rates.

In practice the purchasing power parity model has shown some weaknesses and is a poor predictor of short-term changes in exchange rates.

- It ignores the effects of capital movements on the exchange rate.
- Trade and therefore exchange rates will only reflect the prices of goods which enter into international trade and not the general price level since this includes non-tradeables (e.g. inland transport).
- Governments may 'manage' exchange rates, e.g. by interest rate policy.
- It is likely that the purchasing power parity model may be more useful for predicting long-run changes in exchange rates since these are more likely to be determined by the underlying competitiveness of economies, as measured by the model.

Interest Rate Parity Theory (IRPT)

The IRPT claims that the difference between the spot and the forward exchange rates is equal to the differential between interest rates available in the two currencies.

The forward rate is a future exchange rate, agreed now, for buying or selling an amount of currency on an agreed future date.

e.g

Illustration 2 – IRPT

UK investor invests in a one-year US bond with a 9.2% interest rate as this compares well with similar risk UK bonds offering 7.12%. The current spot rate is $1.5/£.

When the investment matures and the dollars are converted into sterling, IRPT states that the investor will have achieved the same return as if the money had been invested in UK government bonds.

	The UK market		The US market
		Spot \$/£ 1.5 →	
Start	£1m		\$1.5m
	× 1.0712		× 1.092
End	£1.0712m		\$1.638m

In 1 year, £1.0712 million must equate to \$1.638 million so what you gain in extra interest, you lose on an adverse movement in exchange rates.

Any attempt to 'fix' the future exchange rate by locking into an agreed rate now (for example by buying a forward (see section 5 of this chapter for details)), will also fail.

The forward rates moves to bring about interest rate parity amongst different currencies:

$$\frac{\$1.638}{£1.0712} = \$1.5291$$

Rule: IRPT predicts that the country with the higher interest rate will see the forward rate for its currency subject to a depreciation.

If you need to calculate the forward rate in one year's time:

$$F_0 = S_0 \times \frac{(1+i_c)}{(1+i_b)}$$

Where:

F_0 = Forward rate

i_b = interest rate for base currency

i_c = interest rate for counter currency

You are provided with this formula in the exam.

The IRPT generally holds true in practice. There are no bargain interest rates to be had on loans/deposits in one currency rather than another.

However it suffers from the following limitations:

- government controls on capital markets
- controls on currency trading
- intervention in foreign exchange markets.

Test your understanding 5 – IRPT

A treasurer can borrow in Swiss francs at a rate of 3% pa or in the UK at a rate of 7% pa. The current rate of exchange is 10SF/£.

What is the forward rate of exchange for delivery in a year's time?

IRPT

The interest rate parity model shows that it may be possible to predict exchange rate movements by referring to differences in nominal interest rates . If the forward exchange rate for sterling against the dollar was no higher than the spot rate but US nominal interest rates were higher, the following would happen:

- UK investors would shift funds to the US in order to secure the higher interest rates, since they would suffer no exchange losses when they converted $ back into £.
- the flow of capital from the UK to the US would raise UK interest rates and force up the spot rate for the US$.

Four way equivalence

The Fisher Effect

The Fisher Effect was covered in chapter 4 to look at the relationship between interest rates and expected rates of inflation. It is expressed by the formula:

$(1 + i) = (1 + r)(1 + h)$

This states that the money or nominal rate of interest is made up of two parts, the underlying required rate of return (real interest rate) and a premium to allow for inflation.

Countries with high rates of inflation will be expected to have nominal rates of interest in order to ensure investors can obtain a high enough real return.

The International Fisher Effect

The International Fisher Effect claims that the interest rate differentials between two countries provide an unbiased predictor of future changes in the spot rate of exchange.

- The International Fisher Effect assumes that all countries will have the same real interest rate, although nominal or money rates may differ due to expected inflation rates.
- Thus the interest rate differential between two countries should be equal to the expected inflation differential.
- Therefore, countries with higher expected inflation rates will have higher nominal interest rates, and vice versa.

In practice interest rate differentials are a poor unbiased predictor of future exchange rates.

Factors other than interest differentials influence exchange rates such as government intervention in foreign exchange markets.

Expectations theory

The expectations theory claims that the current forward rate is an unbiased predictor of the spot rate at that point in the future.

If a trader takes the view that the forward rate is lower than the expected future spot price, there is an incentive to buy forward. The buying pressure on the forward raises the price, until the forward price equals the market consensus view on the expected future spot price.

In practice, it is a poor unbiased predictor – sometimes it is wide of the mark in one direction and sometimes wide of the mark in the other.

Four-way equivalence

The four theories can be pulled together to show the overall relationship between spot rates, interest rates, inflation rates and the forward and expected future spot rates. As shown above, these relationships can be used to forecast exchange rates.

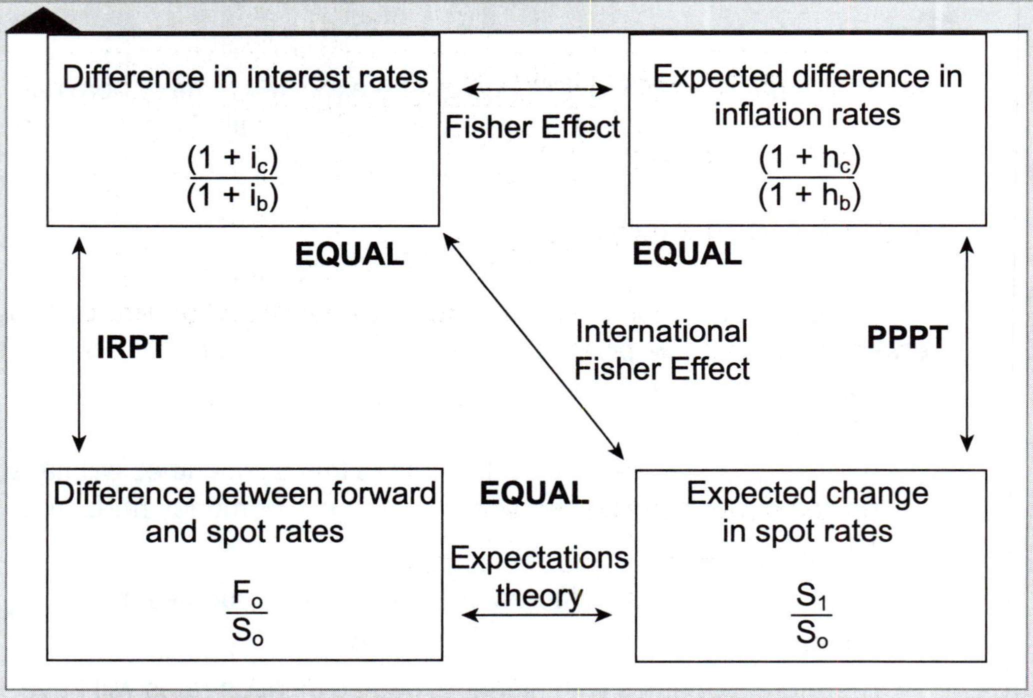

5 Managing foreign currency risk

When currency risk is significant for a company, it should do something to either eliminate it or reduce it.

Taking measures to eliminate or reduce a risk is called:

- hedging the risk or
- hedging the exposure.

Practical approaches

Practical approaches to managing foreign currency risk include:

- Dealing in your home currency
- Doing nothing
- Leading
- Lagging
- Matching receipts and payments
- Netting
- Foreign currency bank accounts
- Matching assets and liabilities

Practical approaches to managing risk

Practical approaches

Deal in home currency

Insist all customers pay in your own home currency and pay for all imports in home currency.

This method:

- transfers risk to the other party
- may not be commercially acceptable.

Do nothing

In the long run, the company would 'win some, lose some'.

This method:

- works for small occasional transactions
- saves in transaction costs
- is dangerous!

Leading

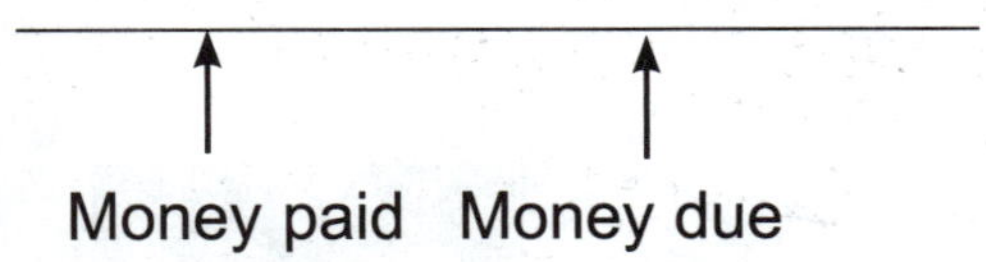

Receipts – If an exporter expects that the currency it is due to receive will depreciate over the next few months it may try to obtain payment immediately.

This may be achieved by offering a discount for immediate payment.

Lagging

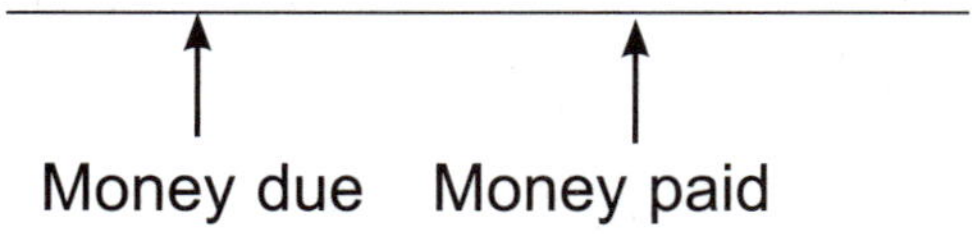

Payments – If an importer expects that the currency it is due to pay will depreciate, it may attempt to delay payment.

This may be achieved by agreement or by exceeding credit terms.

Note: If the importer expects that the currency will in fact appreciate, then it should settle the liability as soon as possible (leading). Or, if an exporter expects the currency to appreciate, it may try to delay the receipt of payment by offering longer credit terms (lagging).

NB Strictly this is not hedging – it is speculation – the company only benefits if it correctly anticipates the exchange rate movement!

Matching payments and receipts

When a company has receipts and payments in the same foreign currency due at the same time, it can simply match them against each other. It is then only necessary to deal on the foreign exchange (forex) markets for the unmatched portion of the total transactions.

Suppose that ABC plc has the following receipts and payments in three months time:

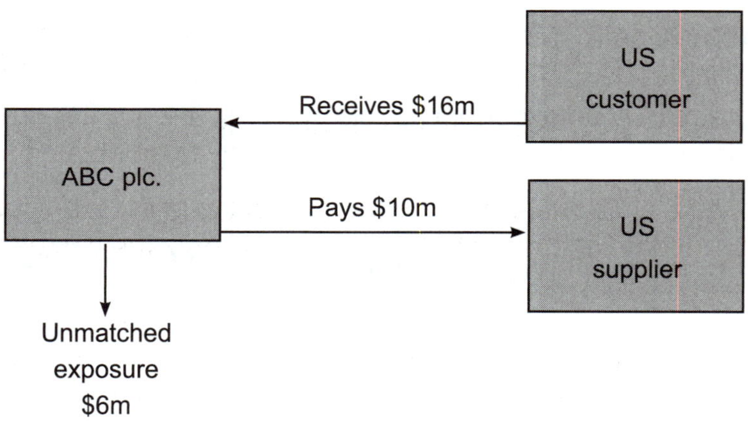

(to be hedged by other methods)

Netting

Unlinked matching, netting is not technically a method of managing exchange risk. However, it is conveniently dealt with at this stage. The objective is simply to save transaction costs by netting off inter-company balances before arranging payment.

Foreign currency bank accounts

Where a firm has regular receipts and payments in the same currency, it may choose to operate a foreign currency bank account.

This operates as a permanent matching process.

The exposure to exchange risk is limited to the net balance on the account.

Matching assets and liabilities (asset and liability management)

A company which expects to receive a significant amount of income in a foreign currency will want to hedge against the risk of this currency weakening. It can do this by borrowing in the foreign currency and using the foreign receipts to repay the loan. For example, Euro receivables can be hedged by taking out a Euro overdraft. In the same way, Euro trade payables can be matched against a Euro bank account which is used to pay the suppliers.

A company which has a long-term foreign investment, for example an overseas subsidiary, will similarly try to match its foreign assets (property, plant etc) by a long-term loan in the foreign currency.

Hedging with forward exchange contracts

Although other forms of hedging are available, forward exchange contacts represent the most frequently employed method of hedging.

e.g

Illustration 3 – Forward exchange contract

It is now 1 January and Y plc will receive $10 million on 30 April.

It enters into a forward exchange contract to sell this amount on the forward date at a rate of $1.60 / £. On 30 April the company is guaranteed £6.25 million.

The risk has been completely removed.

In practice, the forward rate is quoted as a margin on the spot rate. In the exam you will be given the forward rate.

Test your understanding 6 – Hedging with forwards

The current spot rate for US dollars against UK sterling is 1.4525 – 1.4535 $/£ and the one-month forward rate is quoted as 1.4550 – 1.4565.

A UK exporter expects to receive $400,000 in one month.

If a forward exchange contract is used, how much will be received in sterling?

Advantages and disadvantages of forward exchange contracts

Forward exchange contracts are used extensively for hedging currency transaction exposures.

Advantages include:

- flexibility with regard to the amount to be covered
- relatively straightforward both to comprehend and to organise.

Disadvantages include:

- contractual commitment that must be completed on the due date(option date forward contract can be used if uncertain)
- no opportunity to benefit from favourable movements in exchange rates.

Disadvantages of a forward exchange contract

It is a contractual commitment which must be completed on the due date.

This means that if a payment from the overseas customer is late, the company receiving the payment and wishing to convert it using its forward exchange contract will have a problem. The existing forward exchange contract must be settled, although the bank will arrange a new forward exchange contract for the new date when the currency cash flow is due.

To help overcome this problem an 'option date' forward exchange contract can be arranged. This is a forward exchange contract that allows the company to settle a forward contract at an agreed fixed rate of exchange, but at any time between two specified dates. If the currency cash flow occurs between these two dates, the forward exchange contract can be settled at the agreed fixed rate.

Inflexible

It eliminates the downside risk of an adverse movement in the spot rate, but also prevents any participation in upside potential of any favourable movement in the spot rate. Whatever happens to the actual exchange rate, the forward contract must be honoured, even if it would be beneficial to exchange currencies at the spot rate prevailing at that time.

A money market hedge

The money markets are markets for wholesale (large-scale) lending and borrowing, or trading in short-term financial instruments. Many companies are able to borrow or deposit funds through their bank in the money markets.

Instead of hedging a currency exposure with a forward contract, a company could use the money markets to lend or borrow, and achieve a similar result.

Since forward exchange rates are derived from spot rates and money market interest rates, the end result from hedging should be roughly the same by either method.

NB Money market hedges are more complex to set up than the equivalent forward.

Hedging a payment

If you are hedging a future payment:

- buy the present value of the foreign currency amount today at the spot rate:
  - this is, in effect, an immediate payment in sterling
  - and may involve borrowing the funds to pay earlier than the settlement date
- the foreign currency purchased is placed on deposit and accrues interest until the transaction date.
- the deposit is then used to make the foreign currency payment.

Test your understanding 7 – Hedging a payment

Liverpool plc must make a payment of US $450,000 in 3 months' time. The company treasurer has determined the following:

Spot rate $1.7000 – $1.7040

3-months forward $1.6902 – $1.6944
6-months forward $1.6764 – $1.6809

Money market rates:	Borrowing	Deposit	
US$	6.5%	5%	← Annual rates
Sterling	7.5%	6%	← Annual rates

Decide whether a forward contract hedge or a money market hedge should be undertaken.

Note: Money market rates vary according to the length of time the funds are borrowed or lent (see chapter on interest rate risk).

Here the rates quoted are annual rates. Don't forget to adjust these for the period of the loan or deposit (i.e. by dividing by 4 to get a 3 month rate).

Additional question – Hedging a payment

Bolton, a UK company, must make a payment of US$230,000 in three months' time. The company treasurer has determined the following:

Dollar: Sterling Spot rate $1.8250 – $1.8361.

3-months forward $1.8338 – $1.8452

Money market rates:

	Borrowing	Deposit	
US$	5.1%	4.2%	Annual rates
Sterling	5.75%	4.5%	

Ascertain the cost of the payment using a forward contract hedge and a money market hedge.

The answer to this question can be found after the chapter summary diagram at the end of this chapter.

Hedging a receipt

If you are hedging a receipt:

- borrow the present value of the foreign currency amount today:
  - sell it at the spot rate
  - this results in an immediate receipt in sterling
  - this can be invested until the date it was due
- the foreign loan accrues interest until the transaction date
- the loan is then repaid with the foreign currency receipt.

Test your understanding 8 – Hedging a receipt

Liverpool plc is now expecting a receipt of US$1.2m in six months' time and must make a payment of $300,000 in six months' time (leading to a net receipt of $900,000). The company treasurer has determined the following:

Spot rate $1.7000 – $1.7040.
3-months forward $1.6902 – $1.6944
6-months forward $1.6764 – $1.6809

Money market rates:	Borrowing	Deposit	
US$	6.5%	5% ←	Annual rates
Sterling	7.5%	6% ←	

Decide whether a forward contract hedge or a money market hedge should be undertaken.

Note: Money market rates vary according to the length of time the funds are borrowed or lent (see chapter on interest rate risk).

Here the rates quoted are annual rates. Don't forget to adjust these for the period of the loan or deposit (i.e. by dividing by 2 to get a 6 month rate).

Additional question – Hedging a receipt

Bolton is now to receive US$400,000 in 3 months' time. The company treasurer has determined the following:

Spot rate $1.8250 – $1.8361

3-months forward 1.8338 – 1.8452

Money market rates:	Borrowing	Deposit	
US$	5.1%	4.2% ←	Annual rates
Sterling	5.75%	4.5% ←	

Decide whether a forward contract hedge or a money market hedge should be undertaken.

The answer to this question can be found after the chapter summary diagram at the end of this chapter.

Balance sheet hedging

All the above techniques are used to hedge transaction risk.

Sometimes transaction risk can be brought about by attempts to manage translation risk.

Translation exposure:

- arises because the financial statements of foreign subsidiaries must be restated in the parent's reporting currency, for the firm to prepare its consolidated financial statements
- is the potential for an increase or decrease in the parent's net worth and reported income caused by a change in exchange rates since the last transaction.

A balance sheet hedge involves matching the exposed foreign currency assets on the consolidated statement of financial position with an equal amount of exposed liabilities, i.e.:

- a loan denominated in the same currency as the exposed assets and for the same amount is taken out
- a change in exchange rates will change the value of exposed assets but offset that with an opposite change in liabilities.

This method eliminates the mismatch between net assets and net liabilities denominated in the same currency, but may create transaction exposure.

As a general matter, firms seeking to reduce both types of exposure typically reduce transaction exposure first. They then recalculate translation exposure and decide if any residual translation exposure can be reduced, without creating more transaction exposure.

Foreign currency derivatives

Foreign currency risk can also be managed by using derivatives:

Futures

Futures are like a forward contract in that:

- the company's position is fixed by the rate of exchange in the futures contract
- it is a binding contract.

A futures contract differs from a forward contract in the following ways:

- Futures can be traded on futures exchanges. The contract which guarantees the price (known as the futures contract) is separated from the transaction itself, allowing the contracts to be easily traded.
- Settlement takes place in three-monthly cycles (March, June, September or December). i.e. a company can buy or sell September futures, December futures and so on.
- Futures are standardised contracts for standardised amounts. For example, the Chicago Mercantile Exchange (CME) trades sterling futures contracts with a standard size of £62,500. Only whole number multiples of this amount can be bought or sold.
- The price of a currency futures contract is the exchange rate for the currencies specified in the contract.

Because each contract is for a standard amount and with a fixed maturity date, they rarely cover the exact foreign currency exposure.

Futures

When a currency futures contact is bought or sold, the buyer or seller is required to deposit a sum of money with the exchange, called initial margin. If losses are incurred as exchange rates and hence the prices of currency futures contracts changes, the buyer or seller may be called on to deposit additional funds (variation margin) with the exchange. Equally, profits are credited to the margin account on a daily basis as the contract is 'marked to market'.

Most currency futures contracts are closed out before their settlement dates by undertaking the opposite transaction to the initial futures transaction, i.e. if buying currency futures was the initial transaction, it is closed out by selling currency futures.

Effectively a future works like a bet. If a company expects a US$ receipt in 3 month's time, it will lose out if the US$ depreciates relative to sterling. Using a futures contract, the company 'bets' that the US$ will depreciate. If it does, the win on the bet cancels out the loss on the transaction. If the US$ strengthens, the gain on the transaction covers the loss on the bet.

Ultimately futures ensure a virtual no win/no loss position.

Illustration 4 – Futures

It is currently February and a US exporter expects to receive £500,000 in June.

Current spot rate now is	$1.65/£
The quote for June Sterling futures is	$1.65
Standard size of futures contract	£62,500

The US exporter uses futures to hedge its currency risk by selling Sterling futures.

In June, the company receives £500,000

The spot rate in June moved to	$1.70/£
The futures rate in June was also	$1.70

Show the outcome of the futures hedge.

Solution

Number of contracts = £500,000 ÷ £62,500 = 8

Exporter needs to sell futures (sell £s)

In February – the hedge is set up by:

Selling (8 contracts × £62,500) = £500,000 for June delivery at $1.65

In June – the futures position is closed

Buying (8 contracts × £62,500) = £500,000 for June delivery at $1.70

Summary of futures position:

	$
Sell £ for	1.65
Buy £ for	(1.70)
	(0.05)

Loss on futures position = $0.05 / £ × (£62,500 × 8 contracts) = $25,000

The £500,000 received by the US exporter is then sold in June at the prevailing spot rate

£500,000 @ $1.70 = $850,000

Notice that sterling appreciated (the dollar depreciated) in the spot rate over the period, causing an increase in the value of the sterling as follows:

	$
Value of £500,000 – in February @ 1.65	825,000
Value of £500,000 – in June @ 1.70	850,000
Increase in value	25,000

Summary

	$
Increase in value of sterling remittance	25,000
Loss due to futures position	25,000

Thus the futures hedge removes risk – both upside potential (as above) and downside risk.

Note: This example shows a perfect hedge. In reality this is unlikely to happen, due to basis risk (see chapter on interest rate risk) and the standardised nature of futures contracts.

Currency options

Options are similar to forwards but with one key difference.

They give the right but not the obligation to buy or sell currency at some point in the future at a predetermined rate.

A company can therefore:

- exercise the option if it is in its interests to do so
- let it lapse if:
  - the spot rate is more favourable
  - there is no longer a need to exchange currency.

The downside risk is eliminated by exercising the option, but there is still upside potential from letting the option lapse

Options are most useful when there is uncertainty about the timing of the transaction or when exchange rates are very volatile.

Options may be:

PUT ↑ Right to sell currency

CALL ↑ Right to buy currency

Two types of option are available – over the counter options from banks (tailored to the specific wants of the customer and can be used by small and medium sized companies) and exchange traded options (traded on the same exchanges as futures and which can be used by larger companies)

The catch:

The additional flexibility comes at a price – a premium must be paid to purchase an option, whether or not it is ever used.

e.g

Illustration 5 – Options

A UK exporter is due to receive $25m in 3 months time. Its bank offers a 3 month put option on $25m at an exercise price of $1.50 / £ at a premium cost of £30,000.

Required

Show the net £ receipt if the future spot is either $1.60 or $1.40

Solution

Dividing by the smallest $/£ rate gives the highest £ receipt – the premium is paid no matter what so should be ignored for the purposes of determining whether to exercise the option.

Future spot $1.60 – exercise the option. $25m/$1.50 = £16.67m less £30,000 premium gives a net receipt of £16.64m

Future spot $1.40 – abandon the option. $25m/$1.40 = £17.86m less £30,000 premium gives a net receipt of £17.83m

Test your understanding 9

The spot exchange rate

A is the rate today for exchanging one currency for another for immediate delivery

B is the rate today for exchanging one currency for another at a specified future date

C is the rate today for exchanging one currency for another at a specific location on a specified future date

D is the rate today for exchanging one currency for another at a specific location for immediate delivery

Test your understanding 10

Purchasing Power Parity Theory (PPP) refers to

A The concept that the same goods should sell for the same price across countries after exchange rates are taken into account

B The concept that interest rates across countries will eventually be the same

C The orderly relationship between spot and forward currency exchange rates and the rates of interest between countries

D The natural offsetting relationship provided by costs and revenues in similar market environments

Test your understanding 11

An Iraqi company is expecting to receive Indian rupees in one year's time. The spot rate is 19.68 Iraqi dinar per 1 India rupee. The company could borrow in rupees at 10% or in dinars at 15%.

What is the expected exchange rate in one year's time?

A 18.82 Iraqi dinar = 1 Indian rupee

B 20.58 Iraqi dinar = 1 Indian rupee

C 21.65 Iraqi dinar = 1 Indian rupee

D 22.63 Iraqi dinar = 1 Indian rupee

Test your understanding 12

A forward exchange contract is

(1) an immediately firm and binding contract

(2) is for the purchase or sale of a specified quantity of a stated foreign currency

(3) is at a rate of exchange fixed at the time the contract is made

(4) for performance at a future time which is agreed when making the contract

A (1) and (2) only

B (1), (2) and (3) only

C (2) and (3) only

D All of the above

Test your understanding 13

If the underlying transaction gives you ___________, denominated in a foreign currency, the general principal behind a money market hedge states that you need an equivalent liability in the money market to provide a hedge.

A a liability

B an asset

C a forward contract

D a foreign bank account

Chapter summary

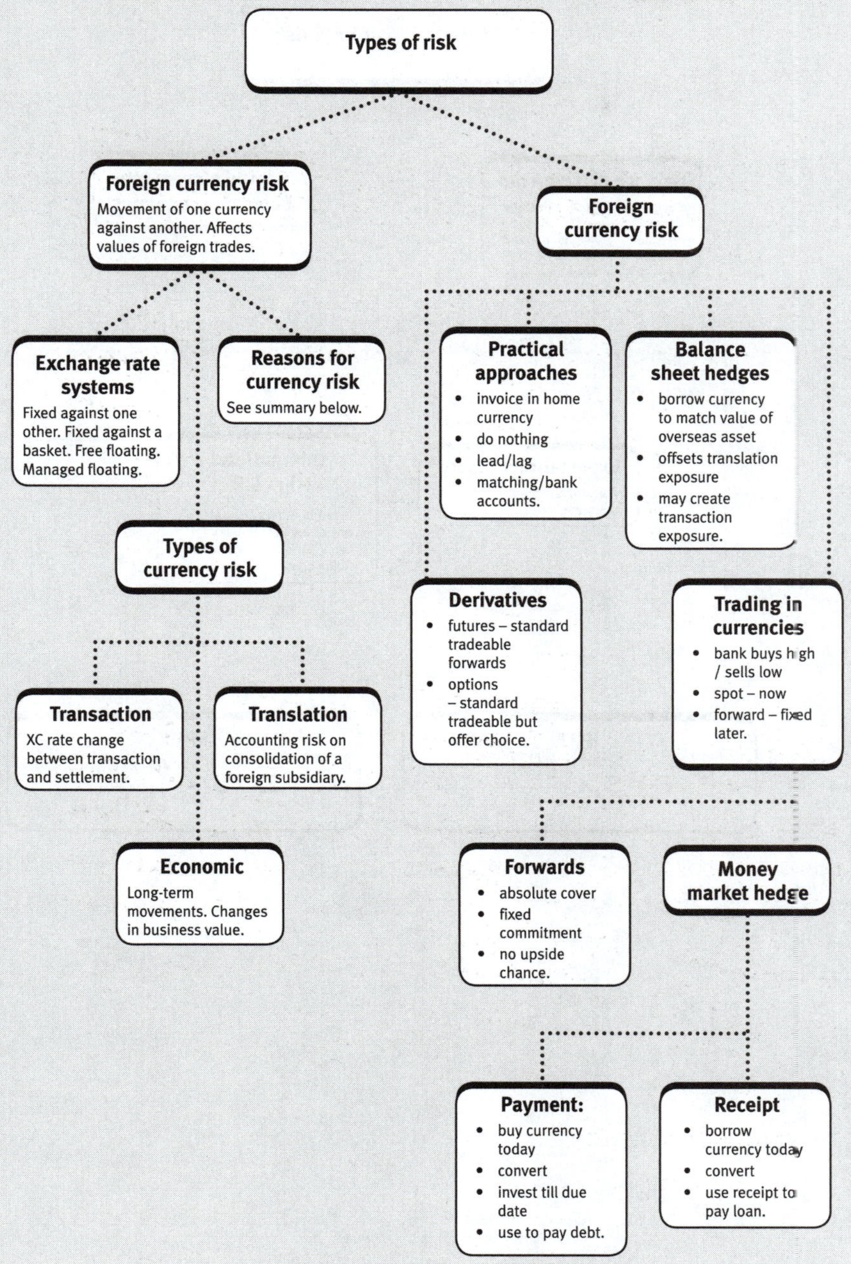

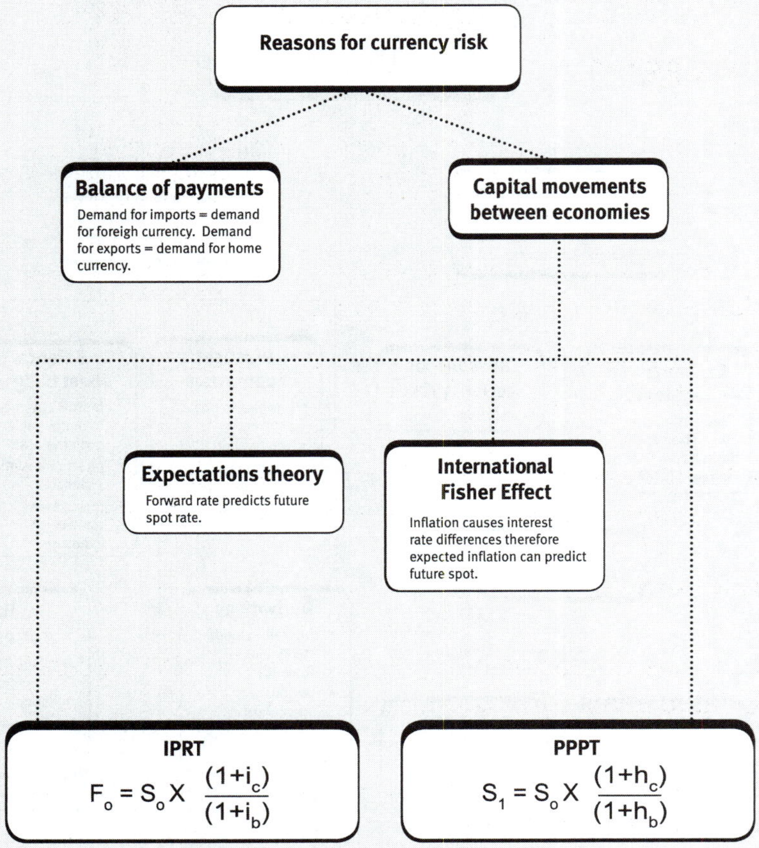
Reasons for currency risk
Balance of payments
Demand for imports = demand for foreigh currency. Demand for exports = demand for home currency.
Capital movements between economies
Expectations theory
Forward rate predicts future spot rate.
International Fisher Effect
Inflation causes interest rate differences therefore expected inflation can predict future spot.
IPRT
$F_o = S_o X \frac{(1+i_c)}{(1+i_b)}$
PPPT
$S_1 = S_o X \frac{(1+h_c)}{(1+h_b)}$

Answer to additional question – Foreign currency implications

A strong pound

The pound has appreciated – therefore other foreign currencies have depreciated relative to the pound:

- UK exporters: Bad news; receipts in currencies that are depreciating; receive fewer pounds.
- UK importers: Good news; payments in currencies that are depreciating; pay fewer pounds.

Note: the alternative for the UK exporter is to put the price up in the foreign currency, but exports then become uncompetitive.

A weak euro

The euro has depreciated – therefore other foreign currencies have appreciated relative to the euro.

- European exporters: Good news; receipts in currencies that are appreciating; receive more euros.
- European importers: Bad news – payments in currencies that are appreciating – pay more euros.

Answer to additional question – Hedging a payment

	Now		**3 mths**	
Payment			($230,000)	**Buy $**
		US deposit rate		
Deposit	$227,610	1.0105 ←	$230,000	
			0	
Buy $ at spot	1.8250 ↓			
Immediate payment	(£124,718)	1.014375 → =	**£126,511** Payment	
		UK borrowing rate		
Forward market hedge:			$230,000/1.8338	
		=	**£125,423**	

Answer to additional question – Hedging a receipt

	Now		3 mths
Receipt			$400,000 **receipt**
		US loan rate	
Loan	$394,964	1.01275 ←	($400,000)
			0
Sell at spot	1.8361 ↓		
Immediate receipt	£215,110	1.01125 →	£217,530
		UK deposit rate	

Forward hedge:

$400,000/1.8452 = £216,779

Test your understanding answers

Test your understanding 1 – Transaction risk

The UK firm faces uncertainty over the amount of sterling they will need to use to settle the US dollar invoice.

The cost of the equipment on 1 January is $\frac{\$300,000}{1.6}$ = £187,500

However on settlement, the cost may be:

(1) = $\frac{\$300,000}{1.75}$ = £171,429

(2) = $\frac{\$300,000}{1.45}$ = £206,897

This uncertainty is the transaction risk.

Test your understanding 2 – Economic risk

The product was previously selling at \$16 × 1.26 = €20.16. After the movement in exchange rates the exporter has an unhappy choice:

Either they must

- raise the price of the product to maintain their profits: 16 × 1.31 = €20.96 but risk losing sales as the product is more expensive and less competitive, or

  maintain the price to keep sales volume but risk eroding profit margins as €20.16 is now only worth €20.16 ÷ 1.31 = \$15.39.

The exporter is facing economic risk.

Test your understanding 3 – Bid and offer prices

Company A wants to buy $100,000 in exchange for sterling (so that the bank will be selling dollars):

- If we used the lower rate of 1.4325, the bank would sell them for £69,808
- If we used the higher rate of 1.4330, the bank would sell them for £69,784.

Clearly the bank would be better off selling them at the lower rate

RULE=> Bank sells lower (remember – this sounds like HELLO!).

Company B wants to sell $200,000 in exchange for sterling (so the bank would be buying dollars):

- If we used the lower rate of 1.4325, the bank would buy them for £139,616
- If we used the higher rate of 1.4330, the bank would buy them for £139,567

The bank will make more money buy at the higher rate:

RULE =>Bank buys high (remember – this sounds like BYE BYE!).

Test your understanding 4 – PPPT

$$1.72 \times \frac{1.03}{1.04} = \$1.7035$$

Test your understanding 5 – IRPT

$$10 \times \frac{1.03}{1.07} = \$9.6262$$

Test your understanding 6 – Hedging with forwards

The exporter will be selling his dollars to the bank and the bank buys high at 1.4565.

The exporter will therefore receive = 400,000 ÷ 1.4565 = £274,631.

Test your understanding 7 – Hedging a payment

Money market hedge:

(1) Create an equal and opposite asset to match the $ liability. Calculate the amount the company needs to deposit now, so that with interest it will generate $450,000 to make the payment in three months' time.

If annual interest rate for a three-month $ deposit is 5%, then interest for three months is 5 × 3 ÷ 12 = 1.25%. The company will want to put 450,000 ÷ 1.0125 = $444,444 on deposit now, so that it will mature to match the payment in three months' time.

(2) The company needs to purchase the required amount of dollars now, at the spot rate, at a cost of $444,444 ÷ $1.70 = £261,438.

(3) In order to compare the money market hedge (MMH) with a forward contract we assume that the company will borrow this money today and repay it in three months' time, with interest.

If annual interest rate for a three-month £ borrowing is 7.5%, then interest for three months is 7.5 × 3 ÷ 12 = 1.875%. So the company will have to repay £261,438 × 1.01875 = £266,340 in three months' time.

Overall result: Liverpool knows today that it will cost £266,340 to settle the $ liability in three month's time.

	Now		3 mths	
MMH				
Payment		3 m rates	($450,000)	**Buy $**
		US deposit rate		
Deposit	$444,444	1.0125	$450,000	
			0	
Buy $ at spot.	1.7000			
Immediate payment	(£261,438)	1.01875	= **£266,340**	
		UK borrowing rate		
				Payment
Forward contract:			$450,000/ 1.6902	
			= **£266,241**	√

The cost of a forward contract is marginally cheaper though this is largely due to rounding differences. In practice because of IRPT, the result should be very similar.

Note that:

- as the payment has been made today, all forex risk is eliminated
- the method presupposes the company can borrow funds today.

Test your understanding 8 – Hedging a receipt

Money market hedge:

(1) Create a liability to match the receipt: borrow an amount now, (\$900,000 ÷ 1.0325 = \$871,671) so that with interest, \$900,000 is owing in 6 months' time.

(2) Convert the \$871,671 borrowed into sterling immediately to remove the exchange risk (\$871,671 ÷ 1.7040) and deposit the £511,544.

(3) In 3 months the \$ loan is paid off by the \$ received from the customer and Liverpool plc realises the £526,890 deposit (£511,544 × 1.03).

Overall result: Liverpool knows today that it will effectively exchange the \$900,000 received for £526,890 in 6 months' time.

	Now		6 mths
		6m rate	
Receipt			\$900,000 **receipt**
		US loan rate	
Loan	\$871,671	1.0325 ←	(\$900,000)
			0
Sell at spot	1.7040 ↓		
Immediate receipt	£511,544	1.03 →	£526,890
		UK deposit rate	
Forward hedge:			
	\$900,000/1.6809 =		£535,427

The forward hedge is the recommended hedging strategy.

Test your understanding 9

Answer A

A spot rate is the exchange rate currently offered on a particular currency. The spot rate is the rate of exchange in currency for immediate delivery.

The forward rate is the rate today for exchanging one currency for another at a specified future date (B).

Test your understanding 10

Answer A

Test your understanding 11

Answer B

Using interest rate parity, the Iraqi dinar is the numerator and the Indian rupee is the denominator.

So the expected future exchange rate dinar/rupee is given by:

$$19.68 \times \frac{(1.15)}{(1.10)} = 20.58$$

Test your understanding 12

Answer D

A forward exchange contract is a binding contract which specifies in advance the rate at which a specified currency will be bought and sold at a specified future time.

Test your understanding 13

Answer B

If you are using a money market hedge to hedge a future receipt (a future foreign currency asset), you must borrow the present value of the foreign currency amount today i.e. set up an equivalent future foreign currency liability.

chapter

14

Interest rate risk

Chapter learning objectives

Upon completion of this chapter you will be able to:

- describe and discuss gap exposure as a form of interest rate risk
- describe and discuss basis risk as a form of interest rate risk
- define the term structure of interest rates
- explain the features of a yield curve
- explain expectations theory and its impact on the yield curve
- explain liquidity preference theory and its impact on the yield curve
- explain market segmentation theory and its impact on the yield curve
- discuss and apply matching and smoothing as a method of interest rate risk management
- discuss and apply asset and liability management as a method of interest rate risk management
- define a forward rate agreement
- use a forward rate agreement as a method of interest rate risk management
- define the main types of interest rate derivatives and explain how they can be used to hedge interest rate risk.

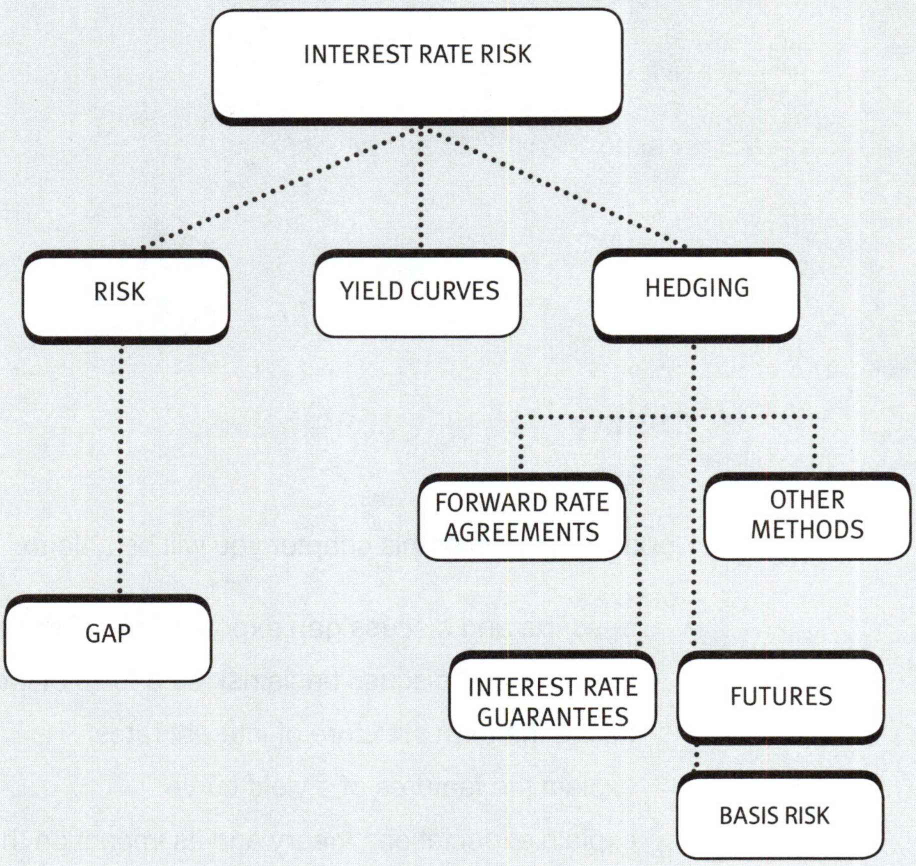

1 Interest rate risk

Financial managers face risk arising from changes in interest rates, i.e. a lack of certainty about the amounts or timings of cash payments and receipts.

Many companies borrow, and if they do they have to choose between borrowing at a fixed rate of interest (usually by issuing bonds) or borrow at a floating (variable) rate (possibly through bank loans). There is some risk in deciding the balance or mix between floating rate and fixed rate debt. Too much fixed-rate debt creates an exposure to falling long-term interest rates and too much floating-rate debt creates an exposure to a rise in short-term interest rates.

It may appear that a company which has size-matched assets and liabilities, and is both receiving and paying interest, may not have any interest rate exposure. However, two floating rates may not be determined using the same basis. For example, one may be linked to LIBOR but the other is not. This makes it unlikely that the two floating rates will move perfectly in line with each other. As one rate increases, the other rate might change by a different amount or might change later.

In addition, companies face the risk that interest rates might change between the point when the company identifies the need to borrow or invest and the actual date when they enter into the transaction.

Managers are normally risk-averse, so they will look for techniques to manage and reduce these risks.

Interest rate exposure

Interest rate risk refers to the risk of an adverse movement in interest rates and thus a reduction in the company's net cash flow.

Adverse Interest Rate Movements

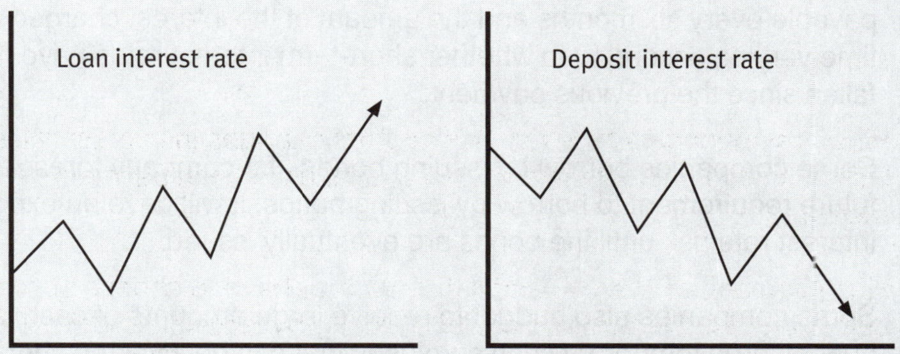

Compared to currency exchange rates, interest rates do not change continually:

- currency exchange rates change throughout the day
- interest rates can be stable for much longer periods

but changes in interest rates can be substantial.

It is the duty of the corporate treasurer to reduce (hedge) the company's exposure to the interest rate risk.

Gap exposure

The degree to which a firm is exposed to interest rate risk can be identified through gap analysis. This uses the principle of grouping together assets and liabilities that are affected by interest rate changes according to their maturity dates. Two different types of gap may occur:

- A negative gap occurs when interest-sensitive liabilities maturing at a certain time are greater than interest-sensitive assets maturing at the same time. This results in a net exposure if interest rates rise by the time of maturity;
- A positive gap occurs is the amount of interest-sensitive assets maturing in a certain period exceeds the amount of interest-sensitive liabilities maturing at the same time. In this situation the firm will lose out if interest rates fall by maturity.

Practical examples of interest rate risk

The following are all practical examples of interest rate risk:

A company might borrow at a variable rate of interest, with interest payable every six months and the amount of the interest charged each time varying according to whether short-term interest rates have risen or fallen since the previous payment.

Some companies borrow by issuing bonds. If a company foresees a future requirement to borrow by issuing bonds, it will have an exposure to interest rate risk until the bonds are eventually issued.

Some companies also budget to receive large amounts of cash, and so budget large temporary cash surpluses that can be invested short-term. Income from those temporary investments will depend on what the interest rate happens to be when the money is available for depositing.

Some investments earn interest at a variable rate of interest (e.g. money in bank deposit accounts) and some short-term investments go up or down in value with changes in interest rates (for example, Treasury bills and other bills).

Some companies hold investments in marketable bonds, either government bonds or corporate bonds. These change in value with movements in long-term interest rates.

Interest rate risk can be significant. For example, suppose that a company wants to borrow $10 million for one year, but does not need the money for another three weeks. It would be expensive to borrow money before it is needed, because there will be an interest cost. On the other hand, a rise in interest rates in the time before the money is actually borrowed could also add to interest costs. For example, a rise of just 0.25% (25 basis points) in the interest rate on a one-year loan of $10 million would cost an extra $25,000 in interest over the course of a year.

2 Why interest rates fluctuate

The yield curve

The **term structure of interest rates** refers to the way in which the yield (return) of a debt security or bond varies according to the term of the security, i.e. to the length of time before the borrowing will be repaid.

The yield curve is an analysis of the relationship between the yields on debt with different periods to maturity.

A yield curve can have any shape, and can fluctuate up and down for different maturities.

There are three main types of yield curve shapes: normal, inverted and flat (or humped):

- normal yield curve – longer maturity bonds have a higher yield compared with shorter-term bonds due to the risks associated with time
- inverted yield curve – the shorter-term yields are higher than the longer-term yields, which can be a sign of upcoming recession
- flat (or humped) yield curve – the shorter- and longer-term yields are very close to each other, which is also a predictor of an economic transition.

The slope of the yield curve is also seen as important: the greater the slope, the greater the gap between short- and long-term rates.

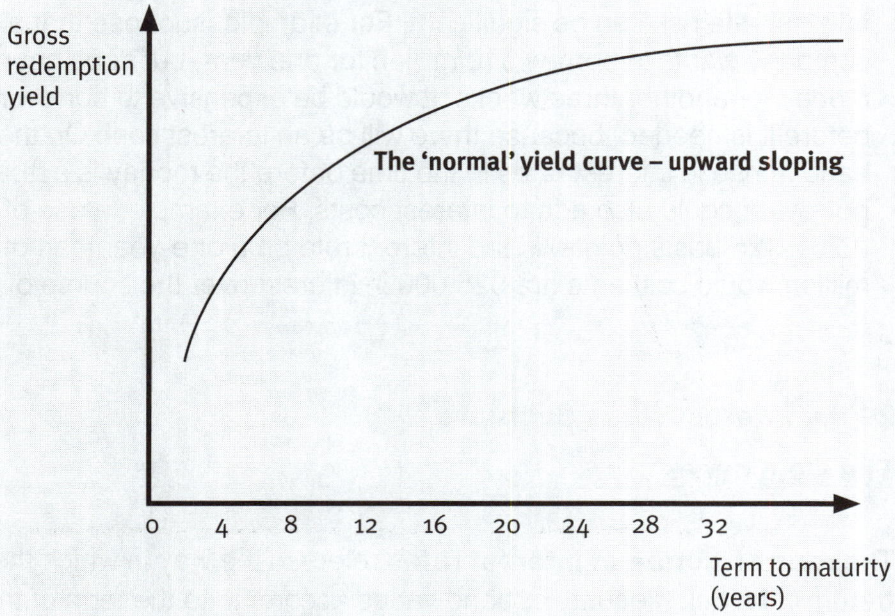

The yield curve

Analysis of term structure is normally carried out by examining risk-free securities such as UK government stocks (gilts). Newspapers such as the Financial Times show the gross redemption yield (i.e. interest yield plus capital gain/loss to maturity) and time to maturity of each gilt on a daily basis.

The return for each instrument is plotted on a graph where the y axis represents the annual return and the x axis represents the instrument's remaining term to maturity. The points plotted on the graph are then joined up to produce a yield curve.

This term structure of interest rates might be shown as a yield curve, as follows.

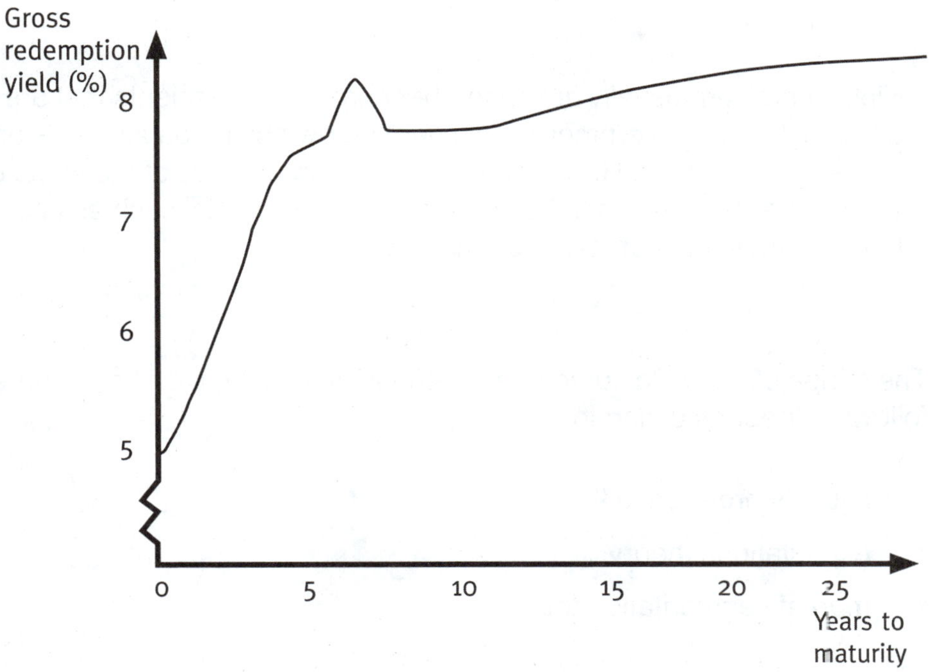

The redemption yield on shorts is less than the redemption yield of mediums and longs, and there is a 'wiggle' on the curve between 5 and 10 years.

A yield curve can have any shape, and can fluctuate up and down for different maturities.

Generally however, yield curves fall into one of three typical patterns.

Normal. A normal yield curve is upward sloping, so that the yield is higher on instruments with a longer-remaining term to maturity. The higher yield compensates the investor for tying up capital for a longer period. Although the yield curve slopes upwards, the gradient of the curve is not steep. A normal yield curve might be expected when interest rates are not expected to change.

Inverse. An inverse yield curve is downward sloping, so that the yield is lower on instruments with a longer-remaining term to maturity. An inverse yield curve might be expected when interest rates are currently high but are expected to fall.

Steep upward-sloping curve. When interest rates are expected to rise, the yield curve is likely to have a steep upward slope, with yields on longer-term investments much higher than the yield on shorter-dated investments.

Yield curves are usually drawn for 'benchmark' investments that are either risk free (government securities) or low risk (such as yields on interest rate swaps). However, they are representative of the slope of the yield curve generally for all other financial instruments, such as inter-bank lending rates and corporate bond yields.

The shape of the yield curve at any point in time is the result of the three following theories acting together:

- liquidity preference theory
- expectations theory
- market segmentation theory.

Liquidity preference theory

Investors have a natural preference for more liquid (shorter maturity) investments. They will need to be compensated if they are deprived of cash for a longer period.

Expectations theory

The normal upward sloping yield curve reflects the expectation that inflation levels, and therefore interest rates will increase in the future.

Market segmentation theory

The market segmentation theory suggests that there are different players in the short-term end of the market and the long-term end of the market.

The yield curve is therefore shaped according to the supply and demand of securities within each maturity length.

Factors affecting the shape of the yield curve

The shape of the yield curve at any particular point in time is generally believed to be a combination of three theories acting together:

- liquidity preference theory
- expectations theory
- market segmentation theory.

Liquidity preference theory

Investors have a natural preference for holding cash rather than other investments, even low-risk ones such as government securities They therefore need to be compensated with a higher yield for being deprived of their cash for a longer period of time. The normal shape of the curve as being upwards sloping can be explained by liquidity preference theory.

Expectations theory

This theory states that the shape of the yield curve varies according to investors' expectations of future interest rates. A curve that rises steeply from left to right indicates that rates of interest are expected to rise in the future. There is more demand for short-term securities than long-term securities since investors' expectation is that they will be able to secure higher interest rates in the future so there is no point in buying long-term assets now. The price of short-term assets will be bid up, the price of long-term assets will fall, so the yields on short-term and long-term assets will consequently fall and rise.

A falling yield curve (also called an inverted curve, since it represents the opposite of the usual situation) implies that interest rates are expected to fall.

In the early 1990s interest rates were high to counteract high inflation. Everybody expected interest rates to fall in the future, which they did. Expectations that interest rates would fall meant it was cheaper to borrow long-term than short-term.

A flat yield curve indicates expectations that interest rates are not expected to change materially in the future.

Market segmentation theory

As a result of the market segmentation theory, the two ends of the curve may have different shapes, as they are influenced independently by different factors.

- Investors are assumed to be risk averse and to invest in segments of the market that match their liability commitments, e.g.
  - banks tend to be active in the short-term end of the market
  - pension funds would tend to invest in long-term maturities to match the long-term nature of their liabilities.
- The supply and demand forces in various segments of the market in part influence the shape of the yield curve.

Market segmentation theory explains the 'wiggle' seen in the middle of the curve where the short end of the curve meets the long end – it is a natural disturbance where two different curves are joining and the influence of both the short-term factors and the long-term factors are weakest.

The significance of the yield curve

Financial managers should inspect the current shape of the yield curve when deciding on the term of borrowings or deposits, since the curve encapsulates the market's expectations of future movements in interest rates.

For example, a normal upward sloping yield curve suggests that interest rates will rise in the future. The manager may therefore:

- wish to avoid borrowing long-term on variable rates, since the interest charge may increase considerably over the term of the loan
- choose short-term variable rate borrowing or long-term fixed rate instead.

The significance of yield curves

Expectations of future interest rate movements are monitored closely by the financial markets, and are important for any organisation that intends to borrow heavily or invest heavily in interest-bearing instruments. A company might use a 'forward yield curve' to predict what interest rates might be in the future. For example, if we know the current interest rate on a two-month and a six-month investment, it is possible to work out what the market expects the four-month interest rate to be in two months' time.

A corporate treasurer might analyse a yield curve to decide for how long to borrow. For example, suppose a company wants to borrow $20 million for five years and would prefer to issue bonds at a fixed rate of interest. One option would be to issue bonds with a five-year maturity. Another option might be to borrow short-term for one year, say, in the expectation that interest rates will fall, and then issue a four-year bond. When borrowing large amounts of capital, a small difference in the interest rate can have a significant effect on profit. For example, if a company borrowed $20 million, a difference of just 25 basis points (0.25% or one quarter of one per cent) would mean a difference of $50,000 each year in interest costs. So if the yield curve indicates that interest rates are expected to fall then short-term borrowing for a year, followed by a 4-year bond might be the cheapest option.

3 Hedging interest rate risk

Forward rate agreements (FRAs)

The aim of an FRA is to:

- lock the company into a target interest rate
- hedge both adverse and favourable interest rate movements.

The company enters into a normal loan but independently organises a forward rate agreement with a bank:

- interest is paid on the loan in the normal way
- if the interest is greater than the agreed forward rate, the bank pays the difference to the company
- if the interest is less than the agreed forward rate, the company pays the difference to the bank.

Test your understanding 1 – FRAs

Enfield plc's financial projections show an expected cash deficit in two months' time of $8 million, which will last for approximately three months. It is now 1 November 20X4. The treasurer is concerned that interest rates may rise before 1 January 20X5. Protection is required for two months.

Now — **Rate agreed**

1 Nov — **1 Jan**

Risk of adverse movement

i.e. that interest rates will increase in this period

The treasurer can lock into an interest rate today, for a future loan. The company takes out a loan as normal, i.e. the rate it pays is the going market rate at the date the loan is taken out. It will then receive or pay compensation under the separate FRA to return to the locked-in rate.

A 2-5 FRA at 5.00 – 4.70 is agreed.

This means that:

- The agreement starts in 2 months time and ends in 5 months' time.
- The FRA is quoted as simple annual interest rates for borrowing and lending, e.g. 5.00 – 4.70.
- The borrowing rate is always the highest.

Required:

Calculate the interest payable if in two months' time the market rate is:

(a) 7% or

(b) 4%.

Test your understanding 2 – FRAs

Able plc needs to borrow £30 million for eight months, starting in three months' time.

A 3-11 FRA at 2.75 – 2.60 is available.

Show the interest payable if the market rate is (a) 4%, (b) 2%.

Interest rate guarantees (IRGs)

An IRG is an option on an FRA. It allows the company a period of time during which it has the option to buy an FRA at a set price.

IRGs, like all options, protect the company from adverse movements and allow it to take advantage of favourable movements.

Decision rules:

If there is an adverse movement	If there is a favourable movement
↓	↓
Exercise the option to protect	**Allow the option to lapse**

IRGs are more expensive than the FRAs, as one has to pay for the flexibility to be able to take advantage of a favourable movement.

If the company treasurer believes that interest rates will rise:

- he will use an FRA, as it is the cheaper way to hedge against the potential adverse movement.

If the treasurer is unsure which way interest will move:

- he may be willing to use the more expensive IRG to be able to benefit from a potential fall in interest rates.

Interest rate futures

Interest rate futures work in much the same way as currency futures. The result of a future is to

- lock the company into the effective interest rate
- hedge both adverse and favourable interest rate movements.

Futures can be used to fix the rate on loans and investments. We will look here at loans.

How they work

As with an FRA, a loan is entered into in the normal way. Suitable futures contracts are then entered into as a separate transaction.

A futures contract is a promise, e.g.:

- if you sell a futures contract you have a contract to borrow money – what you are selling is the promise to make interest payments.

However the borrowing is only notional.

- We close out the position by reversing the original deal, before the real borrowing starts, i.e. before the expiry date of the contract.
- This means buying futures, if you previously sold them, to close out the position. The contracts cancel each other out, i.e. we have contracts to borrow and deposit the same amount of money.
- The only cash flow that arises is the net interest paid or received, i.e. the profit or loss on the future contracts.

As with all futures (as we saw in the previous chapter), each contract is for a standardised amount with a set maturity date. A whole number of contracts must be dealt with.

The price of futures moves inversely to interest rates therefore:

Interest rates rise		**Interest rates fall**	
Loan more expensive	**Loss** from paying extra interest	Loans cheaper	**Gain** cash on interest savings
Futures price falls →	**Profit** made from having sold at one price to open the position and then buy at a lower one to close it.	Futures price rises →	**Loss** made from having sold at one price to open the position and then buying at a higher one to close it.
Net position	**Interest cost effectively fixed**		**Interest cost effectively fixed**

Basis risk

The gain or loss on the future may not exactly offset the cash effect of the change in interest rates, i.e. the hedge may be imperfect. This is known as basis risk.

The risk arises because the price of a futures contract may be different from the spot price on a given date, and this difference is the basis. This is caused by market forces. The exception is on the expiry date, when the basis is zero.

The other main reason why a hedge may be imperfect is because the commodity being hedged (be it currency or interest) must be rounded to a whole number of contacts, causing inaccuracies.

Options

Borrowers may additionally buy options on futures contracts. These allow them to enter into the future if needed, but let it lapse if the market rates move in their favour.

Swaps

An interest rate swap is an agreement whereby the parties agree to swap a floating stream of interest payments for a fixed stream of interest payments and vice versa. There is no exchange of principal.

Swaps can be used to hedge against an adverse movement in interest rates. Swaps may also be sought by firms that desire a type of interest rate structure that another firm can provide less expensively.

Say a company has a $200 million floating loan and the treasurer believes that interest rates are likely to rise over the next five years. He could enter into a five-year swap with a counter-party to swap into a fixed rate of interest for the next five years. From year six onwards, the company will once again pay a floating rate of interest.

e.g

Illustration 1 – Interest rate swaps

Company A wishes to raise $6m and to pay interest at a floating rate, as it would like to be able to take advantage of any fall in interest rates. It can borrow for one year at a fixed rate of 10% or at a floating rate of 1% above LIBOR.

Company B also wishes to raise $6m. They would prefer to issue fixed rate debt because they want certainty about their future interest payments, but can only borrow for one year at 13% fixed or LIBOR + 2% floating, as it has a lower credit rating than company A.

Required

Calculate the effective swap rate for each company – assume savings are split equally.

Solution

Step 1: Identify the type of loan with the biggest difference in rates.

Answer: Fixed (3%)

Step 2: Identify the party that can borrow this type of loan the cheapest.

Answer: Company A

Thus Company A should borrow fixed, company B variable, reflecting their comparative advantages.

Step 3: Work out the potential gain from the swap.

Company A has cheaper borrowing in both fixed and variable. Interest rate differentials are 3% for fixed and 1% for variable. The difference between these (2%) is the potential gain from the swap.

Splitting this equally between the two counter parties, each should gain by 1%.

Step 4: Decide on an appropriate swap arrangement.

	Company A	**Company B**
Market rate on preferred loan type – No swap	LIBOR + 1%	13%
Split the 2% gain	1%	1%
Net payment after swap	LIBOR	12%

In addition to a basic swap, counterparties can also agree to swap equivalent amounts of debt in different currencies. This is knows as a **currency swap**.

The principal is not transferred and the original borrower remains liable in the case of default.

Other practical ways to manage risk

Cash flow matching

An effective, but largely impractical, means of eliminating interest rate risk.

Stated simply, interest rate risk arises from either positive (invested) or negative (borrowed) net future cash flows.

The concept of cash matching is to eliminate interest rate risk by eliminating all net future cash flows.

A portfolio is cash matched if:

- every future cash inflow is balanced with an offsetting cash outflow on the same date
- every future cash outflow is balanced with an offsetting cash inflow on the same date.

The net cash flow for every date in the future is then zero, and there is no risk of interest rate exposure.

Whilst clearly not achievable, it does provide a broad goal that businesses can work towards.

Asset and liability management

Problems arise if interest rates are fixed on liabilities for periods that differ from those on offsetting assets.

Suppose a company is earning 6% on an asset supported by a liability on which it is paying 4%. The asset matures in two years while the liability matures in ten.

- In two years, the firm will have to reinvest the proceeds from the asset.
- If interest rates fall, it could end up reinvesting at 3%. For the remaining eight years, it would earn 3% on the new asset while continuing to pay 4% on the original liability.

To avoid this, companies attempt to match the duration of their assets and liabilities.

Test your understanding 3

Which of the following is not an explanation of a downward slope in the yield curve?

A Liquidity preference

B Expectations theory

C Government policy

D Market segmentation

Test your understanding 4

An inverse yield curve is a possible indication of

A An expected rise in interest rates

B An expected fall in interest rates

C Higher expected inflation

D Lower expected inflation

Test your understanding 5

Which of the following statements, concerning interest rate futures, is incorrect?

A Interest rate futures can be used to hedge against interest rate changes between the current date and the date at which the interest rate on the lending or borrowing is set

B Borrowers buy futures to hedge against interest rate rises

C Interest rate futures have standardised terms, amounts and periods

D The futures price is likely to vary with changes in interest rates

Test your understanding 6

It is 30 June. Greg plc will need a $10 million 6 month fixed rate loan from 1 October. Greg wants to hedge using a forward rate agreement (FRA). The relevant FRA rate is 6% on 30 June.

What is the interest payable/receivable if in 6 months' time the market rate is 9%?

A $150,000 receivable

B $150,000 payable

C $450,000 receivable

D $450,000 payable

Test your understanding 7

An interest rate swap

A allows the company a period of time during which it has the option to buy a forward rate agreement at a set price

B locks the company into an effective interest rate

C is an agreement whereby the parties to the agreement exchange interest rate commitments

D involves the exchange of principle

Chapter summary

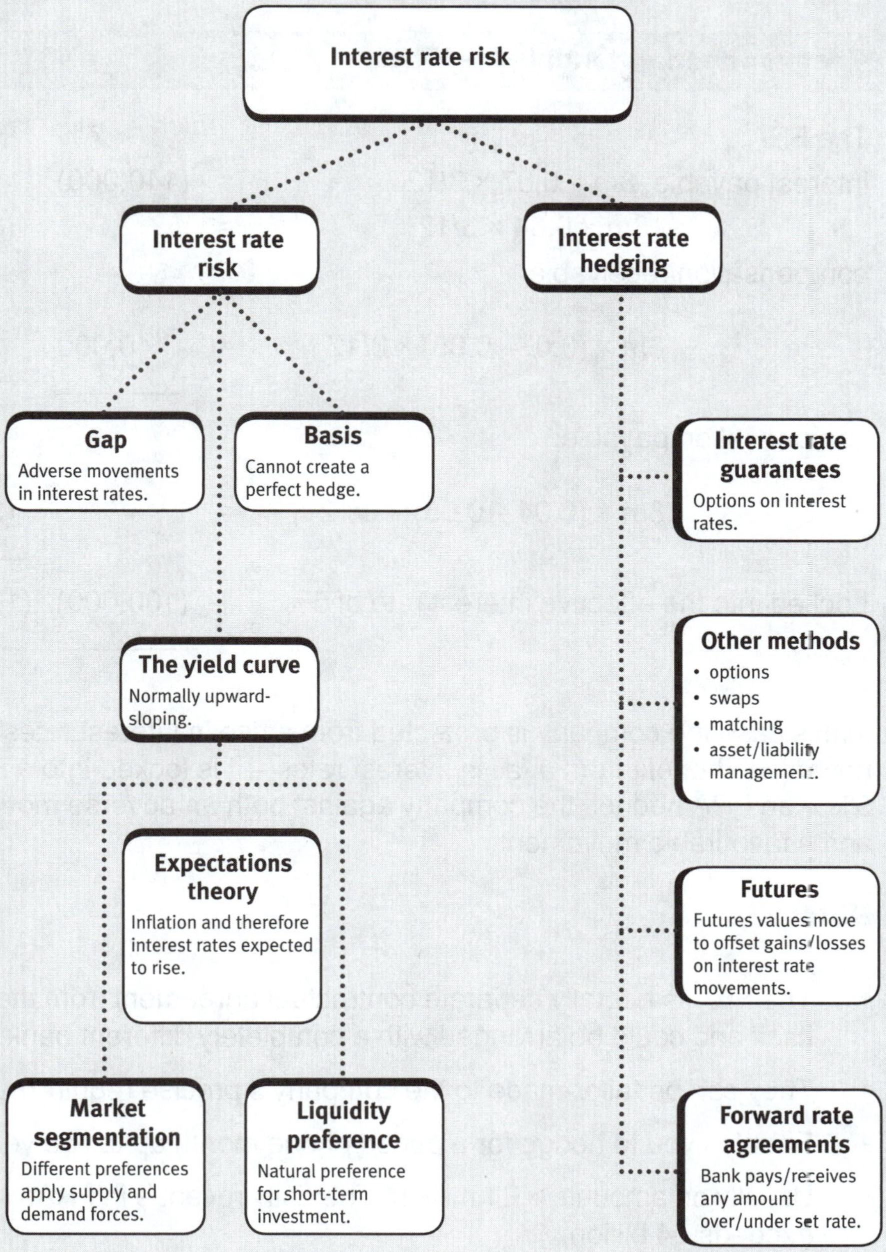

Test your understanding answers

Test your understanding 1 – FRAs

The FRA:		**7%**	**4%**
interest payable: 8m × 0.07 × 3/12	=	(140,000)	
8m × 0.04 × 3/12	=		(80,000)
compensation receivable:			
8m × (0.07– 0.05) × 3/12	=	40,000	
compensation payable:			
8m × (0.04 – 0.05) × 3/12	=		(20,000)
Locked into the effective interest rate of 5%.		(100,000)	(100,000)

In this case the company is protected from a rise in interest rates but is not able to benefit from a fall in interest rates – it is locked into a rate of 5% – an FRA hedges the company against both an adverse movement and a favourable movement.

Note:

- The FRA is a totally separate contractual agreement from the loan itself and could be arranged with a completely different bank.
- They can be tailor-made to the company's precise requirements.
- Enables you to hedge for a period of one month up to two years.
- Usually on amounts > £1 million. The daily revenue in FRAs now exceeds £4 billion.

Test your understanding 2 – FRAs

The FRA:		**4%**	**2%**
Interest payable: 30m × 0.04 × 8 12	=	(800,000)	
30m × 0.02 × 8/12	=		(400,000)
Compensation receivable	=	250,000	
payable	=		(150,000)
Locked into the effective interest rate of 2.75%.		(550,000)	(550,000)

Test your understanding 3

Answer A

Liquidity preference theory (and thus compensating investors for a longer period of time) is an explanation of why the yield curve slopes upwards.

Test your understanding 4

Answer B

An inverse yield curve is downward sloping. It might be expected when interest rates are currently high but expected to fall.

Test your understanding 5

Answer B

Borrowers sell, not buy, futures to hedge against interest rate r ses.

Test your understanding 6

Answer A

The FRA:		
interest payable: 10m × 0.09 × 6/12	=	(450,000)
compensation receivable:		
10m × (0.09 – 0.06) × 6/12	**=**	**150,000**
Locked into the effective interest rate of 6%.		(300,000)

Test your understanding 7

Answer C

An interest guarantee allows the company a period of time during which it has the option to buy an FRA at a set price (A). An interest rate future locks the company into an effective interest rate (B). An interest rate swap **does not** involve the exchange of principal, only the exchange of a floating stream of interest payments for a fixed stream of interest payments and vice versa (D).

chapter

15

Sources of finance

Chapter learning objectives

Upon completion of this chapter you will be able to:

- discuss the criteria which may be used by companies to choose between sources of finance
- explain the relationship between risk and return
- explain the nature and features of different securities in relation to the risk / return trade-off
- discuss increasing the efficiency of working capital management as a source of finance
- discuss the advantages and disadvantages of lease finance as a source of short-term finance
- suggest appropriate sources of short-term finance for a business in a scenario question
- define and distinguish between equity finance and other types of share capital
- discuss the advantages and disadvantages of using retained earnings as a source of finance
- explain the benefits of a placing for an unlisted company
- describe the features and methods of a stock exchange listing including a placing and a public offer
- describe a rights issue
- calculate the theoretical ex-rights price (TERP) of a share
- demonstrate the impact of a rights issue on the wealth of a shareholder
- discuss the advantages and disadvantages of equity finance as a source of long-term finance
- identify and suggest appropriate methods of raising equity finance for a business in a scenario question

- explain the main sources of long-term debt finance available to a business
- discuss the advantages and disadvantages of debt finance as a source of long-term finance
- discuss the advantages and disadvantages of lease finance as a source of long-term finance
- discuss the advantages and disadvantages of venture capital as a source of long-term finance
- suggest appropriate sources of long-term finance for a business in a scenario question
- describe the financing needs of small businesses
- describe the nature of the financing problem for small businesses in terms of the funding gap, the maturity gap and inadequate security
- explain measures that may be taken to ease the financing problems of small and medium enterprises (SMEs), including the responses of government departments and financial institutions
- identify appropriate sources of finance for an SME in a scenario question and evaluate the financial impact of the different sources of finance on the business
- explain the major difference between Islamic finance and other forms of business finance
- explain the concept of interest (riba) and how returns are made by Islamic financial securities
- identify and briefly discuss a range of short and long term Islamic financial instruments available to businesses

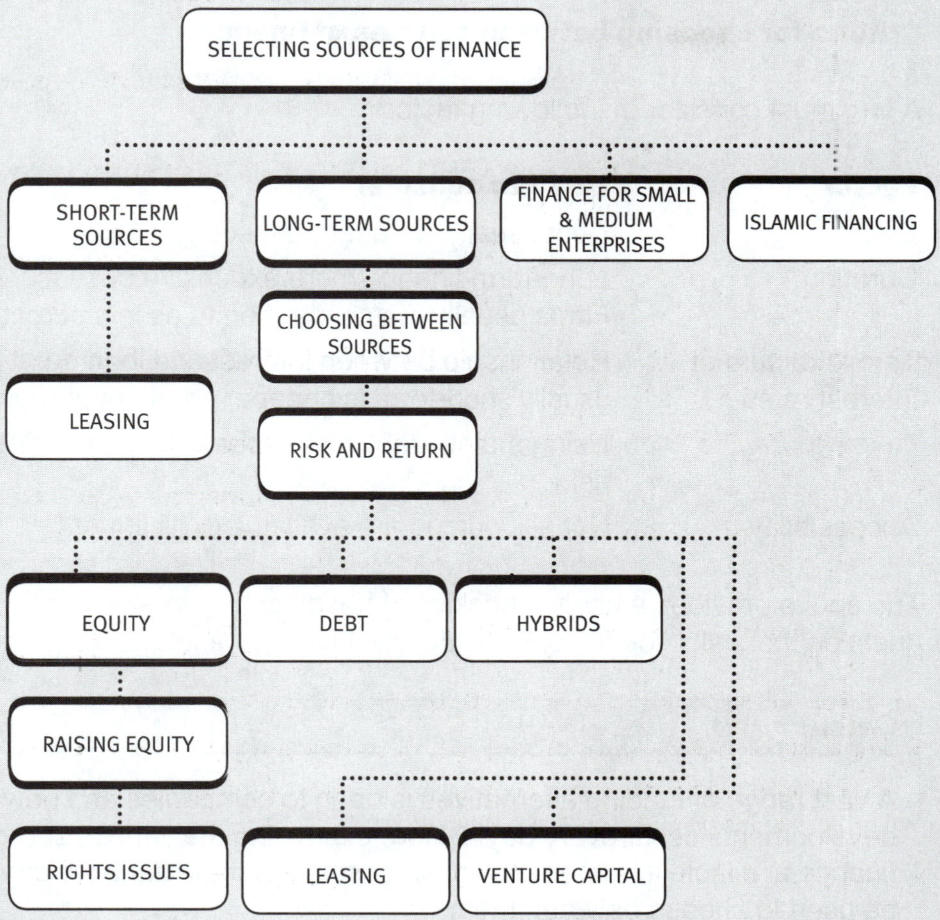

1 Selection of appropriate sources of finance

The need for finance

Firms need funds to:

- provide working capital
- invest in non-current assets.

The main source of funds available is retained earnings, but these are unlikely to be sufficient to finance all business needs.

Criteria for choosing between sources of finance

A firm must consider the following factors:

Factor	Issue to consider
Cost	Debt usually cheaper than equity.
Duration	Long-term finance more expensive but secure. Firms usually match duration to assets purchased.
Term structure of interest rates	Relationship between interest and loan duration – usually short-term is cheaper – but not always!
Gearing	Using mainly debt is cheaper but high gearing is risky.
Accessibility	Not all sources are available to all firms.

The above provides a useful checklist of headings for an examinations question that asks you to consider different types of finance.

Criteria

A vast range of funding alternatives is open to companies and new developments occur every day. Before examining the various sources of finance available it is useful to consider some of the criteria which may be used to choose between them.

Cost

The higher the cost of funding, the lower the firm's profit. Debt finance tends to be cheaper than equity. This is because providers of debt take less risk than providers of equity and therefore earn less return. Interest on debt finance is also normally corporation tax deductible, while returns on equity are not.

Duration

Finance can be arranged for various time periods. Normally, but not invariably, long-term finance is more expensive than short-term finance. This is because lenders normally perceive the risks as being higher on long-term advances. Long-term finance does, however, carry the advantage of security, whereas sources of short-term finance can often be withdrawn at short notice. You should remember 'The Matching Principle' that says:

'Long-term assets should be financed by long-term funds and short-term assets (to some extent) by short-term funds'.

We would generally expect to see working capital financed partly by short-term facilities such as overdraft, whilst fixed assets should be funded by long-term funds. This principle is commonly broken to gain access to cheap short-term funds but the risks involved should be appreciated.

Term structure of interest rates

The term structure of interest rates describes the relationship between interest rates charged for loans of differing maturities.

While short-term funds are usually cheaper than long-term funds, this situation is sometimes reversed and interest rates should be carefully checked.

Imagine the situation where the money markets expected interest rates to fall in the long-term but remain high in the short-term. In this situation borrowing short-term could prove quite expensive.

Gearing

Gearing is the ratio of debt to equity finance. Gearing will be investigated in depth later, but for now we should appreciate that although high gearing involves the use of cheap debt finance, it does bring with it the risk of having to meet regular repayments of interest and principal on the loans. If these are not met, the company could end up in liquidation.

On the other hand, too little debt could result in earnings dilution. For example the issue of a large amount of equity to fund a new project could result in a decrease in earnings per share (EPS), despite an increase in total earnings.

Accessibility

Not all companies have access to all sources of finance. Small companies traditionally have problems in raising equity and long-term debt finance. These problems are investigated later in this chapter but remember that many firms do not have an unlimited choice of funding arrangements.

A quoted company is one whose shares are dealt in on a recognised stock market, so shares in such a company represent a highly liquid asset. This, in turn, makes it much easier to attract new investors to buy new shares issued by the company because these investors know that they can always sell their shares if they wish to realise their investment.

Investment in shares of unquoted companies represents the acquisition of a highly illiquid investment. For this reason it is much more difficult for such a company to raise finance by new share issues.

2 The relationship between risk and return

Investment risk arises because returns are variable and uncertain. An increase in risk generally requires an increase in expected returns.

For example compare:

Building society investment versus Investment in equities

Investment in food retailing versus Investment in computer electronics

In each case an investor would demand higher returns from the second investment because of the higher risk.

It is worth noting the possibility of a reverse yield gap. This refers to the amount by which bond yield (return) exceeds equity yield (return). When the government wants to raise cash it may offer a higher return on government bonds ie. gilts than that offered by shares. A reverse yield gap is likely to occur during periods of high inflation because equities are expected to provide capital gains to compensate for inflation while gilt-edged securites are not. During periods of stable prices the yield gap is usually positive, as mentioned above - a greater yield on equities is needed to compensate investors for their relative riskiness.

Each time an investor demands a higher return on the finance they have provided, this is reflected in a higher cost of that finance to the company.

This is a fundamental principle in the F9 syllabus.

3 Short-term sources of finance

As discussed earlier, working capital is usually funded using short-term sources of finance.

Sources of short-term finance include:

- bank overdrafts
- bank loans
- better management of working capital
- squeezing trade credit
- leasing
- sale and leaseback

Short term finance

With the exception of leasing and sale and leaseback, all other sources of finance have already been covered in the earlier chapters on working capital management.

Leasing as a source of short-term finance

Growing in popularity as a source of finance, a lease is:

- a contract between a lessor and a lessee for the hire of a particular asset
- lessor retains ownership of the asset
- lessor conveys the right to the use of the asset to the lessee for an agreed period
- in return lessor receives specified rentals.

Leasing is a means of financing the use of capital equipment, the underlying principle being that use is more important than ownership. It is a medium-term financial arrangement, usually from one to ten years.

There are two main types of lease agreement:

- operating leases – short-term
- finance leases – long-term.

This section will consider operating leases. Finance leases are considered later in the chapter as a source of long-term finance.

Conditions	Operating lease
Lease period	The lease period is less than the useful life of the asset. The lessor relies on subsequent leasing or eventual sale of the asset to cover his capital outlay and show a profit.
Lessor's business	The lessor may very well carry on a trade in this type of asset.
Risks and rewards	The lessor is normally responsible for repairs and maintenance.
Cancellation	The lease can sometimes be cancelled at short notice.
Substance	The substance of the transaction is the short-term rental of an asset.

Sale and leaseback

A company that owns its own premises can obtain finance by selling the property for cash and renting it back off the acquiror, which would typically be an insurance company or a pension fund.

Although this can provide an immediate source of cash, often more than could be obtained from a mortgage, there are a number of disadvantages including:

- The company loses ownership of the property and will therefore miss out on any appreciation in the property's future value.
- The company will have to sign a rental agreement, usually for at least 50 years, thereby committing the company to occupying the property for many years ahead. This can be restricting.
- The future borrowing capacity of the company will reduce as property is a common asset used to provide security for debt finance.
- Any rent will be subject to regular reviews and will most likely increase over time.

4 Long-term finance – equity

Types of share capital

Equity shareholders are the owners of the business and exercise ultimate control, through their voting rights.

The term equity relates to ordinary shares only.

Equity finance is the investment in a company by the ordinary shareholders, represented by the issued ordinary share capital plus reserves.

There are other types of share capital relating to various types of preference share. These are not considered part of equity, as their characteristics bear more resemblance to debt finance.

Types of share capital

The main types of share capital are summarised in the table below:

Type of share capital	Security or voting rights	Income	Amount of capital
Ordinary shares	Voting rights in general meetings. Rank after all creditors and preference shares in rights to assets on liquidation.	Dividends payable at the discretion of the directors out of undistributed profits remaining after senior claims have been met.	The right to all surplus funds after prior claims have been met.
Cumulative preference shares	Limited right to vote at a general meeting (only when dividend is in arrears or when it is proposed to change the legal rights of the shares). Rank after all creditors but usually before ordinary shareholders in liquidation.	A fixed amount per year at the discretion of the directors. Arrears accumulate and must be paid before a dividend on ordinary shares may be paid. Dividend is not corporation tax deductible.	A fixed amount per share.
Non-cumulative preference shares	Typically acquire some voting rights if the dividend has not been paid for three years. Rank as cumulative in liquidation.	A fixed amount per year, as above. Arrears do not accumulate.	A fixed amount per share.

Ensure you are familiar with the key features of each type of share.

5 Raising equity

There are three main sources of equity finance:

- internally-generated funds – retained earnings
- rights issues
- new external share issues – placings, offers for sale, etc.

Internally-generated funds

Internally-generated funds are earnings retained in the business (i.e. undistributed profits attributable to ordinary shareholders). They are generated as a result of increased working capital management efficiency.

For an established company, internally-generated funds can represent the single most important source of finance, for both short and long-term purposes.

Such finance is cheap and quick to raise, requiring no transaction costs, professional assistance or time delay.

Retained earnings are also a continual source of new funds, provided that the company is profitable and profits are not all paid out as dividends.

Of course, for major investment projects, a greater amount of equity finance may be required than that available from internal sources.

6 Rights issues

A rights issue is an offer to existing shareholders to subscribe for new shares, at a discount to the current market value, in proportion to their existing holdings.

This right of pre-emption:

- enables them to retain their existing share of voting rights
- can be waived with the agreement of shareholders.

Shareholders not wishing to take up their rights can sell them on the stock market.

Advantages:

- it is cheaper than a public share issue
- it is made at the discretion of the directors, without consent of the shareholders or the Stock Exchange.
- it rarely fails.

TERP

The new share price after the issue is known as the **theoretical ex-rights price** and is calculated by finding the weighted average of the old price and the rights price, weighted by the number of shares.

The formula is:

$$\text{Ex-rights price} = \frac{\text{Market value of shares already in issue + proceeds from new share issue}}{\text{Number of shares in issue after the rights issue ('ex rights')}}$$

Test your understanding 1 – TERP

Babbel Co, which has an issued capital of 2 million shares, having a current market value of $2.70 each, makes a rights issue of one new share for every two existing shares at a price of $2.10.

Required:

Calculate the TERP.

Test your understanding 2 – TERP

ABC Co announces a 2 for 5 rights issue at $2 per share. There are currently 10 million shares in issue, and the current market price of the shares is $2.70.

Required:

Calculate the TERP.

The value of a right

To make the offer relatively attractive to shareholders, new shares are generally issued at a discount on the current market price.

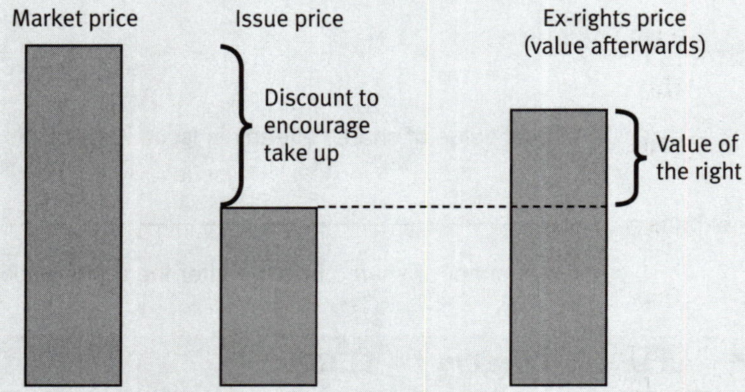

Value of a right = theoretical ex rights price – issue (subscription) price

Since rights have a value, they can be sold on the stock market in the period between:

- the rights issue being announced and the rights to existing shareholders being issued, and
- the new issue actually taking place.

Test your understanding 3 – The value of a right

What is the value of the right in Babbel Co?

Test your understanding 4 – The value of a right

What is the value of the right in ABC Co?

Shareholders' options

The shareholder's options with a rights issue are to:

(1) take up his rights by buying the specified proportion at the price offered

(2) renounce his rights and sell them in the market

(3) renounce part of his rights and take up the remainder

(4) do nothing.

Test your understanding 5 – Shareholders' options

Using the information in test your understanding 1, a shareholder B had 1,000 shares in Babbel Co before the rights offer. Calculate the effect on the net wealth of B of each of the following options:

(1) Take up the shares.

(2) Sell the rights.

(3) Do nothing.

The facts were:

Rights issue 1:2

Cum rights price:	$2.70
Ex-rights price:	$2.50
Issue price	$2.10
Value of right	$0.40

Note:

Cum rights price = market value of the share before the rights issue.

Buyers of shares quoted cum rights are entitled to forthcoming rights.

Additional question – Shareholders' options

Alpha Co has issued share capital of 100 million shares with a current market value of $0.85 each. It announces a 1 for 2 rights issue at a price of 40c per share. It therefore plans to raise $20 million in new funds by issuing 50 million new shares.

Calculate the ex-rights price and for a shareholder, B, holding 1,000 shares in Alpha, consider his wealth if he:

(1) takes up his rights

(2) sells his rights

(3) buys 200 shares and sells the rights to a further 300

(4) takes no action.

The answer to this question can be found after the chapter summary diagram at the end of this chapter.

7 New external share issues

Equity finance can also be raised through the sale of ordinary shares to investors via a new issue.

New share issues

There are several methods of issuing new shares, depending on the circumstances of the company:

Type of company	Company requirement	Method of issue	Type of investor
Unquoted	Finance without an immediate stock market quotation.	• Private negotiation or placing. • Enterprise investment scheme (EIS).	Individuals, merchant banks, finance corporations.
Unquoted or quoted	Finance with an immediate quotation. Finance with a new issue.	• Stock exchange or small firm market placing. • Public offer (fixed price or offer for sale by tender).	The investing public, pension funds, insurance companies and other institutions.
Quoted or unquoted	Limited finance without offering shares to non-shareholders.	• Rights issue.	Holders of existing shares.

Placing

A placing may be used for smaller issues of shares (up to $15 million in value). The bank advising the company selects institutional investors to whom the shares are 'placed' or sold. If the general public wish to acquire shares, they must buy them from the institutions.

Unquoted companies may find it difficult to raise finance because:

- shares are not easily realisable
- it is cheaper to invest in large parcels of shares rather than in many companies
- small firms are regarded as more risky.

However, unquoted companies can arrange for a **placing** of shares with an institution. However, there must usually be at least a prospect of eventually obtaining a quotation on the stock exchange in order for the placing to be successful.

Enterprise investment scheme

See section on finance for small and medium enterprises

Public offer

A public offer is an invitation to apply for shares in a company based upon information contained in a prospectus, either at a fixed price or by tender.

Fixed price offer

Shares are offered at a fixed price to the general public (including institutions). Details of the offer document are published in a prospectus for the issue. The prospectus contains information about the company's past performance and future prospects, as specified by the rules for stock exchange companies. The rule book for UK companies whose shares are listed on the main London Stock Exchange is the UK Listing Rules. These are overseen by the UK Listing Authority, a department of the Financial Services Authority (FSA).

Offer for sale by tender

Shares are offered to the general public (including institutions) but no fixed price is specified. Potential investors bid for shares at a price of their choosing. The 'striking price' at which the shares are sold is determined by the demand for shares.

The price will be either:

(a) the highest price at which the entire issue is sold, all tenders at or above this being allotted in full, or

(b) a price lower than in (a), but with tenders at or above this lower price receiving only a proportion of the shares tendered for, so as to avoid the concentration of ownership in the hands of a few.

Becoming quoted

A company may wish to become listed on the stock exchange to increase its pool of potential investors. Only by being listed can a company offer its shares to the public.

It may start with a quotation on a small firm stock market, such as the Alternative Investment Market (AIM) in the UK, followed by a full listing.

The possible methods of obtaining a stock exchange listing in the UK are:

Method	**Conditions**
Public offer	Offered to public , either at a fixed price or via a tender process where investors 'bid' for shares.
A placing	Offered to institutions.
Introduction	No new issue of shares. Public already holds at least 25%. Shares become listed. Public can then buy on market.

Introduction

Introduction is a process that allows a company to join a stock exchange without raising capital. A company does not issue any fresh shares; it merely introduces its existing shares in the market.

It is used where the public already holds at least 25% of the shares in the company (the minimum requirement for a stock exchange listing). The shares become listed and members of the public can buy shares from the existing shareholders.

Institutional advisers on new share issues

As well as requiring the assistance of accountants in preparing the prospectus, new share issues may require the services of an **issuing house**. An issuing house is an investment bank specialising in new issue of shares.

Issuing houses

A company wishing to raise capital by offer for sale would first get in touch with one of the issuing houses which specialise in this kind of business.

In some cases, the issuing house earns a fee by organising public issues. In others, it purchases outright a block of shares from a company and then makes them an 'offer for sale' to the public on terms designed to bring in a profit to the issuing house.

There are between 50 and 60 members of the Issuing House Association, including all the important merchant banks. The fact that an issue is launched by one of these banks or other houses of high reputation is, in itself, a factor contributing to the chance of success of such a venture.

Investment banks

Investment banks also perform the functions of underwriting, marketing and pricing new issues.

- Underwriting: large share issues are usually underwritten which adds to the cost of raising finance but reduces the risk. An underwriter is someone (usually an investment institution) who is prepared to purchase shares in a share issue that other investors do not buy. For example, suppose that XYZ Co is issuing 50 million new shares at $2.50 each. If the issue is underwritten, the investment bank assisting the company with the issue will find one or more institutions that are prepared to buy up to a given quantity of the shares, if no one else wants them. In return for underwriting a portion of the new issue, an underwriter is paid a commission. If there are just one or two underwriters for an issue, the underwriters might offload some of their risk by getting other institutions to sub-underwrite the issue. Sub-underwriters are also paid a commission.

The effect of underwriting is to ensure that all the shares in a new issue will find a buyer. However, if large quantities of the shares are left in the hands of the underwriters after the issue, the share price is likely to remain depressed until the underwriters have been able to sell off the shares they do not want in the secondary market.

- Marketing: the marketing and selling of a new issue is a business activity in its own right. The investment bank provides the expertise.
- Pricing: one of the most difficult decisions in making a new issue is that it should be priced correctly. If the price is too low, the issue will be over-subscribed, and existing shareholders will have had their holdings diluted more than is necessary. If the price is too high and the issue fails, the underwriters are left to subscribe to the shares. This will adversely affect the reputation of the issuing house and the company. Correct pricing is important, and the investment bank will be able to offer advice based on experience and expertise. One way round the issue price problem is an issue by tender.

What is a stock split?

A stock split takes place when a company divides its existing shares into multiple shares. Although the number of shares increases by a specific multiple, the total monetary value of the shares remains the same compared to pre-split amounts, because the split did not add any real value. The most common split ratios are 2-for-1 or 3-for-1, which means that the shareholder will have two or three shares for every share held earlier.

There are several reasons companies consider carrying out a stock split. Not only will a stock split increase the shares' liquidity but as the price gets higher and higher, some investors may feel the price is too high for them to buy, or small investors may feel it is unaffordable. Splitting the stock brings the share price down to a more 'attractive' level, making the shares more marketable. The effect here is purely psychological as the actual value of the stock does not change, but the lower stock price may affect the way the stock is perceived and therefore entice new investors.

8 Choosing between sources of equity

When choosing between sources of equity finance, account must be taken of factors such as:

(1) the accessibility of the finance

(2) the amount of finance

(3) costs of the issue procedure

(4) pricing of the issue

(5) control

(6) dividend policy – using retained earnings could impact the share price (see chapter on dividend policy).

Because of the relative issue costs and the ease of organisation, the most important source of equity is retained earnings, then rights issues, then new issues.

Choosing between sources of equity

Accessibility to finance

The ability of a company to raise equity finance is restricted by its access to the general market for funds. Thus, whilst **quoted** companies are able to use any of the sources, an **unquoted** company is restricted to rights issues and private placings. The problem of equity finance for smaller companies is examined later in this chapter).

Furthermore, there are statutory restrictions, e.g. those in the UK imposed by the Companies Act 2006. Only public limited companies may offer shares to the general public.

Obviously, the need to raise finance could be combined with a **flotation** (i.e. a private company going public and having its shares quoted on a recognised stock exchange). However, flotations will incur significant costs.

Amount of finance

The amount of finance that can be raised by a **rights issue** from an **unquoted** company is limited by the number and resources of the existing shareholders. It is not possible to provide general estimates of the amounts that may be raised as the circumstances vary. For quoted companies, where rights may be sold, this is less problematic.

Larger sums can be raised by **placings**, but ultimately it is the offer of shares to the general public that opens up the full financial resources of the market.

Costs of issue procedures

Use of internally-generated funds is easily the cheapest and simplest method. For new issues, placings are the most attractive on cost grounds, followed by rights issues, with public offers being by far the most expensive.

However all new share issues will take management and administrative time within the company. This will be much greater for an offer for sale than for the other two alternatives.

Pricing of the issue

One of the most difficult problems in making a **new issue to the public** is setting the price correctly. If it is too high, the issue will not be fully taken up and will be left with the underwriters, and if it is underpriced some of the benefits of the project for which the finance is being raised will accrue to the new shareholders and not to the old.

The same pricing problem exists with a **placing** as with a new issue. There will be no danger of undersubscription, of course, because the placing is agreed before the issue is made. However, the price will have been negotiated so as to be attractive to the subscribing institutions. Almost inevitably, it will be below the issue price that it would obtain in the market, because of the attractions of lower issue costs.

A **rights issue**, on the other hand, completely by-passes the price problem. Since the shares are offered to existing shareholders, it does not matter if the price is well below the traded price. Indeed, it would be normal for this to be so. Any gain on the new shares would, by the nature of a rights issue, go to the existing shareholders.

The pricing of new issues is even more complex when the company is **unquoted**. A company coming to the market for the first time would have no existing market price to refer to and would have to value the shares from scratch.

Control

There is no change in the shareholders with internally-generated funds and rights issues, insofar as they are taken up by existing shareholders. On the other hand, **placings** and **sales** to the general public introduce new shareholders.

Which is preferable depends on the objectives of the fund-raising exercise. If the desire is to retain control for the existing shareholders, then a rights issue is preferable. If diversification of control is desired, then an issue to the public will be preferred.

There can be no rigid rules concerning the choice of finance. Use of internally-generated funds is the best choice, subject to sufficient availability and dividend policy considerations. Of the new issue options, the order of preference will generally be a rights issue, placing and offer for sale to the general public. As funds available are consumed, so the next source is utilised.

9 Long-term finance – debt

Long-term debt (bonds), usually in the form of debentures or loan notes, is frequently used as a source of long-term finance as an alternative to equity.

A bond is a written acknowledgement of a debt by a company, normally containing provisions as to payment of interest and the terms of repayment of principal.

Bonds are also known as debentures, loan notes or loan stock. They:

- are traded on stock markets in much the same way as shares
- are usually denominated in blocks of $100 nominal value
- may be secured or unsecured
- secured debt will carry a charge over:
  - one or more specific assets, usually land and buildings, which are mortgaged in a fixed charge.
  - all assets – a floating charge.

  On default, the loan note holders can appoint a receiver to administer the assets until the interest is paid. Alternatively the assets may be sold to repay the principal.

- may be redeemable or irredeemable.

Irredeemable debt is not repayable at any specified time in the future. Instead, interest is payable in perpetuity. As well as some bonds, preference shares are often irredeemable. It should be noted that, as a form of finance, irredeemable debt is very rare in reality.

If the debt is redeemable the principal will be repayable at a future date.

e.g

Illustration 1 – Long-term finance debt

If a company has '5% 2015 loan notes redeemable at par, quoted at $95 ex-int', this description refers to loan notes that:

- pay interest at 5% on nominal value, i.e. $5 per $100 (this is known as the coupon rate)
- are redeemable in the year 2015
- will be repaid at par value, i.e. each $100 nominal value will be repaid at $100
- currently have a market value of $95 per $100, without rights to the current year's interest payment.

The terms 'loan notes' and 'bonds' are now used generally to mean any kind of long-term marketable debt securities.

10 Characteristics of loan notes and other long-term debt

Advantages:

From the viewpoint of the investor, debt:

- is low risk.

From the viewpoint of the company, debt

- is cheap
- has predictable flows
- does not dilute control.

Disadvantages:

From the viewpoint of the investor, debt:

- has no voting rights.

From the viewpoint of the company, debt:

- is inflexible
- increases risk at high levels of gearing (see chapter 18)
- must (normally) be repaid.

These are the key points for a discussion about the use of debt in an examination question.

Debt finance

Loan notes from the viewpoint of the investor

Debt is viewed as low risk because:

- it often has a definite maturity and the holder has priority in interest payments and on liquidation
- income is fixed, so the holder receives the same interest whatever the earnings of the company.

Debt holders do not usually have voting rights. Only if interest is not paid will holders take control of the company.

Loan note from the viewpoint of the company

Advantages of debt

- Debt is cheap. Because it is less risky than equity for an investor, loan note holders will accept a lower rate of return than shareholders. Also, debt interest is an allowable expense for tax. So if the cost of borrowing for a company is 6%, say, and the rate of corporation tax is 30%, the company can set the cost of the interest against tax, and the effective 'after-tax' cost of the debt would be just 4.2% (6% × 70%).
- Cost is limited to the stipulated interest payment.
- There is no dilution of control when debt is issued.

Disadvantages of debt

- Interest must be paid whatever the earnings of the company, unlike dividends which can be paid in good years and not in bad. If interest is not paid, the trustees for the loan note holders can call in the receiver.
- Shareholders may be concerned that a geared company cannot pay all its interest and still pay a dividend and will raise the rate of return that they require from the company to compensate for this increase in risk. This may effectively put a limit on the amount of debt that can be raised.
- With fixed maturity dates, provision must be made for the repayment of debt.
- Long-term debt, with its commitment to fixed interest payments, may prove a burden especially if the general level of interest rates falls.

Different types of bonds

There are many different types of bonds available. However, a couple of common types that you should be aware of are:

Deep discount bonds

These are loans notes issued at a price that is a large discount to the nominal value of the notes, and which will be redeemable at par (or above par) when they eventually mature.

The low initial price paid by the investor is balanced against a lower rate of return (coupon rate) offered on the bond. Much of the return gained by the investor comes from the capital gain when the bond is redeemed.

Zero coupon bonds

These are bonds that are issued at a discount to their redemption value but no interest is paid on them.

Hybrids – convertibles

Some types of finance have elements of both debt and equity, e.g.:

- convertible loan notes.

Convertibles give the holder the right to convert to other securities, normally ordinary shares at either a:

- predetermined price
  - e.g. notes may be converted into shares at a value of 400c per share
- predetermined ratio
  - e.g. $100 of stock may be converted into 25 ordinary shares.

Conversion premium occurs if:

Market value convertible stock > Market price of shares the stock is to be converted into.

Stock trading at $102, to be converted into 10 shares currently trading at $9 each, has a conversion premium of :

102 – (10 × 9) = $12 or $1.20 per share.

The floor value of a convertible loan note is the minimum market price of the note. Since it attaches no value to the conversion it can be calculated as the present value of the future interest payments plus the present value of the cash redemption value (i.e. the value a straight debenture would have with no conversion rights).

Hybrids – loan notes with warrants

Warrants give the holder the right to subscribe at a fixed future date for a certain number of ordinary shares at a predetermined price.

NB If warrants are issued with loan notes, the loan notes are **not** converted into equity. Instead bond holders:

- make a cash payment for the shares
- retain the loan notes until redemption.

Often used as sweeteners on debt issues:

- interest rate on the loan is low and loan may be unsecured
- right to buy equity set at an attractive price.
- bond holders can sell the warrants after buying the loan notes, thereby decreasing the cost of buying the loan notes

Attractions of convertibles and warrants

Advantage	Reason
Immediate finance at low cost	Because of the conversion option, the loans can be raised at below normal interest rates or with less security.
Attractive, if share prices are depressed	Where companies wish to raise equity finance, but share prices are currently depressed, convertibles offer a 'back-door' share issue method.
Self-liquidating	Where loans are converted into shares, the problem of repayment disappears.
Exercise of warrants related to need for finance.	Options would normally only be exercised where the share price has increased. If the options involve the payment of extra cash to the company, this creates extra funds when they are needed for expansion.

11 Long-term finance – leasing

The key difference between an operating lease (short-term) and a finance lease (medium to long-term) is that the former equates to renting an asset whereas the latter equates to borrowing money in order to purchase the asset.

Long-term lease arrangements are likely to be a finance lease:

Conditions	Finance lease
Lease period	One lease exists for the whole useful life of the asset though may be a primary and secondary period.
Lessor's business	The lessor does not usually deal directly in this type of asset.
Risks and rewards	The lessor does not retain the risks or rewards of ownership. Lessee responsible for repairs and maintenance.
Cancellation	The lease agreement cannot be cancelled. The lessee has a liability for all payments.
Substance	The purchase of the asset by the lessee financed by a loan from the lessor, i.e. it is effectively a source of medium- to long-term debt finance.

Usually the lease period is divided into two:

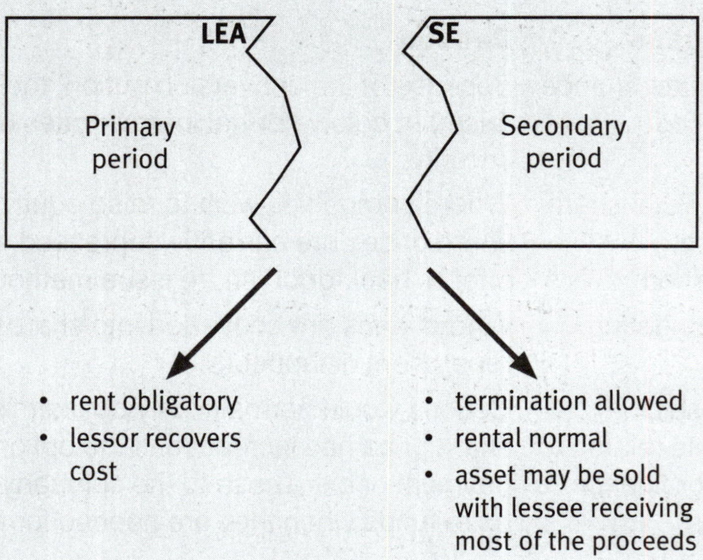

The length of the primary period will vary from asset to asset depending on the total expected economic life.

The decision whether to lease or buy is both a practical and financial one. The financial choice was discussed in the chapter on asset investment decisions.

12 Venture capital

Venture capital is the provision of risk bearing capital, usually in the form of a participation in equity, to companies with high growth potential.

Venture capitalists provide start-up and late stage growth finance, usually for smaller firms.

Venture capitalists will assess an investment prospect on the basis of its:

- financial outlook
- management credibility
- depth of market research
- technical abilities
- degree of influence offered:
  - controlling stake?
  - board seat?
- exit route.

13 Financial impact of sources of finance for small and medium enterprises

Small and medium-sized entities (SMEs) tend to be unquoted with ownership of the business usually being restricted to a small number of individuals. Often the financing needs are beyond the levels of initial seed capital invested by the owner when the business is formed. Capital will be required to invest in non-current assets as well as financing the working capital requirements of the business.

SMEs can often face difficulties when raising finance since investing in an SME is inherently more risky than investing in a larger company due to:

- the lack of business history or proven track record
- the lower level of public scrutiny over accounts and records.

Despite accounting for a significant proportion of economic activity around the world, many SMEs will fail within their first two years of trading, often due to an inability to secure sufficient finance.

The funding gap

As smaller companies tend to be unquoted, it is more difficult for equity investors to liquidate their investment. Typically therefore small firms rely on finance from retentions, rights issues and bank borrowings.

However, Initial ('seed') capital is often from family and friends, seriously limiting the scope for further rights issues.

Bank borrowing doesn't always provide a solution either. To control their exposure, banks will often use credit scoring systems, effectively creating competition amongst SMEs for the available funds. Additional information in the form of business plans will have to be submitted and lenders will very often require additional security to be provided (which the owners may be unwilling or unable to give). Lenders will also want to monitor their investment more closely.

As a result, a funding gap often arises when they want to expand beyond these means of finance but are not yet ready for a listing on the Stock Exchange or Alternative Investment Market (AIM).

This gap may be bridged in a number of ways:

- Financial investors including:
  - Business angels
  - Venture capitalists
- Various government solutions including:
  - increasing the marketability of shares
  - providing tax incentives
  - other specific forms of assistance
- Other practices including:
  - supply chain financing
  - crowdfunding
  - peer-to-peer funding

Financial investors

Small firms are often considered to be more risky. This is a particular issue for newer businesses which may:

- lack proper financial control systems
- have inexperienced management teams
- not have an established track record

- lack sufficient good quality assets to offer as security (it is common for the owners of the business to be asked for personal guarantees).

Although banks remain reluctant to invest heavily in SMEs because of:

- the lack of security
- their risk-averse approach

Investment has become more readily available from:

- venture capitalists – who provide risk-bearing capital to companies with high growth potential
- business angels – wealthy individuals investing in start-up, early stage or expanding firms, at lower levels than a venture capitalist (typically between £10,000 and £250,000 per deal).

Banks

Traditionally, small businesses have borrowed by means of loans and overdrafts from clearing banks. The main problems have always been the **security** required by the bank for granting the loan, and the **risk averse attitude of banks** when faced with a decision relating to a new and untested project. In the UK, the requirement for a personal guarantee from the proprietor to cover the loan or overdraft advance has inhibited the expansion of many small businesses and contributed towards the problem of British ideas being developed abroad.

Whilst the UK government has attempted to make debt investment in small businesses more attractive by the introduction of its Loan Guarantee Scheme, this has not proved very successful due to its relatively high interest rate.

Venture capital funds

The combination of increasing the prospective marketability of SME shares and tax relief schemes has led to the proliferation of venture capital funds, which provide equity capital for small and growing businesses.

One of the original, and still one of the best known, venture capital institutions in the UK is that forming part of the 3i Group. It takes a continuing interest in its client enterprises and does not require to withdraw the capital after, say, a five-year period.

However, in recent years, most major providers of business finance have in some way become involved in the provision of venture capital, usually by setting up or participating in specialist 'venture capital funds'. The main spur to their growth has come from the incentives described above.

The result is that there is now no real shortage of venture capital for viable projects. The range of possible funds includes those run by merchant and other banks, pension funds, individuals and local authorities.

Business angels

Although venture capital companies are the main providers of equity finance to small businesses, they are highly selective and normally do not invest amounts under £100,000 in the UK. An alternative source of smaller amounts of equity capital are private individuals, sometimes known as business angels, who normally have a business background.

Business angels are willing to make investments in small businesses in return for an equity stake. They can also offer the businesses the benefits of their own management expertise. A number of business angel networks operate in the UK to match businesses seeking equity finance with potential investors.

Additional question – Finance for SMEs

Toogood Gardens is a private company that owns and operates a small chain of florists and garden centres in the south west. They have expanded rapidly since they opened 3 years ago, financing the expansion mainly through retained profits.

The directors are now considering a major expansion opportunity as a similar chain in a neighbouring area has become available for sale.

Advise the directors about the best way to raise funds to buy the chain, if a share-for-share deal is not available.

The answer to this question can be found after the chapter summary diagram at the end of this chapter.

Government solutions

Governments have adopted a two-pronged response to increasing the attractiveness of SMEs:

- increasing marketability of shares
- tax incentives for investors.

In addition they have provided specific assistance in a range of areas (see below).

Making shares marketable

A number of SMEs that have good business ideas and growth potential do not fulfil the profitability/track record requirements to obtain a full stock exchange listing.

The development of small firm capital markets, such as the AIM in the UK and the Growth Enterprise Market (GEM) in Hong Kong, is designed to bridge this gap and provide both an exit ground and a venue for further fund-raising for investments.

In addition companies in the UK are now able to purchase their own shares, so a small investor can be bought out as needed.

Tax incentives

The following are the responses of the UK government which illustrate the types of incentives available:

The Enterprise Investment Scheme (EIS)

The Wilson Committee's recommendations led to the development of the current EIS which offers tax relief on investments in new ordinary shares in qualifying unlisted trading companies, including those traded on the AIM. There is a limit on the amount an individual may invest (currently up to £400,000 each tax year) and the investment qualifies for 20% income tax relief.

Any gain on disposing of EIS shares after 3 years is exempt from capital gains tax (CGT). Income tax or CGT relief is available on losses.

The scheme applies to any company carrying out a qualifying trade or business activity wholly or mainly in the UK, provided that the company's gross assets do not exceed £7 million immediately before the shares are issued. It enables companies to raise up to £1m a year. Participating investors may become paid directors of the company and in certain circumstances still qualify for the relief.

Venture Capital Trusts (VCTs)

VCTs are companies listed on the London Stock Exchange and are similar to investment trusts.

At least 70% of the underlying investments must be held in a spread of small unquoted trading companies within three years of the date of launch.

The aim is to encourage individuals to invest indirectly in a range of small higher-risk trading companies whose shares and securities are not listed on a recognised stock exchange. By investing through a VCT, the investment risk is spread over a number of companies.

Income tax relief is available at 30% on new subscriptions by individuals for ordinary shares in VCTs, to a maximum of £200,000 pa. In addition, subject to certain conditions, CGT relief is available on disposal of the shares.

Share incentive schemes

In the UK, there are schemes designed to encourage employees to hold shares in companies by which they are employed. All such schemes require HM Revenue and Customs (HMRC) approval.

Specific forms of assistance

This may take the form of:

- business links – a largely government-funded service that provides information, advice and support to those wishing to start, maintain and grow a business
- financial assistance:
  - loan guarantees
  - grants
  - loans.

Whilst you are not expected to have a detailed knowledge of particular government schemes, you should have a general awareness of the type of assistance offered.

Here we shall concentrate on the financial aspects of government assistance:

Small Firms Loan Guarantee Scheme (SFLGS)

This provides a government guarantee for loans by approved lenders. Loans are made to firms or individuals unable to obtain conventional finance because of a lack of track record or security. The guarantee generally covers 70% of the outstanding loan. This rises to 85% for established businesses trading for two years or more. Loans can be for amounts between £5,000 and £100,000 (£250,000 for established businesses) and over a period of two to ten years.

NB. Not all businesses are eligible for a loan and there are some restrictions on their use.

Regional Selective Assistance (RSA)

This is a discretionary scheme available in those parts of the UK designated as Assisted Areas. It takes the form of grants to encourage firms to locate or expand in these areas. Projects must either create new employment or safeguard existing jobs.

In England, for example, RSA is available for projects involving capital expenditure of at least £500,000.

Enterprise grants

This is a selective scheme for firms employing fewer than 250 people. It is available for high quality projects in designated areas. Businesses may only receive one such grant.

Regional innovation grants

This is available in certain areas of the UK to encourage the development of new products and processes. It is available to individuals or businesses employing no more than 50 people. The scheme provides a fixed grant of up to 50% of eligible costs up to a maximum of £25,000.

Small firms training loans

These are available through the Department for Education and Employment and eight major banks in the UK. The scheme helps businesses with up to 50 employees to pay for vocational education or training, by offering loans on deferred repayment terms:

- firms can borrow between £500 and £125,000 for between 1 and 7 years to cover education and training costs and, with restrictions, costs of consultancy advice on training matters
- the interest on the loan can be fixed or variable, and is paid by the Department for the first 6 to 12 months
- any education or training is eligible provided the firm can show that it will help them achieve their business objectives.

European Investment Bank (EIB) and European Investment Fund (EIF) schemes

The EIB provides loans to banks and leasing companies to help provide finance to small and medium-sized companies. The operators of EIB-supported schemes include finance organisations such as Barclays Mercantile, Lombard Business Finance and Forward Trust.

The EIF provides loan guarantees in conjunction with some finance organisations' own environmental loan facilities. These facilities are designed to assist business to finance investments that produce a quantifiable environmental benefit (energy usage, raw material usage, etc.).

Other practices to bridge the SME funding gap

Supply chain financing

In 2012 the Supply Chain Finance Scheme was introduced which provides cheaper finance for small and medium sized businesses.

The scheme allows large organisations to vouch for their suppliers' incomes. In return, banks will allow the small and medium sized businesses access to credit to improve cash flow and lower costs within the supply chain. This is because larger companies generally have a stronger credit rating and better access to finance than SMEs.

In practice, banks will be notified by the larger company that an invoice is being approved; the bank is then able to offer a 100 per cent immediate advance to the supplier at lower interest rates based upon their customer's credit rating knowing the invoice will be paid.

The sheme helps smaller businesses in two key areas - improving their working capital and tackling the issue of late payments.

Crowdfunding

Crowdfunding is a way of raising finance by asking a large number of people each for a small amount of money. Financing a business, project or venture can typically involve asking a few people for large sums of money. Crowdfunding switches this idea around, using the internet to talk to thousands - if not millions - of potential funders. Typically, those seeking funds will set up a profile of their project on a website. They can use social media, alongside traditional networks of friends, family and work acquaintances, to raise money.

Peer-to-peer financing

Peer-to-peer financing is the practice of borrowing and lending money between unrelated individuals, or 'peers', without going through a traditional financial intermediary such as a bank or other traditional financial institution. There is no necessary common bond or prior relationship betweeen borrowers and lenders. Intermediation takes place by a peer-to-peer lending company and all transactions take place online, with a view to the lender making a profit. Lenders may choose which borrowers to invest in and the loans are unsecured. The emergence of new intermediaries has proven to save time and expenses.

14 Islamic finance

Islamic finance has the same purpose as other forms of business finance except that it operates in accordance with the principles of Islamic law (Sharia).

The basic principles covered by Islamic finance include:

- Sharing of profits and losses.
- No interest (riba) allowed.
- Finance is restricted to Islamically accepted transactions. i.e. No investment in alcohol, gambling etc.

Therefore, ethical and moral investing is encouraged.

Instead of interest being charged, returns are earned by channeling funds into an underlying investment activity, which will earn profit. The investor is rewarded by a share in that profit, after a management fee is deducted by the bank.

The main sources of finance within the Islamic banking model include:

- Murabaha (trade credit)
- Ijara (lease finance)
- Sukuk (debt finance)
- Mudaraba (equity finance)
- Musharaka (venture capital)

Islamic financing

The Islamic economic model has developed over time based on the rulings of Sharia on commercial and financial transactions. The Islamic finance framework seen today is based on the principles developed within this model. These include:

- An emphasis on fairness such that all parties involved in a transaction can make informed decisions without being misled or cheated. Equally reward should be based on effort rather than for simple ownership of capital,
- The encouragement and promotion of the rights of individuals to pursue personal economic wellbeing, but with a clear distinction between what commercial activities are allowed and what are forbidden (for example, transactions involving alcohol, pork related products, armaments, gambling and other socially detrimental activities). Speculation is also prohibited (so instruments such as options and futures are not allowed). Ethical and moral investing is encouraged,
- The strict prohibition of interest (riba). Instead interest is replaced with cash flows from productive sources, such as returns from wealth generating investment activities.

How returns are earned

Riba is defined as the excess paid by the borrower over the original capital borrowed i.e the equivalent to interest on a loan. Its literal translation is 'excess'.

Within the conventional banking system, a bank get access to funds by offering interest to depositers. It will then apply those funds by lending money, on which it charges interest. The bank makes a profit by charging more interest on the money it lends than it pay to its depositers. This process is outlawed under Islamic finance.

In an Islamic bank, the money provided by depositers is not lent, but is instead channelled into an underlying investment activity, which will earn profit. The depositor is rewarded by a share in that profit, after a management fee is deducted by the bank.

For example, in an Islamic mortgage transaction, instead of loaning the buyer money to purchase the item, a bank might buy the item itself from the seller, and re-sell it to the buyer at a profit, while allowing the buyer to pay the bank in instalments. However, the bank's profit cannot be made explicit and therefore there are no additional penalties for late payment.

In effect, the interest is replaced with cash flows from productive sources, such as returns from wealth generating investment activities and operations. These include profits from trading in real assets and cash flows from the transfer of the right to use an asset (for example, rent).

Islamic sources of finance

In Islamic Banking there are broadly 2 categories of financing techniques:

- "Fixed Income" modes of finance – murabaha, ijara, sukuk
- Equity modes of finance – mudaraba, musharaka

Each of these is discussed in more detail below:

Murabaha

Murabaha is a form of trade credit or loan. The key distinction between a murabaha and a loan is that with a murabaha, the bank will take actual constructive or physical ownership of the asset. The asset is then sold onto the 'borrower' or 'buyer' for a profit but they are allowed to pay the bank over a set number of instalments.

The period of the repayments could be extended but no penalties or additional mark up may be added by the bank. Early payment discounts are not welcomed (and will not form part of the contract) although the financier may choose (not contract) to give discounts.

Ijara

Ijara is the equivalent of lease finance; it is defined as when the use of the underlying asset or service is transferred for consideration. Under this concept, the Bank makes available to the customer the use of assets or equipment such as plant, office automation, or motor vehicles for a fixed period and price. Some of the specifications of an Ijara contact include:

- The use of the leased asset must be specified in the contract.
- The lessor (the bank) is responsible for the major maintenance of the underlying assets (ownership costs)
- The lessee is held for maintaining the asset in good shape

An Islamic lease is more like an operating lease but the redemption features may be structured to make it similar to a finance lease.

Sukuk

Within other forms of business finance, a company can issue tradable financial instruments to borrow money. Key feature of these debt instruments are they:

- Don't give voting rights in the company,
- Give right to profits before distribution of profits to shareholders
- May include securities and guarantees over assets
- Include interest based elements

All of the above are prohibited under Islamic law. Instead, Islamic bonds (or sukuk) are linked to an underlying asset, such that a sukukholder is a partial owner in the underlying assets and profit is linked to the performance of the underlying asset. So for example a sukukholder will participate in the ownership of the company issuing the sukuk and has a right to profits (but will equally bear their share of any losses).

Mudaraba

Mudaraba is a special kind of partnership where one partner gives money to another for investing it in a commercial enterprise. The investment comes from the first partner (who is called 'rab ul mal'), while the management and work is an exclusive responsibility of the other (who is called 'mudarib').

The Mudaraba (profit sharing) is a contract, with one party providing 100% of the capital and the other party providing its specialist knowledge to invest the capital and manage the investment project. Profits generated are shared between the parties according to a pre-agreed ratio. In a Mudaraba only the lender of the money has to take losses.

This arrangement is therefore most closely aligned with equity finance.

Musharaka

Musharaka is a relationship between two or more parties, who contribute capital to a business, and divide the net profit and loss pro rata. It is most closely aligned with the concept of venture capital. All providers of capital are entitled to participate in management, but are not required to do so. The profit is distributed among the partners in pre-agreed ratios, while the loss is borne by each partner strictly in proportion to their respective capital contributions.

Test your understanding 6

Which of the following is a key feature of debt as a source of finance?

A Interest must be paid irrespective of the level of profits generated by the company

B Debt holders are repaid last in the case of a winding up of the company

C Debt holders hold full voting rights

D Debt holders suffer relatively high levels of risk, compared to providers of other sources of finance, and therefore debt attracts the highest return

Test your understanding 7

Which two of the following statements are correct?

(1) Bank overdrafts are repayable on demand

(2) Warrants give the holder the right to subscribe at a fixed future date for a certain number of ordinary shares at a predetermined price

(3) Preference dividends are paid before loan interest is paid

(4) Deep discount bonds are issued at a discount to their redemption value and no interest is paid on them

A (1) and (2)

B (1) and (3)

C (2) and (4)

D (3) and (4)

Test your understanding 8

A plc has announced a 1 for 5 rights issue at a subscription price of $2.30. The current cum-rights price of the shares is $3.35.

What is the new ex-div market value of the shares?

A $3.18

B $3.81

C $2.97

D $2.48

Test your understanding 9

Which of the following best describes the term 'coupon rate' as applied to loan notes?

A The rate of stamp duty applicable to purchases of the loan notes

B The total rate of return on the loan notes, taking into account capital repayment as well as interest payments

C The annual interest received divided by the current ex-interest market price of the loan notes

D The annual interest received on the face value of the units of the loan notes

Test your understanding 10

With reference to Islamic finance, the term Riba refers to

A a form of equity where a partnership exists and profits and losses are shared

B the predetermined interest collected by a lender, which the lender recieves over and above the principal amount that it has lent out

C a form of credit sale

D a form of lease

Chapter summary

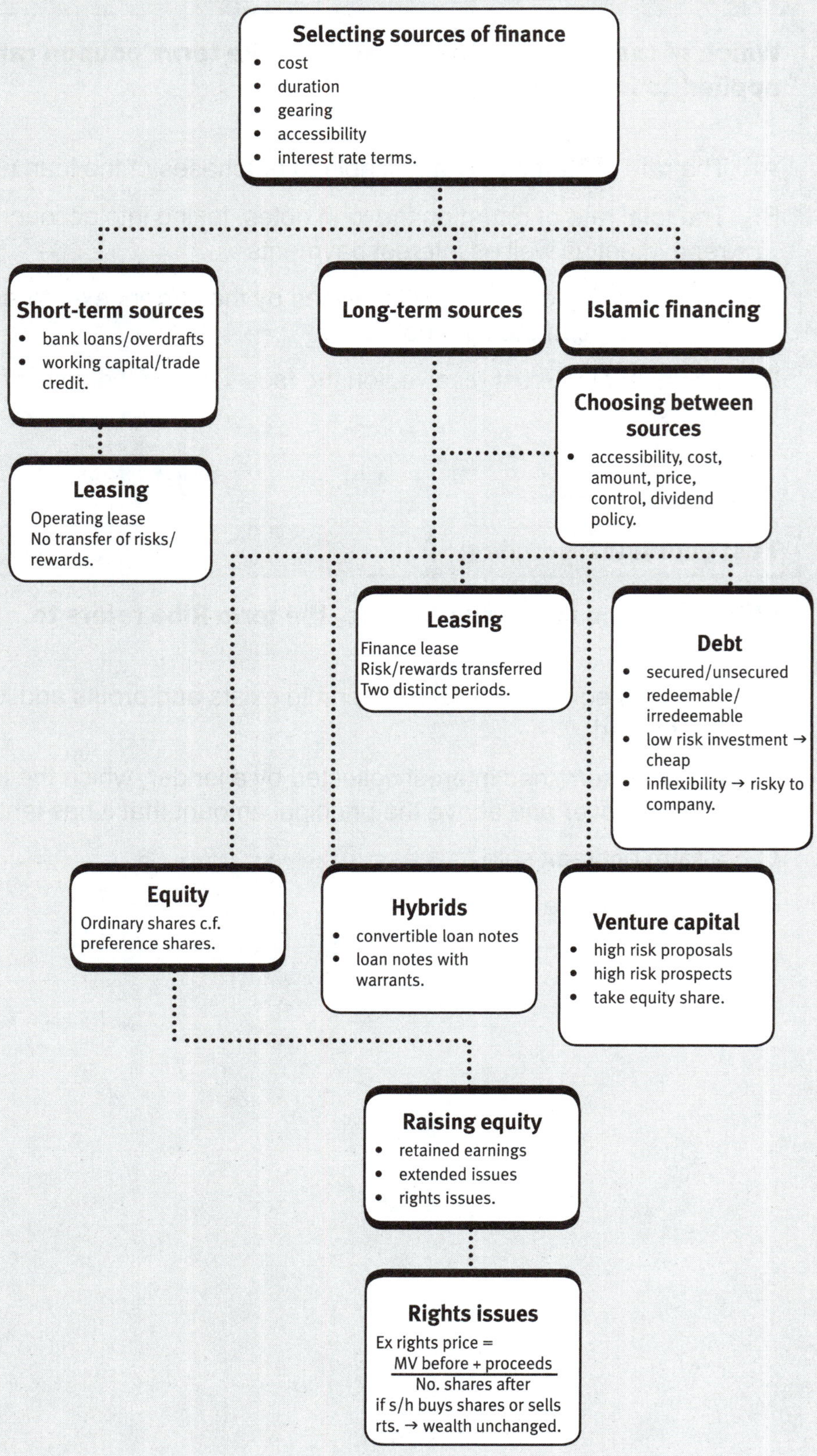

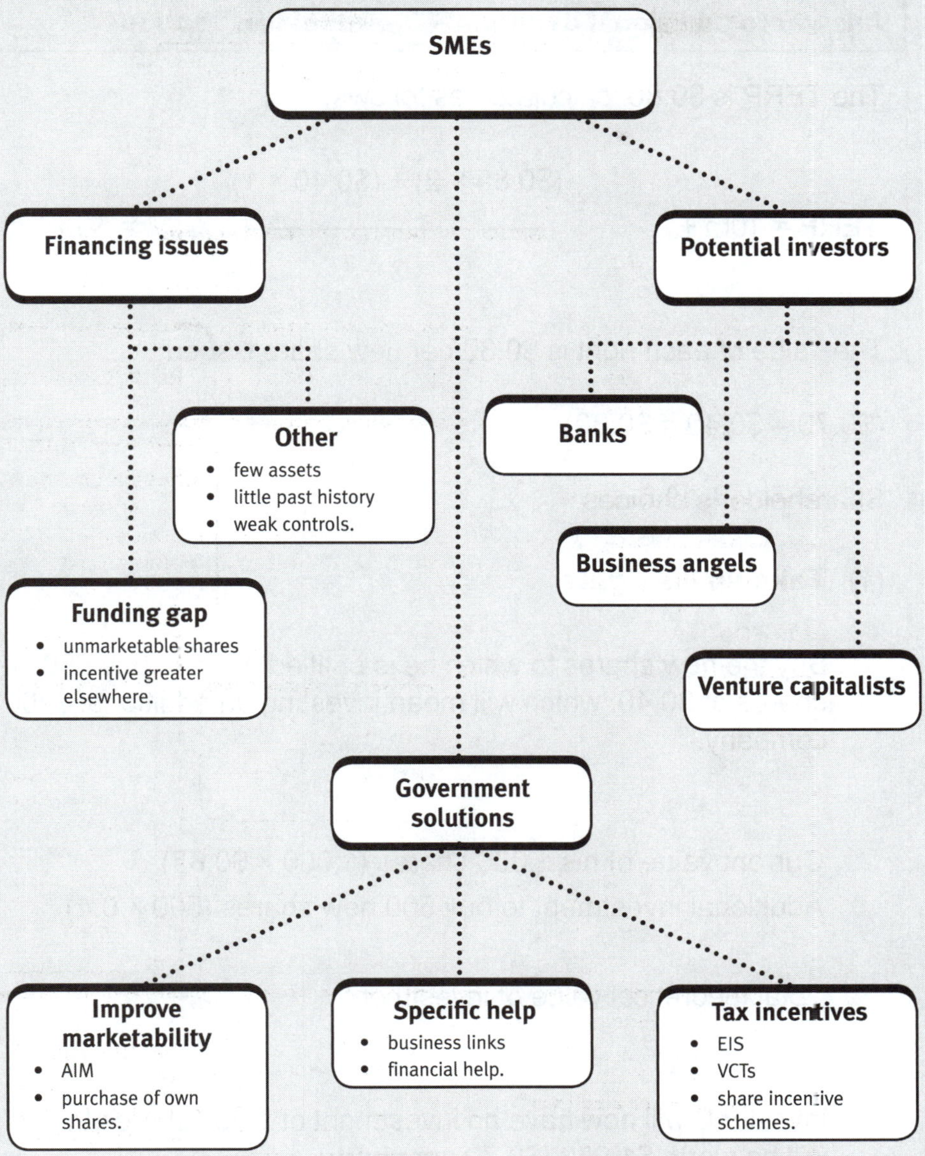
SMEs
Financing issues
Potential investors
Other
few assets
little past history
weak controls.
Banks
Business angels
Funding gap
unmarketable shares
incentive greater elsewhere.
Venture capitalists
Government solutions
Improve marketability
AIM
purchase of own shares.
Specific help
business links
financial help.
Tax incentives
EIS
VCTs
share incentive schemes.

Answer to additional question – Shareholders' options

The TERP is $0.80, calculated as follows:

$$\text{TERP} = 10\text{m} + \frac{(\$0.85 \times 2) + (\$0.40 \times 1)}{3} = \$0.70/\text{share}$$

The value of each right is $0.30 per new share issued

($0.70 – $0.40 = $0.30)

Shareholder's choices:

(1) **Take up his rights**

Buy the new shares to which he is entitled. He can buy 500 new shares at $0.40, which will mean investing an additional $200 in the company.

	$
Current value of his 1,000 shares (1,000 × $0.85)	850
Additional investment to buy 500 new shares (500 × 0.4)	200
Total theoretical value of investment	1,050

Investor B will now have an investment of 1,500 shares that in theory will be worth $1,050 ($0.70 per share).

The value of the total investment has gone up by $200, but this is the amount of the additional investment he has made to acquire the new shares, so his wealth is unchanged.

(2) **Sell his rights**

	$
Current value of his 1,000 shares	850
Theoretical value of his shares after the rights issue (1000 × $0.70)	700
Theoretical loss in investment value	150
Sale value of rights (500 rights × $0.30)	150
Net gain/loss	0

By selling his rights, investor B receives $150, but the value of his investment is likely to fall by $150, leaving him no better and no worse off overall.

(3) **Buys 200 shares and sells 300 rights**

	$
Current value of his 1,000 shares	850
Theoretical value of shares after the rights issue (1,200 × $0.70)	840
Purchase price of 200 new shares (200 × $0.40)	(80)
	760
Sale value of rights (300 rights × $0.30)	90
Net wealth	850

Again his overall wealth is unchanged.

(4) **Take no action**

If investor B takes no action, the value of his shares is likely to fall from $850 before the rights issue to $700 after the rights issue. Taking no action is therefore an inadvisable option, because it results in a fall in investment value without any offsetting benefit from the sale of rights.

However, for those shareholders who do nothing, the company will try to sell the shares to which they are entitled, and if the shares can be sold for more than their rights issue price, the surplus will be paid to the 'do nothing' shareholders.

Answer to additional question – Finance for SMEs

Rights issue

The easiest solution would be a rights issue to existing shareholders. It would:

- retain control
- not increase the financial risk.

However it may not be possible if existing shareholders:

- do not have further funds to invest
- are unwilling to invest further.

Venture capital

Since Toogoods Gardens has fast growth and a proven track record they may be able to attract venture capital funding. However they will need to provide the investors with an exit route, either by:

- agreeing to list on the AIM in the next few years
- buying back their shares at an agreed amount at a future date.

Bank loan

Assuming that the assets of Toogoods Gardens are not already being used as security, a bank loan would be a likely source of funds. It is relatively cheap because of the tax relief on the interest and is a predictable cash flow.

However, they would need to consider the level of financial gearing they have already, and the additional risk they face from business volatility and operating gearing. It would be unwise to take on debt finance if their risk profile was already high, as the increased gearing would amplify the issue.

Grants

If the area for the planned development is one where the government wants to encourage business, a grant may be available.

Test your understanding answers

Test your understanding 1 – TERP

Market value (MV) of shares in issue = 2m × \$2.7 = \$5.4m

Proceeds from new issue = $\frac{2m}{2} \times 1 \times \$2.10 = \$2.1m$

Number of shares in issue ex-rights = $2m + (2m \times \frac{1}{2}) = 3m$

TERP = $\frac{\$5.4m + \$2.1m}{3m} = \$2.50/share$

Note that the calculation can be done on the value of the whole equity or on the basis of the minimum shareholding needed to acquire one extra share:

TERP = $\frac{(\$2.70 \times 2) + (\$2.10 \times 1)}{3} = \$2.50/share$

Test your understanding 2 – TERP

MV of shares in issue = 10m × $2.70 = $27m

$$\text{Proceeds from new issue} = \frac{10m}{5} \times 2 \times \$2.00 = \$8m$$

$$\text{Number of shares in issue ex-rights} = 10m + \frac{10m}{5} \times 2 = 14m$$

$$\text{TERP} = \frac{\$27m + \$8m}{14m} = \$2.50/\text{share}$$

Note: that the calculation can be done on the value of the whole equity or on the basis of the minimum shareholding needed to acquire one extra share:

$$\text{Or TERP} = \frac{(\$2.70 \times 5) + (\$2.00 \times 2)}{7} = \$2.50/\text{share}$$

Test your understanding 3 – The value of a right

Value of a right = $2.50 – $2.10
= $0.40 per new share issued

Test your understanding 4 – The value of a right

$2.50 – $2.00 = 50c per new share issued

Test your understanding 5 – Shareholders' options

			$
Wealth before			
	Shares	1,000@$2.70	**2,700**
Wealth after			
(1) Take up the shares	Shares	1,500@$2.50	3,750
	Less cash paid to buy shares	500 @$2.10	(1,050)
	Total wealth		**2,700**
(2) Sell the rights			
	Shares	1,000@$2.50	2,500
	Plus cash received from sale of rights	500 @$0.40	200
	Total wealth		2,700
(3) Do nothing			
	Shares	1,000@$2.50	2,500
	Total wealth		2,500

Therefore, total wealth under option 3 is $200 less than under options 1 and 2.

*By doing nothing you theoretically eventually forego the right to the new shares.

Note: the wealth of the investor who takes up the rights appears to be unchanged at $2,700. In practice the funds raised would be used to invest in projects with positive NPVs so the wealth of the shareholder is likely to increase.

Test your understanding 6

Answer A

Test your understanding 7

Answer A

Loan interest is paid before preference dividends (statement 3). Zero coupon bonds, as opposed to deep discount bonds, are issued at a discount to their redemption value and no interest is paid on them (statement 4).

Test your understanding 8

Answer A

The new ex-div market value per share = (5 × \$3.35 + \$2.30)/6 = \$3.18

Test your understanding 9

Answer D

The coupon rate gives the annual interest based on the nominal value of the loan notes.

Test your understanding 10

Answer B

Mushuraka is a form of equity where a partnership exists and profits and losses are shared (A). Murabaha is a form of credit sale (C). Ijara is a form of lease (D).

chapter

16

Dividend policy

Chapter learning objectives

Upon completion of this chapter you will be able to:

- explain the impact that the issue of dividends may have on a company's share price
- explain the theory of dividend irrelevance
- discuss the influence of shareholder expectations on the dividend decision
- discuss the influence of legal constraints on the dividend decision
- discuss the influence of liquidity constraints on the dividend decision
- define and distinguish between bonus issues and scrip dividends.

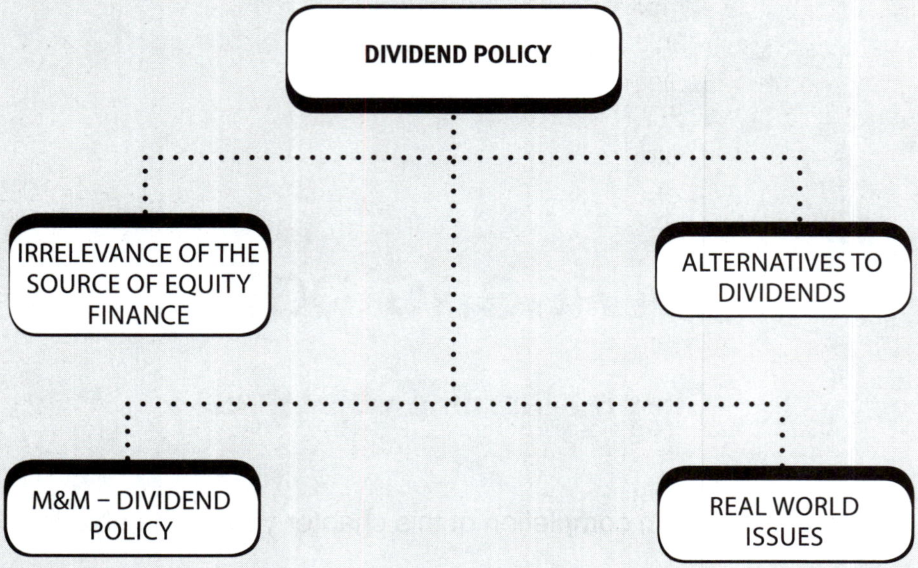

1 The dividend decision

We've already seen in the chapter on sources of finance that retained earnings are an important source of finance for both long and short-term purposes. They have no issue costs, they are flexible (they don't need to be applied for or repaid) and they don't result in a dilution of control.

However, for any company, the decision to use retained earnings as a source of finance will have a direct impact on the amount of dividends it will pay to shareholders.

The key question is if a company chooses to fund a new investment by a cut in the dividend what will the impact be on existing shareholders and the share price of the company?

2 Theories of dividend policy

There are three main theories concerning what impact a cut in the dividend will have on a company and its shareholders.

Dividend irrelevancy theory

The dividend irrelevancy theory put forward by Modigliani & Miller (M&M) argues that in a perfect capital market (no taxation, no transaction costs, no market imperfections), existing shareholders will only be concerned about increasing their wealth, but will be indifferent as to whether that increase comes in the form of a dividend or through capital growth.

As a result, a company can pay any level of dividend, with any funds shortfall being met through a new equity issue, provided it is investing in all available positive NPV projects.

Any investor requiring a dividend could "manufacture" their own by selling part of their shareholding. Equally, any shareholder wanting retentions when a dividend is paid can buy more shares with the dividend received.

Most of the criticism of M&M's theory surrounding the assumption of a perfect capital market.

Dividend irrelevancy theory

M&M's theory states that provided a company is investing in positive NPV projects, it will make no difference to the shareholder (and share price) whether the projects are funded via a cut in dividends or by obtaining additional funds from outside sources.

As a result of obtaining outside finance instead of using retained earnings, there would be a reduction in the value of each share. However, M&M argued that this reduction would equal the amount of the dividend paid, thereby meaning shareholder wealth was unaffected by the financing decision.

Residual theory

This theory is closely related to M&Ms but recognises the costs involved in raising new finance.

It argues that dividends themselves are important but the pattern of them is not.

We'll see in the cost of capital chapter that the market value of a share will equal the present value of the future cash flows. The residual theory argues that provided the present value of the dividend stream remains the same, the timing of the dividend payments is irrelevant.

It follows that only after a firm has invested in all positive NPV projects should a dividend be paid if there are any funds remaining. Retentions should be used for project finance with dividends as a residual.

However, this theory still takes some assumptions that may not be deemed realistic. This includes no taxation and no market imperfections.

Residual theory

A firm pays out a constant dividend of 10c in perpetuity. Its cost of equity is 10%.

The value of the dividend stream to an investor is:

$$\frac{10}{0.1} = 100c$$

- They would need to cancel the T1 dividend of 10c to pay for it.
- The project should earn 10% return, i.e. the 10c would be worth 10 × 1.1 = 11c the following year.

Provided the firm then distributed the additional 11c, the shareholder would have:

T_0	T_1	T_2	T_3
	0	10 + 11	10 ⟶ Perpetuity

$$PV = 10 + 11/1.1^2 + \frac{10}{0.1} \times \frac{1}{1.1^2}$$

$$PV = 17.3554 + 82.6446 = 100c$$

So in theory, provided the firm invests the withheld dividend in projects that at least earn the shareholders' required return, the investors' wealth is unchanged and they will not object.

- Dividends become a residual – firms only pay a dividend if there are earnings remaining after all positive NPV projects have been financed.

Dividend relevance

Practical influences, including market imperfections, mean that changes in dividend policy, particularly reductions in dividends paid, can have an adverse effect on shareholder wealth:

- reductions in dividend can convey 'bad news' to shareholders (dividend signalling)
- changes in dividend policy, particularly reductions, may conflict with investor liquidity requirements
- changes in dividend policy may upset investor tax planning (clientele effect).

As a result companies tend to adopt a stable dividend policy and keep shareholders informed of any changes.

Dividend relevance

In theory the level of dividend is irrelevant and in a perfect capital market it is difficult to challenge the dividend irrelevancy position. However, once these assumptions are relaxed, certain practical influences emerge and the arguments need further review.

Dividend signalling

In reality, investors do not have perfect information concerning the future prospects of the company. Many authorities claim, therefore, that the pattern of dividend payments is a key consideration on the part cf investors when estimating future performance.

For example, an increase in dividends would signal greater confidence in the future by managers and would lead investors to increase their estimate of future earnings and cause a rise in the share price. A sudden dividend cut on the other hand could have a serious impact upon equity value.

This argument implies that dividend policy is relevant. Firms should attempt to adopt a stable (and rising) dividend payout to maintain investors' confidence.

Preference for current income

Many investors require cash dividends to finance current consumption. This does not only apply to individual investors needing cash to live on but also to institutional investors, e.g. pension funds and insurance companies, who require regular cash inflows to meet day-to-day outgoings such as pension payments and insurance claims. This implies that many shareholders will prefer companies who pay regular cash dividends and will therefore value the shares of such a company more highly.

The proponents of the dividend irrelevancy theory challenge this argument and claim that investors requiring cash can generate 'homemade dividends' by selling shares. This argument has some attractions but it does ignore transaction costs. The sale of shares involves brokerage costs and can therefore be unattractive to many investors.

Taxation

In many situations, income in the form of dividends is taxed in a different way from income in the form of capital gains. This distortion in the personal tax system can have an impact on investors' preferences.

From the corporate point of view this further complicates the dividend decision as different groups of shareholders are likely to prefer different payout patterns.

One suggestion is that companies are likely to attract a clientele of investors who favour their dividend policy (for tax and other reasons) e.g. higher rate tax payers may prefer capital gains to dividend income as they can choose the timing of the gain to minimise the tax burden. In this case companies should be very cautious in making significant changes to dividend policy as it could upset their investors.

Research in the US tends to confirm this 'clientele effect' with high dividend payout firms attracting low income tax bracket investors and low dividend payout firms attracting high income tax bracket investors.

3 Other practical constraints

Legal restrictions on dividend payments

- Rules as to distributable profits that prevent excess cash distributions.
- Bond and loan agreements may contain covenants that restrict the amount of dividends a firm can pay.

Such limitations protect creditors by restricting a firm's ability to transfer wealth from bondholders to shareholders by paying excessive dividends.

Liquidity

Consider availability of cash, not just to fund the dividend but also cash needed for the continuing working capital requirements of the company.

4 Alternatives to cash dividends

Share repurchase

- consider using cash to buy back shares as an alternative to a dividend, particularly if surplus cash available would distort normal dividend policy.
- alternative is to pay one-off surplus as a 'special dividend'.

Scrip dividends

A scrip dividend is where a company allows its shareholders to take their dividends in the form of new shares rather than cash.

- The advantage to the shareholder of a scrip dividend is that he can painlessly increase his shareholding in the company without having to pay broker's commissions or stamp duty on a share purchase.
- The advantage to the company is that it does not have to find the cash to pay a dividend and in certain circumstances it can save tax.

Do not confuse a scrip issue (which is a bonus issue) with a scrip dividend.

A bonus (scrip) issue is a method of altering the share capital without raising cash. It is done by changing the company's reserves into share capital.

A bonus issue is not an alternative to a cash dividend. Although these shares are 'distributed' from a company to its shareholders, they do not represent an economic event as no wealth changes hands. The current shareholders simply receive new shares, for free, and in proportion to their previous share in the company.

The rate of a bonus issue is normally expressed in terms of the number of new shares issued for each existing share held, e.g. one for two (one new share for each two shares currently held).

Test your understanding 1

The 'dividends as residuals' view of dividend policy is best described as

A dividends are paid if the company generates profits greater than the previous year (this incremental sum is the residual)

B the profits made by the division of the company in a particular country should be paid to shareholders of the same nationality

C dividends should amount to the entire annual profit less the amount paid in manager incentive schemes

D dividends should only be paid out of cash flow after the company has financed all its positive NPV projects

Test your understanding 2

A scrip dividend is

A a dividend paid at a fixed percentage rate on the nominal value of the shares

B a dividend paid at a fixed percentage rate on the market value of the shares on the date that the dividend is declared

C a dividend payment that takes the form of new shares instead of cash

D a cash dividend that is not fixed but is decided upon by the directors and approved by the shareholders

Test your understanding 3

Modigliani and Miller argue that

A it is better to have the certainty of a known dividend now than the uncertainty of having to wait

B consistency of a company's dividend stream is irrelevant as a means of affecting shareholder wealth

C a reduction in dividend can convey 'bad news' to shareholders

D only when a company has invested in all positive NPV projects should a dividend be paid, if there are any funds remaining

Test your understanding 4

The Mogigliani and Miller proposition concerning dividend policy rests on a number of assumptions. These include

(i) no share issue costs

(ii) no bankruptcy costs

(iii) no taxation

(iv) no financial gearing

A (i) and (ii)

B (ii) and (iv)

C (iii) and (iv)

D (i) and (iii)

Test your understanding 5

Which of the following statements is true?

Statement 1: The traditional school of thought concerning dividend policy implies that managers should adopt as high a dividend policy as possible.

Statement 2: The Modigliani and Miller school of thought implies that managers should adopt as low a dividend policy as possible.

	Statement 1	*Statement 2*
A	True	True
B	True	False
C	False	True
D	False	False

5 Chapter summary

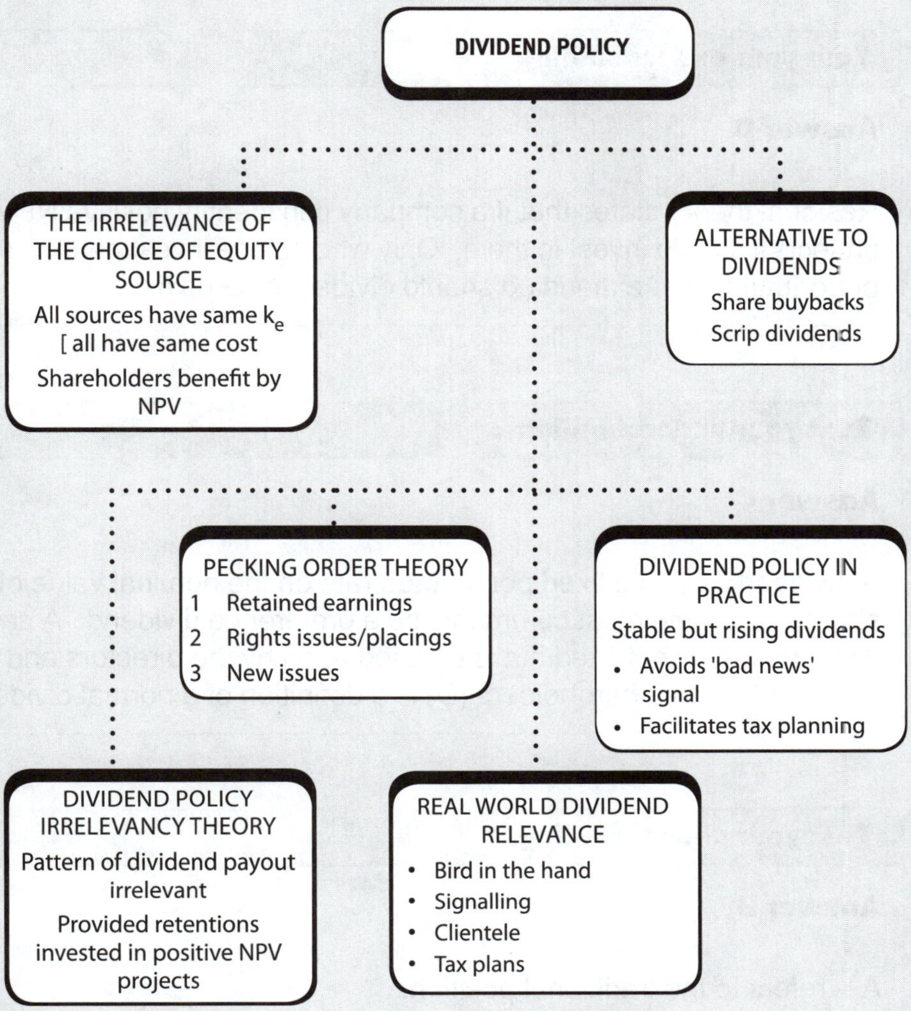

Test your understanding answers

Test your understanding 1

Answer D

Residual theory states that if a company can identify positive NPV projects it should invest in them. Only when these investment opportunities are exhausted should dividends be paid.

Test your understanding 2

Answer C

A dividend paid at a fixed percentage rate on the nominal value of the shares (A) would most commonly be a preference dividend. A cash dividend that is not fixed but is decided upon by the directors and approved by the shareholders (D) is a definition of a normal dividend.

Test your understanding 3

Answer B

A – refers to the traditional position.
C – refers to dividend signalling
D – refers to residual theory

Test your understanding 4

Answer D

Modigliani and Miller assume a perfect capital market (no taxation, no transaction costs, no market imperfections).

Test your understanding 5

Answer B

chapter

17

The cost of capital

Chapter learning objectives

Upon completion of this chapter you will be able to:

- explain the relationship between risk and return in financial investments
- explain the nature and features of different securities in relation to the risk/return trade-off
- explain the relative risk/return relationship of debt and equity and the effect on their relative costs
- describe the creditor hierarchy and its connection with the relative costs of sources of finance
- calculate a share price using the dividend valuation model (DVM)
- calculate cost of equity using the DVM
- calculate dividend growth using the dividend growth model (DGM)
- discuss the weaknesses of the DVM
- define and distinguish between systematic and unsystematic risk
- explain the relationship between systematic risk and return and describe the assumptions and components of the capital asset pricing model (CAPM)
- use the CAPM to find a company's cost of equity
- explain and discuss the advantages and disadvantages of the CAPM
- calculate the cost of finance for irredeemable debt, redeemable debt, convertible debt, preference shares and bank debt
- define and distinguish between a company's average and marginal cost of capital
- calculate an appropriate WACC for a company in a scenario, identifying the relevant data.

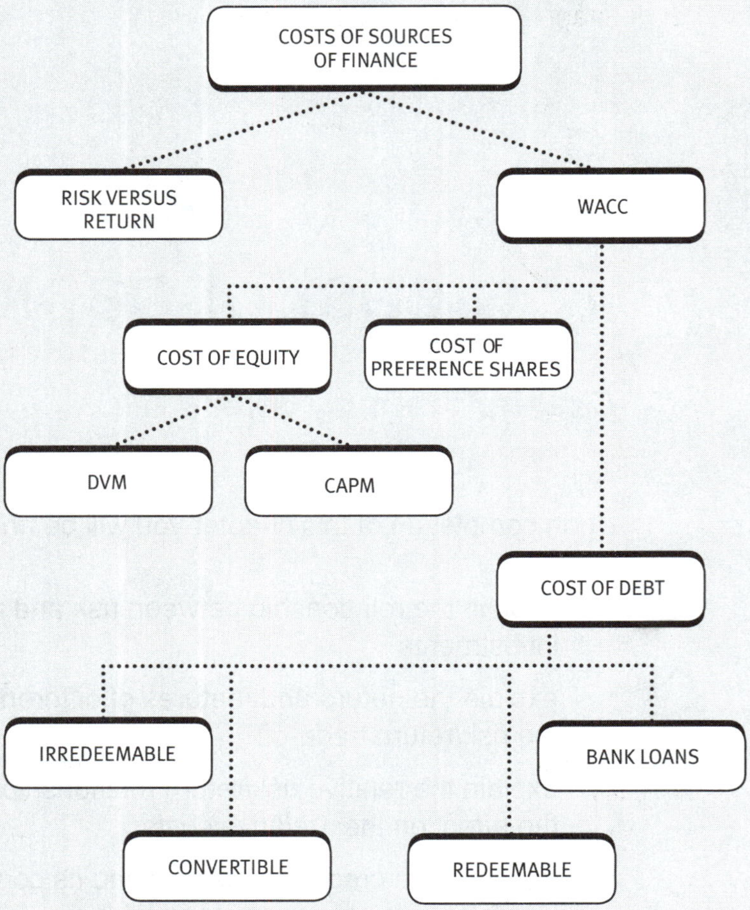

1 The overall approach

We have seen that when appraising investment projects, a firm may evaluate a project's returns using the company's cost of finance (also called the discount rate or cost of capital) to establish the net present value (NPV).

Within the sources of finance chapter we identified the main sources of long term finance within a company as:

- equity (or ordinary shares)
- preference shares
- debt

We also briefly explored the relationship between risk and return. Here we concluded that the greater the risk of an investment, the greater return would be demanded by the investor. The total return demanded by an investor is actually dependent on two specific factors:

- the reward investors demand for the risk they take in advancing funds to the firm
- the prevailing risk-free rate (Rf) of return.

This session will build on all of this by looking at how a firm can identify their overall cost of finance using the technique below:

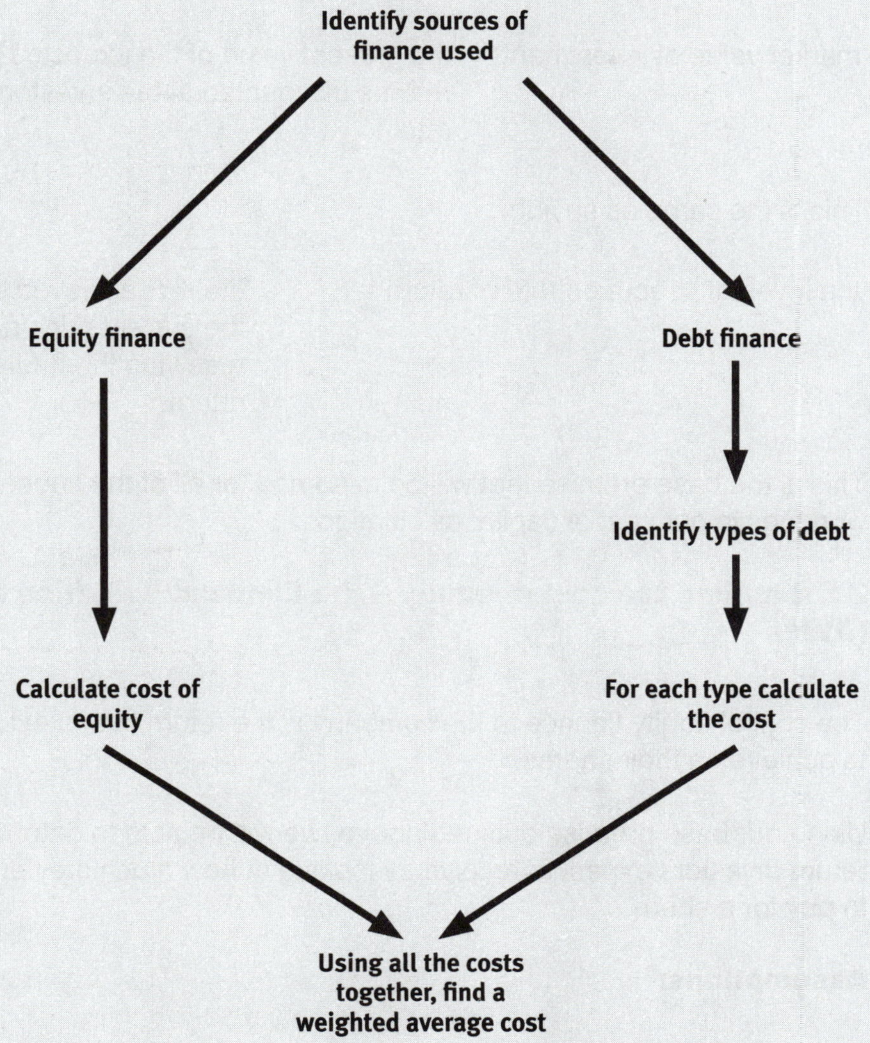

This is the key approach for finding a company's WACC in examination questions.

Calculating returns

The cost of each source of finance to the company can be equated with the return which the providers of finance (investors) are demanding on their investment.

This return can be expressed as a percentage (effectively, an interest rate) that can be used as the overall measure of cost, i.e. the cost of money is the percentage return a firm needs to pay its investors.

To calculate the return being demanded, we will assume that in a perfect market:

market value of investment = the present value of the expected future returns discounted at the investors' required return

This is the same as saying:

the investor's required rate of return = the IRR achieved by investing the current price and receiving the future expected returns

This is the base premise that will be assumed for all of the subsequent workings in our cost of capital calculation.

2 Estimating the cost of equity – the Dividend Valuation Model (DVM)

The cost of equity finance to the company is the return the investors expect to achieve on their shares.

Using our base premise outlined above, we will be able to determine what return investors expect to receive by looking at how much they are prepared to pay for a share.

Assumptions:

DVM states that:

- Future income stream is the dividends paid out by the company
- Dividends will be paid in perpetuity
- Dividends will be constant or growing at a fixed rate.

Therefore:

- Share price = Dividends paid in perpetuity discounted at the shareholder's rate of return.

A discussion of the DVM and its assumptions is likely to be required in an examination question that asks you to calculate cost of equity.

DVM (assuming constant dividends)

The formula for valuing a share is therefore:

$$P_o = \frac{D}{r_e}$$

where:

D = constant dividend from year 1 to infinity

P_o = share price now (year 0)

r_e= shareholders' required return, expressed as a decimal.

For a listed company, since the share price and dividend payment are known, the shareholder's required return can be found by rearranging the formula:

$$r_e = \frac{D}{P_o}$$

Test your understanding 1 – DVM no growth

A company has paid a dividend of 30c for many years. The company expects to continue paying dividends at this level in the future. The company's current share price is $1.50.

Calculate the cost of equity.

DVM (assuming dividend growth at a fixed rate)

Although in reality a firm's dividends will vary year on year, a practical assumption is to assume a constant growth rate in perpetuity.

The share valuation formula then becomes:

$$P_o = \frac{D_o(1+g)}{r_e - g} = \frac{D_1}{r_e - g}$$

where:

g = constant rate of growth in dividends, expressed as a decimal

D_1 = dividend to be received in one year – i.e. at T_1

$D_o(1+g)$ = dividend just paid, adjusted for one year's growth.

Therefore to find the cost of equity the formula can be rearranged to:

$$r_e = \frac{D_o(1+g)}{P_o} + g = \frac{D_1}{P_o} + g$$

Test your understanding 2 – DVM with growth

P Co has just paid a dividend of 10c. Shareholders expect dividends to grow at 7% pa. P Co's current share price is $2.05.

Calculate the cost of equity of P Co.

Test your understanding 3 – DVM with growth

A company has recently paid a dividend of $0.23 per share. The current share price is $3.45.

If dividends are expected to grow at an annual rate of 3%, calculate the cost of equity.

Note how the terms r_e (the shareholder's required return) and k_e (the cost of equity) can be used interchangeably. Don't let this terminology put you off.

The ex-div share price

The DVM model is based on the perpetuity formula, which assumes that the first payment will arise in one year's time (i.e. at the end of year 1). A share price quoted on this basis is termed an ex div share price.

If the first dividend is receivable immediately, then the share is termed cum div. In such a case the share price would have to be converted into an ex div share price, i.e. by subtracting the dividend due for payment.

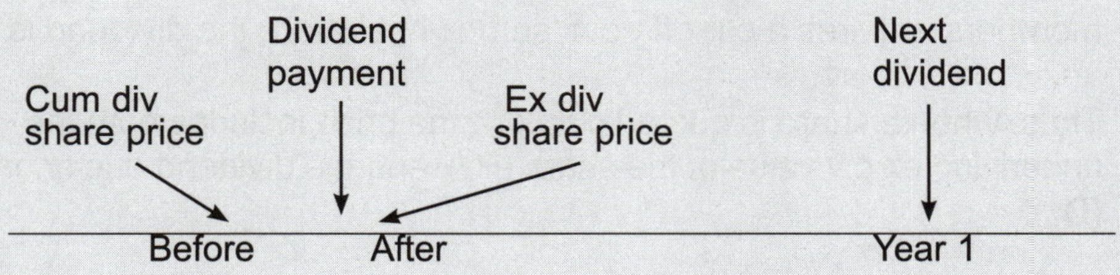

P_0 represents the 'ex div' share price. A question may give you the cum div share price by stating that the dividend is to be paid shortly.

Cum div share price – dividend due = Ex div share price.

The ex div share price

Dividends are paid periodically on shares. During the period prior to the payment of dividends, the price rises in anticipation of the payment. At this stage the price is **cum div**.

Sometime after the dividend is declared the share becomes **ex div**, and the price drops. This may be expressed diagrammatically:

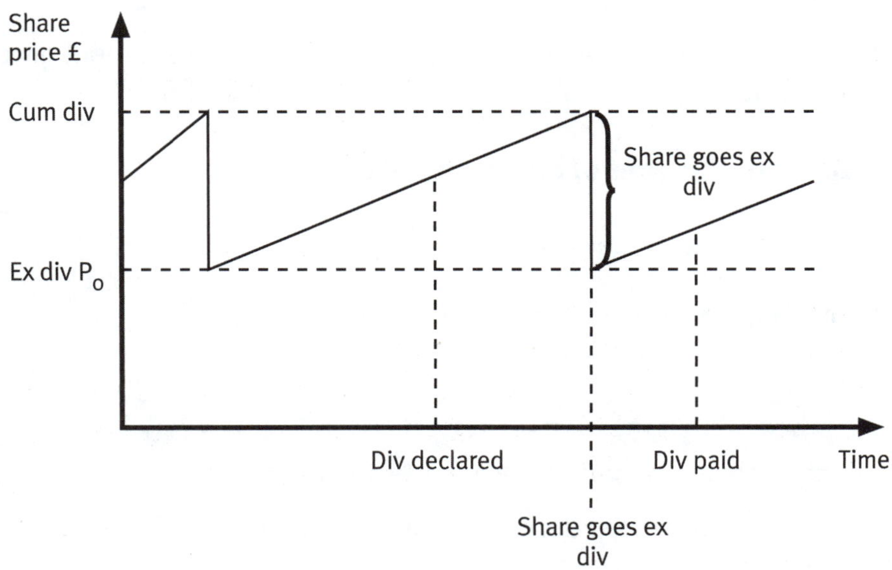

It will be noted that the share goes ex div shortly before the dividend is paid. Any person acquiring the share after this point in time will not receive the dividend, which will be paid to the original shareholder. The reason is that the time it takes for the company to amend its register of members requires a cut-off point somewhat before the dividend is paid.

Thus, when a share is quoted cum div, the price includes both the underlying ex div value of the share (P_o), and the dividend due shortly (D_o).

Use of the dividend valuation model and the formulae developed thus far requires an ex div share price to determine the P_o value.

Test your understanding 4 – The ex-div share price

The current share price is 140c and a dividend of 8c is due to be paid shortly.

Required:

Calculate the value of P_o, the ex-div share price.

Test your understanding 5 – The ex div share price

D Co is about to pay a dividend of 15c. Shareholders expect dividends to grow at 6% pa. D Co's current share price is $1.25.

Calculate the cost of equity of D Co.

Estimating growth

Two ways of estimating the likely growth rate of dividends are:

- extrapolating based on past dividend patterns
- assuming growth is dependent on the level of earnings retained in the business

Past dividends

This method assumes that the past pattern of dividends is a fair indicator of the future.

The formula for extrapolating growth can be written as:

$$g = \sqrt[n]{\left(\frac{D_o}{\text{Dividend n yrs ago}}\right)} - 1 = \left(\frac{D_o}{\text{Dividend n yrs ago}}\right)^{1/n} - 1$$

where:

n = number of years of dividend growth.

Test your understanding 6 – Using past dividends

A company currently pays a dividend of 32c; five years ago the dividend was 20c.

Estimate the annual growth rate in dividends.

Test your understanding 7 – Using past dividends

A company has paid the following dividends per share over the last five years.

20Y0	10.0c
20Y1	11.0c
20Y2	12.5c
20Y3	13.6c
20Y4	14.5c

Calculate the average annual historical growth rate.

The earnings retention model (Gordon's growth model)

Assumption

- The higher the level of retentions in a business, the higher the potential growth rate.

The formula is therefore:

$g = br_e$

where:

r_e= accounting rate of return

b = earnings retention rate.

Test your understanding 8 – The earnings retention model

Consider the following summarised financial statement for XYZ Co

Statement of financial position as at 31 December 20X5

	$		$
Assets	200	Ordinary shares	100
		Reserves	100
	200		200

Profits after tax for the year ended 31 December 20X6 $20

Dividend (a 40% payout) $8

Statement of financial position as at 31 December 20X6

	$		$
Assets	212	Ordinary shares	100
		Reserves 100 + (20 – 8)	112
	212		212

If the company's return on equity and earnings retention rate remain the same, what will be the growth in dividends in the next year (20X7)?

Test your understanding 9 – The earnings retention model

A company is about to pay an ordinary dividend of 16c a share. The share price is 200c. The accounting rate of return on equity is 12.5% and 20% of earnings are paid out as dividends.

Calculate the cost of equity for the company.

Weaknesses of the DVM

The DVM has a sound basic premise. The weaknesses occur because:

- the input data used may be inaccurate:
  - current market price
  - future dividend patterns
- the growth in earnings is ignored.

Make sure you can challenge the assumptions of the DVM for an examination question.

Weaknesses of the DVM

Few would argue with the basic premise of the model that the value of a share is the present value of all its future dividends. Its major weakness stems from limitations in the input data.

Current market price

P_0 – this can be subject to other short-term influences, such as rumoured takeover bids, which considerably distort the estimate of the cost of equity.

Future dividends

For simplicity we usually assume no growth or constant growth. These are unlikely growth patterns. Further, growth estimates based on the past are not always useful; market trends, economic conditions, inflation, etc. need to be considered. In examination questions future dividends are often estimated rather mechanically but it is important to think about influences on future dividends other than past dividends.

Relevance of earnings in the DVM

Earnings do not feature as such in the DVM. However, earnings should be an indicator of the company's long-term ability to pay dividends and therefore in estimating the rate of growth of future dividends, the rate of growth of the underlying profits must also be considered. For example, if dividends grow at 10% whilst earnings grow at 5%, before long the firm will run out of funds with which to pay dividends. Similarly, if dividends grow at 5% and profits at 10%, the firm will soon accumulate excess funds.

3 Estimating the cost of preference shares

Preference shares usually have a constant dividend. So the same approach can be used as we saw with estimating the cost of equity with no growth in dividends.

The formulae are therefore:

$$K_p = \frac{D}{P_o} \qquad P_o = \frac{D}{K_p}$$

where:

D = the constant annual preference dividend

P_o = ex div MV of the share

K_p = cost of the preference share.

The fixed dividend is based on the nominal value of the preference share, which may vary. Do not assume the nominal value is always $1.

Test your understanding 10 – Cost of preference shares

A company has 50,000 8% preference shares in issue, nominal value $1. The current ex div MV is $1.20/share.

What is the cost of the preference shares?

4 Estimating the cost of debt

Types of debt

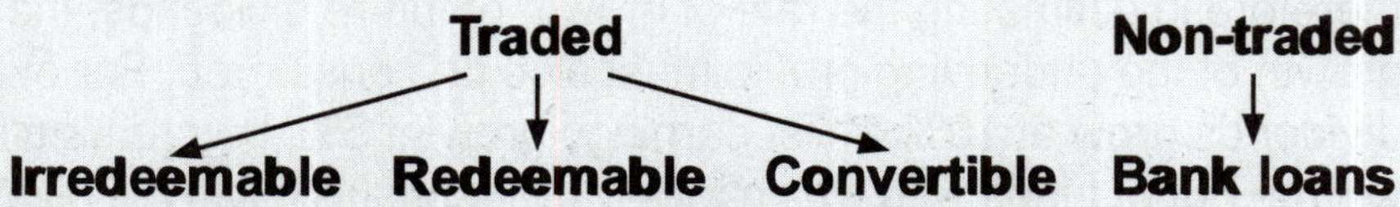

Terminology

- The terms loan notes, bonds, loan stock and marketable debt, are used interchangeably. Gilts are debts issued by the government.
- Irredeemable debt – no repayment of principal – interest in perpetuity.
- Redeemable debt – interest paid until redemption of principal.
- Convertible debt – may be later converted to equity.

Key points to note

- Debt is always quoted in \$100 nominal value blocks.
- Interest paid on debt is stated as a percentage of nominal value – called the coupon rate.
- The terms ex-interest and cum-interest are used in much the same way as ex-div and cum-div was for the cost of equity calculations

The coupon rate

The coupon rate is fixed at the time of issue, in line with the prevailing market interest rate. An 8% coupon rate means that \$8 of interest will be paid on \$100 nominal value block of debt.

The market value (MV) of loan notes may change daily. The main influence on the price of a loan note is the general level of interest rates for debt at that level of risk and for the same period to maturity.

Cost of debt and the impact of tax relief

A distinction must be made between the required return of debt holders / lenders (K_d) and the company's cost of debt ($K_d(1\text{-}T)$). Although in the context of equity the company's cost is equal to the investor's required return, the same is not true of debt. This is because of the impact of tax relief.

The impact of tax relief

Consider two companies, identical apart from the choice of finance: A is all equity financed; B has $10,000 of 10% fixed interest debt.

	A	B
	$	$
Profits before interest and tax (PBIT)	10,000	10,000
Interest cost	–	(1,000)
Profits before tax	10,000	9,000
Tax @ 30%	3,000	2,700

B has paid $300 less tax because of the tax deductibility of the debt interest.

Therefore the net cost of the debt interest to B is:

	$
Interest cost	1,000
Less: Tax saving	(300)
Net cost	700

So B's actual cost of debt is 700/10,000 = 7%

i.e. I (1 – T)

where:

I = coupon rate

T = rate of corporation tax.

Consequently we will use separate terms to distinguish the two figures:

- 'K_d'– the required return of the debt holder (pre-tax)
- 'K_d (1 – T)' – the cost of the debt to the company (post-tax).

Care must be taken since it is not always possible to simply calculate 'K_d (1 – T)' by taking K_d and multiplying by (1 – T). You should therefore regard 'K_d (1 – T)' as a label for the post tax cost of debt rather than as a mathematical formula.

Note also that K_d, the required return of the debt holder can also be referred to as the 'yield', the 'return on debt' and as the 'pre-tax cost of debt'.

Irredeemable debt

The company does not intend to repay the principal but to pay interest forever.

Assumptions:

Market price (MV) = Future expected income stream from the debenture discounted at the investor's required return.

- expected income stream will be the interest paid in perpetuity.

The formula for valuing a loan note is therefore:

$$MV = \frac{I}{K_d}$$

where:

I = annual interest starting in one year's time

MV = market price of the loan note now (year 0)

K_d = debt holders' required return (pre-tax cost of debt), expressed as a decimal.

The required return (pre-tax cost of debt) can be found by rearranging the formula:

$$K_d = \frac{I}{MV}$$

The post-tax cost of debt to the company is found by adjusting the formula to take account of the tax relief on the interest:

$$K_d\,(1-T) = \frac{I(1-T)}{MV}$$

where T = rate of corporation tax.

The MV of the loan notes is set by the investor, who does not get tax relief, and is therefore based on the interest before tax. The company gets corporation tax relief so the cost of debt calculation for the company is based on interest after tax.

Test your understanding 11 – Irredeemable debt

A company has in issue 10% irredeemable debt quoted at $80 ex interest. The corporation tax rate is 30%

(a) **What is the return required by the debt providers (the pre-tax cost of debt)?**

(b) **What is the post-tax cost of debt to the company?**

Test your understanding 12 – Irredeemable debt

A company has irredeemable loan notes currently trading at $50 ex interest. The coupon rate is 8% and the rate of corporation tax is 30%.

(a) **What is the return required by the debt providers (the pre-tax cost of debt)?**

(b) **What is the post-tax cost of debt to the company?**

Redeemable debt

The company will pay interest for a number of years and then repay the principal (sometimes at a premium or a discount to the original loan amount).

Assumptions:

- Market price = Future expected income stream from the loan notes discounted at the investor's required return (pre-tax cost of debt).
- expected income stream will be:
  - interest paid to redemption
  - the repayment of the principal.

Hence the market value of redeemable loan notes is the sum of the PVs of the interest and the redemption payment.

Illustration of redeemable debt

A company has in issue 12% redeemable loan notes with 5 years to redemption. Redemption will be at par. The investors require a return of 10%. What is the MV of the loan notes?

Solution

The MV is calculated by finding the PVs of the interest and the principal and totalling them as shown below.

Annuity Time		**Cash flow**	**Discount Factor (DF) @ 10%**	**PV $**
0	**MV**		Bal. fig	**(107.59)**
1–5	Interest payments	12	3.791	45.49
5	Capital repayment	100	0.621	62.10
	NPV			0

Note that for the investor the purchase is effectively a zero NPV project, as the present value of the income they receive in the future is exactly equivalent to the amount they invest today.

The investor's required return is therefore the internal rate of return (IRR) (breakeven discount rate) for the investment in the loan notes.

The return an investor requires can therefore be found by calculating the IRR of the investment flows:

T_0	MV	(x)
T_{1-n}	Interest payments	x
T_n	Capital repayment	x

Test your understanding 13 – Redeemable debt

A company has in issue 12% redeemable debt with 5 years to redemption. Redemption is at par. The current market value of the debt is $107.59. The corporation tax rate is 30%.

What is the return required by the debt providers (pre-tax cost of debt)?

If it is the post-tax cost of debt to the company that is required, an IRR is still calculated but as the interest payments are tax-deductible, the IRR calculation is based on the following cash flows:

T_0	MV	(x)
T_{1-n}	Interest payments × (1 – T)	x
T_n	Capital repayment	x

Test your understanding 14 – Redeemable debt

Using the same information as given in the previous TYU:

A company has in issue 12% redeemable debt with 5 years to redemption. Redemption is at par. The current market value of the debt is $107.59. The corporation tax rate is 30%.

What is the cost of debt to the company (post-tax cost of debt)?

Additional question – Redeemable debt

A company has in issue 10% loan notes with a current MV of $98. The loan notes are due to be redeemed at par in five years time.

If corporation tax is 30%, what is the company's post-tax cost of debt?

The answer to this question can be found after the chapter summary diagram at the end of this chapter.

Debt redeemable at current market price

In this situation, where the debt is redeemable at its current market price, the position of the investor is the same as a holder of irredeemable debt.

Debt redeemable at current market price illustration

Consider the following investments:

(a) an irredeemable loan note trading at $100 with a coupon rate of 5%

(b) a redeemable loan note trading at $100 with a coupon rate of 5%, due to be redeemed at $100 in 3 years.

The return required by an investor (pre-tax cost of debt) in (a) can be calculated as:

$$K_d = \frac{I}{MV}$$

$$K_d = \frac{5}{100} = 5\%$$

If the investor was instead to invest in (b), they would earn only 3 years of interest rather than receiving it in perpetuity.

The interest for 3 years (using the same required return of 5%) would have a PV of:

= 3 yr AF @ 5% × $5

From our tables, we get:

= 2.723 × \$5 = \$13.60

The \$100 received at T_3 (at a required return of 5%) would have a present value of:

$$\frac{100}{1.05^3} = 86.40$$

Therefore the PV of the overall return = \$13.60 + \$86.40= \$100.

This is the same return as received by the investor in the irredeemable debt!

Therefore where debt is redeemable at its current market price:

$$K_d = \frac{I}{MV}$$

and

$$K_d (1 - T) = \frac{I(1 - T)}{MV}$$

Convertible debt

A form of loan note that allows the investor to choose between taking the redemption proceeds or converting the loan note into a pre-set number of shares.

To calculate the cost of convertible debt you should:

(1) Calculate the value of the conversion option using available data

(2) Compare the conversion option with the cash option. Assume all investors will choose the option with the higher value.

(3) Calculate the IRR of the flows as for redeemable debt

Note: the is no tax effect whichever option is chosen at the conversion date.

Test your understanding 15 – Convertible debt

A company has issued convertible loan notes which are due to be redeemed at a 5% premium in five year's time. The coupon rate is 8% and the current MV is $85. Alternatively, the investor can choose to convert each loan note into 20 shares in five year's time.

The company pays tax at 30% per annum.

The company's shares are currently worth $4 and their value is expected to grow at a rate of 7% pa.

Find the post-tax cost of the convertible debt to the company.

Non-tradeable debt

Bank and other non-tradeable fixed interest loans simply need to be adjusted for tax relief:

Cost to company = Interest rate × (1 – T).

Alternatively, the cost of any 'normal' traded company debt could be used instead

Test your understanding 16 – Non-tradeable debt

A firm has a fixed rate bank loan of $1 million. It is charged 11% pa. The corporation tax rate is 30%.

What is the post-tax cost of the loan?

5 Estimating the cost of capital

The need for a weighted average

In the analysis so far carried out, each source of finance has been examined in isolation. However, the practical business situation is that there is a continuous raising of funds from various sources.

These funds are used, partly in existing operations and partly to finance new projects. There is not normally any separation between funds from different sources and their application to specific projects:

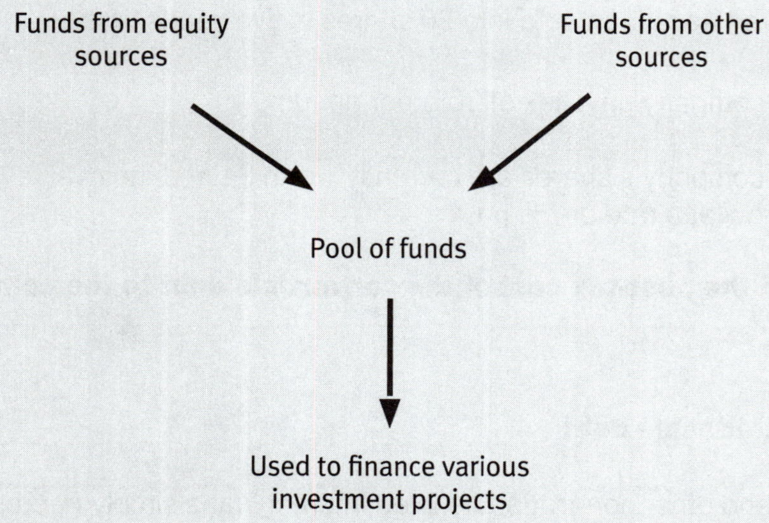

Even if a question tells you that a project is to be financed by the raising of a particular loan or through an issue of shares, in practice the funds raised will still be added to the firm's pool of funds and it is from that pool that the project will be funded.

It is therefore not the marginal cost of the additional finance, but the overall average cost of all finance raised, that is required for project appraisal.

The general approach is to calculate the cost of each individual source of medium-long term finance and then weight it according to its importance in the financing mix.

This average is known as the weighted average cost of capital (WACC).

Average and marginal cost of capital

A firm's average cost of capital (ACC) is the average cost of the funds, normally represented by the WACC. The computed WACC represents the cost of the capital currently employed. This represents financial decisions taken in previous periods.

Alternatively, the cost of raising the next increment of capital can be determined – this is what is termed the marginal cost of capital (MCC). The firm's MCC is the additional cost the firm will pay to raise an additional dollar of capital, assuming the capital is raised using the optimal capital proportions (see chapter on capital structure).

The relationship between MC and AC can be represented graphically, as indicated in the figure below.

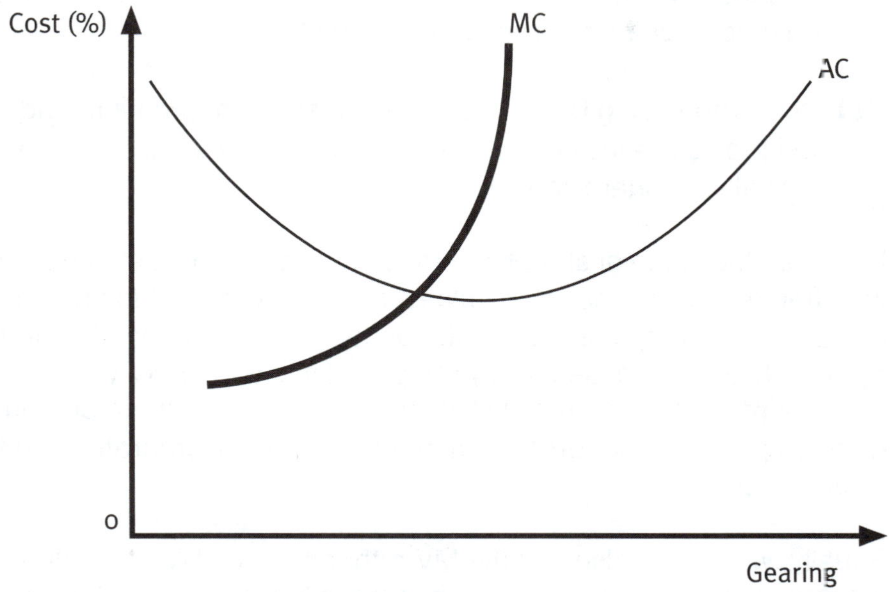

The relationship between ACC and MCC curves can be explained as follows: while the MCC is less than the ACC, the ACC will fall. Once the MCC rises above the ACC, however, the MCC will pull up the ACC, albeit at a slower rate than that at which MCC is rising.

Choice of weights

To find an average cost, the various sources of finance must be weighted according to the amount of each held by the company.

The weights for the sources of finance could be:

- book values (BVs) – represents historic cost of finance
- market values (MVs) – represent current opportunity cost of finance.

Wherever possible MVs should be used.

Choice of weights

If we use the current proportions in which funds are raised, their weights may be measured by reference to BVs or MVs.

Note that when using BVs, reserves such as share premium and retained profits are included in the BV of equity, in addition to the nominal value of share capital.

However, the value of shareholders' equity shown in a set of accounts will often reflect historic asset values, and will not reflect the future prospects of an organisation or the opportunity cost of equity entrusted by shareholders. Consequently it is preferable to use MV weights for the equity. **Note** that when using MVs, reserves such as share premium and retained profits are ignored as they are in effect incorporated into the value of equity.

Equally, we should also use the MV rather than the BV of the debt, although the discrepancy between these is likely to be much smaller than the discrepancy between the MV and BVs of equity.

Calculating weights

When using market values to weight the sources of finance, you should use the following calculations:

Equity = Market value of each share × number of shares in issue

$$\text{Debt} = \frac{\text{Total nominal value}}{100} \times \text{current market value}$$

Calculating the WACC

The calculation involves a series of steps.

Step 1 Calculate weights for each source of capital.

Step 2 Estimate cost of each source of capital.

Step 3 Multiply proportion of total of each source of capital by cost of that source of capital.

Step 4 Sum the results of Step 3 to give the WACC.

All of the above can be summarised in the following formula, which is provided for you in the exam.

$$WACC = \left[\frac{V_e}{V_e + V_d}\right]k_e + \left[\frac{V_d}{V_e + V_d}\right]k_d(1 - T)$$

where:

Ve and Vd are the market values of equity and debt respectively

K_e is the cost of equity

K_d (1 – T) is the post-tax cost of debt

Test your understanding 17 – WACC

Butch Co has $1 million loan notes in issue, quoted at $50 per $100 of nominal value (also equal to their book value); 625,000 preference shares quoted at 40c (book value 30c per share) and 5 million ordinary shares quoted at 25c (book value 20c per share). The cost of capital of these securities is 9%, 12% and 18% respectively. This capital structure is to be maintained.

(a) **Calculate the weighted average cost of capital using market values**

(b) **Calculate the weighted average cost of capital using book values and comment on the difference to your answer from part (i)**

Test your understanding 18 – WACC

B Co has 10 million 25c ordinary shares in issue with a current price of 155c cum div. An annual dividend of 9c has just been proposed. The company earns an accounting rate of return to equity (ROE) of 10% and pays out 40% of the return as dividends.

The company also has 13% redeemable loan notes with a nominal value of $7 million, trading at $105. They are due to be redeemed at par in five year's time.

If the rate of corporation tax is 33%, what is the company's WACC?

When to use the weighted average cost of capital

The WACC calculation is based upon the firm's current costs of equity and debt. It is therefore appropriate for use in investment appraisal provided:

- the historic proportions of debt and equity are not to be changed
- the operating risk of the firm will not be changed
- the finance is not project-specific, i.e. projects are financed from a pool of funds.

or

- the project is small in relation to the company so any changes are insignificant.

If any of these criteria are not met it will not be appropriate to appraise a project using the historic WACC.

6 The impact of risk

The DVM and WACC calculations above assume that an investor's current required return will remain unchanged for future projects. For projects with different risk profiles, this assumption may not hold true.

We therefore need a way to reflect any potential increase in risk in our estimate of the cost of finance.

When considering the return investors require, the trade-off with risk is of fundamental importance. Risk refers not to the possibility of total loss, but to the likelihood of actual returns varying from those forecast.

Consider four investment opportunities: A, B, C and D shown on the risk/return chart below where:

The risk of project A = the risk of project B.

The return from B = the return from C.

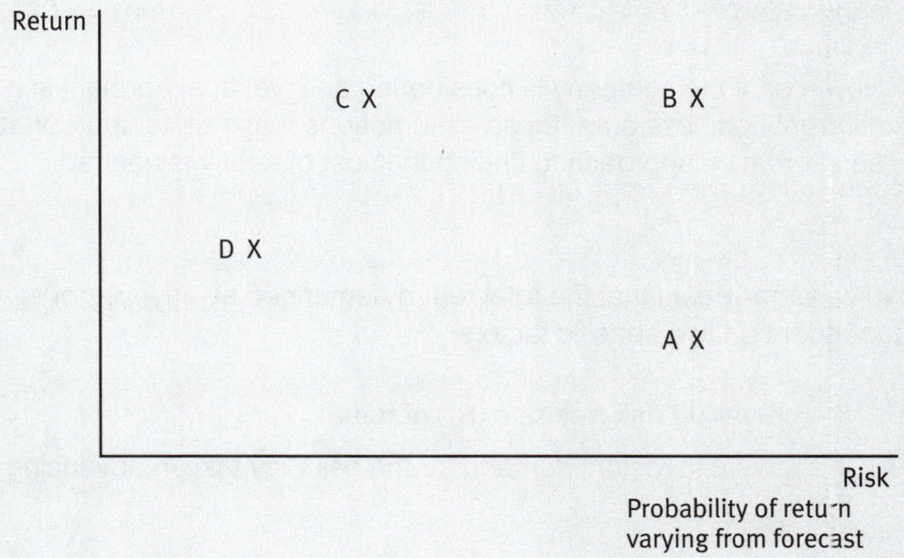

In choosing between the investment opportunities:

B is preferable to A – higher return for the same risk

C is preferable to B – same return for lower risk.

NB. The choice between D and C is less clear-cut. C pays higher returns but this is to compensate for the comparatively higher associated risk. The choice will therefore depend on the investor's attitude to risk and whether the increased return is seen by them as sufficient compensation for the higher level of risk.

The impact of risk

The DVM discussed above, assumes that the return currently being paid to ordinary shareholders will continue to be their required return in the future.

We have seen that the return required is a reflection of the risk the investor faces.

Therefore by using the DVM we are effectively assuming that all future investment projects will be subject to the same risk as those currently undertaken.

However, if the company is considering an investment project in a different business area, these assumptions may not be appropriate and an alternative approach to finding the cost of equity is needed.

We've already said that the total return demanded by an investor is actually dependent on two specific factors:

- the prevailing risk-free rate (Rf) of return
- the reward investors demand for the risk they take in advancing funds to the firm.

Let's look at each of these and how they relate to the different sources of finance.

The risk-free rate of return (Rf)

The Rf is the minimum rate required by all investors for an investment whose returns are certain.

It is given in questions as:

- the return on Treasury bills or
- the return on government gilts.

The risk free rate of return

Once funds have been advanced to a company, an investor faces the risk that they will not be returned. However some investments are less risky than others. For example lending to a government is considered to be extremely low risk as governments are always able to raise funds via taxation to pay back the investor.

The risk is so minimal that government securities are known as risk-free and the return they pay is a minimum benchmark against which all other investments can be measured.

The return is sometimes given in examination questions as the return on Treasury Bills or gilts (gilt-edged securities).

Note that the Rf does include compensation for inflation – i.e. it is a nominal or money rate.

Return on risky investments – loan notes

A risk-free investment has a certain return. Although not risk-free, loan notes are lower risk investments than equities because the return is more predictable. This is because:

- interest is a legal commitment
- interest will be paid before any dividends
- loans are often secured.

If a company issues loan notes, the returns needed to attract investors will therefore be:

- higher than the Rf
- lower than the return on equities.

Return on loan notes

As companies have to make profits in order to honour their loan commitments, loan notes or corporate bonds are not risk-free. Since they are risky investments the company will need to offer a higher return/yield than is paid on gilts to entice investors. The investors will require both a risk-free return and a risk premium.

However as we saw in chapter 15 loan notes are a relatively low-risk investment. Since the loan commitments are legally binding and often secured on company assets they are considered to be less risky than equity investments.

Not all bonds have the same risk. There is a bond-rating system, which helps investors distinguish a company's credit risk. Below is the Fitch and Standard & Poor's bond-rating scales.

Fitch/S&P	**Grade**	**Risk**
AAA	Investment	Highest quality
AA	Investment	High quality
A	Investment	Strong
BBB	**Investment**	**Medium grade**
BB, B	Junk	Speculative
CCC/CC/C	Junk	Highly speculative
D	Junk	In default

Notice that if the company falls below a certain credit rating, its grade changes from investment quality to junk status. Junk bonds are aptly named: they are the debt of companies in some sort of financial difficulty. Because they are so risky they have to offer much higher yields than other debt. This brings up an important point: not all bonds are inherently safer than shares.

The minimum investment grade rating is BBB. Institutional investors may not like such a low rating. Indeed some will not invest below an A rating.

Return on risky investments – equities

Equity shareholders are paid only after all other commitments have been met. They are the last investors to be paid out of company profits.

The same pattern of payment also occurs on the winding up of a company. The order of priority is:

- secured lenders
- legally-protected creditors such as tax authorities
- unsecured creditors
- preference shareholders
- ordinary shareholders.

As their earnings also fluctuate, equity shareholders therefore face the greatest risk of all investors. Since ordinary shares are the most risky investments the company offer, they are also the most expensive form of finance for the company.

The level of risk faced by the equity investor depends on:

- volatility of company earnings
- extent of other binding financial commitments.

Given the link to the volatility of company earnings, it is these investors that will face more risk if the company was to embark on riskier projects.

If we want to assess the impact of any potential increase (or decrease) in risk on our estimate of the cost of finance, we must focus on the impact on the cost of equity.

The return required by equity investors can be shown as

Required return	=	Risk-free return	+	Risk premium

Equities

Equity shareholders are the last investors to be paid out of company profits or in the event of a winding up. The level of risk they face will depend on how volatile the company's earnings are to start with and how great its other commitments are (e.g. how much debt finance is to be serviced – see chapter on capital structure).

After contractual commitments such as debt interest, the profits available for distribution are then used to pay any preference shareholders, before the ordinary shareholders are finally able to participate in any remaining surplus.

What's more, dividends are paid only on the recommendation of the directors, and they may decide, if the business has not had a good year, to pay a reduced dividend or even to withhold a dividend altogether.

7 Estimating the cost of equity – the Capital Asset Pricing Model (CAPM)

In the previous section we said that the required return was equal to the risk free rate of return plus a risk premium; the Capital Asset Pricing Model (CAPM) looks at how to quantify the premium. However, to understand this we need to grasp a number of related ideas first.

Reducing risk by combining investments

An investor, knowing that a particular investment was risky, could decide to reduce the overall risk faced, by acquiring a second share with a different risk profile and so obtain a smoother average return.

Reducing the risk in this way is known as **diversification**.

For example, an investor could combine investment A (for example shares in a company making sunglasses) with investment B, (perhaps shares in a company making raincoats). The fortunes of both firms are affected by the weather, but whilst A benefits from the sunshine, B loses out and vice versa for the rain. Our investor has therefore smoother overall returns – i.e. faces less overall volatility/risk and will need a lower overall return.

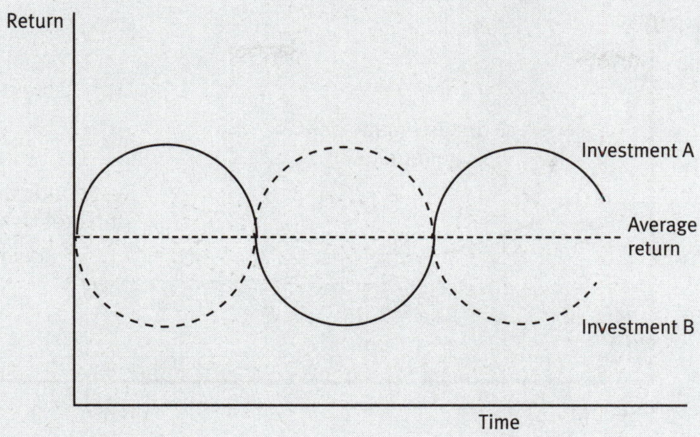

An investor can reduce risk by diversifying to hold a portfolio of shareholdings, since shares in different industries will, at least to some degree, offer differing returns profiles over time.

Reducing risk by combining investments

The returns from the investments shown are negatively correlated – that is they move in opposite directions. In fact they appear to have close to perfect negative correlation – any increase in one is almost exactly matched by a decrease the other.

The diagram above is an exaggeration, as it is unlikely that the returns of any two businesses would move in such opposing directions, but the principle of an investor diversifying a portfolio of holdings to reduce the risk faced is a good one.

However an investor can reduce risk by diversifying to hold a portfolio of shareholdings, since shares in different industries will at least to some degree offer differing returns profiles over time.

Provided the returns on the shares are not perfectly positively correlated (that is they do not move in exactly the same way) then any additional investment brought into a portfolio (subject to a maximum point – see below) will reduce the overall risk faced.

Initial diversification will bring about substantial risk reduction as additional investments are added to the portfolio. However, not all risk can be diversified away as it gets harder and harder to find another investment that responds differently.

As the portfolio increases, risk reduction slows and eventually stops altogether once 15-20 carefully selected investments have been combined.

This is because the total risk faced is not all of the same type.

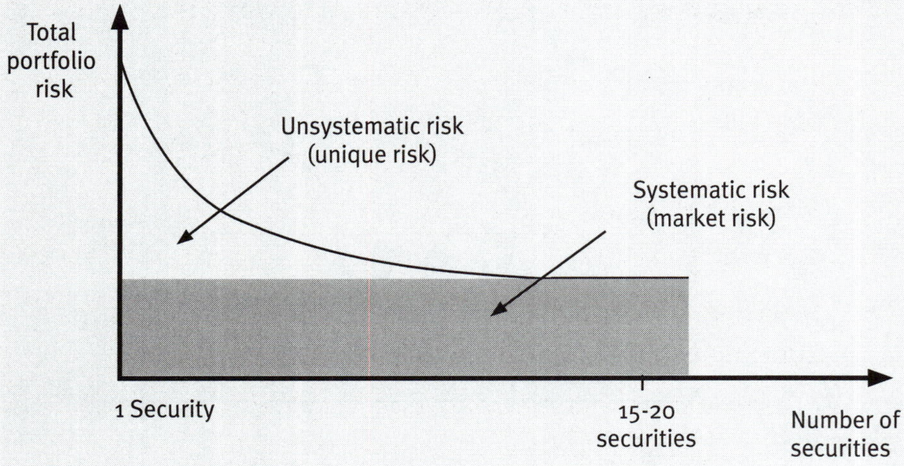

Systematic and unsystematic risk

The risk a shareholder faces is in large part due to the volatility of the company's earnings. This volatility can occur because of:

- systematic risk – market wide factors such as the state of the economy
- unsystematic risk – company/industry specific factors.

Systematic risk will affect all companies in the same way (although to varying degrees). For example, the vast majority of companies suffer in a recession but not necessarily to the same extent – e.g. house-builders typically suffer more than bakers.

Unsystematic risk factors don't affect everyone; indeed, their impact may be unique to an individual company or restricted to a small number of companies, with some being winners and some being losers. For example, the weather – if we have a wet summer then raincoat manufacturers will benefit but sunglasses manufacturers will suffer. However, for the majority of businesses, it won't make any difference. Overall, the stock market is unlikely to be affected much by the weather.

This explains why diversification works, typically there will be winners and losers regarding a particular risk factor but when combined in a portfolio, the impact is cancelled out. Diversification can almost eliminate unsystematic risk, but since all investments are affected in the same way by macro-economic i.e. systematic factors, the systematic risk of the portfolio remains.

The ability of investors to diversify away unsystematic risk by holding portfolios consisting of a number of different shares is the cornerstone of portfolio theory.

Test your understanding 19 – Systematic and non systematic risk

The following factors have impacted the volatility of the earnings of Chocbic Co, a manufacturer of chocolate biscuits and cereals:

- increase in interest rates
- increase in the price of cocoa beans
- legislation changing the rules on tax relief for investments in non-current assets
- growth in the economy of the country where Chocbic Co is based
- government advice on the importance of eating breakfast
- industrial unrest in Chocbic Co's main factory.

Are they sources of systematic or unsystematic risk?

Investors and systematic risk

Rational risk-averse investors would wish to reduce the risk they faced to a minimum and would therefore:

- arrange their portfolios to maximise risk reduction by holding at least 15–20 different investments
- effectively eliminate any unsystematic risk
- only need to be compensated for the remaining systematic risk they faced.

The CAPM

The CAPM shows how the minimum required return on a quoted security depends on its risk.

The required return of a rational risk-averse well-diversified investor can be found by returning to our original argument:

Required return = Risk-free return + Risk premium

This can be further expanded as:

Required return = Risk-free return + relative level of systematic risk × market risk premium for a specific investment

2 The share of the premium an investor requires depends on how the risk of their investment compares to the average.

1 The overall average return on the market (Rm) paid by the stock market in excess of the risk-free rate (Rf) must represent a fair risk premium for systematic risk.

So the formula becomes:

$$E(r)_i = R_f + \beta_i\,(E(r_m) - R_f)$$

where:

$E(r)_i$ = expected return on investment i (often expressed as the required return)

R_f = risk-free rate of return

$E(r_m)$ = the expected average return on the market. This is often simply written as R_m

$(E(r_m) - R_f)$ = equity risk premium (sometimes referred to as average market risk premium)

β_i = systematic risk of investment i compared to the market and therefore amount of the premium needed.

The formula is that of a straight line, y = a + bx, with β_i as the independent variable, R_f as the intercept with the y-axis, $(E(r_m) - R_f)$ as the slop of the line, and $E(r)_i$ (the required return) as the values being plotted on the straight line. The line itself is called the security market line (SML) and can be drawn as:

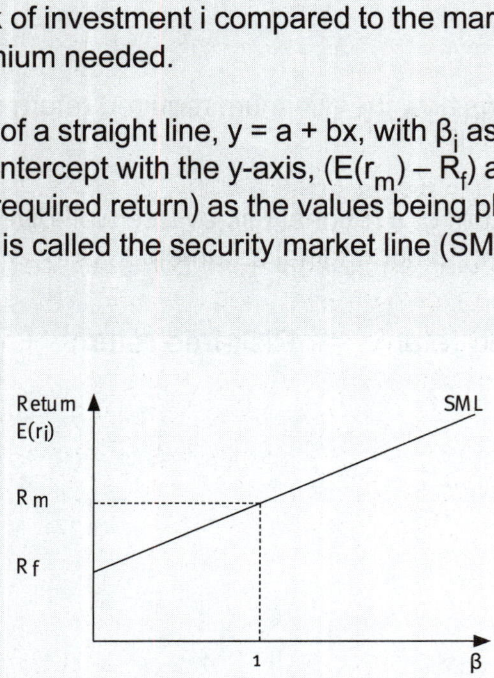

Understanding beta:

If an investment is riskier than average (i.e. the returns more volatile than the average market returns) then the $\beta > 1$.

If an investment is less risky than average (i.e. the returns less volatile than the average market returns) then the $\beta < 1$.

If an investment is risk free then $\beta = 0$.

The CAPM

A security whose returns are highly correlated with fluctuations in the market is said to have a high level of systematic risk. It does not have much risk-reducing potential on the investor's portfolio and therefore a high return is expected of it. On the other hand, a security which has a low correlation with the market (low systematic risk) is valuable as a risk reducer and hence its required return will be lower.

The measure of the systematic risk of a security relative to that of the market portfolio is referred to as its beta factor. In practice industries such as construction are far more volatile than others such as food retailing and would have correspondingly higher betas.

The CAPM shows the linear relationship between the risk premium of the security and the risk premium of the market portfolio.

Risk premium of share = market risk premium × β

i.e. Required return of share = R_f + (market risk premium × β)

or

$$E(r_i) = R_f + \beta_i(E(r_m) - R_f)$$

If an investment is risk free then $\beta = 0$.

The same formula can be applied to compute the minimum required return of a capital investment project carried out by a company, because the company is just a vehicle for the shareholders, who will view the project as an addition to the market portfolio.

In order to use the CAPM, investors need to have values for the variables contained in the model.

The risk free rate of return

In the real world, there is no such thing as a risk-free asset. Short-term government debt (e.g. Treasury bills) is a relatively safe investment and in practice, is used as an acceptable substitute for the risk-free asset.

The market risk premium

Often referred to as the equity risk premium, this is the difference between the average return on the capital market and the risk-free rate of return. It represents the extra return required for investing in equity rather than investing in risk-free assets.

In the short-term, share prices can fall as well as increase, leading to a negative average return. To smooth out such short-term changes, a time-smoothed moving average analysis can be carried out over longer periods of time, often several decades.

Beta

Beta values are found using regression analysis to compare the returns on a share with the returns on the capital market. The beta value for UK companies traded on the UK capital market can be readily found on the internet.

Test your understanding 20 – The CAPM

The current average market return being paid on risky investments is 12%, compared with 5% on Treasury bills. G Co has a beta of 1.2. What is the required return of an equity investor in G Co?

Test your understanding 21 – The CAPM

B Co is currently paying a return of 9% on equity investment. If the return on gilts is currently 5.5% and the average return on the market is 10.5%, what is the beta of B Co and what does this tell us about the volatility of B's returns compared to those of the market on average?

The CAPM is based on a number of assumptions:

- well-diversified investors
- perfect capital market
- unrestricted borrowing or lending at the risk-free rate of interest
- all forecasts are made in the context of a single period transaction horizon.

It is important to be aware of these assumptions and the reasons why they can be criticised.

Assumptions underpinning CAPM

Investors hold diversified portfolios

From the assumptions of CAPM it is deduced that all investors will hold a well-diversified portfolio of shares, known as the market portfolio, which is really a 'slice' of the whole stock market.

This assumption means that investors will only require a return for the systematic risk of their portfolios, since the unsystematic risk has been removed.

Although the market portfolio is not really held by investors, in practice even a limited diversification will produce a portfolio which approximates its behaviour, so it is a workable assumption.

Perfect capital market

This assumption means that all securities are valued correctly and that their returns will plot on to the SML.

A perfect capital market requires:

- no taxes,
- no transaction costs,
- perfect information that is freely available to all investors,
- all investors to be risk averse and rational, and
- a large number of buyers and sellers in the market.

Real-world capital markets are clearly not perfect.

Unrestricted borrowing or lending at the risk-free rate of interest

This assumption provides a minimum level of return required by investors. In reality, this is not possible because the risk associated with individual investors is much higher than that associated with the Government. This inability to borrow at the risk-free rate means the slope of the SML is shallower in practice than in theory.

Single-period transaction horizon

A holding period of one year is usually used in order to make comparable the returns on different securities. A return over six months, for example, cannot be compared to a return over 12. This assumption appears reasonable because even though many investors hold securities for much longer than one year, returns on securities are usually quoted on an annual basis.

Using CAPM in project appraisal

This CAPM formula can be used to calculate a risk adjusted cost of equity for use in situations where the risk associated with the project being appraised is different from the usual operating risk of the company. In this instance, the CAPM formula becomes

$$r_e = R_f + \beta (R_m - R_f)$$

To do this, it is necessary to estimate the beta factor of the new investment project. This is most commonly done by examining the betas of quoted companies in a similar line of business to the new project; these companies are referred to as 'proxy companies', and their betas as 'proxy betas'.

It is important to understand that the CAPM equation only gives us the required return of the shareholders. If the project is to be equity financed, this can be used as the project discount rate. If the project is to be financed with both debt and equity, then the shareholders' required return will need to be combined with the cost of debt to find an appropriate discount rate.

The advantages and disadvantages of CAPM

Advantages:

- works well in practice
- focuses on systematic risk
- is useful for appraising specific projects.

Disadvantages:

- less useful if investors are undiversified
- ignores tax situation of investors
- actual data inputs are estimates and may be hard to obtain.

Advantages and disadvantages of CAPM

In practice, many of the assumptions underlying the development of CAPM are violated. However, rather than being overly critical, it is more sensible to ask 'does the theory work?', i.e. does it explain the returns on securities in the real world?

Fortunately, the answer is yes. Practical empirical tests, whilst showing that betas are not perfect predictors of rates of returns on investments, do show a strong correspondence between systematic risk and rate of return. Certainly CAPM outperforms other models in this area, and in particular it gives a far better explanation of the rate of return on a security than is obtained by looking at its total risk.

Advantages of CAPM

- It provides a market-based relationship between risk and return, and assessment of security risk and rates of return given that risk.
- It shows why only systematic risk is important in this relationship.
- It is one of the best methods of estimating a quoted company's cost of equity capital.
- It provides a basis for establishing risk-adjusted discount rates for capital investment projects.

Limitations of CAPM

By concentrating only on systematic risk, other aspects of risk are excluded; these unsystematic elements of risk will be of major importance to those shareholders who do not hold well-diversified portfolios, as well as being of importance to managers and employees. Hence it takes an investor-orientated view of risk.

The model considers only the level of return as being important to investors and not the way in which that return is received. Hence, dividends and capital gains are deemed equally desirable. With differential tax rates the 'packaging' of return between dividends and capital gain may be important.

It is strictly a one-period model and should be used with caution, if at all, in the appraisal of multi-period projects. Some of the required data inputs are extremely difficult to obtain or estimate, for example:

R_f can be obtained from quoted rates. From the wide range of quoted interest rates, a relevant rate must be decided on. Ideally, the rate ought to relate to a security with the same duration as the project being appraised.

Beta – the measure of systematic risk. Here an estimate is usually required. Such estimates may be derived from subjective judgement, sensitivity analysis or, in some cases, by analysing (and, where necessary, adjusting) the beta coefficient of quoted firms which are thought to display the same risk characteristics as the project being appraised (see chapter on capital structure). Use of regression analysis is subject to statistical error, the presence of unsystematic risk, and the effects of not having a perfect investment market – security prices not always simply reflecting underlying risk.

R_m is extremely difficult to determine as the market is volatile and the expected return is likely to vary with changes in the Rf. Hence, users often attempt to estimate (Rm – Rf), the equity risk premium or excess return on the market. Historically in the UK this excess return has varied between 3% and 9% and similar figures may be used if:

(i) it is felt that historic data is likely to be a good estimate of the future

(ii) the expected excess return is thought to be a constant arithmetic amount above the Rf.

In practice there are certain instances when it is found that the CAPM does not perform as expected, e.g. investments with low betas, investments with low price/earnings (PE) ratios, investments with a strong seasonality.

Generally the basic CAPM is seen to overstate the required return for higher beta securities and understate the required return for low beta securities. However this problem mostly disappears when the effects of taxation are introduced to develop the basic model.

Similarly, CAPM does not seem to generate accurate forecasts for returns for companies with low price earnings ratios and is unable to account for seasonal factors observed in the UK stock market over the years.

January appears nearly always to be an outstandingly successful month for investing in UK shares, but no one can explain why this is the case.

Test your understanding 22

Risk that cannot be diversified away can be described as

A Systematic risk

B Financial risk

C Unsystematic risk

D Business risk

Test your understanding 23

Beta factors (β) measure the systematic risk of a portfolio relative to the market portfolio.

Which of the following statements is true?

(1) If β < 1 the security is less sensitive to systematic risk than the market average

(2) If β > 1 the security is less sensitive to systematic risk than the market average

(3) If β = 1 the security's exposure to systematic risk exactly matches the market average

(4) If β = 0 the security is risk free

A (1) and (4) only

B (2) and (3) only

C (1), (3) and (4) only

D (2), (3) and (4) only

Test your understanding 24

Fonic plc has 10 million 25c ordinary shares in issue with a current price of 175c cum-div. An annual dividend of 10c has been proposed. Annual dividends have been growing at a steady rate of 4% per annum. The company's other major source of funds is $2 million 8% irredeemable loan notes with a market value of $120 per $100 par value.

If Fonic plc pays corporation tax at a rate of 30%, what is the weighted average cost of capital that should be used for assessing projects, rounded to one decimal place?

A 9.6%

B 9.7%

C 9.9%

D 10.0%

Test your understanding 25

The shares of Borough plc have a current market price of 74 cents each, ex-div. It is expected that the dividend in one year's time will be 8 cents per share. The required rate of return from dividends on these shares is 16% per annum.

If the expected growth in future dividends is a constant annual percentage, what is the expected annual dividend growth?

A 0.4% per annum

B 3.5% per annum

C 3.8% per annum

D 5.2% per annum

Test your understanding 26

Which of the following statements are true?

(1) The cost of irredeemable debt is the (post-tax) interest as a percentage of the ex interest market value of the debt

(2) The cost of redeemable debt is given by the internal rate of return of the cash flows involved

(3) The weighted average cost of capital is calculated by weighting the costs of the individual sources of finance according to their relative importance as a source of finance

A (1) only

B (1) and (3) only

C (2) and (3) only

D All of the above

Chapter summary

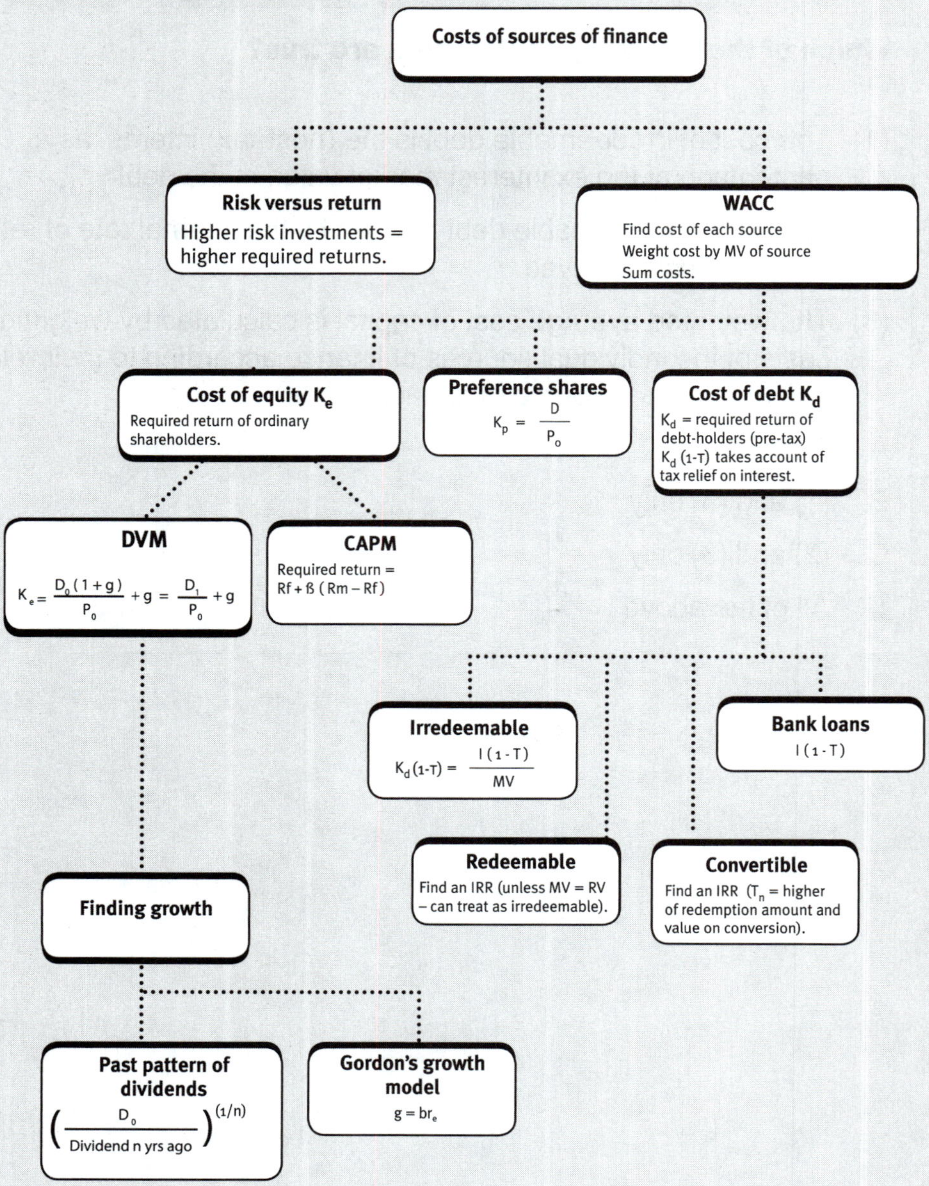

Answer to additional question – Redeemable debt

Time		Cash flow	DF at 10%	PV	DF at 5%	PV
0	MV	(98)	1	(98)	1	(98)
1–5	Interest payments (10 x (1 – 0.3))	7	3.791	26.54	4.329	30.3
	Capital repayment	100	0.621	62.10	0.784	78.40
	NPV			–9.36		10.7

$$IRR = L + \left[\frac{N_L}{N_L - N_H} \times (H - L) \right]$$

$$IRR = 5\% + \frac{10.7}{10.7 - (9.36)} \times (10\% - 5\%) = 7.7\%$$

Therefore the company's cost of debt, K_d (1 – T), is 7.7%.

Test your understanding answers

Test your understanding 1 – DVM no growth

$$r_e = \frac{D}{P_o}$$

$$r_e = \frac{30}{150} = 0.2 \text{ or } 20\%$$

Test your understanding 2 – DVM with growth

$$r_e = \frac{D_o(1+g)}{P_o} + g$$

$$r_e = \frac{0.10\,(1 + 0.07)}{2.05} + 0.07 = 0.122 \text{ or } 12.2\%$$

Test your understanding 3 – DVM with growth

$$r_e = \frac{D_o(1+g)}{P_o} + g$$

$$r_e = \frac{0.23\,(1 + 0.03)}{3.45} + 0.03 = 0.099 \text{ or } 9.9\%$$

Test your understanding 4 – The ex-div share price

Cum-div price – Dividend = Ex-div price

140 – 8 = 132c.

Test your understanding 5 – The ex div share price

$$r_e = \frac{D_o(1+g)}{P_o} + g$$

Since a dividend is about to be paid, the share price given must be cum div. The ex div price is therefore:

125 – 15 = 110c

$$r_e = \frac{15(1 + 0.06)}{110} + 0.06 = 0.205 \text{ or } 20.5\%$$

Test your understanding 6 – Using past dividends

Since growth is assumed to be constant, the growth rate, g, can be assumed to have been the same in each of the 5 years, i.e. the 20c will have become 32c after 5 years of constant growth.

$20c \times (1 + g)^5 =$	32c
or $(1 + g)^5 =$	32/20
	= 1.60

Therefore $1 + g = 1.6^{1/5} \approx 1.1$, so g = 0.1 or 10%

Test your understanding 7 – Using past dividends

dividend with four years growth

20Y0	10.0c
20Y1	11.0c
20Y2	12.5c
20Y3	13.6c
20Y4	14.5c

$$g = \sqrt[n]{\left(\frac{D_o}{\text{Dividend n yrs ago}}\right)} - 1 = \left(\frac{D_o}{\text{Dividend n yrs ago}}\right)^{1/n} - 1$$

The growth rate, g, is therefore:

$$g = \sqrt[4]{\left(\frac{14.5}{10}\right)} - 1 = \left(\frac{14.5}{10}\right)^{1/4} - 1 = 0.097 \text{ or } 9.7\%$$

This is also known as the geometric growth rate.

Test your understanding 8 – The earnings retention model

Profit after tax as a % of capital employed will be 20 ÷ 200 = 10%.

10% × asset value at 31 December 20X6 = 10% × $212 = $21.20.

Dividends will therefore be 40% × $21.20 = $8.48.

This represents a growth of 6% on the year (8.48/8 = 1.06).

This is more directly calculated as:

Note: that the return on equity is calculated with reference to opening statement of financial position values.

g = r (accounting rate of return) × b (the earnings retention rate)

= 10% × 60%

= 6%.

Test your understanding 9 – The earnings retention model

$$K_e = \frac{D_o(1+g)}{P_o} + g$$

where:

P_o ex div = 200 – 16 = 184

D_o = 16

$g = br_e$

b = 1 – dividend payout % = 1 – 0.2 = 0.8

r_e = 12.5%

$g = r_e \times b = 0.125 \times 0.8 = 0.1$

$$K_e = \frac{16\ (1+0.1)}{184} + 0.1 = 19.6$$

Test your understanding 10 – Cost of preference shares

Using $K_p = \frac{D}{P_o}$, $K_p = \frac{8}{120}$ = 0.0667 or 6.67%

Test your understanding 11 – Irredeemable debt

(a) **Pre-tax cost of debt**

$$K_d = \frac{I}{MV}$$

$$K_d = \frac{10}{80} = 12.5\%$$

(b) **Post-tax cost of debt**

$$K_d\,(1 - T) = \frac{I(1 - T)}{MV}$$

$$K_d\,(1 - T) = \frac{10(1 - 0.3)}{80} = 0.0875 = 8.75\%$$

Note - since this is irredeemable debt, a short-cut could be taken by multiplying the pre-tax cost of debt by (1 – T)

$K_d\,(1 - T) = 12.5\%\,(1 - 0.3) = 8.75\%$

Test your understanding 12 – Irredeemable debt

(a) **Pre-tax cost of debt**

$$K_d = \frac{I}{MV}$$

$$K_d = \frac{8}{50} = 16\%$$

(b) **Post-tax cost of debt**

$$K_d(1-T) = \frac{I(1-T)}{MV}$$

$$K_d(1-T) = \frac{8(1-0.3)}{50} = 0.112 = 11.2\%$$

Note – since this is irredeemable debt, a short-cut could be taken by multiplying the pre-tax cost of debt by (1 – T)

K_d (1 – T) = 16% (1 – 0.3) = 11.2%

Test your understanding 13 – Redeemable debt

Time		**Cash flow**	**DF @ 5%**	**PV**	**DF @ 15%**	**PV**
0	MV	(107.59)	1	(107.59)	1	(107.59)
1–5	Interest payments	12.00	4.329	51.95	3.352	40.22
5	Capital repayment	100.00	.784	78.40	.497	49.70
	NPV			22.76		(17.67)

$$IRR = L + \left[\frac{N_L}{N_L - N_H} \times (H - L)\right]$$

$$IRR = 5\% + \frac{22.76}{22.76-(17.67)} \times (15\% - 5\%) = 10.63$$

Therefore the required return of investors is 10.63%.

As the linear interpolation method used to estimate the IRR is an approximation, it does not reconcile back to the 10% required return per the illustration above.

Note: that the rate of corporation tax has been ignored, as the question asked for the return required by the debt holders (pre-tax cost of debt) rather than the post-tax cost of debt to the company.

Test your understanding 14 – Redeemable debt

Time		Cash flow	DF @ 5%	PV	DF @ 15%	PV
0	MV	(107.59)	1	(107.59)	1	(107.59)
1–5	Interest payments (1 – T)	8.40	4.329	36.36	3.352	28.16
5	Capital repayment	100.00	.784	78.40	.497	49.70
	NPV			7.17		(29.73)

$$IRR = L + \left[\frac{N_L}{N_L - N_H} \times (H - L)\right]$$

$$IRR = 5\% + \frac{7.17}{7.17 - (29.73)} \times (15\% - 5\%) = 6.94$$

Therefore the required return of investors is 6.94%.

Test your understanding 15 – Convertible debt

(1) Compare the redemption value (RV) with the value of the conversion option:

Cash RV = $100 × 1.05 = 105

Conversion value = 20 × 4(1.07)^5 = 20 × 5.61 = 112.20

(2) Select the highest of the two values as the amount to be received at T_n.

It is assumed that the investors will choose to convert the debenture and will therefore receive $112.20. **In an exam question, you must assess whether conversion is likely to occur**

(3) Find the IRR of the cash flows to get the cost of debt as normal

Time		Cash flow	DF@ 10%	PV	DF@ 5%	PV
0	MV	(85)	1	(85)	1	(85)
1–5	Interest payments (8 × (1 – 0.3))	5.6	3.791	21.23	4.329	24.24
5	Conversion value	112.20	0.621	69.68	0.784	87.96
	NPV			5.91		27.2

$$IRR = L + \left[\frac{N_L}{N_L - N_H} \times (H - L)\right]$$

$$IRR = 5\% + \frac{27.2}{27.2 - 5.91} \times (10\% - 5\%) = 11.4\%.$$

Test your understanding 16 – Non-tradeable debt

Cost to company = Interest rate × (1 – T).

11 × (1 – 0.3) = 7.7%.

Test your understanding 17 – WACC

S = step

(i)

Security	Market values		Cost of capital (S2)	Weighted cost (S3)
	$	**Proportions (S1)**	%	%
Loan notes	500,000	0.250	× 9.0 =	2.25
Preference shares	250,000	0.125	× 12.0 =	1.50
Ordinary shares	1,250,000	0.625	× 18.0 =	11.25
	2,000,000	1.000		15.00 (S4)

The weighted average cost of capital is therefore 15%. This figure represents an approximate cut-off rate of return on new investments.

Note that the relative costs of the various forms of finance reflect the risk to investors: Debt is cheapest at 9% because it is less risky for the investor and attracts tax relief for the company. Preference shares carry a risk and hence a return that is between that of debt and equity. The 18% return to the ordinary shareholders reflects the fact that their equity is most risky.

(ii)

Security	Book values		Cost of capital (S2)	Weighted cost (S3)
		Proportions		
	$	**(S1)**	%	%
Loan notes	500,000	0.296	× 9.0 =	2.66
Preference shares	187,500	0.111	× 12.0 =	1.33
Ordinary shares	1,000,000	0.593	× 18.0 =	10.67
	1,687,500	1.000		14.66 (S4)

The weighted average cost of capital is therefore 14.66%.

The WACC is lower when we use book values as opposed to market values. We have implicitly assumed that the preference shareholders are happy receiving 12% return on $187,500 (the book value), when in fact they would be expecting 12% return on $250,000 (the current market value). Likewise, we have implicitly assumed that the ordinary shareholders are happy receiving 18% return on $1 million (the book value), when in fact they would be expecting 18% return on $1.25 million (the current market value).

The original investors have the option of selling their investment in the market and investing the proceeds in some other assets of equivalent risk and generating a similar return. So for example, an ordinary shareholder has the option of generating an 18% return on $1.25 million (the current market value) so why would they be content with receiving 18% return on $1 million (the book value)?

Using the book values is therefore against the principle of shareholder wealth maximisation.

Test your understanding 18 – WACC

Information for step 1

MV of equity

10m × ($1.55 – $0.09) = $14.6m

MV of debt

Trading at $105 therefore $7m ÷ 100 × 105 = $7.35m

Total MV of all finance = $14.6m + $7.35m = $21.95m

Step 2

$$K_e = \frac{D_o(1 + g)}{P_o} + g$$

$D_o = 9$

Po = 155 – 9 = 146

g = r × b where r = 0.1 and b = (1 – 0.4)

g = 0.1 × 0.6 = 0.06

$$K_e = \frac{9\ (1.06)}{146} + 0.06 = 12.53\%.$$

Cost of debt is found using an IRR calculation:

Time		**Cash flow**	**DF at 10%**	**PV**	**DF at 5%**	**PV**
0	MV	(105)	1	(105)	1	(105)
1–5	Interest payments (13 x (1 – 0.33))	8.71	3.791	33.02	4.329	37.71
	Capital repayment	100	0.621	62.10	0.784	78.40
	NPV			–9.88		11.11

$$IRR = L + \left[\frac{N_L}{N_L - N_H} \times (H - L) \right]$$

$$IRR = 5\% + \frac{11.11}{11.11 - (9.88)} \times (10\% - 5\%) = 7.65\%$$

$$\text{Therefore the WACC} = \frac{7.35}{21.95} \times 7.65\% + \frac{14.6}{21.95} \times 12.53\% = 10.9\%$$

Note: If calculating cost of capital in the examination, do a reasonableness check to ensure that the cost of debt is less than the cost of equity.

Test your understanding 19 – Systematic and non systematic risk

Factor	**Type of risk**
Increase in interest rates	Systematic
Increase in the price of cocoa beans	Unsystemat c
Legislation changing the rules on tax relief for investments in non-current assets	Systematic
Growth in the economy of the country where Chocbic Co. is based	Systematic
Government advice on the importance of eating breakfast	Unsystemat c
Industrial unrest in Chocbic Co's main factory	Unsystemat c

Test your understanding 20 – The CAPM

Solution

Required return = Rf + β (Rm – Rf)

$r_e = 5 + 1.2\ (12 – 5) = 13.4\%$.

Test your understanding 21 – The CAPM

Required return = Rf + β (Rm – Rf)

9% = 5.5% + β (10.5 – 5.5)

3.5% = 5 β

β = 3.5/5 = 0.7

Since the beta is <1 the returns are less volatile than average.

Test your understanding 22

Answer A

Systematic risk cannot be diversified away.

Test your understanding 23

Answer C

Test your understanding 24

Answer A

Cost of equity = 0.1 (1.04)/(1.75 – 0.1) + 0.04 = 10.30%

Post tax cost of debt = 8 (1 – 0.30) × 100/120 = 4.7%

WACC = (10.3 × 10 × 1.65 + 4.7 × 2 × 1.2)/(10 × 1.65 + 2 × 1.2) = 9.6%

Test your understanding 25

Answer D

Since d_0 (1+g) is the dividend after one year, we have:

74 = 8/(0.16 – g)

74 (0.16 – g) = 8

74g = 3.84

g = 0.052 or 5.2%

Test your understanding 26

Answer D

chapter

18

Capital structure

Chapter learning objectives

Upon completion of this chapter you will be able to:

- define, calculate and explain the significance to a company's financial position and financial risk of its level of the following ratios:
  - operating gearing
  - financial gearing
  - interest gearing
- define company value
- explain the relationship between company value and cost of capital
- explain the traditional view of capital structure theory
- explain the underlying assumptions of the traditional view of capital structure theory
- interpret a graph demonstrating the traditional view of capital structure theory
- explain the assumptions of a perfect capital market
- describe the views and assumptions of Miller and Modigliani (M&M) on capital structure without corporate taxes
- interpret a graph demonstrating the views of M&M on capital structure without corporate taxes
- describe the views and assumptions of M&M on capital structure with corporate taxes
- interpret a graph demonstrating the views of M&M on capital structure with corporate taxes
- identify a range of capital market imperfections and describe their impact on the views of M&M on capital structure
- explain the relevance of pecking order theory to the selection of sources of finance

- discuss the circumstances under which weighted average cost of capital (WACC) can be used in investment appraisal
- identify in a scenario question whether WACC is appropriate for use by a company
- discuss the advantages of the capital asset pricing model (CAPM) over WACC in determining a project-specific cost of capital
- identify in a scenario where CAPM may be suitable to determine a project-specific cost of equity capital
- apply CAPM in calculating a project-specific discount rate.

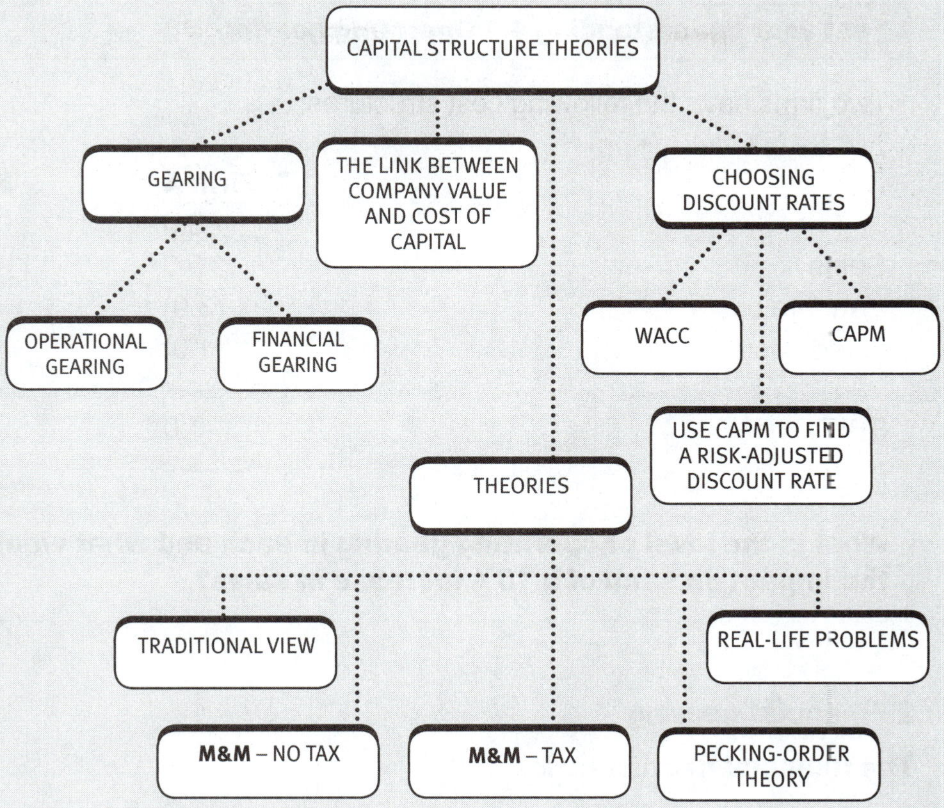

1 Operating gearing

Operating gearing is a measure of the extent to which a firm's operating costs are fixed rather than variable as this affects the level of business risk in the firm. Operating gearing can be measured in a number of different ways, including:

$$\frac{\text{Fixed costs}}{\text{Variable costs}} \quad \text{or} \quad \frac{\text{Fixed costs}}{\text{Total costs}} \quad \text{or even} \quad \frac{\text{\% change in EBIT}}{\text{\% change in revenue}}$$

Firms with a high proportion of fixed costs in their cost structures are known as having 'high operating gearing'.

Thus if the sales of a company vary:

The greater the operating gearing the greater the EBIT variability.

The level of operating gearing will be largely a result of the industry in which the firm operates.

Test your understanding 1 – Operating gearing

Two firms have the following cost structures:

	Firm A	Firm B
	$m	$m
Sales	5.0	5.0
Variable costs	(3.0)	(1.0)
Fixed costs	(1.0)	(3.0)
EBIT	1.0	1.0

What is the level of operating gearing in each and what would be the impact on each of a 10% increase in sales?

2 Financial gearing

The financial gearing ratios

Financial gearing is a measure of the extent to which debt is used in the capital structure.

Note that preference shares are usually treated as debt (see chapter on sources of finance for logic).

It can be measured in a number of ways:

- Equity gearing:

$$\frac{\text{Preference share capital plus long-term debt}}{\text{Ordinary share capital and reserves}}$$

- Total or capital gearing:

$$\frac{\text{Preference share capital plus long-term debt}}{\text{Total long-term capital}}$$

- Interest gearing:

$$\frac{\text{Debt interest}}{\text{Operating profits before debt interest and tax}}$$

NB Since preference shares are treated as debt finance, preference dividends are treated as debt interest in this ratio.

All three ratios measure the same thing, but

- for comparison purposes, the same ratio must be used consistently
- capital gearing is used more often than equity gearing
- interest gearing is a statement of profit or loss measure rather than a financial position statement one. It considers the percentage of the operating profit absorbed by interest payments on borrowings and as a result measures the impact of gearing on profits. It is more normally seen in its inverse form as the interest cover ratio (see below).

Test your understanding 2 – Capital and equity gearing

Statement of financial position for Redknapp Co

	$m	$m
Assets		
Non-current assets (total)		23.0
Current assets (total)		15.0
Total assets		38.0
Equity and liabilities:		
Ordinary share capital		10.0
Ordinary share premium		3.0
Preference share capital		1.5
Reserves		2.5
		17.0
Loan notes 10%		8.0
Current liabilities		
Trade payables	8.0	
Bank overdraft	5.0	
		13.0
Total equity and liabilities		38.0

Calculate the equity gearing and capital gearing of the business.

Book or market values

The ratios can be calculated on either book or market values of debt and equity.

There are arguments in favour of both approaches:

Market values:

- are more relevant to the level of investment made
- represent the opportunity cost of the investment made
- are consistent with the way investors measure debt and equity.

Book values:

- are how imposed gearing restrictions are often expressed
- are not subject to sudden change due to market factors
- are readily available.

Impact of financial gearing

Where two companies have the same level of variability in earnings, the company with the higher level of financial gearing will have increased variability of returns to shareholders.

Test your understanding 3 – The impact of financial gearing

Calculate the impact on Firm C of a 10% fall in sales and comment on your results:

	Firm C
	$000
Sales	10
Variable costs	(2)
Fixed costs	(5)
Operating profit	3
Interest	(2)
Profit before taxation	1

Overall therefore there is a required trade-off between:

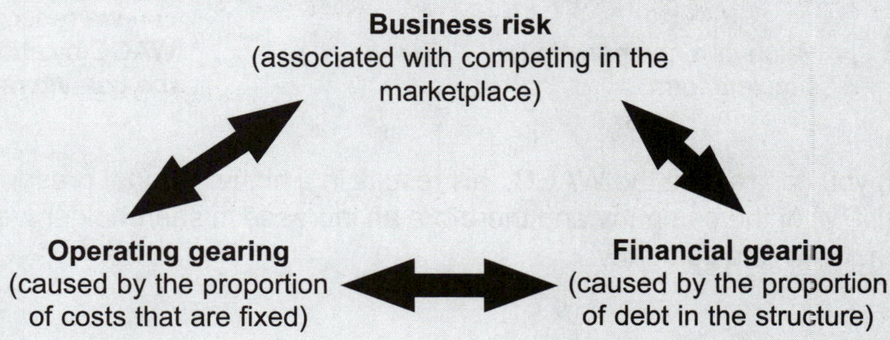

It is a financial manager's role to balance these different risk factors to ensure that the overall risk faced by equity investors is acceptable. It is the level of overall risk that will determine the rate of return an equity investor demands.

In reality, there is little that a financial manager can do to alter the business risk and there may only be limited opportunities for altering operating gearing. It is therefore the risk associated with how the company is financed that is most easily controlled.

A firm must consider the volatility it cannot avoid and ensure that the gearing decisions it takes avoid increasing risks to unacceptable levels.

3 An optimal capital structure? – company value and the cost of capital

The objective of management is to maximise shareholder wealth. If altering the gearing ratio (the extent to which debt is used in the finance structure) could increase wealth, then finance managers would have a duty to do so.

Is it possible to increase shareholder wealth by changing the gearing ratio/level?

- The market value (MV) of a company is the sum of the MVs of its various forms of finance. This equates to the MV of the company's equity plus debt.
- The MV of each type of finance is known to be the PV of the returns to the investor, discounted at their required rate of return.
- If a company distributes all its earnings, it follows that the total MV of the company equates to the present value (PV) of the future cash flows available to investors, discounted at their overall required return or WACC.

MV of a company (perpetuity formula) = **Future cash flows / WACC**

Value of a company in its simplest form

can we reduce the WACC by changing the gearing ratio?

If you can reduce the WACC, this results in a higher MV/net present value (NPV) of the company and therefore an increase in shareholder wealth as they own the company:

$$\text{MV of a company} \quad \frac{100}{0.15} = \mathbf{667} \quad \frac{100}{0.10} = \mathbf{1,000}$$

The WACC is a weighted average of the various sources of finance used by the company.

Debt is cheaper than equity:

- lower risk
- tax relief on interest

but:

increasing levels of debt make equity more risky:

- fixed commitment paid before equity – finance risk
- so increasing financial gearing increases the cost of equity and that would increase the WACC.

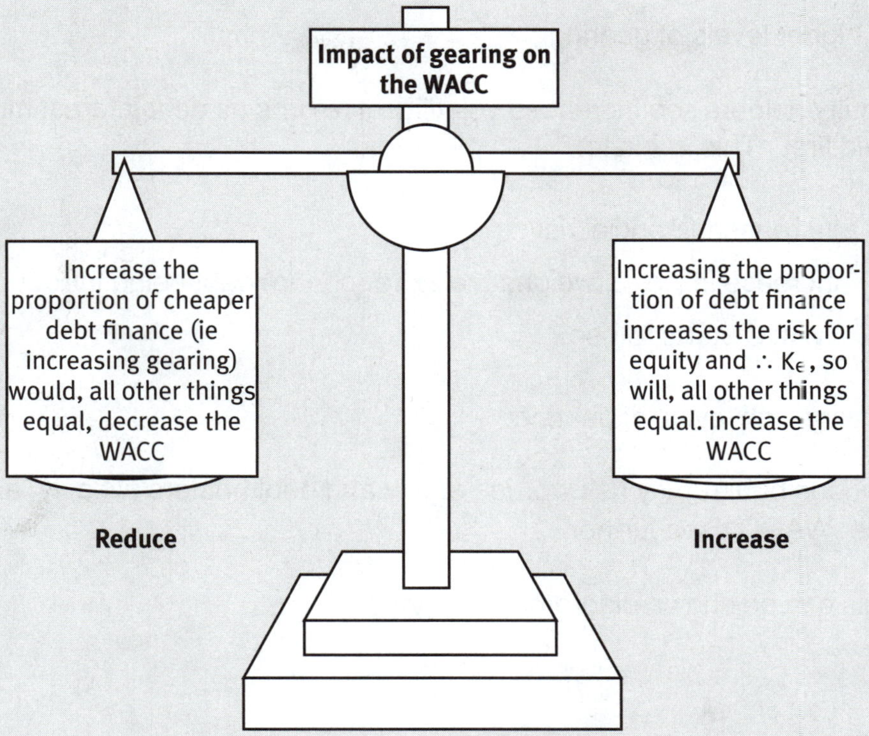

Various theories have attempted to answer the question:

Which has the greater effect on WACC?

The **reduction in WACC** caused by the cheaper debt	The **increase in WACC** by the increase in financial risk and $\mathbf{K_e}$

4 The traditional view of capital structure

Also known as the intuitive view, the traditional view has no theoretical basis but common sense. Taxation is ignored in the traditional view.

At low levels of gearing:

Equity holders perceive risk as unchanged so the increase in the proportion of cheaper debt will lower the WACC

At higher levels of gearing:

Equity holders see increased volatility of returns as debt interest must be paid first. This leads to:

- increased financial risk
- increase in Ke outweighs the extra (cheap) debt being introduced
- WACC starts to rise.

At very high levels of gearing:

Serious bankruptcy risk worries equity and debt holders alike K_e and K_d rise WACC rises further.

This can be shown diagrammatically:

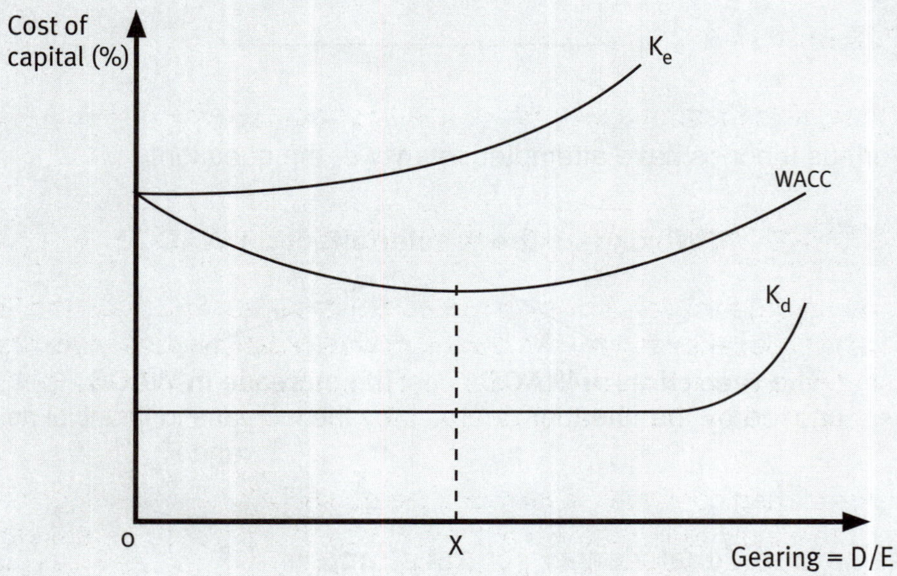

where:

K_e is the cost of equity

K_d is the cost of debt

Conclusion

There is an optimal level of gearing – point X. At point X the overall return required by investors (debt and equity) is minimised. It follows that at this point the combined market value of the firm's debt and equity securities will also be maximised.

Assumptions underpinning the traditional view

- No taxation
- The company pays out all its earnings as dividends
- The earnings of the company are expected to remain constant in perpetuity
- Business risk is constant
- The gearing of a company can be changed immediately by issuing debt to repurchase shares or vice versa. That is to say the capital employed in the business is constant.
- The are no transaction costs for issues

Implication for finance

Company should gear up until it reaches optimal point and then raise a mix of finance to maintain this level of gearing.

Problem

There is no method, apart from trial and error, available to locate the optimal point.

The traditional view of capital structure

As an organisation introduces debt into its capital structure, the WACC will fall because initially the benefit of cheap debt finance more than outweighs any increases in the cost of equity required to compensate equity holders for higher financial risk.

As gearing continues to increase the equity holders will ask for increasingly higher returns and eventually this increase will start to outweigh the benefit of cheap debt finance, and the WACC will rise.

At extreme levels of gearing the cost of debt will also start to rise (as debt holders become worried about the security of their loans), shareholders will continue to increase their required return and this will contribute to a sharply increasing WACC.

As a company begins to 'suffer' from high gearing, problems such as fewer assets left to offer for security on new loans, and restrictive terms from investors, become more likely. Key staff leave to avoid being tainted by a failed company. Uncertainties are placed in the minds of customers and suppliers, which may result in lost sales and more expensive trading terms. Shareholders refuse to invest new funds for positive NPV projects, as they do not wish 'to throw good money after bad'.

If a bankruptcy situation finally occurs, the assets may be sold off quickly and cheaply. A large proportion of management time is spent 'fire fighting', i.e. focusing on short-term cash flow rather than long-term shareholder wealth.

The traditional view therefore claims that there is an optimal capital structure where WACC is at a minimum. This is represented by point X on the above diagram.

At point X the overall return required by investors (debt and equity) is minimised. It follows that at this point the combined MV of the firm's debt and equity securities will also be maximised.

(If investors are offered the same $ return but the % return they require has fallen market pressures will make the value of the securities rise.)

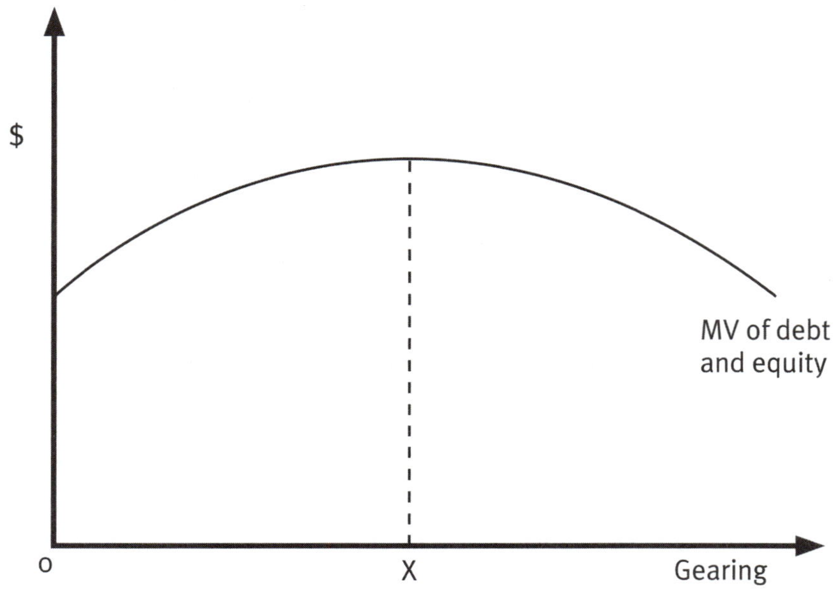

The main support for the traditional view is that it simply accords with 'common sense' and until 1958 it was not questioned.

To address this problem two economists attempted to find the optimal point in 1958.

5 Modigliani & Miller (M&M) – 1958 theory with no taxation

M&M argued that:

- as investors are rational, the required return of equity is directly proportional to the increase in gearing. There is thus a linear relationship between K_e and gearing (measured as D/E)
- the increase in K_e exactly offsets the benefit of the cheaper debt finance and therefore the WACC remains unchanged.

Conclusion

- The WACC and therefore the value of the firm are unaffectec by changes in gearing levels and gearing is irrelevant.
- Implication for finance:
  - choice of finance is irrelevant to shareholder wealth: company can use any mix of funds
  - this can be demonstrated on the following diagram:

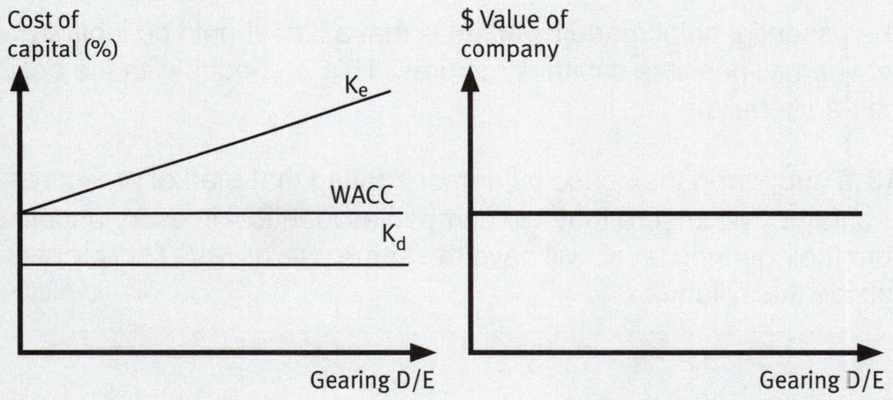

Assumptions underpinning M&M's theory

- No taxation
- Perfect capital markets where investors have the same information, upon which they react rationally.
- No transaction costs
- Debt is risk free

A key part of **M&M**'s theories are the assumptions. Ensure you can discuss them.

Modigliani & Miller: no taxes

The **M&M** view is that:

- companies which operate in the same type of business and which have similar operating risks must have the same total value, irrespective of their capital structures.

Their view is based on the belief that the value of a company depends upon the future operating income generated by its assets. The way in which this income is split between returns to debt holders and returns to equity should make no difference to the total value of the firm (equity plus debt). Thus, the total value of the firm will not change with gearing, and therefore neither will its WACC.

Their view is represented in the above diagrams.

If the WACC is to remain constant at all levels of gearing it follows that any benefit from the use of cheaper debt finance must be exactly offset by the increase in the cost of equity.

The essential point made by **M&M** is that a firm should be indifferent between all possible capital structures. This is at odds with the beliefs of the traditionalists.

M&M supported their case by demonstrating that market pressures (arbitrage) will ensure that two companies identical in every aspect apart from their gearing level, will have the same overall MV. This proof is outside the syllabus.

6 M&M – 1963 theory with tax

A number of practical criticisms were levelled at **M&M**'s no tax theory, but the most significant was the assumption that there were no taxes. Since debt interest is tax-deductible the impact of tax could not be ignored.

M&M therefore revised their theory (perfect capital market assumptions still apply):

In 1963, **M&M** modified their model to reflect the fact that the corporate tax system gives tax relief on interest payments.

The starting point for the theory is, as before, that:

- as investors are rational, the required return of equity is directly linked to the increase in gearing – as gearing increases, K_e increases in direct proportion.

However this is adjusted to reflect the fact that:

- debt interest is tax deductible so the overall cost of debt to the company is lower than in M&M – no tax
- lower debt costs results in less volatility in returns for the same level of gearing which leads to lower increases in K_e
- the increase in K_e does not offset the benefit of the cheaper debt finance and therefore the WACC falls as gearing increases.

Conclusion

Gearing up reduces the WACC and increases the MV of the company. The optimal capital structure is 99.9% gearing.

Implications for finance:

The company should use as much debt as possible.

This is demonstrated in the following diagrams:

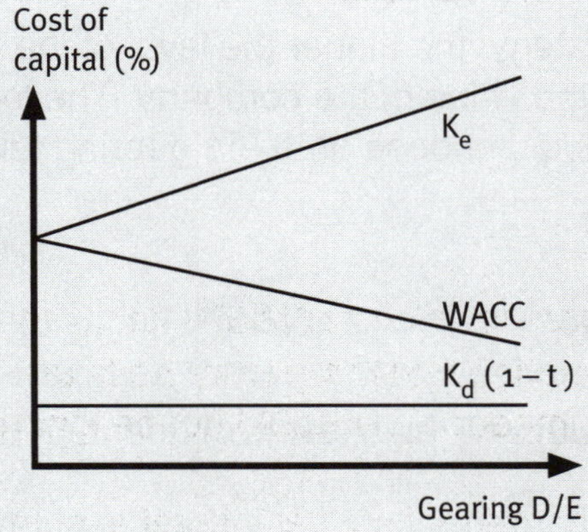

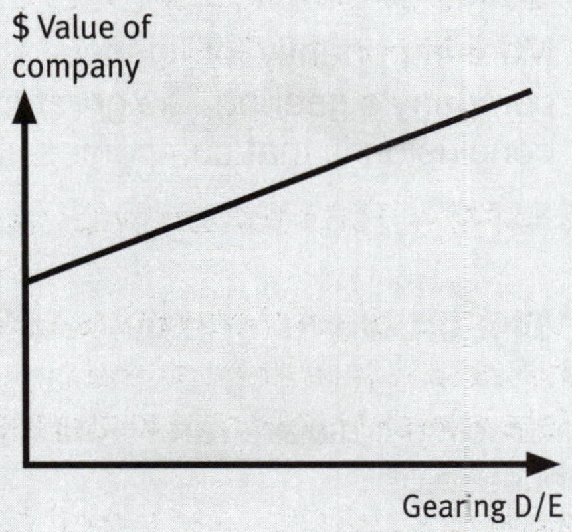

Note: Gearing is measured here using V_d / V_e

Modigliani & Miller: with tax

In their original model **M&M** ignored taxation. In 1963 they amended their model to include corporation tax. This alteration changes the implication of their analysis significantly.

Previously they argued that companies that differ only in their capital structure should have the same total value of debt plus equity. This was because it was the size of a firm's operating earnings stream that determined its value, not the way in which it was split between returns to debt and equity holders.

However, the corporation tax system carries a distortion under which returns to debt holders (interest) are tax deductible to the firm, whereas returns to equity holders are not. **M&M**, therefore, conclude that:

- geared companies have an advantage over ungeared companies, i.e. they pay less tax and will, therefore, have a greater MV and a lower WACC.

Once again they were able to produce a proof to support their arguments and show that as gearing increases, the WACC steadily decreases.

If the other implications of the M&M view are accepted, the introduction of taxation suggests that the higher the level of taxation, the lower the combined cost of capital.

More importantly for financial strategy, the higher the level of the company's gearing, the greater the value of the company. The logical conclusion is that companies should choose a 99.9% gearing level.

7 The problems of high gearing

In practice firms are rarely found with very high levels of gearing. This is because of:

- bankruptcy risk
- agency costs
- tax exhaustion

- the impact on borrowing/debt capacity
- differences in risk tolerance levels between shareholders and directors
- restrictions in the articles of association
- increases in the cost of borrowing as gearing increases.

As a result of these market imperfections, despite the theories, gearing levels tend to be based on more practical concerns and companies will often follow the industry average gearing.

The problems of high gearing

(1) Bankruptcy risk

As gearing increases so does the possibility of bankruptcy. If shareholders become concerned, this will increase the WACC of the company and reduce the share price.

(2) Agency costs: restrictive conditions

In order to safeguard their investments, lenders/debentures holders often impose restrictive conditions in the loan agreements that constrain management's freedom of action, e.g. restrictions:

(i) on the level of dividends

(ii) on the level of additional debt that can be raised

(iii) on management from disposing of any major fixed assets without the debenture holders' agreement.

(3) Tax exhaustion

After a certain level of gearing, companies will discover that they have no tax liability left against which to offset interest charges.

K_d (1 – t) simply becomes K_d.

(4) Borrowing/debt capacity

High levels of gearing are unusual because companies run out of suitable assets to offer as security against loans. Companies with assets which have an active second-hand market, and with low levels of depreciation such as property companies, have a high borrowing capacity.

(5) Difference risk tolerance levels between shareholders and directors

Business failure can have a far greater impact on directors than on a well-diversified investor. It may be argued that directors have a natural tendency to be cautious about borrowing.

(6) Restrictions in the articles of association may specify limits on the company's ability to borrow.

(7) The cost of borrowing increases as gearing increases.

As a result debt becomes less attractive as it is no longer so cheap.

8 Pecking-order theory

In this approach, there is no search for an optimal capital structure through a theorised process. Instead it is argued that firms will raise new funds as follows:

- internally-generated funds
- debt
- new issue of equity.

Firms simply use all their internally-generated funds first then move down the pecking order to debt and then finally to issuing new equity. Firms follow a line of least resistance that establishes the capital structure.

Internally-generated funds – i.e. retained earnings

- Already have the funds.
- Do not have to spend any time persuading outside investors of the merits of the project.
- No issue costs.

Debt

- The degree of questioning and publicity associated with debt is usually significantly less than that associated with a share issue.
- Moderate issue costs.

New issue of equity

- Perception by stock markets that it is a possible sign of problems. Extensive questioning and publicity associated with a share issue.
- Expensive issue costs.

Pecking order theory

Issue cost

Internally-generated funds have the lowest issue costs, debt moderate issue costs and equity the highest. Firms issue as much as they can from internally-generated funds first then move on to debt and finally equity.

Asymmetric information

Myers has suggested asymmetric information as an explanation for the heavy reliance on retentions. This may be a situation where managers, because of their access to more information about the firm, know that the value of the shares is greater than the current MV (based on the weak and semi-strong market information: see chapter 20).

In the case of a new project, managers' forecasts may be higher and more realistic than that of the market. If new shares were issued in this situation, there is a possibility that they would be issued at too low a price, thus transferring wealth from existing shareholders to new shareholders. In these circumstances there might be a natural preference for internally-generated funds over new issues. If additional funds are required over and above internally-generated funds, then debt would be the next alternative.

If management is averse to making equity issues when in possession of favourable inside information, market participants might assume that management will be more likely to favour new issues when they are in possession of unfavourable inside information which leads to the suggestion that new issues might be regarded as a signal of bad news! Managers may therefore wish to rely primarily on internally-generated funds supplemented by borrowing, with issues of new equity as a last resort.

Myers and Majluf (1984) demonstrated that with asymmetric information, equity issues are interpreted by the market as bad news, since managers are only motivated to make equity issues when shares are overpriced. **Bennett Stewart** (1990) puts it differently: 'Raising equity conveys doubt. Investors suspect that management is attempting to shore up the firm's financial resources for rough times ahead by selling over-valued shares.'

Asquith and Mullins (1983) empirically observed that announcements of new equity issues are greeted by sharp declines in stock prices. Thus, equity issues are comparatively rare among large established companies.

Test your understanding 4 – Gearing theories

Answer the following questions:

(a) If a company, in a perfect capital market with no taxes, incorporates increasing amounts of debt into its capital structure without changing its operating risk, what will the impact be on its WACC?

(b) According to M&M why will the cost of equity always rise as the company gears up?

(c) In a perfect capital market but with taxes, two companies are identical in all respects, apart from their levels of gearing. A has only equity finance, B has 50% debt finance. Which firm would M&M argue was worth more?

(d) In practice a firm which has exhausted retained earnings, is likely to select what form of finance next?

Make sure you can explain clearly the two effects of introducing more debt finance and the differing conclusions as to the combined impact these may have on the WACC.

When using diagrams to illustrate your discussion, draw the diagrams carefully and clearly label the axes and all lines illustrating costs of capital.

Summary of gearing theories:

Theory	**Net effect as gearing increases**	**Impact on WACC**	**Optimal finance method**
Traditional theory	The WACC is U-shaped.	At optimal point, WACC is minimised.	Find and maintain optimum gearing ratio.
M&M (no tax)	Cheaper debt = Increase in K_e.	WACC is constant.	Choice of finance is irrelevant – use any.
M&M (with tax)	Cheaper debt > Increase in K_e.	WACC falls.	As much debt as possible.
The pecking order	No theorised process.	No theorised process.	Simply line of least resistance. First internally-generated funds, then debt and finally new issue of equity.

Tutorial note: examination questions concerning the capital structure that minimises the WACC, or maximises the value of the firm are basically asking the same question. Maximising MV and minimising WACC are identical concepts.

9 Capital structure and the choice of discount rate

Use of the WACC in investment appraisal

In the chapter covering cost of capital we learnt how to calculate WACC. It was based upon the firm's current costs of equity and debt. It is therefore appropriate for use in investment appraisal provided:

- the historic proportions of debt and equity are not to be changed
- the operating risk (business risk) of the firm will not be changed
- the finance is not project-specific, i.e. projects are financed from a pool of funds.

or

- the project is small in relation to the company so any changes are insignificant.

Using CAPM in project appraisal

We also saw how the CAPM can be used to help find a discount rate when the project risk is different from that of the company's normal business risk.

The logic behind the CAPM is as follows:

- Objective is to maximise shareholder wealth
- Rational shareholders will hold well diversified portfolios
- Any new project is just another investment in a shareholder's portfolio
- CAPM can set the shareholders' required return on the project

Test your understanding 5 – CAPM

Comhampton Co is an all-equity company with a beta of 0.8. It is appraising a one-year project which requires an outlay now of $1,000 and will generate cash in one year with an expected value of $1,250. The project has a beta of 1.3. r_f = 10%, r_m = 18%.

(a) What is the firm's current cost of equity capital?

(b) What is the minimum required return of the project?

(c) Is the project worthwhile?

CAPM and gearing risk

In chapter 17 we said that to evaluate a project with a different risk profile, a company will need to find a suitable beta factor for the new investment and that these are best estimated with reference to existing companies operating in those business areas.

The reason this approach works is:

- those companies paying above average returns are assumed to have a correspondingly higher than average systematic risk and their beta (the measure of the company's systematic risk compared to the market) is extrapolated accordingly
- the extrapolated beta is then considered a measure of the risk of that business area.

However, the above only considers the business risk. When using betas in project appraisal, the impact of financial gearing (hereafter referred to as "gearing") must also be borne in mind.

Understanding betas

Firms must provide a return to compensate for the risk faced by investors, and even for a well-diversified investor, this systematic risk will have two causes:

- the risk resulting from its business activities
- the finance risk caused by its level of gearing.

Consider therefore two firms A and B:

- both are identical in all respects including their business operations but
- A has higher gearing than B:
  - A would need to pay out higher returns
  - any beta extrapolated from A's returns will reflect the systematic risk of both its business and its financial position and would therefore be higher than B's.

Therefore there are two types of beta:

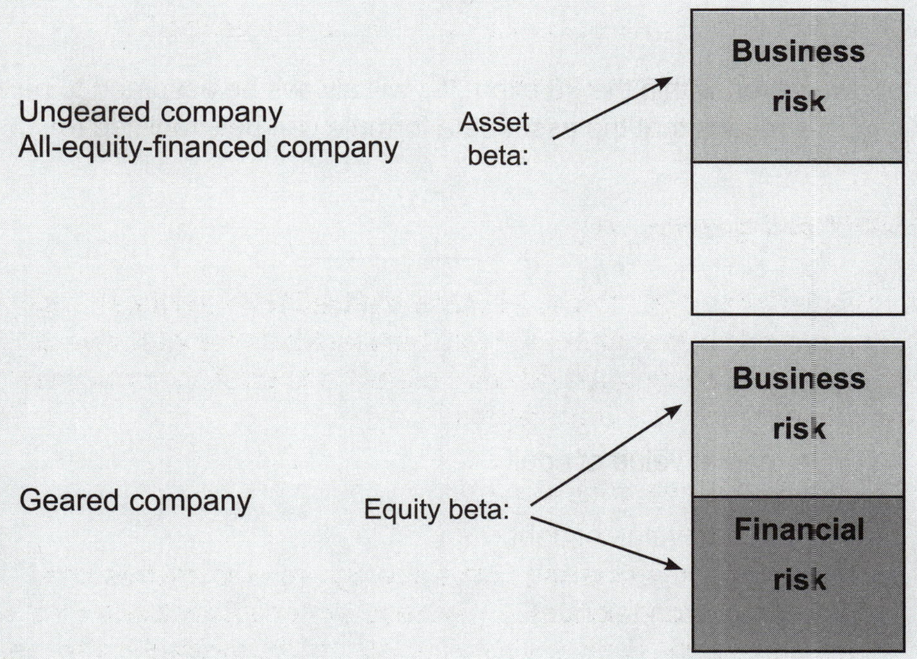

β_{Asset} reflects purely the systematic risk of the business area.

β_{Equity} reflects the systematic risk of the business area and the company-specific financial structure.

Using betas in project appraisal

It is critical in examination questions to identify which type of beta you have been given and what risk it reflects. The steps to calculating the right beta and how to use it in project appraisal are:

(1) Find an appropriate asset beta.

This may be given to you in the question. If not, you will need to calculate it by **de-gearing** a given equity beta. You can do this using the asset beta formula given to you in the exam

$$\beta_a = \left[\frac{V_e}{(V_e + V_d(1-T))}\beta_e\right] + \left[\frac{V_d(1-T)}{(V_e + V_d(1-T))}\beta_d\right]$$

However, within the F9 exam, β_d will always be assumed to be zero. This means that the asset beta formula can be simplified to:

$$\beta_a = \beta_e \times \frac{V_e}{V_e + V_d(1-T)}$$

where:

V_e = market value of equity

V_d = market value of debt

T = corporation tax rate.

A version of this formula is given to you in the exam (the full asset beta formula), the difference being that the above formula assumes debt is risk-free (i.e. debt has a $\beta = 0$).

When using this formula to de-gear a given equity beta, V_e and V_d should relate to the company or industry from which the equity beta has been taken.

(2) Adjust the asset beta to reflect the gearing levels of the company making the investment

Re-gear the asset beta to convert it to an equity beta based on the gearing levels of the company undertaking the project. The same asset beta formula as given above can be used, except this time V_e and V_d will relate to the company making the investment.

(3) Use the re-geared beta to find K_e . This is done using the standard CAPM formula of:

Required return = Rf + β (Rm – Rf)

where:

Rf = risk-free rate

Rm = average return on the market

(Rm – Rf) = equity risk premium (sometimes referred to as average market risk premium)

β = the beta factor calculated in step (2).

Remember that CAPM just gives you a risk-adjusted K_e, so once a company has found the relevant shareholders' required return for the project it could combine it with the cost of debt to calculate a risk adjusted weighted average cost of capital. This is however, outside of the scope of your syllabus.

e.g

Illustration 1 – CAPM & gearing risk

B Co is a hot air balloon manufacturer whose equity:debt ratio is 5:2. The corporate debt, which is assumed to be risk-free, has a gross redemption yield of 11%. The beta value of the company's equity is 1.1. The average return on the stock market is 16%. The corporation tax rate is 30%.

The company is considering a water bed manufacturing project. S Co is a water bed manufacturing company. It has an equity beta of 1 59 and an equity:debt ratio of 2:1. B Co maintains its existing capital structure after the implementation of the new project.

What would be a suitable risk adjusted cost of equity to apply to the project?

Solution

Step 1 – Find an appropriate asset beta

B Co has selected an appropriate equity beta for water bed manufacturing of 1.59, but in order to perform the calculation, this needs to be de-geared into an asset beta to reflect the business risk of the new project/industry. The relevant information is:

- the ß equity (1.59)
- gearing ratio of the new industry (2:1)

$$\beta_a = \beta_e \times \frac{V_e}{V_e + V_d(1 - T)}$$

$$= 1.59 \times \frac{2}{2 + 1(1 - 0.3)}$$

$$= 1.18$$

Step 2 – Adjust the asset beta to reflect the gearing levels of the company

Calculate the equity beta of the new project, by re-gearing:incorporate the financial risk of our company using our gearing ratio (5:2)

$$\beta_a = \beta_e \times \frac{V_e}{V_e + V_d(1 - T)}$$

$$1.18 = \beta_e \times \frac{5}{5 + 2(0.70)}$$

$$1.18 = 0.78\ \beta_e$$

$$\beta_e = \frac{1.18}{0.78} = 1.51$$

Step 3 – Use the re-geared beta to find the risk-adjusted K_e:

Calculate the cost of equity of the project based on CAPM:

$Ke = R_F + ß (R_M - R_F)$

$= 11\% + 1.51 (16\% - 11\%) = 18.55\%$

Test your understanding 6 – CAPM and gearing risk

Hubbard, an all-equity food manufacturing firm, is about to embark upon a major diversification in the consumer electronics industry. Its current equity beta is 1.2, whilst the average equity ß of electronics firms is 1.6. Gearing in the electronics industry averages 30% debt, 70% equity.

Corporate debt is considered to be risk free.

$R_m = 25\%$, $R_f = 10\%$, corporation tax rate = 30%

What would be a suitable risk-adjusted cost of equity for the new investment if Hubbard were to be financed in each of the following ways?

A By 30% debt and 70% equity

B Entirely by equity.

C By 20% debt and 80% equity.

D By 40% debt and 60% equity.

Suitable discount rates for the project should reflect both its systematic business risk and its level of gearing.

Test your understanding 7

Assuming that Modigliani and Miller's theory with tax applies, as gearing increases, which of the following is correct?

	Cost of equity	*WACC*
A	Decreases	No change
B	No change	Decreases
C	Increases	No change
D	Increases	Decreases

Test your understanding 8

Modigliani and Miller (M&M) stated that, in the absence of tax, a company's capital structure would have no impact on its weighted average cost of capital.

M&M made various assumptions in arriving at this conclusion, including

(1) A perfect capital market exists, in which investors have the same information, upon which they act rationally

(2) There are no tax or transaction costs

(3) Debt is risk-free and freely available at the same cost to investors and companies alike

A (2) only

B (1) and (2) only

C (2) and (3) only

D All of the above

Test your understanding 9

Which of the following events is most likely to lead to an increase in a firm's operating risk?

A An increase in the proportion of the firm's operating capital which is debt

B An increase in the proportion of the firm's operating costs which are fixed

C An increase in the proportion of the firm's operating capital which is equity

D An increase in the proportion of the firm's operating costs which are variable

Test your understanding 10

According to the traditional view of capital structure, which of the following statements is incorrect?

A As the level of gearing increases, the cost of debt remains unchanged up to a certain level of gearing. Beyond this level, the cost of debt will increase

B The cost of equity falls as the level of gearing increases and financial risk increases

C The weighted average cost of capital does not remain constant, but rather falls initially as the proportion of debt capital increases, and then begins to increase as the rising cost of equity (and possibly debt) becomes more significant

D The optimal level of gearing is where the company's weighted average cost of capital is minimised

Test your understanding 11

Two companies are identical in every respect except for their capital structure. XY plc has a debt:equity ratio of 1:3 and an equity beta of 1.2. PQ plc has a debt:equity ratio of 2:3. Corporation tax is 30%.

What is an appropriate equity beta for PQ plc?

A 0.93

B 1.43

C 1.62

D 1.76

Chapter summary

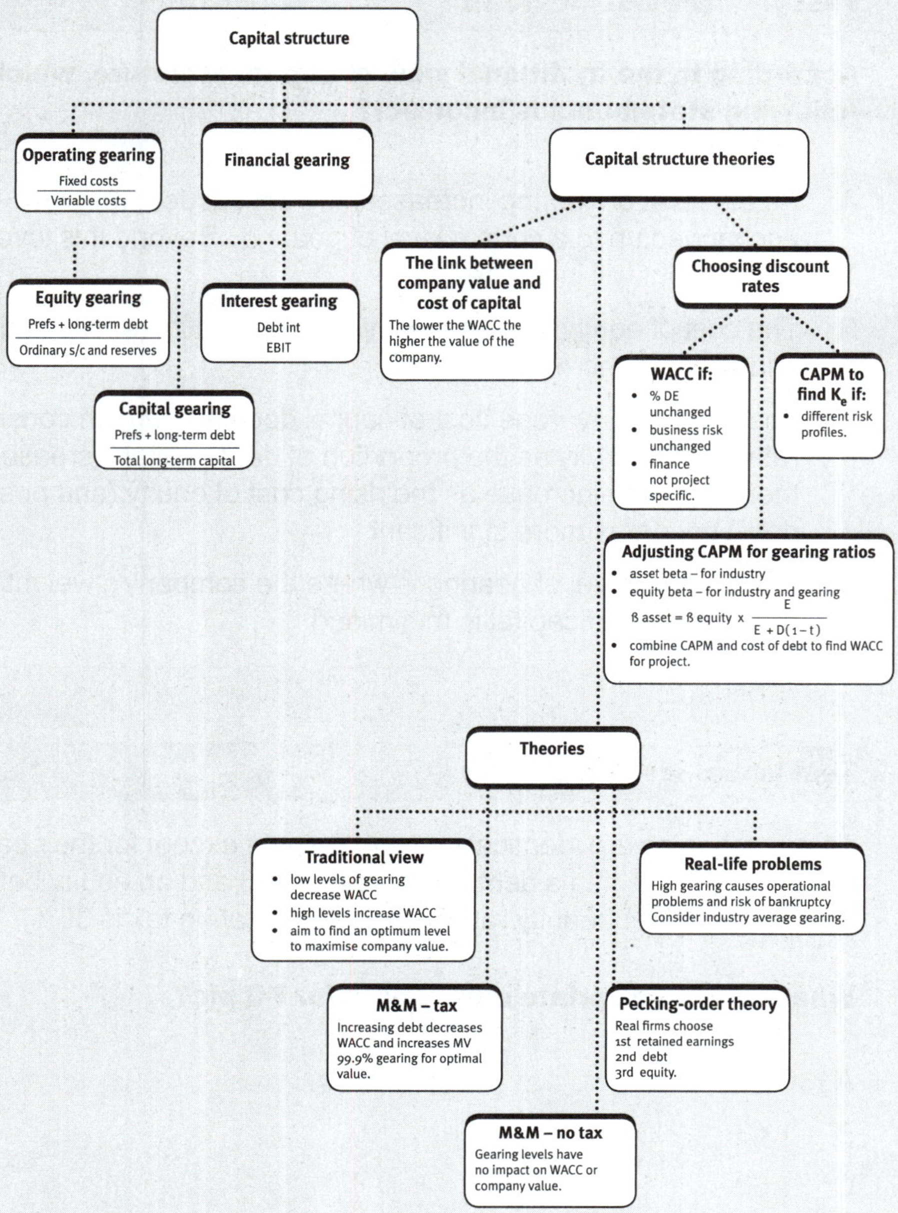

Test your understanding answers

Test your understanding 1 – Operating gearing

Operating gearing can be calculated as follows:

	Firm A	**Firm B**
Fixed costs/Variable costs	1/3 = 0.33	3/1 = 3

Firm B carries a higher operating gearing because it has higher fixed costs.

Its operating earnings will therefore be more volume-sensitive:

	Firm A	**Firm A**	**Firm B**	**Firm B**
	$m	**10% inc**	$m	**10% inc**
Sales	5.0	**5.5**	5.0	5.5
Variable costs	(3.0)	**(3.3)**	(1.0)	**(1.1)**
Fixed costs	(1.0)	**(1.0)**	(3.0)	**(3.0)**
EBIT	1	**1.2**	1	**1.4**

Firm B has enjoyed an increase in EBIT of 40% whilst Firm A has had an increase of only 20%. In the same way a decrease in sales would bring about a greater fall in B's earnings than in A's.

Test your understanding 2 – Capital and equity gearing

If we assume the overdraft is short-term finance (as is usual in these calculations), then the ratios are:

Debt	= \$8m + \$1.5m	= \$9.5m
Equity	= \$10m + \$3m + \$2.5m	= \$15.5m
Equity gearing	= \$9.5m/\$15.5m × 100	= 61.3%
Capital gearing	= \$9.5m/(\$9.5m + \$15.5m)	= 38%

Note: strictly the overdraft is a short-term finance method whereas financial gearing looks at the mix of the company's medium to long-term finance. Where however a company were to consistently operate at an overdraft then there is an argument for including the core amount of the overdraft in long-term debt. In this instance the ratios would become

Debt	= \$5m + \$8m + \$1.5m	= \$14.5m
Equity	as before	= \$15.5m
Equity gearing	= \$14.5m/\$15.5m × 100	= 93.5%
Capital gearing	= \$14.5m/(\$14.5m + \$15.5m)	= 48.3%

Test your understanding 3 – The impact of financial gearing

	Firm C	Firm C – 10% decrease
	$000	$000
Sales	10	9
Variable costs	(2)	(1.8)
Fixed costs	(5)	(5)
Operating profit	3	2.2
Interest	(2)	(2)
Profit before tax	1	0.2

The impact of a 10% decrease in sales has reduced operating earnings by (3 – 2.2)/3 = 26.67%.

The increased volatility can be explained by the high operating gearing in C.

However, C also has debt interest obligations. This financial gearing has the effect of amplifying the variability of returns to shareholders. The 10% drop in sales has caused the overall return to fall by (1 – 0.2)/1= 80%. The additional 53.33% variation over and above the change in operating earnings is due to the use of debt finance.

Test your understanding 4 – Gearing theories

(a) The WACC will remain the same M&M – no tax (see above).

(b) Because the returns to shareholders become more volatile. (Note: this is not just an M&M view but true of all the approaches to gearing).

(c) The company which had geared up M&M – with tax (see above).

(d) Debt Pecking-order theory (see 5 above).

Test your understanding 5 – CAPM

(a) Cost of capital = 10% + (0.8 × (18% – 10%)) = 16.4%

(b) Project required return = 10% + 1.3(18% – 10%) = 20.4%

(c) Expected project return:

$$= \text{Project IRR} \quad \frac{1{,}250 - 1{,}000}{1{,}000} \quad = 25\%$$

Thus the project is worthwhile because its expected rate of return is higher than its minimum required return. This again assumes investors will not want any returns to compensate for the unsystematic risk on the new project, i.e. that they have well diversified portfolios.

Alternatively, the NPV of the project at its minimum required return is:

$	−1,000 + 1,250 /1.204	= $38.20

The NPV shows the gain made by the shareholders if the project is accepted.

Test your understanding 6 – CAPM and gearing risk

In all four situations the best approach is to treat the project as a 'mini-firm' and tailor the discount rate to reflect its level of systematic business risk and financial risk.

(a) **By 30% debt and 70% equity**

In this case the observed equity beta of the electronics industry would reflect the level of business risk and financial risk of the project. No adjustments are therefore required and the average equity β of the electronics industry can be used.

We can therefore jump straight to step (3), using the correct equity beta to find K_e

$$K_e = R_f + \beta\,(R_m - R_f)$$
$$= 10\% + 1.6(25\% - 10\%) = 34\%$$

(b) **Project financed entirely by equity**

To reflect the business risk of the new venture we should start with the equity β of the electronics industry, i.e. 1.6.

As our project is to be ungeared we should then remove the financial risk element:

$$ß_a = ß_e \times \frac{V_e}{V_e + V_d(1 - T)}$$

$$= 1.6 \times \frac{0.7}{0.7 + 0.3\,(1 - 0.30)}$$

$$= 1.23$$

The risk-adjusted cost of equity would then be:

$K_e = R_f + β\,(R_m - R_f)$

= 10% + 1.23 (25% − 10%)

= 28.45%

The project should be evaluated at a rate of 28.45%.

(c) **Project financed by 20% debt and 80% equity**

In this case the equity beta of the electronics industry reflects a higher level of gearing than that for the proposed project. The simplest procedure is to take a two-step approach to the gearing adjustment.

Step 1 Calculate the asset beta for the electronics company (as in (b)).

β asset = 1.23

This is a measure of the pure systematic risk of electronics companies. We now adjust this pure beta in the light of the given financial gearing ratio.

Step 2 Work out the equation 'backwards' to calculate the cost of equity for an electronics company with 80% equity and 20% debt.

$$ß_a = ß_e \times \frac{V_e}{V_e + V_d(1 - T)}$$

$$1.23 = ß_e \times \frac{0.8}{0.8 + 0.2(1 - 0.30)}$$

$$1.23 \times \frac{0.94}{0.8} = ß_e$$

$ß_e = 1.45$

The risk-adjusted cost of equity for such a firm would then be:

$K_e = R_f + ß\,(R_m - R_f)$

$= 10\% + 1.45\,(25\% - 10\%)$

$= 31.75\%$

(d) **Project financed by 40% debt and 60% equity**

In this case the equity beta of the electronics industry reflects a lower level of gearing than that for the proposed project. The process is the same seen in part (c).

Step 1 Calculate the asset beta for the electronics company (as in (b)).

β asset = 1.23

Step 2 Work out the equation 'backwards' to calculate the cost of equity for an electronics company with 60% equity and 40% debt.

$$ß_a = ß_e \times \frac{V_e}{V_e + V_d(1 - T)}$$

$$1.23 = ß_e \times \frac{0.6}{0.6 + 0.4(1 - 0.30)}$$

$$1.23 \times \frac{0.88}{0.6} = ß_e$$

$ß_e = 1.80$

The risk-adjusted cost of equity for such a firm would then be:

$K_e = R_f + ß\,(R_m - R_f)$

$= 10\% + 1.80\,(25\% - 10\%)$

$= 37.0\%$

Test your understanding 7

Answer D

As gearing increases, the cost of equity and equity β will both increase to reflect the additional risk experienced by shareholders. WACC will decrease because of the tax shield effect on interest payments. The asset β is unaffected by the gearing.

Test your understanding 8

Answer D

All of these are assumptions underpinning M&M's theory (1958 theory with no taxation).

Test your understanding 9

Answer B

Operating risk depends on the firm's operating gearing, which is measured by the ratio of fixed to variable costs. Hence, if fixed operating costs rise, as does operating risk.

Test your understanding 10

Answer B

According to the traditional view of capital structure, the cost of equity rises (not falls) as the level of gearing increases and financial risk increases. This is because the company is perceived to be higher risk by shareholders who will start to demand a higher level of return. There is a non-linear relationship between the cost of equity and gearing.

Test your understanding 11

Answer D

$$ß_a = ß_e \times \frac{V_e}{V_e + V_d(1 - T)}$$

$$= 1.20 \times \frac{3}{3 + 1(1 - 0.3)}$$

$$= 0.973$$

$$ß_e = ß_a \times \frac{V_e + V_d(1 - T)}{V_e}$$

$$= 0.973 \times \frac{3 + 2(1 - 0.3)}{3}$$

$$= 1.427$$

chapter

19

Financial ratios

Chapter learning objectives

Upon completion of this chapter you will be able to:

- calculate return on capital employed (ROCE) with data provided
- explain the meaning and usefulness of a calculated ROCE figure
- calculate earnings per share (EPS) and price earnings (PE) ratio with data provided
- explain the meaning and usefulness of an EPS figure and a PE ratio
- calculate return on equity (ROE) with data provided
- explain the meaning and usefulness of a calculated ROE figure
- calculate dividend per share (DPS) with data provided
- explain the meaning and usefulness of a DPS figure
- calculate dividend yield with data provided
- explain the meaning and usefulness of a dividend yield figure
- calculate total shareholder return (TSR) (dividend yield plus capital growth) with data provided
- explain the meaning and usefulness of a TSR (dividend yield plus capital growth) figure
- select appropriate ratios to measure changes in shareholder wealth within a scenario and discuss the relevance of the findings.

- define, calculate and explain the significance to a company's financial position and financial risk of its level of the following ratios:
  - operating gearing
  - financial gearing
  - interest cover
  - interest yield
  - dividend cover
  - dividend per share
  - dividend yield
  - earnings per share (EPS)
  - price/earnings (PE) ratio
- assess a company's financial position and financial risk in a scenario by calculating and assessing appropriate ratios

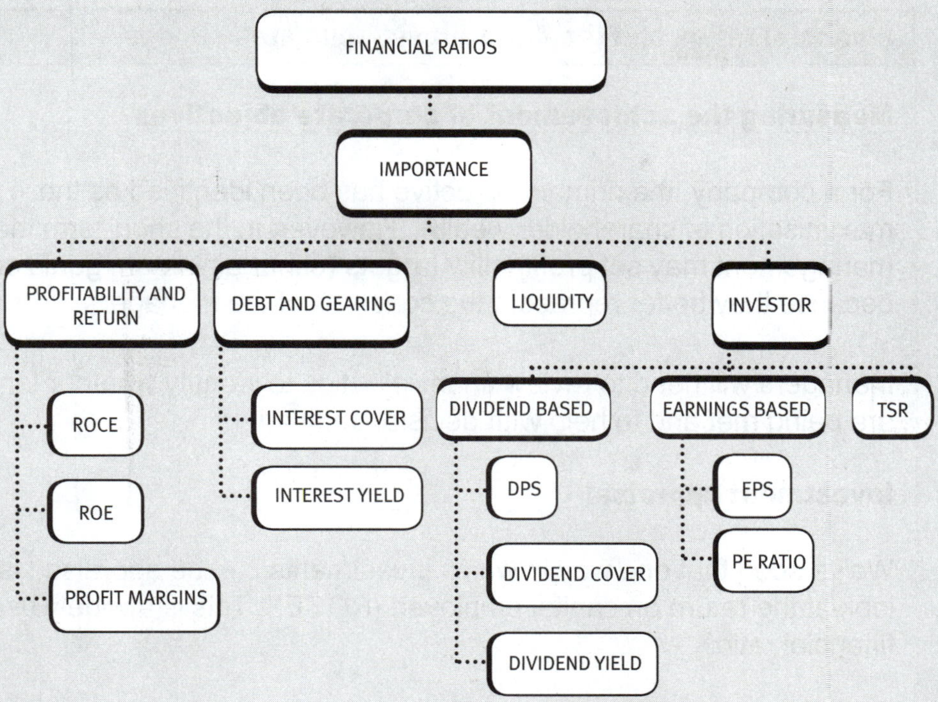

1 The importance of financial ratios

Ratio analysis is the process of comparing and quantifying relationships between financial variables, such as those variables found in the statement of financial position and statement of profit or loss of a company.

The ability to carry out effective ratio analysis and to be able to interpret the meaning of ratios is fundamental to the F9 syllabus.

Financial ratios and ratio analysis are key aspects within all of the following syllabus areas:

- Measuring the achievement of corporate objectives
- Investment appraisal
- Working capital management
- Capital structure
- Business valuations

Financial ratios and the different syllabus areas

Measuring the achievement of corporate objectives

For a company, the primary objective has been identified as the maximisation of shareholder wealth. However, in the short-term the management may set profitability targets (either as interim goals or because they better represent the concerns of the managers).

Managers will need to review financial ratios to identify whether targets are being met and to help with decision making.

Investment appraisal

We've seen that one way in which investments can be appraised is to look at the return on capital employed (ROCE). This is a widely used financial ratio.

In addition to this, managers may need to consider the impact that a new investment may have on the financial ratios of the organisation before deciding whether to invest or not.

Working capital management

We've seen that to assess the length of the cash operating cycle, a number of financial ratios must be calculated and then compared against a benchmark. Again, these ratios are vital for managers to be able to take informed decisions.

Capital structure

Gearing ratios can be a crucial way in which potential investors assess the risk of a business, which in turn will influence their decision over whether to invest or not. Before taking decisions regarding sources of finance, the financial manager must assess the impact of each option on these ratios.

Business valuations

Any potential equity investor or purchaser will review the financial ratios of a business before deciding whether to buy. They will use the ratios to draw conclusions about the worth of the business.

Taken in isolation, the calculations are relatively meaningless. Comparatives such as prior-year information, targets, industry averages and other forms of benchmarking are required if the measures are to be interpreted and the underlying causes investigated.

All the ratios calculated in the chapter are based upon the following information:

Statements of financial position as at 31 May

	20X6	20X5
	$000	$000
Non-current assets	1,800	1,400
Current assets		
Inventory	1,200	200
Receivables	400	800
Cash	100	100
Total Assets	3,500	2,500
Equity and Liabilities		
Ordinary share capital (50c shares)	1,200	500
Share premium	600	0
Reserves	200	100
	2,000	600
Non-current liabilities		
10% Loan notes	1,000	600
Current liabilities		
Loans and other borrowing	200	500
Other payables	300	800
	3,500	2,500

Statements of profit or loss for the year ended 31 May

	20X6	20X5
	$000	$000
Revenue	2,000	1,000
Cost of sales	(1,300)	(700)
Gross profit	700	300
Distribution costs	(260)	(90)
Administration expenses	(100)	(60)
Operating profit	340	150
Interest	(100)	(60)
Profit before taxation	240	90
Taxation	(50)	(20)
Profit after taxation	190	70
Ordinary dividends	(90)	(50)
Retained profit for the year	100	20
Profit and loss b/fwd	100	80
Profit and loss c/fwd	200	100
Share price ($)	1.30	1.26
Market value of loan notes	130	120
Industry information:		
Industry PE ratio	22	20
Industry average growth in EPS (%)	12	8
Industry average ROE (%)	15	12

2 Categories of ratios

The key ratios that you need to be able to calculate and interpret can be broken down into four broad categories:

- Profitability and return
- Debt and gearing
- Liquidity
- Investor ratios

3 Profitability and return

Profitability and return ratios are probably the most widely used. They are key to any financial manager wanting to assess performance against objectives as well as being crucial to the investment decision.

An external investor will also monitor these ratios closely when deciding whether to provide the company with finance and to assess the value of the overall business.

Return on Capital Employed (ROCE)

Considered to be a key ratio, ROCE gives a measure of how efficiently a business is using the funds available. It measures how much is earned per $1 invested.

$$\text{ROCE} = \frac{\text{Profit before interest and tax}}{\text{Capital Employed}} \times 100 = \frac{\text{PBIT}}{\text{CE}} \times 100$$

PBIT = Operating profit

CE = Non-current assets + Current assets - Current liabilities

= Share capital + Reserves + Long-term loans

Disadvantage of ROCE:

- uses profit, which is not directly linked to the objective of maximising shareholder wealth.

Illustration 1 – ROCE

ROCE

$$\text{20X6 ROCE} = \frac{340}{(2{,}000 + 1{,}000)} \times 100 = 11.33\%$$

$$\text{20X5 ROCE} = \frac{150}{(600 + 600)} \times 100 = 12.50\%$$

The company's ROCE has decreased in 20X6, i.e. for every $100 of capital invested the company earned $11.33 in 20X6 compared with $12.50 in 20X5.

ROCE

When assessing company performance, return on capital employed (ROCE) is often broken down as follows:

ROCE

$$\frac{\text{Operating profit}}{\text{Capital employed (CE)}}$$

Operating profit margin X **Asset turnover**

$$\frac{\text{Operating profit}}{\text{Sales revenue}} \quad \times \quad \frac{\text{Sales revenue}}{\text{CE}}$$

Operating profit margin is broken down into:

- **Gross profit margin** $\frac{\text{Gross profit}}{\text{Sales revenue}}$
- **Operating ratios** $\frac{\text{Expenses}}{\text{Sales revenue}}$

Asset turnover is broken down into:

- **Working capital turnover** $\frac{\text{Sales revenue}}{\text{Net working capital}}$
- **Non-current asset turnover** $\frac{\text{Sales revenue}}{\text{Non-current assets}}$

Return on Equity (ROE)

ROE measures how much profit a company generates for its ordinary shareholders with the money they have invested in the company.

It is useful for comparing the profitability of a company with other firms in the same industry.

It is calculated as

$$\text{ROE} = \frac{\text{Profit after tax and preference dividends}}{\text{Ordinary share capital + reserves}} \times 100\%$$

Where there are no preference shares this is simplified to give:

$$\text{ROE} = \frac{\text{PAT}}{\text{Shareholders' funds}} \times 100\%$$

ROE is similar to ROCE except:

- PAT is used instead of operating profit
- Shareholders' funds are used instead of CE (debt + equity).

Disadvantages of ROE:

- it uses profits which are an unreliable measure and not directly linked to shareholder wealth
- it is sensitive to gearing levels – ROE will increase as gearing ratio increases.

ROE

The value of ROE, is that it can help cut through the references to 'achieving record earnings' in many companies' annual reports. Achieving higher earnings each year is straightforward because a successful company generates profits every year. If management simply invested those earnings in a savings account paying 5% pa, they would be able to report 'record earnings' because of the interest they earned. But the shareholders would not be as well off as if the money had been returned to them for re-investment in another business opportunity.

So investors cannot take rising earnings per share each year as a sign of success. However the ROE figure takes into account the retained earnings from previous years, and so tells investors how effectively their capital is being reinvested. It is therefore a far better measure of management's abilities than the annual EPS.

However, apart from the obvious criticism that ROE still relies on the profit figure calculated, it is also sensitive to gearing levels. Assuming that the proceeds of debt finance can be re-invested at a return greater than the borrowing rate, then the greater the levels of debt in the capital structure, the higher the ROE will be.

e.g

Illustration 2 – ROE

ROE		**20X6**	**20X5**
	PAT	190	70
	Shareholders' funds	2000	600
		9.5%	11.7%

The ROE is falling. What is more, it is falling at a time when the industry average has risen from 12% to 15%. This suggests that the company is failing to make the most of the shareholders' investment. This analysis accords with the findings of the ROCE and the PE ratio.

Profit margins

Depending on the format of the statement of profit or loss, you may be able to calculate the gross profit margin and operating profit margin as follows:

$$\text{Gross profit margin} = \frac{\text{Gross profit}}{\text{Revenue}} \times 100$$

$$\text{Operating profit margin} = \frac{\text{Operating profit}}{\text{Revenue}} \times 100$$

A comparison of the changes in the two ratios can often reveal more information about cost control and the changes in operating gearing.

e.g

Illustration 3 – Profit margins

Gross profit margin

	20X6	20X5
Gross profit	700	300
Revenue	2,000	1,000
	35%	30%

Operating profit margin

	20X6	20X5
Operating profit	340	150
Revenue	2,000	1,000
	17%	15%

The 5% increase in gross profit margin is good news for the business as it indicates a wider gap between selling price and cost of sales.

However, the operating margin has only increased by 2% indicating that expenses (distribution and administration) have increased and may require tighter control.

4 Debt and gearing

Ratios that look at debt and gearing are a crucial way of assessing the risk profile of the business.

They will therefore be used extensively by financial managers when taking financing decisions as well as by current and potential investors when assessing the amount of financing to offer and the level of return to demand.

The basic calculations of operating gearing and financial gearing have already been covered in the previous chapter.

Further ratios to be aware of are detailed below.

Interest cover

Interest on loan stock (debenture stock) must be paid whether or not the company makes a profit.

Interest cover is a measure of the adequacy of a company's profits relative to its interest payments on its debt:

$$\frac{\text{Operating profits before debt interest and tax}}{\text{Debt interest}}$$

The lower the interest cover, the greater the risk that profit (before interest and tax) will become insufficient to cover interest payments.

In general, a high level of interest cover is 'good' but may also be interpreted as a company failing to exploit gearing opportunities to fund projects at a lower cost than from equity finance.

Note: the interest cover ratio is the inverse of the interest gearing ratio.

e.g

Illustration 4 – Interest cover

Interest cover

20X6

$$\frac{340}{100} = 3.4 \text{ times}$$

20X5

$$\frac{150}{60} = 2.5 \text{ times}$$

The company is in a strong position as regards the payment of interest. Profit would have to drop considerably before any problem of paying interest arose.

5 Liquidity

All of the liquidity ratios were covered in the chapter on working capital management.

6 Investor ratios

An investor is interested in:

- the income earned by the company for him
- the return on his investment.

For an ordinary shareholder the relevant information will be contained in the following ratios:

Dividends	**Earnings**
DPS	ROE
Dividend cover	EPS
Dividend yield	PE ratio

In general, the higher each of these ratios is, the more attractive the shares will be to potential investors, who will be increasingly confident about the return the shares will give.

Shareholders will also want information on the total shareholder return (TSR).

For a debt investor, they will be interested in the interest yield ratio.

Earnings per share (EPS)

This is the basic measure of a company's performance from an ordinary shareholder's point of view. It is the amount of profit, in cents, attributable to each ordinary share.

The principles of calculating EPS are simple:

$$\text{EPS} = \frac{\text{Profit after interest, after tax and after preference dividends}}{\text{Number of ordinary shares in issue}}$$

EPS can be analysed by studying the growth rate over time – trend analysis.

Disadvantage of EPS.

- EPS does not represent actual income of the shareholder and it uses earnings which are not directly linked to the objective of maximising shareholder wealth.

e.g

Illustration 5 – EPS

		20X6	**20X5**
EPS	PAT	190	70
	No. of shares in issue	2,400	1,000
	(NB Shares were only worth 50c each)	7.92c	7.00c

Solution

The EPS is an improvement on the prior year. It has grown by:

$$\frac{\$0.92}{\$7.00} = 0.13 \qquad = 13\%$$

This is slightly higher than the industry average (12%).

EPS

Although the ratio is simple in principle, in practice there may be a number of complications as both the definitions of **earnings** and **shares in issue** require careful analysis. Accounting treatment may cause the ratios to be distorted, if for example the earnings figure includes the effects of extraordinary items.

When calculating the EPS you cannot compare EPS of one company with EPS of another, as the answer would be meaningless. You should first calculate the growth rate of the EPS and then compare it with the growth of similar companies.

EPS does not represent the income of the shareholder. Rather it represents the investor's share of profit after tax generated by the company according to an accounting formula. Whilst there is obviously a correlation between earnings applicable to individual shareholders and their wealth, they are not equal.

Price Earnings (PE) ratio

A PE ratio gives a basic measure of company performance. It expresses the amount the shareholders are prepared to pay for the share as a multiple of current earnings.

$$PE = \frac{\text{Share price}}{\text{EPS}}$$

A high PE ratio indicates that investors perceive the firm's earnings to be of high quality – usually a mixture of high growth and/or lower risk expectations.

PE ratio

This is the basic measure of a company's performance from the market's point of view. Investors estimate a share's value as the amount they are willing to pay for each unit of earnings. It expresses the current share price as a multiple of the most recent EPS.

If a PE ratio is high, investors expect profits to rise. This does not necessarily mean that all companies on high PE ratios are expected to perform to a high standard, merely that they are expected to do significantly better than in the past. They may have greater growth potential because they are coming from a low base.

Illustration 6 – PE Ratio

PE Ratio		**20X6**	**20X5**
	Share price	130	126
	EPS	7.92	7
		16.4 times	18 times

Investors are willing to buy shares in the company at 16.4 times last year's earnings compared with the previous year's position when they were willing to pay 18 times the earnings.

This fall may be because the company is not expected to grow as much as in the previous year. The industry average PE increased year-on-year from 20 to 22, which may suggest that this company is expected to generate slower growth or carries more risk than the industry average.

Dividend per share (DPS)

The DPS helps individual (ordinary) shareholders see how much of the overall dividend payout they are entitled to.

$$DPS = \frac{\text{Total ordinary dividend}}{\text{Total number of shares issued}}$$

The DPS is usually given in the company's financial statements.

Illustration 7 – DPS

Dividend per share

	20X6	20X5
Dividends for the period	90	50
Total number of shares issued	2,400	1,000
	3.75c	5.0c

The DPS is falling. This would usually be regarded as bad news by investors, although here it is probably related to the share issue in 20X6. If it was a rights issue, e.g. the shareholders will now each own a greater number of shares.

DPS

Since the shareholders are the owners of the business, they are entitled to their share of the profits. This is most simply achieved by paying the amount out as a dividend. It is usually expressed as an amount per share. This is because the total amount a shareholder gets has to reflect their share of the company. If they are only a small shareholder and do not own many shares, they should only get a small share of the profit.

There is a tendency amongst investors to regard the level of dividend payout as a form of information about the company's performance. A falling DPS is regarded as a sign of problems. As a result many companies try to maintain a stable and slowly rising DPS, by resisting making high payouts during particularly good years.

Dividend cover

This is calculated as:

$$\frac{\text{Profit available for ordinary shareholders}}{\text{Dividend for the year (i.e. interim plus final)}}$$

It is a measure of how many times the company's earnings could pay the dividend.

The higher the cover, the better the ability to maintain dividends, if profits drop. This needs to be looked at in the context of how stable a company's earnings are: a low level of dividend cover might be acceptable in a company with very stable profits, but the same level of cover in a company with volatile profits would indicate that dividends are at risk.

Because buyers of high-yield shares tend to want a stable income, dividend cover is an important number for income investors.

Illustration 8 – Dividend cover

20X6		**20X5**	
$\frac{190}{90}$	= 2.1 times	$\frac{70}{50}$	= 1.4 times

The profits available for ordinary shareholders are taken after deduction of the preference dividend. The cover represents the 'security' for the ordinary dividend – in this company the cover is reasonable.

Dividend yield

This provides a direct measure of the wealth received by the (ordinary) shareholder. It is the annual dividend per share expressed as an annual rate of return on the share price.

$$\text{Dividend yield} = \frac{\text{DPS}}{\text{Market price per share}}$$

It can be used to compare the return with that from a fixed-rate investment.

Disadvantage of dividend yield:

- it fails to take account of any anticipated capital growth so does not represent the total return to the investor.

e.g

Illustration 9 – Dividend yield

		20X6	20X5
Dividend yield	DPS / Market price per share	3.75 / 130	5 / 126
		2.9%	4.0%

This return may compare unfavourably with interest rates but is not a full measure of company performance as the investor will also benefit from any increase in share price. As stated before, the low DPS may well be, in part, because of the recent share issue and this will also clearly impact the dividend yield.

Dividend yield

The dividend yield is regarded as being significant in the context of reaching decisions about whether to buy or sell shares. Investors are concerned with the amount of cash, in present value terms, which they will receive from their investment in shares. This cash is the result of:

- dividends received
- proceeds when the shares are ultimately sold.

No ratio provides full information about future cash flows but dividend yield is regarded as being a useful pointer.

Dividend yield is, however, incomplete in that it ignores the capital gain on the share which most shareholders would expect. A better measure would be total shareholder return (TSR).

Total shareholder return (TSR)

This measures the returns to the investor by taking account of:

- dividend income
- capital growth.

$$TSR = \frac{\text{DPS + change in share price}}{\text{Share price at start of period}}$$

TSR makes comparing returns between investments simple, irrespective of the size of the underlying investment.

Illustration 10 – TSR

If we assume that the share price was $1.20 at 31 May 20X4, then the TSR for the two years can be calculated:

		20X6	**20X5**
TSR	DPS +Change in share price	3.75 + (130 – 126)	5 + (126 – 120)
	Share price at start of period	126	120
		6.15%	9.17%

TSR

Probably the best measure of returns to equity, TSR takes account of the dividend income paid to shareholders and the capital growth of the share.

The TSR from an investment can easily be compared between companies or benchmarked against industry or market returns without having to worry about differences in size of the business.

The actual return received by the investor will depend on the shareholder's marginal rate of income tax and the capital gains tax suffered on any realised capital gain. Whether the shareholders prefer high dividend income or high capital gains will therefore depend very much on their tax position.

The TSR can also be calculated as the dividend yield (based on the opening share price) plus the capital gain over the year.

Interest yield

The interest yield is the interest or coupon rate expressed as a percentage of the market price:

$$\frac{\text{Interest rate}}{\text{Market value of debt}}$$

It is a measure of return on investment for the debt holder.

Illustration 11 – Interest yield

		20X6	20X5
Interest yield	Interest	10	10
	Market value of debt	130	120
		7.7%	8.3%

Note: This can be calculated based on one "block" of debt (nominal value = $100) or can be calculated using the total interest payment and the total market value.

The reason for the decline in the interest yield is nothing to do with the company. Instead it reflects a movement in interest rates in the market (and in particular the risk free rate).

Debt investors will still be interested in the level of interest yield as it will help them to assess whether the level of return is sufficiently above the risk free rate to compensate them for the risk associated with the investment.

Being able to select relevant ratios in a given scenario, calculate and interpret them is a key skill that you need to develop for the examination.

7 Combining ratios

When presented with information on some ratios, it is sometimes possible to combine two or more ratios in order to reveal another. For example:

$$\text{P/E ratio} \times \text{Dividend cover} = \frac{1}{\text{Dividend yield}}$$

which can also be written as:

$$\frac{1}{\text{P/E ratio}} \times \text{Dividend payout ratio} = \text{Dividend yield}$$

So, when tackling a question in the exam, if you feel like you're missing a vital piece of information, consider what ratios you have been given, and the elements that go in to each, and this may reveal a way forward.

Test your understanding 1 – Financial ratio analysis

Summarised statement of financial position at 31 December 20X6

		$000	$000
Non-current assets			
Cost *less* depreciation			2,200
Current assets			
	Inventory	400	
	Receivables	500	
	Cash	100	
			1,000
Total assets			3,200
Equity and liabilities			
Share capital			
	Ordinary shares ($1 each)		1,000
	Preference shares (10%) ($1 each)		200
	Reserves		800
			2,000
Non-current liabilities			
	Loan notes (10% Secured)		600
Current liabilities			
	Payables	400	
	Corporation tax	100	
	Dividends	100	
			600
Total equity and liabilities			3,200

Summarised statement of profit or loss for the year ended 31 December 20X6

	$000	$000
Revenue		3,000
Operating profit		400
Interest		(60)
Profit before tax		–––
		340
Taxation		(180)
		–––
Profit after taxation		160
Dividends		
Ordinary – proposed and paid	125	
Preference	20	
	–––	
		(145)
		–––
Retained profit for the year		15
Current quoted price of $1 ordinary shares		$1.40
Price of $1 ordinary shares at 31/12/X5		$1.22

Using the information above, calculate the following ratios and comment on your findings:

(a) ROCE – prior year 11%

(b) EPS – prior year 13.5c, industry average growth 3.5%

(c) PE ratio – industry average 7

(d) ROE – prior year 7%, industry average 7.5%

(e) DPS – prior year 12.5c

(f) Dividend yield

(g) TSR – prior year 20%, industry average 19%.

Test your understanding 2

In the year to 30 September 2014, an advertising agency declares an interim ordinary dividend of 7.4c per share and a final ordinary dividend of 8.6c per share.

Assuming an ex div share price of 315c, what is the dividend yield?

A 2.35%

B 2.73%

C 5.08%

D 4.10%

Test your understanding 3

The price/earnings (P/E) ratio:

A measures how much profits a company generates for its ordinary shareholders with the money they have invested in the company

B is a basic measure of the amount of profit attributable to each ordinary share

C expresses the amount the shareholders are prepared to pay for the shares as a multiple of current earnings

D helps individual ordinary shareholders see how much of the overall dividend payout they are entitled to

Test your understanding 4

Which of the following ratios is represented by the formula shown below?

$$\frac{\text{Profit available for ordinary shareholders}}{\text{Dividend for the year (i.e. interim plus final)}}$$

A Dividend cover

B Dividend yield

C Dividend per share

D Total shareholder return

Test your understanding 5

Which of the following ratios is represented by the formula shown below?

$$\frac{\text{Profit after interest, after tax and after preference dividends}}{\text{Number of ordinary shares in issue}}$$

A Return on capital employed

B Earnings per share

C Total shareholder return

D Financial gearing

Test your understanding 6

A company has the following summarised statement of profit or loss for the year.

	$
Sales revenue	70,000
Less: cost of sales	42,000
Gross profit	28,000
Less: expenses	21,000
Net profit	7,000

What is the company's gross profit margin for the year?

A 10%

B 40%

C 25%

D 17%

Chapter summary

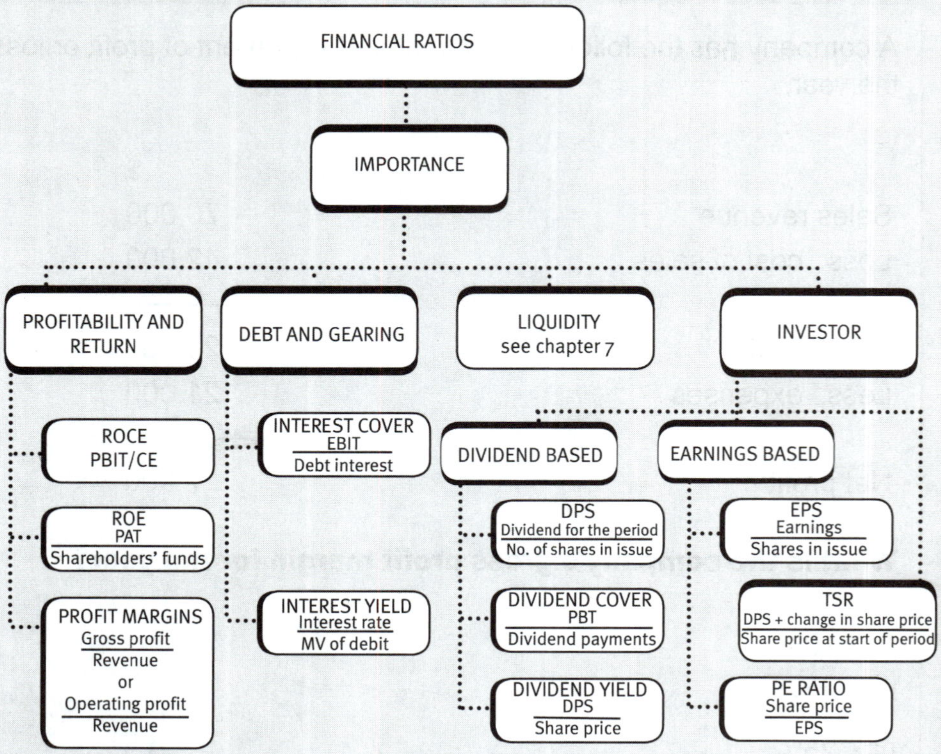

Test your understanding answers

Test your understanding 1 – Financial ratio analysis

(a) **ROCE**

		20X6
PBIT / CE	× 100	400 / 2,600
		15.4%

This short-term measure has improved suggesting the company is improving the efficient use of its funds.

(b) **EPS**

	20X6
Profit available to ordinary shareholders / Number of ordinary shares in issue	(160 – 20) / 1,000
	14c

$$\text{Growth of EPS} = \frac{0.5}{3.5} = 3.7\%$$

The EPS is growing at a rate marginally above the industry average, which suggests an acceptable level of profitability is being achieved.

(c) **PE ratio**

	20X6
Share price	140
EPS	14
	10 times

The PE ratio is higher than the industry average. This may be because the company is perceived to have good growth prospects. It is likely to be seen as having good investment potential since investors are prepared to pay ten times over the current earnings for the shares.

The current growth in EPS is fairly low but the company may be expected to make great improvements in the coming years.

(d) **ROE**

	20X6
PAT and pref. dividend	160 – 20
Shareholders' funds	1,800
	7.8%

The ROE is higher than last year. So in addition to the rising EPS it appears that the company is re-investing the funds it earns effectively. It also appears to be doing better than the industry as a whole. It would be useful to know what the industry average figure was in the previous year in order to determine the trend in its performance.

This finding is in line with the high PE ratio – if the firm is re-investing the funds it earns effectively it will be perceived as likely to develop good growth opportunities.

(e) **DPS**

	20X6
Dividends paid and proposed	125
Total number of shares issued	1,000
	12.5c

The DPS is unchanged despite an increase in EPS. This would make sense, as management are often reluctant to increase dividends too quickly, in case poor trading conditions in future years would then require a dividend cut. Dividend cuts are not well liked by investors.

Since the high PE ratio suggests good growth prospects, management may delay a dividend increase until these come to fruition.

(f) **Dividend yield**

	20X6
DPS	12.5
Market price per share	140
	8.9%

Prior year dividend yield can be calculated as prior year DPS divided by previous share price:

$$\frac{12.5}{122} = 10.2\%$$

It is inevitable that the dividend yield is falling, since the dividend has not been increased whilst the share price has grown. This shows the weakness of dividend yield as a measure – the shareholders are also benefiting from the increased share price but dividend yield does not take account of it.

(g) **TSR**

	20X6
DPS + Change in share price	12.5 + (140 – 122)
Share price at start of period	122
	25%

The overall TSR is above industry average and increasing (prior year = 20%). This can be explained by the increase in share price which supplements the dividends received. This increase is a sign of increased investor expectations of future income.

Overall, this appears to be an efficient growing company with promising prospects recognised by shareholders. Managers are prudently delaying increasing dividend payments too early, to avoid later drops fuelling investor dissatisfaction and a resulting fall in share price.

Test your understanding 2

Answer C

The total dividend per share is 7.4c + 8.6c = 16c

(16/315) × 100 = 5.08%

Test your understanding 3

Answer C

The return on equity (ROE) measures how much profit a company generates for its ordinary shareholders with the money they have invested in the company (A). Earnings per share (EPS) is a basic measure of the amount of profit attributable to each ordinary share (B). Dividend per share (DPS) helps individual ordinary shareholders see how much of the overall dividend payout they are entitled to (D).

Test your understanding 4

Answer A

Test your understanding 5

Answer B

Test your understanding 6

Answer B

Gross profit margin = (Gross profit/Revenue) × 100 = (28,000/70,000) × 100 = 40%

chapter

20

Business valuations and market efficiency

Chapter learning objectives

Upon completion of this chapter you will be able to:

- identify and discuss reasons for valuing businesses and financial assets
- identify information requirements for the purposes of carrying out a valuation in a scenario
- discuss the limitations of the different types of information available for valuing companies
- value a share using the dividend valuation model (DVM), including the dividend growth model
- define market capitalisation
- calculate the market capitalisation of a company using the DVM, including the dividend growth model
- explain the difference between asset- and income-based valuation models
- value a company using the statement of financial position, net realisable value (NRV) and replacement cost asset-based valuation models
- discuss the advantages and disadvantages of the different asset-based valuation models
- value a company using the price/earnings (PE) ratio income-based valuation model
- value a company using the earnings yield income-based valuation model
- value a company using the discounted cash flow (DCF) income-based valuation model
- discuss the advantages and disadvantages of the different income-based valuation models

- value a company in a scenario question selecting appropriate valuation methods
- calculate the value of irredeemable debt, redeemable debt, convertible debt and preference shares.
- explain the concept of market efficiency
- distinguish between and discuss markets that are not efficient at all, weak form efficient, semi-strong form efficient and strong form efficient
- evaluate the efficiency of a market in a scenario
- describe the significance of investor speculation and the explanations of investor decisions offered by behavioural finance
- discuss the impact of the marketability and liquidity of shares in reaching a valuation
- discuss the impact of availability and sources of information in reaching a valuation
- discuss the impact of market imperfections and pricing anomalies in reaching a valuation.

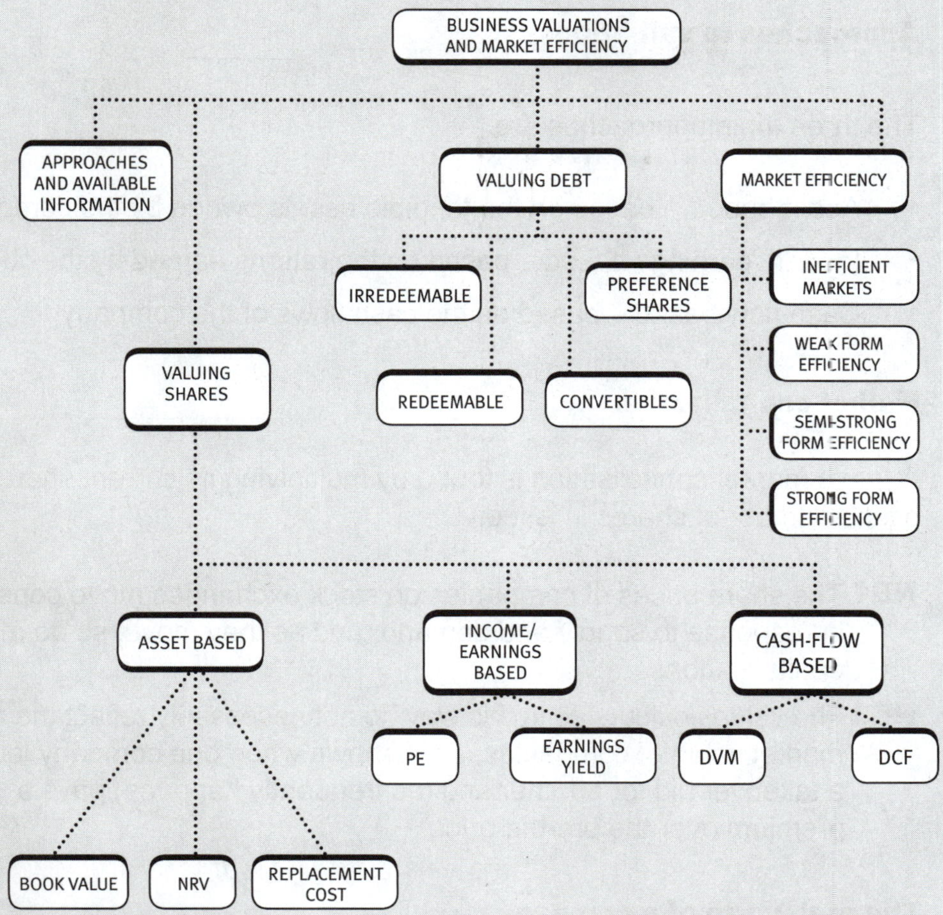

1 Valuing business and financial assets

Valuations of shares in both public and private companies are needed for several purposes by investors including:

- to establish terms of takeovers and mergers, etc.
- to be able to make 'buy and hold' decisions in general
- to value companies entering the stock market
- to establish values of shares held by retiring directors, which the articles of a company specify must be sold
- for fiscal purposes (capital gains tax (CGT), inheritance tax)
- divorce settlements, etc.

Approaches to valuations

The three main approaches are:

- Asset based – based on the tangible assets owned by the company.
- Income/earnings based – based on the returns earned by the company.
- Cash flow based – based on the cash flows of the company

Market capitalisation

A firm's market capitalisation is found by multiplying its current share price by the number of shares in issue.

NB1 The share prices of companies on stock exchanges move constantly in response to supply and demand, and as they move, so do market capitalisations.

NB2 The values calculated in this way do not necessarily reflect the actual market value of companies, as is shown when one company launches a takeover bid for another and (as frequently happens) pays a premium over the pre-bid price.

The real worth of a company

Valuation is described as 'an art not a science'. The real worth of a company depends on the viewpoints of the various parties:

- the various methods of valuation will often give widely differing results
- it may be in the interests of the investor to argue that either a 'high' or 'low' value is appropriate
- the final figure will be a matter for negotiation between the interested parties.

It is important to bring this out in the examination and show the examiner you understand that the valuation is subjective and a compromise between two parties.

Valuation: An art and not a science

The acquisition of a major competitor may enable a company to secure a dominant position in the market place. It is therefore likely to place a higher value on the target company than a potential purchaser from outside the industry.

A realistic valuation will therefore require a full industry analysis rather than an isolated assessment of the business to be valued. In some cases, the circumstances giving rise to the valuation may call for 'a value as would be agreed between a willing buyer and a willing seller' and may often be subject to independent arbitration.

Information requirements for valuation exercises

There is a wide variety of information that may be useful when trying to put a valuation on a business, including:

- Financial statements (including statements of financial position and statement of profit or loss and other comprehensive income, statements of changes in financial position and statements of shareholders equity for past years – maybe as many as five).
- Supporting listings such as non-current assets with depreciation schedule, aged accounts receivable summary, aged accounts payable summary and inventory summary.
- Details of existing contracts (e.g. leases).
- Budgets or projections for the future (again, maybe up to five years depending on the industry).
- Background information on the industry and key personnel.

This list is not exhaustive as much will depend on the situation. However, much of the above information does have limitations which must be accounted for. For example, budgets or projections may be very optimistic and perhaps unrealistic, statements of financial position may be out of date and unrealistic.

Much of the information may be subjective and this can add to the overall subjectivity involved in valuing businesses.

2 Asset-based valuations

Types of asset-based measures

Measure	Strengths	Weaknesses
Book values	• Book values are relatively easy to obtain	• Historic cost value (although could be fair value which is less of a problem)
NRV – assumes a break-up basis (NRV less liabilities)	• Minimum acceptable to owners • Asset stripping	• Valuation problems especially if quick sale • Ignores goodwill

Measure	Strengths	Weaknesses
Replacement cost – going concern	• Maximum to be paid for assets by buyer	• Valuation problems – similar assets for comparison? • Ignores goodwill

Problems with asset-based valuations

The fundamental weakness:

- investors do not normally buy a company for its statement of financial position assets, but for the earnings/cash flows that all of its assets can produce in the future
- we should value what is being purchased, i.e. the future income/cash flows.

Subsidiary weakness:

The asset approach also ignores non-statement of financial position intangible 'assets', e.g.:

- highly-skilled workforce
- strong management team
- competitive positioning of the company's products.

It is quite common that the non-statement of financial position assets are more valuable than the statement of financial position assets.

When asset-based valuations are useful

- For asset stripping.
- To identify a minimum price in a takeover.
- To value property investment companies.

When asset based methods are useful

Asset stripping

Asset valuation models are useful in the unusual situation that a company is going to be purchased to be broken up and its assets sold off. In a break-up situation we would value the assets at their realisable value.

To set a minimum price in a takeover bid

Shareholders will be reluctant to sell at a price less than the net asset valuation even if the prospect for income growth is poor. A standard defensive tactic in a takeover battle is to revalue statement of financial position assets to encourage a higher price. In a normal going-concern situation we value the assets at their replacement cost.

To value property investment companies

The market value of investment property has a close link to future cash flows and share values, i.e. discounted rental income determines the value of property assets and thus the company.

Note: If we are valuing a profitable quoted company, in reality the minimum price that shareholders will accept will probably be the market capitalisation plus an acquisition premium and not the net asset valuation.

Types of asset based measures

Book value – this will normally be a meaningless figure as it will be based on historical costs. However with fair value accounting the book value of many assets and liabilities will be the fair value and therefore will be relevant for valuation purposes.

Break-up value – the break-up value of the assets in the business will often be considerably lower than any other computed value. It normally represents the minimum price which should be accepted for the sale of a business as a going concern, since if the income based valuations give figures lower than the break-up value it is apparent that the owner would be better off by ceasing to trade and selling off all the assets piecemeal. It should be noted that the market values of debt, such as bonds are calculated pre-tax.

Replacement cost and deprival value – this should provide a measure of the maximum amount that any purchaser should pay for the whole business, since it represents the total cost of forming the business from scratch. However, a major element of any business as a going concern is likely to be the 'goodwill'. Since this can only be defined by determining the 'income-based value of business less tangible assets' it may be seen that there is no real way of applying a pure 'asset-based value' to a business – it is always necessary to consider an 'income-based value' as well.

Test your understanding 1 – Asset based measures

The following is an abridged version of the statement of financial position of Grasmere Contractors Co, an unquoted company, as at 30 April X6:

	$
Non-current assets (carrying value)	450,000
Net current assets	100,000
	550,000
Represented by	
$1 ordinary shares	200,000
Reserves	250,000
6% loan notes Z1	100,000
	550,000

You ascertain that:

- loan notes are redeemable at a premium of 2%
- current market value of freehold property exceeds book value by $30,000
- all assets, other than property, are estimated to be realisable at their book value.

Calculate the value of an 80% holding of ordinary shares, on an assets basis.

3 Income/earnings-based methods

Income-based methods of valuation are of particular use when valuing a majority shareholding:

- ownership bestows additional benefits of control not reflected in the dividend valuation model (see later)
- majority shareholders can influence dividend policy and therefore are more interested in earnings.

PE ratio method

PE ratios are quoted for all listed companies and calculated as:

Price per share/Earnings per share (EPS)

This can then be used to value shares in unquoted companies as:

Value of company = Total earnings × PE ratio

Value per share = EPS × PE ratio

using an adjusted PE multiple from a similar quoted company (or industry average).

Problems with the PE ratio valuation

- It may be necessary to make an adjustment(s) to the PE ratio of the similar company to make it more suitable, e.g. if the company being valued:

↓ adjustment	**1** is a private company as its shares may be less liquid **2** is a more risky company – fewer controls, management knowledge, etc.
↑ adjustment	**3** has a higher protected growth level.

Ensure that you explain the reasons why an adjustment is needed. This is essential as it shows you have an understanding of the bigger picture.

Arbitrary rule: Adjusted by 10% per reason – but amounts are less important than the explanation.

- It can be difficult to estimate the maintainable or normal ongoing level of earnings of the company being valued. It may be necessary to adjust these earnings to obtain a maintainable figure, e.g. change a director's emoluments from an abnormal to normal level.

Remember to adjust for tax as the PE ratio is applied to profits after tax.

- PE ratios are in part based upon historical accounting information (the EPS) whereas the valuation should reflect future earnings prospects.

Finding a suitable PE ratio

The basic choice for a suitable PE ratio will be that of a quoted company of comparable size in the same industry.

However, since share prices are broadly based on expected future earnings a PE ratio – based on a single year's reported earnings – may be very different for companies in the same sector, carrying the same systematic risk.

For example a high PE ratio may indicate:

- growth stock – the share price is high because continuous high rates of growth of earnings are expected from the stock
- no growth stock – the PE ratio is based on the last reported earnings, which perhaps were exceptionally low yet the share price is based on future earnings which are expected to revert to a 'normal' relatively stable level
- takeover bid – the share price has risen pending a takeover bid
- high security share – shares in property companies typically have low income yields but the shares are still worth buying because of the prospects of capital growth and level of security.

Similarly a low PE ratio may indicate:

- losses expected – future profits are expected to fall from their most recent levels
- share price low – as noted previously, share prices may be extremely volatile – special factors, such as a strike at a manufacturing plant of a particular company, may depress the share price and hence the PE ratio.

Consequently the main difficulty in trying to apply the model is finding a similar company, with similar growth prospects.

A further difficulty is that the reported earnings are based on historical cost accounts, which in general makes a nonsense of trying to compare two companies. Also it is important to ensure that the earnings in the victim company reflect future earnings prospects. It would be unwise to value a company on freakishly high earnings.

Test your understanding 2 – PE ratio method

You are given the following information regarding Accrington Co, an unquoted company:

(a) Issued ordinary share capital is 400,000 25c shares.

(b) Extract from the statement of profit or loss for the year ended 31 July 20X4

	$	$
Profit before taxation		260,000
Less: Corporation tax		120,000
Profit after taxation		140,000
Less: Preference dividend	20,000	
Ordinary dividend	36,000	
		(56,000)
Retained profit for the year		84,000

(c) The PE ratio applicable to a similar type of business (suitable for an unquoted company) is 12.5.

You are required to value 200,000 shares in Accrington Co on a PE ratio basis.

Earnings yield

The earnings yield is simply the inverse of the PE ratio:

$$\frac{\text{EPS}}{\text{Price per share}}$$

It can therefore be used to value the shares or market capitalisation of a company in exactly the same way as the PE ratio:

$$\text{Value of company} = \text{Total earnings} \times \frac{1}{\text{earnings yield}}$$

$$\text{Value per share} = \text{EPS} \times \frac{1}{\text{earnings yield}}$$

We can incorporate earnings growth into this method as follows:

$$\text{Value of company} = \frac{\text{earnings} \times (1 + g)}{(\text{earnings yield} - g)}$$

This is in effect an adaptation of the dividend growth model where dividend per share has been replaced by earnings per share, the dividend growth rate by earning growth rate and the cost of equity with earnings yield.

Test your understanding 3 – Earnings yield

Company A has earnings of \$300,000, growing at 3% pa. A similar listed company has an earnings yield of 12.5%.

Company B has earnings of \$420,500. A similar listed company has a PE ratio of 7.

Estimate the value of each company.

4 Cash flow based methods

Valuing shares using the dividend valuation model (DVM)

This method can be used for valuing minority shareholdings in a company, since the calculation is based on dividends paid, something which minority shareholders are unable to influence. The DVM was discussed in detail in the chapter on cost of capital. It is summarised again here.

The method

- The value of the company/share is the present value (PV) of the expected future dividends discounted at the shareholders' required rate of return.

Either:

$$P_o = \frac{D}{r_e}$$

or

$$P_o = \frac{D_o(1 + g)}{r_e - g}$$

Assuming: a constant dividend **or** constant growth in dividends

r_e = shareholders' required return, expressed as a decimal

g = annual growth rate

P_o = value of company, when D = Total dividend.

Strengths and weaknesses of the DVM

The model is theoretically sound and good for valuing a non-controlling interest but:

- there may be problems estimating a future growth rate
- it assumes that growth will be constant in the future, this is not true of most companies
- the model is highly sensitive to changes in its assumptions
- for controlling interests it offers few advantages over the earnings methods below.

To use this approach for valuation we need to be able to determine the cost of equity. The examiner will either give the cost of equity directly or give sufficient information so that you can use CAPM to determine the cost of equity.

Test your understanding 4 – Valuing shares: the DVM

A company has the following financial information available:

Share capital in issue: 4 million ordinary shares at a par value of 50c.

Current dividend per share (just paid) 24c.

Dividend four years ago 15.25c.

Current equity beta 0.8.

You also have the following market information:

Current market return 15%.

Risk-free rate 8%.

Find the market capitalisation of the company.

Test your understanding 5 – Valuing shares: the DVM

A company has the following financial information available:

Share capital in issue: 2 million ordinary shares at a par value of $1.

Current dividend per share (just paid) 18c.

Current EPS 25c.

Current return earned on assets 20%.

Current equity beta 1.1.

You also have the following market information:

Current market return 12%.

Risk-free rate 5%.

Find the market capitalisation of the company.

Discounted cash flow basis

This alternative cash flow based method is used when acquiring a majority shareholding since any buyer of a business is obtaining a stream of future operating cash flows.

The maximum value of the business is:

PV of future cash flows

A discount rate reflecting the systematic risk of the flows should be used.

Method:

(1) Identify relevant 'free' cash flows (i.e. excluding financing flows)

- operating flows
- revenue from sale of assets
- tax
- synergies arising from any merger.

(2) Select a suitable time horizon.

(3) Calculate the PV over this horizon. This gives the value to all providers of finance, i.e. equity + debt.

(4) Deduct the value of debt to leave the value of equity.

Test your understanding 6 – Discounted cash flow basis

The following information has been taken from the statement of profit or loss and statement of financial position of B Co:

Revenue	$350m
Production expenses	$210m
Administrative expenses	$24m
Tax allowable depreciation	$31m
Capital investment in year	$48m
Corporate debt	$14m trading at 130%

Corporation tax is 30%.

The WACC is 16.6%. Inflation is 6%.

These cash flows are expected to continue every year for the foreseeable future.

Required:

Calculate the value of equity.

Test your understanding 7 – Discounted cash flow basis

A company's current revenues and costs are as follows: sales $200 million, cost of sales $110 million, distribution and administrative expenses are $20 million, tax allowable depreciation $40 million and annual capital spending is $50 million. Corporation tax is 30%. The current value of debt is $17 million.

The WACC is 14.4%. Inflation is 4%.

These cash flows are expected to continue every year for the foreseeable future.

Calculate the value of equity.

Advantages

- theoretically the best method.
- can be used to value part of a company.

Weaknesses

- it relies on estimates of both cash flows and discount rates – may be unavailable
- difficulty in choosing a time horizon
- difficulty in valuing a company's worth beyond this period
- assumes that the discount rate, tax and inflation rates are constant through the period.

5 Valuation post-takeover

It may be necessary to estimate the value of a company following a takeover of another company. In this situation, when estimating the effect of the takeover on the total value of the company and on the value per share it is important to take into account:

(1) Synergy – any synergy arising from the takeover would be expected to increase the value of the company.

(2) The method of financing the takeover. If cash is used to finance the takeover the value of the company will be expected to fall by the amount of cash needed. If shares are used to finance the takeover then the extra shares issued need to be taken into account when calculating the value per share.

Test your understanding 8 – Valuation in a takeover situation

Boston is an all equity financed company and has 10 million shares in issue. Its share price is 540c per share. It is considering a takeover of Red Socks, a company in the same industry. Red Socks is also all equity financed and has 5 million shares in issue. The share price of Red Socks is 270c per share.

The takeover is likely to result in synergy gains estimated to be worth a total of $5 million.

The financial advisers to Boston have indicated that if an offer is made at a 20% premium to the current market price this is likely to be acceptable to the shareholders of Red Socks.

Required:

(a) If Boston has sufficient cash available to finance the takeover, estimate the total value of Boston post-takeover and the value of each share in Boston.

(b) If Boston offers a share for share exchange for the shares in Red Socks, estimate the total value of Boston post-takeover and the value of each share in Boston.

6 Valuation of debt and preference shares

In chapter 17 we looked at using the DVM to determine costs of capital and saw that many of the equations could be rearranged to give market value. These are summarised below:

Type of finance	**Market value**
Preference shares	$P_o = D/K_p$
Irredeemable debt	MV = I/r
Redeemable debt	MV = PV of future interest and redemption receipts, discounted at investors' required returns

where:

D = the constant annual preference dividend

P_o = ex-div market value of the share

K_p = cost of the preference share.

I = annual interest starting in one year's time

MV = market price of the debenture now (year 0)

PV = present value

r = debt holders' required return, expressed as a decimal

Test your understanding 9 – Valuation of preference shares

A firm has in issue 12% preference shares with a nominal value of $1 each. Currently the required return of preference shareholders is 14%.

What is the value of a preference share?

Test your understanding 10 – Valuation of irredeemable debt

A company has issued irredeemable loan notes with a coupon rate of 7%. If the required return of investors is 4%, what is the current market value of the debt?

Test your understanding 11 – Valuation of redeemable debt

A company has in issue 9% redeemable debt with 10 years to redemption. Redemption will be at par. The investors require a return of 16%.

What is the market value of the debt?

Convertible debt

The market value of a convertible is the higher of its value as debt and its converted value. This is known as its **formula value.**

Additional values you may be asked for regarding convertible debt are:

Floor value	= market value without the conversion option = PV of future interest and redemption value, discounted at the cost of debt.
Conversion premium	= market value – current conversion value.

Test your understanding 12 – Valuation of convertible debt

Rexel Co has in issue convertible loan notes with a coupon rate of 12%. Each $100 loan note may be converted into 20 ordinary shares at any time until the date of expiry and any remaining loan notes will be redeemed at $100.

The loan notes have five years left to run. Investors would normally require a rate of return of 8% pa on a five-year debt security.

Should investors convert if the current share price is:

(a) $4.00.

(b) $5.00.

(c) $6.00.

Test your understanding 13 – Convertible debt calculations

PO Co has in issue 8% bonds which are redeemable at their par value of $100 in three years' time. Alternatively, each bond may be converted on that date into 30 ordinary shares of the company.

The current ordinary share price of PO Co is $3.30 and this is expected to grow at 5% per year for the foreseeable future.

PO Co has a cost of debt of 6% per year.

Required

Calculate the following current values for each $100 convertible bond:

(i) market value

(ii) floor value

(iii) conversion premium

7 Market efficiency

The concept of market efficiency

Opening question:

- If N plc shares are valued at $1.30, is this value reliable (fair, true, accurate)?

Or put another way:

- How efficient is the stock market at valuing the shares of a company?

- An efficient market is one in which security prices fully reflect all available information.

- In an efficient market, new information is rapidly and rationally incorporated into share prices in an unbiased way.

Current position

In the sophisticated financial markets of today, there are

- cheap electronic communications
- large numbers of informed investors.

Conclusion

New information is rapidly (in minutes not days) incorporated into share prices.

Benefits of an efficient market

We need an efficient stock market to

- ensure investor confidence
- reflect directors' performance in the share price.

Benefits of an efficient market

Investor confidence

Investors need to know that they will pay and receive a fair price when they buy and sell shares. If shares are incorrectly priced, many savers would refuse to invest, thus seriously reducing the availability of funds and inhibiting growth. Investor confidence in the pricing efficiency is essential.

Motivation and control of directors

The primary objective of directors is the maximisation of shareholder wealth, i.e. maximise the share price. In implementing a positive net present value (NPV) decision, directors can be assured that the decision once communicated to the market will result in an increased share price. Conversely if directors make sub-optimal decisions then the share price will fall. Like all feedback systems the stock market has a dual function. It motivates directors to maximise share price, whilst providing an early warning system of potential problems.

8 The efficient market hypothesis (EMH)

The EMH states that security prices fully and fairly reflect all relevant information. This means that it is not possible to consistently outperform the market by using any information that the market already knows, except through luck.

The idea is that new information is quickly and efficiently incorporated into asset prices at any point in time, so that old information cannot be used to foretell future price movements.

Three levels of efficiency are distinguished, depending on the type of information available to the majority of investors and hence already reflected in the share price.

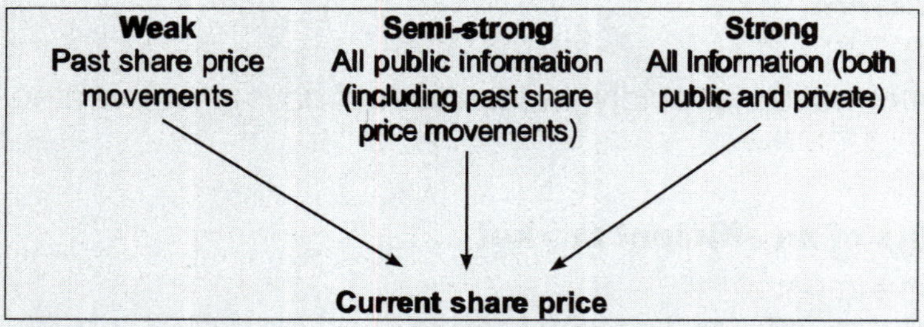

The forms of efficiency are cumulative, so that if the market is semi-strong it is also weak.

9 Types of efficiency

Market inefficiency

An inefficient market is one in which the value of securities is not always an accurate reflection of the available information. Markets may also operate inefficiently, e.g. due to low volumes of trade.

In an inefficient market, some securities will be overpriced and others will be underpriced, which means some investors can make excess returns while others can lose more than warranted by their level of risk exposure.

Weak form efficiency

Information

In a weak form efficient market share price reflects information about **all past price movements.** Past movements do not help in identifying positive NPV trading strategies.

Evidence

Share prices follow a random walk:

- there are no patterns or trends
- prices rise or fall depending on whether the next piece of news is good or bad
- tests show that only 0.1% of a share price change on one day can be predicted from knowledge of the change on the previous day.

Conclusion

The stock market is weak form efficient and so:

- future price movements cannot be predicted from past price movements
- chartism/technical analysis cannot help make a consistent gain on the market.

Weak form efficiency

Random walks

In 1953 **Kendall** presented a paper which examined share price movements over time. He concluded that the prices of shares followed a random walk, i.e. there are no patterns or trends. Any apparent pattern or trend purely occurs by chance.

Why does the random walk occur?

Prices change because of new information. New information is by definition independent of the last piece of new information and thus the resulting share price movements are independent of each other, i.e. the next piece of new information has equal chance of being good or bad, nobody knows.

If a pattern is identified from historical share price movements and this information becomes known in the market, the pattern disappears, as the market buys and sells shares accordingly to take advantage of the pattern.

The market is weak form efficient, as the study of the history of share prices cannot be used to predict the future in any abnormally profitable way.

Semi-strong efficiency

Information

In a semi-strong efficient market the share price incorporates all past information and **all publicly-available** information (i.e. a semi-strong form efficient market is also weak form efficient and public information includes past information).

Evidence

Share prices react within 5–10 minutes of any new information being released and:

- rise in response to breaking good news
- fall in response to breaking bad news.

Conclusion

The stock market is (almost) semi-strong form efficient and so:

- fundamental analysis – examining publicly-available information will not provide opportunities to consistently beat the market
- only those trading in the first few minutes after the news breaks can beat the market
- since published information includes past share prices a semi-strong form efficient market is also weakly efficient.

Strong form efficiency

Information

In a strongly efficient market the share price incorporates **all information**, whether public or private, including information which is as yet unpublished.

Evidence

Insiders (directors for example) have access to unpublished information. If the market was strong form

- the share price wouldn't move when, e.g. news broke about a takeover, as it would have moved when the initial decision was made – in practice they do!
- there would be no need to ban 'insider dealing' as insiders couldn't make money by trading before news became public– it is banned because they do!

Conclusion

The stock market is not strong form efficient and so:

- insider dealers have been fined and imprisoned for making money trading in shares before the news affecting them went public
- the stock exchange encourages quick release of new information to prevent insider trading opportunities
- insiders are forbidden from trading in their shares at crucial times.

Insider dealing

It is well-known that shares can be traded on the basis of information not in the public domain and thereby make abnormal profits. Stock markets are not strong form efficient. The engineer who discovers gold may buy shares before the discovery is made public. The merchant banker who hear's a colleague is assisting in a surprise takeover bid has been known to purchase shares in the target firm.

A breakdown in the fair game perception will damage investor confidence and reduce investment. To avoid a loss of confidence **most stock markets have codes of conduct and most countries have introduced legislation to curb insider dealing**. Insider dealing became a criminal offence in the UK in 1980. However British regulators tend to be less effective than some of their foreign counterparts. American and French regulators rely initially on civil law where the burden of proof is lower than in a criminal case.

Another weapon against insiders is to **make companies release price-sensitive information quickly**. The London Stock Exchange has strict guidelines to encourage companies to make announcements to the market as early as possible, on such matters as current trading conditions and profit warnings. Therefore there is a mechanism to force private information into the public arena to attempt to ensure that share prices are reasonably accurate.

A third approach is to completely prohibit certain individuals from dealing in a company shares at crucial time periods. The stock exchange **Model Code for Directors Dealings** precludes directors of quoted companies (and indeed other employees in the possession of price-sensitive information) from trading shares for a period of two months before the announcement of the annual results. The Code also precludes dealing before the announcement of matters of an exceptional nature involving unpublished information, which is potentially price sensitive.

Conclusions for the market

If the market is semi-strong then a number of key conclusions can be drawn:

- shares are fairly priced – the purchase is a zero NPV transaction (unless you are an insider dealer!)
- managers can improve shareholders' wealth by investing in positive NPV projects and communicating this to the market
- most investors (including professional fund managers) cannot consistently beat the market without inside information.

Conclusions for the market

In an efficient market, shares are priced to give investors the exact return to reward them for the level of (systematic) risk in their shares. As a result the purchase of shares is a zero NPV transaction because the price paid for the share is an accurate reflection of its worth i.e. shares are fairly priced and the concept of an over- or under-valued security does not apply. Therefore the rationale behind mergers and takeovers must be questioned. Semi-strong efficiency implies that mergers could only be successful if synergies can be created, i.e. economies of scale or rationalisation.

Given the fact that well-developed stock markets are weak and semi-strong market efficient most of the time, once new information is communicated to the market it is rapidly reflected in the share price. Thus managers can achieve the overall objective of maximising shareholder wealth by making good decisions and communicating them to the market.

Is it worth acquiring and analysing public information?

If semi-strong efficiency is true, it undermines the work of millions of fundamental (professional and amateur) analysts, whose work cannot be used to produce abnormal returns because all public information is already reflected in the share price.

These analysts study the fundamental factors that underpin the share price, i.e. revenues, costs and risk associated with the company as well as many other sources of public information such as macroeconomic and industry conditions, details of the company personnel, technological changes and so on.

They will then use this information, together with a share valuation model (e.g. like the dividend valuation model – DVM), to estimate the true or intrinsic value of the shares. This value is then compared with the current market price of shares to see if the shares are over- or under-valued (mispriced).

The fundamental analyst is attempting to beat the market to earn an abnormal return by:

- buying under-valued shares before the prices rise.
- selling over-valued shares before the prices fall.

But in an efficient market mis-priced shares do not exist.

Given that there are thousands of sophisticated investors examining the smallest piece of information about each company and its environment, it would seem reasonable to postulate that the semi strong form of EMH is a reality in well-developed stock markets.

Conclusion:

The vast majority of investors (including professional fund managers) cannot consistently beat the market by analysing the information they have available to them, as this public information is already reflected in the share price. So long as the market remains efficient, fundamental analysis is a waste of money and the average investor would be better off by simply selecting a diversified portfolio, thereby avoiding costs of analysis. This message has struck a chord with millions of investors who have placed billions of pounds in low cost Index Tracking Funds, which merely replicate a stock market index, rather than an actively managed fund which tries to pick winners.

The market paradox

In order for the market to remain efficient, investors must believe there is value in assessing information.

Because they assess it continuously the information is reflected in the share price as soon as it is released and an investor cannot beat the market.

The market paradox

The paradox of the EMH is that large numbers of investors have to disbelieve the hypothesis in order to maintain efficiency. The continuous collective actions of fundamental analysts ensure that the market reacts almost instantaneously to the disclosure of new information. Their actions safeguard market efficiency and are thus self-defeating, as they cannot then individually beat the market. Their collective value to the market is that they guarantee its efficiency.

Investor behaviour

Despite the evidence in support of the theory, some events seem to contradict it:

- significant share price volatility
- boom/crash patterns.

e.g. the **stock market crash of October 1987** where most stock exchanges crashed at the same time. It is virtually impossible to explain the scale of those market falls by reference to any news event at the time.

An explanation has been offered by the science of behavioural finance:

- naïve investors see high-performing shares (for example) and rush to buy
- this noise inflates the share price artificially
- informed investors then buy, planning to sell before the inevitable crash.

Investor behaviour

Events such as significant share price volatility and boom/crash patterns seem at odds with the theory of efficient markets because prices are not supposed to deviate markedly from their fundamental value.

One theory behind this seemingly irrational behaviour of the markets is called noise trading by naïve investors. According to this theory there are two types of investors, the informed and uninformed. The informed trade shares to bring them to their fundamental value. The uninformed act irrationally. Perhaps they noticed that certain shares have made investors high returns over the last number of years. So they rush out and buy these shares to get their piece of the action i.e. they chase the trend.

The uninformed investors create lots of noise and push the market up and up. The informed investor often tries to get in on the act. Despite knowing it will end in disaster, the informed investor buys in the hope of selling before the crash. This is based on the idea that the price an investor is willing to pay for a share today is dependent on the price the investor can sell it for at some point in the future and not necessarily at its fundamental value.

A summary

In summary:

✔ Weak form	✔ Semi-Strong form	✘ Strong form
Means that the current share price reflects all information that could be obtained from studying and analysing past share price movements.	Means that the current share price reflects all publicly-available information.	Means that the current share price reflects all information, including that which is privately held.
Evidence: overwhelming in support.	Evidence: substantial in support.	Evidence: stock markets are **not** strong form efficient.
Conclusion: a technical analyst/chartist who studies trends and patterns in past share movements will not make an abnormal gain.	Conclusion: a fundamental analyst will generally not make an abnormal gain, i.e. from analysing publicly-available information. The vast majority of investors cannot consistently beat the market (i.e. earn an abnormal return), as they only have public information available to them and this information is already reflected in the share price.	Conclusion: If the market were strong form efficient an investor could only make abnormal gains by luck. Because the market is only semi-strong efficient, abnormal gains can be made from analysing 'inside information'. Hence the need for legislation to prevent insider dealing, i.e. the 1985 Company Securities (Insider Dealing) Act.

Conclusion:

The stock exchanges of all developed nations are regarded as at least semi-strong efficient for the shares traded actively on those markets.

Test you understanding 14 – Market efficiency

What would you believe about the efficiency of the market if you thought you could make money by:

(1) insider dealing

(2) analysing past price movements

(3) only by pure luck

(4) analysing financial statements, directors' statements, company activities, etc.?

10 Practical considerations in the valuation of shares and businesses

Other factors to consider

Marketability and liquidity of shares

The shares in a private company are often valued by using measures based on the 'fair' share prices of similar listed companies.

However buying a share in an unlisted company is more of a gamble, as the share cannot be easily sold.

This is why the values given by methods such as price/earnings (PE) ratio and earnings yield, are often downgraded.

Available information

We discussed above the importance of information concerning a company being fully available if the share is to be fairly priced.

In unlisted companies, information may be less readily available for a number of reasons such as:

- a weaker control environment
- unaudited financial statements
- fewer compliance regulations apply
- no tradition of sharing information so channels of communication not set up
- less detailed record keeping.

The relative shortage of information in unlisted companies may also cause the initial valuation to be downgraded.

Equilibrium prices

In practice, as discussed above, the market does show sudden price fluctuations that cannot be explained simply by the information being newly released. If a share price is highly volatile, then it is considered not in equilibrium.

Prices used to provide data for the valuation of unlisted shares need to be in equilibrium if meaningful values are to be obtained.

If only a few similar companies exist, and their shares are **not in equilibrium**, any share price calculated must be treated with caution.

Test you understanding 15

Which of the following statements, concerning asset based methods of business valuation, is correct?

A Replacement cost normally represents the minimum price which should be accepted for the sale of a business as a going concern

B Break-up value should provide a measure of the maximum amount that any purchaser should pay for the business

C Book value will normally be a meaningless figure as it will be based on historical costs

D Asset based methods give consideration to non-statement of financial position intangible assets such as a highly skilled workforce and a strong management team

Test you understanding 16

An independent accountant has produced the following valuations of a private company.

	$m
Historical cost adjusted for changes in general purchasing power	3.2
Piecemeal net realisable value	4.1
Cost of setting up an equivalent venture	5.3
Economic value of the business	5.6

Assuming that the above valuations accord with the expectations and risk perceptions of the purchaser, what is the maximum price that should be paid for the private company?

A $3.2m

B $4.1m

C $5.3m

D $5.6m

Test you understanding 17

Company A's latest accounts show earnings of $150k and the company has a P/E ratio of 8.

Company B's latest accounts show earnings of $75k and the company has a P/E ratio of 10.

Company A is considering making a bid for company B. It expects synergies of $10k pa as a result of the merger and expects the market to apply a P/E ratio of 9 to the combined entity.

What is the minimum that Company B's shareholders are likely to accept?

A $915k

B $750k

C $600k

D $1,500k

Test you understanding 18

An investor who bases all his investment decisions solely on an analysis of past share price movements is acting as if he believes that the capital market is

A Strongly efficient

B Semi-strongly efficient

C Weakly efficient

D Not efficient at any level

Test you understanding 19

If the capital market is semi-strong efficient

A Investors will be able to make consistent gains by studying and making use of past share price movements

B Investors will be able to make consistent gains by studying and making use of all available public information about the shares

C Investors will be able to make consistent gains by studying and making use of information which is not available to the pub ic

D Investors will not be able to make consistent gains

Chapter summary

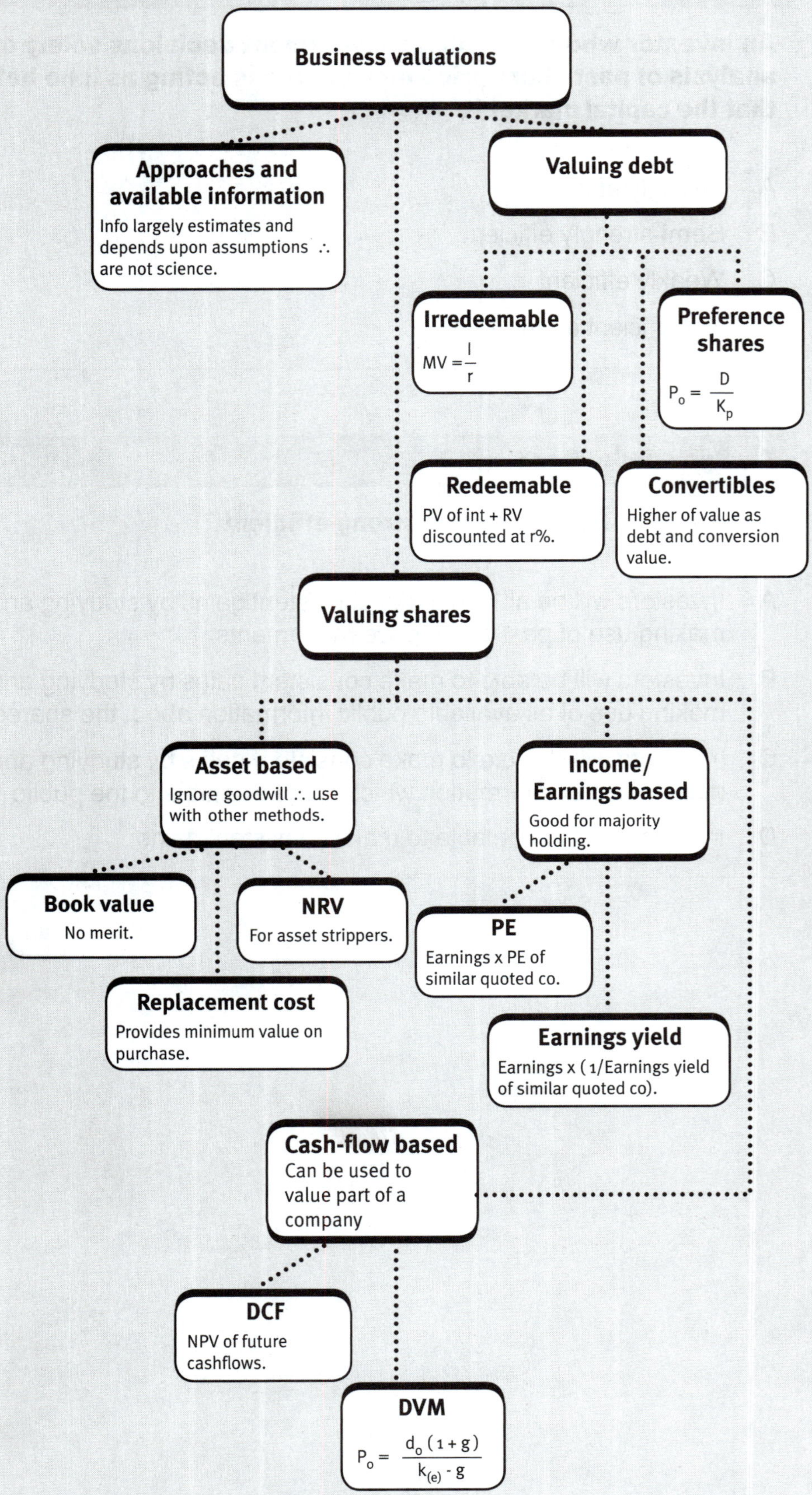

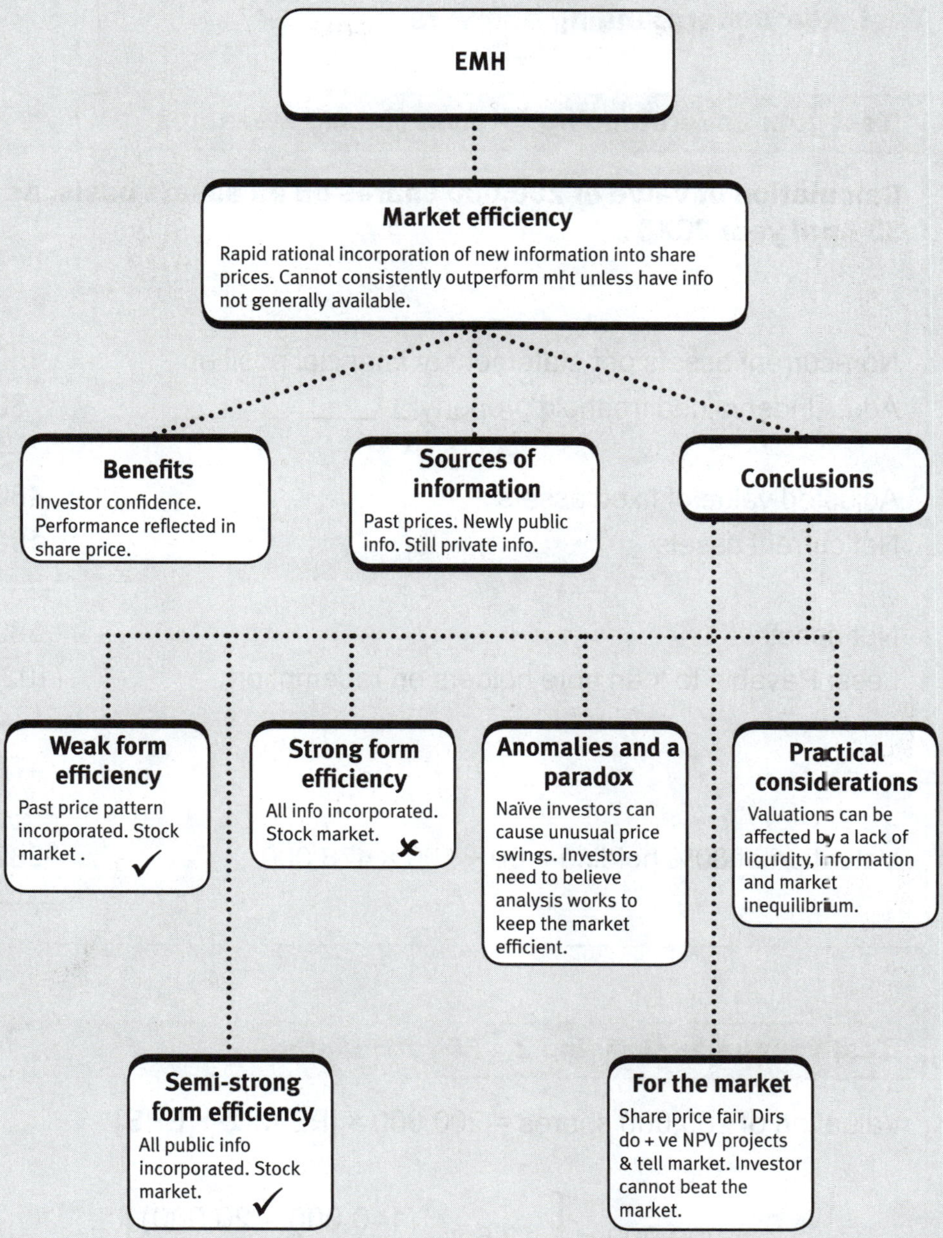
EMH
Market efficiency
Rapid rational incorporation of new information into share prices. Cannot consistently outperform mkt unless have info not generally available.
Benefits
Investor confidence. Performance reflected in share price.
Sources of information
Past prices. Newly public info. Still private info.
Conclusions
Weak form efficiency
Past price pattern incorporated. Stock market. ✓
Strong form efficiency
All info incorporated. Stock market. ✗
Anomalies and a paradox
Naïve investors can cause unusual price swings. Investors need to believe analysis works to keep the market efficient.
Practical considerations
Valuations can be affected by a lack of liquidity, information and market inequilibrium.
Semi-strong form efficiency
All public info incorporated. Stock market. ✓
For the market
Share price fair. Dirs do + ve NPV projects & tell market. Investor cannot beat the market.

Test your understanding answers

Test your understanding 1 – Asset based measures

Calculation of value of 200,000 shares on an assets basis, as at 30 April year 20X6

	$
Non-current assets per statement of financial position	450,000
Add: Undervalued freehold property	30,000
Adjusted value of fixed assets	480,000
Net current assets	100,000
Net assets	580,000
Less: Payable to loan note holders on redemption	(102,000)
	478,000
Valuation of 80% holding = 80 ÷ 100 × 478,000	382,400

Test your understanding 2 – PE ratio method

Valuation of 200,000 shares = 200,000 × [PE ratio × EPS]

$$= 200{,}000 \times \left[12.5 \times \frac{(140{,}000 - 20{,}000)}{400{,}000} \right]$$

= $750,000

Or 50% (12.5 x $120,000) = $750,000.

Test your understanding 3 – Earnings yield

Company A: $\frac{\$300{,}000 \times (1.03)}{0.125 - 0.03}$ = $3,252,632

Company B: $420,500 × 7 = $2,943,500

Test your understanding 4 – Valuing shares: the DVM

The formula

$$P_o = \frac{D_0(1 + g)}{r_e - g}$$

will provide the value of a single share. The market capitalisation can then be found by multiplying by the number of shares in issue.

D_o = 24c

g can be found by extrapolating from past dividends:

$$\sqrt[4]{\frac{24}{15.25}} - 1 = 12\%$$

R_e can be found using CAPM

$R_f + ß (R_m - R_f) =$

8 + 0.8 (15 – 8) = 13.6

Therefore

$$P_o = \frac{24(1 + 0.12)}{0.136 - 0.12} = 1{,}680c = \$16.80$$

The market capitalisation is therefore:

4m × $16.80 = $67.2m

Test your understanding 5 – Valuing shares: the DVM

The formula

$$P_o = \frac{D_0(1+g)}{r_e - g}$$

will provide the value of a single share. The market capitalisation can then be found by multiplying by the number of shares in issue.

D_o = 18c

g using **Gordon's Growth Model**

$g = r \times b$

r = 20%

If dividends per share of 18c are paid on EPS of 25c, then the payout ratio is 18/25 = 72%. The retention ratio is therefore 28%.

So b = 0.28

Therefore g = 0.2 × 0.28 = 0.056.

r_e (using CAPM)

$R_f + ß (R_m - R_f) =$

5 + 1.1 (12 – 5) = 12.7

Therefore

$$P_o = \frac{18(1 + 0.056)}{0.127 - 0.056} = 268c = \$2.68$$

The market capitalisation is therefore:

2m × \$2.68 = \$5.36m

Test your understanding 6 – Discounted cash flow basis

Operating profits = \$350m – \$210m – \$24m = \$116m

Tax on operating profits = \$116m × 0.3 = \$34.8m

Allowable depreciation = \$31m (assumed not included in production or administration expenses)

Tax relief on depreciation = \$31m × 0.3 = \$9.3

Therefore free cash flow = \$116 – \$34.8 + \$9.3 – \$48 = \$42.5

The real discount rate is: $\frac{1.166}{1.06} = 10\%$

The corporate value is = $\frac{\$42.5\text{m}}{0.10} = \$425\text{m}$

Equity = \$425m – (\$14m × 1.3) = \$406.8m.

Note: because the cash flow is a perpetuity we have used the real (uninflated) cash flow and the real discount rate (see chapter on further aspects of discounted cash flows).

Test your understanding 7 – Discounted cash flow basis

Operating profits = \$200m – \$110m – \$20m = \$70m

Tax on operating profits = \$70m × 0.3 = \$21m

Allowable depreciation = \$40m

Tax relief on depreciation = \$40m × 0.3 = \$12

Therefore net cash flow = \$70 – \$21 + \$12 – \$50 = \$11

$$1 + r = \frac{(1 + i)}{(1 + h)} = \frac{1.144}{1.04} = 1.10$$

The real discount rate is: 10%

$$\text{The corporate value is} = \frac{\$11m}{0.10} = \$110m$$

Equity = \$110m – \$17m = \$93m.

Test your understanding 8 – Valuation in a takeover situation

(a) The value of Boston after the takeover can be estimated as the value of Boston before the takeover, plus the value of Red Socks before the takeover, plus the value of any synergy arising from the takeover, less the cash paid by Boston to finance the takeover.

Boston will need to pay \$2.70 × 1.20 = \$3.24 for each share in Red Socks. The total consideration needed to buy the whole of Red Socks will therefore be

5million shares × \$3.24 = \$16,200,000.

The value of Boston post takeover will therefore be:

		$000
Boston pre-takeover	10 million × $5.40	54,000
Red Socks pre-takeover	5 million × $2.70	13,500
Synergy		5,000
less cash consideration		(16,200)
		56,300

Boston will not have issued any new shares and therefore the post takeover share price of Boston will be $56,300,000/10 million = $5.63. This is an increase of 23 cents.

(b) In this case Boston will offer shares worth $16,200,000 to finance the takeover. We can calculate the post takeover share price by considering the split of the synergies.

		$000
Value of consideration given to Red Socks		16,200
Red Socks pre-takeover	5 million × $2.70	13,500
Value of synergy gained by Red Socks		2,700

If the total; synergy from the takeover is $5m, this means Boston must gain the remaining $2.3m ($5m – $2.7m).

As a result, the value of the existing 10 million Boston shares post takeover will be $54m + $2.3m = $56.3 implying a share price post takeover of $5.63 per share.

In order to settle the $16.2m consideration, Boston would therefore need to issue 2.877m new shares ($16.2m ÷ $5.63).

Test your understanding 9 – Valuation of preference shares

$$\text{Using } P_o = \frac{D}{K_p}$$

$$P_o = \frac{12}{0.14} = 85.71 \text{ cents}$$

Test your understanding 10 – Valuation of irredeemable debt

$$MV = \frac{7}{0.04} = \$175$$

Test your understanding 11 – Valuation of redeemable debt

The market value is calculated by finding the PVs of the interest and the principal and totalling them as shown below.

	Time		Cash flow	DF @ 16%	PV
Annuity →	1-10	Interest payments	9	4.833	$43.50
	10	Capital repayment	$100	0.227	$22.70
	Market value				$66.20

Test your understanding 12 – Valuation of convertible debt

Value as debt

If the security is not converted it will have the following value to the investor:

	DF @ 8%	PV
		$
Interest $12/year for 5 years	3.993	47.916
Redemption $100 in 5 years	0.681	68.100
		116.016

Note the PV is calculated at 8% – the required rate of return on a straight debt security.

Value as equity

Market price	Value as equity
	$
4.00	$80 (i.e. 20 × $4)
5.00	$100
6.00	$120

If the market price of equity rises to $6.00 the security should be converted, otherwise it is worth more as debt. The 'breakeven' conversion price is $5.80 per share ($116/20 shares).

The value of the convertible will therefore be $116, unless the share price rises above $5.80 at which point it will be the value of the equity received on conversion.

Test your understanding 13 – Convertible debt calculations

(i) **Market value**

Expected share price in three years' time = \$3.30 × 1.05^3 = \$3.82

Conversion value = \$3.82 × 30 = \$114.60

Compared with redemption at par value of \$100, conversion will be preferred.

The current market value will be the present value of future interest payments, plus the present value of the conversion value, discounted at the cost of debt of 6% per year.

Market value of each convertible bond	= [(\$100 × 8%) × 3 yr 6% AF] + (\$114.60 × 3y r 6% DF)
	= (\$8 × 2.673) + (\$114.60 × 0.840)
	= \$21.38 + \$96.26
	= \$117.64

(ii) **Floor value**

The current floor value will be the present value of the future interest payments, plus the present value of the redemption value, discounted at the cost of debt of 6% per year.

Floor value of each convertible bond	= [(\$100 × 8%) × 3 yr 6% AF] + (\$100 × 3 yr 6% DF)
	= (\$8 × 2.673) + (\$100 × 0.840)
	= \$21.38 + \$84.00
	= \$105.38

(iii) **Conversion premium**

Current conversion value = \$3.30 × 30 = \$99.00

Conversion premium = \$117.64 — \$99.00 = \$18.64

This is often expressed on a per share basis, i.e. \$18.64/30 = \$0.62 per share.

Test you understanding 14 – Market efficiency

(1) It is at most semi-strong.

(2) It is not efficient at all.

(3) It is strong form.

(4) It is at most weak form.

Test you understanding 15

Answer C

The break-up value of the assets normally represents the minimum price which should be accepted for the sale of a business as a going concern (A), since if the income based valuations give figures lower than the break-up value it is apparent that the owner would be better off by ceasing to trade and selling off all the assets piecemeal.

Replacement cost should provide a measure of the maximum amount that any purchaser should pay for the whole business (B), since it represents the total cost of forming the business from scratch.

Asset based measures ignore non-balance sheet intangible assets (D) e.g. a highly-skilled workforce, strong management team and competitive positioning of the company's products.

Test you understanding 16

Answer C

The maximum is the cost to set up an equivalent venture.

Test you understanding 17

Answer B

Value of Company B alone: Company B earnings x Company B P/E ratio = $75,000 × 10 = $750k

Company B's shareholders are likely to accept anything above $750k

Test you understanding 18

Answer D

C cannot be the correct answer since, if the market were weakly efficient, share prices would *already* reflect all information contained in past share price movements. If the investor expects to obtain a return greater than that possible by merely investing in the market portfolio, he must believe that his analysis is *better* than that being carried out by the rest of the market, i.e. he must regard the market as not efficient.

Test you understanding 19

Answer C

The semi-strong form of capital market efficiency implies that all publically available information is reflected in a share price. Therefore, studying that information will not enable an investor to make gains. Only by studying non-public information will an investor be able to make consistent gains (insider trading).

chapter

21

Questions & Answers

1 The financial management function and environment

1 – Stakeholder groups

Private sector companies have multiple stakeholders who are likely to have divergent interests.

Required:

Identify five stakeholder groups for private sector companies and briefly discuss their financial and other objectives.

(10 marks)

2 – Corporate governance

Required:

Examine the extent to which good corporate governance procedures can help manage the problems arising from the divergent interests of multiple stakeholder groups in private sector companies.

(10 marks)

3 – Stakeholder conflict

Minicorp is a mining company. Its mission is to 'maximise profits for shareholders whilst recognising its responsibilities to society'. It is considering a mining opportunity abroad in a remote country area where there is widespread poverty. The mining work will destroy local vegetation and may pollute the immediate water supply for some years to come. The company directors believe that permission for the mining work is likely to be granted by the government as there are few people or animals living in the area and the company will be providing much-needed jobs.

Required:

Identify the likely stakeholders in the company's decision. Consider their possible objectives and describe three likely conflicts in those objectives.

(10 marks)

4 – Measuring performance in NFPs

To some degree the profit motive makes performance measurement easier in profit-seeking private companies than it is in not-for-profit organisations.

Required:

Explain and comment on the problems of measuring performance in a not-for-profit organisation.

(10 marks)

5 – Public sector organisations

"Performance measurement in public sector organisations is often more concerned with value for money rather than profitability."

Required:

(a) Discuss the objectives of a public sector organisation and how performance is measured and controlled.

(10 marks)

(b) Briefly explain the relevance of three measures which may be used to assess performance in public sector services that provide education.

(5 marks)

(Total: 15 marks)

2 Basic investment appraisal

6 – Investment appraisal techniques I

Breccon Co introduced a new product, DV, to its range last year. The machine used to mould each item is a bottleneck in the production process meaning that a maximum of 5,000 units per annum can be manufactured.

The DV product has been a huge success in the marketplace and as a result, all items manufactured are sold. The marketing department has prepared the following demand forecast for future years as a result of feedback from customers.

Year	**1**	**2**	**3**	**4**
Demand (units)	7,000	9,000	11,000	4,000

The directors are now considering investing in a second machine that will allow the company to satisfy the excess demand. The following information relating to this investment proposal has now been prepared:

Initial investment	$20,000
Maximum additional output	5,000 units
Current selling price	$50 per unit
Variable operating costs	$28 per unit
Fixed operating costs	$15,000 per year

If production remained at 5,000 units, the current selling price would be expected to continue throughout the remainder of the life of the product. However, if production is increased, it is expected that the selling price will fall to $45 per unit for all units sold. Again, this will last for the remainder of the life of the product.

No terminal value or machinery scrap value is expected at the end of four years, when production of DV is planned to end. For investment appraisal purposes, Breccon uses a nominal (money) discount rate of 10% per year and a target return on capital employed of 20% per year.

The Production Director has estimated the return on capital employed (accounting rate of return) based on the initial investment for the proposal at 15% and has thus advised it should be rejected. The Finance Director is keen to use discounted cash flows to evaluate the proposal before making a definite decision.

Ignore taxation.

Required:

(a) Calculate the following values for the investment proposal:
(i) net present value
(ii) internal rate of return
(iii) discounted payback period

(11 marks)

(b) Discuss your findings in each section of (a) above and advise whether the investment proposal is financially acceptable.

(4 marks)

(Total: 15 marks)

7 – Investment appraisal techniques II

Required:

Discuss the advantages and disadvantages of the payback and accounting rate of return methods of investment appraisal.

(10 marks)

8 – Investment appraisal techniques III

A company is considering which of two mutually exclusive projects it should undertake. The finance director thinks that the project with the higher NPV should be chosen, whereas the managing director thinks that the one with the higher IRR should be undertaken, especially as both projects have the same initial outlay and length of life. The company anticipates a cost of capital of 10%, and the net after tax cash flows of the projects are as follows:

Year	Project X	Project Y
	$000	$000
0	(200)	(200)
1	35	218
2	80	10
3	90	10
4	75	4
5	20	3

Required:

(a) Calculate the NPV and IRR of each project.

(6 marks)

(b) Recommend, with reasons, which project you would undertake (if either).

(2 marks)

(c) Briefly explain the inconsistency in ranking of the two projects in view of the remarks of the directors.

(2 marks)

(Total 10 marks)

9 – Limitations of NPV

Identify the limitations of Net Present Value techniques when applied generally to investment appraisal.

(10 marks)

10 – Investing in marketing and IT

Investment appraisal techniques need to be adapted to the type of investment being considered.

Required:

Explain how applying discounted cash flow techniques to a marketing or an IT investment decision might differ from an investment in a new machine for a manufacturing facility.

(10 marks)

11 – NPV with taxation

H Co is considering purchasing a new machine to alleviate a bottleneck in its production facilities. At present, it uses an old machine which can process 8,000 units of Product P per week. H could replace it with machine AB, which is product-specific and can produce 20,000 units per week. Machine AB costs $500,000. Removing the old machine and preparing the area for machine AB will cost $20,000.

The company expects demand for P to be 12,000 units per week for another three years. After this, in the fourth year, the new machine would be sold for $50,000. This sale is not expected to take place until later in the fourth year. The existing machine will have no scrap value. Each P sells for $7.00 and has a contribution to sales ratio of 0.2. The company works for 48 weeks in the year. H Co normally expects a payback within two years and its after-tax cost of capital is 10% per annum.

The company pays corporation tax at 30% and receives writing-down allowances of 25%, reducing balance on the investment and any costs incurred in removing the old machine and installing the new machine. Corporation tax is payable one year in arrears.

Required:

(a) Calculate the net present value for the machine.

Make the following assumptions:

(i) The company's financial year begins on the same day that the new machine would be purchased.

(ii) The company uses discounted cash flow techniques with annual breaks only.

(12 marks)

(b) Recommend, with reasons, whether the machine should be purchased. Include any reservations you may have about your decision.

(3 marks)

(Total: 15 marks)

12 – NPV with tax and inflation I

SC Co is evaluating the purchase of a new machine to produce product P, which has a short product life-cycle due to rapidly changing technology. The machine is expected to cost $1 million. Production and sales of product P are forecast to be as follows:

Year	**1**	**2**	**3**	**4**
Production and sales (units/year)	35,000	53,000	75,000	36,000

The selling price of product P (in current price terms) will be $20 per unit, while the variable cost of the product (in current price terms) will be $12 per unit. Selling price inflation is expected to be 4% per year and variable cost inflation is expected to be 5% per year. No increase in existing fixed costs is expected since SC Co has spare capacity in both space and labour terms.

Producing and selling product P will call for increased investment in working capital. Analysis of historical levels of working capital within SC Co indicates that at the start of each year, investment in working capital for product P will need to be 7% of sales revenue for that year.

SC Co pays tax of 30% per year in the year in which the taxable profit occurs. Liability to tax is reduced by tax-allowable depreciation on machinery (tax-allowable depreciation), which SC Co can claim on a straight-line basis over the four-year life of the proposed investment. The new machine is expected to have no scrap value at the end of the four-year period.

SC Co uses a nominal (money terms) after-tax cost of capital of 12% for investment appraisal purposes.

Required:

(a) Calculate the net present value of the proposed investment in product P.

(10 marks)

(b) Advise on the acceptability of the proposed investment in product P and discuss the limitations of the evaluation you have carried out.

(5 marks)

(Total: 15 marks)

13 – NPV with tax and inflation II

ARG Co is a leisure company that is recovering from a loss-making venture into magazine publication three years ago. The company plans to launch two new products, Alpha and Beta, at the start of July 20X7, which it believes will each have a life-cycle of four years. Alpha is the deluxe version of Beta. The sales mix is assumed to be constant. Expected sales volumes for the two products are as follows:

Year	**1**	**2**	**3**	**4**
Alpha	60,000	110,000	100,000	30,000
Beta	75,000	137,500	125,000	37,500

The selling price and direct material costs for each product in the first year will be as follows:

Product	**Alpha**	**Beta**
	$/unit	$/unit
Direct material costs	12.00	9.00
Selling price	31.00	23.00

Incremental fixed production costs are expected to be $1 million in the first year of operation and are apportioned on the basis of sales value. Advertising costs will be $500,000 in the first year of operation and then $200,000 per year for the following two years. There are no incremental non-production fixed costs other than advertising costs.

In order to produce the two products, investment of $1 million in premises, $1 million in machinery and $1 million in working capital will be needed, payable at the start of July 20X7.

Selling price per unit, direct material cost per unit and incremental fixed production costs are expected to increase after the first year of operation due to inflation:

Selling price inflation	3.0% per year
Direct material cost inflation	3.0% per year
Fixed production cost inflation	5.0% per year

These inflation rates are applied to the standard selling price and direct material cost data provided above. Working capital will be recovered at the end of the fourth year of operation, at which time production will cease and ARG Co expects to be able to recover $1.2 million from the sale of premises and machinery. All staff involved in the production and sale of Alpha and Beta will be redeployed elsewhere in the company.

ARG Co pays tax in the year in which the taxable profit occurs at an annual rate of 25%. Investment in machinery attracts a first-year tax-allowable depreciation of 100%. ARG Co has sufficient profits to take the full benefit of this allowance in the first year. For the purpose of reporting accounting profit, ARG Co depreciates machinery on a straight line basis over four years. ARG Co uses an after-tax money discount rate of 13% for investment appraisal.

Required:

Calculate the net present value of the proposed investment in products Alpha and Beta as at 30 June 20X7.

(15 marks)

14 – Lease v buy

Ceder Co has identified a machine that could fulfil the company's future production plans. This machine costs $50,000, payable immediately. The machines would require the input of $10,000 working capital throughout its working life of four years, with no expected scrap value at the end. The forecast pre-tax operating net cash flows associated with the machine are:

Year	**1**	**2**	**3**	**4**
	$	$	$	$
Net operating cash flows	20,500	22,860	24,210	23,410

The company's cost of capital for this investment is 12%.

The company is proposing to finance the purchase of the machine with a term loan at a fixed interest rate of 11% per year.

As an alternative the company has been offered the opportunity to lease the machine over a four-year period at a rental of $15,000 per year, not including maintenance costs.

Taxation at 35% is payable on operating cash flows one year in arrears, and tax-allowable depreciation is available at 25% per year on a reducing balance basis.

Required:

(a) Evaluate whether the company should lease or purchase the machine.

(7 marks)

(b) Comment on your choice of discount rate in (a)

(3 marks)

(Total: 10 marks)

15 – Replacement analysis

Bread Products Co is considering the replacement policy for its industrial size ovens which are used as part of a production line that bakes bread. Given its heavy usage each oven has to be replaced frequently. The choice is between replacing every two years or every three years. Only one type of oven is used, each of which costs $24,500. Maintenance costs and resale values are as follows:

Year	Maintenance per annum	Resale value
$	$	$
1	500	
2	800	15,600
3	1,500	11,200

Original cost, maintenance costs and resale values are expressed in current prices. That is, for example, maintenance for a two year old oven would cost $800 for maintenance undertaken now. It is expected that maintenance costs will increase at 10% per annum and oven replacement cost and resale values at 5% per annum. The money discount rate is 15%.

Required:

Calculate the preferred replacement policy for the ovens in a choice between a two-year or three-year replacement cycle.

(10 marks)

16 – Capital rationing

Quadrant is a highly geared company that wishes to expand its operations. Six possible capital investments have been identified, but the company only has access to a total of $620,000. The projects may not be postponed until a future period. After the projects end, it is unlikely that similar investment opportunities will occur.

Expected investment and net present values are as follows:

Project	**Investment**	**NPV**
A	(246,000)	6,350
B	(180,000)	1,882
C	(175,000)	(2,596)
D	(180,000)	8,356
E	(180,000)	5,490
F	(150,000)	4,993

Projects A and E are mutually exclusive. All projects are believed to be of similar risk to the company's existing capital investments.

Any surplus funds may be invested in the money market to earn a return of 9% per year. The money market may be assumed to be an efficient market. Quadrant's cost of capital is 12% per year.

Required:

(a) Rank the projects based on their NPV.

(1 mark)

(b) Assuming the projects are divisible, calculate the profitability index for each project, and rank the projects to determine how the money would be best invested. Explain briefly why the rankings differ from that in (a) above.

(5 marks)

(c) Now assume the projects are indivisible. Provide advise on how the funds are best invested.

(5 marks)

(d) Briefly explain how uncertainty and risk could be considered in the investment process.

(4 marks)

(Total: 15 marks)

17 – Expected values

Sludgewater, a furniture manufacturer, has been reported to the anti-pollution authorities on several occasions in recent years, and fined substantial amounts for making excessive toxic discharges into the air. Both the environmental lobby and Sludgewater's shareholders have demanded that it clean up its operations.

If no clean up takes place, Sludgewater estimates that the total fines it would incur over the next three years can be summarised by the following probability distribution (all figures are expressed in present values).

Level of fine	Probability
$1.0m	0.3
$1.8m	0.5
$2.6m	0.2

A firm of environmental consultants has advised that spray painting equipment can be installed at a cost of $4m to virtually eliminate discharges. Unlike fines, expenditure on pollution control equipment is tax-allowable via 25% tax-allowable depreciation (reducing balance, based on gross expenditure).

The rate of corporation tax is 30%, paid with a one-year delay. The equipment will have no scrap or resale value after its expected three year working life. The equipment can be in place ready for Sludgewater's next financial year.

A European Union grant of 25% of gross expenditure is available, but with payment delayed by a year. The consultant's charge is $200,000 and the new equipment will raise annual production costs by 2% of sales revenue. Current sales are $15 million per annum, and are expected to grow by 5% per annum compound. No change in working capital is envisaged.

Sludgewater applies a discount rate of 10% after tax on investment projects of this nature. All cash inflows and outflows occur at year ends.

Required:

(a) Assess the proposed investment by calculating the expected net present value.

(10 marks)

(b) Outline the main limitations of your approach in part (a).

(5 marks)

(Total: 15 marks)

18 – Sensitivity analysis

Pheonix is considering the purchase of a new machine to make wood-burning stoves. They have had a market research survey conducted at a cost of $200,000. This predicts demand of 4,000 stoves per annum at a selling price of $750 per stove for 10 years.

The machine will cost $2,000,000, payable in two instalments as follows.

	$
1 January 20X1	1,000,000
31 December 20X2	1,000,000

Depreciation of $180,000 per annum over the next 10 years will be provided to write down the machine to its scrap value.

Use will also be made of some existing equipment which originally cost $150,000, has a book value of $75,000 and would cost $200,000 to replace.

Pheonix is currently negotiating the sale of this machine for $100,000.

Variable cost per stove will be $600, and in accordance with the normal policy $250,000 of fixed overheads will be apportioned to the new product line per annum.

The machine will require its first service one year after purchase, and from then on will be serviced every year. Each service costs $50,000.

The machine will be brought into use immediately to build up inventory, but the first revenues will not be received until 31 December 20X2. Variable costs are payable annually at the same time as the revenues are received.

Required:

(a) Calculate the NPV at the company's cost of capital of 15%.

(5 marks)

(b) Determine the sensitivity of your advice based on the NPV computed in (a) to errors in the estimates of

(i) the required rate of return

(ii) the selling price per unit

(iii) the level of demand.

Your answer should also include a comment on the sensitivities calculated.

(10 marks)

(Total: 15 marks)

3 Working capital management

19 – Cash operating cycle

The following financial information related to Cloud Co:

As at 30 April	**20X1**	**20X0**
	$m	$m
Non-current assets	30.8	26.4
Current assets		
Inventory	22.0	9.5
Receivables	21.0	10.8
Cash	Nil	0.2
	43.0	20.5
Total assets	73.8	46.9
Capital and reserves		
Issued share capital	1.8	1.8
Reserves	38.4	32.7
Equity shareholders' funds	40.2	34.5
Current liabilities		
Bank overdraft	13.1	4.2
Trade payables	20.5	8.2
	33.6	12.4
Total equity and liabilities	73.8	46.9

Other information

(1) Sales for the year to 30 April 20X0 were $89m, yielding an operating profit of $8.7m and a profit before tax (after finance costs) of $8.2m.

(2) At the beginning of the year to 30 April 20X1 the company bought some new manufacturing equipment and recruited six more sales staff.

(3) Sales for the year to 30 April 20X1 were $131m, with an operating profit of $8.5m, and a profit before tax of $7m.

Required:

(a) By calculating the cash operating cycle of Cloud Co, together with any additional calculations that you consider to be relevant, discuss whether or not Cloud Co is overtrading.

(10 marks)

(b) Suggest ways in which Cloud Co might seek to resolve its current funding problems, and avoid the risks associated with overtrading.

(5 marks)

(Total: 15 marks)

20 – Receivables management I

Marton Co produces a range of specialised components, supplying a wide range of customers, all on credit terms. 20% of revenue is sold to one firm. Having used generous credit policies to encourage past growth, Marton Co now has to finance a substantial overdraft and is concerned about its liquidity.

Marton Co borrows from its bank at 13% pa interest. No further sales growth in volume or value terms is planned for the next year.

In order to speed up collection from customers, Marton Co is considering factoring.

Factoring

Factoring will be on a non-recourse basis, the factor administering and collecting payment from Marton Co's customers.

This is expected to generate administrative savings of $200,000 pa and to lower the average receivable collection period by 15 days.

The factor will make a service charge of 1% of Marton Co's revenue and also provide credit insurance facilities for an annual premium of $80,000.

Extracts from Marton Co's most recent accounts are given below:

	($000)
Sales (all on credit)	20,000
Cost of sales	(17,000)
Operating profit	3,000
Current assets:	
inventory	2,500
receivables	4,500
cash	Nil

Required:

(a) Calculate the net benefit to the company of the non-recourse factoring arrangement.

(8 marks)

(b) Briefly comment on any additional factors that must be considered when factoring.

(2 marks)

(Total: 10 marks)

21 – Receivables management II

Marton Co produces a range of specialised components, supplying a wide range of customers, all on credit terms. 20% of revenue is sold to one firm. Having used generous credit policies to encourage past growth, Marton Co now has to finance a substantial overdraft and is concerned about its liquidity.

Marton Co borrows from its bank at 13% pa interest. No further sales growth in volume or value terms is planned for the next year.

In order to speed up collection from customers, Marton Co is considering offering a discount for prompt payment.

Discount

Offering discounts to customers who settle their accounts early. The amount of the discount will depend on speed of payment as follows.

- Payment within 10 days of despatch of invoices 3%
- Payment within 20 days of despatch of invoices 1.5%
- It is estimated that customers representing 20% and 30% of Marton Co's sales respectively will take up these offers, the remainder continuing to take their present credit period.

Extracts from Marton Co's most recent accounts are given below:

	($000)
Sales (all on credit)	20,000
Cost of sales	(17,000)
Operating profit	3,000
Current assets:	
inventory	2,500
receivables	4,500
cash	Nil

Required:

(a) Calculate the net benefit to the company of offering a prompt payment discount to customers.

(8 marks)

(b) Briefly comment on any additional factors that must be considered when offering a discount.

(2 marks)

(Total: 10 marks)

22 – Inventory and cash management

KC Co is currently facing cash flow difficulties. As a small, owner-managed business, it has gradually extended its overdraft over the past three years to its current level of $1m. The company also has a loan from the bank for $1.5m, which is due for repayment in 2 years' time. The loan is secured on the business premises.

KC pay interest on their overdraft at a rate of 15%.

KC's bank has asked KC to reduce the level of its overdraft to $0.5m within the next 2 months, giving the ongoing effects of the banking crisis as the reason for such a tightening of its lending.

The Finance Director (FD) is understandably concerned and considers that better management of working capital could release some much needed cash. He has identified two options for the company:

Option 1: Increase payables

KC currently purchases all of its raw materials from one supplier and obtains a 1.5% discount for settling invoices within 10 days. Standard payment terms are 45 days. The FD is proposing that KC revert to the standard payment terms with this supplier. Total purchases in the year are $6m.

Option 2: Reduce order quantities

Raw materials are currently ordered monthly. For ease the FD has historically placed a fixed order for 100,000 units (costing $0.5m) per month. The supplier charges a fixed fee of $500 per order (regardless of the quantity ordered) and the FD estimates that the cost of holding one unit in stock for a year (including the cost of financing) is $3.00. The FD feels that the company may benefit from ordering a lower number of units per order as it would enable inventory levels to be reduced, thereby releasing further cash.

Required:

(a) If the Financial Controller pursued option 1, calculate the reduction in the overdraft that would result, together with the net effect on profitability (after taking account of the saving in interest payable on the overdraft).

(5 marks)

(b) If option 2 was pursued, again calculate the resulting reduction in the overdraft level and the net effect on profitability.

(7 marks)

(c) Identify the reasons why KC's bank might have tightened its lending policies in the context of the banking crisis.

(3 marks)

(Total: 15 marks)

23 – Cash management I

Thorne Co values, advertises and sells residential property on behalf of its customers. The company has been in business for only a short time and is preparing a cash budget for the first four months of 20X6. Expected sales of residential properties are as follows.

	20X5	20X6	20X6	20X6	20X6
Month	December	January	February	March	April
Units sold	10	10	15	25	30

The average price of each property is $180,000 and Thorne Co charges a fee of 3% of the value of each property sold. Thorne Co receives 1% in the month of sale and the remaining 2% in the month after sale. The company has nine employees who are paid on a monthly basis. The average salary per employee is $35,000 per year. If more than 20 properties are sold in a given month, each employee is paid in that month a bonus of $140 for each additional property sold.

Variable expenses are incurred at the rate of 0.5% of the value of each property sold and these expenses are paid in the month of sale. Fixed overheads of $4,300 per month are paid in the month in which they arise. Thorne Co pays interest every three months on a loan of $200,000 at a rate of 6% per year. The last interest payment in each year is paid in December.

An outstanding tax liability of $95,800 is due to be paid in April. In the same month Thorne Co intends to dispose of surplus vehicles, with a net book value of $15,000, for $20,000.

The cash balance at the start of January 20X6 is expected to be a deficit of $40,000.

Required:

(a) Prepare a monthly cash budget for the period from January to April 20X6. Your budget must clearly indicate each item of income and expenditure, and the opening and closing monthly cash balances.

(10 marks)

(b) Explain how the Baumol model can be employed to reduce the costs of cash management and discuss whether the Baumol cash management model may be of assistance to Thorne Co for this purpose.

(5 marks)

(Total: 15 marks)

24 – Cash management II

Grudem Co makes toys aimed at pre-school children. It was set up two years ago and has already achieved revenue in excess of $500,000 per annum.

It's business model is based around the following:

- Designing a range of toys throughout the year based on focus groups
- In the three months before Christmas extensive research is undertaken to identifying trends in consumer preferences, resulting in production for the top four toys being boosted.

Grudem sells 80% of its output via leading high street stores and 20% via online channels.

Based on latest sales projections for the next year, Grudem Co expects to have cash shortages during November and December, with a peak deficit of $100,000 and large inflows in February and March, resulting in a peak surplus of $300,000.

Required:

(a) Explain why Grudem is experiencing the cash deficit and surplus described.

(4 marks)

(a) Discuss the factors to be considered by Grudem Co when planning ways to invest any cash surplus forecast by its cash budgets.

(6 marks)

(b) Discuss the advantages and disadvantages to Grudem Co of using overdraft finance to fund any cash shortages forecast by its cash budgets.

(5 marks)

(Total: 15 marks)

4 Foreign exchange risk

25 – Forex risk I

FRQ Co is a UK based company which has just begun to make export sales to the Eurozone and is considering starting to purchase from a supplier in Germany. The managing director is aware that the company is likely to face foreign exchange rate risk but is unsure how this could be managed. Additionally the managing director is keen to understand how she could forecast future exchange rates as this would be of assistance when budgeting for the company.

FRQ Co can borrow in euros at 4% and in pounds sterling at 3%. Deposits in pounds earn just 1%. All rates are annual rates.

The current Euro/£ exchange rate is 1.200 +/– 0.005. A 12 month forward contract with a spread of +/– 0.010 will be available.

The company has just won a tender which will result in a receipt of €280,000 in one year's time.

Required:

(a) Briefly explain the methods that could be used to forecast future exchange rates and using the available information calculate a one year forward rate.

(5 marks)

(b) Discuss simple techniques the company could use to minimise the foreign exchange rate risk that it is exposed to and hence reduce the need for hedging.

(3 marks)

(c) Show how the receipt expected in one year's time could be hedged using a forward market hedge or a money market hedge and recommend which hedge should be used.

(7 marks)

(Total 15 marks)

26 – Forex risk II

Toytown is a company which distributes and sells a popular toy train. The company, which is based in Australia, imports trains from the USA which it packages and sells in New Zealand and larger countries in the Far East. The company is also considering establishing a subsidiary in South Africa which would buy products from Toytown and sell within Africa.

Toytown reports its results in its home currency. The company pays for its purchases from the USA in US dollars, but receives payment for the goods which it sells in Australasia and the Far East in local currency. All transactions carried out with the subsidiary in South Africa would be in US dollars. The company generally takes 6 weeks to pay its supplier in the USA and receives payment from debtors within 3 months.

Over the last few years the company has found that sales have been quite predictable and it has been possible to plan sales levels and purchases of goods in advance. However, there is increasing competition from companies in the Far East, which may make this more difficult in the future.

Required:

(a) The company is currently considering whether the foreign currency exposure could be managed more efficiently. Describe the following types of foreign currency exposure, giving examples of how they could impact Toytown, now and in the future:

(i) Economic risk

(ii) Translation risk

(iii) Transaction risk

(6 marks)

(b) Identify the factors which Toytown should consider when deciding which approach to take, and give recommendations on how Toytown should manage its transaction exposure, giving reasons for your recommendations.

(9 marks)

(Total 15 marks)

27 – Forex risk III

Describe the following approaches to managing or hedging transaction risk exposure and the disadvantages and advantages of each method:

(i) Leading and lagging

(ii) Matching

(iii) Forward exchange contracts

(iv) Currency options

(10 marks)

28 – Interest rate risk

A company is also looking into the financing of the establishment of the new subsidiary.

The company estimates that it will need to borrow $2 million US dollars in two months time for a period of six months, but is concerned about expected fluctuation in interest rates and is considering hedging this exposure using a forward rate agreement. The company is able to buy a 2–8 FRA priced at 5.0 – 4.7.

Required:

(a) How could the company use this FRA to hedge the interest rate exposure, what interest would be payable and what additional sum would the company have to pay to or receive from the bank if the market interest rate is:

(a) 4%

(b) 6%?

(5 marks)

(b) Describe how else the company could manage the interest rate risk.

(5 marks)

(Total 10 marks)

5 Sources of finance

29 – Long term finance

Discuss the main factors which should be taken into account when choosing between long-term loan capital and ordinary share capital.

(10 marks)

30 – Rights issue

The Cherry Tree Company has issued 4 million $1 par equity shares, which are at present selling for $3.40 per share. The company needs to raise additional finance in order to undertake a new project. The options being considered are:

- a 1 for 2 rights issue priced at $2.50.
- a five-year $5 million floating rate term loan from a clearing bank, at an initial interest rate of 10%

Required:

(a) Calculate the theoretical ex-rights price of Cherry Tree's equity shares.

(3 marks)

(b) Calculate the theoretical value of a Cherry Tree right before the shares sell ex-rights.

(2 marks)

(c) Explain and evaluate the appropriateness of the following alternative methods of issuing equity finance:

– a placing,

– an offer for sale,

– a public offer for subscription.

(10 marks)

(Total: 15 marks)

31 – Sources of finance

Gad Co, a listed company, operates a fleet of fishing trawlers. In the last financial year, it reported profit after tax of $420,000.

The company has recently signed a long-term contract to supply a large supermarket chain with fresh fish. The new contract will increase profits significantly, but it requires investment in a processing and packaging warehouse costing $2 million. The expected return on investment is 15% per annum. There are two options being considered to finance the required investment.

(1) A two for five rights issue

(2) An issue of 8% convertible loan stock at par.

Gad Co currently has 500,000 $1 ordinary shares in issue with a market price of $11 and has no long term debt finance. Over 50% of the shares are owned by members of the founding Gadus family. The company pays tax at a rate of 30% per year.

Required:

(a) Calculate the theoretical ex rights price per share of Gad Co were the rights issue to go ahead.

(3 marks)

(b) Discuss whether the value of a company, and hence shareholder wealth, can be increased by varying the capital structure.

(6 marks)

(c) Explain the term 'convertible loan stock'. Discuss the advantages and disadvantages of this form of finance from the viewpoint of both the company and investors.

(6 marks)

(Total: 15 marks)

32 – Dividend policy

Discuss the factors to be considered in formulating the dividend policy of a stock-exchange listed company.

(10 marks)

6 Cost of capital

33 – WACC with DVM

The directors of M Co are considering opening a new factory to manufacture a new product at a cost of $3.0 million. During the last 5 years, the company has had 3 million shares in issue. The current market price of these shares (at 31 December 20X8) is $1.45 ex-dividend.

The company pays only one dividend each year (on 31 December) and dividends for the last five years have been as follows:

Year	**Dividend per share (cents)**
20X8	14.1
20X7	14.1
20X6	12.1
20X5	11.6
20X4	11.0

M Co currently has in issue $1 million 7% debentures redeemable on 31 December 20Y2 at par. The current market price of these debentures is $83.60 ex-interest, and the interest is payable in one amount each year on 31 December. The company also has outstanding a $500,000 bank loan repayable on 31 December 20Y7. The rate of interest on this loan is variable, being fixed at 3% above the bank's base rate which is currently 5%.

Required:

(a) Calculate the weighted average cost of capital (WACC) for M Co as at 31 December 20X8

(12 marks)

(b) Briefly advise the directors of M Co on the suitability of using the WACC calculated in (a) above to discount the expected cash flows of the project

(3 marks)

(Total: 15 marks)

Note: Ignore taxation

34 – WACC with NPV

Rupab Co is a manufacturing company that wishes to evaluate an investment in new production machinery. The machinery would enable the company to satisfy increasing demand for existing products and the investment is not expected to lead to any change in the existing level of business risk of Rupab Co.

The machinery will cost $2.5 million, payable at the star t of the first year of operation, and is not expected to have any scrap value. Annual before-tax net cash flows of $680,000 per year would be generated by the investment in each of the five years of its expected operating life. These net cash inflows are before taking account of expected inflation of 3% per year. Initial investment of $240,000 in working capital would also be required, followed by incremental annual investment to maintain the purchasing power of working capital.

Rupab Co has in issue five million shares with a market value of $3.81 per share. The equity beta of the company is 1.2. The yield on short-term government debt is 4.5% per year and the equity risk premium is approximately 5% per year.

The debt finance of Rupab Co consists of bonds with a total book value of $2 million. These bonds pay annual interest before tax of 7%. The par value and market value of each bond is $100.

Rupab Co pays taxation one year in arrears at an annual rate of 25%. Tax-allowable depreciation on machinery is on a straight-line basis over the life of the asset.

Required:

(a) Calculate the after-tax weighted average cost of capital of Rupab Co.

(7 marks)

(b) Prepare a forecast of the annual after-tax cash flows of the investment in nominal terms, and calculate and comment on its net present value.

(8 marks)

(Total: 15 marks)

Ignore taxation.

35 – CAPM

Explain how the capital asset pricing model can be used to calculate a project-specific discount rate and discuss the limitations of using the capital asset pricing model in investment appraisal.

(10 marks)

36 – Discount rates

March Co operates and manages a number of theme parks. The capital structure of March Co as at 1st January 2011 is as follows:

	$m
Issued ordinary shares (25c shares)	250
Bank term loan	200
8% irredeemable debenture	400

The ordinary shares have a current market price of $2 each. Dividends per share (in cents) in the five preceding years were as follows:

2006	2007	2008	2009	2010
6.9	7.2	8.8	9.6	10.5

The dividend for 2010 has just been paid. The bank is currently charging 10% on the term loan. The debenture stock has a market price of $75. The company pays corporation tax at a rate of 30%.

The finance team of March Co is undertaking a financial review of two new projects. The following details are available:

Project 1 – Development and expansion of one of March Co's existing theme parks.

Project 2 – Buying a small chain of recruitment consultants.

The company's overall equity beta is 1.20 and the average equity beta of other recruitment companies is 1.1. The average gearing of other recruitment companies is 70% equity and 30% debt.

The risk free rate is 5% and the estimated market return is 10%. The low risk of debt finance means that the debt beta is negligible. Corporate taxation is at the rate of 30%.

It has not yet been decided how to fund the expansion.

Required:

(a) Calculate a suitable discount rate for the new theme park project.

(10 marks)

(b) Calculate a suitable risk-adjusted cost of equity in order to appraise the investment in the recruitment industry.

(5 marks)

(Total: 15 marks)

37 – Risk

Greg Co is a family-run business specialising in the manufacture of luxury shoes aimed at customers in their 20s and 30s. After three years of static sales, the Directors of Greg Co are now looking for growth and have identified two investment opportunities:

- Buy a rival designer shoe manufacturer, Dan plc, who is known to be experiencing difficulties.
- Diversify into designer clothing to capitalise on the Greg brand.

Alan, the Finance Director, has explained to the board that different discount rates will be required to assess each option:

- The existing company WACC will be used to assess the acquisition.
- A risk adjusted discount rate, calculated using beta factors, will be used to assess the move into clothing.

Required:

(a) Explain the terms business risk and financial risk and the significance of each in deciding whether Greg's existing WACC can be used to assess the acquisition of Dan plc.

(9 marks)

(b) Identify and explain the factors that may change Greg Co's equity beta during the next year assuming it decides to move into designer clothing.

(6 marks)

(Total: 15 marks)

7 Financial ratios

38 – Achieving objectives

The directors of PDQ Inc have commissioned a firm of consultants to conduct a wide-ranging review of the company's public image and market position. Although this is not predominantly a financial review, the consultants need to examine the company's financial performance.

The company has the following summary information for the last five years:

	Year 1	**Year 2**	**Year 3**	**Year 4**	**Year 5**
	$m	$m	$m	$m	$m
Revenue	51.2	58.3	63.9	75.2	78.2
Cost of sales	20.5	22.2	24.3	30.1	30.5
Salaries and wages	15.4	16.8	17.2	15.8	15.2
Other costs	6.1	7.9	9.9	16.3	17.9
Profit before interest and tax	9.2	11.4	12.5	13.0	14.6
Interest	1.5	1.6	1.3	0.3	0.2
Tax	2.5	3.2	3.7	4.2	4.8
Profit after interest and tax	5.2	6.6	7.5	8.5	9.6
Dividends payable	2.1	2.6	3.0	3.4	4.8
Average receivables	10.5	11.7	13.3	14.8	15.2
Average payables	3.8	4.2	5.1	6.7	6.9
Average total assets	41.2	45.2	46.7	63.3	67.1
Shareholders' funds	26.2	30.2	34.7	59.8	64.6
Long-term debt	15.0	15.0	12.0	3.5	2.5
Number of shares in issue (millions)	6.0	6.0	6.0	8.0	8.0
P/E ratio:					
Company	8.0	8.5	9.0	9.2	9.5
Industry	8.5	9.0	9.1	9.0	9.1
Number of employees	1,720	1,750	1,820	1,720	1,690

Notes

(1) Each P/E ratio is the average for the year.

(2) The increased equity in year 4 was partly the result of a share issue which took place at the beginning of the year. Some of the $20m raised was used to reduce debt.

For the past five years, PDQ Inc has stated its objectives as: 'To maximise shareholder wealth whilst recognising the responsibility of the company to its other stakeholders'.

As one of the consultants working on this assignment, you have been asked to assess whether the company has achieved its objectives in the five-year period under review and to discuss the key factors which have determined your assessment.

Required:

(a) to discuss whether the company has met its objectives, based solely on the information available

(10 marks)

(b) to comment on what other financial information you would need in order to provide your client with a more accurate assessment.

(5 marks)

(Total: 15 marks)

8 Business valuations and market efficiency

39 – Valuation methods I

The board of directors of Predator Co, a listed company, is considering making an offer to purchase Target Co, a private limited company in the same industry. If Target Co is purchased it is proposed to continue operating the company as a going concern in the same line of business.

Summarised details from the most recent set of financial statements for Predator and Target are shown below:

	Predator Statement of financial position as at 31 March		**Target Statement of financial position as at 31 March**	
	$m	$m	$000	$000
Freehold property		33		460
Plant & equipment		58		1,310
Inventory	29		330	
Receivables	24		290	
Cash	3		20	
		56		640
Total assets		**147**		**2,410**
Ordinary shares		35		160
Reserves		43		964
Current liabilities		31		518
Medium-term bank loans		38		768
		147		**2,410**

Predator Co 50 cents ordinary shares, Target Co, 25 cents ordinary shares.

Year	Predator Co PAT	Predator Co Dividend	Target Co PAT	Target Co Dividend
	$m	$m	$000	$000
T5	14.30	9.01	143	85.0
T4	15.56	9.80	162	93.5
T3	16.93	10.67	151	93.5
T2	18.42	11.60	175	102.8
T1	20.04	12.62	183	113.1

T5 is five years ago and T1 is the most recent year.

Target's shares are owned by a small number of private individuals. Its managing director who receives an annual salary of $120,000 dominates the company. This is $40,000 more than the average salary received by managing directors of similar companies. The managing director would be replaced, if Predator purchases Target.

The freehold property has not been revalued for several years and is believed to have a market value of $800,000.

The statement of financial position value of plant and equipment is thought to reflect its replacement cost fairly, but its value if sold is not likely to exceed $800,000. Approximately $55,000 of inventory is obsolete and could only be sold as scrap for $5,000.

The ordinary shares of Predator are currently trading at 430 cents ex-div. A suitable cost of equity for Target has been estimated at 15%.

Both companies are subject to corporation tax at 33%.

Required:

(a) Estimate the value of Target Co using the net asset method of valuation

(3 marks)

(b) Estimate the value of Target Co using the dividend valuation model

(4 marks)

(c) Estimate the value of Target Co using the P/E ratio method

(5 marks)

(d) Advise the board of Predator as to how much it should offer for Target's shares.

(3 marks)

(Total: 15 marks)

40 – Valuation methods II

Describe the approach that is normally taken when valuing a company.

Include a discussion of how the purpose and perspective of the valuation and the relevance of the valuation methods used will impact on the valuation process.

(10 marks)

41 – Valuation and market efficiency

VAL Co is a listed company with a stated objective of maximisation of shareholder wealth. It has 70 million ordinary shares in issue with a par value of $1, has no debt finance and currently has nearly $100m in the bank.

Financial information relating to VAL Co for the past three years ending 31 March is as follows:

	2009	**2010**	**2011**	**2012**
Profit after tax for the period ($m)	21.7	27.2	34.6	40.3
Total cash dividend ($m)	15.4	15.4	15.4	–
Share price	4.40	5.25	6.42	6.90

The dividend in respect of the year ending 31 March 2012 has yet to be declared.

VAL Co is considering a major new investment that will be financed using retained earnings. The investment is expected to generate an NPV of $65 million. Information regarding this project has not yet been made public.

AVL Co is a very similar but significantly larger company. AVL Co has 250 million ordinary shares which are currently trading at $4.60. The most recent accounts of AVL Co showed a profit after tax of $85 million.

The directors of VAL Co are concerned that the share price of the company does not accurately reflect the true value of the company. They have established that the market is thought to be semi-strong but do not understand what this means.

Required:

(a) Analyse and discuss whether VAL Co has achieved its stated objective of maximisation of shareholder wealth.

(5 marks)

(b) Calculate an earnings based value of VAL Co in total and per share and discuss your result.

(5 marks)

(c) Explain the levels of market efficiency to the directors and evaluate and comment on the potential impact of the proposed new project on the share price of the company.

(5 marks)

(Total: 15 marks)

Test your understanding answers

1 – Stakeholder groups

Introduction

Stakeholders in a company include amongst others: shareholders, directors/managers, lenders, employees, suppliers and customers. These groups are likely to share in the wealth and risk generated by a company in different ways and thus conflicts of interest are likely to exist. Conflicts also exist not just between groups but within stakeholder groups. This might be because sub-groups exist, for example preference shareholders and equity shareholders within the overall category of shareholders.

Alternatively individuals within a stakeholder group might have different preferences (e.g. to risk and return, short term and long term returns). Good corporate governance is partly about the resolution of such conflicts. Financial and other objectives of stakeholder groups may be identified as follows:

Shareholders

Shareholders are normally assumed to be interested in wealth maximisation. This, however, involves consideration of potential return and risk. For a listed company, this can be viewed in terms of the changes in the share price and other market-based ratios using share price (e.g. price/earnings ratio, dividend yield, earnings yield).

Where a company is not listed, financial objectives need to be set in terms of other financial measures, such as return on capital employed, earnings per share, gearing, growth, profit margin, asset utilisation, and market share. Many other measures also exist which may collectively capture the objectives of return and risk.

Shareholders may have other objectives for the company and these can be identified in terms of the interests of other stakeholder groups. Thus, shareholders as a group may be interested in profit maximisation; they may also be interested in the welfare of their employees, or the environmental impact of the company's operations.

Directors and managers

While executive directors and managers should attempt to promote and balance the interests of shareholders and other stakeholder groups, it has been argued that they also promote their own individual interests and should be seen as a separate stakeholder group.

This problem arises from the divorce between ownership and control. The behaviour of managers cannot be fully observed by the shareholders, giving them the capacity to take decisions which are consistent with their own reward structures and risk preferences. Directors may therefore be interested in their own remuneration package. They may also be interested in building empires, exercising greater control, or positioning themselves for their next promotion. Non-financial objectives of managers are sometimes inconsistent with what the financial objectives of the company ought to be.

Lenders

Lenders are concerned to receive payment of interest and eventually re-payment of the capital at maturity. Unlike the ordinary shareholders, they do not share in the upside (profitability) of successful organisational strategies. They are therefore likely to be more risk averse than shareholders, with an emphasis on financial objectives that promote liquidity and solvency with low risk (e.g. low gearing, high interest cover, security, strong cash flow).

Employees

The primary interests of employees are their salary/wage and their security of employment. To an extent there is a direct conflict between employees and shareholders as wages are a cost to the company and income to employees.

Performance-related pay based on financial or other quantitative objectives may, however, go some way toward drawing the divergent interests together.

Suppliers and customers

Suppliers and customers are external stakeholders with their own set of objectives (profit for the supplier and, possibly, customer satisfaction with the good or service from the customer) that, within a portfolio of businesses, are only partly dependent on the company in question. Nevertheless it is important to consider and measure the relationship in term of financial objectives relating to quality, lead times, volume of business, price and a range of other variables in considering any organisational strategy.

2 – Corporate governance

Corporate governance is the system by which organisations are directed and controlled.

Where the power to direct and control an organisation is given, a duty of accountability exists to those who have devolved that power. Part of that duty of accountability is discharged by disclosure of both performance in the annual report and accounts and also the governance procedures themselves.

Corporate governance codes are usually voluntary, and operate on a comply or explain basis. Thus, any requirements are to disclose governance procedures in relation to best practice, rather than comply with best practice, and to explain/justify any divergence from best practice.

The decision-making powers in a company rest mainly with the board of directors. Much of corporate governance regulation has therefore focused on governance principles and best practice relating to this stakeholder group. The principles and guidelines in the UK Corporate Governance Code, for example, are aimed largely at trying to ensure that the directors act responsibly and in the interests of the other stakeholder groups, particularly the shareholders, rather than themselves. Ideally, the interests of directors and other stakeholders should be aligned and consistent with each other.

Some companies, such as those in the UK, have a unitary board structure, with one board consisting of both executive and non-executive directors. This contrasts with the two-tier board structure in Germany for instance where there is more independence between the two groups of directors. In a two-tier structure, non-executives on a supervisory board and executive directors on a management board which reports to the supervisory board.

Typical corporate governance proposals (such as those written into the UK Corporate Governance Code) include the following:

(1) Independence of the board with no covert financial reward

(2) Adequate quality and quantity of non-executive directors to act as a counterbalance to the power of executive directors.

(3) Remuneration committee controlled by non-executives, to decide the remuneration of the executive directors.

(4) Appointments committee consisting of non-executives, to recommend new appointments to the board.

(5) Audit committee consisting of non-executives, with responsibilities for audit matters, including negotiating the fee of the external auditors.

(6) Separation of the roles of chairman and chief executive to prevent concentration of power in one person.

(7) Full disclosure of all forms of director remuneration including shares and share options.

(8) Better communication between the board of directors and the shareholders, particularly institutional investors.

(9) Greater prominence for risk management, which is specified as a particular board responsibility.

Overall, the visibility given by corporate governance procedures goes some way toward discharging the directors' duty of accountability to stakeholders and makes more transparent the underlying incentive systems of directors.

3 – Stakeholder conflict

Stakeholder groups would include:

Potential employees, local residents, wider community, environmental pressure groups, government, company directors/managers and prestige shareholders

Possible conflicts between their objectives would include:

Local residents/ pressure groups & Managers/ shareholders
Local damage will have lasting impact on the environment. Local people/pressure groups may consider this unacceptable whilst shareholders may think that provided compensation is paid it is a reasonable consequence.

Company directors/ managers & Employees/Pressure groups
Company directors may do only the minimum to comply with any health and safety legislation in order to save money. Potential employees may be desperate for work and un-informed and may therefore take risks with their own health. The wider community and pressure groups will focus on employee health as a priority.

Shareholders & Government
Shareholders will want to see their own wealth increased by way of a return on their investment. The government may regard the wealth as belonging to the country and seek to prevent profits being taken out.

Note: Again any number of possible conflicts could be identified here. The scenario demonstrates the danger of focussing on improving share wealth to the exclusion of all other objectives.

4 – Measuring performance in NFPs

Not-for-profit organisations include public sector bodies such as the National Health Service or local councils, charitable bodies e.g. Oxfam, and other organisations whose purpose is to serve the broader community interests, rather than the pursuit of profit. In broad terms, such organisations seek to serve the interests of society as a whole, and so they give non-financial objectives priority of place.

It is reasonable to argue that they best serve society's interests when the gap between the benefits they provide, and the cost of that provision is greatest. This is commonly termed value for money, and it is not dissimilar to the concept of profit maximisation, but for the fact that public welfare is being maximised rather than profit.

In practice it is incredibly difficult to quantify, for example, the benefits from an operation such as the UK's National Health Service. How does one put a value on a life which has been prolonged by 'x' number of years, or on the easing of pain which is brought about by the replacement of an arthritic joint? The benefits extend beyond factors which can be measured in purely financial terms. Nonetheless, financial criteria can be used to appraise the extent to which such organisations offer value for money, and hence make good use of the funds provided to them.

The major difficulty for public sector bodies lies in precisely how to measure the achievement of the non-financial objectives. Value for money as a concept assumes that there is a yardstick against which to measure success, i.e. achievement of objectives. In reality, the indicators of success are open to debate. For example, in a health service is success measured in terms of fewer patient deaths per hospital admission, shorter waiting lists for operations, average speed of patient recovery and so on? As long as objectives are difficult to specify, so too will it remain difficult to specify where there is value for money. Comparative performance measures are useful, but care must be taken not to read too much into limited information.

5 – Public sector organisations

(a) The profit motive is not applicable in most public sector situations. Instead we must measure the services provided, in relation to the cost of providing those services. In recent years successive governments have been concerned with measuring service provision. They have employed a VFM (value for money) audit that aims to get 'the best possible combination of services from the least possible resources'. This is done by pursuing the three Es:

Effectiveness: this is the achievement of the objectives. For example, in the waste management department of a local council the task is to collect household waste. An effective service provision will have few customer complaints and all refuse collected on a regular basis. In this situation customer complaints could be a performance measure.

Economy: this is reducing costs. The organisation should have a system of cost control to ensure that costs are kept to a minimum. In the past, public sector organisations in the United Kingdom had poor cost control, but more recently systems have been put in place to reduce the costs of the organisations. Performance can be measured by calculating various cost statistics.

Efficiency: this is the achievement of objectives at minimum cost – a combination of the other two aims. For example, the local council referred to above may look at the cost per household to clear refuse and compare it to what was achieved in previous years or what other councils have achieved. They may also look at the number of bins emptied per day as an efficiency measure as the more emptied the lower the annual cost of this service.

(b) To ensure that the scarce resources which have been placed at their disposal are used efficiently and effectively, public sector services such as education need to place a high priority on their financial control and performance. There has always been a quest for 'yard sticks' in such organisations, i.e. ways in which performance can be measured, compared and evaluated.

One of the measures which tends to be used in education is the amount spent on each pupil/student i.e. the cost per pupil/student for each school or college, etc. It should be noted, however, that the amount spent per head is no indication that the amount involved has been spent wisely and is not necessarily a measure of efficiency. It can be used in two ways:

– to support the view that it is possible to provide a similar service at a lower cost, or

– by political parties who point to the fact that, in their areas of influence, more is spent per pupil/student on education.

Where the educational establishment provides a meals service, comparisons can be made using the cost of each meal served or on a cost per pupil/student basis. Such comparisons would only be valid if the meals mix and volume of meals served were similar. Where the meals service was revenue earning, performance could also be evaluated using ratios for profitability, etc.

In cases where the educational establishment provides a library, cost comparisons could be made with similar sized libraries using the cost per book, or cost per pupil or cost of new books.

6 – Investment appraisal techniques I

(a) (i) **Calculation of NPV**

\$000	t_0	t_1	t_2	t_3	t_4
Investment	(20)				
Income (W1)		65	155	200	(20)
Operating costs (W2)		(71)	(127)	(155)	(15)
Net relevant cash flow	(20)	(6)	28	45	(35)
Discount factor at 10%	1	0.909	0.826	0.751	0.683
Present value	(20.00)	(5.45)	23.13	33.80	(23.91)

NPV = \$7,570 > 0 therefore accept

Workings

(W1) **Calculation of income**

$	t_1	t_2	t_3	t_4
Total income with new machine (demand × $45)(Note – Yr 3 restricted to 10,000 capacity)	315,000	405,000	450,000	180,000
Current income (5,000 units × $50)(Note – Yr 4 only 4,000 units)	250,000	250,000	250,000	200,000
Additional income	65,000	155,000	200,000	(20,000)

(W2) **Calculation of operating costs**

	t_1	t_2	t_3	t_4
Variable cost ($/unit)	28.00	28.00	28.00	28.00
Additional units per year	2,000	4,000	5,000	0
Variable costs ($/year)	56,000	112,000	140,000	0
Fixed costs ($/year)	15,000	15,000	15,000	15,000
Operating costs ($/year)	71,000	127,000	155,000	15,000

(ii) **Calculation of internal rate of return**

$000	t_0	t_1	t_2	t_3	t_4
Net relevant cash flow	(20)	(6)	28	45	(35)
Discount factor at 20%	1	0.833	0.694	0.579	0.482
Present value	(20.00)	(5.00)	19.43	26.06	(16.87)

Net present value $3,620

Internal rate of return = 10 + [(7,570/(7,570 – 3,620)) × (20 – 10)] = 10 + 19.2 = 29.2%

(iii) **Calculation of discounted payback**

$000	t_0	t_1	t_2	t_3	t_4
Present value	(20.00)	(5.45)	23.13	33.80	(23.91)
Cumulative present value	(20.00)	(25.45)	(2.32)	31.48	7.57

Discounted payback period = 2 + (2.32/33.80) = 2 + 0.07 = 2.07 years

(b) The investment proposal has a positive net present value (NPV) of $7,570 and is therefore financially acceptable. The results of the other investment appraisal methods do not alter this financial acceptability, as the NPV decision rule will always offer the correct investment advice.

The internal rate of return (IRR) method also recommends accepting the investment proposal, since the IRR of 27.5% is greater than the 10% return required by Breccon Co. If the advice offered by the IRR method differed from that offered by the NPV method, the advice offered by the NPV method would be preferred.

The calculated return on capital employed of 15% is less than the target return of 20%, but as indicated earlier, the investment proposal is financially acceptable as it has a positive NPV. The reason why Breccon Co has a target return on capital employed of 20% should be investigated. This may be an out-of-date hurdle rate that has not been updated for changed economic circumstances.

The discounted payback period of 2.07 years is a significant proportion of the forecast life of the investment proposal of four years, a time period which the information provided suggests is limited by technological change. The sensitivity of the investment proposal to changes in demand and life-cycle period should be analysed, since an earlier onset of technological obsolescence may have a significant impact on its financial acceptability.

7 – Investment appraisal techniques II

The payback period is the time taken to recover initial investment.

Advantages	Disadvantages
(1) Simple to understand and calculate.	(1) It does not consider the time value of money.
(2) A simple measure of risk: the longer the payback, the higher the risk.	(2) There is no measure of return.
(3) May be important to companies with limited cash resources for budgeting purposes.	(3) Ignores cash flows after the payback period.
(4) Uses cash flows that are less open to manipulation than profits.	
(5) Emphasises cash flow in the early years.	

The accounting rate of return is a percentage measure. It is the ROCE of an investment.

Advantages	Disadvantages
(1) Simple to understand and calculate.	(1) It does not consider the time value of money.
(2) Widely used.	(2) It is based upon (subjective) accounting profit.
(3) Can be calculated from available accounting data.	(3) It is not an absolute measure of return.
(4) It considers the whole of the investment, and is some measure of (accounting) return.	

8 – Investment appraisal techniques III

(a) **Project X**

Year	CF	DF	PV	DF	PV
	$000	10%	$000	20%	$000
0	(200)	1.000	(200.000)	1.000	(200.000)
1	35	0.909	31.815	0.833	29.155
2	80	0.826	66.080	0.694	55.520
3	90	0.751	67.590	0.579	52.110
4	75	0.683	51.225	0.482	36.150
5	20	0.621	12.420	0.402	8.040
		NPV (10%) =	29.130	NPV (20%) =	(19.025)

Project Y

Year	CF	DF	PV	DF	PV
	$000	10%	$000	20%	$000
0	(200)	1.000	(200.000)	1.000	(200.000)
1	218	0.909	198.162	0.833	181.594
2	10	0.826	8.260	0.694	6.940
3	10	0.751	7.510	0.579	5.790
4	4	0.683	2.732	0.482	1.928
5	3	0.621	1.863	0.402	1.206
		NPV (10%) =	18.527	NPV (20%) =	(2.542)

$$\text{IRR (X)} = 10 + \frac{29.13}{29.13 - (-19.025)} \times (20 - 10) = 16.05\%$$

$$\text{IRR (Y)} = 10 + \frac{18.527}{18.527 - (-2.542)} \times (20 - 10) = 18.79\%$$

NPV (X,10%) = $29,130

NPV (Y, 10%) = $18,527

(b) Project X, when discounted at the cost of capital 10%, has the highest NPV. However, Project Y has a higher IRR than Project X. When a conflict arises between the NPV and IRR criteria, select the project with the highest NPV. Therefore Project X should be accepted in preference to Project Y.

(c) Project Y's cash flow occurs mainly in year 1, whilst most of X's comes in the years 2 to 4. This is the reason for Y's higher IRR, because the IRR calculation assumes that any monies reinvested during the life of the project are reinvested at the project's IRR rather than at the company's cost of capital (the latter being the assumption of the NPV calculation).

9 – Limitations of NPV

General limitations of Net Present Value when applied to investment appraisal

NPV is a commonly used technique employed in investment appraisal, but it is subject to a number of restrictive assumptions and limitations which call into question its general relevance. Nonetheless, if the assumptions and limitations are understood then its application is less likely to be undertaken in error.

Some of the difficulties with NPV are listed below:

(i) NPV assumes that firms pursue an objective of maximising the wealth of their shareholders. This is questionable given the wider range of stakeholders who might have conflicting interests to those of the shareholders.

(ii) NPV is largely redundant if organisations are not wealth maximising. For example, public sector organisations may wish to invest in capital assets but will use non-profit objectives as part of their assessment.

(iii) NPV is potentially a difficult method to apply in the context of having to estimate what is the correct discount rate to use. This is particularly so when questions arise as to the incorporation of risk premia in the discount rate, since an evaluation of the riskiness of the business, or of the project in particular, will have to be made but may be difficult to discern. Alternative approaches to risk analysis, such as sensitivity and decision trees are, themselves, subject to fairly severe limitations.

(iv) NPV assumes that cash surpluses can be reinvested at the discount rate. This is subject to other projects being available which produce at least a zero NPV at the chosen discount rate.

(v) NPV can most easily cope with cash flows arising at period ends and is not a technique that is used easily when complicated, mid-period cash flows are present.

(vi) NPV is not universally employed, especially in a small business environment. The available evidence suggests that businesses assess projects in a variety of ways (payback, IRR, accounting rate of return). The fact that such methods are used which are theoretically inferior to NPV calls into question the practical benefits of NPV, and therefore hints at certain practical limitations.

(vii) The conclusion from NPV analysis is the present value of the surplus cash generated from a project. If reported profits are important to businesses, then it is possible that there may be a conflict between undertaking a positive NPV project and potentially adverse consequences on reported profits. This will particularly be the case for projects with long time horizons, large initial investment and very delayed cash inflows. In such circumstances, businesses may prefer to use accounting measures of investment appraisal.

(viii) Managerial incentive schemes may not be consistent with NPV, particularly when long time horizons are involved. Thus managers may be rewarded on the basis of accounting profits in the short term and may be incentivised to act in accordance with these objectives, and thus ignore positive NPV projects. This may be a problem of the incentive schemes and not of NPV; nonetheless, a potential conflict exists and represents a difficulty for NPV.

(ix) NPV treats all time periods equally, with the exception of discounting far cash flows more than near cash flows. In other words, NPV only accounts for the time value of money. To many businesses, distant horizons are less important than near horizons, if only because that is the environment in which they work. Other factors besides applying higher discount rates may work to reduce the impact of distant years. For example, in the long term, nearly all aspects of the business may change and hence a too-narrow focus on discounting means that NPV is of limited value and more so the further the time horizon considered.

(x) NPV is of limited use in the face of non-quantifiable benefits or costs. NPV does not take account of non-financial information which may even be relevant to shareholders who want their wealth maximised. For example, issues of strategic benefit may arise against which it is difficult to immediately quantify the benefits but for which there are immediate costs. NPV would treat such a situation as an additional cost since it could not incorporate the indiscernible benefit.

10 – Investing in marketing and IT

Forecasting cash flows

With investments in machinery for manufacturing facilities companies are able to calculate and measure with some degree of accuracy the net cash benefits of purchasing the new machine:

- the current machine capacity
- the new machine capacity
- the expected demand
- the current unit contribution.
- the annual cost of running a machine
- the estimated useful life of the machine

The forecast NPV obtained should thus be a reasonable figure that managers can have some confidence in.

Management will usually be aware of the (high) initial costs associated with an IT or marketing decision but quantifying the cash benefits is much more difficult. For example, the predicted benefit may be an 'improvement in corporate image' or 'advancement in technology' but converting these into cash flows are tricky, both in terms of amount and timing.

The importance of non-financial aspects

All investment opportunities involve both financial and non-financial aspects. For example, when choosing a new machine the NPV must be considered along with likely pollution, noise levels and safety records for the machine.

However, marketing and IT investment opportunities are more difficult to assess because the non-financial aspects may be more significant and hence the issues surrounding quantification more important.

If a new IT system is installed, how can the firm put a value on the benefits to the staff and the company? With marketing, if customer perception and the product's profile improve, how can this be measured? The benefits are often subjective, qualitative and intangible.

It is thus more difficult to use NPV analysis to obtain a meaningful assessment of benefits.

Choice of discount rate

You could argue that the above uncertainties mean that investments in marketing, say, are inherently more risky than those in manufacturing and hence a higher discount rate should be used to assess them.

11 – NPV with taxation

(a) Initial investment = \$500,000 + \$20,000 = \$520,000

Tax-allowable depreciation schedule:

Time		\$	Tax saving @ 30%	Timing of tax relief
T_0	Initial investment	520,000		
T_1	Tax benefit @ 25%	(130,000)	39,000	T_2
	Written down value	390,000		
T_2	Tax benefit @ 25%	(97,500)	29,250	T_3
	Written down value	292,500		
T_3	Tax benefit @ 25%	(73,125)	21,938	T_4
	Written down value	219,375		
T_4	Sale proceeds	(50,000)		
T_4	BA	169,375	50,813	T_5

Contribution:

Current production	8,000	units per week
New capacity	20,000	units per week
Demand	12,000	units per week
So, increase in production and sales	4,000	units per week (up to demand)
Unit contribution ($7.00 × 0.2)	× $1.040	
Increase in contribution	$5,600	
	× 48 weeks	
Increase PER ANNUM	$268,800	

Net present value calculation ($000)

Time	T_0	T_1	T_2	T_3	T_4	T_5
	$000	$000	$000	$000	$000	$000
Contribution		268.80	268.80	268.80		
Tax payable (30%)			(80.64)	(80.64)	(80.64)	
Initial investment	(520.00)					
Scrap proceeds					50.00	
Tax-allowable depreciation			39.00	29.25	21.94	50.81
Net cash flows	(520.00)	268.80	227.16	217.41	(8.70)	50.81
DF@ 10%	1.000	0.909	0.826	0.751	0.683	0.621
PV	(520.00)	244.34	187.63	163.27	(5.94)	31.55

NPV = $100,850

(b) The NPV is greater than zero, suggesting the project should be accepted.

The problem is the payback period = 2 years 1 month (W), which is slightly outside the company's target payback period.

Working

(W) After two years, cash inflow is $495,960. Another $24,040 is required for payback. In the third year, time to recover investment = 24/217 × 12 = 1.3 months.

Despite the project exceeding the normal payback period of two years, the project should be accepted. There is a predicted NPV of $100,850 – a good return on the investment.

One reservation is that the company is purchasing a product specific machine with a capacity far in excess of requirement. They would be advised to find a cheaper machine with lower capacity, which may give a better return.

12 – NPV with tax and inflation I

(a) **Calculation of net present value**

Year	0	1	2	3	4
	$	$	$	$	$
Total contribution		287,000	445,200	645,750	317,160
Taxation		(86,100)	(133,560)	(193,725)	(95,148)
Tax-allowable depreciation tax benefit		75,000	75,000	75,000	75,000
Initial investment	(1,000,000)				
Working capital	(50,960)	(29,287)	(37,878)	59,157	58,968
Net cash flows	(1,050,960)	246,613	348,762	586,182	355,980
Discount factor at 12%	1.000	0.893	0.797	0.712	0.636
Present value	(1,050,960)	220,225	277,963	417,362	226,403

NPV = $90,993. The positive NPV indicates that the investment is financially acceptable.

Workings

Sales revenue

Year	1	2	3	4
Selling price ($/unit)	20.80	21.63	22.50	23.40
Variable cost ($/unit)	12.60	13.23	13.89	14.59
Contribution ($/unit)	8.20	8.40	8.61	8.81
Sales (units/year)	35,000	53,000	75,000	36,000
Total contribution ($/year)	287,000	445,200	645,750	317,160

Total investment in working capital

Year 0 investment =	$20.80 × 35,000 × 0.07 =	$50,960
Year 1 investment =	$21.63 × 53,000 × 0.07 =	$80,247
Year 2 investment =	$22.50 × 75,000 × 0.07 =	$118,125
Year 3 investment =	$23.40 × 36,000 × 0.07 =	$58,968

Incremental investment in working capital

Year 0 investment =	$20.80 × 35,000 × 0.07 =	$50,960
Year 1 investment =	$80,247 – $50,960 =	$29,287
Year 2 investment =	$118,125 – $80,247 =	$37,878
Year 3 recovery =	$58,968 – $118,125	$59,157
Year 4 recovery =	$58,968	

(b) **Acceptability of the proposed investment in Product P**

The NPV is positive and so the proposed investment can be recommended on financial grounds as it should increase shareholder value.

Limitations of the investment evaluations

The NPV evaluation is heavily dependent on the production and sales volumes that have been forecast and so SC Co should investigate the key assumptions underlying these forecast volumes. It is difficult to forecast the length and features of a product's life cycle so there is likely to be a degree of uncertainty associated with the forecast sales volumes. This is particularly true given the short product life-cycle due to rapidly changing technology.

Scenario analysis may be of assistance here in providing information on other possible outcomes to the proposed investment.

The inflation rates for selling price per unit and variable cost per unit have been assumed to be constant in future periods. In reality, interaction between a range of economic and other forces influencing selling price per unit and variable cost per unit will lead to unanticipated changes in both of these project variables. The assumption of constant inflation rates limits the accuracy of the investment evaluations and could be an important consideration if the investment were only marginally acceptable.

Since no increase in fixed costs is expected because SC Co has spare capacity in both space and labour terms, fixed costs are not relevant to the evaluation and have been omitted. No information has been offered on whether the spare capacity exists in future periods as well as in the current period. Since production of Product P is expected to more than double over three years, future capacity needs should be assessed before a decision is made to proceed, in order to determine whether any future incremental fixed costs may arise.

13 – NPV with tax and inflation II

(a) **NPV calculation for Alpha and Beta**

Year	1	2	3	4
	$	$	$	$
Sales revenue	3,585,000	6,769,675	6,339,000	1,958,775
Material cost	(1,395,000)	(2,634,225)	(2,446,750)	(761,925)
Fixed cost	(1,000,000)	(1,050,000)	(1,102,500)	(1,157,625)
Advertising	(500,000)	(200,000)	(200,000)	
Taxable profit	690,000	2,885,450	2,569,750	39,225
Taxation	(172,500)	(721,362)	(642,438)	(9,806)
Tax-allowable depreciation tax benefit	250,000			
Fixed asset sale				1,200,000
Working capital recovery				1,000,000
Net cash flow	767,500	2,164,088	1,927,312	2,229,419
Discount factor at 13%	0.885	0.783	0.693	0.613
Present value	679,237	1,694,481	1,335,626	1,366,634

	$
Sum of present values	5,075,978
Initial investment	3,000,000
Net present value	2,075,978

The positive NPV indicates that the investment is financially acceptable.

Workings

Alpha sales revenue

Year	1	2	3	4
Selling price ($/unit)	31.00	31.93	32.89	33.88
Sales (units/year)	60,000	110,000	100,000	30,000
Sales revenue ($/year)	1,860,000	3,512,300	3,289,000	1,016,400
Beta sales revenue				
Selling price ($/unit)	23.00	23.69	24.40	25.13
Sales (units/year)	75,000	137,500	125,000	37,500
Sales revenue ($/year)	1,725,000	3,257,375	3,050,000	942,375
Total sales revenue ($/year)	3,585,000	6,769,675	6,339,000	1,958,775

Alpha direct material cost

Year	1	2	3	4
Material cost ($/unit)	12.00	12.36	12.73	13.11
Sales (units/year)	60,000	110,000	100,000	30,000
Material cost ($/year)	720,000	1,359,600	1,273,000	393,300
Beta sales revenue				
Material cost ($/unit)	9.00	9.27	9.55	9.83
Sales (units/year)	75,000	137,500	125,000	37,500
Material cost ($/year)	675,000	1,274,625	1,193,750	368,625
Total direct material cost ($/year)	1,395,000	2,634,225	2,466,750	761,925

(b) The evaluation assumes that several key variables will remain constant, such as the discount rate, inflation rates and the taxation rate. In practice this is unlikely. The taxation rate is a matter of government policy and so may change due to political or economic necessity.

Specific inflation rates are difficult to predict for more than a short distance into the future and in practice are found to be constantly changing. The range of inflation rates used in the evaluation is questionable, since over time one would expect the rates to converge.

Given the uncertainty of future inflation rates, using a single average inflation rate might well be preferable to using specific inflation rates.

The discount rate is likely to change as the company's capital structure changes. For example, if the company was to fund this investment entirely via debt or equity finance, the gearing of the company will change.

Looking at the incremental fixed production costs, it seems odd that nominal fixed production costs continue to increase even when sales are falling. It also seems odd that incremental fixed production costs remain constant in real terms when production volumes are changing. It is possible that some of these fixed production costs are stepped, in which case they should decrease.

The forecasts of sales volume seem to be too precise, predicting as they do the growth, maturity and decline phases of the product life-cycle. In practice it is likely that improvements or redesign could extend the life of the two products beyond five years. The assumption of constant product mix seems unrealistic, as the products are substitutes and it is possible that one will be relatively more successful. The sales price has been raised in line with inflation, but a lower sales price could be used in the decline stage to encourage sales.

Net working capital is to remain constant in real terms. In practice, the level of working capital will depend on the working capital policies of the company, the value of goods, the credit offered to customers, the credit taken from suppliers and so on. It is unlikely that the constant real value will be maintained.

The net present value is heavily dependent on the terminal value derived from the sale of non-current assets after five years. It is unlikely that this value will be achieved in practice. It is also possible that the machinery can be used to produce other products, rather than be used solely to produce Alpha and Beta.

14 – Lease v buy

(a) **Lease v buy decision**

	Year 0	1	2	3	4	5
Buy:	$	$	$	$	$	$
Asset purchase	(50,000)					
Tax-allowable depreciation (W1)			4,375	3,281	2,461	7,383
Net cash flows	(50,000)	0	4,375	3,281	2,461	7,383
Discount factor at 7.15% (W2)	1.000	0.933	0.871	0.813	0.759	0.708
Present value	(50,000)	0	3,811	2,667	1,868	5,227

Net present value = ($36,427)

	Year 0	1	2	3	4	5
Lease:	$	$	$	$	$	$
Lease payments	(15,000)	(15,000)	(15,000)	(15,000)		
Tax relief on lease			5,250	5,250	5,250	5,250
Net cash flows	(15,000)	(15,000)	(9,750)	(9,750)	5,250	5,250
Discount factor @ 7.15% (W2)	1.000	0.933	0.871	0.813	0.759	0.708
Present value	(15,000)	(13,995)	(8,492)	(7,927)	3,985	3,717

Net present value = ($37,712)

Both net present values are negative as we are just looking at the costs of financing the projects. As the net present value of the buying option is less negative, it appears that the purchase of the machine is the recommended alternative.

Note: the operating and working capital cash flows will be the same irrespective of whether or not he machine is leased or bought, so are not relevant/incremental.

Workings

(W1)

Time		**$**	**Tax saving @ 35%**	**Timing of tax relief**
T_0	Initial investment	50,000		
T_1	Tax-allowable depreciation @ 25%	(12,500)	4,375	T_2
	Written down value	37,500		
T_2	Tax-allowable depreciation @ 25%	(9,375)	3,281	T_3
	Written down value	28,125		
T_3	Tax-allowable depreciation @ 25%	(7,031)	2,461	T_4
	Written down value	21,094		
T_4	Sale proceeds	(0)		
T_4	BA	21,094	7,383	T_5

(W2)

The discount rate is the after-tax cost of the equivalent loan, 11% (1-0.35) = 7.15%.

(b) **Discount rate**

The choice of discount rates in lease versus buy analysis is contentious.

The approach used here is to regard the lease as an alternative to purchasing the machine using debt finance. The discount rate is, therefore, the amount that the company would have to pay on a secured loan on the machine, the loan being repayable on the terms that are implicit in the lease rental schedule.

This discount rate is only likely to be valid if leases and loans are regarded by investors as being equivalent, and all cash flows are equally risky.

15 – Replacement analysis

Two-year cycle for replacement: (Cash flows are inflated according to their individual inflation rates)

Year	**0**	**1**	**2**
	$	$	$
Original cost	24,500		
Maintenance		550	968
Resale values			(17,199)
Net total cost	24,500	550	(16,231)
Discount factor at 15%	1.000	0.870	0.756
Present value	24,500	479	(12,271)

Net present value of costs = $12,708

Equivalent annual cost = 12,708/(annuity factor at 15% for two years) = 12,708/1.626 = 7,815.

Three-year cycle for replacement: (Cash flows are inflated according to their individual inflation rates)

Year	**0**	**1**	**2**	**3**
	$	$	$	$
Original cost	24,500			
Maintenance		550	968	1,997
Resale values				(12,965)
Net total cost	24,500	550	968	(10,968)
Discount factor at 15%	1.000	0.870	0.756	0.658
Present value	24,500	479	732	(7,217)

Net present value of costs = $18,494

Equivalent annual cost = 18,494/(annuity factor at 15% for three years) = 18,494/2.283 = 8,101.

The conclusion is that a two-year replacement cycle is preferable.

16 – Capital rationing

(a) **Ranking of projects:**

Rank	Project	NPV
		$
1	D	8,356
2	A	6,350
3	E	5,490
4	F	4,993
5	B	1,882
6	C	(2,596)

(b) **Profitability index is:**

Project	Initial outlay	NPV	Profitability index (NPV / outlay)
	$	$	
A	(246,000)	6,350	0.0258
B	(180,000)	1,882	0.0105
C	(175,000)	(2,596)	(0.0148)
D	(180,000)	8,356	0.0464
E	(180,000)	5,490	0.0305
F	(150,000)	4,993	0.0333

Ranking of projects:

Rank	Project
1	D
2	F
3	E
4	A
5	B
6	C

The money should therefore be invested as follows:

Project	Initial investment	NPV
D (Ranked 1)	$180,000	$8,356
F (Ranked 2)	$150,000	$4,993
E (Ranked 3)	$180,000	$5,490
A (ignored since A & E are mutually exclusive)		
Total	$510,000	
B (Ranked 5) (Note 1)	$110,000	$1,150
C	$620,000	$19,989

Note 1: At this point there is only $110,000 left to invest. This will therefore be invested into part of project B. Given that only $110k out of $180k is being invested, the return generated will only be $1,150 ($1,882 × $110k ÷ $180k)

The rankings differ from (a) because NPV is an absolute measure whereas the profitability index is a relative measure that takes into account the different investment cost of each project.

(c) The objective is to select a combination of investments that will maximise NPV subject to a total capital outlay of $620,000. Projects A and E are mutually exclusive, and project C has a negative NPV. The following are potential combinations of projects:

Project combinations	Total outlay	NPV	Total NPV
	$	$	$
A, B, D	(606,000)	6,350 + 1,882 + 8,356	16,588
A, B, F	(576,000)	6,350 + 1,882 + 4,993	13,225
A, D, F	(576,000)	6,350 + 8,356 + 4,993	19,699*
B, D, E	(540,000)	1,882 + 8,356 + 5,490	15,728
B, D, F	(510,000)	1,882 + 8,356 + 4,993	15,231
D, E, F	(510,000)	8,356 + 5,490 + 4,993	18,839

* Best option

Note: It is not possible to combine four projects within the constraints outlined above, and expected NPV cannot be increased by combining two projects.

Accepting projects A, D and F will maximise NPV

This combination will require a total capital outlay of $576,000, and the unused funds will be invested to yield a return of 9%. Since the money market is an efficient market, the NPV of funds invested here will be zero.

(d) Risk and uncertainty may be considered in several ways. For example:

Adding a risk premium to the discount rate

A premium may be added to the usual discount rate to provide a safety margin. Marginally profitable projects (perhaps the riskiest) are less likely to have a positive NPV. The premium may vary from project to project to reflect the different levels of risk.

Payback period

Estimates of cash flows several years ahead are quite likely to be inaccurate and unreliable. It may be difficult to control capital projects over a long period of time. Risk may be limited by selecting projects with short payback periods.

Sensitivity analysis

Sensitivity analysis typically involves posing 'what if' questions. For example, what if demand fell by 10%, selling price was decreased by 5%, etc. Alternatively, we may wish to discover the maximum possible change in one of the parameters before the project is no longer viable. This would be calculated for each input individually to identify which estimates are most important and hence where potential errors pose the most risk.

Using probability distributions

A probability distribution of expected cash flows may be determined, and hence the expected NPV (EV) may be found together with risk analysis e.g. best possible outcome, worst possible outcome, probability of a negative NPV.

A more sophisticated measure of risk is to calculate the standard deviation. This considers the degree of dispersion of the different possible NPVs around the expected NPV. The greater the spread of outcomes around the expected NPV, the higher the potential risk.

The coefficient of variation should be calculated to compare projects.

17 – Expected values

(a) The expected present value of the fines is equal to:

EV = (0.3 × \$1.0m) + (0.5 × \$1.8m) + (0.2 × \$2.6m) = \$0.3m + \$0.9m + \$0.52m = \$1.72 million.

Calculation of the net present value of the investment requires computation of the capital cost plus incremental production costs as set out in the following table:

Year	0	1	2	3	4
	\$m	\$m	\$m	\$m	\$m
Equipment purchase	(4.0)				
European Union grant (25% of cost)		1.000			
Increased production costs		(0.315)	(0.331)	(0.347)	
Tax saving at 30%			0.095	0.099	0.104
Tax savings on tax-allowable depreciation (see note 3 below)		0.300	0.225	0.169	0.506
Net cash flow	(4.0)	0.985	(0.011)	(0.079)	0.610
Discount factor at 10%	1.000	0.909	0.826	0.751	0.683
Present value of cash flow	(4.0)	0.895	(0.009)	(0.059)	0.417
Net Present Value = (\$2.756m)					

Notes:

(1) The consultant's charge has already been incurred and (as a committed cost) is therefore irrelevant to the current cecision.

(2) Increased production costs

Year	**Sales**	**Extra production costs (2%)**
	\$m	\$m
1	15.750	0.315
2	16.538	0.331
3	17.364	0.347

(3) **Tax-allowable depreciation:**

Year	Written down value	Tax-allowable depreciation (25%)	Tax saved (one year in arrears, at 30%)
0	4.00	1.000	0.300
1	3.00	0.750	0.225
2	2.25	0.563	0.169
3	1.687 (balance)	0.506	

The negative NPV on the investment in spray painting equipment exceeds the present value of the fines which Sludgewater might expect to pay. It therefore seems that the project is not viable in financial terms, and it would be cheaper to risk payment of the fines.

(b) The limitations of the approach used in part (a) include the following:

Limitations of expected values

There are three main problems with the use of expected values for making investment decisions:

(i) The investment may only occur once. It is certainly very unlikely that there will be the opportunity to repeat the investment many times. The average of the anticipated returns will thus not be observed.

(ii) Attaching probabilities to events is a highly subjective process.

(iii) The expected value does not evaluate the range of possible NPV outcomes.

Objectives

By focussing on the net present value, we are assuming that the primary objective is to maximise shareholder value. However, it can be argued that Sludgewater has a moral and community responsibility to install anti-pollution equipment as long as the cost of installation does not jeopardise the long-term survival of the company.

In addition, the company needs to think about its long-term strategic objectives, and its stance on anti-pollution systems in relation to these objectives. The market positioning of the company over the longer term is likely to be affected by decisions made in the short term, and so even if not investing in the project makes short-term financial sense, it may be more attractive from a long-term viewpoint.

It is also possible that technological and legal circumstances will change over time, and such changes need to be anticipated in current decisions.

Limitations in the figures used

The figures above suggest that the project is not wealth-creating for Sludgewater's shareholders, because the value of the expected saving in fines ($1.72 million) is below the expected cost of the project ($2.756 million). However, if the level of fines were to rise substantially, then the optimal choice (in financial terms) might change. Given the company is a persistent offender, and the green lobby is becoming more influential, it is not unreasonable to anticipate that the fines will rise in the future as a result of political pressure.

Note: While not explicitly asked for, sensitivity analysis would be a useful tool here:

The difference between the expected value of the fines and the cost of the project is currently just over $1 million. This means that the fines would need to rise by nearly 60% (1/1.72 × 100) before the project becomes financially worthwhile. Changes in the size of the fines would be very difficult to predict as it is a political issue.

18 – Sensitivity analysis

(a) **NPV @ 15%**

Year	**Narrative**	**Cash flow**	**DF @ 15%**	**PV**
		$000		$000
0	Deposit	(1,000)	1.000	(1,000)
0	Sales proceeds foregone	(100)	1.000	(100)
2	Instalment	(1,000)	0.756	(756)
2 – 11	Contribution	600	4.367 (W1)	2,620
1 – 10	Service costs	(50)	5.019	(251)
10	Scrap proceeds	200	0.247	49
				562

Since the NPV is positive, the project should be accepted.

(W1) AF 2–11 = AF 1–10 × DF 1 yr
= 5.019 × 0.870
= 4.367

(W2) AF 2-11 = AF 1-10 × DF 1 yr
= 4.192 × 0.833
= 3.492

$$IRR = 15 + \frac{562}{562 - 123} \times (20 - 15) = 21.4\%$$

(f) **Sensitivity**

(i) **the required rate of return**

$$\frac{21.4\% - 15\%}{15\%} \times 100\% = 42.7\%$$

(ii) **the selling price per unit**

The relevant cash flow affected is the present value of sales revenue. This equals:

$750 × 4,000 units × AF2-11

= $750 × 4,000 × 4.367 = $13,101k.

Therefore:

$$\frac{\$562k}{\$13,101k} \times 100\% = 4.3\%$$

(iii) **the level of demand**

The relevant cash flow affected is the present value of contribution. Therefore:

$$\frac{\$562k}{\$600k \times 4.367} \times 100\% = 21.4\%$$

(iv) **Comment on the sensitivities calculated.**

The actual return is 42.7% higher than the estimated cost of capital. This suggests there is ample buffer and should not be a cause of concern.

The level of demand could fall by 21.4% (from 4,000 units per annum to 3,142) before the project would no longer be worthwhile. Whilst this may seem like a relatively high margin of safety, stoves are a luxury product and will be more likely to suffer a drop in demand during economic downturns. It is therefore suggested that the market research is thoroughly reviewed to ensure the reasonableness of the conclusions drawn.

The greatest concern is over the selling price. If this fell by more than 4.3% (from $750 to just $718), the project would no longer be worthwhile. Again, it is recommended that the market research report is revisited in an attempt to assess the probability of this happening.

19 – Cash operating cycle

(a) **Cash operating cycle**

		20X1	**20X0**
Inventory days (W1)	(365 × 9.5)/80.3		43 days
	(365 × 22)/122.5	66 days	
Receivables days	(365 × 10.8)/89		44 days
	(365 × 21.0)/131	59 days	
Payables days (W1)	(365 × 8.2)/80.3		(37 days)
	(365 × 20.5)/122.5	(61 days)	
Length of operating cycle		64 days	50 days

(W1) **Cost of sales**

Assuming that cost of sales is the difference between sales and operating profit
20X1: = $131m – $8.5m = $122.5m
20X0: = $89m – $8.7m = $80.3m

Other relevant Financial analysis

		20X1	20X0
Current ratio	20.5/12.4		1.65 times
	43.0/33.6	1.28 times	
Quick ratio	11.0/12.4		0.89 times
	21.0/33.6	0.63 times	
Sales / net working capital	89/8.1		11 times
	131/9.4	14 times	
Revenue increase	131/89	47%	
Non-current assets increase	30.8/26.4	17%	
Inventory increase	22.0/9.5	132%	
Receivables increase	21.0/9.5	94%	
Payables increase	20.5/8.2	150%	
Overdraft increase	13.1/4.2	212%	

Discussion

Overtrading or undercapitalisation arises when a company has too small a capital base to support its level of business activity. Difficulties with liquidity may arise as an overtrading company may have insufficient capital to meet its liabilities as they fall due. Overtrading is often associated with a rapid increase in revenue and Cloud Co has experienced a 47% increase in revenue over the last year. Investment in working capital has not matched the increase in sales, however, since the sales/net working capital ratio has increased from 11 times to 14 times.

Overtrading could be indicated by a deterioration in inventory days. Here, inventory days have increased from 43 days to 66 days, while inventory has increased by 132% compared to the 47% increase in revenue. It is possible that inventory has been stockpiled in anticipation of a further increase in revenue, leading to an increase in operating costs.

Overtrading could also be indicated by deterioration in receivables days. In this case, receivables have increased by 94% compared to the 47% increase in revenue. The increase in revenue may have been fuelled in part by a relaxation of credit terms.

As the liquidity problem associated with overtrading deepens, the overtrading company increases its reliance on short-term sources of finance, including overdraft and trade payables. The overdraft of Cloud Co has more than doubled in size to $13.1 million, while trade payables have increased by $12.3 million or 150%. Both increases are much greater than the 47% increase in revenue. There is evidence here of an increased reliance on short-term finance sources.

Overtrading can also be indicated by decreases in the current ratio and the quick ratio. The current ratio of Cloud Co has fallen from 1.65 times to 1.28 times, while its quick ratio has fallen from 0.89 times to 0.63 times.

There are clear indications that Cloud Co is experiencing the kinds of symptoms usually associated with overtrading. A more complete and meaningful analysis could be undertaken if appropriate benchmarks were available, such as key ratios from comparable companies in the same industry sector, or additional financial information from prior years so as to establish trends in key ratios.

(b) **Current funding problems**

Cloud Co needs to re-organise the funding of its business in a way which reduces its exposure to short-term debt. This could be done either by converting the bank overdraft into a long-term loan or by increasing the equity investment.

Conversion of the overdraft would alter the overall level of financial gearing within the business and so would bring some additional risks for both equity investors and suppliers. Increasing the equity investment is the better alternative. The issued share capital is low given the current level of sales. However, the ability of Cloud to do this will depend on whether the existing shareholders are willing to invest more money or whether new shareholders could be found.

At the same time, Cloud could look carefully at its current levels of working capital and aim to reduce the level of inventory and receivables as a means of releasing capital. In 20X1, receivables and inventory levels stood at 16.0% and 16.8% of sales value respectively. If the 20X0 levels had been maintained (12.1% and 10.7%), the company's investment in these two current assets could have been reduced from $43m to $30m, a saving of $13m. The cash freed up by tighter working capital controls may then provide sufficient capital to pay for further sales expansion in the future, without the need to look for additional outside funding.

Additionally the company could restrict further growth in order to avoid overtrading.

Cloud would appear to have exhausted its sources of working capital, and any further increases in sales would therefore place the company under a great cash strain. By reorganising its financing, and increasing the long-term equity investment, Cloud could regain access to additional short-term borrowing, and so avoid the risk of overtrading.

20 – Receivables management I

(a) **Factoring**

Reduction in receivables days	=15 days	
Reduction in receivables	= 15 ÷ 365 × $20m =	$821,916
Effect on profit before tax:		
Finance cost saving	= (13% × $821,916) =	$106,849
Administrative savings	=	$200,000
Service charge	= (1% × $20m) =	($200,000)
Insurance premium	=	($80,000)
Net profit benefit	=	$26,849

(b) The factoring calculation relies on the factor lowering Marton Co's receivables days. If the factor retains these benefits for itself, rather than passing them on to Marton Co, this will raise the cost of the factoring option. The two parties should clearly specify their mutual requirements from the factoring arrangement on a contractual basis.

There is also a risk that some customers may view the factoring arrangement as an indication that Marton Co is having financial difficulties and so may be reluctant to trade going forwards.

21 – Receivables management II

(a) **The discount**

With year-end receivables at $4.5 million, the receivables collection period was: $4.5m ÷ $20m × 365 = 82 days.

The scheme of discounts would change this as follows:

10 days for 20% of customers

20 days for 30% of customers

82 days for 50% of customers

Average receivables days become:

(20% × 10) + (30% × 20) + (50% × 82) = 49 days

Hence, average receivables would reduce from the present $4.5 million to:

49 × $20m ÷ 365 = $2,684,932

Finance cost saving = 13% × ($4.5m – $2.685m) = $235,950

The cost of the discount:

(3% × 20% × $20m) + (1.5% × 30% × $20m) = ($210,000)

The net benefit to profit before tax: $25,950

(b) This result relies on the predicted proportions of customers actually taking up the discount and paying on time. It also neglects the possibility that some customers will insist on taking the discount without bringing forward their payments. Marton Co would have to consider a suitable response to this problem.

22 – Inventory and cash management

(a) **Revert to standard terms on payment of supplier**

Cost = lost discount.
\$6m × 1.5% = \$90,000

Benefit = increase in payables balance leading to reduction in overdraft and savings in interest payable
Current payables balance = 10 ÷ 365 × \$6m = \$164,384
Revised payables balance = 45 ÷ 365 × \$6m = \$739,726
Increase in payables (reduction in overdraft) = \$575,342
Saving in overdraft interest = \$575,342 × 15% = \$86,301

Net reduction in profitability = \$90,000 – \$86,301 = \$3,699

(b) **Reduce number of units per order**

Cost per unit = \$500,000 ÷ 100,000 = \$5 per unit

Under the current policy of ordering 100,000 units per order, the average inventory level of raw materials would be:
100,000 ÷ 2 × \$5 = \$250,000

Theory suggests that the order quantity should be reduced to the economic order quantity (EOQ)
CO = \$500
CH = \$3.00
D = 100,000 × 12 = 1,200,000 units p.a.
EOQ = $\sqrt{((2 \times \$500 \times 1{,}200{,}000) \div \$3.00)}$
EOQ = 20,000 units

If the quantity per order was reduced to the EOQ, average inventory levels would fall to:
20,000 ÷ 2 × \$5 = \$50,000

This would give a net reduction in the level of inventory (and therefore a decrease in the overdraft balance) of \$250,000 – \$50,000 = \$200,000

This in turn would save interest of \$200,000 × 15% = \$30,000

The specific costs associated with inventory would alter as follows:

	Old policy		New policy	
		$		$
Ordering costs	(1,200,000 ÷ 100,000 × $500)	6,000	(1,200,000 ÷ 20,000 × $500)	30,000
Holding costs	(100,000 ÷ 2 × $3.00)	150,000	(20,000 ÷ 2 × $3.00)	30,000
		–––––		–––––
Total costs		156,000		60,000

This is a reduction in inventory costs of $96,000 and an overall net increase in profitability of $126,000.

(c) **The role of banks**

The role of banks as financial intermediaries is to provide short-term finance for use by business organisations by providing a link between investors who have surplus cash and borrowers who have financing needs.

The banking crisis began in early 2008 and resulted in a loss in confidence in the banking system, causing many banks to suffer a run on their reserves, meaning the cash reserve ratio was insufficient to cover the demand from investors to withdraw cash.

This in turn led to the so called 'credit crunch', a financial crisis where banks refused to issue credit or, where they would lend, they charged very high interest rates.

Even though governments and central banks around the world have taken steps to restore confidence and liquidity, there is still some way to go before lending policies reach the relaxed state prior to the banking crisis. It is therefore not unusual even now for banks to reassess their lending and, at times tighten policies.

23 – Cash management I

(a) **Cash Budget for Thorne Co:**

	January	**February**	**March**	**April**
Receipts	$	$	$	$
Cash fees	18,000	27,000	45,000	54,000
Credit fees	36,000	36,000	54,000	90,000
Sale of assets				20,000
Total receipts	54,000	63,000	99,000	164,000
Payments				
Salaries	26,250	26,250	26,250	26,250
Bonus			6,300	12,600
Expenses	9,000	13,500	22,500	27,000
Fixed overheads	4,300	4,300	4,300	4,300
Taxation				95,800
Interest			3,000	
Total payments	39,550	44,050	62,350	165,950
Net cash flow	14,450	18,950	36,650	(1,950)
Opening balance	(40,000)	(25,550)	(6,600)	30,050
Closing balance	(25,550)	(6,600)	30,050	28,100

Workings

Month	**December**	**January**	**February**	**March**	**April**
Units sold	10	10	15	25	30
Sales value ($000)	1,800	1,800	2,700	4,500	5,400
Cash fees at 1% ($)	18,000	18,000	27,000	45,000	54,000
Credit fees at 2% ($)	36,000	36,000	54,000	90,000	108,000
Variable costs at 0.5% ($)		9,000	13,500	22,500	27,000

Monthly salary cost = (35,000 × 9)/12 = $26,250

Bonus for March = (25 – 20) × 140 × 9 = $6,300 Bonus for April = (30 – 20) × 140 × 9 = $12,600.

(b) The Baumol model is derived from the EOQ model and can be applied in situations where there is a constant demand for cash or cash disbursements. Regular transfers are made from interest-bearing short-term investments or cash deposits into a current account. The Baumol model considers the annual demand for cash (D), the cost of each cash transfer (C), and the interest difference between the rate paid on short-term investments (r_1) and the rate paid on a current account (r_2), in order to calculate the optimum amount of funds to transfer (F). The model is as follows.

$$F = ((2 \times D \times C)/(r_1 - r_2))^{0 \cdot 5}$$

By optimising the amount of funds to transfer, the Baumol model minimises the opportunity cost of holding cash in the current account, thereby reducing the costs of cash management.

However, the Baumol model is unlikely to be of assistance to Thorne Co because of the assumptions underlying its formulation. Constant annual demand for cash is assumed, whereas its cash budget suggests that Thorne Co has a varying need for cash. The model assumes that each interest rate and the cost of each cash transfer are constant and known with certainty. In reality interest rates and transactions costs are not constant and interest rates, in particular, can change frequently. A cash management model which can accommodate a variable demand for cash, such as the Miller-Orr model, may be more suited to the needs of the company.

24 – Cash management II

(a) **Reasons for cash behaviour**

Deficit

Grudem Co clearly experiences seasonal trends in its business - toy sales are higher in the run up to Christmas.

This results in large cash outflows in November and December, made more pronounced as

- Large high street retailers are likely to take months to pay Grudem.
- Grudem's business model of boosting production just before Christmas makes the cash outflow more severe.
- Grudem is seeing its business grow.

Surplus

Once Grudem gets to February and March production costs are lower and it will start receiving cash from large high street customers, resulting in the large surplus.

(b) **Dealing with a surplus**

Based on the argument above, a significant proportion of any cash surplus is therefore likely to be short-term in nature.

Short-term cash surpluses should be invested with no risk of capital loss. This limitation means that appropriate investments include treasury bills, short-dated gilts, public authority bonds, certificates of deposit and bank deposits.

When choosing between these instruments Grudem Co will consider the length of time the surplus is available for, the size of the surplus (some instruments have minimum investment levels), the yield offered, the risk associated with each instrument, and any penalties for early withdrawal.

A small company like Grudem Co is likely to find bank deposits the most convenient method for investing short-term cash surpluses, although the sums involved also make certificates of deposit attractive.

The company must also consider how to invest longer-term surpluses. As a new company Grudem Co is likely to want to invest surplus funds in expanding its business, but as a small company it is likely to find few sources of funds other than bank debt and retained earnings. There is therefore a need to guard against capital loss when investing cash that is intended to fund expansion at a later date.

(c) **Dealing with a cash deficit**

In the two months before Christmas Grudem Co has a cash deficit, with the highest cash deficit being $100,000. This cash deficit would most likely be financed by an overdraft.

An advantage of an overdraft is that it is a flexible source of finance, since it can be used as and when required, provided that the overdraft limit is not exceeded. In addition, Grudem Co will only have to pay interest on the amount of the overdraft facility used, with the interest being charged at a variable rate linked to bank base rate.

A disadvantage of an overdraft is that it is repayable on demand, although in practice notice is given of the intention to withdraw the facility. The interest payment may also increase, since the company is exposed to the risk of an interest rates increase. Banks usually ask for some form of security, such as a floating charge on the company's assets or a personal guarantee from a company's owners, in order to reduce the risk associated with their lending.

25 – Forex risk I

(a) The methods that could be used to forecast future exchange rates include:

PPPT – Purchasing Power Parity Theory – This states that the future spot rate between two currencies is a function of the current spot rate and the differential in the inflation rates between the two countries. It is often called 'the law of one price' as it assumes that an item will always cost the same in all markets. Hence where inflation rates differ between countries the exchange rate will move to eliminate any price difference caused by the differential inflation rates.

IRPT – Interest Rate Parity Theory – This states that the forward rate between two currencies is a function of the current spot rate and the differential in the interest rates between the two countries. Although the theory calculates the forward rate this is thought to be an unbiased predictor of the future spot rate.

Forward rate & forecast future spot rate:
1.200 Euro/£ x (1 + 0.04)/(1 + 0.03) = 1.212 Euro/£

(b) Simple techniques the company could use include:

- Dealing only in pounds. This would involve insisting that all overseas customers are invoiced in and pay in pound sterling and that all overseas suppliers invoice in and accept receipts in pound sterling. Whilst this would pass all the forex risk to the overseas customers and suppliers, this method may well not be acceptable to them.
- Netting off. This would involve the company netting off Euro amounts due from overseas customers against Euro amounts payable at the same point in time to the German supplier. For instance if FRQ Co expects to receive €230,000 in 4 months but also expects to have to pay €190,000 in 4 months then the payment can be entirely funded from the receipt and only the net receipt of €40,000 needs to be hedged. Indeed if the €40,000 is not considered material the company may decide not to hedge.

(c)

One year forward rate – 1.212 Euro/£ +/- 0.0010
One year forward rate spread – 1.202 – 1.222 Euro/£

Forward market hedge:
€280,000/1.222 = £229,133 receipt in one year

Money market hedge:
Have a Euro asset so therefore a matching Euro liability is created.
Borrow sufficient Euros so that in one year €280,000 is owed.
280,000/1.04 = €269,231
Convert the Euros borrowed into £ immediately.
Spot spread – 1.195 – 1.205 Euro/£
€269,231/1.205 = £223,428 receipt
Calculate the equivalent £ receipt in one year.
(assume the company has cash balances)
£223,428 × 1.01 = £225,662 receipt

Recommendation – the forward market hedge should be used as it will produce the biggest receipt in £ and it is the simplest to do.

26 – Forex risk II

(a) (i) **Economic risk**

Economic risk is the variation in the value of the business (i.e. the present value of future cash flows) due to unexpected changes in exchange rates. It has a long-term impact.

For an export company it could occur because:

- the home currency strengthens against the currency in which it trades
- a competitor's home currency weakens against the currency in which it trades.

Toytown would face problems if the Australian dollar strengthens against the other local currencies. The company would then have to consider either decreasing the profit margin on products, or increasing the sales price to maintain profit levels. The second option could result in a loss of sales. The likelihood of this would be increased if Toytown faced more competition from local companies who are not exposed to the same risk.

(ii) **Translation risk**

Translation risk is an accounting risk rather than a cash-based one. It arises when the reported performance of an overseas subsidiary is translated into the home-based currency terms in order that they can be consolidated into the group's financial statements and is distorted because of a change in exchange rates.

Unless managers believe that the company's share price will fall as a result of showing a translation exposure loss in the company's accounts, translation exposure will not normally be hedged. The company's share price, in an efficient market, should only react to exposure that is likely to have an impact on cash flows.

In the case of Toytown, if the subsidiary company were established, a variation in the Australian dollar to US dollar exchange rate would cause a variation in the reported valuation of the subsidiary. For example, if the Australian dollar strengthened against the US dollar, the reported value of the subsidiary would decrease.

(iii) **Transaction risk**

Transaction risk is the risk of an exchange rate changing between the transaction date and the subsequent settlement date, i.e. it is the gain or loss arising on conversion. This type of risk is primarily associated with imports and exports. If a company exports goods on credit then it has a figure for receivables in its accounts. The amount it will finally receive depends on the foreign exchange movement from the transaction date to the settlement date.

Transaction risk has a potential impact on the cash flows of a company. The degree of exposure involved is dependent on:

- the size of the transaction (is it material?)
- the time period before the expected cash flows occurs
- the anticipated volatility of the exchange rates.

In the case of Toytown, if the Australian dollar strengthens against the US dollar during the six weeks before it pays the supplier for purchases from the USA, the company will make a gain. If the Australian dollar strengthens against local currencies before it is paid by customers, the company will make a loss.

(b) Factors which Toytown will need to consider include:

- the cost of different options, for example, this would be lower for a forward exchange contract than for currency options
- the expertise of staff and the capacity of the company's management to arrange and manage different means of hedging
- whether receipts and payments in US dollars are likely to coincide enough for them to be matched
- how reliably the company can predict payment dates from customers – they have control over payment dates to the US supplier
- the likely volatility of exchange rates – the company needs to try to predict them as accurately as possible
- the availability of different methods – whether all products are available for all currencies.
- The risk appetite of the company - for example, would it prefer to fix the future cash flow or pay extra for currency options and still be open to the potential for exchange gains?

If the company does set up a subsidiary as planned, then it may be possible to match US dollar transactions if these become stable and predictable. However, in the early stages of a new business they are likely to be less predictable and matching may not be possible.

At the current time the company is able to forecast the timing of receipts and payments so forward contracts are likely to be the most suitable method. They should be available in most of the currencies the company deals in and are easy for staff to understand.

If in the future cash flows become uncertain, the company may want to reconsider the use of currency options.

27 – Forex risk III

(i) **Leading and lagging**

Leading and lagging are means used to alter the time period between the transaction and settlement dates to avoid exchange rate losses or increase the likelihood of a gain.

If an exporter expects that the currency it is due to receive will depreciate over the next few months, it may try to obtain payment immediately, perhaps by offering a discount for immediate payment. This is leading.

Lagging is an attempt to delay payment if the importer expects that the currency it is due to pay will depreciate. This may be achieved by agreement or by exceeding credit terms.

Strictly speaking this is not hedging the exposure, it is speculation. The company only benefits if it correctly anticipates the exchange rate movement.

(ii) **Matching**

When a company has receipts and payments in the same foreign currency due at the same time, it can simply match them against each other. It is then only necessary to deal on the foreign exchange (forex) markets for the unmatched portion of the total transactions.

Where a firm has regular receipts and payments in the same currency, it may choose to operate a foreign currency bank account. This operates as a permanent matching process and the exposure to exchange risk is limited to the net balance on the account.

The scope for matching is limited unless there are flows in both directions.

(iii) **Forward exchange contracts**

Forward exchange contracts are the most frequently used method of hedging. Such a contract is a binding agreement to buy or sell currency at a fixed future date for a predetermined rate, the forward rate of exchange.

Advantages are that companies have flexibility with regard to the amount to be covered and that the contracts are relatively straightforward both to comprehend and to organise. The agreement on a fixed rate eliminates downside risk.

However there are disadvantages – the company makes a contractual commitment that must be completed on the due date and has no opportunity to benefit from favourable movements in exchange rates. They are not available in all currencies.

(iv) **Currency options**

Options are similar to forwards, but with one key difference – they give the right, but not the obligation, to buy or sell currency at some point in the future at a predetermined date. A company can therefore exercise the option if it is in its interests to do so, or let it lapse if the spot rate is more favourable or there is no longer a need to exchange currency.

The advantage of options is that they eliminate downside risk but allow participation in the upside. Options are most useful when there is uncertainty about the timing of the transaction, or when exchange rates are very volatile.

However the additional flexibility comes at a price – a premium must be paid to purchase an option, whether or not it is ever used.

28 – Interest rate risk

(a) A forward rate agreement is an over-the-counter agreement between a bank and a customer. A customer can buy an FRA to fix the interest rate for a short-term loan starting at a future date. The FRA relates to a specific borrowing period. In the example given in the question the company can borrow for a period of 6 months starting in 2 months time at a simple annual interest rate of 5.0%. This locks the company into an effective interest rate of 5.0% whatever the market rate.

The company enters into a normal loan but independently organises a forward with a bank:

– interest is paid on the loan in the normal way

– if the interest is greater than the agreed forward rate, the bank pays the difference to the company

– if the interest is less than the agreed forward rate, the company pays the difference to the bank.

The FRA:

		6%	4%
		$	$
Interest payable	2m × 0.06 × 6/12	(60,000)	
	2m × 0.04 × 6/12		(40,000)
Compensation receivable		10,000	
Payable			(10,000)
Locked into the effective interest rate of 5%	2m × 0.05 × 6/12	(50,000)	(50,000)

In this case Toytown is protected from a rise in interest rates, but is not able to benefit from a fall in interest rates – it is locked into a rate of 5%. The FRA hedges the company against both an adverse movement and a favourable movement.

(b) Other ways of managing the risk include the following:

- Do nothing – borrowing the money when required at the prevailing interest rate may result in a cheaper loan but exposes the company to the possibility of a higher expense, so will be unacceptable here.
- Interest rate guarantees – IRGs are an option on a FRA, giving the company the option to change its mind and not adopt the FRA should rates move in its favour. This has the advantage of allowing the company to benefit from a favourable movement in interest rates while still be protected from adverse movements, albeit at a cost.
- Interest rate futures effectively fix the rate with the gain or loss on the futures position offsetting the loss or gain on the actual loan. Futures contracts are similar to FRAs except have standardised sizes and contract dates.

29 – Long term finance

Factors to consider when choosing between debt and equity:

Cost	The cost of equity is higher over the longer term than the cost of loans. This is because equity is a riskier form of investment for the investor. Moreover, loan interest is tax deductible whereas dividend payments are not. However, when profits are poor, there is no obligation to pay equity shareholders whereas the obligation to pay lenders will continue.
Financial risk (gearing)	Loan capital increases the level of risk to equity shareholders who will in turn require higher rates of return. If the level of gearing is high in relation to industry norms the credit standing of the business may be affected, although a highly geared firm may achieve high returns if the ROCE is higher than the cost of servicing the loans. Managers, although strictly concerned with the interests of shareholders, may feel their own positions are at risk if a high level of gearing is obtained. However, they may be more inclined to take on additional risk if their remuneration is linked to the potential benefits which may flow from higher gearing.
Cash flows	If the company is not going to be a good cash generator for a while, then it is likely that equity will be more suitable.
Security	If a company has good security available, then it may be able to raise more debt.

Control	Issuing equity may change control whilst issuing debt will not impact upon control.
Business risk	If business risk is high and/or operational gearing is high, then high levels of debt should be avoided.
Track record	If Cherry Tree Company has a good track record, then raising debt and equity will be easier. A business/entrepreneur with no track record will find it hard to raise finance and will probably need to find a provider of equity willing to take the high risk.
Amount	Raising small amounts by equity is not normally cost effective. Where the amount to be raised relative to the existing finance in the company is large, then the impact on gearing must be considered.
Issue	Debt is normally cheaper, easier, and quicker to raise, and has more certainty.
Covenants	Debt may often have covenants attached. Are they acceptable?

30 – Rights issue

(a) **TERP**

Market value (MV) of shares in issue = 4 million × \$3.40 = \$13.6 million

$$\text{Proceeds from new issue} = \frac{4\text{ million}}{2} \times \$2.50 = \$5\text{ million}$$

$$\text{Number of shares in issue ex-rights} = 4\text{ million} + (4\text{ million} \times \frac{1}{2}) = 6\text{ million}$$

$$\text{TERP} = \frac{\$13.6\text{ million} + \$5\text{ million}}{6\text{ million}} = \$3.10\text{/share}$$

Note: that the calculation can be done on the value of the whole equity or on the basis of the minimum shareholding needed to acquire one extra share:

$$\text{TERP} = \frac{(\$3.40 \times 2) + (\$2.50 \times 1)}{3} = \$3.10\text{/share}$$

(b) **Value of a Cherry Tree right**

Value of a right	= \$3.10 – \$2.50
	= \$0.60 per new share issued

(c) **Alternative methods of issuing equity finance**

Placing

A placing is where an issuing house undertakes to find purchasers for the shares and places the shares with these clients. Issue costs are much cheaper as there are no underwriting costs or prospectus costs. However, there are limitations on the amount of capital that can be raised using this method and shares tend to be placed in larger bundles. This will dilute the control of current shareholders as shares are more likely to be placed with large financial institutions.

Offer for sale

Shares are sold to an issuing house which then offers the shares for sale to the general public either at a fixed price or by tender. If the sale is by tender then a minimum price is set and the actual issue price determined when all of the tenders have been received. The issues are always underwritten and this fee is payable to the issuing house and will vary with the degree of risk relating to the issue. There is no restriction on the amount of capital that can be raised using this method but issue costs are likely to be higher than a rights issue and existing control may be diluted.

A public offer for subscription

Shares are sold directly to the public by the company. Issue costs are likely to be high as the company must advertise and administer the process. Specialist advisors are used to determine the issue price and underwriting fees may be high. This method enables a company to access a wider market for funds but they may not have the in house expertise to administer the process and the issue costs may be prohibitively high for a relatively small issue of shares.

31 – Sources of finance

(a) **TERP**

Market value (MV) of shares in issue = 500,000 × \$11 = \$5.5 million

Proceeds from new issue = \$2 mil ion

Number of shares in issue ex-rights = $500{,}000 + \left(500{,}000 \times \frac{2}{5}\right) = 700{,}000$

$$\text{TERP} = \frac{\$5.5\text{ million} + \$2\text{ million}}{700{,}000} = \$10.71/\text{share}$$

Note: that the calculation can be done on the value of the whole equity or on the basis of the minimum shareholding needed to acquire one extra share:

Subscription price per share = Proceeds ÷ number of shares to be issued

= \$2 million ÷ 200,000 = \$10 per share

$$\text{TERP} = \frac{(\$11 \times 5) + (\$10 \times 2)}{7} = \$10.71/\text{share}$$

(b) **Impact of capital structure on company value**

Evidence on the importance of capital structure to a company's value is not conclusive. There is general agreement that, as long as a company is in a tax paying position, the use of debt can reduce the overall cost of capital due to the interest on debt being a tax allowable expense in almost all countries. This was suggested by two Nobel prize winning economists, Miller and Modigliani. However, high levels of debt also bring problems, and companies with very high gearing are susceptible to various forms of risk, sometimes known as the costs of financial distress.

A common perception about capital structure is that as capital gearing is increased the weighted average cost of capital falls at first. However, beyond a certain level of gearing the risk to both providers of debt and equity finance increases, and the return demanded by them to compensate for this risk also increases, leading to an increase in the weighted average cost of capital. There is a trade-off between the value created by additional tax relief on debt and the costs of financial distress. Overall, there is therefore an optimal capital structure, which will vary between companies and will depend upon factors such as the nature of the company's activities, realisable value of assets, business risk etc. According to the theory, companies with many tangible assets should have relatively high gearing, companies with high growth, or that are heavily dependent on R&D or advertising would have relatively low gearing.

Not all companies behave as if there is an optimal capital structure, and on average, in countries such as the UK and USA, the average capital gearing is lower than might be expected if companies were trying to achieve an optimal structure. It must however be remembered that moving from one capital structure to another cannot take place overnight. The cost of debt, via interest rates, and the cost of equity, can change quite quickly. It is therefore not surprising that companies do not appear to be at an optimal level.

If value can be created by a sensible choice of capital structure then companies should try to achieve an optimal, or almost optimal, capital mix, as long as this mix does not have detrimental effects on other aspects of the company's activities.

(c) Convertible loan stock provides the investor with the right, but not the obligation, to convert the loan stock into ordinary shares at a specified future date and a specified price. The investor will only exercise this option if the market value of the shares is above the 'exercise price' at the specified date. The investor will change status from that of lender to that of owner when the option to convert is exercised.

The main benefit to the investor is that if the company is successful the investor will be able to participate in that success. This participation is not possible with straight debt. For the investor then, convertible loan stock offers the best of both worlds – relatively low risk debt, but with participation in a successful company. Because of this finance is relatively easily raised.

If the company is successful, the convertible loan stock will be self-liquidating, which can be convenient for the company. The company may also be able to negotiate lower rates of interest or fewer loan restrictions because of the potential gains on conversion.

Convertible loan stock is often used in takeover deals. The target company shareholders may find this form of finance attractive if they are uncertain as to the future prospects of the combined business. The investors will be guaranteed a fixed rate of return and, if the combined business is successful, they will be able to participate in this success through the conversion process. However, convertible loan stock can be viewed as part loan and part equity finance, and some investors may find it difficult to assess the value to be placed on such securities.

32 – Dividend policy

Formulating dividend policy

There are a number of factors that must be considered when formulating the dividend policy of a stock-exchange listed company:

Liquidity

A company needs access to sufficient cash in order to pay a proposed dividend. The same is true if a company is considering withholding a dividend payment in order to invest in a new project; that investment requires cash and if the company doesn't have cash available, retained earnings will not represent a potential source of finance.

Legal and other restrictions

A dividend can only be paid in accordance with statutory requirements. For example, in the United Kingdom dividends must be paid out of accumulated realised profits.

The signalling effect of dividends

In a less than perfectly-efficient market, directors have access to more information about a company than the shareholders do. Given this information asymmetry, dividend decisions convey new information to the market and can therefore provide signals around the current position of the company and its future prospects. The signalling effect also depends on the dividend expectations in the market. A company should therefore consider the likely effect on share prices of the announcement of a proposed dividend.

The need for finance

There is a close relationship between investment, financing and dividend decisions, and the dividend decision must consider the investment plans and financing needs of the company. If a company is looking at additional investment, say, then the need for external finance can be reduced if the dividend payment is reduced.

The level of financial risk

If financial risk is high due to a high level of debt finance within the capital mix, maintaining a low level of dividend payments will result in a higher level of retained earnings, which will reduce gearing by increasing the level of reserves. Over time this will help to reduce the level of financial risk to a more acceptable level.

33 – WACC with DVM

(a) **Calculation of weighted average cost of capital**

Definitions:

K = weighted average cost of capital
ke = cost of equity capital
kd = cost of debenture capital
kL = cost of bank loan
E = Total ex-dividend market value of equity
D = Total ex-interest market value of debt
L = Total value of outstanding bank loan

(i) **Calculation of ke**

Assuming an underlying dividend growth of g per annum, the average growth rate between 20X4 and 20X8 is given by:

$$g = \sqrt[4]{\frac{14.1}{11.0}} - 1$$

g = 6.4%

Assuming that shareholders take past dividend growth as a reasonable approximation to future dividend growth, then using the dividend growth model,

$$k_e = \frac{D_0(1 + g)}{P_0} + g$$

$$k_e = \frac{14.1(1 + 0.064)}{145} + 0.064 = 16.75\%$$

(ii) **Calculation of kd**

kd is the discount rate which equates the present value of future income ($7 per annum) and redemption ($100) to the current market price ($83.60).

Time		Cash flow	DF @ 10%	PV	DF @ 15%	PV
0	MV	(83.60)	1	(83.60)	1	(83.60)
1–4	Interest payments	7.00	3.170	22.19	2.855	19.99
4	Capital repayment	100.00	0.683	68.30	0.572	57.20
	NPV			6.89		(6.41)

$$IRR = 10 + \frac{6.89}{6.89 + 6.41} \times (15 - 10) = 12.6\%$$

Therefore the required return of investors is 12.6%.

Note: this question states that taxation should be ignored. If this was not the case, the interest payments in years 1 – 4 should be net of tax.

(iii) **Calculation of cost of bank loan**

The current cost of debt is taken as the best estimate of the future cost of debt, i.e. 8%.

Note: if the question included taxation, this rate should be reduced by (1 – T).

(iv) **Calculation of the weighted average cost of capital**

Security	**MV**		**Cost of capital**	**Weighted cost**
		Proportions		
	$m		%	%
Bank loan	0.5	0.088	× 8.0 =	0.704
Debentures	0.836	0.147	× 12.6 =	1.852
Ordinary shares	4.35	0.765	× 16.75 =	12.814
	5.686	1.000		15.370

(b) **Advice to directors**

The situation outlined in the question is such that the project being considered could hardly be thought of as marginal. The cost of the project ($3m) is nearly 70% of the existing market value of the company. In these circumstance k could only be used as a target discount rate if its business risk were the same as that of existing projects and it were to be financed in the same way as existing projects. This is unlikely to be the case, and as a generalisation it is probably unwise to use the existing k to evaluate such a major investment opportunity.

34 – WACC with NPV

(a) **Calculation of weighted average cost of capital**

Cost of equity = 4.5 + (1.2 × 5) = 10.5%

The company's bonds are trading at par and therefore the before-tax cost of debt is the same as the interest rate on the bonds, which is 7%.

After-tax cost of debt = 7 × (1 – 0.25) = 5.25%

Market value of equity = 5m × 3.81 = $19.05 million
Market value of debt is equal to its par value of $2 million
Sum of market values of equity and debt = 19.05 + 2 = $21.05 million

WACC = (10.5 × 19.05/21.05) + (5.25 × 2/21.05) = 10.0%

(b) **Net present value calculation ($000)**

Time	**0**	**1**	**2**	**3**	**4**	**5**	**6**
	$000	$000	$000	$000	$000	$000	$000
Cash inflows		700.4	721.4	743.1	765.3	788.3	
Tax payable (25%)			(175.1)	(180.4)	(185.8)	(191 4)	(197.1)
Initial investment	(2,500)						
Tax-allowable depreciation			125.00	125.00	125.00	125.00	125.00
Working capital	(240)	(7.2)	(7.4)	(7.6)	(7.9)	270.1	
Net cash flows	(2,740)	693.2	663.9	680.1	696.7	992.0	(72.1)
DF@ 10%	1.000	0.909	0.826	0.751	0.683	0.621	0.564
PV	(2,740)	630.1	548.4	510.8	475.9	616.0	(40.7)

NPV = $500

The investment is financially acceptable, since the net present value is positive. The investment might become financially unacceptable, however, if the assumptions underlying the forecast financial data were reconsidered. For example, the sales forecast appears to assume constant annual demand, which is unlikely in reality.

Workings

Tax-allowable depreciation tax benefits

Annual tax-allowable depreciation (straight-line basis) = $2.5m/5 = $500,000

Annual tax benefit = $500,000 × 0.25 = $125,000 per year

Working capital investment

Year	0	1	2	3	4	5
	$000	$000	$000	$000	$000	$000
Working capital	240	247.2	254.6	262.2	270.1	
Incremental investment	(240)	(7.2)	(7.4)	(7.6)	(7.9)	270.1

35 – CAPM

Using CAPM

The capital asset pricing model (CAPM) can be used to calculate a project-specific discount rate in circumstances where the business risk of an investment project is different from the business risk of the existing operations of the investing company. In these circumstances, it is not appropriate to use the weighted average cost of capital as the discount rate in investment appraisal.

The first step in using the CAPM to calculate a project-specific discount rate is to find a proxy company (or companies) that undertake operations whose business risk is similar to that of the proposed investment. The equity beta of the proxy company will represent both the business risk and the financial risk of the proxy company. The effect of the financial risk of the proxy company must be removed to give a proxy beta representing the business risk alone of the proposed investment. This beta is called an asset beta and the calculation that removes the effect of the financial risk of the proxy company is called 'un-gearing'.

The asset beta representing the business risk of a proposed investment must be adjusted to reflect the financial risk of the investing company, a process called 're-gearing'. This process produces an equity beta that can be placed in the CAPM in order to calculate a required rate of return (a cost of equity). This can be used as the project-specific discount rate for the proposed investment if it is financed entirely by equity. If debt finance forms part of the financing for the proposed investment, a project-specific weighted average cost of capital can be calculated.

Limitations of CAPM

The limitations of using the CAPM in investment appraisal are both practical and theoretical in nature. From a practical point of view, there are difficulties associated with finding the information needed. This applies not only to the equity risk premium and the risk-free rate of return, but also to locating appropriate proxy companies with business operations similar to the proposed investment project. Most companies have a range of business operations they undertake and so their equity betas do not reflect only the desired level and type of business risk.

From a theoretical point of view, the assumptions underlying the CAPM can be criticised as unrealistic in the real world. For example, the CAPM assumes a perfect capital market, when in reality capital markets are only semi-strong form efficient at best. The CAPM assumes that all investors have diversified portfolios, so that rewards are only required for accepting systematic risk, when in fact this may not be true. There is no practical replacement for the CAPM at the present time, however.

36 – Discount rates

(a) **Calculation of weighted average cost of capital**

Definitions:

K = weighted average cost of capital
ke = cost of equity capital
kd = cost of debenture capital
kL = cost of bank loan
E = Total ex-dividend market value of equity
D = Total ex-interest market value of debt
L = Total value of outstanding bank loan

(i) **Calculation of ke**

Assuming an underlying dividend growth of g per annum, the average growth rate between 20X4 and 20X8 is given by:

$(10.5 \div 6.9)^{0.25} - 1 = 0.11$

g = 11%

Assuming that shareholders take past dividend growth as a reasonable approximation to future dividend growth, then using the dividend growth model,

$$k_e = \frac{D_0(1 + g)}{P_0} + g$$

$$k_e = \frac{10.5(1 + 0.11)}{200} + 0.11 = 16.83\%$$

(ii) **Calculation of kd**

Debenture = irredeemable debt so therefore:
$Kd(1 - t) = 8 \times (1 - 0.3)/75 = 7.47\%$

(iii) **Calculation of cost of bank loan (kL)**

$10\% \times (1 - 0.3) = 7\%$.

(iv) **Calculation of the weighted average cost of capital**

Security	**MV**		**Cost of capital**	**Weighted cost**
	Workings	$m	%	$m
Bank loan		200	× 7.0 =	14.00
Debentures	400m × 75 ÷ 100	300	× 7.47 =	22.41
Ordinary shares	250 ÷ 0.25 × $2	2,000	× 16.83=	336.60
		2,500		373.01

WACC = $373.01m ÷ $2,500m × 100 = 14.9%

(b) Assuming the systematic risk of the recruitment industry is accurately reflected by the beta equity of other recruitment companies, this risk may be estimated by un-gearing the equity beta of the other recruitment companies and re-gearing it to take into account the different financial risk of March Co.
As corporate debt is assumed to be risk free:

$$ß_a = ß_e \times \frac{V_e}{V_e + V_d(1 - T)}$$

$$ß_a = 1.1 \times \frac{70}{70 + 30(1 - 0.3)} = 0.85$$

Current capital structure of March Co = $2,000m : $500m (see above) or 80:20.

$$0.85 = ß_e \times \frac{80}{80 + 20(1 - 0.3)}$$

$$0.85 = ß_e \times 0.85$$

$$ß_e = \frac{0.85}{0.85} = 1.00$$

K_e = 10% = R_m as the beta is 1.

37 – Risk

(a) **Business risk and financial risk**

In this context, it is useful to separate the total risk of the company into business risk and financial risk.

- The business risk is the risk inherent in the nature of the company's operations.
- The financial risk is a function of a company's gearing.

The weighted average cost of capital should only be used as the target discount rate for appraising investment opportunities whose acceptance will not alter the weighted average cost of capital.

Since the cost of any type of capital can be regarded as a function of a risk-free rate and a risk premium, this implies that k should not be used to evaluate opportunities which have significantly different risk characteristics from the average risk borne by the company prior to acceptance of the project.

For a project to be evaluated using the WACC, its acceptance must not alter the company's overall business risk nor must it alter the financial risk. Therefore, it must be of a similar nature to existing projects and it must be financed in such a way that the gearing ratio is unchanged and hence the financial risk is unaltered. In practice may also be used to evaluate small or marginal projects whose acceptance is unlikely to alter overall corporate risk.

In the case of the suggested acquisition, the target company is a shoe manufacturer like Greg Co, so it could be argued that they share the same level of business risk. However, the fact that Dan plc is experiencing difficulties could suggest it has a higher level of risk, perhaps due to inferior products or poor marketing.

We are not told how the acquisition will be financed. It may be possible for Greg Co to use a mixture of debt and equity to keep its gearing ratio constant but if this is not feasible, then the financial risk would also change.

Either or both of these concerns could be significant enough to compromise the validity of the company WACC as a suitable discount rate.

(b) **Factors that may change the equity beta**

Greg Co's equity beta measures the risk attached to equity returns. These risks have two elements:

- The business risk of the underlying earnings; and
- The additional gearing risk which effectively amplifies the earnings risk in arriving at overall risk.

Any factors that affect either of these two risk elements will affect Greg's equity beta. In particular:

- The new project will carry a different level of business risk in its earnings stream. Even though one would expect a reasonably high correlation between existing and project earnings, there will still be some diversification of unsystematic risk. However, this is irrelevant when looking at the beta as this is concerned only with systematic risk. The effect on the overall beta of Greg Co will be determined by the project's own beta which relates to the project return risk and market return risk.
- The financing of the project may result in an increase in the gearing of the company which will have a knock on effect on the equity beta, which may rise. Alternatively, gearing may fall which will reduce the equity beta.
- Other changes in the economy in general or the recruitment industry in particular may affect the variability in future equity returns in relation to those of the market. Betas will therefore fluctuate over time even without specific operational or financing changes.
- Also, a change in the mix of Greg's existing activities, away from the current mix would impact the current equity beta of the company.

38 – Achieving objectives

(a) **Stakeholders**

Introduction

The company states its objectives as 'to maximise shareholder wealth whilst recognising the responsibility of the company to its other stakeholders.' Since we are only given financial information in the question, we can only assess whether the company has met its objectives with respect to its shareholders and other financial stakeholders (suppliers, customers, employees, loan creditors and the government) and not to its non-financial stakeholders (journalists, the public, etc).

Shareholders

Consider first the shareholders.

	Year 1	Year 2	Year 3	Year 4	Year 5
Market capitalisation ($m) (Profit after tax × P/E ratio)	41.6	56.1	67.5	78.2	91.2
Earnings per share (cents) (Profit after tax ÷ number of shares)	87c	110c	125c	106c	120c
Dividends per share (cents)	35c	43c	50c	43c	60c
(Total dividends ÷ number of shares)					

The share issue of $20m at the start of year 4 seems to have disturbed the favourable trends in earnings and dividends per share for that year. However the overall pattern looks very satisfactory over the 5 year period; the company has succeeded in increasing shareholder wealth as it hoped.

By year 5 the share price stands at $91.2m/8m = $11.40 per share compared with only $41.6m/6m = $6.93 in year 1.

Employees

We can see that payments to employees fell substantially after year 3, together with the absolute number of employees. The average wages per employee has fallen since year 2, suggesting that the mix of employees is shifting towards less-skilled workers which could bring problems in the future.

	Year 1	Year 2	Year 3	Year 4	Year 5
Average wages per employee ($)	8,950	9,600	9,450	9,190	9,000

Loan creditors

The loan creditors have received lower interest payments in years 4 and 5, but this arises purely because of the reduction in long-term debt made possible by the rights issue at the start of year 4.

Conclusion

It appears that individual employees have received less of the financial benefits accruing to the company than the shareholders. While the average wages per employee has fallen over the last four years (suggesting perhaps that certain senior employees have been made redundant), dividends per share have risen substantially over the same period.

It is not possible to judge, purely from the information available, whether the company has or has not met its objectives. The additional information that would be helpful is discussed below.

(b) **Further Information required**

Other financial information which would be needed to assess more accurately whether the company has met its objectives includes the following:

– What investment possibilities were rejected by management?

The analysis above seemed to show that shareholders did well over the period, but was their return maximised, i.e. the best possible? To decide this it would be necessary to assess the alternative courses of action that were rejected during the course of the year; if any of these would have been more profitable than what was actually decided, then the shareholders' return was not the maximum possible.

– How did securities markets in general fare over the period?

A shareholder should view his investment in shares in the company in the light of other returns available on similarly risked securities in the market. If better returns were available elsewhere at no more risk than the rational risk averse investor should dispose of their shares.

– What was the inflation rate over the period?

Growth in money amounts of dividends and earnings might look less impressive if the trend is deflated by the inflation rate and only real increases are examined.

- Details of the company's workforce.

  Why has the payroll cost reduced in the last two years, by cutting wage rates or by losing high-paid employees? If there has been a formal programme of rationalisation and redundancies, an assessment of future prospects would be valuable.

- Volatility of share prices.

  We are given an average P/E ratio for each year, but how volatile has this and the share price been during each year? Companies should seek to reduce volatility by keeping markets informed so that analysts appreciate what the management are trying to do. This should support the share price.

- Amounts spent on environmental and social issues.

  A progressive company in today's business environment recognises its responsibilities to society on top of its other duties. Projects to ensure the minimum of pollution and support of local communities will serve to discharge these responsibilities.

  Amounts spent on employee communications and staff welfare would similarly support the good reputation of the company.

39 – Valuation methods I

(a) **Net asset valuation**

Target is being purchased as a going concern, so realisable values are irrelevant.

	$000
Net assets per accounts $(1,892 – 768)	1,124
– adjustment to freehold property $(800 – 460)	340
– adjustment to inventory	(50)
Valuation	**1,414**

Say $1.4m

(b) **DVM**

The average rate of growth in Target's dividends over the last 4 years is 7.4% on a compound basis.

$85 (1 + g)^4 = 113.1$ hence g = 7.4%

The estimated value of Target using the DVM is therefore:

$$\text{Valuation} \quad \frac{\$113{,}100 \times 1.074}{0.15 - 0.074} = \$1{,}598{,}282$$

Say $1.6m

(c) **P/E ratio method**

A suitable PE ratio for Target will be based on the PE ratio of Predator as both companies are in the same industry.

$$\text{PE of Predator} \quad \frac{70 \times \$4.30}{\$20.04\text{m}} \text{ or } \frac{430}{28.63} = \mathbf{15.02}$$

The adjustments: – Downwards by 20% or 0.20, i.e. multiply by 0.80.

(1) Target is a private company and its shares may be less liquid.

(2) Target is a private company and it may have a less detailed compliance environment and therefore may be more risky.

A suitable PE ratio is therefore 15.02 × 0.80 = 12.02

(multiplying by 0.80 results in the 20% reduction).

Target's PAT + Adjustment for the savings in the director's remuneration after tax:

$183,000 + ($40,000 × 67%) = $209,800

The estimated value is therefore $209,800 × 12.02 = $2,521,796

Say $2.5m

(d) **Advice to the board**

On the basis of its tangible assets the value of Target is $1.4 million, which excludes any value for intangibles.

The dividend valuation gives a value of around $1.6 million.

The earnings based valuation indicates a value of around $2.5 million, which is based on the assumption, that not only will the current earnings be maintained, but that they will increase by the savings in the director's remuneration.

On the basis of these valuations an offer of around $2 million would appear to be most suitable, however a review of all potential financial gains from the merger is recommended. The directors should, however, be prepared to increase the offer to maximum price.

40 – Valuation methods II

Introduction

When valuing a company, the normal approach taken is to create a range of values using the various valuation methods possible given the available information. This range of values may vary significantly, especially if the company is a hard company to value. This may be the case if the company is in an unusual trade or if it is growing rapidly for instance.

An appropriate value can then be decided upon given the range of values calculated, the reason or purpose of the valuation, the perspective and the relevance of the valuation methods to the particular circumstances of the company.

Purpose – why do we need a valuation?

The purpose of the valuation will impact on the valuation process:

For instance, if a company is being valued with a view to its sale then a higher value will be desired.

If a company is being valued for tax or divorce reasons then a lower value may be desired.

Furthermore, those valuing a company with a view to its purchase will often seek a lower value.

A related factor here is whether the sale is for all the shares or a minority stake. A dividend based value will have less relevance when valuing a majority stake in a company as a majority shareholder will control the earnings, cash flows and assets of the company, whereas it could be useful for a minority stake.

Perspective – who is the valuation for?

Most valuation methods can be adapted depending on whether the valuation is required for the buyer or the seller.

For example, if using an asset based approach, then a net realisable value basis will give a minimum price for the seller, while a replacement basis can be used to give an upper price limit for the buyer.

Similarly if using an earnings approach the buyer and seller may estimate sustainable earnings differently depending on their expectations of future growth, possible cost savings and other synergies.

Relevance of methods used

The relevance of the valuation methods to the type of company being valued must also be considered:

For instance a value based on the current tangible assets of a company is likely to have little relevance to a company which has significant intangible assets or which has significant future growth prospects.

A valuation based on the present value of future cash flows is considered particularly relevant where a company has significant growth prospects as this growth can be reflected in the estimates of the future cash flows.

As stated earlier, an appropriate value only can be decided (or often negotiated if the valuation is for a sale & purchase transaction), as there is no scientific way of accurately valuing a company. Hence it is often said that valuation is an art and not a science.

41 – Valuation and market efficiency

(a)

	2009	2010	2011	2012
Growth in profit for the period	–	25.3%	27.2%	16.5%
Payout ratio	71%	57%	45%	–
Earnings per share (cents)	31.0	38.9	49.4	57.6
Price/earnings ratio (times)	14.2	13.5	13.0	12.0
Dividend per share (cents)	22	22	22	–
Dividend yield (on opening price)	–	5%	4.2%	–
Share price growth	–	19.3%	22.3%	7.5%
Total shareholder return	–	24.3%	26.5%	–

It is clear that VAL Co has recently been through a period of exceptional growth, with the profit for the period and EPS growing substantially each year.

However, not everything is as positive as it might initially seem. The price earnings ratio has been falling from a high of 14.2 down to its current level of 12.0. Whilst this may be due to a decline in share prices more generally, a comparison against AVL Co (a very similar albeit larger company) shows that this is unlikely; AVL are currently trading on a P/E ratio of 13.5 (250 million × \$4.60 ÷ \$85 million) which is the level previously seen by VAL Co back in 2010.

Share price growth has fallen significantly in 2012 meaning that if a similar level of dividend were to be declared in 2012, the total shareholder return would also fall. Dividend yield has also been falling.

Perhaps the biggest cause of this will be the Board's apparent reluctance to invest in new projects. For a company to sit on such a large cash balance does not provide the best growth potential and does not maximize returns for shareholders. Undoubtedly shareholders would like to either see the surplus cash invested in positive NPV projects or returned to the investors by way of higher dividends. For this reason, it would not appear as if VAL Co is achieving its objective of maximization of shareholder wealth.

(b) P/E ratio of AVL Co (a suitable proxy co):

EPS – $85m/250m = $0.34
P/E ratio – $4.60/$0.34 = 13.5 times

(We had already calculated the P/E ratio in part (a))

Value of VAL Co using the P/E ratio of AVL Co:

EPS – $40.3m/70m = $0.576
Value per share – $0.576 × 13.5 = $7.78
Total company value – $7.78 × 70m = $544.6m

As the current market value of a share is $6.90, the P/E ratio value calculated indicates that VAL Co may be undervalued by S0.88 ($7.78 – $6.90) per share. As noted above, this undervaluation is most likely due to the market's lack of confidence in the investment decisions being made by the company.

However the P/E value calculated is rather simplistic and a number of other factors should be considered in addition to those noted in part (a):

VAL Co has achieved significant growth in recent years and hence it may well have a better future than AVL Co once it does start investing. Hence the valuation of $7.78 could itself be an under valuation.

VAL Co is smaller than AVL Co. The market capitalisation of AVL Co is $1,150m (250m × $4,60) whilst the market capitalisation of VAL Co is $483m (70m × $6.90). Due to this the market may view AVL Co as a more stable company than VAL Co in which case a value for VAL Co based on the P/E ratio of AVL Co may be an over valuation. However, the fact that the market has previously valued VAL Co based on a higher P/E ratio may suggest this isn't the case.

Carrying out a valuation of VAL Co using the P/E ratio of just one other company is potentially unwise as although AVL Co is said to be very similar, but larger, there are bound to be other differences. Hence it may be better to use an industry average P/E ratio.

The fact that the market is currently unaware of the new project that VAL Co is considering will mean that the value of that project is not currently reflected in the market value given the efficiency of the market. Hence the market value may be an under valuation. If the market does not know that the company intends to use their cash productively the market may be marking down the value of VAL Co as it seems to be under utilising its cash resource.

(c) The three levels of market efficiency can be explained as follows:

Weak form efficiency – the market fully reflects all information contained in past share price movements. Hence the market price of a share will only change when new information which impacts on the company is received by the market.

Semi – strong form efficiency – the market fully reflects all publicly available information. This implies that the market price of a share will immediately respond to any new release of information into the public domain. Therefore, the only way in which an investor could consistently beat the market would be if they had access to insider information.

Strong form efficiency – the market fully reflects all information. That is it reflects both information which is publicly known and information which is not yet publicly known.

As the market is semi-strong but information regarding the project has not yet been made publicly available, the value of the project is not currently included in the share price of the company. Hence if the company were to make information regarding the project publicly available then the value of the company will rise by the $65m NPV of the project. This assumes that the market agrees with the evaluation of the project and considers that the NPV calculated is accurate.

Assuming this occurs then the value per share will rise by $0.93 ($65m/70m). Hence the share price will rise to $7.83 ($6.90 + $0.93).

Index

Index

Index

Index